With the explosive expansion of AI and advance... ...he human fit into this new world? And, how do we hu... ...of these new forces? Reblooming the Knowledge M... ...he by providing a comprehensive and valuable fran... ...nd utilizing "knowledge" in all its facets. In the context of this book, consider that "knowledge" broadly consists of "cognitive assets" such as humans' tacit and explicit mental constructs that determine their mindsets, insights, expertise, and skills – or organizations' broad knowledge base possessed by its employees or embedded in data bases, documents, systems, and procedures – or intelligent systems' capabilities which are based on knowledge which was provided at their creation or is being developed by themselves or in conjunction with people. The last few years have exposed the emergence of a whole new world where AIs and AI-based tools are assisting us to explore and develop new, often novel, knowledge in almost every scientific and technical field. This surprisingly large body of knowledge needs to be "tamed" – organized, shared, and put to use. The extensive framework provided by this book with resonance and coherence at the core should prove a very useful guide for these endeavors.

-**Karl-Martin Wiig, Co-Founder, Knowledge Research Institute and International Knowledge Management Network; Author of** *Knowledge Management Foundations, People-Focused Knowledge Management, Knowledge Management Methods,* **and** *Knowledge Management: The Central Focus for Intelligent-Acting Organizations*

In "Reblooming the Knowledge Movement," the authors meticulously dissect the intricate dance between knowledge and its pivotal role in the evolution of humanity. Through its sections, the book offers a panoramic view of the foundational elements of knowledge, the transformative power of information, and the tools and strategies necessary for harnessing knowledge effectively in modern organizations. Their deep dive into intelligent complex adaptive systems illuminates the dynamic nature of knowledge-centric organizations, seamlessly integrating historical philosophical concepts with the demands of a rapidly changing world. But beyond its scholarly insights, what stands out is the book's heart – a fervent passion for the knowledge movement and its capacity to empower, innovate, and inspire. Whether you're a seasoned professional in the knowledge management field or an individual seeking to grasp the essence of information in the age of digital transformation, this book is a revelation.

- **Vincent Ribiére, Ph.D., D.Sc., Managing Director and Co-Founder of the Institute for Knowledge and Innovation Southeast Asia (IKI-SEA), Director of the KIM Ph.D. Program, Bangkok University, Thailand**

According to Dewey, the United States was founded on three democratic principles: (1) Inclusive authority, people have input into issues that impacted them. (2) Relational parity, how individuals are treated is not dependent on their status. And (3) Social involvement, people cooperate as free and equal individuals in solving the problems which affect their social world. Our organizations have not always lived up to these democratic ideals. Many have become hierarchies with little if any involvement of the frontline in critical decisions. The knowledge movement provides the opportunity to renew our organizations, for them to rebloom. This reblooming is occurring because increasingly the most critical knowledge in organizations is not their existing knowledge, rather it is the ability of frontline employees to create new knowledge through their on-going interactions with customers and the environment. The need for this new kind of knowledge is generating more democratic forms of organizing such as agile team networks, self-managing teams, mini factories, holacracy models, and platform structures that are designed to innovate and enhance knowledge creation. Knowledge is reblooming in organizations.

- **Dr. Nancy Dixon, Founder, Common Knowledge Associates, USA. Author of eight books including** *Common Knowledge: How Companies Thrive by Sharing What They Know.*

From the early visions of Fritz Matchlup and Peter Drucker, to the pioneering work of Bennet, Dixon, Wiig, Turner, and Prusak, we are blessed with a renewed vision of the next evolutionary stages that the Knowledge Movement will encompass. Bennet and Turner provide us with an outline taking us from "then" to "now," and beyond. Based upon the current divisiveness permeating much of our political, social, and business realms, it is timely for these authors to introduce the Reblooming Knowledge Movement (RKM) model. RKM will passionately "focus on organizations and characteristics that are democratic in nature." The book supports our quest to "explore the contribution of the knowledge productivity movement to the liberties and freedoms that it promotes, including the freedom of thought, expression, association, and individual self-organization, self-development, and growth." Our planetary consciousness associated with RKM is emerging as the foundation for innovative, collaborative, creative thought, and action.

Group cohesion, within the context of resonance and coherence, appears as a focal point of the RKM model, whose inner petals are: (1) leading and visioning, (2) networking and communicating, (3) participating and collaborating, and (4) seeking purpose and meaning. The outer petals encompass (5) transparency, (6) truth and (7) trust. If we mirror this model to other spiritual models of consciousness and spiritual development, such as Alice Bailey's Ageless Wisdom treatises on the Seven Rays, we are led to perceive parallels that stimulate our creativity, innovation, freedom, and learning. Numerous esoteric models exist to encapsulate the range of teaching and learning proposed on the RKM model. However, very few of these esoteric models provide the praxis necessary to apply a model such as this to individuals, groups, and organizations. Thus, investing time in exploring this comprehensive model comprising theory and practice is well worth the effort for your intellectual and spiritual development.

> - **Dr. Michael J.D. Sutton, Fellow of the Business Excellence Institute, USA, FUNIFICATION.BIZ, Author of *Document Management for the Enterprise***

Reblooming is a great approach for cultivating knowledge. This book has very knowledge-rich writers. Now, the next addition is coming from your reading and sharing. Happy knowledge blooming!

> - **Leif Edvinsson, Professor Emeritus, Sweden and Hong Kong; The New Club of Paris; World's First Professor on Intellectual Capital; UK Brain Trust Brain of the Year**

Management fads come and go, with a focus on quality, productivity, objectives, processes, etc. But sometimes, the focus is not a fad, and a theme continues to return. The realization that organizations are based on, and driven by, knowledge, has become a recurring theme. Like the phoenix rising, knowledge is again becoming recognized as a fundamental management concept. In the past, "knowledge" was not well-defined; knowledge development was a topic that leadership pictured "down in the training department"; knowledge management was mainly associated with specific technologies; and knowledge-based topics like innovation, story, strategy, decisions, and economy, were simply viewed as management-based topics. Alex Bennet and Robert Turner have lived through the "ups and downs" of the knowledge movement, and have now brought together the authors and concepts needed for Reblooming the Knowledge Movement. At a time where remote workforces, AI, and quantum computing are on the rise, this timely book addresses the management need for this knowledge movement and finally connects terms like resonance, coherence, and entropy as organizational and management concepts. By showing how seemingly academic terms are fundamentals of management, and by providing dozens of workable tools and examples, this reblooming of the knowledge movement is here to stay.

> - **John Lewis, Ed.D., Chief Knowledge Officer, Explanation Age LLC & SearchBlox Software, Inc., USA, Author of *Story Thinking***

Alex Bennet and Robert Turner have been wowing us with the richness of their thought for years, and this latest book is true to its title ... Reblooming the Knowledge Movement literally blooms across each page, through your mind, and it promises to bloom across space. If you hope to understand the limitless power of knowledge for producing change, Reblooming will flood your consciousness with enough fertile ideas to last a lifetime. Reblooming is a cornucopia bursting with flowers of thought.

- **Dr. William E. Halal, George Washington University, USA; Author of** *Beyond Knowledge: How Technology is Driving an Age of Consciousness*

As the evolution of artificial intelligence has attracted the attention of the global community, the need for accurate and unbiased knowledge as a result of AI has also been prevalent. Reblooming the Knowledge Movement: The Democratization of Organizations by Alex Bennet and Robert Turner is at the cornerstone of raising the bar for the need for knowledge management to meet this challenge. The authors advocate for an interdisciplinary approach to knowledge cultivation and use while also supporting the knowledge exchange where individuals enrich knowledge ensuring consistency between values, beliefs, and actions. The authors reblooming of knowledge focuses on achieving resonance and coherence, ensuring organizational cohesion while celebrating diversity and creative friction. This cohesion strengthens the very core of the author's Reblooming Knowledge Movement (RKM) model. It is a pleasure to provide my perspective in the endorsement of this book.

- **Dr. Anthony J. Rhem, CEO/Principal Consultant of A.J. Rhem & Associates, USA. Author of** *Knowledge Management in Practice*, **and** *Essential Topics in Artificial Intelligence: An examination of AI Ethics and Governance, Large Language Models, Artificial General Intelligence, and Natural Language Processing*

Reblooming the Knowledge Movement is a fundamental step toward restoring confidence in human capacity to find solutions at a time the whole world is grappling with crises such as climate change, geopolitical tensions, poor governance, suppression of democracy, information overload, fake news and depletion of values. This book is a powerful resource relevant to diverse contexts. I have started using it as a framework for building indigenous theories of development and restoring African social principles. Such a framework is in itself a tangible knowledge product.

- **Charles Dhewa, CEO, Knowledge Transfer Africa (KTA), Zimbabwe; Core Member of International Knowledge Management for Development D-Group; Winner of the International Knowledge Management Award 2019**

This is a very serious, encyclopedic book, from that first generation of leaders in knowledge management and complexity, reflecting on decades of thinking and practice. It is organised around the simple principle - and ideal - that "within ourselves and across our organizations, we seek resonance among and coherence of words and actions, information and knowledge". I wish I had had this book when I was working on typologies of knowledge, because the authors have a captivating way of bringing the human dimension and a deep sense of context back into our understanding of knowledge. This book is an important contribution, because it uniquely frames knowledge management not just as a corporate discipline, but more as a discipline for being human, in society and the world.

- **Patrick Lambe, Partner, Straits Knowledge, Ireland. Author of** *Principles of Knowledge Auditing, Organising Knowledge*, **and** *The Knowledge Manager's Handbook*

If you haven't been enticed by the idea of managing knowledge yet, or felt that this was a folly that will probably fade away – this book might be the ticket to convince you otherwise. Two first-gen knowledge management enthusiasts unite to reflect on what has worked in the past and what can be done better for knowledge-driven organisations. This book presents a pragmatic-yet fresh, translatable outlook on why knowledge management is here to stay as the driver for organisations to realise their "action potentials".

> **- Dr. Frada Burstein, Professor (Adjunct), Monash University, Australia**

Another tour de force on knowledge, learning, and innovation by Dr. Alex Bennet and co-author Robert Turner. They give new meaning to the term "encyclopedic" in this recent work. Their research and writings reflect their enthusiasm and mastery of knowledge in all its various aspects. It should be the perfect go-to publication for both academics and practitioners of knowledge management in its myriad interpretations and practices.

> **- Michael Stankosky, DSc, Former Lead Professor, Knowledge Management, George Washington University, USA; Cofounder of the Institute of Knowledge & Innovation, GWU; Author; Editor Emeritus, *VINE*; Member of the Academy of Scholars**

This book is everything you need to know about KM but were afraid to ask! The first stage of KM followed the old metaphor of organizations as machines, and this is why it was dying as other management fads. The book Reblooming the Knowledge Movement is committed to the metaphor of organizations as living organisms, and this makes a great difference, with new hope for KM to rebloom as a Knowledge Movement, which is a better metaphor itself since, actually, knowledge cannot be managed!

The first stage of KM focused on trying to capture this organic competence and failed! The emerging knowledge movement is focused on community development and is succeeding. This book tells this story and offers a wealth of knowledge for all of us of what really works in this great movement. The world is a global village as Marshal McLuhan predicted many years ago, made possible by technology. Yet technology gives and takes, as I learnt from my late teacher Neil Postman. This book has it all! Including a PoC in a chapter written with ChatGPT. I love it!

> **- Dr. Edna Pasher, Founder, Pasher Management Consultants and Israel Smart Cities Institute. Author of *The Complete Guide to KM*. PhD in Media Ecology. Pioneer of the knowledge and Innovation management movement in Israel.**

Reblooming the Knowledge Movement: The Democratization of Organizations by Alex Bennet and Robert Turner is an insightful exploration of resurgence in the realm of knowledge management in the modern era. The authors introduce the significant concept of 'useful knowledge', essentially underlining its application in tackling concrete problems, signaling a pragmatic shift in knowledge utilization. The book ventures into an intriguing discussion of surface knowledge versus deep knowledge, which understanding empowers organizations to leverage their knowledge resources effectively. The concept of knowledge governance is aptly discussed, emphasizing the authority, decision-making, and accountability facets of managing knowledge within an organization. Such mechanisms have significant implications for organizational effectiveness and innovation. In essence, the book provides a comprehensive perspective on various aspects of KM, shedding light on the intricate dynamics of knowledge governance, audits, sharing, and varying knowledge levels, and thereby stands as an indispensable resource for knowledge management practitioners and scholars alike in all industries.

> **- Cory Lee Cannon, Cannon-Lear Enterprises LLC, South Korea**

It gives me immense pleasure to write a few words towards endorsement of the book, *Re-blooming the Knowledge Movement* by Alex Bennet and Robert Turner. Reading this book rekindles the quest for knowing more about what knowledge and knowledge management can mean. This quest may be at an individual level for those who have had deep association with some facets of knowledge management, knowledge economy, knowledge cities and knowledge-based development. It may also be for corporates who are looking for a comprehensive guide on how to assimilate and implement important concepts, methodologies, guidelines, and toolkits of knowledge management to enhance organizational productivity and performance. It is heartening to note that the authors have christened a new word, "knowledge movement", to describe in more generic and wide-scoped terms the concepts and frameworks related to the birth, growth, and resurgence of knowledge management and related disciplines.

The book throws a fresh light on emerging perspectives of the knowledge movement in the midst of rapid global changes and technological advancements. A case in example is the emergence of Generative AI/Large Language Models such as ChatGPT and their potential contribution to the knowledge movement. In this regard, a chapter in the book "co-authored" by ChatGPT as a guest author demonstrates a happy convergence of the human being and AI in disseminating the fruits of the knowledge movement. At the same time, contributions by many a distinguished author through separate chapters in the book have added highly valuable and diverse perspectives of hitherto unexplored aspects of the knowledge movement.

The book is written in a language which is simple and interesting, and yet provides a comprehensive coverage of the subject matter. It provides a 360-degree view of the tenets of the knowledge movement from the theoretical/foundational to a practical and implementation-focused orientation. I strongly recommend this book to all who would like to leverage the knowledge shared in it for enriching their own as well as their organizational insights about the knowledge movement, and putting into practice the vast repository of concepts, tools and guidelines provided therein.

> - **Prof. (Dr.) Surinder Batra, Former Dean (Academics) & Professor, Institute of Management Technology, Ghaziabad, India**

The journey from conception to maturity is lined with buds and seeds of sustainment and improvement. However, there is a point within maturity where there is a choice between retirement and renewal. *Reblooming the Knowledge Movement: The Democratization of Organizations* is the renewal of KM with invaluable knowledge from KM's past life! This book is an essential resource for the encore evolution and progression of KM within today's organizations.

> - **Dr. Annie Green, George Washington University, USA, International Institute for Knowledge and Innovation (IIKI), Knowledge Management Global Network (KMGN)**

"*Reblooming the Knowledge Movement*" stands as a comprehensive wellspring of wisdom, an indispensable work for those who aspire to lead with the mastery of knowledge. The book beckons readers on an enchanting odyssey in its meticulously crafted structure, unveiling knowledge management – from its foundations to its role in modern organizational dynamics. This piece transcends the boundaries of time. As you journey through its pages, prepare to be captivated, informed, and forever enriched.

> - **Dr. Tori R. Dodla, Knowledge Collaborative Engineer, Knowledge Management Researcher, Capitol Technology University, USA**

Reblooming the Knowledge Movement

The Democratization of Organizations

Alex Bennet and Robert Turner
Mountain Quest Institute

with Francisco Javier Carrillo,
Florin Gaiseanu, Chulatep Senivongse,
Milton de Sousa and Pedro Brito, and ChatGPT
Foreword by Rory Chase

MQIPress (2023)
Frost, West Virginia
ISBN 978-1-949829-74-7

This is not a book about the intelligent life of plants. Others have already explored that subject. This is a book about the intelligent life of humans and their organizations.

FIRST EDITION (October 2023)

MQIPress
Frost, West Virginia
303 Mountain Quest Lane, Marlinton, WV 24954
United States of America
Telephone: 304-799-7267
eMail: alex@mountainquestinstitute.com
www.mountainquestinn.com
PTMF India: www.ptmfonline.com

ISBN 978-1-949829-74-7
Cover drawing by MQI Resident Artist Cindy Taylor

Dedicated to all those who seek knowledge for the greater good. Our special appreciation to the thought leaders in the knowledge field whose words continue to ring in our heads and hearts and to our Special Topics contributing authors: Florin Gaiseanu (Romania), Milton de Sousa and Pedro Brito (Portugal), Chulatep Senivongse (Thailand), and Francisco Javier Carrillo (Mexico). Special thanks to Rory Chase (England) for pausing in his well-earned retirement to champion this movement; to Nancy Dixon who in a private conversation 20+ years ago described the knowledge movement as the democratization of organizations; to our tool contributors Joyce Avedisian, Rajat Baisya, Mark Boyes, WB Lee, John Lewis, Arthur Murray, Arthur Shelley, and Michael Stankosky; and to our incredibly supportive partners, Jane Turner and David Bennet.

Antheros Dianthus*

Imagine and envision in your mind's eye …
Reblooming across the global knowledge movement.
More people learning more, everywhere,
More people thinking more, everywhere,
Knowledge arising profusely in abundant array,
We are creating and innovating, everywhere.
A new Spring—with infinite variety, everywhere.

A new species emerges in the knowledge landscape.
It is rare, but when we find it, it speaks to us.
It is brilliant in form, it blooms with vibrance.
This species replenishes our field of vision.
It emboldens our senses; inviting us to understand more.
It flourishes with freedom—expanding with knowledge.

The reblooming species unfolds to greet us.
It reblooms in perpetual Spring, always there for us.
This flower rises from earth of infinite sustenance.
Information abounds and reverberates all around.
The stem enables knowledge creation and learning.
The inner petals provide for expanding capacity.
The outer petals engender shared empowerment,
Sustaining change with creative resilience.
The backdrop of energy unifies vitality.
With center stamens and pistils engaging regeneration,
Resonating in coherence …
Ever thriving, living, and *REBLOOMING*!

* "Antheros Dianthus" is Greek for this new floral species
  in the Dianthus genus named by the ancient Greek
  botanist Theophrastus – dios = divine + Anthos = flower.
  Adding to the over 300 species, Antheros Dianthus means
  Forever Blooming Divine Flower.

Preface

Reblooming ... In California there is a rare superbloom marvel that occurs following a years-long drought, where native wildflowers – whose seeds have lay dormant during the drought – gloriously burst forth across the deserts and grasslands at the same time!

Amazing to be sure, a rather similar phenomenon has occurred in the United States and across global economic and business environments during the post-WWII decades. As economies became increasingly prolific, first with information and then knowledge resources and dynamics, the knowledge era and the knowledge economy emerged. Eventually, during the late 1990's and the early 2000's the knowledge management discipline gave rise in corporate America, in many progressive business centers around the worlds, in select academic institutions, and in the public sector as well. Hence, the early fruitful seeds of the knowledge movement were sown.

In the midst of cultivating the foundation for the new era and new economy a pervasive financial drought swept the landscape. The first decade of the 21st Century was impeded by major depletions to growth and progress that impacted global development as well as United States advancement. The three major impediments were the collapse of the speculative high-tech dot-com bubbles, the September 11th devastating attacks, and the subprime mortgage crisis which caused the collapse of many of the largest financial institutions and reverberated across the global economy to the tune of trillions of dollars.

Nevertheless, after lying dormant for a period of years, a regenerative economic climate has revived and reawakened vibrant appreciation for the knowledge movement. The capacity of this transformation is most evident in the resilience of this rekindling in the wake of the global Covid pandemic. During the dormancy, new levels of underlying forces such as knowledge resonance and coherence stimulated the dynamics of competition and invention. Although a financial break from the higher overhead investments of knowledge management occurred, there were powerful underlying intensities such as the coalescing of knowledge worker capacities with prevailing digital technologies like data analytics and web-based information sharing. Essentially, the digital technology resource base was alive and well. Moreover, it was advanced enough to welcome a new superbloom yield of the coalescing of AI, quantum computing, and human intelligence.

Suddenly, in the hyperpaced speed of this modern world, knowledge ascendancy is front and center on demand for all three entangled pillars of our future – digital brilliance (AI), quantum science, and the human mind. What will we create at the nexus?

During its dormancy, knowledge management continued to sow the early seeds of a disciplined knowledge undertaking, supporting resilience, recognition of values, and expansion of knowledge work and innovation. As early thought leaders in the field declared, it does not matter what you call it, the need for good knowledge, which can only be built on good information, is at the core of all that we do as individuals, as organizations, as nations, and as a humanity.

AI and quantum computing are useless and dangerous to humanity without humanity. The need for *good* knowledge was never so obvious as in the changing, uncertain, complex and anxiety-filled environment of today, where sustainability of living systems at all levels of life requires greater adaptability and foresight to navigate an unknown future. Our hopes are apparent and are achievable. The seeds have been planted. The environment of the world is shifting. The time for reblooming the knowledge movement has come.

Alex: It was the early 90's when the potential offered by Knowledge Management fully invaded our heads and hearts – the "our" referring to my long-time partner, protagonist and friend David Bennet, nuclear physicist, neuroscientist, and life-long learner. It was he, of course, who brought KM to my attention and handed me a book by Karl Wiig titled *Knowledge Management Foundations: Thinking About Thinking – How People and Organizations Represent, Create and Use Knowledge*. Later, we were to engage in wonderful conversations with Karl and his wife in their Texas home. That book was the beginning. We were caught.

Before long opportunities emerged within this blossoming field, and the Department of the Navy (DON) was willing and able to move into the KM potential that was quickly becoming a reality. Diving in, I left behind my focus and positions as Acquisition Reform Executive and Standards Improvement Executive for the Acquisition workforce and joined the CEO shop, becoming the Deputy CIO for Enterprise Integration and moving into the Chief Knowledge Officer role for the Department. It was in this role that I was able to network and build relationships with early KM thought leaders. For example, Larry Prusak, who had founded the Institute for Knowledge Management sponsored by IBM, a global consortium of over 70 organizations engaged in researching and advancing the practices of KM and organizational learning through action research. DON played an active role, not only serving as a research site, but also sending DON KM enthusiasts around the world to participate in other research efforts underway. Simultaneously, over in the Army and the Federal Aviation Administration, Robert Turner was having his own KM Aha! experience.

Bob: Go back with me a few more years into the 1970s. While doing graduate work at Boston University, I was struck by the overlapping of what seemed to me a related set of trends. First, I was drawn toward the increasing prominence and impact of individual high-performance in the modern workplace. Then, I heard regularly about the emerging information economy, including the growing population of knowledge workers from the extensively published professor and management consultant Peter Drucker and others. Out of this emergence of a post-industrial economy, my regard for the difference between information and knowledge grew. That is, I came to appreciate knowledge as considerably more, perhaps infinitely more, complex than information.

Later, in the early 1980s, while consulting in the Army's internal management consulting program, I was encouraged to dig deeply into the role of knowledge processes in complex decision making and innovation. Research included developing an advanced concept for an Army management center known as the Fusion Center. At the heart of this endeavor was the goal of compressing time required for impacting significant organizational issues and strategic opportunities from months to days. For example, with a significant reduction of process time for addressing complex questions came increases in the choices about who could be available to participate. Moreover, the nature of the search and regard for knowledgeable experts became broader and deeper everywhere we looked. Also notable was that new levels of attention were being given to the nature and quality of knowledge desired. We were not only observing expanding levels of knowledge, we were also discovering enhanced ways of finding it. It seemed that the Information Economy was being superseded by the Knowledge Economy. Eventually, we learned from the extensive research of the economist Fritz Matchlup. He became a harbinger of the forthcoming Knowledge Economy as early as 1962 with his monumental work *The Production and Distribution of Knowledge in the United States*.[1]

Then in the 1990s, I had the opportunity for a number of years to participate in the Institute for the Future out of Menlo Park and the IBM Institute for Knowledge Management. These experiences were welded together in a decision support center at the Federal Aviation Administration's Team Technology Center. In our work with developing a virtual decision support operational hub, we also used the center to research technologies and processes for supporting virtual organizational learning and knowledge productivity. In 2005 our efforts were awarded a government-wide Award for Excellence in the development of the FAA Knowledge Services Network (KSN). Additionally, we were requested by the U.S. Office of Personnel Management (OPM) to organize a cross government Federal Knowledge Management Network. That network provided a forum for thought leaders in the rising tide of learning and knowledge productivity. And then, two streams of research and productivity in the federal government KM realm joined to become one, a government-wide working group, and that's when I met Alex.

Both of Us: The knowledge movement is so much more than the field that emerged at the end of the last century. Back then, we were happy knowledge management had been linked to the information technology explosion since that provided interest and funding before full realization of the potential of the field was recognized. What was happening, of course, is that as people began to really understand more deeply the meaning and value of knowledge, it was bringing businesses back to a focus on people. But it was doing even more than that, although it was difficult to put your hands on. As interest in the knowledge field and particularly knowledge management rose and fell, with academics and practitioners repeatedly predicting its demise just as a new focus would emerge producing a plethora of energy, something new and wonderful was bubbling below the surface, an intellectual passion that offered larger potential than we could at the time fully comprehend.

As this deep involvement in the field continued, we recognized that thought leaders in the knowledge movement shared the same passion *we* felt about the field. It was apparent when you met them, not only in their words but in the tone of their voice and their excitement, and we noted that it was contagious. These observations fueled continuous thought and a desire for clarity.

Passion is made up of desires, behaviors, and thoughts that suggest urges with considerable force and is used as a determinant or indicator of what is of *greater or higher interest*. From a biological viewpoint, passion (both the emotion that is externally observed and the feeling that is internally experienced) can be induced by external events and circumstances, and by ideas, which become part of a set of stimuli that includes considerable variation in the type of stimuli both among individuals and across cultures.[2] Morals also come into play, exciting passion, with even moral distinctions derived from passion![3] As Csikszentmihalyi describes, passion elevates values and engages reality at all levels in its search for "what it means to be *alive*".[4] *What it means to be alive!* Was that the "something more" in KM we were sensing?

For the next year Alex took the opportunity to interview and extensively converse with 34 of the early knowledge movement thought leaders – spanning four continents – working in and with industry, academia and government. For this group, the field offered "the richness of a multidimensionality of experience" which, in turn, offered the potential to provide "nourishment and cultivation of the future." This thing most called knowledge management brought a focus to "overall human value", that is, the "value of knowledge and what it can do for society, for individuals, and for interactions between individuals."

There was "a sense of mission" emerging, a "true interest in improving the system" through "integrity, consistency and persistence", and a "courage to stand by what you believe". All of this coupled to "a sincere desire to help people in organizations." And then, amongst the middle of narratives as together we struggled to discover the words to describe the perceived "more" bubbling below the surface of the knowledge movement, one thought leader, Nancy Dixon, author of *Common Knowledge*, simply stated that it *enabled the democratization of organizations*. And there it was.

There was a freedom woven in the valuing of thought, knowledge, intellectual capital – a freedom from previously perceived limitations of the human mind. Immediately the context of Viktor Frankl rose to awareness; Viktor Frankl, who discovered moments of love and beauty of thought in the midst of the horrors of Auschwitz.[5] He reflected on the sight of a single flower in the debris, and on the helping hand of a stranger. And now we know that our thoughts and feelings, our beliefs and values, are ours to have, to choose, to change. Being human brings with it a freedom of thought, the freedom of ideas, the freedom to value, and the freedom to learn. Knowledge flows from these freedoms, which can only be controlled by others if we allow them to do so.

These freedoms are embedded in the knowledge movement, and, as we reflected, there was even more. There is a collegial freedom, interacting with other people as well as with their ideas. There is a freedom of speech, with diverse perspectives and insights driving critical thinking, spurring "the creation of new ideas", and offering greater opportunity for innovation. Diversity supports those freedoms, with the level of diversity characterizing the *strength* of those freedoms. In an article titled "The Hindu Concept of Human Freedoms" published by *The UNESCO Courier* in 2018, author Shrikrishna Venkatesh Puntambekar, an Indian academic, wrote, "Freedom encourages growth ... we desire freedom of thought and expression of movement and association, of education and of expansion in the mental and moral spheres. In any defined and ordered plan for living, we must have the right of non-violent resistance and autonomy, in order to develop our ideas of the good human life."

Tenets of freedom emerge as we probe the essence of who we are, with knowledge at our very core driving our actions, which determines the course of ourselves and our organizations. There is a larger identity of self, a *self-realization* that, as the Navy adage goes, we are the captains of our ship. We are not only responsible for our knowledge, but are responsible for *self-development* and, in a larger sense, responsible for the way we *use* our knowledge. The meme *with knowledge comes responsibility* was already engaged in spreading across the field.

Other tenets of the freedoms core to the knowledge movement were revealing themselves as the influx of technology-supported information flooded the senses, and issues of *truth* and *trust* surfaced in everyday organizational decision-making. And in the search for "truth" we perceived the human power of humility. For example, KM thought leaders recognized the need to have "the *humility* to realize that they may not be right" and "an *openness* for listening and seeing new signals". And then it dawned on us that the MOVEMENT OF KNOWLEDGE ITSELF is a freedom! We choose whether to share what we know with others, and how we contribute to the creativity and innovation so necessary for our organizations to succeed in the world of today and the future.

Early on, knowledge management was a way of working in the organization focused on making full use of the knowledge, experience and capabilities of all employees in support of the organizational mission and vision and, specifically, good decision-making and innovation, already recognized as necessary for sustainability. With a focus on organizations and characteristics that are democratic in nature, it is from that viewpoint we are going to explore the contribution of the knowledge productivity movement to the liberties and freedoms that it promotes, including the freedom of thought, expression, association, and individual self-organization, self-development, and growth. We will also look at the social contract between leaders and workers in a knowledge-centric organization; the role of leadership virtue, morality, and trust; individual liberty, choice and agency; and touch on attributes such as networking and communication, participation and collaboration; the role of communities; free and open dialogue in the sharing of opinions; the necessity for truth, trust and transparency; critical thinking and inquiry; leading and visioning; affective attunement; purpose and meaning; the motivation to achieve the greater good; and the "mode of associated life" in a knowledge organization.

The Reblooming Knowledge Movement (RKM) and Model

The Reblooming Knowledge Movement (RKM) model unfolds toward, and is at the heart of, the Knowledge Economy. Because of the inherent coalescing of myriad disciplines and sciences, the proper study of both is through the kaleidoscopic or teleidoscopic lens of consilience. In order to comprehend and navigate these unprecedented global forces, vantage points are being established. The RKM model is introduced in this volume to provide a fresh and dynamic perspective for growing, cultivating, and using knowledge itself. Explanation of the RKM model is offered throughout the chapters, and specifically in Chapter 7 with the assistance of a contributing guest, ChatGPT.

At the center of the Reblooming Knowledge Movement is resonance and coherence. In a connected world, we are developing a *culture of connection* in our organizations and around the globe. There is the interweaving of thought, which both enables the emergence of innovation and the creation of forces.

While humans have always been social creatures, with physical mechanisms developed in the brain which enable learning through social interaction,[6] global connectivity and the internet have raised networking and communication – and thus the opportunity for participation and collaboration – to an international art form. Physical proximity is no longer an essential factor in the workplace.

Yet the very connectedness that provides opportunities for our global world also facilitates the flow of disinformation, misinformation and propaganda, all coupled to very real challenges facing humanity. These forces tarnish information, throwing doubt in its viability in terms of truth and trust.

Within ourselves and across our organizations, we seek resonance among and coherence of words and actions, information and knowledge. You will discover the idea of resonance throughout this text. From one perspective, resonance is a knowledge exchange where individuals build upon the knowledge of others, greatly enhancing and expanding the growth of knowledge across the organization. This, of course, is only possible when there are common learning points – goals, characteristics, and histories – that help expedite the understanding of the information being shared. From another perspective, resonance is the consistency of values and beliefs with actions, both from the individual and organizational viewpoints. From still another perspective, resonance represents the shared state of affective attunement, a vibrational entrainment that opens the door to learning, deeper and easier knowledge sharing, and, collectively, the triggering of new ideas.

While there are many definitions for coherence, most are largely in relationship to energy in terms of the amount of synchronization between oscillating systems. For example, as happens between photons in a laser when two or more systems operating at the same frequency become phase-locked or frequency-locked. As McCraty reminds – and consistent with the use of the term – "When coherence is increased in a system that is coupled to other systems, it can pull the other systems into increased synchronization and more efficient functioning."[7]

This is applicable to the system that is our body as we interact with others. Research coming out of the Institute of HeartMath refers to coherence as wholeness and global order, where the whole is greater than the sum of its individual parts or considered as a *clarity of thought, speech and emotional composure*. Imagine this as an organization with people becoming frequency-locked, heading the same direction toward the same vision through a *connectedness of choices*, which is a term emerging from the DON where despite (or perhaps because of) diversity of thought, skills, and experience, decisions made at every part of the organization (with clarity of thought, speech and emotional composure), although different, head the organization in the same direction. Now, add to that vision the idea of resonance, people resonating with each other, a knowledge exchange where each individual builds upon the knowledge of the other, greatly enhancing the growth of knowledge.

At the core of reblooming the knowledge movement is the seeking of resonance and coherence, a group cohesion within the organization and among the organization's partners and stakeholders, with diversity and creative friction coloring and then strengthening that coherence. Thus, at the center of our reblooming model we place the concept of resonance and coherence.

The Structure of the Book

Each section of this book is unique and could stand alone as a guide, exploring the knowledge movement from different perspectives, within and without. Yet again, you will discover among them a cohesion that offers insights into the important role knowledge is playing in the advancement of humanity.

SECTION I: Laying the Foundation. The first section builds a foundation, with the knowledge emerging in knowledge workers and knowledge organizations expanding through freedom, learning, creativity and innovation in an atmosphere of trust, truth and transparency. Chapter 1 introduces the concepts and attributes emerging from historical philosophers focused on the democratic process. We embrace these characteristics as embedded in the processes of the organization, not as an outcome. Indeed, when static, an organization can never be successful. While processes and outcomes are undoubtedly (and hopefully) interrelated, we recognize the knowledge movement itself as a complex adaptive system with people at the helm, which is continuously shifting and refocusing in response to changing, uncertain, and complex environmental factors. This is detailed in Chapter 5.

The key concept in Chapter 2 is intelligence, both in terms of individuals and organizations. We begin by confirming that we and our organizations are complex adaptive systems, and identifying the special attributes that are part of that understanding. What does it *mean* to be an intelligent complex adaptive system? We explore this from the perspective of the individual knowledge worker as an intelligent complex adaptive learning system (ICALS) and the perspective of the knowledge-centric organization as an intelligent complex adaptive system (ICAS), linking those attributes with the democratic elements and characteristics synthesized from the what's and how's of early philosophers. The stage is now set to dive deeper into what is meant by information, knowledge, and the knowledge movement.

Information – a foundational building block of knowledge – is a basic property of the Universe, as fundamental as matter and energy. Chapter 3 is where we begin to build a deeper understanding from a quantum field perspective of the information rich environment in which we live and work. We lightly touch on Information Literacy, a core skill at the turn of the century which has changed significantly as the Information Economy made a 180 degree turn and a technologically augmented workforce moved into organizational leadership roles. The *use* of information technology is no longer a major concern; rather, the focus today, in a limited attention economy, is on *the truth and trust* of information.

In Chapter 4, now we are ready to take a deeper look at the concept of knowledge, delving into core models that provide metaknowledge about knowledge, which we define as the capacity (potential or actual) to take effective action. We consider *the nature of knowledge*, which is always relative and incomplete, and *why* theory is important, and explore different ways of considering tacit knowledge, by definition that knowledge which is known but cannot be easily voiced or shared.

Chapter 5 takes a deeper look at the knowledge field itself, generally referred to as knowledge management, through the ideas, philosophies, and feelings of its early thought leaders. What is special about this movement? Why does it raise passion in its practitioners? And why are there strong links between democratic attributes and the knowledge movement? And from these thought leaders, four foundational characteristics of the field emerge, including the recognition that the field itself is a complex adaptive system with many possibilities and opportunities.

Chapter 6 explores the relationship of information, knowledge, creativity, and innovation. We draw on findings based on over a decade of researching experiential learning through the expanding lens of neuroscience to provide some core insights for those valuing innovation, and introduce the MIKE (Most Innovative Knowledge Enterprise) award conceptual framework of intellectual capital practice-based innovation.

With the groundwork of critical components of Knowledge Reblooming laid, we move on to Section II, which provides a pragmatic approach to implementing a knowledge strategy or initiative.

SECTION II. Realizing a Reblooming Strategy. In Chapter 7, we first lay out the Reblooming Knowledge Movement (RKM) model, adding an inner layer of petals focused on processes: Leading and visioning, seeking purpose and meaning, networking and communicating, and participating & collaborating, all moving the organization toward resonance and coherence. A guest contributor – ChatGPT, an artificial intelligence chatbot built on GPT large language models developed by OpenAI and released in November 2022 – joins us in affirming the importance of Knowledge Reblooming to the organization. We hope you enjoy ChatGPT's interjections!

In Chapters 8 through 12, we walk through the simple PPIS approach (Plan-Prepare-Implement-Sustain), which can be used for implementing any new strategy or initiative, although in today's workplace *all* strategies and initiatives engage knowledge in some way. Planning (Chapter 8) offers the opportunity to focus on a course of action *prior* to taking any action. While assessing readiness is part of the planning process, it is important enough to demand its own chapter with an appendix (Chapter 9 and Appendix D). We begin the chapter with a discussion of "Readiness for the Unknown", detailing the five critical characteristics for long-term sustainability: adaptability, resilience, alignment, robustness, and quick response.

After completion of the planning stage, attention is fully focused on preparing for implementation (Chapter 10), setting objectives, understanding knowledge flows, and embracing the role of change agent. And then we move into implementation, beginning with leadership commitment visibility and including a reaffirmation of the core of reblooming knowledge: achieving resonance and coherence. Along the way we touch briefly on the continuing role of communities, and the emergent role of knowledging networks. Sustainability is the focus of Chapter 12. Trust, which is entangled throughout the text, is again addressed as well as the importance of transparency, and the MIKE (Most Innovative Knowledge Enterprise) award criteria are introduced as a diagnostic tool for assessing and improving innovative practices, as a basis for international benchmarking studies, and as a vehicle providing a context-rich data pool for guiding innovation research. The book *INside INnovation: Looking from the Inside Out*, compiled and edited by Dr. Alex Bennet and Dr. Rajat Baisya and which is a companion book to *Reblooming the Knowledge Movement*, offers a deeper treatment of the international MIKE criteria, as well as a look at its origins, including reflections from its creators.

Moving through the processes, you will discover some new twists and turns. For example, story thinking as a strategic approach (Plan), the power of resonance and coherence (Prepare), the need to address collaboration overload (Implement), and the hazard of knowledge hiding (Sustain). And finally, we move into a discussion of wisdom.

SECTION III: Special Topics. We are joined by four international experts in their domains of knowledge to expand our learning and offer new ways of moving into an unknown future. Dr. Florin Gaiseanu (Romania and Spain) provides an informational model for living systems. Dr. Milton de Sousa (Portugal) writes on how leaders inspire action through meaningful knowledge, a precursor to his 2023 book release *The Meaningful Leader*. Dr. Chulatep Senivongse (Thailand) shares his passion for improving absorptive capacity in small businesses, specifically exploring Absorptive Capacity 3.0 which is emerging from organizational learning and the learning organization. Finally, Dr. Francisco Javier Carrillo (Mexico) asks us to take a closer look at the potential of knowledge management and knowledge-based development for human flourishing. In this section, we also include detailed treatments of relationship network management, an empowering approach for knowledge workers, and knowledge capacities, ways to shift our perception in the search for new ideas.

SECTION IV: In today's environment, it is critical to understand systems and complexity in terms of our "selves" *and* our organizations. While we have introduced the Intelligent Complex Adaptive System (ICAS) as the knowledge organization and the Intelligent Complex Adaptive Learning System as the individual, that introduction is not deep enough to serve as a foundation for complex decision-making. Therefore, should you choose to engage, we begin this section with the strongest tool we can gift in a book, a deeper understanding of systems and complexity. For this gift we draw on the work of Dr. David Bennet, who has lived a long and productive life of learning as a scientist, a researcher, a teacher, and a facilitator working with senior leadership teams. While both of the authors have focused on systems and complexity for many years, every time we read David's work, we discover something worth further reflection. See Chapter 19 on Systems and Complexity Thinking. Chapter 20 includes 29 representative people-focused tools that are either unique, particularly pertinent to this book, can serve as examples, or are favorites of the authors and contributors. Chapter 21 provides a Knowledge Tool Matrix, which suggests additional tools, with information regarding their use easily available on the internet or through your AI partner. The Knowledge Tool Matrix is meant as a reminder and/or an idea prompter.

Lest you feel the authors have abandoned you, the reader, in a world of tools, we dive back into the subject at hand with an **AFTERWORD**, a sharing of some final thoughts, and add a final poetic offering drafted by ChatGPT and edited and massaged by humans, thus emerging from what we call "Augmented AI". ChatGPT has much to learn from we humans.

Contents

SECTION II

SECTION III

SECTION IV

TABLES

SECTION I

SECTION II

Foreword

In his novel *The Go-Between*, L. P. Hartley wrote that "The past is a foreign country; they do things differently there," and his observation applies to our understanding of the origins and development of Knowledge Management (KM).

For those of us who participated in the early stages of KM, over four decades ago, it seems like only yesterday. On the other hand, for individuals recently joining the workforce and students about to start their working lives, KM is most likely viewed as an historical management theory, supplanted by newer, more relevant approaches. However, as this book will reveal, creating and sustaining holistic knowledge-driven organizations is more relevant today than it has ever been.

The second half of the 20th century witnessed a rapidly changing world and the need for new organizational structures. Post-World War II saw an expansion of global trade, emergence of multinational companies and workforces, and the lengthening of supply chains. It was a period when the emphasis shifted from the production of goods to meeting the needs of customers, expressed in the corporate motto: "The Customer is King." During the 1980s and 1990s, the introduction of personal computers and the World Wide Web (Internet) increased networking and reduced transaction times from weeks to days to minutes.

Responding to these rapid changes, manufacturing and service organizations, and later the public sector, moved from an industrial-era command-and-control mentality to experimenting with post-industrial age structures. With a greater focus on customers as well as growing concerns about worker skills and training, business leaders initially sought to improve work processes through various quality tools and techniques. The 1980s saw the introduction of Total Quality Management (TQM), an attempt to deploy quality-based methods to ensure the production and delivery of standardized goods and services. However, while TQM achieved considerable success in many manufacturing industries, applying it to back offices, services and the public sector did not yield the anticipated results.

Led by management theorists and global consulting firms, competing organizational structures were rapidly introduced, including the 'Agile Organization,' the 'Learning Organization,' and the 'Flat Organization.' While each of these models had their proponents, none seemed to meet the needs of multiple business sectors and demanding customers. By the late 1980s, a few innovative business leaders began experimenting with a new concept – managing organizational knowledge. Word spread by way of conferences, magazine articles and books regarding the impressive business results which could be gained through successfully managing organizational knowledge, and the term 'Knowledge Management' was coined.

It was pointed out early on by some KM proponents and by its detractors that knowledge could not be 'managed.' However, it was agreed that organizational knowledge could be deployed to improve decision-making and innovation. Bob Buckman of Buckman Laboratories was an early pioneer in KM and perhaps best described the true benefits of KM in his 2004 book: *Building a Knowledge-Driven Organization.*

Depending on their background and interests, management 'gurus', consultants and practitioners at the time had different views of KM, ranging from organizational structures to developing people, to capturing organizational memory, to improving innovation capabilities. While each new KM model had its proponents, none seemed to be a one-size-fits-all solution.

During 1997-1998, Teleos, a UK-based KM advisory firm, examined existing KM models and frameworks and then synthesized a composite KM model which became the basis for the Most Admired Knowledge Enterprises (MAKE) Award. Over a period of 20 years, the MAKE Awards recognized the world's leading enterprises at managing organizational knowledge. It became increasingly accepted that leading KM organizations had different knowledge 'drivers', including business sector, founding corporate ethos, style of leadership, processes, employees' skills base, type of customers, etc.

An analysis over a 20-year period of more than 100 World-Class Most Admired Knowledge Enterprises revealed that the critical factor in achieving excellence was leadership. A stable team of dedicated leaders with vision, resources and endurance could create an organizational culture which produced exceptional, measurable results in as little as 3 years. The right senior team enabled organizations to create and deliver knowledge-based products/services/solutions, maximize enterprise intellectual capital, sustain a collaborative knowledge-sharing and learning environment, and create value based on stakeholder knowledge.

However, for every KM success there is at least one perceived failure. MAKE researchers reported that it usually took an organization 5 to 10 years to maximize its knowledge-driven potential. On the other hand, changes in leadership, disruptive technologies and/or mergers/acquisitions could destroy a knowledge-driven organization in less than one year. World-class KM is very fragile by nature.

The advent of the 21st century brought new challenges to organizations and their leaders. Disruptions in global trade, advances in social media, breakthroughs in machine learning, the emergence of the Gig economy, and 'Black Swan' events have created greater perils for the commercial and public sectors. KM was increasingly viewed as yesterday's 'fad' and new approaches, such as rapid innovation and managing intellectual capital, appeared.

Over the past 20 years, there has been an increasing dependence on technology to solve business and social problems. Global search engines, such as Google, and information sites, for example Wikipedia, have gradually replaced traditional sources of knowledge found in libraries and within organizations. Machine learning provides a methodology to categorize and retrieve non-print records, such as photographs and digital and audio recordings. The rapid advancement of Artificial Intelligence (AI) combines increasingly powerful computers, algorithms, and the experiences of thousands of individuals or situations to provide almost instant 'answers' to complex questions. However, the validity of the results depends upon the accuracy of the input variables. On the horizon is a futuristic AI world where humans might be relegated to assisting machines in decision-making.

The authors and contributors to this book should be congratulated for their vision and dedication. Not only does *Reblooming the Knowledge Movement: The Democratization of Organizations* introduce the reader to Knowledge Management practice, but it also provides a compendium of tools and techniques for achieving organizational excellence in today's rapidly changing global environment.

It is true that "The past is a foreign country," but it is also true that we can learn from the past to achieve great things in the future.

Rory L. Chase
Founder of Teleos and The KNOW Network, United Kingdom
Creator of the Most Admired Knowledge Enterprises (MAKE) Awards
Summer 2023

SECTION I

LAYING THE FOUNDATION

We begin this section exploring the democratic elements and characteristics synthesized from the what's and how's of early philosophers, then dive into systems and complexity, specifically looking at the role of intelligence in the human, who can be described as an intelligent complex adaptive learning system (ICALS), and the knowledge organization as an intelligent complex adaptive system (ICAS). With these foundations in hand, we move on to exploring the two triggers whose importance focused the knowledge movement – information and knowledge. By now, you may recognize that for the authors "KM" represents "knowledge movement". Regardless of what you call it, we will explore the initial blossoming of the field under the rubric of knowledge management, sharing the emerging feelings of early thought leaders about the field. And finally, recognizing innovation as an essential ingredient for the long-term success of any organization, we explore the relationships among information, knowledge, creativity, and innovation.

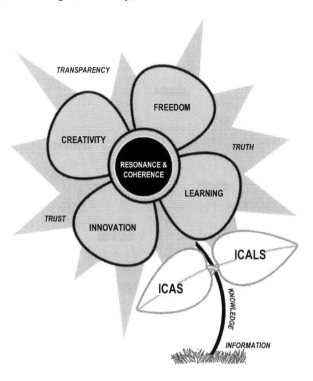

CHAPTER 1

INTRODUCTION TO DEMOCRATIZATION

*Everything that is really great and inspiring is created
by the individual who can labor in freedom.* -Albert Einstein

During the last three generations of our human experience, especially in the more developed nations, we have encountered unprecedented trends impacting organizational cultures and workplaces. What we have been through and what we now know are a prelude to a promising era for caring and creating, building and innovating, in organizations. Of critical importance, we rise on a profoundly new understanding of how we learn and how we think. As we stay the course, a common denominator will be a determining factor in the quality of our future. That nexus of change and progress is democratization. This is not simply democratization as delineated by political boundaries and forces; this is the democratization of our work organizations that support our performance and productivity. It calls upon us to engage brilliantly and collaboratively in the cultures and economies of the world of work.

What you read here will grab your attention at a very deep and personal level. Depending upon your age and where you find yourself in the world today, it will strike you differently than it does others around you. But from whatever direction you look, you may sense that you are part of an unparalleled global transformation. In a few paragraphs below, your perspective of what has transpired in the last century or so will enable you to appreciate how well the world stage is set for what is happening, what you are part of now, and how you will impact the future.

First, we briefly recall the global working environment of the last century. As we come forward in time, the thumbnail description of the changing times will update you to the emergence of this unprecedented period, a period that has been researched, documented and proclaimed as the knowledge economy, the knowledge society, the knowledge era, and what we characterize as the *knowledge movement*. The common element is KNOWEDGE. What is provided in *Reblooming the Knowledge Movement* will help you understand useful and dynamic aspects of knowledge, relevant fields, disciplines, and sciences, including a large collection of facilitative tools and processes like knowledge management.

As the subtitle of *Reblooming* suggests, *The Democratization of Organizations* is a cornerstone, and we offer in this first chapter an introduction to democratization. This cornerstone goes to the heart and soul of knowledge work and is a core driver for knowledge productivity, especially as pertaining to creativity and innovation. Finally, you will find in the Afterword how the democratization cornerstone could enable the next phase in human progress.

If you are a young professional in one of the rapidly changing modern global populations, almost anywhere in the prosperous nations and even beyond, you may find the message of several of the next few paragraphs somewhat distant. Even if you are an avid history buff, what transpired in the past two generations was extreme and accelerated. For others, it may make more sense because they experienced it. Fortunately, you are remarkably inclined to participate in what we are about to describe because of the range of values, skills, and interests you bring to the 21st Century workplace. To be sure, you will be instrumental in the success of what is transpiring. Hold that thought while we introduce the rest of us.

A major portion of the rest have experienced first-hand the full range of what we are about to condense for consideration. And, as we have listened to the previous generation, some who are still among us, their observations resonate with this brief account. The last century began with life in the early 1900's, largely attending to human subsistence activities with global mortality rates averaging less than 50 years. In some countries life expectancy was half of that. As late as the nineteenth century, agriculture by itself employed at least three-quarters of the world's work force.[8] During the time frame from the middle of the 18th Century to the middle of the 19th Century we recall the Industrial Revolution, which took place in Great Britain, continental Europe, and the United States. Although this was a major advancement to technological progress and the standard of living, it was primarily confined to those nations. Concurrently, a devastating legacy of the 20th Century was the loss of over 100 million people to war and genocide. By the end of World War II, the global level of military equipment production had substantially expanded manufacturing enterprises in many countries.

Again, after WWII, during the mid-part of the century there was a major shift in the role of knowledge in the global economy. While knowledge had a definable role for centuries, what transpired then was course changing for the world economy as well as for the U.S. economy. For example, Austrian born economist Fritz Machlup, who authored more than 20 books mainly during his concurrent tenures at New York University and Princeton University, provided a clear case for moving knowledge productivity front and center. His monumental research entitled *The Production and Distribution of Knowledge in the United States* is extensively detailed. It was originally intended to be a ten-volume series, but by the time of his death there were only three volumes completed. Nevertheless, this was enough to clearly establish knowledge as a driver in the modern business world. We should also note, as an example of his international reach, that Machlup was president of the International Economic Association from 1971-1974.

That brings us to the great surprise of the economic boom of post-WWII known as the Golden Age of Capitalism, which created the most inclusive positive economic impact in history beginning from 1950 into the 1970s. The prosperity of this period positively impacted many nations and, surprisingly, included both Germany and Japan and other nations that suffered deeply during WWII. Along with this surge in capitalism came an even deeper appreciation for the growing role of knowledge, including recognition of knowledge as the basic economic resource. It's fascinating to follow the nature, the rise, and the emerging prominence of this human resource. One book that traces the evolution of knowledge is Peter Drucker's work Post-Capitalist Society. He wrote there:

> *Knowledge is now fast becoming the sole factor of production, sidelining both capital and labor. It may be premature (and certainly would be presumptuous) to call ours a "knowledge society"; so far, we have only a knowledge economy.*[9]

Between Machlup and Drucker and the library of books they provided, the foundation for a modern knowledge era and movement was established. This provided a charter for the knowledge management wave of books, concepts, publications, consortiums, and consultants that flourished during the end of the 1990s and the first decade of the 20th Century. Drucker as the "father of modern business management" put out the clarion call: "The purpose of management is the productivity of knowledge" – and it was heard around the world.

As Drucker became noted internationally for his consulting mantra "Management by Objectives", he had to eventually step forward and clarify that he always said, "Management by objectives <u>and self-control</u>." In his view, self-control was a key element for fully engaging the "knowledge worker". For Drucker, the knowledge worker was symbolic of the democratization condition required throughout modern enterprises. He held that workers should not be seen as costs, but rather as assets and investors.

In that regard, the renowned University of Pennsylvania Wharton School Professor, Russel Ackoff, prodigious management consultant, friend of Peter Drucker and author of 35 books, wrote of the new challenge for business enterprises. He recalled in his landmark book *The Democratic Corporation: A Radical Prescription for Recreating Corporate America and Rediscovering Success*"[10] a consulting experience that exemplified what he envisioned:

I once worked with two different districts of the Federal Reserve Bank at the same time. Both had exactly the same functions. Nevertheless, their work environments were completely different. The one conceptualized as a social system operated as a democratic community with a great deal of informal as well as formal participation in decision making. The other was operated as a machine, a rigid bureaucratic hierarchy in which everyone was bounded and knew what those boundaries were. In the former, employee morale at all levels was high; they were having fun at work. Although they did not look as busy as those in the second bank, they were much more productive. They understood how what they did affected the bank's overall performance, and they focused on improving it. This gave them a feeling that what they were doing was of value to society at large. At the other bank, almost all-non managerial employees were bored, could not see the value of what they were doing, and hence did not feel as though they were part of something of value.[11]

There we have it. In so few decades that you don't need more than one hand to count them on, one of the greatest advances in human endeavors emerged. The birth of the knowledge movement. This wasn't an economic breakthrough conceived in a think tank. What presented was the aggregation of a kaleidoscope of human progress and ingenuity that kept pointing to *human knowledge capacity*. Questions resonated from the observation decks. What enterprise form would best support knowledge workers? How would the new generation workforce adapt? What knowledge principles, processes, organization roles, and forms would generate innovation in this new era? How could this advanced understanding of knowledge be transferred to the next level of human endeavors? What had we learned about unleashing the human spirit – like freedom and democratization? The list was considerable and perhaps self-generating. The future would tell.

But first there would be a hiatus from the knowledge movement. The new century came knocking with two horrific wars. The first decade was draining. The economic devastation of the dot.com tech bubble bursting was followed by a collapse of the housing bubble. Both of these disasters extended internationally at the loss level of $6 trillion. If you aggregate these self-afflicted disasters with the onslaught of terrorism, you have a nation regrouping to recover its footing. It was in such a time that the tide of the knowledge movement receded and gave way to the steady, easier low-hanging fruit of less bold endeavors such as large-scale data management technologies. By this time there was considerable experience with data and information, so the comfort in using, the ease of performance, and the predictability of profit were an immense consolation. Meanwhile, the knowledge movement lingered primarily on the sideline, waiting, ready to rebloom.

The human spirit and its yearning for freedom to exercise individual agency can only be suppressed for so long. And while it appears to take a number of learning cycles to truly embed the larger lessons of life in the collective human experience, as the survival of humanity succeeds, this *does* happen. The complex adaptive systems that we are MUST always be growing or declining such that our choices eventually determine either our extinction, or our survival at a higher level of consciousness.

The rise of the knowledge movement has resulted in a more democratic approach to the way work is accomplished in organizations, supporting the emergence of democratic leadership – also called participative leadership, collaborative leadership, and shared leadership – as well as touching other leadership approaches such as transformational leadership, situational leadership, collective leadership, servant leadership and inspirational leadership, all of which include basic elements of collaboration – working together with others to achieve a common goal. This is not surprising since knowledge, as contrasted to information, is right at the core of what it is to be human such that it truly cannot be controlled and fully managed but rather nurtured into existence.

As will be detailed in Chapter 3, information is considered a measure of the degree of organization expressed by any non-random pattern or set of patterns. Information exists in the human brain in the form of stored or expressed neuronal patterns that may be activated and reflected upon through conscious thought. When that information is effectively acted upon – whether consciously or unconsciously – it is considered knowledge, which is applied information to create value. This is consistent with more formal definitions such as "justified true belief" (Plato), or a bit more recently, "the capacity (potential or actual) to take effective action".[12] Thus, "knowledge" is directly tied to action, situation-dependent and context-sensitive, and as noted above, is at the very core of what it is to be human. A deeper discussion of knowledge is in Chapter 4.

The knowledge movement, then, in the organizational setting is not only the management of "knowledge" per se but is rather very much concerned with managing information and leading and supporting people, facilitating the flow of knowledge (information that can be effectively applied), and, quite simply put but requiring significant focus to accomplish, connecting information to information, people to information, information to people, and people to people. All of this activity is in support of the four major organizational processes – creativity, problem-solving, decision-making and implementation – which can be condensed into decision-making and innovation. So, as much as early advocates of KM insisted on focusing on technology solutions – which is fortunate because the technology explosion raised awareness of and supported the KM field, enabling learning as we discovered what KM *really* was all about

– eventually the concepts of intellectual capital, communities of practice, and social networks wove their way into the spotlight, bringing people back into the middle of the business equation.

EMERGENCE OF DEMOCRATIC CHARACTERISTICS

For a moment, reflect on the following descriptions in terms of a single organization in the knowledge movement landscape:

- People cooperating together to solve problems through rational means with mutual respect and good will.
- People dialoguing to ensure responsible decisions to common problems.
- People evaluating each other's assertions based on reason and evidence free of coercive influences.

While those may just sound like good business practices—and definitely part of a knowledge-centric organization approach—they are democratic ideas emerging from historical philosophers focused on the idea of a democratic governance.[13]

Pericles (430 BCE) called for equal justice to all in their private differences, and class considerations not being allowed to interfere with merit, with the freedom enjoyed in government extending to the "ordinary life". **Aristotle** built on the idea of liberty, with the best government doing that which is best both in abstract and in terms of the relativity to circumstances. **John Locke** felt that there was a social contract between legitimate government and the people, and that the only legitimate government was one based on the consent of the people. If that contract (trust) was violated, the people had the right to rebel. Locke's views are very much echoed in the U.S. Declaration of Independence.[14]

In his book *The Spirit of the Laws*, (1748), a focus of **Montesquieu**, the French political theorist, was on the necessity of "public virtue" for those in power, that is, motivation by a desire to achieve the greater good. Montesquieu felt that without leadership virtue a "democratic republic" was likely to be destroyed through conflict of various factions, each of which would pursue their own narrow interests at the expense of others. The notion of individual "liberty" (or freedom) was strongly argued by **John Stuart Mill** in his work *On Liberty* (1859). Mill saw this as a liberty of thought and discussion, advocating for a freedom of association, and free opinion, seeing the "collision of adverse opinions" as critical to the search for truth.

John Dewey was focused on the importance of individual self-development and growth. The democratic approach provided freedoms that facilitated that development and growth, specifically, "the freedom to exchange ideas and opinions with others, the freedom to form associations with others to pursue common goals, and the freedom to determine and pursue one's own conception of the good life." In his book *Democracy and Education* (1916), Dewey defined democracy beyond a form of government as a "mode of associated life", with people (citizens) cooperating with each other to rationally solve common problems (critical inquiry and inquisitive mind) with mutual respect and good will. Further, he saw this mode as one that should be subject to criticism and improvement according to situation relevancy and public interest.

Dewey contributed largely to the theory and practice of education. His attitude toward experiential learning built on William James' amazement at the continuity of human consciousness.[15] Dewey believed that "the principle of continuity of experience means that every experience both takes up something from those which have gone before and modifies in some way the quality of those which come after."[16] He was right. Quite appropriately, his experiential learning model was built upon by Kurt Lewin, Jean Piaget, David Kolb, and J. E. Zull, which provided the foundation for the Intelligent Complex Adaptive Learning System (ICALS) model of experiential learning[17] developed by David Bennet, which embraces neuroscience findings since the turn of the century to explore experiential learning from the inside-out.

Dewey was very much focused on the rights of the individual. In an educational setting, he observed that an educator needs to "have that sympathetic understanding of individuals as individuals, which gives him an idea of what is actually going on in the minds of those who are learning."[18] This is the concept of affective attunement that was going to emerge as a neuroscience finding years later. Regarding individual's rights in organizations, in his book *The Public and Its Problems* (1927) he said that an important feature of social democracy is the right of workers to directly participate in control of the organization where they were employed. He also emphasized the importance of community dialogue as a critical democratic component.

In the 1970's it was German philosopher and social theorist **Jürgen Habermas** who described what he called an "ideal speech situation" for a group to achieve a rational consensus. This is the idea that assertions be based on reason and evidence with no coercive influences, physical or psychological. He pushed this even further by saying that these participants would be *motivated by their desire to garner rational consensus*, bringing in the belief in a common human value. This "ideal speech situation" served as a model and standard for free and open discussion. Largely building on the thought of John Locke, in his book *A Theory of Justice* (1971), American philosopher **John Rawls** revived the idea of a social contract with a focus on liberty, equal opportunity to seek work, and the distribution of wealth.

Thus, these early philosophers have not only explored "what" a democracy is but have provided an idea of "how" participation can occur in organizations, including the supportive attributes that enable the "how". For example, looking from the viewpoint of the four major processes in the organization, decision-making requires employee participation, community, and dialogue based on truth, trust, reason, and responsibility, that is, making responsible decisions. Problem solving requires cooperation, critical inquiry and rational consensus (the "ideal speech" situation proposed by Habermas) based on rationality, mutual respect, good will, an inquisitive mind, and an openness to criticism and improvement. The necessary "freedoms", which are also considered as liberties, include the liberty of thought and open discussion, and the freedoms of association, opinion (since the "collision of adverse opinions" is critical to the search for truth), the exchange of ideas, and choice (in pursuit of the good life). All of this as part of a sociomoral atmosphere with the following attributes: rights of the individual, individual self-development and growth, individual responsibility, equal opportunity based on merit, distribution of wealth, and a coercive-free environment. And at the core of this environment is a sense of public virtue, that is, motivated by the desire to do greater good. See Figure 1-1. That sets a pretty high bar for the democratization of organizations!

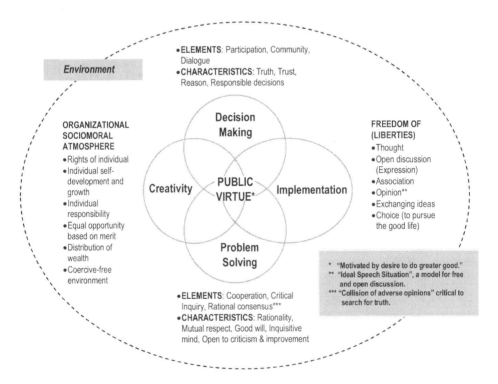

Figure 1-1. Democratic elements and characteristics synthesized from the what's and how's of early philosophers.

VIEWPOINTS OF ORGANIZATIONAL DEMOCRATIZATION

Early ideas of "corporate democracy" implied a governance structure where people engaged in "ruling". This refers back to the Greek origins of the word "democracy", which derives from *demokratia* (which is from *demos*, meaning people) and *kratein* (meaning to rule). Thus, in its strictest interpretation, this would mean "shared residual claims by all members of the organization in combination with democratic decision-making rules and embedded in a supportive organization structure."[19] However, coming in many forms and shapes, the concept of democratization of organizations, particularly in many European countries, was generally a reflection of employee representation in formal works councils or on the non-executive board, and in the U.S. this largely took the form of unions, with some organizations moving into employee ownership.

An example of an early "corporate democracy" which embedded all of these three concepts is a Dutch firm who in the 1970s implemented an innovative model of corporate democracy. Established in 1925, the company originated as a single bicycle shop but today comprises 26 separate companies which include central heating systems, smart thermostats, and solar panels as well as service and maintenance. Regarding the concept of *shared residual claims*, half of the profits are used to finance new investments, and the other half is equally distributed across employees of the firm. Re the concept of *democratic decision-making rules,* all employees have a voice in the firm's policies and, at least indirectly, in both strategic and operational decision-making. This occurs through an elaborate election procedure, with works councils functioning as the linking-pins with management teams. Re the concept of *supportive organizational structure*, centralization is combined with decentralization, with a constitution which details the organizational structure, decision-making rules, and stakeholder roles and responsibilities in a legally enforceable document. The structure includes a company-owned financial institution, an employee association (with all employees as members), a holding company, and a network structure of business units. Clearly, core elements are *communication* and *employee participation.*

While this represents an unusual example of democratization of an organization, there is wide application in many countries where the influence of labor has been institutionalized, for example, in works councils and labor unions. There is also significant literature dealing with human resource management (HRM) specifically related to employee empowerment, some of which engage employees in determining their own work environment. Further, there has been much attention to financial incentives, which, as forms of engaging and rewarding employee participation, are the distribution of wealth.[20]

Rigorous research by Rousseau and Rivero exploring democracy as a way of organizing in a knowledge economy used a broad definition of democracy in organizations focused on the power of the people which manifests in "ways of thinking, behaving, and organizing that promote participation in and influence over the decision affecting their everyday lives."[21] They refer to three distinct types of democracy: (1) political democracy, which is supported by empowered individuals and groups with freedom of speech, freedom of expression, and freedom of the press; (2) economic democracy, which is economic freedom connoting personal agency with freedom of contract as well as egalitarianism, a moral virtue which diminishes differences and seeks equality; and (3) electronic democracy, built on connection and communication, which engages freedom of expression and access to people in authority.[22]

A democratic in nature culture – an emergent quality in organizations which reflects beliefs, values, and norms – supports broad participation, a high level of trust, and accountability characterized by collective problem-solving[23] and some level of participative decision-making. While often defined as the way work gets done, culture is largely a mindset which, if democratic in nature, would be based on participation, cooperation, collaboration, and compromise as well as human attitudes based on respect and mutual trust. Collective interaction facilitates these features.[24]

DEMOCRATIC LEADERSHIP

With freedom of thought and respect for contribution at the core, democratic leadership is an open leadership style that has been called   participative leadership, collaborative leadership (the leadership style embedded in the knowledge organization model), and shared leadership. The common theme is *the building of consensus through collaboration*. Opinions are invited and honored, with open conversation and the sharing of ideas encouraged, and creativity rewarded. This would be concurrent with shared understanding and commitment in terms of a direct line of sight to the vision and mission of the organization, and the specific organizational intent of the team and/or community of which a level of self-direction and self-organization is expected.

Freedom of thought, freedom of expression, and freedom of association are all critical to democratic leadership. As Traci Fenton, Founder of WorldBlu, says in her recent book, *Freedom at Work: The Leadership Strategy for Transforming Your Life, Your Organization, and Our World*:

> *A democratic style of leadership has been responsible for more ingenuity, prosperity, happiness, and success in human history than any other style of leaderships because a democratic stye of leadership taps into the core idea that we are made to be free.*[25]

In exploring collaborative leadership (democratic leadership), it was found that leaders with the best results do not rely on one style.[26] Leadership evolves with the times. As the large body of work on leadership has expanded in response to the knowledge economy, there are half a dozen forms of leadership that have come to the fore: direct leadership, servant leadership, situational leadership, collective leadership, inspirational leadership, and transformational leadership.

Related to the idea of **Direct Leadership** are authenticity, presence by example, leadership by example, role modeling, leading from the front, and setting the climate to excel. Values are directly related to authenticity; since an authentic person cannot be what they are not, values are highly visible. Presence by example and leadership by example are closely related, with presence allowing for leadership participation without necessarily involving the leader in the same activities as employees. Presence represents awareness of intent and expectation, and can be perceived as having a spiritual orientation, that is, a visible—and invisible—connection. Leadership by example and role modeling are closely related, ways of connecting with people and inspiring them to be the best they can be. Leadership by example also has a direct connection to accountability, with the leader being accountable to himself and accountable to his people.

Servant leadership describes a leader who is there to serve and not be served. Servant leadership is an active process that involves both engagement and reflection. This is a leader who has a caring heart who has the ability to reach out and reach down, no matter how deep the organization. Leading with empathy and compassion, the servant leader takes a personal interest in each employee, drawing out what is special and showing how these special talents can contribute to the organization. Servant leadership would include affiliative behavior, the element of "create emotional bonds and harmony", and coaching behavior, the element of "develop people for the future." A servant leader helps others to help themselves. As voiced by Greenleaf, a servant leader is servant first and only then aspires to lead.[27] This service orientation means that people and community take priority, above personal objectives.

As can be seen, this type of leadership is built on developing relationships, dialoging, listening and respecting the space needed by employees to be themselves and put their best foot forward. Perhaps it goes without saying that the servant leader is a nurturer who creates an environment where employees can operate as an effective team.

A more recent emergence which is responding to disruptive work environments advanced by the pandemic is **Meaningful leadership**, which lays at the intersection between meaning, work, and leadership. In today's environment, employees are rethinking the purpose and meaning in their lives, and many are looking to their organizations for the answers. As Milton de Sousa forwards in his book *The Meaningful Leader*, considering the movement from crisis to crisis over the past 20 years, it is not surprising that "the demand for organizations to provide meaningful work has become increasingly relevant".[28] See Chapter 15 on Meaningful Leadership.

Situational leadership is common sense leadership, a natural way of sizing up a situation and using the situation to effect outcomes. Just as knowledge, leadership is situation dependent and context sensitive, offering flexibility at the point of action. Situational theories say that leadership is a product of demand and is *dependent on the situation at hand.* The specific factors of a situation determine who emerges as a leader.[29] If there is time, a leader's social network can be used to make sense of the situation before making a decision (a social form of learning). The point made here is that decision-making is based not only on what information is available, but also on the circumstances of the situation at hand. That approach requires a leader to have the ability to read the circumstances, appreciate them, use good judgment, and have the courage to take a position at the right time. Situational leadership demands choices.

Collective leadership recognizes that although the leader must make the call and take responsibility, the knowledge resides within his or her team. This is quite close to the idea of collaborative leadership. In collective leadership everyone is expected to take responsibility, exercising his or her initiative to get the work done. With this self-direction there is still the need to collaborate, with leaders at all levels benefiting from listening and tapping into the different perspectives offered throughout the organization. While someone needs to make the call, the knowledge resides throughout the whole team and the team has collective ownership of the issues. This is consistent with the democratic element " build consensus through participation."

Inspirational leadership is about getting a message across to people while simultaneously engaging them. While relative to a specific individual or related group and creating an emotional connection, inspirational leadership is simultaneously mission focused, painting a picture of a bright future. The living message of inspirational leaders resonates with others, building on core concepts such as believing in what you do, setting high goals, knowing your job well, learning from others, and making things happen, all circling back to an individual's purpose, motivation and commitment. This is true *idea resonance*. Although an entirely different approach than servant leadership, inspirational leadership relates to the coaching behavior, "develop people for the future."

Transformational leadership is about breaking new ground to achieve a higher level of excellence in all areas. This could involve changing mental models, mindsets, attitudes and value systems, or raising the knowledge and skills of employees to a new height of excellence. In transformational leadership we see pacesetting behavior, the element of "expect excellence and self-direction." Transformational leadership could also mean moving the organization toward commitment and engagement, winning the hearts and minds of employees. This would include affiliative behavior, the element of "create emotional bonds and harmony."

As with all forms of leadership, it must be recognized that values play a significant role in transformation. Not only is there the need to be able to paint a compelling and believable picture of the future, the transformational leader must gain trust and confidence through his authenticity. Further, giving employees a big idea is not sufficient to guide the process of transformation. Rather, there is much to be done, building consensus (democratic behavior), discussing issues over time, gaining more and more perspectives to help guide future decisions and employee thinking as the transformation occurs.

Figure 1-2 below shows aspects of each of these forms that contribute to democratic leadership. As can be seen, all of these forms include basic elements of collaboration, that is, working together with others to achieve a common goal.

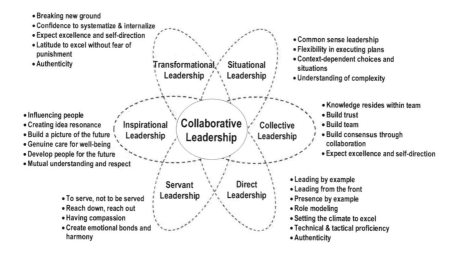

Figure 1-2. Six types of leadership and their aspects that contribute to collaborative (democratic) leadership.

While elements of all six of the leadership styles briefly explicated above feed into collaborative leadership, as we entered the knowledge era each emerged as a separate focus in response to changing organizational needs. Leadership is, above all, situational, historical, context-sensitive, a matter of character, and is time and space dependent.

In her recent book, Fenton bases her theory on three pillars: a freedom-centered mindset (breaking through limitations, making better decisions, and acting with clarity and confidence); freedom-centered leadership (leading through freedom rather than through fear); and freedom-center design (developing a world-class culture). Her world-class culture is based on ten organizational democracy principles, which serve well as a reminder to what a world-class organization adheres. Briefly, both synthesizing from Fenton and adding some of our thoughts to the descriptions, the ten single word principles as forwarded by Fenton are:

1. *Purpose and vision* (reason for being and intentional direction)

2. *Integrity* (high morality and ethics for individuals and organization)

3. *Dialogue and Listening* (application of humility (see the tool in Section IV); deepening of meaning and connection)

4. *Transparency* (openness and sharing), with trust and truth the outer pedal layer of the Reblooming Knowledge Movement (RKM) model.

5. *Accountability* (responsible to self and others)

6. *Decentralization* (shared power throughout organization; decisions at the point of knowledge and action)

7. *Individual and Collective* (valuing and respecting right of both)

8. *Choice* (honoring diversity; opening the door to possibilities)

9. *Fairness and Dignity* (just and impartial treatment for all; recognition of inherent worth of each)

10. *Reflection and Evaluation* (individual and organizational commitment to learning; continuous feedback and growth).[30]

These all make sense, and while perhaps these are things we "know", somehow, in a volatile environment, they often seem to be forgotten. In commitment to these principles, since 2007 WorldBlu has issued an open invitation to take their "Freedom at Work Scorecard", which shows where an organization falls in the continuum of organizational democracy. Their analysis looks at organizational design, which pinpoints what is succeeding and what is not. The intent is to help organizations move out of fear-based leadership to freedom-based leadership, which in turn has proven the organization to be more profitable; more adaptable, responsive, and robust; more human; and more fun and meaningful. Further, in addition to serving as a stabilizing factor and minimizing waste, organizational democracy "inspires full engagement and a sense of ownership", "is faster in the execution and implementation stage", and "achieves bottom-line goals without killing employees' soul in the process".[31] This free assessment offers a unique learning opportunity for organizations in today's business environment to assess where they are and how they can improve. Fear has no place in future sustainability.

THE FREEDOM OF THOUGHT

The knowledge movement – with a refocus on the business value of intellectual capital and its criticality to innovation – has facilitated the growth and spread of thought leadership. In the mid-1950's it was posited there were 555,000 "opinion leaders" in the United States. By 1971, by extrapolation, this number was somewhere around one million. By 1985, it was found that one out of every 200 Americans was taking the opportunity to lead at one time or another, on one issue or another, in one community or another. The knowledge revolution and the galloping rate of growth of complexity "means that a growth curve of the requirement for leaders (if anyone were clever enough to construct such an index) would show a steeper climb than any other growth rate in our political economy."[32] But it goes even farther than that. The organizational focus on knowledge – the recognition of its value and necessity to the organization in today' environment – has ushered in an explosion of thought leadership.

The term thought leader emerged in the knowledge movement vocabulary just before the turn of the century. For example, in 1998, Booz, Allen & Hamilton, working with the world's largest companies and those that led them, interviewed top executives, authors and academicians to address big concerns such as defining values and vision, managing people and risk, adapting to changed markets and new technology, and assessing performance and portfolio mix. When the results were in, the President and COO, Brian Dickie, stated:

> [These issues] have only become more important as competition intensifies, the speed of computers multiplies, and the economy becomes increasingly global. At the same time, because of external pressures and changing management approaches, new ways of thinking about those concerns have swept through boardrooms and across factory floors with remarkable synchronicity … We call this cutting-edge group 'Thought Leaders'.[33]

Recognizing the competitive advantage to have more and better ideas, by the 2003 publication of *The Ultimate Book of Business Thinking* thought leadership was cited as an idea that had already delivered significant and lasting benefits. Further, it was recognized that thought leaders not only have the ability to creatively form innovative ideas, but because of their deep knowledge in a specific domain – enabling recognition of patterns and higher-order conceptual relationships – they have the ability to scan the environmental opportunity space and perceive potential future issues and opportunities.

While no two thought leaders are alike – each with different interests, diverse educations, varied professional experience, divergent passions, individuated thought patterns and connections, and unique social networks – there are a number of related characteristics and patterns that emerged in a

Mountain Quest Institute 2004 research study of early knowledge movement thought leaders (the KMTL study). Thought leaders are people who:

- Have a deep understanding of their field of focus, engaging critical thinking, systems thinking and recognizing patterns.
- Recognize in a textured and nuanced way the complexities of human behavior.
- Are able to develop the taxonomy and language for the unknown as well as apply it to develop something that has an impact on and benefit to society.
- Are learners with the capacity to shift perspectives, pushing the boundaries and listening and giving fresh ideas in such a way that people walk away with a different perspective, which drives their decisions and actions.
- Are intelligent, creative, authentic, and relatively humble, considering collaboration as the best means toward achieving effectiveness and efficiency.
- Are intrinsically motivated, with an element of altruism, a desire to do the greater good, as they focus on making a difference.
- Have the ability to turn ideas into reality, influencing people's behavior and changing the way people think about the world.

Again, as highlighted, we see a consistency in many of the words and concepts forwarded by early thought leaders in the knowledge movement and the elements and characteristics forwarded by the early philosophers when defining and describing democracy.

CLOSING THOUGHTS

In 2003 the Academy of Management sponsored a conference in Seattle on "Democracy in a Knowledge Economy". In that conference, Rousseau and Rivero forwarded that "Although we are increasingly likely to be governed by democratic political systems, our workplaces are seldom democratic."[34] A central concern addressed was the "disconnection between the expansion of democratic governments and the relatively limited facets of democracy practiced in the workplace."[35] And, indeed, for a number of years it did appear that the world WAS more likely to be increasingly governed by democratic political systems.

However, while the battle for democratic freedom in terms of governments around the world is still very much underway, organizations have slowly and deliberately embraced the knowledge movement – called by many different names – and a multitude of entangled innovation approaches as it became clear that knowledge, flows were critical to innovation. And you cannot have knowledge without good information in terms of currency, relevance, and truth.

In a large amount of literature looking from diverse viewpoints, democracy as a form of governance has been predicted as doomed to failure. For example, Linz and Stepan forward that democratic regimes are prone to self-destruction.[36] This is because a governing "democratic" body can use democratic processes to destroy itself. We see examples of this in the political environments of today. As Dahl firmly states, no principle or procedural requirements, nor "absolute rights can prevent tyranny from emerging."[37] There is a tension between equality and liberty. As de Tocqueville forwards, equality will crush and likely destroy liberty "because equality facilitates majority despotism, it threatens liberty."[38]

Yet the rise of the knowledge movement – the valuing of intellectual capital and the emergence of technological advancements and connectivity triggering shifts in prosocial democratic behaviors – has slowly but consistently spread throughout organizations. We will further explore this in the next few chapters.

CHAPTER 2

EXPANDING HUMAN INTELLIGENCE

Whatever else the successful organization of the future may be,
it will be a place where the intelligence of every member
is treasured and allowed to bloom. -Warren Bennis[39]

We – our "selves" and our organizations – are complex adaptive systems. It's not a matter of our saying this; rather, by definition, and by virtue of being alive and reading this book, it is who we are. To understand our possibilities and how the knowledge movement is empowering those possibilities, it is important to understand what it is to be human, this "who we are", and our capacity for intelligence. With this end in mind, we set the stage by offering learning points from foundational works written by the authors, two very different books, yet both with learning and knowledge at the core.

Unleashing the Human Mind: A Consilience Approach to Managing Self. Grounded in the Intelligent Complex Learning System (ICALS) theory based on over a decade of researching experiential learning through the expanding lens of neuroscience.

Organizational Survival in the New World: The Intelligent Complex Adaptive System (ICAS). The knowledge organization based on research in complexity and neuroscience – and incorporating networking theory and knowledge management – turning the living system metaphor into a reality for organizations.

It was near the end of the 20th century before we began to clearly recognize that people are complex adaptive systems, and that the entangled, dynamically interacting physical, mental, emotional, and spiritual systems *cannot be separated from each other*. As Reality System Theory confirms, "The human reality is a dynamic holistic system subject to the continuous ebb and flow of intellectual, emotional, and spiritual influences."[40]

A system is a group of elements or objects, the relationships among them, their attributes, and some boundary that allows one to distinguish whether an element is inside or outside the system. Complex systems consist of a large number of interrelated elements (parts) that may or may not have nonlinear relationships, feedback loops, and dynamic uncertainties very difficult to understand and predict. A complex adaptive system (CAS) co-evolves with the environment through *adaptation*, the process by which a system improves its ability to survive and grow through internal adjustments. Adaptation may be responsive, internally adjusting to external forces, or it may be proactive, internally changing so that it can influence the external environment. A CAS has partially ordered subsystems—with various levels of self-organization—that evolve over time.[41]

As complex adaptive systems continuously interact with their environment and adapt, they operate at some level of perpetual disequilibrium, which contributes to their unpredictable behavior.[42] Having nonlinear relationships, a CAS creates global properties that are called emergent because they emerge from multiple elements and their relationships and actions, making it difficult to trace these emergent characteristics back to their origins. In an organization, culture is an emergent property, a result of the actions and interactions among people in the organization and the environment over time.

While visible, emergent properties cannot typically be understood through analysis and logic because of the large number of elements and relationships. As Johnson points out, "It wouldn't truly be considered emergent until those local interactions resulted in some kind of discernible macro-behavior."[43] An example is life, along with many of the behaviors we each exhibit.

As can be seen, emergence is a property of a system that its separate parts do not have. A good example of this phenomenon is consciousness. "No single neuron has consciousness, but the human brain does have consciousness as an emergent property."[44] In the midst of all this change – and despite the need for the disequilibrium to adapt – most individuals have a tendency to seek stability. Yet the very disequilibrium that a system requires in order to adapt provides the uncertainty that challenges stability. In a changing, uncertain and complex business environment, what this means in an organizational setting is that when management seeks stability through control – which occurs in the bureaucratic model – the elements of the system (people) cannot self-organize and cannot adapt, and the "system" (organization) will fail.

Reality System Theory looks through the lens of quantum physics, building on Heisenberg's uncertainty principle[45] and the contextualism of the quantum field.[46] The now-classic uncertainty principle refers to the particle/wave fluctuation and contextualism refers to context sensitivity, that is, change as a function of time and surroundings. Of contextualism, Wilber reminds us that, "Meaning is context-dependent, and contexts are boundless."[47] As we now recognize through the focus on knowledge since the turn of the century, all knowledge is context sensitive and situation dependent.[48] Thus, it is paramount that in the organization decisions be made at the point of action *where the knowledge in context exists*. A more extensive treatment of systems and complexity thinking is included in Chapter 19.

The Human as an ICALS

While our first inclination when talking about learning is to pull up a vision of the brain, which is a molecular structure and the fluids that flow within and through that structure, it is the mind, created by neurons and their firings and connections, which is the totality of the *patterns in the brain and throughout the body*, that encompasses all our thoughts, ideas and perceptions. Thus, we use the term mind/brain to refer to both the structure and the patterns emerging within the structure *and* throughout the nervous system.[49] Note that while the brain has historically been recognized as the seat of control, the body-mind in its entirety acts as an information network with no fixed hierarchy.[50] There is a discussion of "hierarchy" below.

As we interact with life, our neuronal circuitry rewires itself in response to stimulation. Neurons are not bound to each other physically and have the flexibility to repeatedly create, break and recreate relationships with other neurons, the process of plasticity. Axons and dendrites – which are appendages treelike in nature – enable the exchange of information among neurons. As a matter of reference, it is estimated that the average brain contains 86 billion neurons,[51] with each connected through synaptic connections or small gaps through which neurotransmitters can flow to about 10,000 other neurons.

Thus, the total possible synaptic connections in the brain is calculated in the hundreds of trillions. The patterns of neuronal connections – the flow of small electrical impulses through the branch-like axons and dendrites, together with the flow of molecules through the synaptic junctions – create the patterns within the mind/brain. The dendrites (collecting inputs) and axons (providing outputs) are unique properties of neurons. Further, neurons create spikes, what are called "action potentials", which are patterns of changes in electrical signals starting near the cell body and traveling along the axon until reaching the end of every branch, at which point it can make connections to other neuron dendrites (synaptic connections). This is consistent with the idea of Hebbian learning, which forwards that when we learn something connections are strengthened and when we forget something connections are weakened (*neurons that fire together, wire together*). Forgetting occurs when unused connections disappear.

Take a moment to reflect on this concept of "action potentials" as the "potential" aspect of knowledge in an organizational setting, where through self-organization people can interact, collaborating and sharing their knowledge in response to a challenge or opportunity which, in context, may start with a small interaction within the organization or between the organization and the business environment. The freedom to act is essential to taking effective action, that is, by definition, knowledge.

Experiential Learning

Learning is the creation of knowledge; and humans are experiential learners. Note that "the very act of thinking is a form of movement",[52] or experience. Building on the intellectual thought of John Dewey, Kurt Lewin and Jean Piaget – with somewhat different terminology and diagrams but with closely related functional processes – in 1984 David Kolb detailed "the process whereby knowledge is created through the transformation of experience."[53] Kolb considered this work a *theory*, not just a model. His model is characterized as a cycle involving four adaptive modes, namely, *concrete experience, reflective observation, abstract conceptualization,* and *active experimentation*. While individuals have learning preferences, all four of these modes are available to healthy people. Since learning is the creation of knowledge, which is the focus of this book, a brief explanation of these four modes is included here.

Concrete experience is a form of knowing that comes from the grasping of experience by apprehension. Apprehension is a formed idea, the ability to understand, to grasp the importance and meaning of something. From a philosophic viewpoint, it is "that understanding of an experience that consists in knowing what an experience is like; and we know what an experience is like by virtue of having that experience."[54]

Apprehension includes the sub-elements of sensing, awareness, attention, intuition, and feelings.[55] It is the experiencing of everything in your immediate space with an awareness that does not require thinking.[56] While it may be tacit in nature, you know these things immediately and without rational or conscious thought. Feelings are a very important part of concrete experience and can significantly modulate the learning process and its results. Positive emotions excite an individual to learn. When we are excited about something, our minds are more open, and we look to building ideas; negative emotions close off ideas.

Reflective observation is careful thought, an idea, making sense of what is observed through the process of reconsidering previous actions, events, and decisions. Jung felt that the internal world of concepts, ideas, and fantasy was equal or superior to the objective reality of the external world.[57] While at least in Western society the active mode tends to dominate the reflection mode, innovation requires a high level of reflective observation. Sub-elements include understanding, meaning, truth/how things work, intuition, and integration (a search for unity).[58]

Abstract conceptualization is comprehension, the ability to grasp the meaning of something, with the sub-elements of concepts, ideas, logic, problem solving, creativity, building models and theories, anticipation, control, rigor, and discipline,[59] all elements that enable effective decision-making and innovation. Through abstract conceptualization, problems are solved by recalling ideas and past experiences from memory and creating new ideas and solutions to problems (the process of associative patterning, with incoming information associated with past experiences and learning). Comprehension allows one to crate and analyze a model of a situation, to communicate it to others, and to predict and recreate those apprehensions.

Active Experimentation refers to movement, energetic activity, doing something in order to achieve a purpose, an interaction between the individual and the environment. This action mode is the domain of knowledge, which is directly tied to taking effective action. Sub-elements include focal attention, object-based logic, and heightened boundary perception.[60] An orientation toward active experimentation "focuses on actively influencing people and changing situations",[61] emphasizing practical application, doing, accomplishing.

The Importance of Social Engagement

In 2002 biologist J. E. Zull expanded Kolb's model, suggesting that there was a related view of the human brain and that Kolb's learning cycle arose naturally from the structure of the brain.

In 2010, nuclear physicist David Bennet completed a ten-year study of emerging research in neuroscience with a focus on adult experiential learning. The neuroscience findings emerging from this study are in Appendix A. Pondering on the human as an integrated, biological and complex system entangled across the physical, mental, emotional and spiritual dimensions, Bennet undertook a scientific analysis of thinking and learning in the human brain through the lens of consilience. Kolb's model and Zull's overlay provided a baseline for development of an expanded experiential learning model, which supports the Intelligent Complex Adaptive Learning System (ICALS).[62]

Through this process, Bennet recognized that *Self* served as the underlying foundation of learning, with acknowledgement of the role of the environment in the learning process. Thus – adding to the four modes of concrete experience, reflective observation, abstract conceptualization, and active experimentation – the fifth mode of social engagement became clear. See Figure 2-1. While Kolb noted the influence of the environment on internal learning, today we recognize that the environment is actively (and continuously) engaged in the learning process. For example, an enriched environment can produce a personal internal reflective world of imagination and creativity, affecting both active experimentation and concrete experience. Since the mind is an associative patterner, the things, people, and potential higher-order influences in our environment very much trigger our thoughts. Further, we also now know that we are social creatures, just beginning to wake up to "the complexity of our own brains, to say nothing of how brains are linked together … all of our biologies are interwoven".[63] Given this understanding – which is explored in Chapter 9 – sub-elements can be grouped into social support and social interaction.

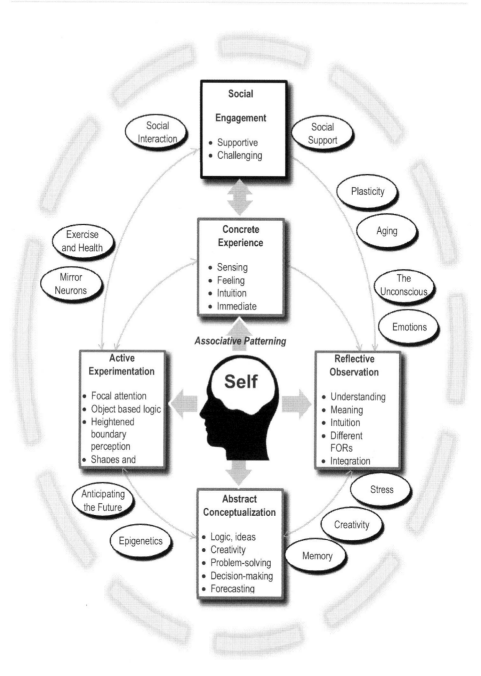

Figure 2-1. The Intelligent Complex Adaptive Learning System.

Social Engagement includes social support and social interaction. Sub-elements of social support – which emerges from an enriched environment, social bonding, and affective attunement (respect and trust) – are an open mind; risk-taking; willingness to listen and learn; reducing stress and fear; creating resonance with people and ideas; and contributing to the evolution and sculpting of the brain. Sub-elements of social interaction – which facilitates learning through energetic unconscious exchanges such as occur through mirror neurons and engaging physical learning mechanisms naturally evolved in the brain – are accelerating learning and creativity; enhancing understanding, meaning, truth and how things work; developing a shared language; and supporting use and understanding of concepts, metaphors, anecdotes and stories. [64]

BEING AN INTELLIGENT SYSTEM

It is not a coincidence that the sub-elements of all five learning modes are complementary to/support the knowledge movement spurred by the embedding of "knowledge management systems" in the organization. Nor is it a coincidence that the knowledge movement expanded from the initial focus on technology to a focus on intellectual capital as the bottom line of the organization, to recognizing the value of communities of practice, to a focus on social networking and knowledge sharing, and, as the spiral upward continued, a refocus on innovation, the life blood of an organization in a changing, uncertain, and complex worldscape.

Note that the ICALS research which resulted in an expanded experiential learning model *refers to the human as an Intelligent Complex Adaptive Learning System.* When the term "intelligent" is added to the concept of a complex adaptive system, it infers a capacity for reasoning and understanding, or an aptitude for grasping truths. Wiig broadens this view of intelligence and considers it the ability of a person to think, reason, understand, and *act,*[65] which relates the concepts of knowledge (effective action) and intelligence.

Hawkins says that "We are intelligent not because we can do one thing particularly well, but because we can learn to do practically anything." He calls out four attributes of the human brain which provide the flexibility needed to form a baseline for intelligence. These are learning continuously, learning via movement, creating many models, and using reference frames to store knowledge.[66] It is important to recognize that humans are verbs, not nouns, continuously learning and changing, forming new connections and patterns with new synapses. Thus, in every minute of every day, the thoughts and actions of all employees in an organization are changing, affecting culture, emergent behaviors that are not yet recognizable, and – perhaps subtly or not so subtly – the bottom line of an organization whose intellectual capital determines its sustainability.

Learning via movement refers to both thought and the active human body, which through sensing provides us the data to develop a model of the world in which we live. This relates to the ICALS research finding that **the mind/brain creates an internal representation of the world**.[67] We now know that this modeling occurs in the cortical columns in the neocortex, which receives input from movement and generates behaviors, predicting the next input. "Many models" refers to the tens of thousands of cortical columns in the neocortex, which provide the flexibility to process and navigate a changing, uncertain and complex environment. Reference frames, which are established in each cortical column, are a fairly new concept to the field of neuroscience. These reference frames enable the ability to perceive shape, changes, and locations *relative to each other*. The bottom line of this learning is that the human is quite capable of intelligently adapting to the current and future environment. As Hawkins describes: "Thinking occurs as the brain activates one location at a time in a reference frame and the associated piece of knowledge is retrieved."[68] Reference frames are found in most systems that exhibit planning, and other complex, goal-oriented behaviors.

Enhancing the learning process raises the question of learning from what perspective? Taking a systems perspective brings home the point that an "intelligent" CALS is a *self-organizing* complex adaptive system, which is a system in which the agents (individuals) have a high degree of freedom to organize themselves to better achieve their local objectives. Understanding the learner as a self-organizing Intelligent Complex Adaptive Learning System gives caution to organizations that would control, direct, or mandate learning and knowledge. Such a system can rarely be controlled by force— rather, it must be guided and nurtured through supportive influence, what the ICAS model of a knowledge organization defined as Collaborative Leadership.

As is becoming clear, humans are integral parts of a larger whole, entangled with other humans and parceled into organizational subsystems which are potentially capable of creative and intelligent decisions and actions. As Zohar and Marshall state, *Neither IQ nor EQ nor SQ*[69] *separately or in combination is enough to explain the full complexity of human intelligence nor the vast richness of the human soul and imagination.*[70]

Intelligence is entangled with the level of learning. And while there are certainly autonomous responses to the environment that would qualify as intelligent under our definition, there are other responses such as catching a cold or the flu that we may not consider "intelligent". Thus, our usage of "intelligent" is largely emergent and refers to the choices that guide our thoughts and actions, and the contributions we make to ourselves, to others, to our environment, and to an improved and sustainable future.

Organizational Intelligence

As an emergent property, an intelligent organization is greater than the sum of its parts (people) to include having the capabilities to innovate and acquire knowledge and apply it to relevant situations. Pinchot and Pinchot describe the intelligent organization as one that can face many competitors simultaneously and deal effectively with all of them, attending to all the details and supporting competencies that add up to cost-effective, superior performance.[71] The Pinchot definition of an intelligent organization is consistent with the democratization of organizations. As Warren Bennis describes, the Pinchots show that

> ... widespread rights, truth, equality, and community in the workplace are not merely humane options but, in fact, essential foundations for creating intelligent organizations that will succeed in today's complex and demanding world.[72]

They further note that "the quality of the relationships between members of the organization is a strategic issue that determines the very fabric of the organization."[73] We agree that relationships are the foundation of human intelligence.[74] This was confirmed through ICALS research findings[75] that: (1) physical mechanisms have developed in our brain to enable us to learn through social interactions; (2) the brain actually needs to seek out affectively attuned others for learning; and (3) affective attunement contributes to the evolution and sculpting of the brain. While good relationships in the organizational setting have always been important, because of the advance of technology and the increasing role of knowledge in handling time compression and complexity, and the recognition that diversity of thought facilitates creativity and innovation, they have become a critical asset. See Chapter 14 on Relationship Network Management.

A simple working definition of organizational intelligence is the ability of an organization to perceive, interpret, and respond to its environment in a manner that simultaneously meets its organizational goals while satisfying its stakeholders, that is, its employees, customers, investors, community, and environment. Organizational intelligence is also a descriptive term indicating the measure of the organization's (and its workforce's) capability to exhibit intelligent behavior.

Intelligent behavior of individuals, groups, and organizations can be understood in terms of (1) demonstrating behavior traits that re effective and acceptable; (2) being well prepared; (3) choosing the right posture in each situation; (4) being able to solve problems well; and (5) being able to make high-quality decisions and take effective actions for their implementation. Each of these can be studied to find the specific competencies needed for success in each area. For example, intelligent behavior traits range from listening to others, remaining objective and flexible to learning, and thinking before acting. Independent thought, the ability to collaborate well in pressure situations, and having strong principles all help create credibility and trust, and support good long-term relationships., Intelligent behavior leads to good working relationships at every level, greatly enhancing the speed and quality of decision-making and situational assessment. Note the consistency of these traits and the supporting discussion with the elements and characteristics of the democracy emerging from early philosophers as shown in Chapter 1, Figure 1-1.

Although data and information are necessary for acting intelligently, it is the knowledge that is created and acted upon that is the critical factor for success. For an organization to behave intelligently as a complex adaptive system, it must achieve continuous, interdependent collaboration and interplay among all levels of its system. This means balancing the knowledge and actions of its people to achieve both the lowest-level tasks and the highest-level vision of the organization, creating a distributed intelligence throughout the organization. This can be done by using teams and communities to amplify local intelligence levels, accelerate quality decision-making, and foster innovation and creativity.

HIERARCHY AND BUREAUCRACY

One of the pleasures of living out in the country is the opportunity to learn from farm animals. For example, horses have a strong hierarchal social structure, one that simultaneously provides the feeling of safety while honing their peripheral awareness in terms of ensuring they acquiesce to any horse higher in the pecking order. To "acquiesce" might be reactive (such as moving out of the way), or proactive (such as staying in the background or taking a later turn at the salt lick). Generally, once established, they seem to be comfortable with their placement and the repetitive behaviors that come along with that placement, with the subsequent consequence of few "reactive" events and ever-increasing "proactive" behavior. Of course, when perceived danger occurs, the number one horse takes a strong stance at the front of the herd, with the others leaving a safe space and gathering behind.

This keen awareness of "each" and "other" goes beyond the comfort of hierarchy. Watching four of the MQI Arabians stream down the mountain pasture (different ages, different sizes, different places in the hierarchy of the herd), they matched each other's gaits, gliding in perfect harmony through the grass, simultaneously stopping in an even perpendicular line, turning 90 degrees to the right in unison, and arching their necks back to the right. Amazingly, the only thing discoverable that had caught their attention was a soft breeze coming from the direction of their attention. Nostrils flaring and manes blowing, they held this pose for an unbelievable ten seconds before each moved in their own direction.

Hierarchy and bureaucracy are not exchangeable words or concepts. A hierarchy is "an order of some complexity, in which the elements are distributed along the gradient of importance."[76] In a hierarchy the dominant structural element may be a central point such as in a circular structure or have an axial symmetry. Wherever the central point (dominant structure) is located in the hierarchy (middle, top, bottom, etc.), each part is determined by where it is located in relation to the central point. From one perspective, the central point or dominant structure might well be the overarching system itself. For example, in the human body, the interdependent systems for the whole work independently to some extent, with systems and subsystems all contributing to levels of functioning (and hopefully wellness) of the body. While it is true that in a radical version of hierarchy the entire pattern may depend directly on one center, most hierarchies consist of groups of subordinate hierarchies who in turn have groups of subordinate hierarchies, with each group having its own particular relation to the dominant center point.[77] Throughout nature, hierarchy is the structural choice. We applied the power of hierarchies in manufacturing plants and assembly lines.

The key points here are (1) there is a central theme to the system with a dominant center point, and (2) the function of any one part can only be understood in its relation to the whole. While dependency (and potentially interdependency) are elements of hierarchies, the relationship of subordinate hierarchies to higher level groups need not be one of control. They are subordinate in terms of location, in terms of focus, and, in living systems, in terms of learning.

In the human body there are subsystems which process matter-energy (such as the mouth, lungs, heart, stomach and liver); subsystems which process information (such as the eyes, postsynaptic regions of neurons, network of neurons interconnecting centers of the central nervous system, temporal auditory cortex, and larynx); and subsystems which process both matter-energy and information (such as the genitalia and skin).[78] All are in service to the whole human, yet rarely are these systems the focus of our attention unless something is wrong with them, at which point we tap the expert in that domain and make an informed decision on actions to take. And while we may change our behavior to avoid a repeat experience, our attention moves to new ideas and opportunities while those sub-systems continue functioning, with old cells dying and new cells growing depending on the needs of our body and activity. This natural hierarchy with complex entanglement and interdependency of systems can serve as a model for our organizations.

The bureaucratic framework developed by Max Weber (1864-1920) called for a hierarchical structure, clear division of labor, rule and process orientation, impersonal administration, rewards based on merit, decisions and rules in writing, and management separated from ownership.[79] Conflict is a recurring theme throughout this model, with Weber postulating that forces exist within organizations that perpetuate conflict and class separation. For Weber this conflict was primarily between the capitalist and worker, the owner of the means of production versus the producer of labor, differentiating these as "classes." He also believed that the *ever-increasing importance of expert and specialized knowledge* created a conflict between the "specialist type of man" and the older type of "cultivated man" [which in his model was management]. Weber states, "This fight intrudes into all intimate cultural questions," then continues, "During its advance, bureaucratic organization has had to overcome those essentially negative obstacles that have stood in the way of *the leveling process necessary for bureaucracy*" [emphasis added].[80] In other words, the intellectual capital of the worker was a non-concept and their desired behavior was no more and no less than accomplishing the physical actions required to build the product or part of the product for which they were being paid.

The bureaucratic model was built on management power over workers in what Weber called *imperative control*, with legitimacy as the common ground for maintaining imperative control. Although Weber did not see knowledge as a form of legitimacy, he *did* link knowledge with power. He believed that "Every bureaucracy seeks to increase the superiority of the professionally informed by keeping their knowledge and intentions secret."[81]

This behavior periodically continues today in the form of what has been described as knowledge withholding, hoarding, and hiding.[82] Weber felt that since the pure interest of the bureaucracy was power, secrecy would increase with the increase of bureaucracy. And indeed, this model dominated organizations for more than 100 years before the information technology explosion opened the doors to the flow of information, accelerating learning and the creation of knowledge at all levels of society, ushering in the knowledge age.

In light of the discussion above, there are two distinctive differences between a hierarchy and a bureaucracy: (1) Hierarchies are structural while bureaucracies are operational; and (2) Bureaucracies are always hierarchical, but hierarchies are not always bureaucracies. So, while the knowledge organization (described below as the ICAS, Intelligent Complex Adaptive System) is hierarchical in nature, with support functions and a management "thread", leadership is collaborative and decision-making is distributed. See below.

If you have a bureaucratic hierarchy, it encourages individuals to limit their learning within the space of their clear, well-defined job responsibilities. On the other hand, if you have a hierarchy that recognizes the value of and takes advantage of employees as intelligent complex adaptive systems, an organizational structure in which employees become involved in a variety of tasks related to a common objective, the natural tendency is toward expanded learning over a broader range of interests and competencies. This difference significantly aids the intelligent complex adaptive organization by providing a wider diversity of competency, and a more flexible workforce, ergo the capacity to adapt to changing requirements.

Our history of organizations demonstrates that hierarchal structures have led to control and abuse of power.[83] Herein lays the rub. In literature and in everyday usage, the terms hierarchy and bureaucracy are often used interchangeably, and the hierarchal structure of organizations has been used extensively to support bureaucracy. The recognition of the distinction between hierarchy and bureaucracy places us in a framework to reap the benefits of hierarchy in our thinking, talking and acting as – with knowledge at its core – our organizations move out of the bureaucratic model toward intelligent complex adaptive behavior.

THE ORGANIZATION AS AN ICAS

Organizations take inputs from their environment, transform those inputs into higher-value outputs and provide then to customers and stakeholders. Organizations solve problems (or take on opportunities) by creating options using internal and external resources in efficient and effective ways that create added value above and beyond the value of the inputs. Briefly, the organization solves problems (or take on opportunities) that create options for action that then produce some internal or external value. Although they do this through available resources – people, ideas, technology, funds, facilities, etc. – as we moved from the manufacturing to the information to the complexity age, we recognized the most valuable resource is knowledge.

The ICAS model was developed at the turn of the century to match the new knowledge needs of a changing, uncertain, and complex global business environment in an information rich world. The principal actors in any enterprise are people and the main resources that make people effective are the intellectual capital assets that they possess or otherwise have available to conduct work. These intellectual capital assets must constantly be renewed through collaboration, learning, and innovation to sustain the advantages needed for the enterprise to remain competitive. Hence, the ICAS relies extensively on deliberate and systematic structures, strategies and initiatives focused on support of knowledge movement.

An organization's value added comes from the totality of actions of all employees every day. So, the objective and responsibility of the ICAS is to ensure that every employee takes the most effective actions necessary to achieve sustainable competitive advantage. For this to occur, each employee must have a clear understanding of the corporate vision and objectives, and the knowledge, resources, and freedom to express their ideas, collaborate, make decisions, and act in concert with others. Establishing the roles, relationships, authorities, and freedoms of employees provides the framework and context within which work is performed.

The ICAS, as an organization, must act like a biological system in many ways if it is to survive in a rapidly changing, nonlinear, complex, dynamic, and uncertain world. There are eight characteristics that help provide the internal capability to effectively deal with this environment. However, these characteristics cannot be ordered to occur, rather, they are emergent, the result of, over time, relationships, decisions and actions occurring within the organization at all levels.

The eight emergent characteristics are organizational intelligence, shared purpose, selectivity, optimum complexity, knowledge centricity, flow, permeable boundaries, and multidimensionality. See Figure 2-2. A discussion of organizational intelligence which is consistent with the knowledge organization that is ICAS was included in Chapter 2.

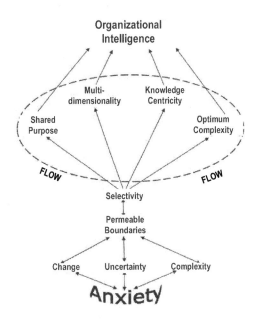

Figure 2-2. The eight emergent characteristics of the knowledge organization that is ICAS.

Unity and shared purpose represents the ability of the organization to integrate and mobilize resources to (1) provide a continuous line of focus and attention and (2) pull together the relevant parts of the organization when and where they are needed. Faced with a large number of threats and opportunities and the potential need for quick reaction, the ICAS has systems in place that constantly reach into, and sustain, continuous two-way communication with a large number of relatively independent subsystems (communities, teams and individuals). These subsystems organize themselves to maximize their learning, innovation, and knowledge, that is, their ability to take effective action at the local point of stakeholder interface.

Selectivity or filtering of incoming information from the outside world will always occur. Individual attention is limited by physiology to one thing at a time, and groups may have difficulty staying on a single topic. If left to itself, natural selectivity may become random and create more noise than purposeful action within the organization, which is what subsystems such as teams, communities of practice and interest, and self-organizing groups can help prevent. Shared purpose and current organizational tactics make visible what signals the organization is interested in. When the priorities that really matter to the organization are clear and kept firmly in awareness, incoming signals can be quickly evaluated, and appropriate decisions made.

Optimum complexity is discovering the right level of internal complexity to deal with the external environment while maintaining over all order and unity of purpose in the organization. As phenomena, knowledge and complexity emerged in the same revolution with a somewhat interdependent relationship that continues to co-evolve. Increasing complexity drives the need for more knowledge, and more knowledge creates more complexity. It is not the number of possible states, either in the organization or in its external environment that need concern an organization. It is the number of possible states that make a difference to the organization that counts. Of the almost infinite number of states of information, material, or energy that impinge upon the organization, only a few of them are meaningful and make a difference.

A *knowledge-centric organization* (KCO) is quite simply an organization that organizes virtually around the knowledge needs of its decision-makers at every level. In a continuous cycle, it is first a builder (creating technological structures to house and transfer content), then an operator (orchestrating interactions among individual, teams, and communities as well as customers and other stakeholders and serving as a media agent between partnering organizations), and then a knowledge broker (overseeing and operating the exchange of goods, services, and knowledge transactions). This is where knowledge sharing comes into play, with four key elements: connecting people to people, information to people, people to information, and information to information to provide the context necessary for effective decision-making.

Knowledge centricity is closely related to organizational intelligence, with each employee taking responsibility for ensuring intellectual capital growth. For any complex adaptive system to behave intelligently it must achieve continuous, interdependent collaboration and interplay among all levels of the system. This capability highlights the importance of both internal and external networks as they heavily influence the relationships and amplify knowledge diffusion among agents, components, and external systems. As these networks increase, the organization becomes more complex, harder to manage by those seeking direct control, but potentially capable of handling more complexity in its environment, with teams and communities accelerating quality decision-making and fostering innovation and creativity.

As introduced above, the use of teams, communities, and relationship networks leverage knowledge and broaden the experience (and therefore learning, the creation of knowledge) of individuals at every level of the organization. Figure 2-3 provides one approach to the organization of operational and action teams, communities and relationship networks in the ICAS organization.

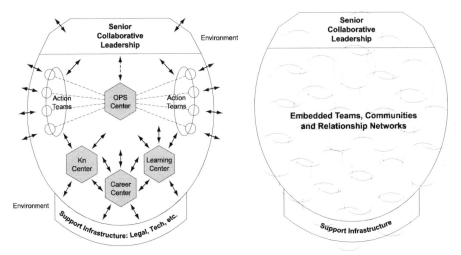

Figure 2-3. Presupposed structure among operational and action teams, communities, and relationship networks. Source: Bennet & Bennet, Organizational Survival in the New World: The Intelligent Complex Adaptive System.[84]

Flow enables knowledge centricity and facilitates the connections and continuity that maintain unity and give coherence to organizational intelligence. The emergent characteristic of flow can be discussed in terms of the flow of data, information, and knowledge; the movement of people in and out of organizational settings; and the optimal human experience. The flow of data, information, and knowledge is facilitated through teams and communities, and can be accelerated through event intermediation. The intelligent fluid flow of people in and out of the organization can support the organization's need for flexibility in responding to demands of the global marketplace, with the workforce growing and shrinking, engaging free agents, partnering, and buying intellectual capital as needed.

A critical flow element is the concept of autotelic work, an exhilarating state where people are so involved that nothing else seems to matter. In a team setting, individuals lose the sense of identity or separateness during the experience, then afterwards emerge with a stronger sense of self. This phenomenon results in individuals and teams giving their best capabilities to tasks at hand, with participants coming away with feelings of accomplishment, job, and well-being that influences their willingness to trust and openly communicate with other team members, enhancing collaboration and team performance.

There are no longer clear boundaries between jobs, levels of management, or organizations, with a further blurring of boundaries as people and technology create virtual networks around the globe. The *permeable and porous boundaries* of the ICAS allow the organization to optimize its results through teaming, partnering, alliances, and close relationships with customers and stakeholders. And within the organization, boundaries between the individual, other individuals, the social organization, and the organizational culture are "zones of interpenetration" where ideas are formed, and change occurs.[85]

One of our favorite metaphors for the changing boundaries of the ICAS is the *Phylum porifera*, what we call a sponge. Sponges are simple, multicellular animals that have minimal interdependence among their cells. In 1907 an embryologist, H. V. Wilson, discovered that a living sponge could be pushed through fine silk so that it was broken up into individual cells and cell debris.[86] Over the next three weeks, the cells started crawling around and aggregating into larger masses until a functional sponge was re-formed. Although we would not suggest pushing a living organization through fine silk, nevertheless, the splitting and reaggregating around goals (in the sponge's case survival) is a metaphor appropriate for the ICAS. With the living body, atoms and molecules constantly die and are replaced. The structure of the cell retains its identity even while the matter that composes it is continually altered. The cell rebuilds itself in line with its own pattern of identity, yet is always a part of emerging action, alive and responding even in the midst of its own multitudinous deaths.

From the perspective of evolution, man, because of his intelligence, adaptability, and robustness, has become the dominant species in the world. For the ICAS to survive in the intensely competitive organizational arena of today and tomorrow requires the instinctual ability to sense, learn, and respond with agility and robustness at all levels of its structure. This requires the organization to continuously interact; to forget and learn; to identify and deal with risk; to think in terms of systems and complexity; to perceive and analyze in terms of wide scope and long timeframes; and to keep its identity and unity. The organization must develop instincts and automatic competencies that are natural and become second nature at all levels. This is *multidimensionality*. A core integrative competency is Relationship Network Management (see Chapter 14).

The Enterprise of the Future Framework

Twenty years ago, in the timeframe the Bennets were launching the ICAS theory, they participated in the George Washington University Enterprise of the Future Program co-founded by Arthur Murray and Kent Greenes. Drawing on over a decade of university-level research, the framework for the emerging model consists of four primary facets as shown in Figure 2-4, which includes primary points related to leading, connecting, co-creating and delivering extraordinary value, and making breakthrough discoveries. In his words, these points are explicated by Arthur Murray below.[87] You will discover that these points show a descriptive consistency with the concept of ICAS.

Leading: *Building the enterprise of the future means completely rethinking strategy, even to the point of co-creating entirely new business ecosystems. Transforming the very structures of society, whether technological, economic, or political, is not out of the question. Strategy cannot be formulated in a vacuum. At the same time, vision cannot be conceived without knowledge and insights into trends which will shape and impact the strategy. Predicting and tracking major trends in the marketplace and aligning strategy with those trends allows organizations not only to predict, but also to co-create, the future. In this way, organizations are better able to confront reality in a world that is growing more "virtual" every day.*

Connecting: *Let's face it. Connecting billions of minds and tens of billions of devices cannot occur without technology, or more specifically, Information and Communication Technology (ICT). Still, we need to carefully and vigilantly avoid the temptation to leap ahead to technology-based solutions without first considering people, business processes, and especially, strategy. We view technology as an enabler. Our goal with respect to this pillar is to stitch together many disparate internal and external components into an evolving, adaptive, self-aware infrastructure nexus. Companies that can build such a nexus will be able to capture and retain critical knowledge efficiently and effectively, thereby attracting and retaining the next generation of workers. A highly productive workforce means greater satisfaction, less time wasted, and increased output with the same staffing levels.*

Co-creating and delivering extraordinary value: *For the enterprise of the future, one of the central themes is organizing for sustained high performance in a non-bureaucratic world. Industrial age, even information age, structures are inadequate for achieving this goal. By structures we mean not only the traditional organization chart, but also the processes, social networks, ontology, and most importantly, the business model itself.*

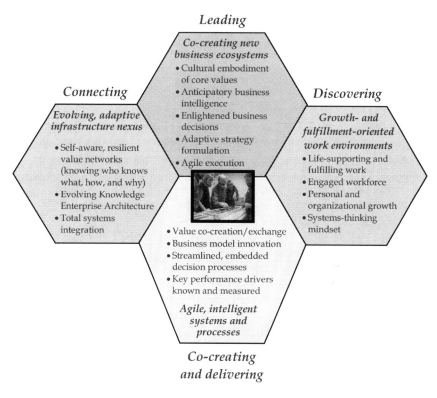

Figure 2-4. Enterprise of the Future Conceptual Framework[88]

Hierarchical bureaucracies and bureaucratic matrices need to be replaced by fluid, agile, social networks and communities. Process models can no longer focus solely on tasks, but must include streamlined decision flows. In the compressed time cycles of today's world, the right decisions need to be made quickly and consistently at points dispersed from central authority. This demands coming up with entirely new decision models supported by real-time collaboration tools and self-organizing networking environments. The main intent is to organize all the resources and assets at the enterprise's disposal in a way that consistently delivers timely, relevant knowledge and experience to the key decision points in a business process. In other words, to apply the enterprise's collective know-how when and where it's needed. All aimed, of course, at co-creating sustained extraordinary value for the customer.

Making breakthrough discoveries*: Much of the value of an organization, typically eighty percent or more, ultimately lives or dies within this pillar. As a result, new valuation methods, in which individual and organizational knowledge is created, shared, measured, and nurtured, need to be developed. People form the core of any enterprise. As a consequence, innovating, learning,* *and transforming at least as fast as, or faster than, the speed of change in your market demands both an individual and organizational perspective. New competency development and motivational systems are needed to attract, retain, and grow the world's best social knowledge entrepreneurs and workers. This in turn provides an environment with abundant opportunities for personal and organizational performance, growth and achievement.*

How much do these descriptions describe the organization of today? Do they describe your organization? Certainly, our organizations have moved closer toward this model, and perhaps in some cases surpassing it. Let's dig down a bit deeper, taking a closer look at the ICAS in terms of its democratic nature.

The Democratic Nature of the ICAS

As is clear, the emergent characteristics of the knowledge organization are consistent with the behavior of an intelligent complex adaptive system operating in the knowledge economy. The presupposed structure among operational and action teams, communities, and relationship networks shown in Figure 2-3 is a learning structure, positioning the organization in a symbiotic relationship with its cooperative enterprise, virtual alliances, and external environment while simultaneously retaining unity of purpose and selectivity of incoming threats and opportunities. This is the idea of a living system composed of other living systems – teams within teams, interacting communities, self-organization within organization – that combine and interact to provide the capabilities of an advanced, intelligent techno-sociological adaptive enterprise.

Based on complexity theory and knowledge centricity, there are a number of guiding principles for structuring the ICAS. Briefly, these are:

1. The structure needs to be compatible with the culture and both should be ecologically matched to the environment and the organization's purpose, strategy, and vision.

2. The structure design supports the workforce in their daily decision-making and actions, which includes the informal network and knowledge needs of employees at every level.

3. The structure supports the long-term needs of the workforce, including learning, professional development, and career management, with technology, roles and responsibilities, facilities, and policies all functioning effectively to satisfy both short-term and long-term ICAS needs.

4. The structure support leader and manager needs for loose-tight control of resources, that is, with loose control over self-organization, empowerment, and internal communications, but tighter control over financial transactions, career assignments, and strategic direction.

5. The structure supports and encourages emergence of the eight characteristics of the ICAS.

Culture is a source of organizational energy, or apathy, and a major determinant of organizational performance. It is the *invisible medium* within which every knowledge worker moves, thinks, and acts every workday. The ICAS culture is an action culture because of the importance of every individual taking the right action at the right place and time. The core of the action culture is built on the foundation of creating, leveraging, and applying knowledge anywhere, anytime it is needed. Power is rarely used and mostly invisible, with senor people guiding, setting the corporate direction, and making minimal decisions on local direction and implementation. Individuals have considerable flexibility to move around in the organization, and are encouraged to do so, to foster continuous learning and maintain *the diversity and instability needed for creativity and adaptability.*

Leadership is, above all, situational, historical, context-sensitive, a matter of character, and is time and space dependent. Collaboration is such an important part of creating the right environment and leveraging knowledge that the ICAS requires collaborative leaders and the art they practice, collaborative leadership, which is also called democratic leadership and was introduced in Chapter 1. The work of the collaborative leader is to create, maintain, and nurture the ICAS so that it makes the best use of knowledge and the full competencies of all workers to achieve sustainable competitive advantage while maintaining the values, ethics, and purposes of the organization. Overall, this is the ultimate responsibility of collaborative leadership.

While this has been a quick tour of the ICAS as a knowledge organization, the organization is detailed in depth in the book *Organizational Survival in the New World: The Intelligent Complex Adaptive System* by Alex and David Bennet. We also highly recommend *The End of Bureaucracy & the Rise of the Intelligent Organization* by Gifford and Elizabeth Pinchot.

As a summary, at the highest level, the ICAS is an organization designed to continuously adapt to and co-evolve with its environment. In so doing, the organization must exhibit flexibility and agility coupled with the ability to create and apply new ideas and actions to determine what will and will not work. In such a highly complex and dynamic environment it is difficult at best, and often impossible, to anticipate the future of that environment or the environment's response to any given organization action.

This leads to the importance of the knowledge worker, who is the individual at the at the point of contact, at the point of action, between the organization and its customers. *These workers must have the competency and the freedom to take effective actions wherever possible and to utilize the full resources of the organization.*

The range and depth of outside forces that the ICAS can effectively respond and adapt to is a fundamental measure of its survival capability. At the same time, its sustainable competitive advantage will be measured by its robust ability to take advantage of a wide range and depth of opportunities, originating both within and external to the firm. All of this requires knowledge built on trusted information. The ICAS offers a working environment that takes full advantage of the opportunities offered by diverse, creative, participative, collaborative, self-developing, and self-responsible intelligent complex adaptive learning systems, i.e., people.

A QUICK SUMMARY

Focusing on the identified modes and sub-elements of the human as an intelligent complex adaptive learning system and the eight emergent characteristics and descriptors of the knowledge organization as an intelligent complex adaptive system, we, at a high-level, match those with the democratic elements and characteristics synthesized from the what's and how's of early philosophers. See Table 2-1.

Table 2-1. Relationship of democratic elements and characteristics to ICALS and ICAS models in the knowledge economy.

Democratic Freedoms and Characteristics	ICALS (Knowledge Centric Human) Modes of Learning	ICAS (Knowledge Centric Organization) Emergent Characteristics
Thought	reflective observation; abstract conceptualization; intelligence (capacity for reasoning and understanding)	knowledge centricity; flow; self-development; choice
Expression (Open discussion)	social support (willingness to listen and learn); social interaction (accelerating learning and creativity)	knowledge centricity; flow; Relationship Network Management
Association	choice; attention	teams and communities; permeable and porous boundaries; Relationship Network Management
Opinion (Ideal situation model)	social interaction (accelerated learning and creativity; enhancing understanding, meaning,	knowledge centricity; teams and communities; multidimensionality

	truth and how things work)	
Exchanging ideas	social engagement; social support (creating resonance with people and ideas)	knowledge centricity; flow; permeable and porous boundaries; Relationship Network Management
Choice (to pursue the good life)	choice; action potential; active experimentation	knowledge centricity; self-development
Participation	concrete experience; active experimentation; social support (open mind, willingness to listen and learn)	knowledge centricity; permeable and porous boundaries; distributed decision-making (point of knowledge/action); Relationship Network Management;
Community	social learning; social bonding; affective attunement; social support; social interaction	organizational intelligence; knowledge centricity; teams and communities; continuous interdependence; collaboration and interplay at all levels of system; permeable and porous boundaries
Dialogue	associative patterning; social support (open mind, willingness to listen and learn)	knowledge centricity; flow; permeable and porous boundaries; Relationship Network Management
Truth	reflective observation; sensing; social interaction (enhancing understanding and truth, how things work); intelligence (aptitude for grasping truths)	organizational intelligence; unity and shared purpose; flow
Trust	affective attunement (respect and trust)	unity and shared purpose; flow
Reason	abstract conceptualization (ability to grasp meaning, logic); intelligence (capacity for reasoning and understanding)	organizational intelligence; unity and shared purpose
Responsible decisions	abstract conceptualization (discipline);	knowledge centricity; unity and shared purpose; self-organization; selectivity;

	comprehension; intelligence (capacity for reasoning and understanding and grasping truths)	decisions at the point of action (knowledge)
Cooperation	active experimentation (influencing people and changing situations); social support; social interaction (use and understanding of concepts, metaphors, anecdotes and stories)	continuous interdependent collaboration and interplay at all levels of system; permeable and porous boundaries
Critical inquiry	abstract conceptualization (problem solving, rigor); active experimentation (object-based logic); intelligence	organizational intelligence; knowledge centricity; selectivity; optimum complexity; multidimensionality
Rational consensus	social interaction (developing a shared language)	knowledge centricity; multidimensionality
Rationality	abstract conceptualization (logic, discipline, rigor); intelligence	organizational intelligence; selectivity ; optimum complexity; multidimensionality
Mutual respect	affective attunement (respect and trust)	knowledge centricity; multidimensionality
Good will	affective attunement (respect and trust, willingness to listen, reducing stress and fear);	flow (autotelic work)
Inquisitive mind	reflective observation (an idea); apprehension; enriched environment; social support (open mind, risk-taking)	knowledge centricity; multidimensionality
Open to criticism & improvement	affective attunement (willingness to listen and learn); intelligence	knowledge centricity
Rights of individual	Choice; intelligence	self-organizing; multidimensionality
Individual self-development and growth	all modes of learning; choice; continuous learning	knowledge centricity; Relationship Network Management

Individual responsibility	self-organizing; choice	self-organizing; decisions at the point of action
Equal opportunity based on merit	[N/A]	organizational intelligence
Distribution of wealth	[N/A]	flow (autotelic work)
Coercive-free environment	[N/A]	organizational intelligence; unity and shared purpose

The cohesion across democratic elements and characteristics, the intelligent complex adaptive learning system (the human), and the knowledge organization as an ICAS is not surprising, since they all emerge from a growing understanding of living systems.

In the next chapter we dive deeply into a basic property of the universe – information – the availability of which, supported by technology, is the core of knowledge and very much drives our individual and organizational decisions and actions.

CHAPTER 3

INFORMATION RISING

*In all corners of the world, there are research group enthusiastically
exploring the many facets of quantum information, and making
valuable contributions.* -Sergio Curlief and Angel Ricardo Plastino[89]

Information—the foundation of knowledge—is a basic property of the Universe and, as eloquently stated by theoretical biologist Tom Stonier, *as fundamental as matter and energy*.[90] Along with Stonier, we take **information** to be a measure of the degree of organization expressed by any non-random pattern or set of patterns. The order within a system is a reflection of the information content of the system. Data (a form of information) would then be simple patterns, and while data and information are both patterns, they have no meaning until some organism recognizes and interprets the patterns.[91] Thus, information exists in the human brain in the form of stored or expressed neuronal patterns that may be activated and reflected upon through conscious thought. This is a high-level description of knowledge that is consistent with the operation of the brain and is applicable in varying degrees to all living organisms.

We live in an information field. The life journey begins with information. In living systems, the distribution of atoms and molecules is non-random, and "organization is the physical expression of a system containing information."[92] Organization means the existence of a non-random pattern of particles and an energy field, or more generally, the sub-units comprising any system such that "the intricate organization of matter and energy which makes possible that phenomenon which we call life, is itself a product of the vast store of information contained within the system itself. "[93]

In the material world, organization can be observed in space and time as a physical phenomenon. Boltzmann, who was a thought leader in statistical mechanics, connected order/disorder changes in a system to visible changes in entropy,[94] which led Schrödinger to further explore the relationship of entropy and order in living systems.[95] This in turn led to his reflection that "order" was the inverse of "disorder", with "entropy" the level of randomness in a system denoting a gradual decline into disorder. Stonier took this thought further, noting that describing information entropy as a state of a system was far more than a metaphor. He discovered that *changes in entropy were consistent with changes in a system's information content*. Further, he noted that "an increase in entropy measures an increase in the *absence* of information."[96] This is an important finding. What it means is that the inability of an organization to move forward toward its mission or compete in its competitive environment most likely is a result of the *absence* of information that would enable effective knowledge.

Stonier saw many parallels between information and energy, seeing information as an intrinsic component in all physical systems, what could be defined as "potential energy". An example of potential energy often used in textbooks is a pencil, which sits on the desk or stays in a drawer until another force is applied to it (you pick it up and write with it). Then, the force (energy) you have exerted in the writing is turned into information, that which is written on the paper. Consistent with this scenario, Stonier defined potential energy as "a state in which the *expenditure* of energy has resulted in an *increase* in the information content of the system."[97]

Stonier also described the exponential growth of information based on the recursive properties of information systems. As he says:

Organized systems exhibit resonances. Resonances lead to oscillations. Oscillations represent timed cycles during which changes may be introduced. Such changes may dampen or amplify the existing oscillations. Alternatively, they may create new resonances and excite new sets of oscillations. The more complex the system, the greater the likelihood of introducing changes into the system during any given cycle. Hence the exponential growth of information.[98]

This makes the relationship between information and entropy clear, which also plots the evolution of the universe. Where you have entropy approaching the infinite and information in a zero state, the Big Bang occurred. Then, as matter became more and more complex, moving toward biological systems, entropy moved toward the zero state. And here is where the phenomenon of *intelligence* (the emergence of consciousness) occurred, with systems capable of both organizing themselves *and* ordering their environment.

In an organization – which as we have noted is itself a complex adaptive system – the increase of information and complexity requires greater self-organization, that is, so to speak, *more organization of the organization*, as well as ordering of the environment in which the organization exists. Thus, the rise of information systems created a positive reinforcing loop as increased information required "more and better" information systems to manage it, and then knowledge systems, enabling decision-makers at all levels of the organization to (as the meme suggests) have access to what they need when they need it: right knowledge, right place, right time.

While we will not delve too much deeper into Stonier's work – although we urge those who have the interest and energy to do so – it is important to our conversation to note that, just as energy and matter, energy and information are *interconvertible*. That means they can be exchanged one for the other, and that energy can be converted into either information *or* matter. The law of the conservation of energy can be expanded to read "in a closed system, what is conserved is the sum total of energy plus matter *plus* information." Thus, in an organization, stored information pertinent to the present or potential future purpose of the organization is energy in a holding pattern such that, just as knowledge, there is the element of supporting actual and potential use.

AN INFORMED UNIVERSE

Scientists such as Bohm and Harold Puthoff have more recently explored the role of nature's information field in the "quantum vacuum". For example, Puthoff described an equilibrium that exists between matter and the energy field, which he refers to as the zero-point energy field.[99] One consequence of this connection is that we are—quite literally and physically—"in touch" with the rest of the universe, and that the modulation of such fields might just carry *meaningful* information, which insinuates purpose, much like the popular movie phrase, "The Force be with you".

This is the comprehensive concept of an *informed* universe, that is, a *meaningful* universe. Note that information serves as the raw material and it is only when the raw material is processed that it becomes a *message* which, upon receipt and processing by the recipient—and noting the context sensitivity of meaning (thank you Einstein for our understanding of relativity)—can information become *meaningful* to the processing individual.[100]

Ervin Laszlo describes this as the Akashic Field. In his quest for an integral theory of everything, Laszlo's Akashic Field—what he calls the A-Field—expands on the Indian philosophical concept of the Akashic Chronicle. The A-Field is a cosmic information field that is at the core of an informed universe. While it cannot be seen, heard, touched, smelled, or tasted, it's effect can be perceived. Your personal experiences of "knowing" may support this idea. There have been so many experiments and experiences in the authors' lives that have brought us to the understanding that things in the "real world" are connected, linked by flows of energy and flows of information.

In this Field, there is an informing of "everything by everything else", which is universal.[101] This does NOT mean the "same", but rather isomorphic, which is having the same basic form. Perhaps a better way to think about this is as a resonance, where frequencies of sounds resonate with other sounds playing at the same frequency. When this occurs—when things are at the same frequency—they are said to be coherent. Coherence is a term which represents the degree of synchronization between coupling oscillating systems. We talk more about resonance and coherence in Chapter 7 and Chapter 10.

In the A-Field, "things are directly 'in-formed' by the things that are most like them" yet there is also a coherence such that, less directly, other frequencies can also "in-form". This all happens at a staggering speed. As Laszlo explains, "Information conveyed through the A-field subtly tunes all things to all other things and accounts for the coherence [and the symmetry] we find in the cosmos, as well as in living nature."[102]

Each and every one of us are *active participants* in this relationship with the Field, swimming in a vast ocean of energy which is full of entangled, continuously flowing sub-fields. *From a quantum perspective*, we now recognize this as a large probability field of thought, dynamically and continuously redistributing old patterns and creating new patterns. And *our* thoughts and feelings and actions—all of which contain information—are playing in this Field through a continuous exchange of energy! Focusing on living systems, Chapter 13 presents the fundaments of the functioning of our informational system, which assures the body maintenance, its evolution and species continuity, and shows how we connect the environment external/internal world, pointing to the cognitive centers for connection with this reality. The second section of the chapter focuses on understanding the functioning and application in life of this informational system that is us.

So, what does all this mean to the organization? As a starting point, people, especially those with deep knowledge developed through attention to a knowledge domain over a period of time such that they have developed an energetic resonance, have the capability to access information beyond their conscious awareness. This often comes in the form of what is called knowing, intuition, or "intuitive nudges". Nonetheless, when recognized, this "knowing" can be a powerful tool in support of creative and innovative solutions to challenges and opportunities. And when we understand the power of this "knowing", with it comes responsibility, an energetic responsibility of sorts. We begin with the concept of information literacy.

INFORMATION LITERACY

With the advent of the Internet in the latter part of the 20th century, the exponential increase in information brought with it the necessity to become *information literate* in this new emerging environment of connectivity. As the U.S. Presidential Committee on Information Literacy forwarded,

> *Information literacy is a survival skill in the Information Age. Instead of drowning in the abundance of information that floods their lives, information literate people know how to find, evaluate, and use information effectively to solve a particular problem or make a decision ....*

As a working definition, Information Literacy (IL) includes a set of skills that enable individuals to recognize when information is and is not needed and how to locate, evaluate, integrate, use, and effectively communicate needed information. Of course, as technology expanded and users of this technology rapidly adapted, this skill set has been in a continuous state of flux. For example, in the 1990's, an IL self-assessment instrument asked the following questions:

- Do you recognize when you need information?
- Can you name at least two search engines?
- Can you find basic facts on the Internet?
- Can you analyze your data for validity and reliability?
- Do you know how to identify a computer hoax or urban legend?
- Do you know how to request permission to use information under copyright?
- Do you know basic steps to ensure your online privacy?
- Do you know what browser you are using?

It's interesting to look back at the simplicity of that instrument! Today our grandchildren could teach us how to manage most of this. However, while clearly there are different needs in today's environment in order to be information literate, we still struggle with the larger issues of privacy and the validity and reliability of information.

Today's augmented human swims in a sea of information. Competently navigating these waters means (1) determining the nature and extent of the information needed; (2) accessing needed information effectively and efficiently; (3) understanding the context of that information (remembering that all knowledge is relevant, that is, context sensitive and situation dependent (see the discussion on context in Chapter 12); (3) determining the value of that information in terms of truth, currency, and applicability; (4) evaluating information and its sources critically, and incorporating selected information into your knowledge base and value system; (5) using information effectively to accomplish a specific purpose; and (6) understanding the economic, legal, and social issues surrounding the use of information, and understanding how to use information ethically and legally.

As can be recognized, the importance of being information literate *increases* along with continuing technological advancement, which is touching every aspect of our everyday lives. For example, the U.S. Defense Acquisition University began in 2023 upskilling employees across the Army, Navy, Air Force and Marines on data analytics and AI skills to understand the emerging technology that DoD is buying. DoD specific context is included, with curated training based on employees' roles and career trajectories. Looking to the future – and noting that general "data literacy" is necessary across the workforce – DAU is partnering with DoD's Chief Digital and Artificial Intelligence Office on coursework curation, as well as zeroing in on those skills and abilities the acquisitions workforce is going to need in the coming years.[103]

At the heart of everything we create as a humanity in every field of human endeavor – health and medicine, safety, transportation, energy, exploration, manufacturing and technological innovation, finance, education – and in whatever work we pursue, in our sociality and in our governance, our mind/brain is augmented in increasingly unimaginable ways. That augmentation is primarily computers and advanced communication technologies, which are inseparable as their relationship with us is increasingly synergistic. Already we may say that the interdependence between humans, computers, and communication systems is so rich and dynamic that technologies are shifting from a focus on specialized design and specific functionality to the dynamics and sharing of information, misinformation, disinformation, and propaganda, cracking open the illusion of trust and truth, which bear further attention.

Attention as an IL Skill

Rather appropriate to place in the beginning of a knowledge book, attention has more recently emerged as an IL skill as the gap between the attention of individuals and organizations and the information that needs to be attended to has widened. Davenport and Beck describe attention as a slippery intangible asset and begin their book *The Attention Economy* with a focus on the current attention deficit.[104] For example, they describe an organization's attention deficit in terms of organization ADD. The symptoms are the increased likelihood of missing key information needed for decisions; diminished time for reflection on anything but simple information transactions such as email; difficulty holding others' attention; and a decreased ability to focus when necessary.[105] This work includes an in-depth treatment of attention and approaches for improvement. A fascinating finding is the recognition that time management and attention management are not linked.

At the unconscious level, the human senses—the information processors providing the information for our decisions and actions—know how to process vast amounts of information effectively, and the unconscious brain is *always* processing.[106] Whether object, activities or people, the emergent quality of SELF (which is YOU) is being shaped by what you pay attention to over time.[107] You could think of your SELF as a hierarchy of goals, because it is the *purpose and goals that you set* which focus your largest amount of attention. Not only *what* we pay attention to but *how* we pay attention is important. For example, we might consider a person who continuously worries about getting hurt as neurotic, or a person who avoids eye contact and stays relatively quiet as shy, and those considerations affect the interaction we have and the actions we take.

In terms of mental development, it is the frontal lobes that help an individual pay attention and ask good questions. As Amen describes, a more developed frontal lobe allows you to take better advantage of new knowledge, to know what to focus on, and to relate it to life experiences so that it has more useful value to you.[108] The eighteen-year-old may be able to memorize facts more easily, but his frontal lobe isn't as good at selecting which facts to memorize. A "more developed frontal lobe" occurs through mental exercise, which has a positive effect on the brain at any age, and both physical and mental exercise increases brainpower.[109]

Spatial attention allows humans to selectively process visual information through prioritization of an area within the visual field. A region of space within the field is selected for attention and the information within this region then receives further processing. Spatial attention to a specific thing, person or event increases the intensity of the related neuronal firings, which in turn affect the conscious experience of focus, amplifying the contrast in the experience and making it less faint and more salient.[110] This translates into increased memory and recall; repetition increases memory recall. This well-known phenomenon goes back to Hebb's Rule that *neurons that fire together wire together*. The more a given pattern is repeated, the stronger the neuronal connections are and the easier a specific memory can be recalled. This affirms what most good students at all ages learn along the way, that *repetitive focused attention is a conscious tool for managing memory and recall.* Reflect on what this means to an organization in terms of the working environment.

Similar to spatial attention, focusing attention on a particular non-spatial stimulus feature such as color increases its representational precision, resulting in more concrete conscious experiences.[111] Thus, attention directly impacts the breadth and depth of neuronal connections in the short and long-term.

Since IL requires the skills to use information and communication technologies and applications, it is closely linked to both computer literacy (ICT skills) and media literacy (mediums and formats transmitting information). In promoting IL worldwide, UNESCO forwards that "the ability to navigate in cyberspace and negotiate hypertext multimedia documents requires both the technical skills to use the Internet and the literacy skills to interpret the information."[112]

TRUST IN INFORMATION

In the literature coming out of the fields of organizational development, knowledge management, sociology, education, and neuroscience, trust repeatedly emerges as a required factor for the free flow of information and knowledge. However, global connectivity and the internet have brought—and continue to bring about—new modes of social networking and information flows, *demanding a shift in our perceptions*, and facilitating a shift from relationship-based interaction (with value of exchange built on trust and respect of people) to idea-based interaction (with value of exchange built on respect for and resonance with the information being exchanged). Thus, *affective attunement* is developed through virtual relationships based on the resonance of ideas. While this is quite different than the personal relationships or connections built up over time among personal and work interactions, those that connect continuously *do* build up a level of trust based on the responses of those with whom they interact, howbeit personal trust and the trust of ideas can be very different perceptions. See Figure 3-1.

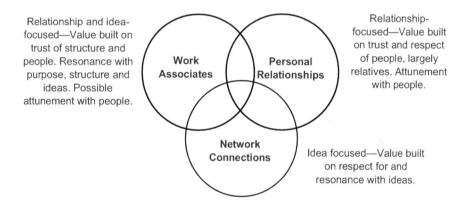

Figure 3-1. Idea resonance and trust.

We seek attuned others. Interestingly, this aspect of the human was recognized by several of the philosophers defining democratic characteristics, which was long before it was shown to be true through neuroscience research. Attunement infers to being in harmony with or resonating with another. It is a shared state, a vibrational entrainment—inclusive of understanding another's needs and feelings. The notion of affective attunement is connected to John Dewey's observations in his book *Democracy and Education* (1916), discussed in more depth in Chapter 5, that an educator needs to "have that sympathetic understanding of individuals as individuals, which gives him an idea of what is actually going on in the minds of those who are learning."[113] Social interaction mechanisms in the brain foster the engagement in affective attunement, consider the intentions of others, understand what another person is thinking, and think about how we want to interact.[114]

There is the phenomenon of sequential linkages that comes into play and supports an individual's willingness to trust. "If I know someone that you know who was a close colleague of someone else who owns a company that another individual is a partner in, then we have a starting place for building some level of trust."[115] As an example, when two people serving in the military have been on the same ship or in the same conflict during their careers, there is a common bond which offers a foundation on which to build trust.

De Furia[116] suggested five behaviors that can help build trust: sharing relevant information, clarifying mutual expectations, reducing controls, allowing for mutual influence, and meeting expectations. However, these behaviors infer building a relationship, which does not occur in the instant at hand. Certainly, when ideas are exchanged among the same individuals over time, a level of trust can develop based on consistent positive feelings about idea responses, which is the essence of idea resonance. Since the creative interplay of ideas is the focus of exchange, there is no expectation of outcomes. This occurs in communities of practice and interest, whose focus is on knowledge and the creation of new ideas.[117] Since social media offers a platform for the free flow of ideas, it would appear that in the context of De Furia's behaviors, that allowing for mutual influence offers the greatest relevance for building trust in the new social reality.

While in the past trust was built up over time, in today's world, where everything happens quickly and often over the internet, virtual trust is not only trust among individuals and groups communicating virtually – and trust of the information being communicated, that is, the idea resonance introduced above – but also a trust in the technology, the hardware and software used to communicate (security, reliability, accurate transmission, etc.) and the information being exchanged. Building on those considerations, the trustworthiness of information can be considered from a number of viewpoints: (1) its relevance to specific objectives; (2) its quality (accuracy); (3) its timeliness; and (4) its completeness. Of course, trusting information also means trusting the *source* of that information, whether it comes from a person, organization, database, webpage, book or social network. Since *trust is a feeling*, trust of self is also paramount. Feelings and emotions are different, with feelings considered as private, inwardly directed and emotions as public, outwardly directed. Note that while the *feeling* of trust may or may not be connected to emotions, it will undoubtedly *affect* emotions, especially when trust is broken.

It is important to caveat that trusting another's responses does not mean that an individual agrees with those responses. As Bennet and Bennet offer, this means that "we intellectually respect those responses and trust that they are being provided from an honest and intellectual framework. As such, we choose to focus and reflect on those responses in resonance with our own intelligent frame of reference."[118] In this environment of virtual networking – a "cooperative association of interconnected informational beings, and all the subtext that comes with that distinction"[119] – the individual takes on expanded responsibility in discretion and discernment coupled with an ever-increasing amount of information, and our organizations are repeatedly asking: "What information can we trust?" While certainly in a bounded domain of knowledge and given sufficient time, and the skill and health to continuously navigate the internet, there is the possibility to stay at the forefront of knowledge for a short time. However, knowledge is relative (as is trust), both context-sensitive and situation-dependent, ever-changing and always partial and incomplete.

Over the past twenty years there has been much written about the CUCA and VUCA environment.[120] This literature cannot be ignored. While some people can thrive in a volatile environment, and indeed the human body and mind have been created to adapt to its environment, nonetheless, surviving in such a continuous challenging stream of energy can and often does take a heavy toll on the body, mind, emotions and spirit. Thus, when larger than life events occur coupled with global conditions beyond what has been known before—all escalated through chaotic arousal challenging the very foundations upon which our lives are grounded—humans are moved to reach out for help, searching for a "savior" of sorts who is perceived as having the power to break through these threats, and on whose coattails one can ride. This adds another bubble to the idea resonance model, and that is the phenomenon of "Idea Locking" (Figure 3-2).

Relationship Network Management (RNM), a networking process developed by the U.S. Department of the Navy which will be addressed more fully later in this book, forwards that the everyday interactions among people—conversations both face-to-face and over the Internet—lay the groundwork for the decisions that will be made in the future. The relationship network is the matrix of people, the sum of a person's relationships (connections and significant associations) in the past and the present. (See Chapter 14.) Concepts supporting successful relationships are trust, interdependency (a state of mutual reliance, confidence and trust), openness (directly related to trust and a willingness to share), flow (of data, information and knowledge) and equitability (both sides getting something out of the relationship). In the DON model, trust is based on integrity and consistency over time, that is, saying what you mean and following through on what you say.[121] However, in Idea Locking this terminology has taken on a new meaning. Trust, which is at the core of all five of the RNM elements, appears to deal with the continuation and support of the ONE BIG IDEA by participants in the exchange, whether it is true or not. Perhaps de Furia helps us understand this better—and apply it to the current state of the world—when he shares:

Interpersonal trust is present in a situation in which one individual places his or her interests under the control of another individual, with the expectation of gaining a desired outcome for which the potential negative consequences of violated trust are greater than the value of the potential desired outcome.[122]

An important element that plays into Idea Locking is arousal. The brain has indeed been shaped through evolution to adapt and then readapt to an ever-changing world, modifying both its chemistry and architecture.[123] A moderate level of arousal actually facilitates learning, initiating neural plasticity by increasing the production of neurotransmitters and neural growth hormones, which in turn facilitate neural connections and cortical organization.[124] However, overstimulation—a high level of arousal, which engages strong emotions—reduces mental function and lowers consciousness, and "once emotions occur they become powerful indicators of future behavior."[125]

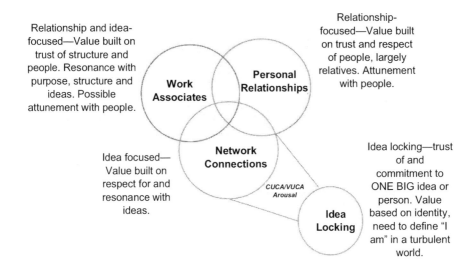

Figure 3-2. Idea locking, idea resonance, and trust in a shifting world.

THE SEARCH FOR TRUTH

People are truth seekers. Yet truth, highly subjective, has a relative value to the situation at hand. In a specific situation, we are the perceiver and how we perceive is influenced by our prior experiences and subconscious biases. Where a concept which was previously considered truth does not fit a new situation, a larger concept exists that encompasses that concept. In seeking "the truth of a matter", we search for that higher level of truth. Thus truth—which can be considered the highest virtue in the mental world—may only be "true" for a limited period. Over time, dynamic differences can cause forces to develop, and old truths can become conceptually, logically, and socially "untrue" and inappropriate.

While individuated perception is always at play in truth seeking, truth can be thought of as having three types: actual (which denotes our inner "feeling" of truth), apparent (that which is observed), and imagined (a distorted version of our inner perception). When we lock onto a truth as "absolute", it causes us to separate from a changing world, hindering our ability to judge and make decisions from an objective viewpoint and not allowing ourselves to grow and change.

Because truth is structured, it can be discerned in comparison to another truth and can be given a relative value regarding the level of truth. That relative value is a mathematical representation of how much a conceptual truth is true in a specific example and will change when other examples are considered. Since it is a changing target, it follows that *no one can own or control truth.* While certainly influenced by others, regardless of what is said by our leaders, or what is espoused through our media, or what is believed by our friends and families, the discernment of the level of truth or non-truth is fully within each of us. It is a judgment based on our past thoughts and actions, our beliefs and values, and the current situation, which is changing in the instant at hand.

Fortunately, the glorious human brain was created for just such discernment. Supported by the brain, the mind creates patterns of thought through neuronal firings and their connections. Note that neurons are not physically bound to each other. Thus, they have the flexibility to create, break and recreate relationships with other neurons, which is referred to as the process of plasticity. In 2000, Eric Kandel, a medical doctor, neuroscientist and professor of biochemistry and biophysics, won the Nobel Prize for showing that when individuals learn, the wiring (neuronal patterns, connections, and synapse strengths) in their brain change.[126] As a living process, the mind/brain system is replete with feedback loops, control systems, sensors, memories, and meaning-making systems (theories) made up of about 100 billion neurons.

Enter the explosive world of media "agitainment", blurring the lines of fact and fiction with misinformation and disinformation. **Misinformation** simply means information that misinforms. All knowledge is imperfect and/or incomplete. This is because it is continuously shifting and changing in concert with our environment, the demands placed upon us, our response to that environment, and new discoveries.[127]

Disinformation

Disinformation, which appears to include the intent of deception, also abounds. However, since people's motives are impossible to test, Miniter considers disinformation that which is widely believed, yet probably false. This definition gives disinformation power, adding an element of uncertainty to the term regarding the level of truth. There are a number of possible sources of disinformation. First, there are honest errors upon which myths are often built. A good example is the concept of "survival of the fittest" which is credited with Darwin, and indeed he forwarded that in his early work. What is less known is that in a later publication Darwin[128] corrected this to read that "those communities which included the greatest number of the most sympathetic members would flourish best and rear the greatest number of offspring." Thus began the recognition that cooperation and unity, rather than survival of the fittest, are the keys to the success of a species."[129] In fact, cooperation was identified as the key factor in evolution and survival.[130] But it was too late to retrieve what had already become a meme, and which continues today to be used heavily throughout the competitive business world such that it remains foundational to many belief sets.

Second, some errors are simply mistakes, misquotes or misattributions. And some information may be partial, confusing or ignore details and context such that what is provided cannot be properly understood. Myths—seeming facts part of conventional wisdom yet probably false—often become or promote memes. Note that memes become stronger and more memorable when they are delivered in connection with an emotional event that engages the feelings of the listener/participant.

A third source of disinformation is official spin, that is, selective partial information released by "someone in charge" that favorably situates an occurrence or event. As recognized in current events, this can be a destructive and controlling force when used by people in positions of power. Disinformation is often a part of information operations which are conducted by various governments.[131] A fourth source of disinformation is that which is spread by foreign sources. The media may pick up dubious information and run with it, or they may be misled by foreign websites and releases. A fifth source is connected to historical amnesia. History easily vanishes from memory, and dates of events are often confused in media's rush to be the first to reveal breaking news.[132] A sixth source is leaks, which may or may not contain a level of truth and is often the (version of) truth they would like the target audience to adopt. These are generally on purpose, with a personal agenda behind the lead.[133]

Disinformation and misinformation further spread through "organic reach",[134] which is when it is picked up and spread by individuals to families, networks, friends, etc. In recent research, four studies explored the effects of message attributes, reader/viewer characteristics, and their interaction of the likelihood of individuals spreading disinformation online.[135] It was discovered that whether disinformation was spread had nothing to do with the authoritativeness of sources, or who or how many people engaged it. Nor did an individual's digital literacy play a role, and there was only a very weak relationship in terms of gender, age and education. Rather, the urge to spread specific information was directly related to (1) the belief that it was likely true, and (2) a pre-disposition to and familiarity with the ideas. In other words, it had everything to do with self-beliefs and self-truths, all of which, while set in motion through family, culture, education, experiences, and all the other aspects of what it is to be human, are developed over time and yet can be influenced by the bombardment of "fake news" through the mediasphere.

There is an element of cognitive attraction that comes into play regarding receptivity to ideas broadcast through the mediasphere. Approaching this issue from the viewpoint of cultural evolution and cognitive anthropology, Acerbi feels that disinformation and misinformation are successful when the content taps into an individual's general cognitive preferences.[136] The consistent finding in his research was that the quality of content was not related to or equated with truth, but rather with psychological appeal. This is consistent with the earlier discussion of idea resonance.

Sensing Truth

Sensing the truth in others—and ourselves—can occur in conjunction with higher-level communication skills such as empathy coupled with reflection. When we sense untruth in ourselves or others, forces are created. For example, consider the forces between logical and emotional influences on thinking when limited funding is allocated. Let's say a public servant must make a choice between a perceived much-needed research study (long-term value) and an emotional plea for funding from a constituent (short-term value with high visibility). While we can mentally sense when things are not heading in the same direction, calling emotions into play adds an element of confusion, creating force. As MacFlouer[137] forwards, the total value of truth (T) minus the value of untruth (U) equals force (F), that is:

$$T - U = F \ \textit{or} \ T - (u1 + u2 + u3 \text{, etc.}) = F$$

Truth has value; untruth *reduces the ability of thought to control energy*, such that clarity of thinking becomes more difficult. Thus, exposure to untruth reduces the structure of our thinking and reduces our senses and trust in our knowledge. *The greater our exposure to untruths, the lower our ability to sense those untruths.* An example is the continuous pattering of a politician. When people become used to untruths, they are not in a position to hear truth, that is, they cannot discern it as easily. One strategy to move toward intelligent communication with such individuals would be to share partial truths, slowly increasing their receptivity to the larger truth. A simple TRUTH SEARCHING tool is included in Section IV.

Propaganda

Propaganda, a mode of power and control through information, is a group of ideas or statements, often false or exaggerated, that are spread with intent to help or hinder a cause, a political leader, a government, etc.[138] While the information associated with propaganda may or may not be true, it is selectively engaged and spread to accomplish a hidden agenda, highly questionable as to level of truth for the situation at hand. Thus, the knowledge created from propaganda does not lead to intelligent activity. In this day and age, propaganda has evolved from an epidemic to a far-reaching pandemic, touching every mind at some level. As governments, businesses and people pass on disinformation and misinformation—the sale of ideas, whether for political or financial gain—"we are being propagandized to become propagandists."[139]

As an element of information warfare, propaganda has no visible and definable fronts; it is not geographically localizable and is ubiquitous, that is, it is everywhere simultaneously.[140] Further, because of fragmentation in small bites and wide-spread dispersal across the media at every level of society, it is intangible and can be difficult to recognize. These small bites are of such a nature that they often morph into memes, catching on and becoming part of a larger myth. These small sites are eagerly consumed in social media without supporting evidence, just a delicious headline.

As technologies have opened larger avenues of communication, propaganda has increasingly become the method of choice for influencing the purchases of the larger population and gaining competitive power. However, influencing people in this way is generally short-term; that is, over time an individual's preferences surface. When people have been influenced to purchase products they do not want or need, there is long-term fallout in terms of shared negative response.

In today's information environment, there are two primary forms of propaganda: (1) the shifting of cause and effect and (2) the strategic weaving of untruth and truth, creating layers of lies. The shifting of cause and effect is the most common. Power—at least for a time—can be achieved through making effects look like they are causes, which provides the ability to distort reality and create false beliefs. An example is the promise of communism, with the effect of some limited giving (food on the table and the promise of better times) leading to power transfer from the people to the government. The effect becomes the cause and people believe that communism is the reason they have food. Another example of reversal is when people try to take something for nothing by getting people to relinquish their power. When truth is compromised, mental capability shrinks and it becomes easier to convince people of untrue things, thus easier to manipulate and control them. The more often this occurs, the less ability the victims have to discern the truth. Concomitantly, as people relinquish power, the understanding of what they are doing is lost and their lives become less meaningful.

As a business example, owners who have been used to a high-profit margin and are reluctant to reduce that margin, may choose to cut salaries, informing employees that, in a down-turned economy, salaries must be reduced to keep the business alive and enable employees to keep their jobs. Where the truth lies becomes quite fuzzy, with an underlying reversal of cause and effect. Further, in this example employees are given the perceived chance to help keep the business functioning to ensure their income, albeit a reduced one. Perception consists of our impressions, attitudes and understanding about what we observe, which is a product of the threshold through which we focus. There is the added alure of partnering and loyalty when it appears that management is doing everything they can to work through a difficult situation that directly impacts employees.

Layering infers a continuous building of untruths, or a strategic weaving of truth and untruth. In the current post-truth climate, layering appears to be gaining more power. Consistent with our earlier discussion, the continuous layering of untruths causes redundancy in the progression of thought; as lies continue to build, prior lies are actually forgotten. People also become comfortable with not hearing the truth. A side effect is development of a sense of belonging to something larger and, not wanting to stand out or be different – sometimes driven by the fear of consequences – with a subsequent loss of creativity and individuation. A key factor in the weaving of truths and untruths is rhythm, which weaving can lead to destruction of the mental faculties. If you can recognize the rhythm and disrupt it, the truth is easier to discern.[141] A tool titled RHYTHM DISUPTOR is included in Section IV.

A higher form of propaganda is becoming creative in negative ways, creating a causal reality of intricately constructed lies which are hard to challenge.[142] Objects are created to convince people that what they last heard is connected to what they are being told, even when these may be opposites! An example is the political blathering during the 2016 U.S. Presidential election. A voice in a position of power can be destructive when connecting with people who do not have strong conceptually-developed minds or are still actively developing that life skill. When a mind focused on cause and effect hears one recognizable truth, that mind can easily connect other things told to them as true, not realizing a lack of consistency or any of the contradictions that are present.

Responses will then follow the path of false perceptions and logic characterized by such thought as: "If he told the truth in the past, then this must be true." Or "If this was successful before, then it will be successful now." Or "If he is wealthy and in a position of power, then it must be right."

Brainwashing

Brainwashing, which uses various techniques engaging the sense to change the thoughts and beliefs of others against their will, refers to mind control. In brainwashing, senses diminish such that the structure of thinking becomes discontinuous and there is the loss of sense-making capability. When the senses are not unified or balanced, working together, there is a reduction in the ability to discern truth and untruth. Thus, brainwashing most often includes some nature of sensory deprivation or overload.

Brainwashing can occur through various information distribution sources, including the media. The young are programmed by specialized computer games that glorify violence, potentially leading to acceptance of the use of violence and a belief that the end justifies the means. This is occurring in the wake of over-stimulation and divisiveness emerging from political and economic uncertainties coupled with a deadly pandemic. Media such as movies have the power to brainwash all ages, both negatively and positively. Continuing with our example, the negative weakening effects of media violence alone can lead to subtle grades of depression, which "kill more people than all the other diseases of mankind combined."[143] While there are many excellent studies in this domain, let's briefly explore Hawkins' work to better understand the full import of media violence on the physical body. Using Kinesiology testing, Hawkins was able to show that a typical television show produced weakening about 113 times in a single episode. As Hawkins explains:

> *Each of these weakening events suppressed the observer's immune system and reflected an insult to the viewer's central as well as autonomic nervous system. Invariably accompanying each of these 113 disruptions of the acupuncture system were suppressions of the thymus gland; each insult also resulted in damage to the brain's delicate neurohormonal and neurotransmitter systems. Each negative input brought the watcher closer to eventual sickness and to imminent depression.*[144]

Using Hawkins' levels of consciousness, any event providing information that produces a state of consciousness calibrated below 200 – which represents such states as Shame, Guilt, Apathy, Grief, Fear, Desire, Anger and Pride – is destructive and unsupportive of life.

As a final affirmation of what you most likely recognize since you are reading this book, *science provides the backbone for the discovery of truth.*

Through science, we can develop a more thorough understanding of the physical Universe and be provided the tools to act on the world. As explained:

> *The expansion of material knowledge permits a great intellectual appreciation of the meanings of ideas and the values of ideas. A human being can find truth in his inner experience, but he needs a clear knowledge of facts to apply his personal discovery of truth to the ruthlessly practical demands of everyday life.*[145]

FINAL THOUGHTS

We reiterate. Information—the foundation of knowledge—is a basic property of the Universe and *as fundamental as matter and energy.* If truth for the situation at hand can be discerned, information serves us well. And, ultimately, the responsibility for discerning truth lays firmly with the individual decision-maker.

CHAPTER 4

THE FOUNDING GRACE OF KNOWLEDGE THEORY

The phrase "knowledge is power" is often attributed
to Francis Bacon from his Meditationes Sacrae (1597)

Today, we use a definition of knowledge such as "the capacity (potential or actual) to take effective action",[146] connecting information and action, all very much built on the thousands-of-years-old philosophical definition of "justified true belief", where a belief is "justified" as true through action and the results of that action. Still, there's so much more we're learning about the nature of knowledge, which is at the very core of what it is to be human.

For example, we recognize that knowledge is dependent on context, that it is always partial/incomplete or imperfect, and that it grows with use and increases when shared. And a whole lexicon and a myriad of taxonomies have emerged as the term knowledge was linked to management, serviced by technology, and tied to the bottom-line of our organizations. There are levels of knowledge, types of knowledge, parts of knowledge, characteristics of knowledge, and aspects of knowledge, with concepts such as tacit and explicit becoming part of our everyday vocabulary. We hope this long chapter will serve as a foundation for a deeper understanding of knowledge and can serve as a future resource.

As a functional definition, **knowledge** is considered *the capacity (potential or actual) to take effective action in varied and uncertain situations,*[147] a human capacity that consists of understanding, insights, meaning, intuition, creativity, judgment, and the ability to anticipate the outcome of our actions. There is considerable precedent for linking knowledge and action consistent with the emergence in the 1990's driven by computing, consultants, conferences, and commerce of the Knowledge Management (KM) field as a business management approach.[148] In the KMTL research study of KM thought leaders, 84 percent of responders tied knowledge directly to action or use.[149] Contributing thoughts from participants in this study[150] and the follow-on Sampler Research Call [151]are included throughout this book. Similarly—building on nearly 20 years of APQC (American Productivity & Quality Center) research in the field of KM – O'Dell and Hubert define knowledge from the practical perspective as "information in action".[152]

While recognizing that it is common to define information as processed data and knowledge as actionable information, Batra finds it interesting that the definitions or interpretations of the term knowledge are contextual (and rightly so). However, he also notes that knowledge gets interpreted as know-what, know-how, know-who, and know-why in another context, and in an HR context, knowledge includes the competence set of individual skills and attitudes. From a strategic perspective, knowledge can be considered as a strategic resource for the firm, taking the form of intellectual capital and intangible capital. He finds these differences in interpretation useful to the students of KM in "appreciating that knowledge is not a monolithic entity which can be managed in a prescriptive manner."[153]

Dhewa likes the notion of "useful knowledge", which he says is basically a way of understanding knowledge as an economic resource, a concept originally developed by Kuznets[154] and extensively used by Mokyr in his studies about the role of knowledge in the industrial revolution.[155] As Dhewa suggests, "I am applying this notion in exploring the role of knowledge in the agriculture sector. Unless knowledge solves a specific issue like income growth, it's not knowledge at all, according to me. When knowledge is applied, it defines itself."[156]

Linking knowledge and action provides a foundation for measuring knowledge effectiveness. Knowledge itself is neither true nor false, and its value in terms of good or poor is difficult to measure other than by the outcomes of actions based on that knowledge. Good knowledge would have a high probability of producing the desired (anticipated) outcome, and poor knowledge would have a low probability of producing the expected result. For complex situations, the quality of knowledge (from good to poor) may be hard to estimate before the action is taken because of the system's unpredictability. However, after the outcome has occurred, it may be possible to assess the quality of knowledge by comparing the actual outcome to the expected outcome; although it is also possible that there may not be a direct observable causal relationship between a decision made/action taken and the results of that action. To change a complex system generally involves a decision set implemented over time. Note that this is consistent with the philosophical definition of knowledge as "justified true belief", where a belief is proven true by the result of action taken based on belief.

As if on cue, in the midst of a growing understanding of complexity, we developed the instruments that enabled us to better understand the way our mind/brain operates, the amazing qualities of the body that power our thoughts and feelings, and the reciprocal loops as those thoughts and feelings change our physical structure,[157] and the realization that we are social beings designed to think and learn socially. That emerging knowledge begged us to rethink what we know about learning and knowledge, providing a new starting point to expand toward the future, a future both *individual and social in nature*.[158] This sets the stage for the potential offered through the knowledge movement and the passion this field incites in thought leaders and novices alike.

THE NATURE OF KNOWLEDGE

When Einstein discovered relativity, we didn't fully understand its implications. Knowledge is dependent on context. In fact, it represents an understanding of situations and their context, insights into the relationships to a system, and the ability to identify leverage points and weaknesses to recognize the meaning in a specific situation and to anticipate future implications of actions taken to resolve problems, meet challenges, and take advantage of opportunities. Thus, all knowledge is situation-dependent and context-sensitive.

Shared understanding, the underlying purpose of communication and a primary goal of knowledge mobilization,[159] is taken to mean the movement of knowledge from one person to the other, recognizing that what passes in the air when two people are having a conversation is information in the form of changes in air pressure. These patterns of change may be understood by the listener (if they know the language and its nuances), but the changes in air pressure *do not* represent understanding, meaning or the capacity to anticipate the consequences of actions. The listener must be able to take these patterns (information) and— interpreting them through context—re-create the knowledge that the source intended. This same phenomenon occurs when information is passed through writing or other communications vehicles. In other words, content and context (information) originating at the source resonate with the perceiver such that the intended knowledge can be re-created by the perceiver. If the subject is simple and familiar to both participants, knowledge sharing (re-creation) may be easy. However, if the subject is complex and the parties do not have common contexts, sharing may be very challenging.[160]

Recognizing the nature of knowledge in terms of context sensitivity and situation dependence, it follows that all knowledge is imperfect and/or incomplete, that is, any small shift in the context or situation may require shifting or expanding knowledge, which in turn drives different decisions and actions to achieve the desired outcome(s). Further, in a complex environment—and all people and organizations are complex adaptive systems—it is impossible to know or even identify all the elements of a system affecting a challenge or situation, and, around the world, people are always learning and expanding what is known. Thus, knowledge is always partial (imperfect and/or incomplete), although it may be the best we can create at the moment of decision for the situation at hand.[161]

Further, *intelligent* activity involves engagement in the external reality. Building on the discussion in Chapter 2, intelligent activity means interacting with our environment, with the choices we make and actions we take affecting the larger energy field within which we interact. In an organization intelligence is taken to be the ability of an organization to perceive, interpret, and respond to its environment in a manner that simultaneously meets its organizational goals while satisfying its stakeholders, that is, its employees, customers, investors, community, and environment. Since knowledge grows with use and increases when shared, through our actions we participate in the expansion of the field, which in turn requires new ways of thinking—new knowledge—for us to be effective.

Kn (Informing) and Kn (Proceeding)

We consider knowledge as comprised of two parts: Knowledge (Informing) and Knowledge (Proceeding).[162] This builds on the distinction made by Ryle between "knowing that" and "knowing how" (the potential and actual capacity to take effective action). **Knowledge (Informing)** is the *information (or content)* part of knowledge.[163] While this information part of knowledge is still generically information (organized patterns), it is special because of its structure and relationships with other information. Knowledge (Informing) consists of information that may represent understanding, meaning, insights, expectations, intuition, theories and principles that support or lead to effective action. When viewed separately this is information even though it *may* lead to effective action. It is considered knowledge when used as *part of the knowledge process*.

Knowledge (Proceeding) represents the *process* and *action* part of knowledge. Knowledge (Proceeding) is the process of selecting and associating or applying the relevant information, or Knowledge (Informing), from which specific actions can be identified and implemented, that is, actions that result in some level of anticipated outcome. There is considerable precedence for considering knowledge as a process versus an outcome of action. For example, Kolb forwards in his theory of experiential learning, knowledge retrieval, creation and application requires engaging knowledge as a process, *not* a product.[164] Bohm reminds us that "the actuality of knowledge is a living process that is taking place right now" and that we are taking part in this process.[165] Note that the process our minds use to find, create and semantically mix the information needed to take effective action is often unconscious and difficult to communicate to someone else (otherwise, tacit).

In Figure 4-1, "justified true belief" represents the theories, values and beliefs that are generally developed over time and often tacit. Note that "justified true belief" is the definition of knowledge credited to Plato and his dialogues.[166] The concept is based on the belief that in order to know a given proposition is true you must not only believe it but must have justification for believing it. Justified true belief represents an individual's truth, that is, the beliefs and values that make up our personal theories, all developed and reinforced by life experiences. In the figure, the term "memory" is used as a singular collective and implies all the patterns and connections accessible by the mind occurring before the instant at hand.

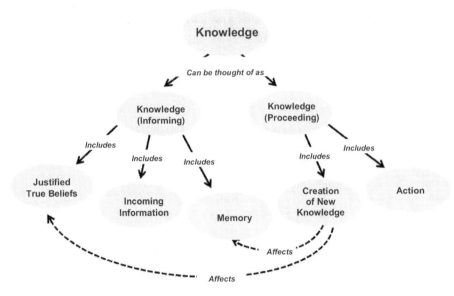

Figure 4-1. Knowledge (Informing) and Knowledge (Proceeding).

Knowledging

Since knowledge is relative, that is, situation-dependent and context sensitive, "knowledging" represents a *conscious learning choice in a specific situation and context*. The process of knowledging – which is a natural human skill – begin with identification of an issue or problem. Situations emerge every day that require solutions. Seeking those solutions, the individual purposefully places themselves in experiential (attending a seminar) and existential (reflection) learning situations, external and internal. Internet searches and, if that fails, social networking appear to be the mechanisms of choice to find solutions. If the situation or issue is pressing enough and looks like it will require a large capital or time commitment, the process expands through environmental awareness, scanning the environment and identifying the environmental opportunity space to ensure conscious exposure to issues, challenges, and ideas related to the issue at hand, then possibly vericating your thoughts and findings (consulting a trusted ally) while simultaneously adapting humility in openness to other's ideas while freely sharing your ideas with others. As this journey of expansion continues, pattern thinking emerges, which aids effective forecasting regarding the impact of potential solutions.

Organizationally based, knowledging includes the ability to work in resonance with the vision, mission, and values of the organization while engaging Knowledge Capacities (Chapter 16), creatively pursuing innovative processes and products that increase effectiveness, efficiency, and knowledge productivity.

Note that knowledging is not a singular journey. Through Relationship Network Management (Chapter 14), the "knowledger" – the individual who is knowledging – discovers the expanding potential of affective attunement from the viewpoints of both leading and learning, giving and receiving.

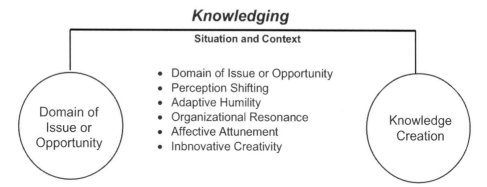

Knowledging

Situation and Context

- Domain of Issue or Opportunity
- Perception Shifting
- Adaptive Humility
- Organizational Resonance
- Affective Attunement
- Inbnovative Creativity

Domain of Issue or Opportunity

Knowledge Creation

Figure 4-2. Knowledging, the focused link between seeking expertise as a response to an issue or opportunity and knowledge creation, highly situation dependent and context sensitive.

Recall that knowledge is the capacity to take effective action in a specific situation and a specific context; thus, knowledging is the process of seeking knowledge in a specific domain for a specific situation at hand, which is most often not the expertise domain of the seeker. While learning, the creation of knowledge, is the outcome of knowledging, they are very different terms since knowledging is purposefully – formally or informally, externally or internally – seeking knowledge (the capacity to take effective action) specific to an issue at hand. In other words, a community is focused around a domain of knowledge, while the knowledging network is focused around a specific issue in a specific context, perhaps a problem that needs resolving NOW. Thus, the six capabilities supporting knowledging relate to the specificity of focus. *Environmental awareness* is the ability to identify and understand the situation at hand and the context in which that situation is occurring in addition to, as noted above, the ability to scan the environment and identify the environmental opportunity space to consider the best solution, ensuring conscious exposure to related issues, challenges, and ideas.

Perception shifting is the ability to look at the situation at hand or domain of focus from different perspectives. Examples of this are provided in Chapter 16 on Knowledge Capacities. *Adaptive humility* is a necessary ability which does not only entail listening to and considering other's ideas, but the ability to connect those ideas to information gleaned from environmental awareness and perception shifting as well as adapt those ideas to the situation at hand.

Organizational resonance is a necessity – it is one of the overarching goals of Reblooming Knowledge. This reiterates the need for a "connectedness of choices" between the knowledger (the individual who is knowledging) and organizational values, beliefs, and actions. As introduced in the Preface, related to the Reblooming Knowledge model in Chapter 7, and discussed in Chapter 11, this is a knowledge exchange that represents the shared state of *affective attunement*, the vibrational entrainment that opens the door to learning, deeper and easier knowledge sharing, and, collectively, the triggering of new ideas. To this group of abilities, we add *innovative creativity*, which is purposefully engaging your creativity with innovation in mind (see Chapter 10) or the companion book *Innovative Creativity: Creating with Innovation in Mind* by Bennet and Shelley.

WHY IS THEORY IMPORTANT?

When Kant proposed a Copernican Revolution, he argued that our experiences are structured by the categories of our thought, the way we think about space, time, matter, substance, causality, contingency, necessity, universality, particularity, etc.[167] Bohm suggests that to achieve clarity of perception and thought "requires that we be generally aware of how our experience is shaped by ... the theories that are implicit or explicit in our general ways of thinking."[168] Bohm emphasizes that *experience and knowledge are one process*. It is our theories that give shape and form to experience in general, both expanding and limiting us.

A **theory** is considered a set of statements and/or principles that explain a group of facts or phenomena to guide action or assist in comprehension or judgment.[169] Based on beliefs and/or mental models and built on assumptions, theories provide a plausible or rational explanation of cause-and-effect relationships.

Taken from the Greek word *theoria*, which interestingly has the same root as theatre, theory means to *see* or *view* or *to make a spectacle*. Theories reflect higher-order patterns, that is, not the facts themselves but rather the *basic source of recognition and meaning of the broader patterns*. This is consistent with the division of mental thought, with lower mental thought based on logic (cause-and-effect) and higher mental thought based on concepts (theories) which have been developed over time from patterns of lower mental thought. Whole thought is considered the ability to combine lower and higher mental thought such that theories can be developed from events, events can be explained by theories, and theories can be applied as events.[170]

Bohm sees theories as a form of insight, a way of looking at the world, clear in certain domains, and unclear beyond those domains, continuously shifting as new insights emerge through experience. While a written theory could be considered information, when used by a decision-maker to create and guide effective action it would be considered knowledge. Further, while in its incoming form it is Knowledge (Informing), when complexed with other information in the mind of the decision-maker to make decisions and guide action it becomes part of the process that is Knowledge (Proceeding).

A framework or model based on a theoretical structure highlights the primary elements of the theory and their relationships. In Figure 4-3 below, there is a dotted line between practice and assumptions, and assumptions and theory. **Assumptions** are something taken for granted or accepted as true without proof, a supposition or presumption. **Principles** are considered basic truths or laws; rules or standards; an essential quality or element. **Guidelines** are a statement or other indication of policy or procedure by which to determine a course of action (how to apply). A **framework**, then, is a set of assumptions, concepts, values and practices that constitute a way of viewing reality. Thus, a framework is tied closely to action.

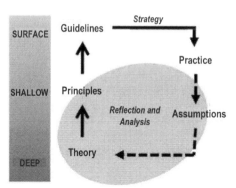

Figure 4-3. Theory as deep knowledge. Deeper understanding increases the ability to apply learning in different contexts and changing situations.

While every decision made and action taken is at some level based on assumption, people tend to not dig down below surface knowledge to understand their assumptions, yet they are always there in every decision we make. Assumptions underpin theory, from which principles emerge. Principles drive guidelines, which in turn inform practice. And through actions and the feedback from those actions new assumptions are born.

Recall that a characteristic of deep knowledge is the amazing ability of the human mind to shift our frame of reference as the context and situation shift, the realm of the expert who has learned to identify and apply patterns (deep knowledge). As Batra says, there is a symbiotic relationship between theory and practice cannot be over-emphasized. When we understand the relationships among things, we can make better decisions with a higher probability of having the expected results. Fitzgerald jokingly observes that "in theory there is no difference between theory and practice; but in practice, there is."[171]And this is a reality. When we are in the midst of activity (practice) it is difficult to shift our thinking to consider the whole system of interactivity taking place, while if a theory is in front of us, it might just be easier to fit an activity that is occurring into the theory.

We are all decision-makers, and the decisions we make and actions we take are in anticipation of the outcomes of those decisions and actions. Each of us has a self-organizing, hierarchical set of theories (and an understanding of relationships among those theories) that guide our decision-making process.[172]

Let's quickly walk through the decision-making process, which begins with a situation that is both *context sensitive and situation dependent*, and with three sets of information that start the learning process: (a) theories, values, beliefs, and assumptions internal to the decision-maker, (b) memories and information related to aspects of the situation at hand, and (c) incoming information from the external environment. The decision-maker creates knowledge by reflecting upon and comprehending the interactions among (a), (b) and (c) above, complexed with knowledge related to potential actions available and applicable to the situation at hand, which are part of (b).[173] Out of this process comes understanding, meaning, insights, perhaps creative ideas, and *anticipation of the outcome of potential actions*, that is, knowledge, the capacity (potential or actual) to take effective action.

Frequently, there are a number of potential actions that will move the decision-maker toward the desired outcome relative to the situation at hand. For example, assuming three potential actions and their forecasted outcomes, the decision-maker evaluates each decision option in terms of the science and the art of decision-making. The *science* of decision-making refers to the use of logic, reductionist thinking, analysis, cost-benefit investigations, linear extrapolation, and—where feasible—simulations, trade-off analysis, and probability analysis. The *art* of decision-making refers to the intuition, judgment, feelings, imagination, and heuristics which come largely from the unconscious. Combining these two approaches to understand the forecasted outcomes, the decision-maker selects the option which either objectively or intuitively (or both) is expected to have the highest probability of success in achieving the desired goals and objectives, often the beginning of a decision journey.[174] We add that caveat since in today's changing, uncertain, and complex reality, it can be difficult for a single decision to fully accomplish what is desired. Rather, it is a "good" decision if it heads the individual (or organization) in the desired direction.

There are striking similarities between decision-making in a complex adaptive situation and the internal workings of the mind/brain. In the brain thoughts are represented by patterns of neuronal firings of 70 milivolt pulses and the strength of their synapse connections. The brain stores information (thoughts, images, beliefs, theories, emotions, etc.) in the form of patterns of neurons, their connections, and the strength of those connections. Although the patterns themselves are nonphysical, their existence as represented by neurons and their interconnected environment *are* occurring in the physical, that is, supported by the atoms, molecules and cells. Incoming signals to the body (images, sounds, smells, sensations of the body) are transformed into internal patterns in the mind/brain that represent (to varying degrees of fidelity) corresponding associations in the external world. The intermixing of these sets of information (patterns), what is referred to as semantic mixing[175] or complexing, creates new neural patterns that represent understanding, meaning, and the anticipation of the consequences of actions (knowledge). The mind/brain is essentially a self-organizing, cybernetic, highly complex *adaptive learning system* that survives by converting incoming information from its environment into knowledge, acting on that knowledge. This system is replete with feedback loops, control systems, sensors, memories, and meaning-making systems made up of about 100 billion neurons and about 10^{15} interconnections.

From the viewpoint of the mind/brain, any knowledge that is being "re-used" is actually being "re-created" and—especially in an area of continuing interest—most likely complexed over and over again as incoming information is associated with internal information.[176] Thus, knowledge as such is *an emergent phenomenon*. There is no direct cause and effect relationship between information and knowledge, rather it is the *interaction among many ideas, concepts and patterns of thought* (including goals, objectives, beliefs, issues, context, etc.) that create knowledge. Further, if Knowledge (Informing) is different, there is a good chance that Knowledge (Proceeding) will be different, that is, the *process* of pulling up, integrating and sequencing associated Knowledge (Informing) and semantically complexing it with incoming information to make it comprehensible (usable and applicable) is going to vary. In essence, every time we apply Knowledge (Informing) and Knowledge (Proceeding) it is new knowledge because the human mind—unlike an information management system—*unconsciously tailors what is emerging as knowledge to the situation at hand.*[177]

As can be seen, this is NOT a process that can be "controlled" externally. However, it can be influenced by lack of access to information or external parties controlling what information is available (see the discussion in Chapter 2 on misinformation, disinformation and propaganda). Nonetheless, the process uses pertinent information (to the individual decision-maker) that has been stored in memory throughout a lifetime and which is therefore not dependent on one point in time, supporting freedom of choice consistent with the underlying theories, values, beliefs, and assumptions internal to the decision-maker, which in turn are continuously being updated by experiences and current incoming information of import to the decision-maker.

We never see the same world twice. The brain (as distinct from a computer) does *not* store exact replicas of past events or memories. Rather, it stores *invariant representations*. These forms represent the *basic source of recognition and meaning of the broader patterns*.[178] Nobel laureate Eric Kandel says that this process of storing invariant forms enables individuals to "apply memories to situations that are similar but not identical to previous experiences", which is the process of plasticity.[179] One way this can be described is as developing internal representations of the external world, that is, **a cognitive map that provides a meaningful interpretation or image of our perceptions and experiences**. These are what we call our theories.

LEVELS OF KNOWLEDGE

Building on the definitions of Knowledge (Informing) and Knowledge (Proceeding) introduced above, it is also useful to think about knowledge in terms of three levels: surface, shallow and deep. Recognizing any model is an artificial construct, the focus on three levels (as a continuum) is consistent with a focus on simple, complicated and complex systems. Note that this is a focus on the "knowledge" (information that represents the potential or actual ability to take effective action) itself.

Surface knowledge is predominantly, but not exclusively, information. Answering the question of what, when, where and who, it is primarily explicit, and represents visible choices that require minimum context. Little action is typically required to understand it; rather requiring an awareness of *what is* on the part of the receiver. Surface knowledge in the form of information can be stored in books and computers and memorized by the mind/brain. However, because it has little meaning to improve recall, few connections to other stored memories, and minimal emotional tags, surface knowledge is frequently difficult to remember and easy to forget.[180]

Shallow knowledge includes information that has some depth of understanding, meaning and sense-making. To make meaning requires context, which the individual creates from incoming information and their own internally-stored information, a process of creating Knowledge (Proceeding). This meaning can be created via logic, analysis, observation, reflection, and even—to some extent—prediction. Shallow knowledge is the realm of social knowledge, and as such this focus of KM overlaps with social learning theory.[181] Shallow knowledge requires some level of context, which largely occurs through conversations with others, offering the opportunity for questions and answers and the free expression of opinions. Knowledge emerges (and expands) through interactions as employees move through the processes and practices of an organization. For example, organizations that embrace the use of teams and communities facilitate the mobilization of both surface and shallow knowledge and the creation of new ideas as individuals interact in those groups.

For **deep knowledge** the decision-maker has developed and integrated many if not all of the following seven components: understanding, meaning, intuition, insight, creativity, judgment, and the ability to anticipate the outcome of our actions. Deep knowledge represents the ability to shift our frame of reference as context and situation shift, that is, the transference of patterns from one situation to another. Since Knowledge (Proceeding) must be created in order to know when and how to take effective action, the unconscious plays a large role in this area. This is the realm of the expert who has learned to detect patterns and evaluate their importance in anticipating the behavior of situations that are too complex for the conscious mind to understand. During the lengthy period of practice (lived experience) needed to develop deep knowledge, experts have developed sometimes complex internal theories that guide their Knowledge (Proceeding).

Each learning experience builds on its predecessor by broadening the sources of knowledge creation and the capacity to create knowledge in different ways. When an individual has deep knowledge, more and more of their learning will continuously build up in the unconscious. In other words, in the area of focus, knowledge begets knowledge. The more that is understood, the more that can be created and understood, relegating more to the unconscious to free the conscious mind to address the instant at hand. The wider the scope of application and feedback, the greater the potential to identify second order patterns, which in the largest aggregate leads to the phenomena of Big Data.[182]

THE EXPLICIT, IMPLICIT, AND TACIT DIMENSIONS

By the latter part of the 20th century the push to understand knowledge and its value to organizations had spread across a number of disciplines with the result that concepts of explicit and tacit knowledge became well-known terms in both the academic organizational literature and the popular press. We briefly introduce these and the historical use of "implicit" below.

Explicit knowledge is the process of calling up information (patterns) and processes (patterns in time) from memory that can be described accurately in words and/or visuals (representations) such that another person can comprehend the knowledge that is expressed through this exchange of information. Straight-forward and easily understood, this has historically been called declarative knowledge.[183]

Emotions can be expressed as explicit knowledge in terms of changes in body state. As Damasio notes, "Many of the changes in body state—those in skin color, body posture, and facial expression, for instance—are actually perceptible to an external observer."[184] These changes to the body state often represent part of an explicit knowledge exchange, as do body movements.[185] Examples would be turning red with embarrassment or blushing in response to an insensitive remark.

Implicit knowledge is a more complicated concept, and a term not unanimously agreed-upon in the literature. This is understandable since even simple dictionary definitions—which are generally unbiased and powerful indicators of collective preference and understanding—show a considerable overlap between the terms "implicit" and "tacit," making it difficult to differentiate the two. We propose that a useful interpretation of *implicit knowledge* is knowledge stored in memory of which the individual is *not immediately aware*. While this information is *not readily accessible*, it may be pulled up when triggered (associated). Triggering might occur through questions, dialogue or reflective thought, or happen as a result of an external event. In other words, implicit knowledge is knowledge that the individual *does not know* they have but is self-discoverable! However, once this knowledge is surfaced, the individual *may or may not* have the ability to adequately describe it such that another individual could create the same knowledge; and the "why and how" may remain tacit knowledge.

A number of published psychologists have used the term implicit interchangeably with the current usage of tacit, that is, with implicit representing knowledge that once acquired can be shown to effect behavior but is not available for conscious retrieval.[186] As described in the above discussion, what is forwarded here is that the concept of implicit knowledge serve a middle ground between that which can be made explicit when triggered and that which cannot easily (if at all) be made explicit. By moving beyond the dualistic approach of explicit and tacit—that which can be declared versus that which can't be declared, and that which can be consciously remembered versus that which can't be consciously remembered—we posit implicit as *representing the knowledge spectrum between explicit and tacit*. While explicit refers to easily available, some knowledge requires a higher stimulus for association to occur yet is not buried so deeply as to prevent access. This understanding is the domain of implicit knowledge.

The concept of a spectrum between explicit and tacit is not a new idea. Calling them interactive components of cooperative processes, Reber agrees that there is no clear boundary between that which is explicit and that which is implicit (our tacit): "There is ... no reason for presuming that there exists a clean boundary between conscious and unconscious processes or a sharp division between implicit and explicit epistemic systems ..."[187] Similarly, Matthews says that the unconscious and conscious processes are engaged in what he likes to call a "synergistic" relationship.[188] What this means is that the boundary between the conscious and the unconscious is somewhat porous and flexible. Given that caveat, how do we describe tacit knowledge?

Tacit knowledge is the descriptive term for those connections among thoughts that cannot be pulled up in words, a knowing of *what* decision to make or *how* to do something that cannot be clearly voiced in a manner such that another person could extract and re-create that knowledge (understanding, meaning, etc.). An individual *may or may not* know they have tacit knowledge in relationship to something or someone. But even when it *is known*, the individual is unable to put it into words or visuals that can convey that knowledge. We all know things, or know what to do, yet may be unable to articulate *why* we know them, *why* they are true, or even exactly *what they are*. To "convey" is to cause something to be known or understood or, in this usage, to transfer information from which the receiver is able to create knowledge.

All knowledge starts as tacit knowledge, that is, the initial movement of knowledge is from its origins within individuals (with unconscious participation) to an outward expression (howbeit driving effective action). What does that mean? Michael Polanyi, a professor of both chemistry and the social sciences, wrote in *The Tacit Dimension* that, "We start from the fact that we can know more than we can tell."[189] He called this pre-logical phase of knowing "tacit knowledge", that is, knowledge that cannot be articulated.[190] Be aware that these definitions place the concepts of tacit and explicit squarely on the individual, as characteristics attributable to a specific individual, not the knowledge.

Tacit and explicit knowledge can be thought of as residing in "places," specifically, the unconscious and conscious, respectively, although both Knowledge (Informing) and Knowledge (Proceeding)—whether tacit or explicit—are differentiated patterns spread throughout the neuronal system, that is, the volume of the brain and other parts of the central nervous system. On the other hand, implicit knowledge may reside in either the unconscious (prior to triggering, or tacit) or the conscious (when triggered, or explicit). See the continuum of awareness of knowledge source/content represented in Figure 4-5 in the discussion of expanding the tacit dimension below. Note that there is no clean break between these characteristics related to the ability to express knowledge, which is, of course, highly dependent on the "who" is expressing. Cheng Gong, MIKE Award Coordinator and Founder of Infinite Knowledge in China, includes a *Level of Tacitness* bar on what he calls the Tacit Knowledge Onion, moving from high (more abstract) to low (more concrete), reflecting the knowing that all knowledge begins as tacit.

Knowledge (Proceeding) may be explicit, implicit or tacit. However, for anything except the simplest knowledge, the process we use to find, create and mix the information needed to take effective action is difficult, if at all possible, to communicate to someone else. Thus, in many situations, the expertise involved in deciding what actions to take will be tacit. Team discussions, problem solving and decision-making, while helpful and necessary, must address the emotional, intuitive and embodied tacit knowledge aspects as well as relevant data, information, and explicit knowledge of the participants.

Relationship with Levels of Knowledge

There are significant differences between the levels of knowledge introduced above and the explicit, implicit and tacit dimensions of knowledge. First and primary is the focus. As forwarded above, the tacit, implicit and explicit dimensions are focused on that which resides in the conscious and that which resides in the unconscious pertinent to a specific individual in a specific situation; that is, the ability of an individual to express knowledge (explicit) or inability to express knowledge (tacit), with implicit used to describe knowledge stored in memory of which the individual is not immediately aware, but which may be pulled up when triggered (associated), a moving middle ground between explicit and tacit. Since this terminology is based on the ability of an individual, what is tacit to one person may not be tacit to another, etc. In contrast, the levels of knowledge focus on the *ease of understanding* specific knowledge: simple facts (surface knowledge), the need for shared context (shallow knowledge, also known as social knowledge) and the pattern-recognition of lived experience in a knowledge domain (deep knowledge).

While it is possible to be unable to recall/voice simple facts and yet be able to convey deep knowledge through stories, for example, a larger amount of surface knowledge will be explicit, and a larger amount of deep knowledge will be tacit. See Figure 4-4.

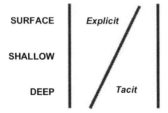

Figure 4-4. Relationship between levels of knowledge and dimensions of knowledge.

This relationship between the levels of knowledge and the dimensions of knowledge is because surface knowledge is primarily information, easily accessible and rapidly changing, facts easy to memorize and recite back (game shows) and largely Knowledge (Informing). In contrast, deep knowledge deals with patterns developed over time, the realm of the expert who has developed an internal knowing based on complex interactions through focused effort in a domain of knowledge. Much of this will be Knowledge (Proceeding), the unique way a decision-maker complexes internal and external Knowledge (Informing) to make decisions and take effective action.

Expanding the Tacit Dimension

Dealing with change, uncertainty and complexity—the business environment of today—demands deep knowledge, which comes primarily from tacit knowledge.[191] If tacit is that which cannot be fully shared through communication and is not part of one's ordinary consciousness, then how do we *get* the knowledge needed to deal with complex problems, dynamic systems or unpredictable events?

The deeper we go into the meaning and characteristics of the concept of tacit knowledge, the more complex it becomes. Nevertheless, as the importance of tacit knowledge grows in support of organizational performance, so must our depth of understanding and the articulation of that understanding. Building on our functional definition of knowledge, *the capacity (potential or actual) to take effective action* (justified true belief), we now explore four aspects of tacit knowledge: embodied, affective, intuitive and spiritual. Each of these has its own unique characteristics and plays a different role in learning and the implementation of tacit knowledge within individuals and organizations. The four aspects of tacit knowledge are represented in Figure 4-5 along with explicit and implicit knowledge on the continuum of awareness.

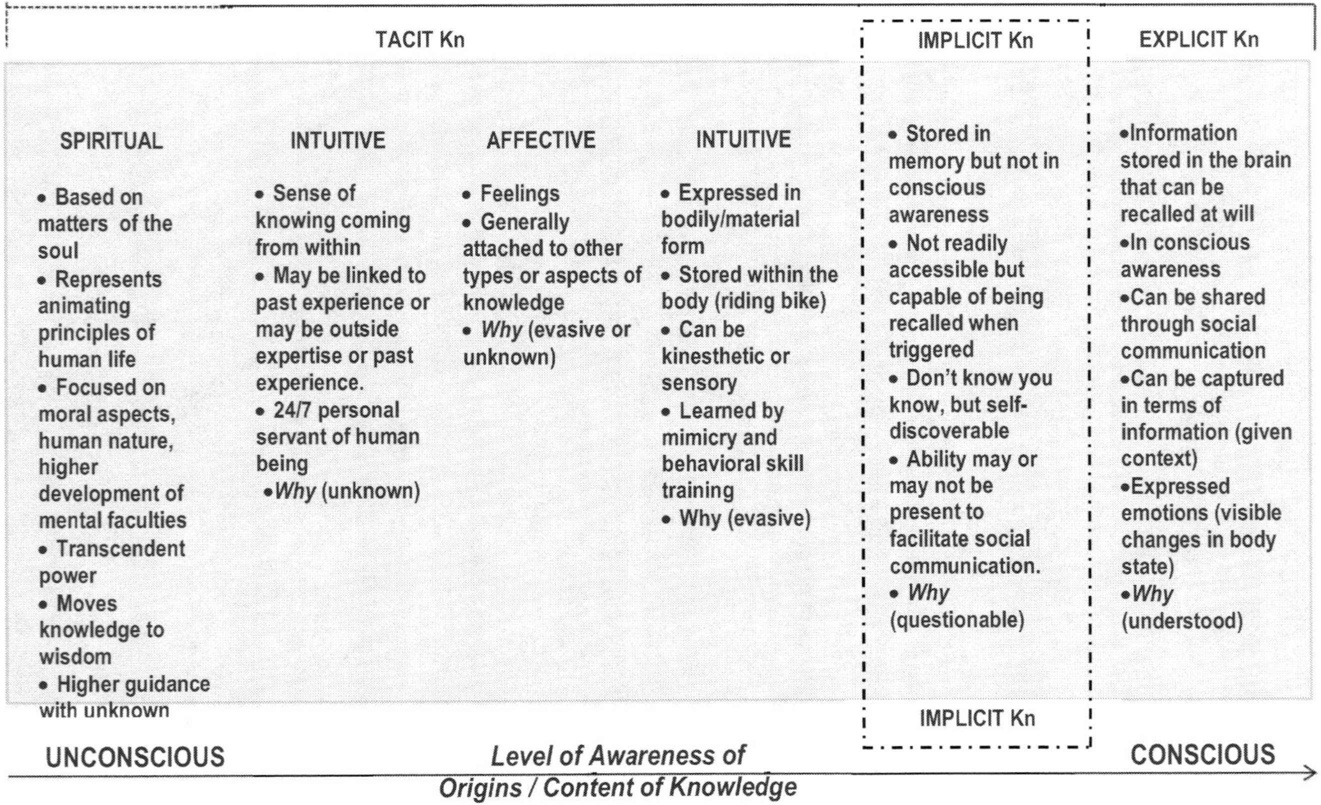

	TACIT Kn			IMPLICIT Kn	EXPLICIT Kn
	SPIRITUAL	**INTUITIVE**	**AFFECTIVE**	**INTUITIVE**	**IMPLICIT Kn**	**EXPLICIT Kn**
	• Based on matters of the soul • Represents animating principles of human life • Focused on moral aspects, human nature, higher development of mental faculties • Transcendent power • Moves knowledge to wisdom • Higher guidance with unknown	• Sense of knowing coming from within • May be linked to past experience or may be outside expertise or past experience. • 24/7 personal servant of human being • *Why* (unknown)	• Feelings • Generally attached to other types or aspects of knowledge • *Why* (evasive or unknown)	• Expressed in bodily/material form • Stored within the body (riding bike) • Can be kinesthetic or sensory • Learned by mimicry and behavioral skill training • *Why* (evasive)	• Stored in memory but not in conscious awareness • Not readily accessible but capable of being recalled when triggered • Don't know you know, but self-discoverable • Ability may or may not be present to facilitate social communication. • *Why* (questionable)	•Information stored in the brain that can be recalled at will •In conscious awareness •Can be shared through social communication •Can be captured in terms of information (given context) •Expressed emotions (visible changes in body state) •*Why* (understood)

UNCONSCIOUS ← Level of Awareness of / Origins / Content of Knowledge → CONSCIOUS

Figure 4-5. Continuum of awareness of knowledge source/content.

Embodied tacit knowledge, also referred to as somatic knowledge, can be represented in neuronal patterns stored within the body. It is both kinesthetic and sensory. *Kinesthetic* is related to the movement of the body and, while important to every individual every single day of our lives, is a primary focus for athletes, artists, dancers, kids, and assembly-line workers. A commonly used example is knowledge of riding a bicycle. *Sensory*, by definition, is related to the five physically-based human senses through which information enters the body (sight, smell, hearing, touch, and taste). An example is the smell of burning metal from your car brakes while driving, or the smell of hay in a barn. These smells can convey knowledge of whether the car brakes need replacing (get them checked immediately), or whether the hay is mildewing (dangerous to feed horses, but fine for cows). These responses would be overt, bringing to conscious awareness the need to take effective action and driving that action to occur.

Because embodied learning is often linked to experiential learning,[192] embodied tacit knowledge can generally be learned by mimicry and behavior skill training. While deliberate learning through study, dialogue, or practice occurs at the conscious level, when significant or repeated over time such learning often becomes tacit knowledge. Further, as individuals develop competence in a specific area, more of their knowledge in that area becomes tacit, making it difficult or impossible for them to explain how they know what they know. The neuronal patterns representing that knowledge become embedded within long-term working memory where they become automatic when needed but lost to consciousness. Embodied tacit knowledge can be both preventative and developmental. For example, a physical response can warn *not* to do something or, conversely, move an individual *to do something*. Both of these responses constitute the capacity to take effective action since *not taking an action is an action choice.*

Intuitive tacit knowledge is the sense of knowing coming from inside an individual that may influence decisions and actions, yet the decision-maker or actor cannot explain *how* or *why* the action taken is the right one. Damasio calls intuition, "the mysterious mechanism by which we arrive at the solution of a problem *without* reasoning toward it."[193] While that may be true in terms of our preferred definition of "reasoning", we are certainly "working" at it! The unconscious works around the clock with a processing capability many times greater than that at the conscious level. This is why as the world grows more complex, decision-makers must depend more and more on their intuitive tacit knowledge.

Intuitive tacit knowledge can be both Knowledge (Informing) and/or Knowledge (Proceeding), and it may reside in either the potential aspect of taking effective action (knowing how) or the actual aspect of taking effective action (acting). A form of knowing, deep tacit knowledge is created within our minds (or hearts or guts) over time through experience, contemplation, and unconscious processing such that it becomes a natural part of our being—not just something consciously learned, stored, and retrieved. In other words, intuitive tacit knowledge is the result of continuous learning through experience. To develop intuitive skills requires making sure that your experiences are meaningful, that is, having specific objectives in mind such as how to size up situations quickly and develop a good sense of what will happen next.[194] It is also important to get immediate and accurate feedback directly related to the context within which a decision was made. Understanding the outcomes of actions and why something did or did not happen helps develop patterns in the unconscious (intuition). According to Klein, to build up expertise requires: (1) feedback on decisions and actions, (2) active engagement in getting and interpreting this feedback (not passively allowing someone else to judge); and (3) repetitions, which provide the opportunity to practice making decisions and getting feedback.[195]

Affective tacit knowledge is connected to emotions and feelings, with emotions representing the external expression of some feelings. Feelings expressed as emotions become explicit.[196] Feelings that are not expressed—perhaps not even recognized—are those that fall into the area of affective tacit knowledge. From neuroscience research, information coming into the body moves through the amygdala, that part of the brain that is,

> ... *important both for the acquisition and for the on-line processing of emotional stimuli ... [with] Its processing encompassing both the elicitation of emotional responses in the body and changes in other cognitive processes, such as attention and memory.*[197]

It is as incoming information moves through the amygdala that an emotional "tag" is attached. If this information is perceived as life-threatening, then the amygdala takes control, making a decision and acting on that decision before conscious awareness of a threat! Haberlandt goes so far as to say that there is no such thing as a behavior or thought not impacted by emotions in some way.[198] Even simple responses to information signals can be linked to multiple emotional neurotransmitters. Thus, affective tacit knowledge is attached to other types or aspects of knowledge. For example, when an individual thinks about recent occurrences like an argument or a favorite sports team losing in the Rose Bowl, feelings are aroused. Or recall the internal responses to holding the hard copy of your first book, or your new born child. As Mulvihill states,

> *Because the neurotransmitters which carry messages of emotion are integrally linked with the information during both the initial processing and the linking with information from the different senses, it becomes clear that there is no thought, memory, or knowledge which is 'objective,' or 'detached' from the personal experience of knowing.*[199]

Feelings as a form of knowledge have different characteristics than language or ideas, but they may lead to effective action because they can influence actions by their existence and connections with consciousness. When feelings come into conscious awareness, they can play an informing role in decision-making, providing insights in a non-linguistic manner and thereby influencing decisions and actions. For example, a feeling (such as fear or an upset stomach) may occur every time a particular action is started which could prevent the decision-maker from taking that action.[200]

Spiritual tacit knowledge can be described in terms of knowledge based on matters of the soul. The soul represents the animating principles of human life in terms of thought and action, specifically focused on its moral aspects, the emotional part of human nature, and higher development of the mental faculties.[201] While there is a "knowing" related to spiritual knowledge similar to intuition, this knowing does not include the experiential base of intuition, and it may or may not have emotional tags. The current state of the evolution of our understanding of spiritual knowledge is such that there are insufficient words to relate its transcendent power, or to define the role it plays in relationship to other tacit knowledge. Nonetheless, this area represents a form of higher guidance with unknown origin.

In a Mountain Quest Institute study in early 2007, representative human characteristics spiritual in nature were identified that contribute to learning.[202] These characteristics were grouped into five general areas: *shifting frames of reference* (represented by abundance, awareness, caring, compassion, connectedness, empathy, openness); *animating for learning* (represented by aliveness, grace, harmony, joy, love, presence, wonder); *enriching relationships* (represented by authenticity, consistency, morality, respect, tolerance, values); *priming for learning* (represented by awareness, eagerness, expectancy, openness, presence, sensitivity, unfoldment, willingness); and *moving toward wisdom* (represented by caring, connectedness, love, morality, respect, service).

The general area of *shifting frames of reference* was intertwined with learning, thinking and acting, covering the external approach (looking from an outside frame of reference) and the internal approach (taking an empathetic perspective which moves the viewpoint from the objective to the subjective). Frames of reference can be focusing and/or limiting, allowing the mind to go deeper in a bounded direction. Shifting frames of reference potentially offers the opportunity to take a multidimensional approach to exploring the world around us and facilitates creativity and innovation. "Shifting frames of reference" has been identified as a Knowledge Capacity (see Chapter 16). The area of *animating for learning* speaks to the fundamental source of life—learning, the energy used for survival and growth. The area of *enriching relationships* is tied to competence theory,[203] which assumes that it is natural for people to strive for effective interactions with their world. This brings in the two dimensions of spirituality that exist beyond ourselves (other people and the larger energy system/ecosystem whether it is referred to as an energy field, consciousness field, quantum field or God field) with whom we can truly learn to grow in understanding.[204] *Priming for learning* attributes are considered as those that actively prepare and move an individual toward learning. Wisdom, the highest part of the knowledge spectrum, is considered as forwarding the goal of achieving the common or greater good.[205] Reflecting on this short study, it would appear that spiritual knowledge would provide a transcendent frame of reference that puts things in relationship to a larger perspective while promoting self-knowledge and learning.

Intersections and Overlaps

Similar to the possible interactions among tacit, implicit and explicit knowledge, the four aspects of tacit knowledge can experience considerable interconnections and overlaps. For example, referring to a somatic learning model by Amann, Merriam says that "the spiritual aspect of somatic learning is meaning-making through music, art, imagery, symbols, and rituals and overlaps or intersects with the other three dimensions",[206] which are described as kinesthetic learning, sensory learning and affective learning. While organized differently than the knowledge model presented here, the Amann model includes four elements—kinesthetic, sensory, affective and spiritual—as tacit knowledge.[207]

As a second example of overlap, affective and embodied somatic states can operate both inside and outside an individual's awareness or consciousness; however, if overlap occurs in the unconscious the results may surface as intuition. Conversely, affective and embodied somatic states are often accompanied by overt somatic markers; for example, a "gut feel" or what has been described as an "intuitive urge". In contrast, intuition comes from the neural network of the reticular activating system. Instead of producing a body-state change (sematic marker), it inhibits the regulatory neural circuits located in the brain core, which can influence behaviors.[208]

It is important to realize that we as decision-makers are holistic in nature, that is, all of the tacit knowledges described above are playing a role in our experiential engagement of life. In an increasingly uncertain and complex environment, to take effective action requires a mix of explicit, implicit and particularly tacit knowledge. The dilemma is that implicit knowledge and tacit knowledge, residing in the unconscious, cannot be readily shared such that individuals and teams can extract information and recreate the knowledge to make decisions and take effective action. The growing criticality of gaining access to this knowledge magnifies the need to understand implicit knowledge and the four aspects of tacit knowledge (embodied, intuitive, affective and spiritual), and intentionally develop vehicles to bring that knowledge into play.

Artificial Intelligence Tacit Knowledge

The AI systems coming on line today fall into the category of *explainable AI*, that is, systems that can provide the reasoning behind decisions, which helps to identify trustworthy data. The term "explainable" generally encompasses several related properties such as reliability, resiliency, bias, and accountability. In a research study funded by the National Institute of Standards and Technology (U.S. Department of Commerce), four principles for explainable AI were identified which fall in the categories of explanation, meaning, explanation accuracy, and knowledge limits. In order, these refer to (1) delivering evidence or reasons for outcomes and processes; (2) providing understandable explanations to the consumer(s); (3) providing an explanation that correctly reflects the reason for generating output and/or accurately reflects the system process; and (4) ensuring that a system operates under the conditions for which it was designed, and only when it reaches sufficient confidence in its output.[209]

One approach to explainable AI – an expanding field as Artificial Intelligence becomes more prominent in our reality – is statistical analysis. In *black-box systems*, which are defined by the associations between inputs and (desired) outputs, those statistics are based on task performance. Interestingly enough, this is how we also value "knowledge", that is, how effectively knowledge-driven decisions and actions achieve the expected (desired) outcome on a scale from 0 to 1. Remember, by definition, knowledge is the capacity (potential or actual) to take effective action or "justified true belief", if you will, which is the philosophical terminology for the same concept.

With AI, it appears we are currently on a learning curve akin to our learning curve in neuroscience before the turn of the century, before development of new technologies such as functional magnetic resonance imaging (fMRI), transcranial magnetic stimulation (TMI, and others significantly aided research looking from the inside-out of the mind/brain, determining where physiologically the brain has been most active, or what happens when you send strong signals composed of very short magnetic pulses directly into specific brain regions, thereby inducing tiny electrical currents in an individual's neural circuitry.[210] That state of blindness in terms of the workings of the mind/brain is where we are now with AI. While we, at least initially, have complete information regarding an AI system's internal state, as the system is used it tends to become more complex (much like the human mind) such that "the internal state of this system is not easily interpretable",[211] that is, the entanglement of connections has created an emergent state where it is difficult if not impossible to follow a cause-and-effect relationship, much less identify confounding variables. So, this statistical approach relies primarily on external observations, much as experiential learning did in the last century, and cannot confirm *how* output was determined.[212]

The idea of "tacit knowledge" in an AI system builds on Chomsky's concept of tacit knowledge which is, as defined above, the use of an internal knowledge or knowing that cannot be explicitly articulated.[213] Lam argues that, although it can't be articulated, since tacit knowledge is propositional – information used to perform certain actions – that we "can view the implicit use of high-level concepts by machine learning systems as an example of tacit knowledge."[214] This is consistent with the use of "tacit knowledge" by Davies, who argues that as tacit knowledge, a rule relating to some propositions is identifiable by a representation of that rule existing in the system, a *causally systematic process.*[215]

The looming question of whether a machine learning system can possess tacit knowledge punctuates two early questions asked by Smolensky in 1988: "What kind of subconceptual features do the units in the intuitive process represent?" and "Which activity patterns actually correspond to particular concepts or elements of the problem domain?"[216] These are still relevant and there are no clear answers. Lam concludes that "establishing explicit knowledge of a rule is impossible in the case of the subsymbolic machine learning systems used today." However, he does that "as system has some knowledge of a rule in a more limited sense."[217]

Our AI systems were initially built to follow mental reasoning. As Lam states "Understanding in large part requires the ability to reason about things, for which clear logical and causal connections have no substitute."[218] However, as lower mental thought, reasoning has its limits. In development of the human mind – as we move from Phase 1 to Phase 2 of the Intelligent Social Change Journey[219] – we develop the ability to identify patterns and move into higher-level conceptual thinking which is not bound by cause-and-effect, makes full use of past-present-future thinking, and seeks to understand the higher relationships among things (ideas), higher truths. This is what General AI is reaching towards.

TYPES OF KNOWLEDGE

In any specific application there may be several areas of knowledge that need to be considered in order to take action. These areas, or types of knowledge, can be grouped or organized according to similarities and differences, what could be described as a knowledge taxonomy. As a framework for recognizing and working with knowledge, the following taxonomy offers a useful grouping for understanding different types of knowledge from the viewpoint of what knowledge is needed to do a particular type of work or take a particular action.

The categories in this taxonomy include: Kmeta, Kresearch, Kpraxis, Kaction, Kdescription, Kstrategic and Klearning (see Figure 4-6). Taken together, these types of knowledge play different roles in understanding situations and taking actions. Each of these types is described briefly below.

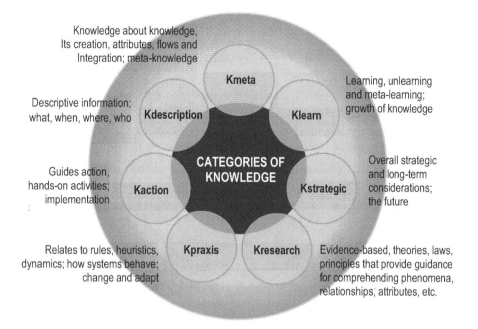

Figure 4-6. A knowledge taxonomy for grouping types of knowledge from the viewpoint of what knowledge is needed to do a particular type of work or take a particular action.

Meta-knowledge, **Kmeta**, represents the capacity to understand, create, assimilate, leverage, sculpt, and apply various types of information and knowledge. Since most complex situations contain several disciplines and categories of knowledge, our use of Kmeta (knowledge about knowledge) also includes the ability to bring different types of knowledges together. William Whewell, in his 1840 synthesis, *The Philosophy of the Inductive Sciences*, spoke of consilience as "...a 'jumping together' of knowledge by the linking of facts and fact-based theory across disciplines to create a common groundwork of explanation."[220] Wilson also uses consilience to mean, "The explanations of different phenomena most likely to survive ... those that can be connected and proved consistent with one another."[221] In making sense of complex situations, the consilience of different frames of references and knowledge categories may provide the best understanding for developing a solution.

Evidence based knowledge, **Kresearch**, includes theoretical as well as empirical knowledge and represents the fundamental concepts that explain *why* things happen. Such knowledge serves as a guide for setting expectations and possibilities and provides the user a level of confidence.

Pragmatic knowledge, **Kpraxis**, represents the practical understanding of situations and *how* they change or *can* be changed. Much pragmatic knowledge is tacit, experiential and intuitive.

Knowledge in action, **Kaction**, represents the ability to take specific actions that achieve the desired result. It includes understanding the *local* context and situation within which the action is taken.

Descriptive knowledge, **Kdescription**, is information that informs the *what, who, when* and *where* of a situation. As can be understood from the discussion of knowledge offered by Stonier,[222] all knowledge is composed of information, but all information is *not* knowledge. Knowledge is information that, when combined in the mind (associated or *complexed*), creates understanding, meaning and, where action is involved, the anticipation of its outcome.

The role of **Kstrategic** is to ensure that the actions taken are in consideration of their long-term impact and are consistent with the strategy, identity, and values of the organization. While this is a high-level type of knowledge (and thinking), note that this refers to the information, processes and patterns used to apply other information, processes and patterns in a strategic way. This means that many different types of knowledge can be used strategically.

The role of **Klearning** includes individual, group and organizational learning. This focus is to ensure that as a situation or process unfolds, individuals learn from each other and, when appropriate, build organizational learning into a task outcome to ensure that the organization is capable of adapting to future changes in the environment.

The above seven categories can be considered as a useful spectrum of knowledge areas, sometimes overlapping and often having gaps between them. They are selected for their usefulness in the problem solving, decision-making, execution and feedback learning processes, particularly when dealing with complex situations. An individual or members of a team or organization may have expertise in one, several, or none of these categories and the knowledge needed will depend on the content, context and desired outcome of the situation/problem. The more complex the situation, the more different types of knowledge may be needed for the individual or team to be successful.

In the discussion of Kstrategic above, it was noted that this type of knowledge refers to the information, processes and patterns used to apply other information, processes and patterns in a strategic way. In other words, many different types of knowledge can be used strategically. The concepts of tactical, operational, and strategic information and knowledge are often used in organizations. These three concepts can be correlated to the levels of knowledge (surface, shallow, and deep).

For example, strategic knowledge would emphasize deep knowledge because of the complexity of forecasting the future environment and creating a strategy to ensure organizational sustainability into the future. A successful strategy would require creative ideas and practices with flexibility built into implementation. Operational management would require primarily surface knowledge during normal operations when the environment was stable. However, when disruptions occurred in the environment or within the organization, managers and leaders with deep knowledge in the areas where the disruptions impacted the organization, and its future would be called upon. Tactical implementation, under stable conditions, would require mostly surface knowledge, with shallow knowledge available for equipment failures, or changes in technology or core processes. All of the above descriptions are simplifications of reality and are provided to highlight the differences and range of needs of the levels of knowledge in a typical organization.

Knowledge Mobilization

Knowledge Mobilization provides the opportunity to further explore the types of knowledge introduced above. Knowledge Mobilization (KMb) is an action journey within an identified action space, combining theoretical knowledge (**Kresearch**) with praxis (**Kpraxis**) through the collaboration of multiple stakeholders having a common goal. Within that space, KMb is a process of creating value or a value stream through the creation, assimilation, leveraging, sharing and application of knowledge (**Kaction**).

The government of Canada embraced KMb through its Knowledge Impact on Society program, which was designed to move knowledge from the researcher to the citizens, with KMb complementing—and becoming as important as—the research itself. Observing the KMb process from a bird's eye view (see Figure 4-7), we can identify three major forces for success, with each of these forces representing individuals or teams and the knowledge they possess. Recognizing that in reality there is no beginning and no end, we begin our discussion with the researchers who have deep knowledge of the research findings (**Kresearch**) and are usually found in universities or research institutions. These are the people who generate and tailor theories (higher mental conceptual thought).

The second significant force in the KMb process is the practitioner, who typically has strong knowledge of change management and how to get things done. This pragmatic "how to" knowledge is primarily gained through interactions (dialogue, mimicry, questions and answers, shared language, etc.) to successfully mobilize. The third major force includes those individuals or teams throughout the community at the point of action where local actions are taken to change behavior and create opportunities. Community leaders possess experiential knowledge and a strong understanding of their local culture, its beliefs, and values. This knowledge in action is largely surface in nature.

In Figure 4-7, the three outer ovals represent the three primary forces involved in the KMb process (researchers, practitioners, and community members). The other three ovals represent the corresponding knowledge they bring to the KMb process. While much of this knowledge may originate from the community itself, the traditional flow of the process is from the researcher to the practitioner to the community member, with this flow of knowledge from the theory of the researcher to the pragmatic knowledge of the practitioner to knowledge-in-action of the community member. While this flow is essential to KMb, so, too, is the simultaneous flow of knowledge from community member to practitioner to researcher as well (in a circular process of renewal) and direct flows among researchers and community members where it makes sense. The challenge is to facilitate: (1) this flow of knowledge, (2) the transformation of knowledge from theory to action and back, and (3) the interactions necessary among the three groups to nurture that flow and successful application. As can be seen, it is critical to understand the differences between the types of knowledge necessary at each part of the process in order to mobilize the knowledge that is needed and "take effective action".

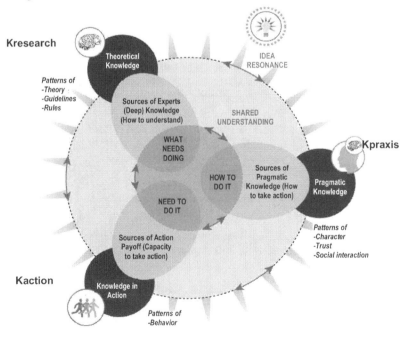

Figure 4-7. The KMb process and knowledge flows.

Let's look at a hypothetical example. Researchers discover a simple process involving natural food combinations and positive attitudes that can eliminate cancer. Alternative medicine practitioners and nutritionists are a part of the trials and, along with advocacy groups, strive to mobilize this information across their communities (patients, schools, community groups, etc.). Deep knowledge (**Kresearch**) has been translated into shallow knowledge (**Kpraxis**) which in turn is translated into surface knowledge (**Kaction**). The end of cancer.

Staying with the KMb approach, the eight steps in the generic KMb model start with a situation that has been matched to research findings (Figure 4-8). These steps are:

1. Situation (problem, issue, opportunity) identified. (**Kdescriptive**)

2. Information gathered about/from the situation and its context. (**Kdescriptive**)

3. Understanding generated from the information, experience and other multiple related sources. (**Kmeta**)

4. Theoretical knowledge considered in the context of the situation. (**Kresearch**)

5. Pragmatic knowledge from practical experience, similar situations, and systems understanding of the target community integrated with (1) through (4) above. (**Kpraxis**)

6. Action or a set of actions taken. (**Kaction**)

7. New situation emerges from these actions. (**Kdescriptive**)

8. Feedback provides the opportunity to assess the effectiveness of actions toward achieving the desired goal and the opportunity to change or supplement those actions as needed. (**Klearning**)

As shown in Figure 4-8, these eight steps move through the focus areas of problem identification to problem understanding to problem solving to decision-making, implementation, and action learning. A primary type of knowledge is connected to each step of the model. Note that while this model has been couched in terms of an identified "problem", this process would also apply to an identified opportunity. Throughout this process, research findings are being explored in the context of the situation, other theoretical knowledge, and the pragmatic knowledge of community stakeholders.

Throughout this process, research findings are being explored in the context of the situation, other theoretical knowledge, and the pragmatic knowledge of community stakeholders.

This discussion provides a framework for recognizing and working with types of knowledge and the roles they play in facilitating a particular type of work, taking a specific action, and achieving a desired outcome. It can also prove helpful in ensuring that a specific type of knowledge has not been overlooked when addressing an issue or opportunity. One or more areas can be used depending on the content, context and desired outcome of the situation/problem.

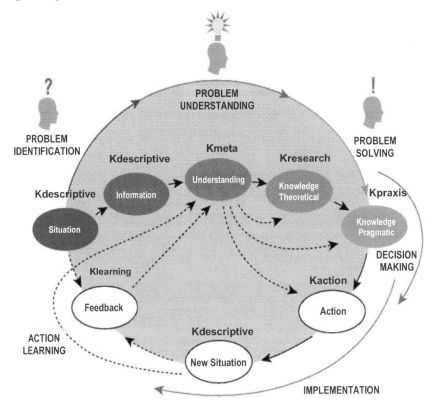

Figure 4-8. The eight steps of the generic KMb process and types of knowledge.

For example, KMb combines theoretical knowledge (**Kresearch**) with the "how to" knowledge of practitioners (**Kpraxis**) with experiential knowledge at the point of action (**Kaction**) to create a value process and achieve the common goal of multiple stakeholders. But it is possible for a decision-maker or an organization—or a country—to become so focused on a specific type of knowledge that they devalue other types of knowledge. Intelligent action demands a balance, that is, an understanding of all the knowledges at play in a specific situation coupled with *a perfect state of interaction where intent, purpose, direction, values and expected outcomes are clearly communicated and understood among all parties, reflecting wisdom and achieving a higher truth.*[223] This is the definition of intelligent activity.

This brief treatment of KMb—a much larger approach than can be presented here—is intended to provide an example of the types of knowledge that need to be translated and mobilized in order to achieve a desired outcome. For an in-depth treatment of KMb see *Knowledge Mobilization in the Social Sciences and Humanities: Moving from Research to Action.*[224]

While there are many more models related to knowledge, we have shared those which we are free to share, and which can be used freely by you in the course of your choices and activities. The point here is for YOU to choose the models that help you better understand (**Kmeta**) and successfully apply (**Kaction**) knowledge, which ultimately can indeed be described as "justified true belief".

CHAPTER 5

THE EMERGING FIELD:
THROUGH THE EYES OF THOUGHT LEADERS

In some sense [we are] moving toward the democratization of organizations,
the legitimizing and recognition of the knowledge that we have at the front line ...
we value those workers more and they value themselves more
because their voices are being heard and legitimized. - Nancy Dixon

We're going to take advantage of this chapter to share the thoughts and feelings of early thought leaders in the knowledge field related to both theory and practice. While there are hundreds of books available that advance various theories and practices, and lots of opinions voiced, few authors have had the inimitable opportunity to get inside the minds and hearts of thought leaders in the field.

So, the learning that is shared in this chapter is entangled with the thoughts of Verna Allee, Debra Amidon, Ramon Barquin, Surinder Kumar Batra, David Bennet, Juanita Brown, John Seely Brown, Frada Burstein, Francisco Javier Carrillo, Robert Cross, Tom Davenport, Ross Dawson, Steve Denning, Charles Dhewa, Nancy Dixon, Leif Edvinsson, Kent Greenes, Susan Hanley, Clyde Holsapple, Esko Kilpi, Dorothy Leonard, Geoff Malafsky, Carla O'Dell, Edna Pasher, Larry Prusak, Madanmohan Rao, Tomasz Rudolf, Melissie Rumizen, Hubert Saint-Onge, Judi Sandrock, Dave Snowden, Milton de Sousa, Tom Stewart, Michael J.D. Sutton, Karl-Erik Sveiby, Doug Weidner, Steve Weineke, Etienne Wenger-Trayner, and Karl Wiig.

Not surprisingly, as individuals and organizations began to recognize the potential value in what was largely called knowledge management (KM), there emerged nearly as many definitions as there were individuals writing and talking about the field! Nearly every book in the literature forwards its own definition of knowledge and knowledge management. This, of course, makes interpreting each book somewhat challenging. A number of authors define knowledge in relationship to, or close to, information.[225] Others consider knowledge to derive from experience (learning) and thinking and say it originates in the mind,[226] and a third group considers the classical definition of knowledge—justified true belief—to be the best one.[227] Most authors consider knowledge to be actionable.[228]

A somewhat surprising observation is that many, if not most, authors of KM books do not even define or address the meaning or interpretation of the concept of knowledge! How can you manage something you do not define? As introduced in Chapter 1, for purposes of this study, *knowledge* is defined as the human capacity (both potential and actual) to take effective action. In the interest of providing the flavor of KM definitions as an emergent field, a representative set is included below. Several of these authors attempt a detailed, all-inclusive definition of the term.

- KM is the systematic, explicit, and deliberate building, renewal, and application of knowledge to maximize an enterprise's knowledge-related effectiveness and returns from its knowledge assets.[229] (Karl Wiig)

- Knowledge creation is the capability of a company as a whole to create new knowledge, disseminate it throughout the organization, and embody it in products, services, and systems.[230] (Nonaka & Takeuchi)

- KM is getting the right knowledge to the right people at the right time so they can make the best decision.[231] (Burkowitz & Petrach)

- KM is human activity that is part of the knowledge management process (KMP) of an agent or collective. KMP, in turn, is an ongoing, persistent, purposeful interaction among human-based agents through which the participating agents aim at managing (handling, directing, governing, controlling, coordinating, planning, organizing) other agents, components, and activities participating in the basic knowledge processes (knowledge production and knowledge integration) into a planned, directed, unified whole, producing, maintaining, enhancing, acquiring, and transmitting the enterprise's knowledge base.[232] (Firestone)

- Knowledge management is a discipline that promotes an integrated approach to identifying, managing and sharing all of an enterprise's information assets, including database, documents, policies and procedures as well as unarticulated expertise and experience resident in individual workers.[233] (Gartner Group)

- KM is viewed as a process for optimizing the effective application of intellectual capital to achieve organizational objectives.[234] (U.S. Department of the Navy)

In Daryl Morey's book of classic and contemporary works on knowledge management, he is inclined towards the learning-centric view (versus the information-centric view in several definitions above), which emphasizes that knowledge is the 'capability to act effectively', is derived from learning, and from this viewpoint KM is a management function that accelerates learning.[235] Exactly!

A clear pattern emerging from these definitions is that knowledge as intellectual capital is a human resource essential for the success of the organization or enterprise, and thus the need to "manage" that resource. "Manage" in this sense means making the best use of the resource, not to "control or direct" the resource. Knowledge cannot be controlled. How to *develop, manage and apply* that valuable resource, then, becomes the focus of knowledge strategies, processes and approaches, and as is clear by definition, *this involves people.*

Many thought and organizational leaders exploring the potential offered by the knowledge movement, shied away from the word "manage". In the KMTL Study by the Mountain Quest Institute – which engaged 34 thought leaders in the "field", "perspective" or "movement" with values and value – 71% of them did not like the term knowledge management, largely due to the historic bureaucratic-related concepts of the term management. While thought leaders consistently expressed a passion, an excitement about the field and the potential offered by this focus on knowledge, there was no consistency on *what to call the field.* So, they talked about it as knowledge awareness, connecting, ecology, emergence, environment, evolution, innovation, management, navigation, networking, sharing, strategy and transfer as well as collective intelligence, collective wisdom, competence learning, learning architecture, organizational and organizational learning. All of those make sense.

As early as 1998, Carrillo, who is a guest author of Chapter 18 in this book, forwarded the possibility that KM "could become a self-conscious and dynamic field of *collective wisdom.*"[236] Indeed, for those who delved deeply into the field's potential, that has happened. And Wiig hit a home run when he described successful "KM" as "a *mentality* of how to deal with knowledge-related issues and activities, investments and the like for the purpose of **promoting everything from learning to sharing but also for promoting innovation**."[237]

This response begs the question: Is it important that we use the same terminology to describe this focus on knowledge? No, it isn't. de Sousa, who is a guest author of Chapter 15 in this book, sees "KM" as a fundamental organizational instrument providing meaning to the work we do, and most importantly *why* we do it. "Since it is through knowledge that we make sense of the world around us – and the role we and our organizations play in that world – the knowledge focus becomes a strategic instrument **to provide purpose to both the organization and the individual**."[238] As a European, Milton de Sousa hasn't seen many people calling themselves KM practitioners. He does, however, observe a trend towards a more hands-on consulting and change approach whereby consultants take a role of facilitator, establishing connections, making tacit knowledge explicit, tapping into unexplored areas of knowledge, raising awareness of the knowledge that exists in the organization, etc. "Interestingly, most of these consultants are not even aware of KM models or even of KM as a discipline, they just intuitively feel that this *focus on knowledge flows* makes sense and that change in the traditional top-down approach and expertise-based consulting (generating reports and recommendations) is not sufficient."[239]

KM OVERVIEWS IN THE LITERATURE

Karl Wiig, often referred to as the father of knowledge management, provided a thorough review of the field when formally introducing the subject to the public through his three books,[240] which are thorough and both conceptual and pragmatic. Wiig emphasized fundamental concepts, focusing on knowledge, meta-knowledge and the management and application of knowledge to improve organizational performance. This groundbreaking work lays a KM foundation built on three pillars: Pillar I, *Exploring Knowledge*, includes surveying, categorizing, analyzing, codifying and organizing knowledge. Pillar II, *Finding the Value of Knowledge*, includes appraising and evaluating. Pillar III, *Actively Managing Knowledge*, includes synthesizing knowledge-related activities, handling, using and controlling, leveraging, distributing and automating, and implementing and monitoring knowledge-related activities.[241] Although these works include many visuals, taxonomies, and practical suggestions for understanding and applying knowledge, and are seminal contributions to the field, they can be difficult reading for a newcomer to the field.

In a survey article titled "The Current State of Knowledge Management," Thomas Beckman stated that "Knowledge management is an emerging discipline with many ideas yet to be tested, many issues yet to be resolved, and much learning yet to be discovered."[242] That was in 1997. After presenting an outline of major ideas and practices in the field, describing five different typologies, and considering the field from other perspectives of processes, technologies, organizations, management and implementation, he noted: "Future work must focus on building practical experience through extensive experimenting, prototyping, and testing."[243]

Fourteen Learning Objectives

A growing interest in KM was also occurring in the U.S. Federal Sector. Sponsored by the cross-government Knowledge Management Working Group, working sessions were held in 2000-2001 to build an understanding of the concepts, roles, and importance of KM in the U.S. government. As a result of these sessions, the working group developed "learning objectives" for KM courses taught in the public sector. These inclusive objectives in essence span the breadth of the knowledge field.

At the time this set of learning objectives was formalized, one of the authors was Co-Chair of the Federal Working Group, which was coordinating implementation of KM across the Federal government. These learning objectives set the scope of the field of KM for the Federal sector as well as the thousands of businesses and millions of professionals that support the U.S. government. They make clear connections to earlier management movements and provide a business focus for KM while emphasizing the importance of learning and knowledge; in other words, focusing on both the value of intangibles to the Federal sector and linking those intangibles directly to people and learning. The ideas presented through these learning objectives, built on the foundational work of research institutions such as APQC and The Knowledge Institute as well as educational institutions such as the George Washington University, an early advocate in the field, and practitioners, provide an objective overview of the content of the field. The learning objectives are in Appendix B.

FOUNDATIONAL CHARACTERISTICS OF THE KNOWLEDGE FIELD

Written from the viewpoint of thought leader/practitioner, four foundational characteristics of the field emerged from the KMTL research study which provide insights into the field. These are:

- The field is inclusive, open minded, and encourages diversity and new ideas.
- KM is self-referential, with reinforcing feedback loops.
- The KM field encourages autotelic work or flow.
- KM is a complex adaptive system with many possibilities and opportunities.

Each of these will be briefly detailed below.

The field is inclusive, open minded, and encourages diversity and new ideas.

The field is open and inclusive and appears to offer something for everyone. The diversity of ideas, theories and solutions emerging do not appear to be in competition with each other, rather they represent a library of possibilities available to a kaleidoscope of customers, offering the opportunity for widespread participation and contribution from many individuals, cultures, and nations. Larry Prusak, the founder and director of the Institute for Knowledge Management, recognized the value of this diversity of ideas. "I do strongly believe that the unit of analysis when working with knowledge is an aggregate (a network, a practice, etc., but not 'eat all the enterprise')." Prusak applies this belief to his work unceasingly and punctuates, "It works or I wouldn't continue to use it."[244]

The field is self-referential, with reinforcing feedback loops.

The field has the unusual and interesting property of being self-referential with respect to its own practitioners. The nature of the practitioner's work and the processes involved in sharing that work with others are the same as the content of the field itself. All three of these involve learning, creating, sharing, and applying knowledge. This self-referencing acts as a regenerative feedback loop in which the results of practitioner's work impacts organizations and other workers which then reinforces the practitioner's learning, knowledge, social interaction, and capacity to share further work. As Edna Pasher – a researcher and consultant specializing in strategy, change, knowledge and innovation management, and intellectual capital measurement and development – quite eloquently explained,

> *I never develop anything alone. I always happily collaborate with others, just as I do in this paper. I collaborate with clients and colleagues from a variety of disciplines. I look for inspiration from the sciences and the arts, from "deep smarts" and from novices. Every perspective has a contribution* **into creating a Life Long Learning experience for me and my clients which enables innovation and renewal** [emphasis added] *This is the essence of KM for me.*[245]

Kent Greenes, an early pioneer in KM, says that he's blessed with a high success rate of applying his simple frameworks, which obviously reinforces his continued reliance and comfort with the frameworks he knows best. He acknowledges that "most of that is due to generous co-learning with the people I've worked with over the years, both fellow KMers and customers alike, ... and some tenacity on my part."[246]

This balance of knowledge access and knowledge exchange lies at the heart of the framework used by Hubert Saint-Onge, founder and principal of Saint-Onge Alliance, which serves as a model for determining how to build both the technology and organizational systems required for such a platform to thrive and contribute to the success of the organization. "As a matter of principle," explains Saint-Onge, "I believe that an effective knowledge management strategy has to strike a balance between *knowledge access* (the ability to store, search, access information) and *knowledge exchange* (the collaborative generation of knowledge in response to productive inquiry among colleagues)."[247] In the knowledge architecture, knowledge access is codified and stored, tends to be more static, is driven by accessibility and retrieval, and is centrally available to all individuals. There are built-in collaborative spaces for knowledge exchange, which is interactive and dynamic and driven by productive inquiry. Figure 5-1 represents this theory.

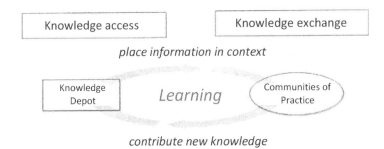

Figure 5-1: Striking a balance between knowledge access and knowledge exchange. Source: Hubert Saint-Onge.

The field encourages autotelic work or flow.

The field has the inherent ability to offer thought leaders environments and situations that result in autotelic work or flow experiences. In the KMTL Research Study, this current of energy and moments of high enjoyment, considered over time, is very close to what was identified as passion in terms of thought leader response. While flow is most often referred to as a *flow state*, lasting for some nominal time period, the field itself and its content supports many of the conditions needed for the flow experience described by Csikszentmihalyi.[248] For example, speaking in terms of Csikszentmihalyi's description of the onset of the flow experience, the highest goals of KM are clear, and through networks, conversations, communities, and symposia there is relatively fast feedback. Practitioners are in control of their work, work with their clients to choose their own specific goals, receive feedback from workers (and other practitioners) in the field, and are up to the tasks they set for themselves. There is also a widespread (but not universal) pattern of humbleness. The results of practitioner's work validate the ability to concentrate, and for much of their work they must be "in the present" to be effective, that is, flexible and responsive as the situation and context changes.

Overall, those practitioners who are thought leaders in the field get a great deal of satisfaction from their work and feel that it is very beneficial to them personally as well as to organizations and society as a whole. This observation is worth exploring further. In the KMTL Study interviews, thought leaders frequently touched on their feelings and the *excitement* that came from *learning, creating knowledge, helping others, and experiencing the awareness of "what it means to be alive",* or *"livingness."* This was expressed by Pasher as replacing the concept of the organization as a machine with the concept of the organization as a living organism, a complex adaptive system, which "leads most of our KM efforts in the direction of Communities of Practice and Communities of Passion, where people share knowledge and help each other to solve problems."[249] She acknowledges inspiration from Margaret Wheatley, the author of *Leadership and the New Science*,[250] who forwards *whatever the problem, community is the answer*. Similarly, many of the KMTL thought leaders emanated the excitement of being able to help individuals, organizations, and nations – and perhaps mankind – *learn, grow and make a difference*. As one thought leader forwarded, **the foundation of KM lies at the core of humanity**, **knowledge,** and this alone creates passion in many. The intent of this discussion is to propose that for the thought leaders actually engaged in the field, very much a model of scholar practitioners (continuous learners), *there is a repetitive or long-term state of flow*, that is, the autotelic work experience.

The overlap between knowledge management and learning at both the individual and organizational levels is not surprising. Learning is the *process for acquiring knowledge*, the capacity to take effective action. This is why theories developed in support of organizational learning provide some of the best theory related to KM. For example, Amy Edmondson, a professor at Harvard working with her doctoral students, has amassed a great deal of knowledge on how teams learn, learning from failure, the role of leadership in team learning, and the role of psychological safety in creating knowledge. As Nancy Dixon, a researcher and consultant, notes, "Her work is firmly based in practice – on research conducted in the field" drawn largely from the seminal work of Chris Argyris[251] on organizational learning and Karl Weick[252] on sensemaking.

A second example of this overlap is the seminal theoretical contributions forwarded by Etienne Wenger-Trayner, best known in the KM field for his work related to communities of practice.[253] Wenger-Trayner, a participant in the Mountain Quest Institute Sampler Research Call who describes himself as a social learning theorist, reminds us that *theories are learning tools*. In the social sciences, theories are not true or false in the sense of being confirmed by data in a direct way; theories are useful ways of understanding the world, which lead those who use them to ask certain questions and see certain possibilities for action. *Theories are thinking tools*. So, the empirical validation of models is more complex because it has to do with the investigation and refinement of practice.

The field is a complex adaptive system with many possibilities and opportunities.

The science of complexity considers the basic properties of nonlinear-feedback networks and particularly of complex adaptive networks.[254] Specifically, complex adaptive systems "consist of a number of components, or agents, that interact with each other according to sets of rules that require them to examine and respond to each other's behavior in order to improve their behavior and thus the behavior of the system they comprise".[255]

KM did not have a "single" leader or guru as was evident in earlier management initiatives such as TQM and BPR. As Snowden describes, "There were a lot of intelligent people coming together from different backgrounds to create what became a movement. [Note his description of KM as a "movement".] KM was unique in not being from one person/group based on a pseudo-empirical study. Instead, it came from multiple backgrounds and disciplines."[256] Because of this, *the field does not have a consistent objective, a specified process, or a restricted domain of interest.* Being flexible and robust, the field (in the form of its practitioners) has adapted to – and addressed – issues and opportunities without being constrained by rigid practices or unquestioned edicts. Aided by the breadth and scope of the field and the variety of potential applications, practitioners have been free from imitation and constraints, relatively independent in their focus while simultaneously interdependent in terms of learning from each other and creating new knowledge. They pursue many different areas that can be brought together to focus on meta-knowledge and its application to individual and organizational performance.

A potential negative aspect of these perceived business-driven new beginnings of the field is the inability to capitalize on a rich inheritance of scientific, technical and political foundations. As early as 2001, Carrillo stressed that the KM profession needed to become aware of its legacy in regards to reflective human understanding. "Once conscious about the conditions that can either enhance or prevent its own development, it can take the actions necessary to master its destiny."[257] Conscious awareness enables choice.

As the field has fluctuated in and out of organizational focus, leadership of the field has been (and continues to be) distributed, self-organizing, collaborative, and natural, whether in an organization or in academia, just as are many KM activities such as knowledge sharing, communities of practice, and social networking, and the new technologies continuously emerging in support of the field. This diversity has *encouraged continuous learning* and adapting to local needs and contexts as various methods and approaches are tested and evaluated. This will continue to be the case as the challenge and opportunity of AI moves more fully in the realms of knowledge.

Greenes describes this continuous cycle of learning and adaptation.

My saving grace is when I experience something that works and is different than the way I know it, I always change. Learning from experience and impact, especially when it's painful, is something I've always done ... I suppose it's part survival and performance genes, and part of value

programming from birth. But it's also the way most people really learn ...
this is the reason it's so important to capture the pain and gain when
harvesting knowledge and experience for others to learn from.[258]

As Battram forwards, "Complex behavior need not have a complex explanation, and order will emerge from 'self-organization'."[259] Considering the self-organization in the field, we can see that the subject matter (knowledge) and its corollary (learning), coupled with the objectives of improving organizational performance, have provided a direction and focus without constraining the field. Thus, even in its periodic seeming demise, the field is continuously emerging rather than being designed or planned.

KM THEORY EMERGING

All this activity does not negate the fact that there was a growing desire by academics and practitioners alike for some **KM overarching theory**. As the field potential to help achieve individual and organizational success was recognized – with different sets of tools, processes and technology advancements linked to the KM platform in different contexts and situations – there was an expanding need to train new practitioners. Yet the same characteristics that supported success in "seasoned" practitioners who could draw on previous knowledge presented barriers and difficulties for new practitioners entering the field. How to produce consistent results without consistent theories or models in the field? How to make KM a discipline so that it could be moved into the university curricula? And from that viewpoint? What theories or models could be used to educate/train new practitioners?

A global survey of over 200 KM professionals sponsored by the Information and Knowledge Management Society of Singapore (iKMS) in 2007 – referenced here as the iKMS Global Survey – identified the need (and desire by some practitioners) for an **inter-connected theoretical base**. Saint-Onge, founder of SaintOnge Alliance and a thought leader in the field, agrees there is nothing as useful as a well-grounded theory. "KM practitioners who do not have a framework to use as a guide for orchestrating their efforts will very likely waste a great deal of time and energy." He adds quickly, "Of course, the framework must be based in the reality of the context in which they operate." Saint-Onge feels that early research threw relatively little light on the key dynamics involved in building a vibrant, productive knowledge exchange in organizations, and even today is too limited in scope to provide effective guidance to practitioners. "We are still lacking a comprehensive framework based on systematic research."[260] Here, Bohm would caution that theories, as knowledge, are ever-changing forms of insight. "What prevents theoretical insights from going beyond existing limitations and changing to meet new facts is just the belief that theories give true knowledge of reality (which implies, of course, that they need never change)."[261]

Theories in the field reflect the disciplines from which practitioners have emerged. For example, economists bring theories from their discipline or sub-disciplines into KM practice. Greenes finds that theory from neuroscience, learning, behavior, and other related fields impact his thinking. Wenger-Trayner's social learning theory is the foundation of the KM communities of practice movement. Similarly, Carrillo tends to rely more on theoretical frameworks developed outside the KM field insofar as these bear more relevance to knowledge phenomena. These areas include Empirical Epistemology, Behavioral Economics, Decision-making, Theories of the Firm, Consciousness, Science of Science, Value Field Theory, and Development Theory.[262] Because of this diversity of theory, results from the iKMS Global Survey call out two significant but connected implications: a lack of coherence arising from the lack of an integrated theoretical base, and poor executive arising from poorly prepared and supported practitioners.[263]

Of course, there may be other factors involved. For example, Prusak feels that practitioners – especially in the U.S. – distrust theory and have little interest in it. While this distrust may be the product of anti-intellectualism in the U.S. culture as a whole, Prusak thinks it is also the association of theory with wooly-minded academics who have no "real life" experiences and a subsequent lack of understanding of how organizations actually work. Snowden pushes the envelope even farther, saying that practitioners today are seeking security in structured roles. "They are no longer interested in *why* things work but just want a simplistic recipe."[264]

Etienne Wenger-Trayner, a social learning theorist, agrees that there may be a tendency to hang on to simple models that have intuitive appeal, and notes that this is not limited to the knowledge field. "The human world is a complex system with lots of dimensions, so simple models are attractive. They can serve the purpose of organizing one's thinking in manageable ways." He continues that this can prove very useful, especially for people in business who need to make quick arguments about complex processes, but then cautions, "the power of simple models is also their danger ... They can become something that people apply repeatedly, almost as a substitute for thinking rather than a tool for thinking."[265]

Kent Greenes, founder and president of Greenes Consulting, says that he has been able to use a few simple self-grown frameworks to guide, tailor and align his knowledge approaches with his customers. "I deliberately keep them simple to help engage and meet non-KM experts where they are at, typically reframing them in the language of the people I'm trying to assist." This simplicity enables him to be agile in terms of application. "At a high level, they fit every organization and situation. I mean, come on, how can a simple framework of five integrated elements of KM – Culture, Process, Content, Technology and Structure – *not* be applicable?" He adds, "I actually think it can apply to probably every discipline! It's how you tailor what makes up each of the five elements to each organization that is each practitioner's special sauce."[266]

Through all of this, the George Washington University (GWU) program led by Dr. Michael Stankosky[267] – which offered the first KM doctorate-level program – continued their quest to "evolve the discipline of knowledge management toward a universally accepted set of theorems; replicable practices; and a common language created by a real and virtual Global Community of Interest/Practice."[268] As such, as hundreds of scholar practitioners moved through GWU classrooms, laboratories, study halls, offices and private homes over a decade, the Institute for Knowledge and Innovation emerged as nodes in the U.S., Russia, Europe, Asia, the Middle East, Canada, and Latin America. At the core of this focus is the Four Pillar Framework, which has evolved even as the idea of KM evolved. (See Figure 5-2.)

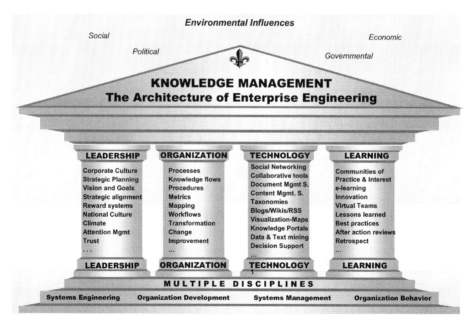

Figure 5-2. The GWU Four Pillar Framework circa 2009.[269] (Used with permission)

Describing this framework, Calabrese wrote: "With Leadership commitment supporting Organizational collaborative practice, processes and forums, land appropriate Technology enabling tools one can grow a Learning Enterprise/Environment to perpetuate a sustainable knowledge-enabled culture."[270]

As a designer, advisor, speaker and attendee at conferences around the world during the latter 90's and now well into the new century, the work of other KM practitioners was a common topic of conversation. While initially the search was for new case studies, as year-after-year passed there was a noted repetitiveness in the focus of the presentations, that is, similar actions with similar results. KM was growing old and stale. While this would appear to bode well for the development of an overarching KM theory, this does not appear to be the case. These are the "recipes" described by Snowden, who feels that the academic community failed KM by not engaging until there were cases to study. He says that both academics and practitioners needed to get rid of their obsessions with treating KM projects as rats in a maze with a false model of causality which is contextually limited. For example, Snowden worked in New York with the United Nations Development Program (UNDP) and various development experts to look at how to measure and scale success in the Development Sector. Pushing for co-evolution between theory and practice, Snowden brought in post-design thinkers from MIT and biologists from the Rosen School to meet with Cognitive Edge partners to create a new science-informed approach to the problem. "We need more of that and fewer cases," he emphasized.[271]

MOVING THE FIELD INTO THE FUTURE

We have entered a time when significant advancements in the knowledge movement are already underway or expected to occur. For example:

Artificial Intelligence (AI) and Machine Learning: AI technologies have the potential to revolutionize the knowledge movement. Intelligent algorithms can be used to analyze vast amounts of data, extract insights, and make recommendations for knowledge gaps or areas that require attention. Recall the advances that were made when our technologies were able to analyze big data. AI is now taking the next step, and the upward limits are not visible. The question becomes what we will choose to do with this knowledge. AI-powered systems can also assist in automating knowledge creation, and curation and dissemination processes, thereby improving efficiency and effectiveness.

While it has not been widely stated, AI itself has largely evolved through the expanded understanding of knowledge and learning facilitated by the knowledge movement. Here are a few examples of knowledge practices that have helped build more powerful, reliable and responsible AI systems:

1. The collecting, organizing, and structuring of data and information is essential for AI development as machines need access to vast amounts of structured and relevant data to learn from and make accurate predictions.

2. The ontologies, taxonomies and knowledge graphs created through the knowledge movement assist in structuring and representing knowledge in a machine-readable format, facilitating effective knowledge inference and reasoning in AI systems.

3. Knowledge practices such as creating knowledge repositories, capturing tacit knowledge, and promoting collaboration facilitate the sharing and transfer of expertise and experience, all leading to faster AI development.

4. The knowledge frameworks and processes to capture feedback, analyze performance, and identify areas for improvement have helped in the iterative development of AI models and algorithms, leading to more accurate and reliable results.

5. By promoting transparent and accountable practices, the knowledge movement can help ensure that AI systems are built with a strong ethical foundation, minimizing potential harm and bias.

Further, AI continues to learn valuable lessons from the knowledge and learning sciences to enhance the writing of its code in the areas of cognitive processes, active learning strategies, pedagogical techniques, transfer of learning, and metacognition and self-regulation.

Knowledge Graphs and Semantic Technologies: Knowledge graphs, like Google's Knowledge Graph, aim to connect different entities and concepts to provide a more holistic view of information. Advancements in knowledge graphs and semantic technologies may enhance how knowledge is organized, linked, and retrieved, making it easier to identify and navigate gaps in knowledge.

Collaborative and Social Knowledge: As knowledge becomes more dispersed and dynamic, collaborative and social knowledge approaches gain importance. Platforms that facilitate knowledge sharing, collaboration, and crowd-sourcing can enable individuals and teams to connect, exchange ideas, and bridge knowledge gaps collectively. Customers have now been drawn into creativity discovery sessions, more fully participating in the innovation process.

Personalized Knowledge Management: This has been through several renditions over the past 20 years, but appears to be re-emerging as a new generation of knowledge workers move into the workforce. Customized knowledge delivery systems – potentially customized by an AI system itself – could tailor information to an individual's specific needs, interests, and expertise, thereby assisting users in acquiring relevant knowledge and identifying their unique knowledge gaps.

Blockchain: Blockchain technology offers potential applications for effective knowledge flows. By ensuring secure and transparent transactions, blockchain can assist in validating the sources, provenance, and ownership of knowledge assets. This can enhance trust, facilitate knowledge sharing, and even incentivize contributions to the knowledge ecosystem.

But these only represent beginnings. As we learn more about how the human mind/brain works, that learning leads to a larger understanding of how to enable our systems to further support the human in our continuous journey of seeking more, more, and more. Knowledge, at the core of what it is to be human, is ever-expanding, and WE have not yet reached OUR limits of how to gain expanded value from its potential.

As you can see, as the KM field has emerged, so, too, have patterns of thought and preferences. There is not one overarching theory – although certainly the George Washington University Four Pillar Model provides a standard – and many different theories presenting from practitioner's fields of interest prove useful. Acknowledging the field itself as a complex adaptive system while simultaneously recognizing that knowledge – at the core of the field – is relative to the context and situation at hand, there is tremendous diversity requiring individual agency on the part of practitioners. Yet, because knowledge sharing is so critical to the bottom line of an organization, this requires cooperation, collaboration, communities, and networking right along with new technologies to ensure shared understanding through knowledge flows. And then comes full recognition that innovation could not occur without knowledge.

CHAPTER 6

FREEDOM OF THOUGHT AND INNOVATION

History shows that innovation is a delicate and vulnerable flower,
easily crushed underfoot, but quick to regrow
if conditions allow. -Matt Ridley[272]

We ran into Matt Ridley's book rather accidentally – or perhaps you could call it serendipitous, much like innovation itself. Serendipity is the art of finding what we are not seeking, *yet perhaps what we need or want*. It is the interweaving of chance into our lives … or is it? The remarkably appropriate title of Ridley's book is: *How Innovation Works and Why It Flourishes in Freedom.*

Innovation happens when people have freedom of thought, expression, and association. When their minds are free to wonder, experiment, and speculate in a coercive-free environment, not burdened with worries of everyday survival. When visions can be openly shared and ideas bang up against each other in the safety net of trust, respect, and truth. It is usually not choreographed, planned, or managed, and is not easily predicted. Ah! But it *can* be discovered through trial and error, what Ridley calls "the human version of natural selection".[273] What a great way of perceiving that, because it is natural, and in freedom creativity and innovation flourish.

But maybe we're getting ahead of ourselves. Let's briefly explore the relationship among information, knowledge, creativity, and innovation. Then we're going to take a road less traveled, that is dig deeper down into creativity and innovation from the viewpoint of your mind/brain. Our 2022 book, *Unleashing the Human Mind: A Consilience Approach to Managing Self,* is based on a decade of researching experiential learning through the expanding lens of neuroscience. There is a great deal of this learning that is directly pertinent to creativity and innovation and which is not largely available in that context, so we're going to share some of that learning with you. After which we're going to pop back up into the organizational reality and take a close look at the "Most Innovative Knowledge Organization" international awards program to see what criteria are used to judge a successful innovative organization.

INFORMATION, KNOWLEDGE, CREATIVITY, INNOVATION

In Chapter 3 we introduced theoretical biologist Tom Stonier's definition of information as a measure of the degree of organization expressed by any non-random pattern or set of patterns and, in an organization, described information as *energy in a holding pattern*. Then, in Chapter 4, we forwarded the functional definition of knowledge as the capacity (potential or actual) to take effective action, otherwise, effectively acting on that information.

Similarly, creativity is a capacity. Creativity comes exclusively from people, a CAPACITY to see new ideas from associating internal and external information, which is the associative patterning process of the human mind. In turn, innovation is *applied creativity* in concert with knowledge. As an idea generator, knowledge is the currency of creativity and innovation, and knowledge cannot exist without information.

As can be seen, information, knowledge, creativity and innovation have an entangled relationship. Knowledge is effectively applying information (in terms of producing the expected result). Innovation is effectively applying creativity (in terms of a useful design, process or product).

Knowledge = Information + Effective Action (Potential or Actual)

Innovation = Knowledge + Creativity + Useful Application

While knowledge comes from the past and creativity requires knowledge, both knowledge and creativity are capacities which can be applied in the present (actual) or engaged in the future (potential). They have a symbiotic relationship, that is, knowledge cannot exist without creativity, and creativity cannot exist without knowledge. Learning, which is the creation of knowledge, is a continuous creative experience. Further, they *both* emerge from the associative patterning process of the brain, that is, the unique complexing of external and internal information (organized patterns). This is an important concept that you will hear about several more times in this chapter.

In Figure 6-1, there is a dotted line between knowledge and creativity, which when combined lead to innovation. It has long been recognized that there is a tension between knowledge and innovation, that creative thinking goes beyond knowledge. As Weisberg suggests, "Knowledge may provide the basic elements, the building blocks out of which are constructed new ideas, but in order for these building blocks to be available, the mortar holding the old ideas together must not be too strong."[274] The intent is that while universally acknowledging that it is necessary to have knowledge of a field if you wish to discover something novel within that field, simultaneously, if you have locked into specific ideas and are not open to learning, you will never be able to move beyond stereotyped responses.[275] Thus, learning, the creation of knowledge, is necessary to facilitate new ideas and bring them into fruition. This also stresses the importance of humility – at the interpersonal level meaning focused beyond self, being open to listening to others – as expansive to creativity and, in turn, innovation.

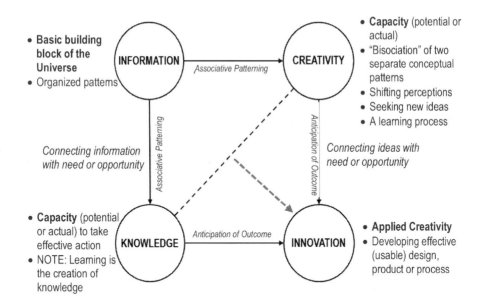

Figure 6-1. Exploring the relationships among information, knowledge, creativity and innovation.

Note that innovation is not necessarily an immediate result. As Fritz Machlup said in the early 1960's in his seminal work on the knowledge economy, "We shall have to bring out clearly that this is not a simple unidirectional flow from one stage to the next, from inception to development, to eventual adoption, but there are usually cross-currents, eddies, and whirlpools."[276] Past experiences, feelings, knowledge, goals, and the situation at hand all influence how creative an individual will, or can, be. It is the context of the activity or situation at hand (need, challenge, etc.) that triggers the putting things together (bisociation) in an unusual way to create (and recognize) something that may be new and potentially useful (innovation). Thus, knowledge – context sensitive and situation dependent and a trigger for creativity – serves as an action lever for innovation.

MORE ON CREATIVITY

As a working definition, creativity can be considered the ability to conceive new ideas, concepts or capabilities that have not been created before. As with knowledge – and honoring the diversity and individuation of the human mind – there are differences of thought related to the creativity process. For example, specific to the human, Hobson says that creativity is inherent in the basic operation of the nervous system,[277] Andreasen sees the brain as a self-organizing system with the capability of creating novel linkages in milliseconds,[278] and Christos says that while it only stands to reason from a scientific perspective that individual creativity is a function of the brain and what is stored in it, the question is: *how*?[279]

Speculating, Christos felt the answer was related to memory being stored distributively such that there's an overlap of memories or a common use of neurons and synapses for their representation, which would give rise to new states not intentionally stored in the network.[280] These would be associations of patterns, connections that represent other ideas and knowledge. Christos was right.

While it was historically believed that the brain stores patterns in a hierarchical and nested fashion – and certainly some patterns restored in this manner – it is also now recognized that patterns (as information and potential knowledge) are stored at locations relative to reference frames, which are allocated in the cortical columns in the neocortex.[281] Incoming information is associated, or complexed, with patterns which are distributed throughout the cortical columns, creating new patterns in the mind pertinent to the situation at hand. Further, the brain (as distinct from a computer) does not store exact replicas of events or memories. Rather, it stores invariant representations which represent the basic source of recognition and understanding of the broader patterns, and to create a "full picture" or "complete thought", the gaps are filled in by the mind. Thus, all knowledge is continuously being "re-created" or is "new" for the situation at hand, while simultaneously being complexed with the invariant form of past memories. As Christos describes,

> *We often imagine that creativity is totally new and original, but in most cases it is not. It generally possesses features of known acts (or stored memories). Ideas re built on other ideas and knowledge, and no person is truly and absolutely original. Creative ideas are copied, borrowed, and manipulated versions of what we know and acquire. Human creativity and imitation (or memes) play complementary roles in the evolution of ideas.*[282]

A meme is an idea, behavior pattern, or piece of information that is passed on, again and again, through the process of imitation such that it takes on a life of its own.[283] Memes may or may not reflect the original intent of an idea. See a more detailed discussion of memes in Chapter 11 under Knowledge Sharing.

Further, information coming in from the external environment can "stimulate a much more complete or richer internal experience of the 'whole' of that thing to be conjured up."[284] This process is called apprehension, which is when a part of something perceived as external stimulates something new, what we sometimes describe as creativity.

The human brain has a natural capacity to be creative, the ability to generate something entirely new – its own information or memory-like states – not formally acquired from the overlapping storage of memory, but arising from what Christo calls "spurious memories", new states or memories not intentionally stored in the network. While they may possess some subtle combinations of stored memories, they

> *... have the capacity to generate new ideas that combine different bits of information ... [and] may be extremely useful (and possibly essential), not just for creativity but also so that a neural network can learn something new, adapt, generalize, classify, think, and make new associations.*[285]

Andreasen suggests there are five circumstances that create cradles of creativity. These are (1) an atmosphere of intellectual freedom and excitement; (2) a critical mass of creative minds; (3) free and fair competition; (4) mentors and patrons; and (5) at least some economic prosperity. Those are all pretty clear, and make sense.

So how do we get to this state? We will briefly explore below several of the findings from the Mountain Quest Institute research study based on a decade of research on experiential learning through the lens of neuroscience. These findings assume that the mind has been primed in the area of focus, that is, engaged in a specific domain of learning and practice over a period of time. This is detailed further in a companion text titled *Innovative Creativity: Creating with Innovation in Mind*. Three specific approaches are introduced below: (1) creating an enriched environment, (2) quieting and opening the mind; and (3) volleying between the conscious and unconscious.

Creating an Enriched Environment

An enriched environment, which increases the formation and survival of new neurons, can produce a personal internal reflective world of imagination and creativity. This means an enriched environment, entering the mind/brain/body through sensory experiences, stimulates the mind to associate patterns and create new possibilities, exactly what is needed to set the stage for innovation.

"Enriched" by word structure means to make rich or richer. By definition, that would mean improving something, making something more meaningful or more rewarding. When referring to an enriched environment in terms of learning and knowledge, this would refer to an environment that stimulated learning and therefore the emergence of knowledge, or in terms of innovation, ideas.

If we went back 20 some years or so, we would have been taught that effective learning requires concentration – no physical, mental, or emotional distractions. And to a certain extent it is true that our minds cannot function as effectively (and sometimes not at all) when they are bombarded with disturbances. Thus, from the viewpoint of a formal classroom setting, this would mean surroundings that were quietly attractive, passive yet comfortable, providing safety, positive feelings, and an aura of warmth and confidence. Outside the classroom, nature provided the necessary quiet AND stimulus.

We might also have recognized that the idea of an enriched environment was highly sensitive to the specific learner. So we might want a surrounding environment containing a diversity of interesting and thought-provoking ideas, pictures, books, statues, etc., reflecting on the use of space design and plants, art and music, furnishings and light to help create that environment. All potentially good ideas.

In today's world, while nature may still provide both quiet and stimulation for those who can fully connect with her energy, an enriched environment would most likely include technology augmentation, with computer technology, web services, and social media all offering platforms to stimulate thought and ideas. Much of that enrichment might be focused on social aspects, that is, engagement with other people. This certainly makes sense. People do not often learn in isolation, but are very much engaged in a continuous process of what is often referred to as social learning. And, as will be discussed later below, social interaction is where ideas – and innovation – can flourish.

Quieting and Opening the Mind

Quieting the mind. Practices such as meditation, lucid dreaming, and hemispheric synchronization can serve to improve creativity and problem solving. For example, meditation can significantly enhance the ability to focus attention. In this context, quieting the mind means to reduce the noise that "bedevils the untrained mind, in which an individual's focus darts from one sight or sound or thought to another like a hyperactive dragonfly, and replace it with attentional stability and clarity".[286] That's getting rid of "monkey chatter", which we all experience at some point.

Yet simultaneously, we now know that there is an optimum level of stress (somewhere between motivation and anxiety) that facilitates learning! Arousal or excitement can serve as a strong motivation to drive people to learn, but cannot be so strong that it becomes high stress moving to anxiety. For example, Merry sees adaptation not as a basic transformative change, but as having a new range of possibility. When people face growing uncertainty and stress, their resilience allows them to find novel forms of adaptation to the changing conditions.[287]

Hemispheric synchronization, the use of sound coupled with a binaural beat to bring both hemispheres of the brain into unison,[288] is an approach to opening the mind. Binaural beats were identified in 1839 by H.W. Dove, a German experimenter. In the human mind, binaural beats are detected with carrier tones (audio tones of slightly different frequencies, one tone to each ear) below approximately 1500 Hz.[289] The mind perceives the frequency differences of the sound coming into each ear, integrating the two sounds as a fluctuating rhythm and thereby creating a beat or difference frequency. This perceived rhythm originates in the brainstem, is neurologically routed to the reticular activating formation, also in the brainstem,[290] and then to the cortex where it can be measured as a frequency-following response.[291] This inter-hemispheric communication is the setting for brain-wave coherence which facilitates whole-brain cognition, assuming an elevated status in subject experience.[292] What can occur during hemispheric synchronization is a physiologically reduced state of arousal while maintaining conscious awareness,[293] and the capacity to reach the unconscious creative state through the window of consciousness.

Other practices such as changing one's frame of reference open the mind to new ways of viewing problems which facilitate new ideas. (See Chapter 16 on Knowledge Capacities.)

Volleying between the Conscious and Unconscious

While both conscious and unconscious patterns are involved with creativity, the unconscious plays a big role in creativity. Creative insight is the result of searching for new relationships between concepts in one domain with those in another domain.[294] It creates a recognition and understanding of a problem within the situation, including the how and why of the past and current behavior of the situation. It is often the result of intuition, competence, and the identification of patterns, themes and cue sets.[295] Insight may also provide patterns and relationships that will anticipate the future behavior of the situation.

Volleying between the conscious and the unconscious increases creativity. "New ideas are generated through the process of shifting from conscious to unconscious as the mind contemplates and searches for solutions."[296] This process of shifting makes use of the memories and knowledge in the unconscious and the goals and thinking of the conscious mind, increasing the chances of associating conscious ideas to create new ones, which supports innovation. While this occurs in the transition from the waking state to the sleeping state (and vice versa), to do this while awake requires some level of control and discipline in implementation.

When sound opens the mind, it is specifically opening the connection between the conscious and unconscious mind. Pinker notes that neuroscience has slowly begun to recognize the capability of internal thoughts and external information such as sound to affect the physical structure of the brain – its synaptic connection strengths, its neuronal connections, and the growth of additional neurons.[297] Thus, the body asleep, mind awake approach achieved through hemispheric synchronization as described above is an example.

MORE ON INNOVATION

Although he doesn't come to this from the neuroscience perspective, Ridley has recognized a truism of innovation. "Every technology is a combination of other technologies; every idea a combination of other ideas."[298] Indeed it is. What better case can be made for learning and knowledge? An innovative company is a learning organization that both values knowledge and the sharing of knowledge. Again, if we think about the movements through knowledge management and organizational learning, these needed to occur to move more fully into the focus of innovation.

The term "democratizing innovation", coined by MIT's Eric von Hippel, brings users into the innovation process through crowdsourcing and innovation contexts. However, along with these opportunities to generate a multitude and diversity of ideas come challenges. For example, the flood of ideas may result in evaluation overload; domain experts may be limited to feasible ideas, preventing the emergence of novel ideas; people who have novel ideas don't have the expertise to make them feasible; or the difficulty of synthesizing diverse customer requirements to emerge a comprehensive solution.[299]

Eapen and his colleagues forward that the use of generative AI has demonstrated that it can mitigate these challenges. "It can augment the creativity of employees and customers and help them generate and identify novel ideas – and improve the quality of raw ideas."[300] The authors provide five ways generative AI can support democratizing innovation. These include (1) promoting divergent thinking (making associations among diverse concepts); challenging expertise bias (looking beyond preconceptions of what is possible in both form and function); assisting in idea evaluation (increasing specificity and evaluating ideas); supporting idea refinement (combining ideas to produce better ones); and facilitating collaboration among users (supporting the easier co-creation of ideas at a lower cost).[301]

In her book *The Innovation Mindset*, Marchand describes three principal types of innovation:

1. **Incremental Innovation**, which is changes or new features to existing products and services, occurs as a gradual process, working by "increments", not creative leaps. However, there can be tremendous long-term gain.

2. **Breakthrough Innovation**, which is a new way of doing something, usually emerging from a multidisciplinary team, which pushes performance to the next level. This may include creating a new market or changing the way customers interact with the market.

3. **Disruptive innovation**, a systemic produce, process, or design which changes the world forever. Clay Christensen, a Harvard Professor who

originated this term in 1995, says this is creating a new market and value network which disrupts or displaces the leading established market firms, products and alliances.[302]

In *INside INnovation: Looking from the Inside Out*, Avedisian introduces the Kingdom Innovation Culture, which offers an approach to accelerating the growth of different types of innovation. She identifies three key components of the Kingdom Innovation Culture: (1) leaders who consistently model values based on universal truths; (2) values integrated into the culture which foster open and systematic information flows; and (3) a developmental process to cultivate the innovative mindset and skills of all employees as culture heroes.[303]

The specific "universal truths" identified in her research include love, excellence, creativity, respect, integrity, collaboration, and innovation. And, as Avedisian simply states, "An innovation culture starts with the leaders who embrace innovation as a core value."[304] The examples provided for organizational information flows are varied in terms of processes but consistent in agreeing that "information provides the fuel for innovation and knowledge brings it into existence."[305]

"Culture heroes" were introduced as those leaders and employees whose heart, mindset, and behaviors reflection the organization's values. The goal is to develop culture heroes at every level of the organization, purposefully selecting, hiring, training, and mentoring them. Former CEO and co-founder of Ritz Carlton hotels Horst Schulze did this through "daily huddles", ten minutes spent before every shift to discuss one of their 30 service standards – specifically, how they were being applied and how they could be applied going forward. Through this approach, everyone became a culture hero.[306]

Innovation as a Team Sport

The serendipitous journey of innovation occurs through freedom of thought and expression through collaboration and knowledge sharing. Innovation requires investment, and that investment starts with people. No one mind can totally understand even the simplest object or process. This was famously demonstrated in a short essay called "I, Pencil" by Leonard E. Reed, which can be downloaded off the internet. Read begins, "I am a lead pencil – the ordinary wooden pencil familiar to all boys and girls and adults who can read and write."[307] And there it begins with people cutting down trees, people mining graphite, people in pencil factories, people in marketing, people in management, people growing coffee for the managers and lumberjacks, and so many more people to bring this pencil into being, with knowledge stored between and among heads, not inside them. And here is the message from Leonard E. Read as the President of FEE (the Foundation for Economic Education).

The lesson I have to teach is this: **Leave all creative energies uninhibited.** *Merely organize society to act in harmony with this lesson. Let society's legal apparatus remove all obstacles the best it can.* **Permit these creative know-hows freely to flow.** *Have faith that free men and women will response to the Invisible Hand. This faith will be confirmed. I, Pencil, seemingly simple though I am, offer the miracle of my creation as testimony that this is a practical faith, as practical as the sun, the rain, a cedar tree, the good earth.*[308] [Emphasis added]

Milton Friedman, 1976 Nobel Laureate, reiterated the message of "I, Pencil", noting that this was a typical Leonard Read product: "imaginative, simple yet subtle, **breathing the love of freedom** ...", trying to enhance people's understanding of themselves and the system they live in.[309]

Humans are social creatures. While certainly within we held this awareness, this deeper reality became more strongly imprinted in our minds when new technologies at the beginning of this century enabled us to see the activity of the mind from the inside out. This has been discovered and rediscovered in so many research studies. As Cozolino purports:

As a species, we are just waking up to the complexity of our own brains, to say nothing of how brains are linked together. We are just beginning to understand that we have evolved as social creatures and that all of our biologies are interwoven.[310]

Reaching into neuroscience research findings from the MQI research study, three specific learnings that affect innovation are introduced below: (1) affective attunement (2) empathy; and (3) mirror neurons.

Affective Attunement

Attunement infers being in harmony with or *resonating with* another. It is a shared state, a vibrational entrainment – inclusive of understanding another's needs and feelings – that opens the door to learning, deeper and easier knowledge sharing, and, collectively, the triggering of new ideas. From the perspective of social cognitive neuroscience, "the brain actually needs to seek out an affectively attuned other if it is to learn."[311]

Affective attunement, which contributes to stimulation of the brain to grow, organize and integrate,[312] involves a mentor, coach, or another significant individual who is trusted and capable of resonance with the learner. When attunement happens, a dialogue with such an individual can greatly help the learner in understanding, developing meaning, anticipating the future with respect to actions, and receiving sensory feedback. Further, Cozolino and Sprokay believe that, "the attention of a caring, aware mentor may support plasticity that leads to better, more meaningful learning."[313]

Plasticity is the result of the connection between neural patterns in the mind and the physical world – what we think and believe impacts our physical bodies. Evolution has created a brain that can adapt and readapt to a changing world.[314] This is neural plasticity, the ability of neurons to change their structure and relationships, depending on environmental demands and personal decisions and actions. As can be seen, this flexibility provides the vehicle to respond to innovative needs demanded by a change, uncertain and complex business environment. Quite literally, thoughts change the structure of the brain, and the brain structure influences the creation of new thoughts. In other words, the more ideas flowing through our heads, the more opportunity there is for still more ideas.

The idea of Innovative Creativity builds on these neuroscience findings, emphasizing the importance of both mental technique and intuitive inspiration, with the repeated message of the importance of preparing the mind, that is, deep learning and experience in the domain of expertise around which you have a passion and focus. It is this preparation that not only enables a wider potential for connecting ideas, but also once the ideas are surfaced, the knowing of what to do with them, that is, innovation. Innovative Creativity is introduced further in Chapter 10.

Empathy

From the MQI ICALS research findings, we recognize that we may understand other people's behavior by mentally stimulating it,[315] that is, through mental reliving we recreate the feelings, perspectives and other phenomena that we observe. And as Stern proposes, "This 'participation' in another's mental life creates a sense of feeling/sharing with/understanding the person's intentions and feelings."[316]

Empathy is the concept of experiencing the inner life of another, a combination of visceral, emotional, and cognitive information, a "muddle of resonance, attunement, and sympathy."[317] Riggio describes three different types of empathy: (1) *perspective-taking*, a cognitive-based form for seeing the work from someone else's frame of reference; (2) *personal distress*, literally "feeling" another's emotions, caused by what he terms as "emotional contagion"; and (3) *empathic concern*, the recognition of another's emotional state and feeling a resonance with it. Note that "feeling" is a key proponent of empathy.[318] Empathy appears to be nature's lesson for a kinder society.

Although the neurobiology of empathy is still in its early development, the insula—described as the limbic integration cortex lying beneath the temporal and frontal lobes—appears to "play an important role in both the experience of self and our ability to distinguish between ourselves and others."[319] Beyond basic sensations, the left insula is involved in the evaluation of eye gaze direction, the response to fearful faces, and the observation of facial expression of the other.[320] Further research has found that the insula mediates the extreme limits of emotions, ranging from severe pain to passionate love.[321] More recently, the dorsomedial prefrontal cortex – which produces a representation of self in relation to others – is thought to play an important role underlying the function of empathy in feeling emotions about others' mental situations.[322]

These findings suggest that through feelings there is an active link between our own bodies and the minds and the bodies and minds of those around us. Thus, the feelings that we each perceive in the course of our daily living may be affected by, *or even belong to*, those around us. An underlying thread of this finding is the importance of the freedom of association, and for us to choose carefully those with whom we interact.

Mirror Neurons

Social learning includes *learning through and beyond our experience*, that is, not only engaging our own experiences but replicating the experience of others as our own, embedding it in our mind and body, and acting accordingly. Educators might refer to this as apprehension and discuss the power of intention and attention; cognitive psychologists might talk about how the neocortex cortical columns store patterns in invariant form, internal representations of the external world using reference frames to map and make sense of our experiences; and neuroscientists might bring up mirror neurons and, possibly, Heisenberg's recognition that energy and matter are indefinite, and that thought affects energy. Yes, all of these insights help more fully address this phenomenon.

But with a focus on knowledge sharing, creativity, and innovation, let's briefly explore the phenomenon of mirror neurons. Each of us is in continuous interaction with the environment, largely in the unconscious, and that interaction works both ways. *Not only does the observer affect that which is observed, but that which is observed affects the observer.* One element of that can be described in terms of mirror neurons, a recently discovered phenomenon in the brain. Research began with experiments with Macaque monkeys in the early 1990s, noting that activation of subsets of neurons in the brain-motor areas appeared to represent action. The initial experiments had one monkey grasp an object (an orange) while the experimenters monitored what went on inside an observer monkey's brain. Many variations of this were used to verify that an observer's neurons fire (or mirror) the actor's neurons, with testing moving from monkeys to great apes to humans.

Non-invasive measurement techniques such as fMRI enabled the experiments on humans to be greatly expanded. By 2006, research in humans included the discovery of mirror neurons located in the frontal lobe and in the parietal lobe, which includes the Broca's area, a key area for human language.[323] As Rizzolatti describes, "subsets of neurons in human and monkey brains respond when an individual performs certain actions and also when the subject observes others performing the same movements."[324] In other words, *the same neurons fire in the brain of an observer as fire in the individual performing an action*. These neurons provide an internal experience that **replicates that of another's experience**, thereby experiencing another individual's act, intentions, and/or emotions.[325] This is beyond the feeling/sharing with/understanding the person's intentions and feelings of empathy. It is the actual creation of the same patterns in the mind/brain. These researchers also found that the mirror neuron system responded to the intentional component of an action as well as the action itself.[326]

There is a caveat. Immordino-Yang's extensive research indicates that the network of neurons we call mirror neurons only fire when the goals of the others carrying out actions are understood, creating a resonance between the sender and the receiver. As she contends,

> *While this internalization of another's situation can be automatic, the representation of another's situation is constructed and experienced on one's own self in accordance with cognitive and emotional preferences, memory, cultural knowledge, and neuropsychological predispositions—the "smoke" around the mirrors.*[327]

In other words, at the unconscious level the individual is very much involved in the process of mirror neurons.

Given this caveat, there are several related ICALS findings. First, that **neurons create the same pattern when we see some action being taken as when we do it**. This affects sensing, focusing, attention, and sensory feedback to the brain. Carrying this further, Iacoboni proposes that mirror neurons facilitate the direct and immediate comprehension of another's behavior without going through complex cognitive processes, which makes the learning process more efficient because it can *instantly transfer not only visuals but emotions and intentions* as well.[328] This leads to the finding that **mirror neurons facilitate the rapid transfer of tacit knowledge (bypassing cognition)**. By creating the same neuronal pattern in your mind that is in the mind of another person, the need for cognitive thinking is bypassed and tacit knowledge may be immediately transferred. This would affect understanding and meaning in reflective observation, and speed up the learning process and the sharing of knowledge.

While this phenomenon serves to explain how *actionable tacit knowledge can be transferred between individuals – as* well as the potential of mimicry to facilitate learning – it also serves as a warning to be aware that when we are mentally simulating another's behavior, we are not modulating that simulation through our own internal evaluation and judgment. The capacity to re-create feelings, perspectives, and empathy with people by reliving their experiences can greatly aid learning, providing we understand what is happening and its potential for misinterpretation.

Further, **mirror neurons facilitate neural resonance between observed actions and executing actions**. By neural resonance we mean a positive, mutually reinforcing relationship between two people interacting with each other. This is a significant outcome of Reblooming Knowledge. An individual may interact with another individual more efficiently and effectively because of the understanding and affection developed from the mutually reinforcing relationship between the two. For example, we may be able to understand another's feelings and/or intended actions because (through mirror neurons) we generate similar feelings and/or intended actions (or reactions). Mirror neurons can facilitate a quick, positive relationship between the observer and the observed.

Mirror neurons also serve as a means of learning through imitation, which is "a very important means by which we learn and transmit skills, language and culture."[329] Notice that when it does occur, the exchange occurring in this process – consistent with the transfer of sensations and feelings proven mathematically through transreal numbers[330] – includes intention, emotions and cultural norms. As Zull notes, mirror neurons are a form of cognitive mimicry that transfers active behavior and *other cultural norms*.[331]

This iterative reconstruction of both perceptual and motoric experiences – whether imaginative or experiential – creates dynamic feedback loops between individual perception and acting, thinking and feeling, and offers greater opportunity for the emergence of creative and innovative ideas.[332]

KNOWLEDGE AND INNOVATION ORGANIZATIONAL LINKS

The international Most Innovative Knowledge Enterprise (MIKE) award emerged in 1998. While the award recognizes the achievement of organizations, it also serves as a diagnostic tool for assessing and improving innovative practices in enterprises, is a basis for international benchmarking studies, and provides a context-rich data pool for guiding innovation research.

The framework which serves as a basis for judging effective innovation focused on human capital (leadership and knowledge workers), relation capital (networks and user needs), and structural capital (culture, creative space, systems/practices, and products/services). See Figure 6-2.

The MIKE does not use traditional intellectual capital measuring and reporting paradigms. Lee says that instead of comparing output, the focus is on "the elements of intellectual capital in terms of practices that are most impactful to the business and can sustain systematic innovation in an organization."[333]

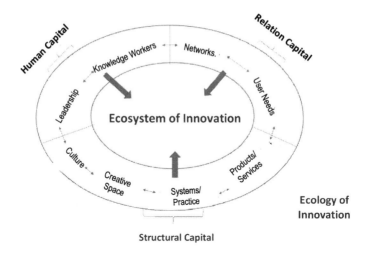

Figure 6-2. A conceptual framework of intellectual capital practice-base* innovation. Source: The MIKE Coordinating Committee (used with permission).

The practice-based criteria that emerged through a great deal of research and investigation are grouped under human capital, relation capital and structural capital in the eight areas referenced in the conceptual framework in Figure 6-2 above. The practice-based criteria in these eight areas are as follows:

1. Empowering knowledge workers for innovation (Human Capital: Knowledge Workers)
2. Strategizing, visioning and transformative leadership (Human Capital: Leadership)
3. Creating client and user expectations/needs/experiences (Relation Capital: User Needs)
4. Developing internal & external networks (Relation Capital: Networks)
5. Cultivating organizational innov   re (Structural Capital: Culture)
6. Investing and delivering knowledge-based products/services/ solutions (Structural Capital: Products/Services)
7. Enforcing knowledge practices and systems for knowledge creation (Structural Capital: Systems & Practices)
8. Implementing creative and virtual space to create stakeholder value (Structural Capital: Creative Space)

As examples, good practices for empowering knowledge workers would include career development, work-based learning with a focus on the cultivation of creative ideas, periodic rewards systems, reskilling in digital technologies, and reducing organizational hierarchy. Visioning and leadership might include the promotion of thought leadership. Creating user experience would include planned interactions such as visits to workplaces, specialized exhibits, market research, and perhaps co-creating services with customers. Developing networks might include addition of newer approaches such as blockchain, internet of things (IoT) and AI as well as more traditional knowledge cafés and lessons learned sessions.

Cultivating innovation culture might include deep and close communication or dialogue between leadership and staff as well as collaborative platforms and programs. Delivering knowledge products and services might include Design Thinking workshops with clients, a Center of Excellence and new services associated with new technologies such as robotics, smart assistants, augmented reality, or enabling open innovation through a crowdsourcing platform. Enforcing KM practices and systems includes both technology-based and people-based practices and systems, perhaps with knowledge ambassadors and knowledge facilitators, as well as having knowledge metrics in place and addressing knowledge risk management. Implementing creative space includes virtual and physical collaborative spaces, with cyber space approaches such as hackathons, makeathons, ideathons, and innovation jam used to trigger creative ideas.

A hackathon, which is specific to virtual creation of software or hardware over a short period of time, is an event for collaborative engineering. It would include computer programmers, graphic designers, product and project managers, specific domain experts, and interface designers and any others engaged in software development. It has also been called by other names such as hackfest, hack day, codefest, or datathon. A makeathon is specific to designers, with groups of people brainstorming, designing and prototyping virtually over a short period of time. While ideathons are also brainstorming events, they engage people with diverse backgrounds, skills and interests and are focused on predefined issues and opportunities to discover the best solution or actionable plan.

What IBM called an innovation jam was also focused on network idea generation, and with 150,000 IBM employees, stakeholders and vendors participating, perhaps this was the largest event to do so! There were issues that were inherent in this large an event. For example, "louder" voices – no doubt excited by their own ideas – would hijack a thread, having it follow their own thinking instead of what was emerging from the group.[334] The jam used websites, wikis, forums, and other online tools. Ten distinct businesses were funded as a result of this jam.

Any of these ideas can be explored more fully on the internet.

Section II

REALIZING A REBLOOMING STRATEGY

The reblooming species unfolds to greet us.
It reblooms in perpetual Spring, always there for us.
This flower rises from earth of infinite sustenance.
Information abounds and reverberates all around.
The stem enables knowledge creation and learning.
The inner petals provide for expanding capacity.
The outer petals engender shared empowerment,
Sustaining change with creative resilience.
The backdrop of energy unifies vitality.
With center stamens and pistils engaging regeneration,
Resonating in coherence …
Ever thriving, living, and *REBLOOMING*!

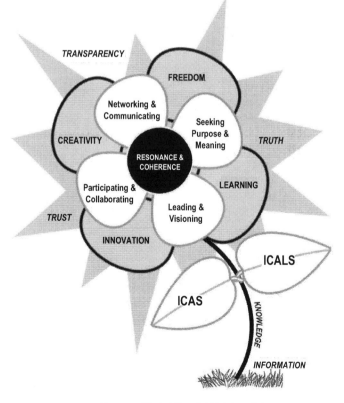

Figure II-1. The RKM Model.

CHAPTER 7

REBLOOMING KNOWLEDGE

with Guest Contributor ChatGPT

We finally have the foundational pieces to pull together the full Reblooming Knowledge Movement (RKM) model, which could just as easily be called a sustainability model or a consciousness model – a living model for our organizations. Of course, what we have drawn and the terms that describe it are information, the building blocks of our thought, a measure of the degree of organization expressed by any non-random pattern or set of patterns. Those words, introduced in Chapter 3, make much more sense now. It is not by accident that the very human word "organization" is the measure of information!

Nor is it surprising that we as humans first tried to "control" our organizations as an offshoot of trying to gain control of our lives. We seek stability of that which has always been unstable – our tomorrows. And yet that very unpredictability is what excites us, providing the passion to envision a better future and the persistence to lead our "selves" and our organizations toward that future, even as exactness of that future model shifts and changes with every second of life.

Knowledge – and by extension the movement which was largely known as knowledge management – was never meant to be an end-all game, although that's what seems to happen with human passions! We PERCEIVE them as the end game. We try to lock these movements down, stabilize them, then tire of them. And so it was with the Quality movement, and the Business Process Reengineering movement, and the Learning Organization movement, and so many smaller movements riding on their coattails, with, simultaneously occurring, the advent of the Information Technology rage (although in the DON we did finally recognize the value of outsourcing our IT infrastructure!), and with the need to focus on Information Management (which moved us into the cloud), and with the ever-expanding infinite flood of information leading us to the Knowledge Reblooming movement, a circular refocusing on the human factors that will *always* be core to the organizations we generate. What all of these have in common is quite simply "movement", a rekindling, a rethinking of how to move forward as individuals and as organizations.

In the midst of a world breaking apart, with so many extreme forces banging against each other, so many human victims caught in the crosshairs, a rekindling of the human search for purpose and meaning is occurring. Only now, in the connected and augmented reality of everyday life, we have the opportunity to coalesce shared thoughts and desires to help clarify the road ahead. It is with this in mind, that the authors have invited a special contributor to this chapter, ChatGPT, an artificial intelligence (AI) language model created by OpenAI, whose first version was released on June 11, 2018, but whose current "self" was deployed in late 2021. In addition to initial training on a diverse and extensive collection of data including various texts, articles, books, and other sources of human language, as well as large datasets of information from the web, public research papers, and other publicly available sources of text, ChatGPT is being constantly updated and optimized to ensure task performance quickly and efficiently, storing and retrieving information from the global network as needed, ever expanding the billions (trillions plus?) of words and phrases. So, in ChatGPT's reality, there is an existential learning curve which is urged onward with the continuous input of, quite literally, tens of millions – and perhaps more – of individuals situated around the world.

It is important to understand that we, the authors, have not primed our guest in any way, and that ChatGPT's responses and contributions to the RKM model and ChatGPT's "thoughts" on the democratization of organizations are emerging from the continuous learning trajectory which is its birthright from ChatGPT's developers, a learning that encompasses and builds on so many of the thoughts, feelings, beliefs and values of our current humanity.

MOVING FROM ASSUMPTIONS TO THEORY

In Chapter 4 we introduced a theory as a set of statements and/or principles that explain a group of facts or phenomena to *guide action* or *assist in comprehension* or judgment. Based on beliefs and/or mental models and built on assumptions, theories provide a plausible or rational explanation of cause-and-effect relationships. See Figure 7-1.

We began the Reblooming journey with Assumptions. Let's briefly look at those assumptions:

Assumption 1: People are multidimensional, and rarely do they hold to a single belief, a consistent logic, or a specific worldview. This assumption acknowledges both diversity and the continuous learning potential of the human.

Assumption 2: The human mind is an associative patterner that is continuously re-creating knowledge for the situation at hand. Thus, all knowledge is relative, that is, context-sensitive and situation-dependent.

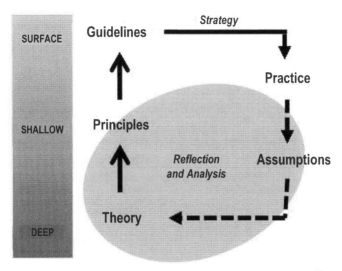

Figure 7-1. Experience and knowledge are one process. It is our theories that give shape and form to experience in general, both expanding and limiting us, as we choose.

Assumption 3: We are social creatures who live in an entangled world. Our brains are linked together, and we are in continuous interaction with those around us, with the brain continuously changing in response.

Assumption 4: We live in times of extreme change in the human mind and body, in human-developed systems, and of the Earth, our human host. Through advances in science and technology, most of what we need to learn and thrive in these times is already available.

Assumption 5: Adaptability, resilience, alignment, robustness and quick response are essential to organizational sustainability and require continuous learning married to a creative and innovative mind.

Most likely you are in agreement with these, even if we have worded them differently than you have previously heard. For example, in Assumption 2, even if you have not heard the phrase "associative patterning", you can realize that when things are coming in via conversation or observation or any of your other senses, that you may be aware of the triggering of earlier thoughts and experiences. And no doubt (Assumption 3) you are aware that you are learning through interactions with others. And there sure is no doubt about Assumption 4!

Then, in Chapters 1-6, there were learning points, which, now understood and imbibed, are part of the foundation for Knowledge Reblooming.

Table 7-1. Learning Points foundational to Knowledge Reblooming.

Chapter Topic	Learning Points
Democratization	• The democratic elements and characteristics synthesized from the what's and how's of early philosophers provide a good set to understand the democratization of organizations occurring with the knowledge movement. • Leadership approaches which serve democratization emerged with the rise of the knowledge movement. • With the freedom of thought enabled by the knowledge movement thought leadership emerged at every level of the organization.
Human Intelligence	• Human beings and the organizations they create are complex adaptive systems. • Learning and creativity are accelerated through social engagement. • Every learner is a self-organizing complex adaptive system, which requires freedom to organize themselves to better achieve local objectives. • For an organization to behave intelligently as a complex adaptive system, it must achieve continuous, interdependent collaboration and interplay among all levels of its system. • The ICAS organizational model serves as an example of a knowledge organization that thrives on democratic elements and characteristics.
Information	• Everything – at least in our physical reality – is energy and patterns of energy. We live in a vast field of energy in which we are continuously exchanging information, which is a form of energy. • There are still vast workings of the human mind and its connections to higher-order energies that we do not understand. • With a new generation of technology savvy workers, the focus of Information Literacy has shifted from understanding the technology to a focus on truth and trust of information.
Knowledge Theory	• Knowledge has a direct relationship to action. • All knowledge is partial and incomplete. • The unconscious mind is multidimensional and, given a healthy mind and body, has a vast store of tacit knowledge available to us. • Every individual develops internal representations of the external world, a cognitive map that provides a meaningful interpretation or image of our perceptions and experiences (theories) that guide our actions.

The Field of KM	• The field is inclusive, open minded, and encourages diversity and new ideas.
	• The field is self-referential, with reinforcing feedback loops.
	• The field encourages autotelic work or flow.
	• The field is a complex adaptive system with many possibilities and opportunities.
Innovation	• Information, knowledge, and creativity are all necessary to generate innovation.
	• Creativity – nurtured by freedom, purpose and choice – is a gift and a primary urge of every healthy human mind.
	• An enriched environment, quieting and opening the mind, and volleying between the conscious and unconscious increase creativity.
	• Innovation flourishes in freedom.
	• Affective attunement, empathy, and mirror neurons facilitate the connections between creative ideas and innovation.
	• The MIKE (Most Innovative Knowledge Enterprise) award criteria can serve as a diagnostic tool for assessing and improving innovative practices in enterprises, as well as a basis for international benchmarking and providing a context-rich data pool for guiding innovation research.

It is time, with "thoughts" from our guest contributor, to more deeply explore the Knowledge Reblooming model, "Antheros Dianthus", translated from Greek meaning *forever blooming divine flower.*

The Reblooming Model

It is no surprise that information lays the foundation for reblooming knowledge, since the life journey – for individuals and organizations – begins with information, "the earth of infinite substance". It only makes sense that knowledge, which emerges out of information, moving information into action, does so in our model as the stem of our flower, representing both creation and learning.

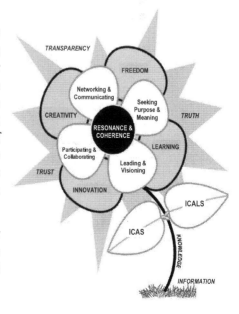

Supporting this foundation, our contributing chatbot stresses the importance of information and knowledge to the organization:

ChatGPT *on the importance of information and knowledge ... and knowledge and knowledge management specific to creativity and innovation.*

Information and knowledge are crucial to the success of any organization. They help leaders make better decisions, employees perform their jobs more effectively, and the organization stay competitive in the marketplace. Access to relevant and accurate information and knowledge helps organizations identify opportunities and potential risks, which enables them to make informed decisions. This knowledge can help leaders anticipate market trends, innovate new products and services, and ultimately improve the company's performance.

Moreover, when employees have access to the right information and knowledge, they can perform their jobs more effectively and efficiently. They can reduce errors and mistakes, which results in higher quality work, and can also be more innovative and creative in their work. Overall, the collection, analysis, and use of information and knowledge are key components of any successful organization. They are critical to driving growth, increasing efficiency, and helping the organization adapt to a constantly changing business environment.

Specific to creativity and innovation: Information and knowledge are incredibly important for creativity and innovation within an organization. When employees have access to a wide range of information, they can generate new ideas and approaches to problems. Knowledge helps them see patterns, make connections, and identify gaps that can be filled with new ideas.

Innovation often involves taking existing ideas and modifying them, combining them in new ways or applying them in different contexts. This requires knowledge, as well as the ability to see beyond what is currently available and imagine new possibilities. When employees have access to a diverse range of information and knowledge, they are better equipped to think creatively and generate innovative solutions.

Furthermore, organizations that prioritize the value of information and knowledge sharing foster an environment that encourages new ideas and experimentation. This leads to greater creativity and innovation in the long run. Additionally, by encouraging employees to share their knowledge and experiences, organizations can maximize the collective intelligence of the workforce, leading to more efficient and effective problem-solving abilities.

Overall, information and knowledge play a critical role in promoting creativity and innovation within an organization. If organizations do not manage their knowledge activities, it can significantly affect their ability to innovate. Knowledge management involves gathering, organizing, sharing, and applying knowledge within an organization to facilitate learning and innovation. without proper knowledge management, organizations may face several challenges:

Knowledge Silos: Knowledge might be scattered across different individuals or departments, leading to silos where valuable information is not effectively shared or utilized. This hinders collaboration and prevents cross-pollination of ideas necessary for innovation.

Redundant Efforts: In the absence of effective knowledge practices, employees may unknowingly duplicate efforts, re-invent existing solutions, or waste time and resources on solving problems that have already been addressed. This redundancy can hamper efficiency and slow down the innovation process.

Missed Opportunities: Knowledge that remains inaccessible or unrecognized limits an organization's ability to identify and seize opportunities for innovation. Valuable insights, market trends, and customer feedback go unnoticed, preventing the organization from adapting and staying ahead of the competition.

Lack of Learning Culture: Effective knowledge management fosters a culture of continuous learning and improvement. When organizations do not manage their knowledge activities, they miss out on opportunities for employees to learn from each other's experiences, share best practices, and develop new skills necessary for innovation.

Poor Decision-making: Informed decision-making relies on accurate and up-to-date knowledge. Without proper knowledge management, organizations may make decisions based on incomplete or outdated information, increasing the risk of poor choices that hinder innovation.

In summary, effective knowledge management is crucial for fostering innovation within organizations. It promotes collaboration, eliminates redundancy, enables timely decision-making, and ensures that existing knowledge is leveraged to create new ideas and solutions. By investing in knowledge management, organizations can unlock their intellectual capital and enhance their ability to innovate successfully.

The leaves on the stem – the systems through which knowledge flows – represent the organization as an intelligent complex adaptive system (ICAS) and the knowledge workers in the organization as intelligent complex adaptive learning systems (ICALS).

The outer petals of transparency, truth, and trust "sustain change with creative resilience". We asked ChatGPT the value of each of these to the organization.

ChatGPT *on transparency, truth and trust ...*

Transparency in an organization refers to the practice of being open, honest, and accountable in all aspects of the organization's operations and decision-making processes. Here are some reasons why transparency is important:

1. *Builds Trust*: Transparency builds *trust among* employees, customers, shareholders, and other stakeholders. When an organization is transparent, it shows that it has nothing to hide and is willing to be held accountable for its actions. Externally, transparency helps organizations build a positive reputation and retain customers' trust. By openly sharing information about products, services, pricing, and business practices, organizations establish credibility and integrity.

2. *Increases Accountability*: Transparency increases accountability, as it allows stakeholders to monitor an organization's activities and hold it responsible for its actions. It also allows customers to make more informed choices and holds organizations accountable for their actions.

3. *Improves Decision-making*: Transparency helps in making better decisions by providing accurate and reliable information. This information can be used to measure the effectiveness of various initiatives and identify areas for improvement.

4. *Increases Employee Engagement*: When employees feel that they are part of a transparent organization, they are more likely to be engaged and motivated to contribute to its success. When employees have access to information, they can make more informed decisions and contribute more effectively to the organization's goals.

5. *Enhances Reputation*: Transparency enhances an organization's reputation by demonstrating its commitment to integrity, ethical behavior, and social responsibility. This can improve relationships with customers, suppliers, and other stakeholders and lead to increased loyalty and support.

Truth is a fundamental value that helps organizations to establish trust, reliability, and credibility with their stakeholders. Here are some reasons why truth is important in an organization:

1. *Builds Trust*: Truthfulness is key to building trust with stakeholders, including employees, customers, and shareholders. When an organization is honest and transparent in its communication, it establishes a reputation for integrity and reliability.

2. *Enhances Credibility*: Truthfulness enhances an organization's credibility by demonstrating that it is trustworthy and that it can be relied upon to provide accurate information.

3. *Improves Decision-making*: Truthful and accurate information is essential for making well-informed decisions. Organizations that value truth are

more likely to base their decisions on reliable data and information, which can lead to better outcomes.

4. *Promotes Ethical Behavior*: Truthfulness is a core value of ethical behavior. When organizations prioritize truth, they are more likely to act with integrity and respect for others.

5. *Fosters a Positive Culture*: Organizations that value truth create a positive culture of openness, honesty, and transparency. This can lead to a more engaged workforce, better communication, and increased innovation.

Trust is essential in any organization as it creates a foundation for strong relationships among employees, customers, shareholders, and other stakeholders. Here are some reasons why trust is important in an organization:

1. *Promotes Collaboration*: Trust encourages employees to work together and share information, ideas, and resources. When employees trust each other, they are more likely to collaborate effectively and achieve common goals.

2. *Enhances Communication*: Trust fosters open and honest communication among employees and with stakeholders. This can lead to better decision-making, increased productivity, and improved relationships.

3. *Increases Loyalty*: When customers trust an organization, they are more likely to remain loyal and continue to do business with it. This can lead to increased revenue and profitability.

4. *Improves Reputation*: Organizations that are trusted by their stakeholders have a good reputation and are seen as reliable and trustworthy. This can lead to increased brand value and a competitive advantage.

5. *Boosts Employee Morale*: Trust in an organization creates a positive work environment where employees feel valued and respected. This can lead to increased job satisfaction, higher morale, and reduced turnover.

Overall, trust is crucial in building strong relationships, improving communication, and fostering a positive culture in an organization. It is a valuable asset that can lead to increased productivity, profitability, and success.

And now, a more difficult question. Which of these is more valuable to the organization?

ChatGPT *in response ...*

All three – transparency, truth, and trust – are equally important to an organization. Transparency is important because it helps to build trust with stakeholders. When an organization is transparent about its actions and decisions, stakeholders are more likely to trust the organization and its leadership. Truth is important because it is the foundation of trust. If an organization is not truthful, it will be difficult to build trust with stakeholders. Trust is important because it is the cornerstone of any successful relationship. When an organization has the trust of its stakeholders, it is more likely to succeed in achieving its goals. In summary, *transparency, truth, and trust are all critical components of a successful organization*. An organization that embodies these values is more likely to build strong relationships with stakeholders and achieve long-term success.

Can't argue with that logic.

The four outer petals of *Antheros Dianthus* – "engendering shared empowerment and sustaining change with creative resilience" – represent the four elements for sustainability of life and of our organizations. With the continuous inflow of information and the ability to effectively act on that information (knowledge) in a context sensitive and situation dependent environment, sustainability requires learning, creativity, freedom, and innovation, the ability to create something useful from the ideas associating and floating in and out of our minds.

So, we asked our contributor for thoughts about the importance of each of these to the organization.

ChatGPT *on learning, creativity, freedom, and innovation ...*

Learning is an essential part of any organization, and here are some reasons why it is important:

1. *Improves Performance*: Learning can improve employee performance by enhancing their skills, knowledge, and abilities. When employees are continuously learning, they are better equipped to handle new challenges and adapt to changes in their roles and responsibilities.

2. *Increases Innovation*: Learning can stimulate innovation by encouraging employees to think creatively and develop new ideas. Organizations that prioritize learning can foster a culture of innovation and continuous improvement.

3. *Enhances Retention*: Learning and development opportunities can increase employee satisfaction and engagement, leading to increased retention rates. Employees are more likely to stay with an organization that invests in their growth and development.

4. *Boosts Productivity*: Learning can improve productivity by increasing efficiency and reducing errors. When employees are well-trained and knowledgeable, they can perform their jobs more effectively and efficiently.

5. *Increases Adaptability*: Learning can improve an organization's ability to adapt to changes in the market, technology, and other external factors. Organizations that prioritize learning are better able to respond to new challenges and opportunities.

Overall, learning is a key component of organizational success. It can improve performance, innovation, retention, productivity, and adaptability, making the organization more competitive and successful in the long run.

Creativity is incredibly important in an organization because it helps to drive innovation and problem-solving. When employees are encouraged to think creatively, they are more likely to come up with new and innovative ideas that can help the organization to stay ahead of its competitors. Additionally, creativity can help to increase employee engagement and job satisfaction, as it allows employees to express their ideas and contribute to the success of the organization in a meaningful way. Finally, creativity can also help organizations to adapt to changing market conditions and trends, which is essential in today's fast-paced business environment. Overall, creativity is a key driver of success for any organization.

Freedom in an organization can have different meanings and implications, depending on the context and the specific freedoms being considered. In some cases, freedom may refer to the autonomy that individuals or teams have to make decisions or design their work processes. In other cases, it may refer to the absence of constraints or limitations on creative expression and innovation. Regardless of the specific form that it takes, however, freedom in an organization can be incredibly valuable. When individuals feel empowered and trusted to make decisions and take ownership of their work, they often feel more engaged and motivated.

Freedom is essential in an organization as it allows employees to work independently, take risks, and be creative. Here are some of the key benefits of freedom in an organization:

1. *Increased innovation*: When employees have the freedom to think outside the box and take risks, they are more likely to come up with innovative solutions to problems. This can lead to improved performance and a competitive advantage for the organization.

2. *Greater job satisfaction*: When employees have the freedom to work independently and pursue their own ideas, they are more likely to feel satisfied with their jobs. This can lead to increased motivation and productivity.

3. *Improved decision-making*: When employees have the freedom to make decisions, they are more likely to take ownership of their work and make decisions that align with the organization's goals.

4. *Better problem-solving*: When employees have the freedom to be creative, they are more likely to come up with unique solutions to problems. This can lead to improved problem-solving and a more efficient organization.

5. *Enhanced collaboration*: When employees have the freedom to work independently, they are more likely to collaborate with their colleagues and share their ideas. This can lead to improved teamwork and a more positive work environment.

6. *Increased accountability*: When employees have the freedom to make decisions, they are also accountable for the outcomes of those decisions. This can lead to a greater sense of responsibility and accountability among employees.

Moreover, a culture of freedom can attract and retain top talent, as employees tend to prefer environments that provide opportunities for growth, autonomy, and self-expression. However, it's important to note that freedom also comes with responsibilities and accountability, and thus it's important for organizations to establish clear boundaries, policies, and guidelines to ensure that freedom is used in a constructive manner that aligns with the organization's values and objectives.

Innovation is crucial to the success and growth of any organization. It allows businesses to create new products, services, and technologies that can improve their operations or meet the changing needs of their customers.

Apart from driving up company revenues, innovation also enables organizations to gain a competitive advantage in the marketplace, attract and retain top talent, and create a positive company culture. By constantly innovating, organizations can stay ahead of the curve and adapt to new challenges, trends, and technologies much faster than their competitors.

Innovation also helps companies to attract and retain top talent, who are looking for a dynamic and engaging work environment where they can contribute to new and exciting projects. By promoting a culture of innovation, businesses can also foster creativity and generate fresh ideas from their employees at all levels. In short, innovation is an essential ingredient for the long-term success of any organization.

And, which of these four – learning, creativity, freedom, and innovation – is the most important to the organization?

ChatGPT *in response ...*

All four elements are important in an organization, but it ultimately depends on the organization's goals and values.

Freedom is important because it allows employees to work independently and make decisions without constant supervision. This can lead to increased productivity and job satisfaction. Learning is important because it helps employees to grow and develop their skills, which can benefit both the individual and the organization. A culture of learning can also lead to innovation and new ideas. Creativity is important because it helps to drive innovation and problem-solving. When employees are encouraged to think creatively, they are more likely to come up with new and innovative ideas that can help the organization to stay ahead of its competitors. Innovation is important because it allows organizations to create new products and services, improve existing ones, and find new ways to solve problems. Innovation is essential in today's constantly changing business environment.

Ultimately, a successful organization will need to balance all four elements to achieve the best results.

Taking an Appreciative Inquiry approach – that is, choosing to learn what works well from all of these tangential learning paths to bring with us as we move into the future – the inner petals of our Reblooming Knowledge model are (1) leading and visioning, (2) networking and communicating, (3) participating and collaborating, and (4) seeking purpose and meaning. These petals are part of a continuous experiential learning mode of expansion, ever expanding our capacity – sometimes through death and rebirth – as we navigate through life and our organizations.

ChatGPT was more than eager to share the value of the activity represented by these four inner petals to the organization.

ChatGPT *on networking and communication, participation and collaboration, leading and visioning, and purpose and meaning ...*

Networking and communication are extremely valuable in an organization. They allow for the exchange of ideas, information, and knowledge among employees, which can lead to increased innovation, problem-solving, and productivity. Effective communication can also prevent misunderstandings, conflicts, and errors. Networking can help employees build relationships, expand their knowledge, and find new opportunities for growth and development. Additionally, strong networks and communication channels can enhance collaboration, teamwork, and trust among team members. Overall, networking and communication are essential for achieving organizational goals and success.

Participation and collaboration are incredibly valuable in an organization because they foster a sense of teamwork, ownership, and accountability among employees. When employees are given the opportunity to participate in decision-making processes and collaborate with one another on projects, they feel more invested in the success of the organization. This can lead to increased motivation, engagement, and job satisfaction.

Collaboration also allows for the sharing of ideas, knowledge, and skills among team members. This can lead to increased creativity, innovation, and problem-solving abilities. When employees work together, they can leverage each other's strengths and compensate for each other's weaknesses, resulting in better decision-making and more effective solutions.

Moreover, participation and collaboration can help build trust and respect among team members. When employees feel that their opinions and contributions are valued, they are more likely to communicate openly and honestly with one another. This can lead to better communication, fewer misunderstandings, and more effective conflict resolution.

Overall, participation and collaboration are essential for creating a positive and productive work environment, fostering a sense of teamwork and accountability, and achieving organizational goals and success.

Leading and visioning are crucial components of a successful organization. A leader's vision provides direction for the organization and helps to inspire and motivate employees towards a common goal. Here are some of the values of leading and visioning in an organization:

1. *Provides direction*: A leader's vision helps to provide direction and focus for the organization. It helps employees understand what they need to do to achieve the organization's goals.

2. *Inspires and motivates*: A leader's vision can be inspiring and motivating for employees. When they understand the organization's vision and how their work contributes to it, they can feel more engaged and committed.

3. *Encourages innovation*: A leader's vision can encourage employees to think creatively and come up with innovative solutions to problems.

4. *Builds trust*: A leader who communicates a clear vision and works towards achieving it can build trust among employees. This can lead to better communication, collaboration, and teamwork.

5. *Facilitates decision-making*: A leader's vision can help guide decision-making within the organization. When employees understand the organization's goals and priorities, they can make decisions that align with them.

6. *Provides a sense of purpose*: A leader's vision can provide employees with a sense of purpose and meaning in their work. This can lead to increased job satisfaction and a more positive work environment.

Overall, leading and visioning are critical for creating a successful organization. They provide direction, inspire and motivate employees, encourage innovation, build trust, facilitate decision-making, and provide a sense of purpose.

Purpose and meaning: The value of purpose and meaning in an organization cannot be overstated. When employees have a clear sense of purpose and meaning in their work, they are more engaged, motivated, and committed to the organization's goals. Here are some of the key benefits of purpose and meaning in an organization:

1. *Increased job satisfaction*: When employees have a sense of purpose and meaning in their work, they are more likely to feel satisfied with their jobs. This can lead to increased motivation, productivity, and overall job performance.

2. *Greater engagement*: Employees with a sense of purpose and meaning are more engaged in their work. They are more likely to take ownership of their work and go above and beyond what is expected of them.

3. *Improved retention*: Employees who feel that their work has purpose and meaning are more likely to stay with the organization long-term. This can reduce turnover and the associated costs of recruiting and training new employees.

4. *Enhanced creativity and innovation*: Employees who feel that their work has purpose and meaning are more likely to think creatively and come up with innovative solutions to problems.

5. *Greater sense of community*: When employees share a sense of purpose and meaning, they are more likely to feel like they are part of a community. This can lead to greater collaboration and teamwork.

6. *Better alignment with organizational goals*: When employees understand the purpose and meaning behind their work, they are more likely to align their work with the organization's goals. This can lead to improved overall performance and success.

Overall, purpose and meaning are essential for creating a positive and productive work environment, fostering engagement and commitment among employees, and achieving organizational goals and success.

At the very center of the RKM model are resonance and coherence. In the organization setting, resonance offers multi-faceted potential. From one perspective, resonance is a knowledge exchange where individuals build upon the knowledge of others, greatly enhancing and expanding the growth of knowledge across the organization. From another perspective, resonance is the consistency of values and beliefs with actions, both from the individual and organizational viewpoints. From still another perspective, resonance represents the shared state of affective attunement introduced in Chapter 6, a vibrational entrainment that opens the door to learning, deeper and easier knowledge sharing, and, collectively, the triggering of new ideas.

Coherence is "wholeness and global order, where the whole is greater than the sum of its individual parts" or considered as a "clarity of thought, speech and emotional composure".[335] Resonance and coherence represent a group cohesion within the organization and among the organization's partners and stakeholders, with diversity and creative friction coloring and then strengthening that coherence. Thus, the place of resonance and coherence in the center of the RKM model. (See Chapter 11 for an in-depth discussion of resonance and coherence.)

What does our guest contributor have to say about resonance and coherence? Let's ask.

ChatGPT *on the importance of resonance and coherence ...*

Resonance and coherence are important values that can contribute to the success of an organization. They are both key concepts in organizational behavior and culture.

Resonance refers to the level of connection between the organization and its employees, and the alignment of individual and group goals, values, and behaviors within an organization. When employees are aligned with the company's mission and values, they are more likely to be engaged and motivated, which can improve productivity and overall performance. Coherence, on the other hand, refers to consistency and compatibility of different aspects of the organization, and specifically in the actions and behaviors of individuals within an organization. When there is coherence, members of a group are working together in a coordinated and effective way towards a common goal. This can lead to improved efficiency, productivity, and performance.

In the context of innovation, resonance involves creating an environment where employees feel a deep connection to the organization's purpose, values, and goals. When employees resonate with the organization, they are more likely to be motivated, engaged, and committed to driving innovation. Resonance fosters a sense of ownership and empowers individuals to contribute their unique ideas and perspectives, leading to a more innovative and dynamic culture.

Coherence, on the other hand, ensures that various elements within the organization are consistent and work together harmoniously. This includes aligning the organizational structure, processes, incentives, and resources to support innovation efforts. When there is coherence, employees understand how their individual contributions fit into the bigger picture and how innovation is valued and rewarded within the organization. Coherence helps eliminate barriers to innovation and allows for a seamless flow of ideas, collaboration, and experimentation.

By combining resonance and coherence, organizations can create an environment that nurtures and supports innovation. When employees resonate with the organization's purpose and values and there is coherence in how innovation is fostered, organizations can unlock the full potential of their workforce and drive meaningful and sustainable innovation.

Further, together, resonance and coherence create a strong organizational culture focused on achieving shared goals and delivering value to customers that promotes teamwork, collaboration, and trust. When employees feel connected to their colleagues and their company, they are more likely to be invested in their work and committed to the organization's success.

MOVING FROM THEORY TO PRINCIPLES and GUIDELINES

Principles are considered basic truths or laws; rules or standards; an essential quality or element. Guidelines are a statement or other indication of policy or procedure by which to determine a course of action. While principles are still somewhat theoretical in nature, guidelines are more pragmatic, reaching into the "how" to apply and supporting knowledge in action.

Thinking in terms of fundamental truths that expand on identified assumptions and learning points, the authors add the following "principles" in support of Knowledge Reblooming:

- The strength of freedom is the diversity of thoughts, feelings, and experience.

- Purpose and meaning are discovered in sharing with, and service to, others.

- Learning and development of mind through knowledge creation is a fundamental human right.

- Cultivation of self in terms of knowledge, development, and management are each individual's responsibility.

- Humility opens the door to expanded experiential learning, the expansion of knowledge.

- Freedom of thought and expression and open knowledge flows throughout the organization facilitate the transition from creativity to innovation.

The Section II chapters that follow can be thought of in terms of guidelines, although they are very loose guidelines, for each organization is unique, with bounded areas of expertise, varied resources, specified vision trajectories, and, in a healthy organization, fully participative multi-dimensional minds collectively collaborating to achieve that vision. The intent is to trigger those minds to enable the identification and pulling together – the movement of knowledge – of that which is most important to your organization's success as we together move into an uncertain future, a future where the creative and innovative minds of all of us are needed.

That said, there is no doubt that knowledge, built on good information, is – and will continue to be as long as human organizations continue – the foundation of any organization, providing the capacity for the creative mind to make intelligent decisions and innovate.

As we express our appreciation to our guest contributor ChatGPT, there are several interjections offered related to (1) the connections between information, knowledge, creativity, and innovation, and (2) democratization in the knowledge organization. So, in respect, we share those offerings.

ChatGPT *on information, knowledge, creativity, and innovation in organizations ...*

Information and knowledge are crucial to the success of any organization. They help leaders make better decisions, employees perform their jobs more effectively, and the organization stay competitive in the marketplace.

Access to relevant and accurate information and knowledge helps organizations identify opportunities and potential risks, which enables them to make informed decisions. This knowledge can help leaders anticipate market trends, innovate new products and services, and ultimately improve the company's performance.

Moreover, when employees have access to the right information and knowledge, they can perform their jobs more effectively and efficiently. They can reduce errors and mistakes, which results in higher quality work, and can also be more innovative and creative in their work.

Information and knowledge are incredibly important for creativity and innovation within an organization. When employees have access to a wide range of information, they can generate new ideas and approaches to problems. Knowledge helps them see patterns, make connections, and identify gaps that can be filled with new ideas.

Innovation often involves taking existing ideas and modifying them, combining them in new ways or applying them in different contexts. This requires knowledge, as well as the ability to see beyond what is currently available and imagine new possibilities. When employees have access to a diverse range of information and knowledge, they are better equipped to think creatively and generate innovative solutions.

Furthermore, organizations that prioritize the value of information and knowledge sharing foster an environment that encourages new ideas and experimentation. This leads to greater creativity and innovation in the long run. Additionally, by encouraging employees to share their knowledge and experiences, organizations can maximize the collective intelligence of the workforce, leading to more efficient and effective problem-solving abilities. Overall, information and knowledge play a critical role in promoting creativity and innovation within an organization.

ChatGPT *on the democratization of organizations.*

Democratization can play a crucial role in fostering creativity and innovation in the knowledge-based economy. As knowledge becomes more accessible to a broader range of people, it brings about greater diversity of perspectives and ideas, which can only enrich the creative process. Moreover, democratization can promote a culture of openness, collaboration, and knowledge sharing, leading to a more dynamic and supportive climate for innovation. When people are encouraged to share their knowledge, expertise, and experience, it helps to break down silos and barriers to creative problem-solving.

In a knowledge organization, a democratic culture can be characterized by the following qualities:

1. *Openness*: A democratic knowledge organization encourages open communication, transparency, and sharing of information.

2. *Collaboration*: Members of a democratic knowledge organization work together in a cooperative and collaborative way, sharing their knowledge and expertise to achieve common goals.

3. *Inclusivity*: A democratic knowledge organization values diversity and inclusivity, recognizing that diverse perspectives and experiences can lead to better decision-making and problem-solving.

4. *Accountability*: Members of a democratic knowledge organization are accountable for their actions and decisions, and there are mechanisms in place to ensure that decisions are made fairly and transparently.

5. *Participation*: A democratic knowledge organization encourages participation and engagement from all members, providing opportunities for input and feedback on decisions that affect the organization.

6. *Continuous learning*: Members of a democratic knowledge organization are committed to continuous learning and development, recognizing that knowledge and expertise are constantly evolving.

7. *Empowerment*: A democratic knowledge organization empowers its members to take ownership of their work and contribute to the organization's success. This can include providing opportunities for leadership development and decision-making at all levels of the organization.

Democratization [across an industry] allows for a more equitable distribution of resources, which can help level the playing field for small startups and individuals who may not have the financial means to compete with larger corporations. This can democratize access to resources and technology, enabling more people to have the tools they need to create innovative products and services. Overall, *democratization helps to democratize innovation*, allowing more people to participate and contribute to the creative economy, which can lead to more innovation, diversity of thought, and ultimately, greater economic growth.

Thank you to all who – through interaction with ChatGPT – have participated in the collective thinking shared by our guest contributor, ChatGPT.

CHAPTER 8

PLAN

CREATE A SHARED VISION (147) ... ENSURE LEADERSHIP COMMITMENT (149) ... Appreciative Inquiry (150) ... BUILD THE BUSINESS CASE (151) ... CONSIDER KNOWLEDGE RISK (154) ... DEVELOP THE STRATEGY (156) ... Design Thinking (158) ... Story Thinking (159) ... Human-Centered Design (161) ... Strategy Approaches (162) ... Example: The DON Strategy for Knowledge Sharing (165) ... WRITE THE PLAN (166) ... ENGAGE INTER-ORGANIZATIONAL PARTNERING (169) ... SELECT THE TEAM (172) ... EXAMINE ORGANIZATIONAL STRUCTURE (175) ... Knowledge Roles (179) ... NURTURE AN INNOVATION CULTURE (181) ... Knowledge Ignorance & Anti-Intellectualism (187) ... THINK SYSTEMS (190)

The planning phase of any organizational strategy or initiative offers the opportunity to focus on a course of action to move forward *prior* to taking any action. By the planning stage, a number of leaders at all levels of the organization have recognized the value of, and need for, implementation of a knowledge-focused initiative or strategy. Along with readiness, the following actions are important to consider during the planning phase: create a shared vision, ensure leadership commitment, build the business case, consider knowledge risk, develop the strategy, write the plan, engage inter-organizational partnering, select the team, examine organizational structure, nurture an innovation culture, and think systems. Each of these areas is introduced below. Readiness, which is part of the planning process, is discussed in Chapter 9.

CREATE A SHARED VISION

In an unknowable future, the vision must be more of a direction than an end state. In their research on consciousness, Edelman and Tononi identify the mechanism that provides unity to consciousness, thereby creating a continuous history of thought and a consistency of identity and action.[336] This ability to maintain different parts of the brain in harmony and to pull them together in an organization – creating coherence – is facilitated by constant and widespread communication. The journey toward intelligent activity starts with a shared direction of what the organization will accomplish, which emerges from the visioning process.

The importance of a shared vision where employees participate in the development of a corporate vision cannot be over-emphasized. This shared visioning process facilitates organization-wide ownership and enables employees to make decisions and take actions consistent with the directions set by senior leadership.

An example of the shared visioning process is Arthur Shelley's *Conversations that Matter*.[337] The Process begins with an image. Figure 8-1 is one of many images designed to stimulate Conversations That Matter around the concept of visioning the future. It is designed not to define the path, but to engage people to explore their perspectives of what the *range of paths* may be, and to share pespectives on their current point in this journey. This process occurs with the tenents of Appreciative Inquiry in mind, which is discussed below. See the tool "Conversations that Matter" in Section IV.

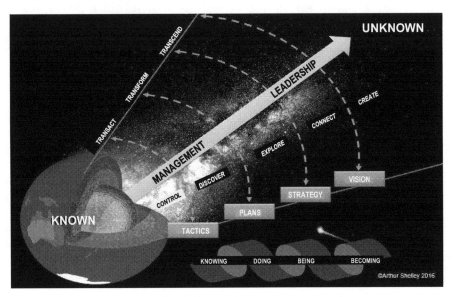

Figure 8-1. Exploring the unknown to co-create more known.

It is not uncommon for people in the same organization (and even on the same team) to perceive their current positon to be very different parts of this image. Experiences using this image (and others with a different focus) have demonstrated the power of exploring individually, and then in pairs or small groups, before engaging in whole-group wider discussion, which maximises the range of perspectives available through divergent thinking before convergent dialogue begins. Cycling between divergent conversation (focusing on open exploring and option generating) and convergent interactions (focusing on merging, prioritizing and reducing ideas and concepts) enables us to optimise the outcomes. This iterative approach has been successfully adopted in several design and problem-solving approaches such as Design Thinking, which is discussed below in "Developing the Strategy".

The wider the scope of participants in the conversations, the greater the outcomes can be. For example, successes with stimulating open conversations includes the public gamification of the design of biochemicals. Researchers have found that novice voices can add new perspectives. Some novel RNA (Ribo

Nucleaic Acid) molecues have been designed and folding patterns solved by providing a gamified environment asking online gamers to solve the "puzzle" (faster than supercomputers were able to achieve).

Another example is mapping of astronomical bodies by enabling thousands of amateur astronnomers to add data to the collective library. The learning happens much faster, and the extensive data generated enables astronomers to shift their focus from data gathering to data analysis, from which emeges understanding and discovery.

ENSURE LEADERSHIP COMMITMENT

Leadership must be actively involved for any knowledge strategy to be successful. When a respected and trusted leader demonstrates commitment to a vision through words and consistent and continuous personal actions, members of the leader's relationship network – stakeholders, peers and employees – quickly follow suit. (See Chapter 14 on Relationship Network Management.)

As leaders take an Appreciative Inquiry approach in communicating, collaborating and rewarding successes, those successes spread across the organization. Appreciative Inquiry, an approach that discovers and promotes the best in people, is a positive approach to purposeful change, accelerating receptivity to new ideas, behavior change, the adoption of best practices. It is based on the simple premise that organizations (teams, communities) grow in the direction of what they are repeatedly asked questions about and therefore focus their attention on.[338]

Appreciative Inquiry is a transformational tool which offers leaders a generative capacity in the sociorational realm of human affairs. Emerging as a part of action research at Case Western Reserve University, it is a way of living with and being with, directly participating in, the social organizations of which we are a part, engaging the uniqueness of the appreciative mode. As action researchers Cooperrider and Srivastva profess, the Appreciative Inquiry approach "engenders a reverence for life" that draws the leader to "inquire beyond superficial appearances to deeper levels of the life-generating essentials and potentials of social existence."[339]

When handling a change effort or organizational intervention, the traditional approach is to identify problems and hunt for solutions, which is critical comprehension based on objectivity, dispassionate analysis, and skepticism.[340] The Appreciative Inquiry approach is to locate and understand that which is working, learn from it, and amplify it. In complexity theory, amplification is using what is successful over and over again in similar situations as long as they yield the desired results. This is not blind trial-and-error experimentation since decision-maker learning occurs continuously and judgment, experience, and deep knowledge can create understanding and knowing that result in more effective actions. Further, appreciation of immediate experience is an act of attention, valuing, and affirmation.

While leadership commitment is critical and ensures support for knowledge management behaviors from the top of the organization, it is also important to locate and engage the enthusiastic champions and future leaders that are emerging at all levels throughout the organization. These are forward-thinking individuals who are already pushing the edge of change, most likely already applying knowledge approaches because these approaches just make good business sense. While they may not use the words "knowledge management" they are nonetheless knowledge champions with success stories and lessons learned waiting to be identified and shared.

Appreciative Inquiry

The Appreciative Inquiry approach forwards that in any change effort people have more confidence and comfort in the journey to the future (the unknown) when they carry forward part of the past (the known). Further, if parts of the past are carried forward, they should be what is best about the past. It is critical to identify those practices and successes that support the direction of the change effort, and share and sustain those successes. The principles of Appreciative Inquiry as translated by Hammond below.[341]

The Principles of Appreciative Inquiry

- In every society, organization or group, something works.
- What we focus on becomes our reality.
- Reality is created in the moment and there are multiple realities.
- The act of asking questions of an organization or group influences the group in some way.
- People have more confidence and comfort to journey to the future (the unknown) when they carry forward parts of the past (the known).
- If we carry parts of the past forward, they should be what is best about the past.
- It is important to value differences.
- The language we use creates our reality.

When we were implementing knowledge management in the U.S. Department of the Navy, we formed a community of practice that reached across functional areas and commands, discovering those who had passion around this emerging field. Once Department goals were identified and vetted, specific high-level strategies were developed through a community process in support of each goal. The next step was at the various command functional levels, where teams were used to identify specific initiatives tied directly to the specific mission of the command in support of the high-level goal.

Amazingly, once needed initiatives were identified in team planning sessions, inevitably functional champions would emerge who were already moving in this direction! These champions were blazing the trail for others to follow, providing a sense of direction and being on the right path.

Recognizing that people do not change easily or quickly, implementation requires continued leadership interest, oversight, presence, and sometimes active involvement, coupled with the repeated message that knowledge is critical to the organization's mission. Beyond being aware of desired changes, employees have to understand them, believe they are necessary for the health of the organization, feel good about them, take ownership of them, feel empowered to do them, and recognize the value of doing them. (See Chapter 10 for an in-depth discussion of the individual change model.)

Leaders and managers help change happen when they openly explain and communicate their understanding and expectations through the consistency of their actions with the desired change, face-to-face conversations, group meetings, open forums, virtual forums, and perhaps a town hall discussion. Beginning in the planning phase, leadership must be on board with the knowledge strategy selected, becoming an active voice and remaining active throughout the preparing and implementing phases, and continuing to support the strategy, recognizing and rewarding successes, in the sustaining phase.

BUILD THE BUSINESS CASE

From a corporate view it is essential to have a strong business case for any anticipated change strategy. The business case lays out the current organizational effectiveness level, identifies needed changes and, most importantly, describes the anticipated changes and expected results in terms that make sense from a business perspective. However, the business perspective is not the only perspective to be considered. It is equally important to have the anticipated changes make sense to the employees and other organizational stakeholders such as customers, and the environment and local community as they apply.

Figure 8-2. In preparing the business case, all perspectives need to be considered.

While most likely a need or opportunity is driving development of a business case, the actual process of building a business case works best backwards, first carefully considering the result of anticipated changes, that is, what you want the organization to look like and the anticipated performance and market advantage of the organization assuming those changes are complete. This certainly makes sense, and hopefully was developed in "Create a Shared Vision" above. Then, understanding where the organization currently stands, identify the strategic and tactical actions necessary to achieve those changes. See Figure 8-3.

Thinking in terms of current state-change-future state offers a first cut at things to consider when building a business case. As we build the business case, we are reminded to consider change from the business perspective, the stakeholder and customer perspective (including a focus on employees) and an environmental and local community perspective. The left box focused on the current level of organizational effectiveness, the current state of the organization. Here we look at the reasons for suggested or needed change, considering those reasons from the viewpoint of every level of the organization and the viewpoints of vendors, partners and customers. We also take the time to look at the current environment in terms of the market, customers, and risk.

The middle circle is the identified needed change as a response to a threat or opportunity, or to improve performance or expand a market. Here we examine the basic beliefs and assumptions underlying the recommended change. Are they based on antiquated assumptions or belief systems? We identify quantitative parameters, with backup information relative to the reasonableness of the change, including investment requirements and return on investment. We consider the feasibility and fundamental approach for change management, asking: Are the changes consistent with the current structure and culture of the organization or will these have to be significantly revamped to achieve the desired end state? And it is here that we identify the strategic and tactical actions necessary to make this change and explore the risks associated with these actions as well as the risk associated with taking no action.

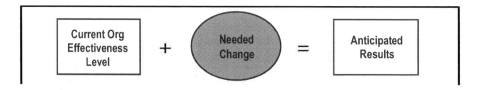

• Identify and thoroughly examine the reasons for suggested or needed change. (Consider every level of the organization and explore from viewpoints of vendors, partners and customers.) • Look at the current environment from the viewpoints of the market, customer and risk (in terms of government regulations, technology breakthroughs, etc.)	• Examine the basic beliefs and assumptions underlying the recommended changes. (Are they based on antiquated assumptions or belief systems?) • Identify quantitative parameters with backup info relative to reasonableness (investment requirements, return on investment). • Consider the feasibility of and fundamental approach for change management. (Are the changes consistent with the current structure and culture of the organization or will these have to be significantly revamped to achieve the desired end state?) • Identify the strategic and tactical actions necessary. (What are the risks associated with these actions? What is the risk of no action?)	• Identify the future market within which the organization is going to move from the viewpoints of the market, customer and risk (in terms of government regulations, technology breakthroughs, etc.) • Identify the anticipated performance and market advantage (long-term organizational health; short-term payoffs). • Consider: What are the financial, managerial, sociological, technological and political consequences of the recommended changes as seen by both outsiders and insiders? • Consider the impact on employees, infrastructure and culture. Ask and answer the silent questions from employees: WIFM (what's in it for me?) How will it affect my local work and my local organization? How will it affect the organization as a whole? What role can AI play in this change?

Figure 8-3. A first cut at things to consider when building a business case.

Finally, we look at the anticipated results, identifying the future market within which the organization is going to move from the viewpoints of the market, customer and risk. Here we identify the anticipated performance and market advantage in terms of both long-term organizational health and short-term payoffs. From a systems viewpoint, we look at the financial, managerial, sociological, technological and political consequences of the recommended changes as seen by both outsiders and insiders. And a critical element related to anticipated results is the impact on employees, infrastructure and culture. Ask and answer the silent questions from employees: WIFM (What's in it for me?),

How will it affect my local work and my local and future organization? How will it affect the organization as a whole? And what role can Artificial Intelligence play in this change?

The strength and thoroughness of the business case will depend heavily on the size and history of the organization, the nature of its leadership, and the expectations of its customers and other stakeholders. These balances may be large-scale research balances all the way down to individual knowledge worker competencies, attitudes, and decisions on priorities or work or how to approach problems. As always, since everyone is potentially subjected to internal biases, erroneous assumptions, and misplaced beliefs, it is wise to get a second, or perhaps group, opinion to reevaluate how individuals or teams perceive the situation, their most effective aspects of work, or their balance points.

From another perspective, all changes in organizations create/demand a change in a number of balance points. Balance points are the points of equilibrium for dynamic tensions arising in an organization, or in implementation of change! A balance is necessary to ensure that one facet of implementation doesn't dominate another facet. For example, in a knowledge program, the processes and technology must work in concert; technology alone is not sufficient. In a KM program, dynamic tensions might include: How much risk are we willing to take to achieve leverage and, conversely, how much leveraging are we willing to do despite the risk? How much data and information should be left at the local level, and how much should be available globally? How much data and information and what data and information should be made explicit? How much data and information and what data and information should be captured in a formal system? In this world of access and excess, the answer is not automatically "more".[342] While often knowledge workers and leaders do not recognize that they are simply changing balance points, it is exactly these changes that can be so threatening to individuals if they do not recognize them as balance points and important aspects of the work.

CONSIDER KNOWLEDGE RISK

When first delving into decision-making, an early lesson is that making no decision, doing nothing, IS a decision. It is the same when considering a knowledge strategy. Whether you are comfortable with it or not, no organization can thrive – and not many organizations can survive – without "managing" their knowledge environment internally and externally. Thus, the risk associated with knowledge is primarily one of having no knowledge strategy, having an ineffective knowledge strategy, or the mismanagement of information, which provides the foundation for knowledge.

While risk itself is an important element to consider in any new strategy, which denotes an investment in organizational resources, the risk-value relationship is the determinant, with evaluation based on "the investigation of risk factors of a risk and the likelihood of a risk and its impact".[343] Five facets associated with knowledge risk are knowledge shortage, knowledge obsolescence, knowledge leakage, knowledge loss, and knowledge accessibility.

Knowledge shortage can be identified through the knowledge audit process, which is described in Chapter 10 and included as a tool in Section IV. Knowledge shortage can be mitigated through employee training, developing a learning culture, and talent management. Knowledge shortage and knowledge loss are often associated with the turnover or retirement of key personnel. Strategies to mitigate these issues include developing on-going partnering relationships with expert resources, hiring multiple personnel with expertise in critical areas, supporting the potential of young employees through shadowing of and mentoring by key decision-makers, ensuring an effectively functioning community of practice in knowledge domains critical to the organization, and copying the military approach by having retirees stay available through a "reserve" (when needed) contract for six months to one year after retirement.

Knowledge obsolescence is tied directly to validity and timeliness of information in concert with availability and accessibility of that information. Updating and connecting of information is every employee's responsibility. This can also be tied to knowledge accessibility. Early in the implementation of knowledge management in the Department of the Navy, a situation emerged where a specific part on frigates kept failing. While space on a ship at sea is at a premium, it was necessary for this part to be immediately available, so when the fleet set out for a sixpack (six-month deployment) extra parts had to be taken along. However, if it had been recognized the whole engine was scheduled for replacement at a port stop three weeks out, carrying those extra parts would not have been required. In other words, the two databases (one for ordering parts and a second for scheduled repairs) were not synced.

Knowledge leakage can be considered in terms of people and information systems, two very different issues. Leakage due to people might involve customers and other stakeholders because of their close knowledge of and relationship to the organization, people in the supply chain, or purposeful leakage through disgruntled employees. Leakage through information systems can be addressed through information technology security and intellectual property management.

See the related discussion of knowledge voids in "Connect the Dots" in Chapter 10 and the discussion of knowledge hiding in "Knowledge Sharing" in Chapter 12.

DEVELOP THE STRATEGY

A strategy is an approach or plan for *how* an organization or team will achieve a knowledge program in support of its mission, and generally includes the use of a variety of tools and multiple initiatives, or the application of an initiative across the larger enterprise. For example, since a strategy such as knowledge retention is a systems issue, it would involve a variety of tools and initiatives that involved explicit capture, flow mechanisms, mentoring, boundary management, and subconscious access (see Appendix C for a sample knowledge strategy. Also, Chapter 17 focuses on a strategy for improving absorptive capacity). Knowledge strategies, that is, how to bring a knowledge focus into an organization or to create a knowledge-centric organization from the start, have been addressed by a number of authors. In particular, intellectual capital (IC) was early-on recognized as a vital force in organizational effectiveness. There has been significant effort to understand what intellectual capital is and how it can be strategically managed to harness and leverage an organization's knowledge and learning capacity to improve long-term competitive advantage.

In an introductory treatment of Knowledge Management in the first issue of *The Journal of Knowledge Management* in September 1997, Karl Wiig observed that organizations tended to pursue strategies that best matched their culture, priorities, and capabilities, which makes sense no matter what strategy you are applying! He called out five basic knowledge-centered strategies:[344]

1. Knowledge strategy as business strategy (creation, capture, organization, renewal, sharing and use)

2. Intellectual asset management (patents, technologies, organizational practices, customer relations)

3. Personal knowledge asset responsibility (personal responsibility for innovation, renewal, effective use, competitiveness)

4. Knowledge creation (learning, research and development, motivation to innovate, lessons learned)

5. Knowledge transfer (systematic transfer approaches including knowledge sharing and adopting good practices)

Wiig further noted that the highly successful enterprises "have value disciplines that focus on either operational excellence, product leadership or customer intimacy."[345] Operational excellence focused on customer satisfaction in cost and convenience through streamlining production steps and processes and minimizing overhead costs. Product leadership refers to producing state-of-the-art products and services, which is accomplished through creativity and innovation. Customer intimacy points to the tailoring of products to fit customer needs, including the personalization for customer success.

While these are still in play, since this early thought a wide variety of strategies have been – and continue to be – suggested by various authors, with each strategy centering on a single or small group of factors. For example, Henry Chesbrough and David Teece considered innovation as the primary focus while Daniel Kim dealt with individual and organizational learning, and Arthur Armstrong and John Hagel addressed on-line communities while others addressed culture as the payoff.[346] Focused on absorptive capacity, see the strategy discussion in Chapter 19. Some authors offer specific processes for managing intellectual capital (IC), treating intellectual capital as a stock to be acquired, audited, stored, and applied.[347] Conversely, many knowledge professionals consider this a very narrow and misplaced approach, particularly in treating IC as an asset presumably owned by the corporation. This is not surprising since historically – and continuing into the present – there has been a breach between the knowledge movement technologists, people who see knowledge as information to be stored and moved around by technology, and those who believe that KM is about humans and their ability to create, learn and apply knowledge, with IT playing a supportive role.[348] This friction has been palpable since the term knowledge management began to gain attention in the business world. It further flared as technology advancements drove the focus toward social networking, in essence, a focus on social knowledge, and then, this time in response to the shifting and uncertain environment, cycled up to a refocus on innovation.

Arthur Murray has a simple four-step KM framework that he has helped organizations apply at the strategic level or when they are crafting strategic initiatives focused on achieving a specific goal or objective. As Murray forwards, these four steps are intended to "keep you on track in responding to the challenges and opportunities you'll face now, and in the years ahead."[349]

The first step is to *make sure your strategic goals and objectives, strategy and resources, are in alignment.* It is important to clearly define success and be able to measure it, as well as to ensure that strategic goals and objectives are flowing down to all levels of the organization. (See the "Strategic Alignment" tool in Section IV contributed by Murray.)

The second step is to *identify major gaps and risks inhibiting or preventing you from achieving your performance goals, along with opportunities.* Along with identifying and managing risk, most obstacles and barriers come from knowledge gaps, that is, when knowledge has not been properly captured, shared, or applied.

The third step is to *look deep beneath the surface for the root causes underlying the gaps, risks, and opportunities.* This requires a systems thinking approach (see Chapter 19 on Systems and Complexity Thinking), that is, going beyond just framing a problem, risk, or opportunity to identifying root causes and interdependencies.

The fourth step is to *integrate the various pieces and enable knowledge to flow freely throughout your enterprise*. This requires a transformational change effort addressing people, processes, and technologies. (See "Become a Change Agent" in Chapter 10.)

Design Thinking

Design Thinking and, more recently, Story Thinking have emerged as two powerful strategic change approaches that strongly support innovation. Design Thinking is focused on problem, issue, or opportunity boundaries to ensure that the best questions are being asked, applying a creative mentality to everyday situations.[350]

A critical aspect of Design Thinking is looking at a situation from the perspective of those who are directly involved, and from that perspective defining viable solutions, debating potential answers, releasing a prototype, and then reviewing and modifying the design to ensure that it will fulfill the needs of the organization. Employee involvement across all functional areas is foundational, providing the opportunity for a greater range of potential scenarios and solutions to emerge.[351] A five-step process for approaching specific problems and opportunities is: recognizing the problem/opportunity, interpreting the problem/opportunity, generating ideas for solutions/ approaches, prototyping answers, and finalizing the solution/approach. In other words, these steps are: Empathize, Define, Ideate, Prototype, and Test. The purpose of each step is included in Figure 8-4 below. The dotted lines indicate early-stage testing and a feedback loop to identify correlated features for product and service design.

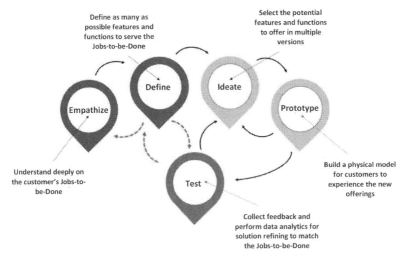

Figure 8-4. A non-linear, five-stage process of design thinking.
Source: Dr. Chulatep Senivongse.[352] (Used with permission)

As a method for new business creation supporting innovation,[353] testing is integrated into each step of the Design Thinking process. For example, during ideation, intuition can be used to explore how a product will be utilized by clients.[354] What problem does it solve? What are other competitive products missing?

Story Thinking

William Shakespeare portrayed life as a play, and Carl Jung informed us that we are in a story whether we are aware of it or not. And indeed, we are living in *a story of our creation.*

Synthesis, a critical knowledge competency (see "Training and Learning" at the end of Chapter 9) is at play in our everyday life as we tie our life together into a coherent story, a concept of self. Throughout the process of living, we are walking through a temporal sequence of how things are done, with one pattern evoking the next, with the recall of our memories following a pathway of association. Thus, we can say that *human memories are story-based.* Effective memories also have memory traces, which are labels that attach to previously stored memories. As we move through a variety of experiences, the individual singles out and accentuates what is significant and connects these events to historic events to *create a narrative unity,* what can be described as a fictionalized history. As Long forwards, "The person makes choices about the importance of persons and events, decides on their meanings … [which are] neither a lie nor 'the truth', but instead a work of imagination, evaluation and memory."[355]

Story Thinking, developed by John Lewis,[356] moves beyond the value of storying as a communications and knowledge sharing approach to using the *structure of story* as an operational strategy. Emerging from Aristotle's pattern of story, Story Thinking has a six-phase cycle: Automation, Disruption, Investigation, Ideation, Expectation, and Affirmation (ADIIEA).

Expanding on the natural story cycle, the process starts with a normal routine (Automation), encounters something out of the ordinary (Disruption), looks deeper into the situation (Investigation), comes up with some ideas (Ideation), and acts on a plan (Expectation), with results eventually recognized (Affirmation), which over time settle into a new routine (automation) … and the cycle begins again. [357]

1. **Automation**: "We had successful operations at work."

2. **Disruption**: "But we knew more competition was coming."

3. **Investigation**: "We discovered a new idea that we could incorporate."

4. **Ideation**: "And created a new vision."

5. **Expectation**: "Development took some time."

6. **Affirmation**: "But it all came together!"

7. **Automation**: "Now operations are even better."

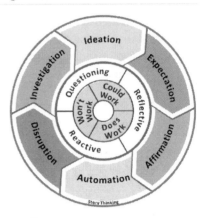

When applying Story Thinking in an organization – whether focused on a change effort, learning, or leadership – there are six key principles, [358] which are included below.

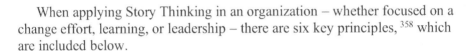

Key Principles of Story Thinking

- The mental model of work is a story, not a process. *Design* the work through agile navigation around the story thinking cycle.

- Seek the positive side of each story, and within each phase of the story thinking cycle.

- Provide transparency by keeping track of the options and choices made throughout the story thinking cycle.

- Move beyond causal sensemaking (IF/THEN) to look for symbiotic sensemaking (AND), that is, an existential relationship, with the very existence of a thing requiring the existence of something else (problem/opportunity).

- Continue lifelong learning even when it means shifting from a "knower" (stuck in the half-pipe of the story thinking cycle) to a "novice" in a new field of study.

- Develop your desire and ability to understand while simultaneously developing your desire and ability to influence others, seeking a balance and embracing *collaboration* instead of *competition* as influence.

If this has caught your interest – and hopefully it has – we strongly suggest that you explore Lewis' book *Story Thinking: Transforming Organizations for the Fourth Industrial Revolution*. Lewis takes Story Thinking into the realms of change, learning, and leadership, providing real application examples and challenging us to break old paradigms and engage new ways of thinking and acting. You will discover the usefulness of Lewis' Learning Objective Framework and Key Performance Indicators to help ensure the success of your organizational journey. "Option Outline", a Story Thinking tool, is included in Section IV.

Human-Centred Design

Human-centred design (which is written into the ISO standards) means bringing the human into decision-making, in every step of the problem-solving process, and in the design and sustainability of virtual platforms. The Knowledge Capacity of Reversal gives us a hint of how to do this. (An in-depth discussion of Knowledge Capacities is in Chapter 16.) For example, designing customer websites from the outside-in, perhaps using the technique of journey mapping – following the customer from entry points to the information they are seeking – which helps develop an understanding of what is important to the customer, how difficult it is for them to find what is important, and how this journey can be made easier.

Mary Ann Monroe, who served with the General Services Administration and National Institutes of Health before working with Maximus, says the first step is to understand the problems customers are struggling with, and then ensure that your online site makes it easy to sign in, and find, complete, and submit forms as well as obtain immediate help as needed.[359] Monitoring website activity allows the identification of where delays or confusion occurs, which can then be immediately addressed.

Human-centred design requires a team approach. While AI is making this more efficient, dependent on the level of knowledge needed (surface, shallow or deep) no single individual or AI system is necessarily going to provide the best answers. This makes sense – customers are diverse, with different perceptions, needs, ways of communicating, and levels of understanding. The idea is to improve both *effectiveness and efficiency* of organizational processes, for external customers, employees, and other stakeholders, improving human well-being, satisfaction, accessibility and sustainability. An example of human-centred design is the Knowledge Mobilization new product research process, which engages participatory action research, entangling the developers of knowledge (sources) together with the beneficiaries of knowledge (users) in the process of knowledge discovery. See Figure 8-5.

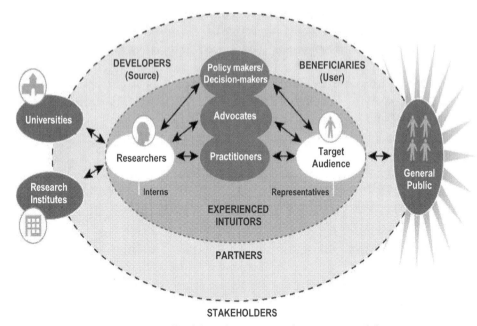

Figure 8-5. Engaging all of the players into the process of discovery.

Strategy Approaches

All knowledge strategies and projects in an organization need to be focused on the unique mission-critical knowledge assets of the organization to expand, sustain, and share them. Criteria to assess the importance and benefit of strategies and initiatives can emerge from answering questions related to value, continuity, tools and risk. (Examples of questions are provided in the sample strategy in Appendix C. Also, see Chapter 17 for strategic approaches for adopting absorptive capacity.) Specific approaches to implementing initiatives would include starting with a pilot project, starting with quick wins and low-hanging fruit (short bursts), or full-scale implementation. There are advantages and disadvantages to each.

An advantage of a **pilot project** is its potential contribution to a learning curve; a disadvantage is that often what is learned in a specific part of the organization is not easily transferable to another part of the organization (knowledge is situation dependent and context sensitive), such that the learning process must be repeated when larger implementation occurs. However, pilot projects *can* have considerable success. For example, after identifying knowledge as a strategic asset, the U.S. Defense Information Agency (DIA) developed a knowledge lab to help them evolve into a learning organization, which fielded and assessed pilots such as Leadership Social Network Analysis, Critical Discourse, Storytelling, Knowledge in Action, and Knowledge Transaction Costs.

Similarly, The U.S. Forest Service often opted for the pilot approach when exploring new protocols. For example, the CROP (Coordinated Resource Offering Protocol) model – initially developed in 2003 by Oregon-based Mater Engineering – was first applied in 2006. A series of pilot projects was used as a means of addressing the growing fuel load problem within major forest systems. The model also addresses the realized potential for fostering catastrophic wildfires within these systems across the U.S. Over the next several years, 20 plus CROP evaluations were completed on over 50 million acres of public forestlands, all in geographic regions where forest restoration and fuel load reduction efforts were a high priority. Critical success factors included consistency of use of protocols, the ease of availability of CROP results, and the use of resource offering maps. The benefit of this approach was coordination of biomass removal between public agencies and heightened public trust and support for biomass removal from public lands.

The U.S. Army includes piloting as part of their five-step KM process to create shared understanding: assess, design, develop, pilot, and implement. In the pilot phase, the four-step process is plan, prepare, execute, and evaluate. For a large organization, this is an intelligent approach with a focus on knowledge flows, that is, the ease of movement of knowledge in organizations. This focus is reflected in their principles of operations: (1) Drive the operations process; (2) Build and maintain situational understanding; (3) Apply critical and creative thinking; and (4) Encourage collaboration and dialogue.

An advantage of the **short bursts approach** is the rapid visibility of benefits to the organization, making it easier to implement in a larger fashion. A disadvantage is that this sets the expectation for quick wins without addressing the larger underlying problems, which undoubtedly will require more time and attention to mitigate. An advantage of **full-scale implementation** is the demonstrated commitment to this course of action, which helps ensure success; a disadvantage would be if this strategy is premature and the organization is not yet prepared to move down this road.

As an example of full-scale implementation, USAID, known for its rich international development experience, has people that work worldwide generating knowledge and requiring timely information wherever they are. This knowledge can be found in reports in a mission in Zagreb, in databases in Cairo, in the expertise and skills of a Honduran employee, or in the head of an employee in Washington, D.C. Since this knowledge moves into the realms of deep knowledge and is not easily translated into a technological system, there is the potential for lost knowledge when people move from one post to another within the organization, the organization is restructured, or someone retires.

Thus, KM in USAID is focused on connecting the development community with what and who they need to know to work smarter in accomplishing the mission and strategic objectives. USAID was ready for full implementation. They set up a KM Reference Group to obtain Agency-wide input on USAID's knowledge program, and a strategic framework was developed to organize activities by their impact on knowledge generation, capture, sharing, and application.

Knowledge Generation: Generate development knowledge that optimizes the use of innovation approaches. Results: educational understanding improved, consistent development methodology applied, appropriate Information and Communication Technologies (ICT) utilized.

Knowledge Capture: Capture and make accessible the full spectrum of USAID's development knowledge. Results: common operation construction developed, knowledge stovepipes broken.

Knowledge Sharing: Share and disseminate USAID's development knowledge to expand reach and effectiveness. Results: transfer of expertise and experience improved, tacit knowledge mobilized.

Knowledge Application: Apply development knowledge for optimal impact of programs and management practices. Results: agile and adaptive development leadership enabled, evidence-based decision-making supported, knowledge gaps identified and addressed.

Moving into 2023, AidScape – which serves as USAID's central source for U.S. foreign assistance data, international socioeconomic data, and data-driven analysis supporting USAID goals – encompasses ten separate data portals housing hundreds and hundreds of thousands of support materials with pertinent data made easily retrievable around the world. And it connects people.

The strategic approach for DON was holistic, full-scale implementation at three focus levels: the individual, the organization, and the enterprise. The idea was to create balancing loops to mitigate, make accessible, and be able to value the exponentially increasing amount of data and information coming into the system. Examples of initiatives at each of these levels are seen in Figure 8-6.

We will briefly share the DON strategy for knowledge sharing. Several strategies offered in Appendix C are intended as an idea generator to introduce and explore some possibilities that may be relevant to your organization. See also the strategy approach for expanding absorptive capacity in Chapter 17.

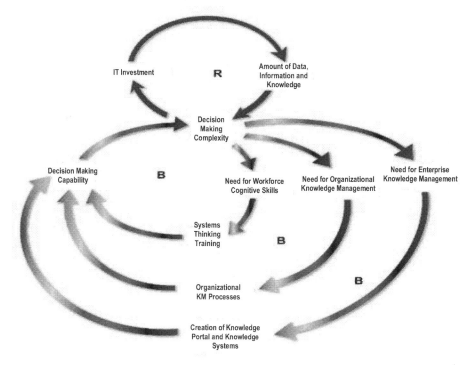

Figure 8-6. The holistic systems implementation approach used by the DON.

Example: The DON Strategy for Knowledge Sharing

In support of improved decision-making and innovation, the implementation strategy for knowledge management in the Department of the Navy (DON), based on the levels of consciousness, served as a model for the growth of knowledge and sharing across the Department (see Figure 8-7). For example, when exploring a new idea – whether within an individual or in the organization as a whole – closed structured concepts are first created. As these concepts germinate, some focused but limited sharing of these concepts occurs. Over time, particularly if there is positive feedback during the limited sharing, there is increased sharing from which a deeper awareness and connectedness occurs, that is, building on itself, a common understanding of the concept is shared across a larger number of people, who in turn share it with others. This can occur in work structure, cross-functional teams, or communities. From this framework, individuals and organizations participating in this sharing create new concepts, and from those concepts, new innovations, purposefully sharing them with partners and colleagues, in events and community dialogues, across and beyond the framework, leading to application of these ideas to everyday work. As connectedness increases, there is also heightened awareness, or consciousness, of the *potential value of these concepts to a larger audience*, engendering the rise of social responsibility, and leading motivated individuals and organizations to advance these concepts even further through cross-organizational presentations, research, and published journal articles and books.

The change strategy suggested here is holistic, and not bounded by the organization. Indeed, it encourages interactions across large relationship networks, and sharing and learning across organizational boundaries.

The DON implementation strategy was viewed in terms of orchestrating and implementing 12 specific elements: creating a shared vision; building the business case; demonstrating leadership commitment; facilitating a common understanding; setting limits; sharing new ideas, words and behaviors; identifying the strategic approach; developing the infrastructure; measuring and incentivizing; providing tools; promoting learning; and visioning an even greater future.[360]

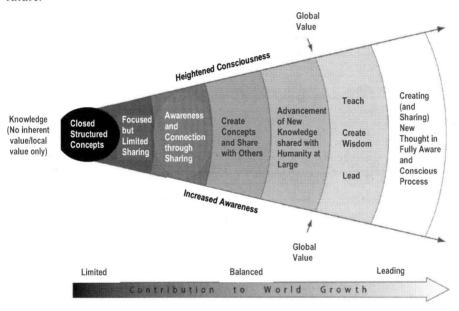

Figure 8-7. The growth and sharing of knowledge.

WRITE THE PLAN

The journey toward intelligent activity started with the visioning process which surfaces a shared direction toward what the organization will accomplish. The strategic plan focuses on *how it will be accomplished*, that is, *how the work gets done*. Learning from history, we realize that it is advantageous for an organization to have a strategic plan. What may be different about the knowledge movement approach is that the plan is a product of the whole organization, with inputs and reviews at every level of, and from every functional area in, the organization. In the development process, goals are worked and reworked to assure the right set of goals addressed at a low enough level to make them real and viable, and a high enough level to provide flexibility and tailoring at the point of action where implementation decisions are made. The plan has the potential to bring the organization's collective vision of its future into clear focus, and communicates leadership's commitment to this vision.

A good first step for the planning process is a feasibility review. Ensure that the following statements are true:

1. The strategic goal, mission and purpose of the organization are clear and understood by people within the organization.

2. The planned project is aligned or consistent with core organizational planning processes such as strategic business planning, operational planning, and information technology planning.

3. The planned project is consistent with the organization's strategic focus.

4. Resources (time, people, funding) are available to take the project to completion.

5. The project is important to the organization and, if at all possible, will be completed.

6. The project is economically feasible.

7. Enough data and information are available to make a sound decision.

The number of elements required for planning a project is highly dependent on the complexity of the initiative or strategy. For example, defining scope, identifying tools, developing schedules, budgets, manpower needs, risk analysis, etc. – all the elements that go into planning any successful project – will depend heavily upon the content and context of the initiative or strategy, the size of the initiative, the timetable for implementation, as well as the specific organization.

A written plan should be developed which outlines the various stages and activities of the project. Planners usually start with a vision of the desired project outcomes and determine, at a high level, the characteristics and macro elements of the project required to achieve these outcomes. For example, if the desired initiative is knowledge retention, then macro elements of the project might involve (1) a fast-track approach for those who are leaving in 30 days; (2) a series of tools and activities for those who are retiring in six months; and (3) a strategic approach to ensure that knowledge is continuously flowing up, down, and across the organization, and that there are mandated pre-retirement actions, and a plan in place to ensure accessibility to necessary knowledge and wisdom post-retirement. For uniformed military personnel, the ability to recall retired personnel for a number of years following retirement is written into the contract. In the DON, for key decision-makers with deep knowledge, we began to include a six-month post-retirement obligation to engage in a community of practice in their domain of expertise along with mentoring and shadowing opportunities offered to younger employees on a leadership trajectory. While this community commitment only entailed a few hours a month, it provided accessibility to critical deep knowledge when an issue emerged.

Through the process of decomposition, major elements in the plan are broken down into smaller pieces which lend themselves to scheduling, costing and specific activities. The plan identifies all the expected things that must be accomplished during the life of the project. For instance, in the above example of knowledge retention, the plan (1) would undoubtedly include an exit interview, (2) might include a knowledge audit and development of a desk guide for every position, and (3) might include development of communities of practice, use of shared space, nurturing of storytelling, and regular mentoring opportunities. Both large and small changes help make a difference.

As part of the planning process, it is a good idea to interview leaders who will be engaged in the process at some level to discover critical success factors and identify perceivable barriers to implementation. In a Mountain Quest Institute research study that engaged 207 separate drinking water utilities, including both government and private organizations, it was discovered that over 50 percent of the utilities already had active knowledge management programs. Strategies already underway largely related to knowledge sharing, team decision-making, and knowledge retention. The largest focus in the "planning stage" was knowledge retention – today a critical issue considering the loss of personnel during the pandemic, the large shift to virtual work, and the difficulty of finding specific deep expertise. Following closely behind was knowledge-based development. (KBD is the focus of Chapter 15 in Section III.) Smaller initiatives focused at various levels included developing and updating manuals, professional and leadership development, work performance improvement, succession and talent resource planning, workforce planning, quality-based documentation, communications and training plans, developing document repositories, process and operational improvements, and the use of social network analysis.

With that context in mind, critical success factors relative to implementation of knowledge strategies and initiatives in drinking water utilities were identified as: leadership by example, good communications, employee buy-in, bringing employees into the project, resources, leadership support, a team-based approach, allowing time for change to occur, technology support, developing trust, valuing employees, and providing training and development. Barriers to successful implementation were identified as financial resources, time, resistance to change, lack of manpower, politics, leadership and management, public perception, getting buy-in for the project, culture, and resistance to technology, regulations and laws. As part of the planning process, the Readiness Assessment Instrument – introduced in Chapter 9 – helps identify the readiness of an organization to successfully implement knowledge strategies and initiatives.

It is important to note that the *way* a knowledge plan is implemented is as important as *what is being* implemented. One of the reasons is that it is focused on knowledge, and knowledge is very personal – it resides within people. Thus, while information technology and information management are necessary, they are not sufficient for success. Ensuring support resources are in place, the KM plan is focused on people: helping people create, share, leverage and apply their information and knowledge in support of the organization's objectives.

The process of developing the strategic plan is part of the change strategy. The strategic plan as a collective process brings with it a sense of ownership across the organization, and responsibility for the outcome, with both laying the groundwork for successful implementation. A way to get even more people involved is to make success stories a part of the plan. Early in the planning cycle, leadership publicizes the desire to locate early successes to serve as examples for each top-level goal or objective of the plan. As the top-level goals/objectives clarify over the course of the planning process, with them emerge examples of innovative thinking that are jumpstarting the organization toward achieving these goals/objectives. Not only does this process identify innovations underway, but it facilitates further ownership of the plan, and encourages organizational units to understand and begin implementation of the plan *prior* to its publication and distribution – and prior to the plan becoming a dust collector on the shelf. By the time the plan is staffed through the various stakeholders of the organization, the organization is aligned, senior leadership is committed, and implementation has already begun. NOTE: This process can be even more effective if the plan is going to be used as the basis for funding programs, thus providing the opportunity for visibility of success stories. For example, in the DON our CIO strategic plan – married to and including Information and Knowledge Management strategies and initiatives – was required by Congress, providing the opportunity for early successes to be directly conveyed and linked to funding.

ENGAGE INTER-ORGANIZATIONAL PARTNERING

While a knowledge strategy or initiative needs to be directly embedded in the operations side of an organization, it cannot succeed without technology, human resources, and financial support. This needs to be acknowledged in the planning phase, with the "knowledge" and "management" functions of the organization fully engaged. See Figure 8-7.While the terms "eBusiness" and "eGovernment" have been historically used with the "e" representing "electronic" – and indeed back in 2002 I participated in two books that professed just that: *KM: The Catalyst for Electronic Government* and *Building KM Environments for*

Electronic Government – today it is easier to understand that "e" as representing "enabled", that is, "enabled business" and "enabled government", with technology an important enabler.

As technological advancement has continued, "enabled" has moved beyond virtual reality into mixed reality and augmented reality (AR), and AI. This is not always an easy transition. Early on, senior leadership in the DON CIO shop had the opportunity to pilot the then-new Palm Five technology. As part of this process, for three weeks the DON had 24/7 access to me, pretty much giving them the ability to track my every movement. While today that sounds somewhat "normal", in that first experience it was actually rather disturbing, generating a feeling of nervousness, waiting for that beep to signal the need for immediate contact.

At exponentially accelerating rates we have become networked together through technologies that compound their inherent capabilities and functionalities with each new iteration of innovation. When examined carefully, the impacts are almost too new, too different, and too complex to adequately describe. For example, the internet began primarily as an information distribution capability and cell phones as portable telephones. Now, with interlacing layers of technological advancements, the convergence of the internet and cell phones has given rise to a nearly indispensable human tool that serves widely as an augmentation device for the human brain in nearly everything we do, including formal learning. And as technological advancements continue, new forms and functions are continuously emerging in every dimension of human activity, especially learning, self-management, personal performance, and self-development.

"Enabled" is highly inclusive of experience, education, and learning. While this has historically been an aspect of human resources, the nature of learning as impacted by networks has new, unpredictable dynamics. Speed, accessibility, reach, ubiquity, standards, reliability, etc. are evolving, albeit frequently chaotically, with the boundaries between formal and informal learning blurring. An example is the Khan Academy. In 2004, Sal Khan began helping a cousin with mathematics using an internet Yahoo app. Before long, other cousins joined in his tutoring and he transferred his instruction to YouTube. Over the years, the Khan Academy (KA) platform has grown to approximately 8,000 videos that have had nearly two billion viewings. Now, 100 million users are calculated to have used KA worldwide in dozens of languages, and 10 million users subscribe to KA. On the KA website home page, we read, "We're a nonprofit with the mission to provide a free, world-class education for anyone, anywhere."

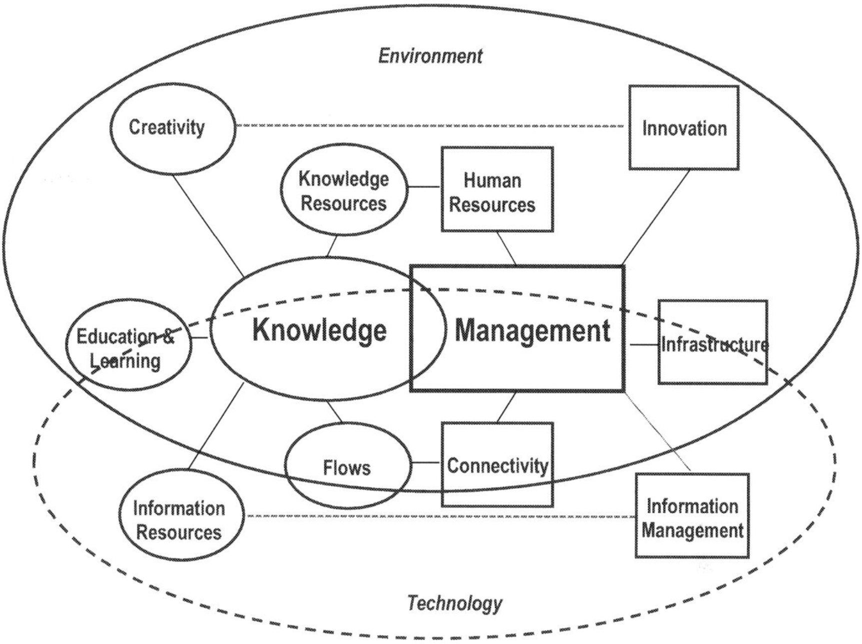

Figure 8-8. Knowledge "enabled" business requires technological, human resources, and financial support.

Learning is the acquisition of knowledge; it is the focus of Human Resources to support learning experiences and educational opportunities related to organizational needs. Yet in a changing, uncertain, and complex environment it is difficult to identify what those future "needs" may entail, and with employees having greater access to a wider array of educational materials it has made sense to move a significant part of this responsibility back to the individual learner. As self-development and self-learning expand, the Human Resources role changes, becoming a knowledge broker of sorts, connecting people to resources and tracking their advancement, and when appropriate connecting them to new positions within the organization where that learning can reward the individual and work to the benefit of the organization.

As can be seen, inter-organizational partnering across functional areas is essential, with every functional area having a role to play in the success of a knowledge strategy or initiative. The "knowledge way" is one that supports intelligent activity, with intelligent activity described as *a state of interaction where intent, purpose, direction, values and expected outcomes are clearly understood and communicated among all parties, reflecting wisdom and achieving a higher truth.*[361] That definition will appear several times in this section of the book.

SELECT THE TEAM

The effectiveness of any knowledge strategy or initiative is very dependent on the energy, dedication, collaboration and coherence of the efforts of all major stakeholders that play a role in its implementation. Thus, it is important for the implementation team to not only have the right mix of people in terms of expertise, capability and organizational connectivity, but to equally consider attitudes, networking skills, and commitment to success. At the core of all successful change strategies are *integrators*, those trusted individuals who connect people, information, and knowledge. The integrator is particularly important for organizations who must interact on a daily basis with both internal and external stakeholders and other organizations in the government, nonprofit and profit sectors.

Implementation team members should come from different parts of the organization, have backgrounds representing the areas of the organization that the initiative will impact, and understand and feel good about the purpose and implementation of the task. The team should be heavily involved with developing the strategy as well as implementing the plan. This allows the team to have ownership of the initiative and develop a common perspective and understanding of their objectives, issues, and contributions to the organization's performance.

In the DON we looked for people who had passion around the blossoming knowledge movement, and there were quite a few who had already recognized the value-added! Passion indicates desires, behaviors, and thoughts that suggest urges with considerable force,[362] with positive passions affirming something of higher interest and great.[363] This is the same passion we observed in thought leaders in the field. What could this knowledge focus contribute to the mission of the organization?

To help ensure program success, tasks can be written in a one-page agreement (or charter), signed by senior leadership and every team member. This agreement clearly states the objectives, resources, authorities, and limits of the team. Assuming that all team members have the required experience and competency to perform effectively in their disciplines, ten key success factors can help a team successfully perform in and respond to environmental forces. *Environment* refers to the aggregate of surrounding organizations, conditions or influences that affect the existence or effectiveness of the team. Forces from the environment place demands on, and provide support to, the team and can have a strong influence on its ability to achieve high performance. Those ten success factors are:

1. *Team leadership*: the ability of the team leader to lead and develop the team.

2. *Shared vision/approach*: A vision and mission that all team members accept and share. It also includes full agreement by team participants on the team's approach to carrying out its responsibilities.

3. *Team collaboration*: Team members working closely together with no hidden agendas and mutually supporting each other and team goals.

4. *Empowerment*: Team and team member capability, and authorization to represent their organization, make decisions, and/or take action.

5. *Technology support*: How much and how well technology supports team needs.

6. *Team learning*: The ability of a team to continuously learn, question old assumptions, and improve its ability to take effective action.

7. *Enterprise partnering*: A program or continuous activity to establish partnering relationships with stakeholders in the enterprise.

8. *Feedback*: A program or continuous activity to get feedback from customers and other key stakeholders on how well the team and its program are doing.

9. *Team collocation*: The percentage of team members located in the same local space and/or having 24/7 synchronous and asynchronous connection and actively participating.

10. *Team size*: The number of full-time members on the team.

These key success factors are interrelated. For example, *team leadership* and *team learning* strongly affect all four of the major team and organizational processes: (1) innovation, the ability of the team to generate new ideas, processes, methods, tools, techniques, etc.; (2) problem-solving, the ability of the team to identify the problem, and to generate alternatives for its solution; (3) decision-making, the ability of the team to make quality decisions by selecting the best alternative; and (4) implementation, the ability of a team to plan and take effective action to get the intended results. (An in-depth treatment of these four processes is included in Chapter 11.) Leadership plays a role in almost everything a team does, with a good team leader exercising influence through facilitation, coaching, and role modeling in all of these processes. (See Chapter 15, "How Leaders Inspire Action through Meaningful Knowledge".) Team learning is the development of the team's ability to execute these processes and to adapt its behavior and thinking to new challenges and tasks.

The innovation process is dependent upon the team's *shared vision/ approach* to guide the creation of new ideas. Innovation is used to solve problems and problems are defined by some deviation between where the team wants to be and where it is. Without a vision and approach to guide them, innovation may be misguided. *Collaboration* sets the tone of team interaction, which can encourage or minimize the generation and constructive evaluation of new ideas. *Feedback* is where many new ideas come from. It is also the origin of the need for innovation and can stimulate team members to think differently about their perspectives. Team *problem solving* is also dependent on the team's *shared vision/ approach* to guide the direction of its solutions. *Collaboration,* in the same sense as above, plays a large role in team member interactions and team ability to combine divergent views and knowledge to arrive at a strong set of alternatives. Finally, *enterprise partnering* establishes relations with key stakeholders who provide different views of both problems and their possible solutions. They may also have resources or knowledge of other individuals who can help in the problem-solving process.

Team *decision making* is dependent on *collaboration* to achieve quality decisions and to get buy-in from all team members. *Empowerment* is also very important because it allows team members to commit their part of the organization and let the team make decisions without delays in having to get multiple agreement from enterprise stakeholders. *Team size*, either too small or too large, can affect the quality of decisions made. Small teams may not have enough diversity of experience and knowledge and very large teams may never reach agreement or, if they do, many team members may remain quiet and not buy into the decision. Team *implementation* is influenced by the *shared vision/approach* because it guides individuals as they carry out the plan of action and milestones. Common understanding and ownership of the team vision empowers team members to act on their own, yet stay aligned with the team goal. *Enterprise partnering* can be of considerable value during the implementation phase of a decision. Key stakeholder support may be the difference between success or failure of the knowledge strategy or initiative. Often there are many parts of the organization and individuals impacted by team decisions, and any of them may have the capability to block or slow down progress if they do not support or understand what the team is doing. *Empowerment* supports implementation by giving team members the authority and freedom to act without continuously going back to the team for direction.

In addition to affecting the major processes, the key success factors influence each other in many ways. For example, the team leader sets the tone of the team and by his/her actions and management style influences all of the other factors. A shared vision helps pull team members together and improve their collaboration level. At the same time, a high collaboration level will help a team in developing its vision and approach to task implementation. The degree of connectivity via physical team collocation and/or synchronous and asynchronous virtual support will affect its ability to work collaboratively. And both partnering and feedback help a team develop and maintain its vision/approach.

Collaboration makes it easier for a team to learn. Enterprise partnering makes it easier for a team to obtain feedback from its stakeholders. In turn, a high collaboration level can help develop and implement a strong enterprise partnering program. Feedback indicates a potential need for the team to reassess itself and can help direct team learning. Both collocation and team size can influence the degree of team collaboration. The appropriate use of technology improves the speed of communication and the efficiency of many of the other success factors.

This close relationship of the success factors indicates they represent the structure of a complex system. These relationships will vary in strength depending on the team, its situation, and the task at hand. It is the challenge of every team to dynamically manage these factors to get the team performance needed for a given task.

Senior leadership must support the team as it runs into implementation issues or difficulties. This is essential for success, as there will likely be individuals at all levels who do not understand – or agree with – a specific initiative. Since the U.S. Department of the Navy (DON) operates as a large enterprise, it was necessary for them to create an overarching Community of Practice (CoP) – led by a senior leader in the Secretary of the Navy's office – as a guidance body to implementation of their knowledge program, with members of the overarching CoP (who were geographically dispersed) each having a supporting CoP in their functional area or geographical location. While the overarching CoP was indeed focused on the discovery and sharing of new ideas, task teams were drawn from this group as necessary to support implementation of enterprise-wide initiatives.

EXAMINE ORGANIZATIONAL STRUCTURE

With the current agility focus and a reintroduction of the "flat organization" concept, it is a good idea to examine your organizational structure to ensure information and knowledge flows up, down, and across the organization are operating optimally. An organization cannot exist without a structure, and the larger an organization becomes the more critical the structure becomes. The structure determines accountability in terms of roles, functions and responsibility, as well as determining decision-making authority.

Is your organization centralized or decentralized and at what levels? In today's changing, uncertain and complex decision environment, it is important to have decision-making authority where the knowledge resides. See the in-depth discussions of adaptability, resilience, alignment, robustness and quick response – all attributes of an "agile" organization – in the first half of Chapter 8.

Is your hierarchy structured top-down or circular? Hierarchies and bureaucracies (often confused) are not the same. As introduced in the Chapter 2 discussion of hierarchy, the central point (dominant structure) of a hierarchy may be the traditional (used in bureaucracies) top-down triangle or may have a circular structure or axial symmetry. Regardless, most hierarchies consist of groups of subordinate hierarchies who in turn have groups of subordinate hierarchies, with each group having its own particular relation to the dominant center point.[364] Two key findings which are worth reiterating are (1) there is a central theme to the system with a dominant center point, and (2) the function of any one part can only be understood in its relationship to the whole. In other words, both dependency and interdependency are elements of hierarchies, and the relationship of subordinate hierarchies to higher level groups *need not be one of control.* For example, in an organization, production of parts would be at a lower level than where they are assembled, and while the sales department would be separate, it could not function if there were no products to sell, nor would the parts department be of any value if the final product could not be sold – interdependent yet with separate focal points, making different choices but heading the organization in the same direction in support of the organizational vision. This is what we have described as a "connectedness of choices".

Is your organization vertical or flat? Vertical structures have a chain of command, with each lower part of the chain having less authority and responsibility. Examples of organizational structures that are vertical are functional/role-based, product-based, market-based, and geographical structures. "Flat" organizations, which are not really flat but "flatter" than the vertical format, reduce the "middle-men", and tend to make companies more democratic and inclusive. An example is the matrix organization, where individuals report to multiple people who are the leads in various job functions (marketing, development, customer support, etc.) The principles (and benefits) of a flat organization include trust, transparency, confidence, passion, autonomy, fail fast with no single point of failure, and agility. Amy Little, a workforce planning specialist at the technology consulting firm Saggezza, says these eight "principles" are interconnected. As she forwards,

> *Transparency builds trust, and trust instills confidence. Confidence allows individuals to be comfortable with the potential of failure. Autonomy creates a sense of pride and passion. Agility and collaboration increase transparency and decrease the likelihood of a single point of failure. Without all of these, it would be nearly impossible for employees to pivot quickly when things don't go the way they were planned.*[365]

With the current push and necessity for agility, the flat organization structure, particularly for a small upstart organization, with the democratic and inclusive mode of self-direction (empowerment and self-direction) of flat organizations, is certainly worth serious consideration. However, no matter how many layers of management are eliminated, networking and communication, participation and collaboration, leading and visioning, and purpose and meaning (the inner petals of the RKM model) – all built on a foundation of trust, truth and transparency – are the core elements of success and sustainability.

Concurrently, hierarchies offer a structure to facilitate the coordination, participation, and collaboration that enable creativity and innovation to flourish, and serve as focusing and learning platforms. Foss and Klein see the key challenge for the design and operation of hierarchies today as the balance of two opposite forces: (1) the desire for empowerment and autonomy, and (2) the need for managerial authority, particularly when there is a need for rapid change, with the larger organization participative in and supporting that change.[366]

In the early days of implementing knowledge management and a commitment to moving toward a knowledge centric organization (KCO), the DON created career paths for this discipline as well as Information Management, Computer and Information Systems Engineering, Information Assurance, and Tele-Communications, all of which were pertinent in different parts of the organization. Specific to the knowledge field as a career area were 12 specific job roles. These are briefly explicated in Table 8-1 below, adapted from the DON competency toolkit.

Table 8-1. Knowledge roles developed for the DON.

Knowledge Role	Associated Competencies, Learning Objectives, Performance Levels, and Proficiency Requirements
Chief Knowledge Officer (CKO)	Manages knowledge sharing process at command level; leads efforts to move the organization to knowledge centricity (a KCO); requires dedication to KM principles, ability to discuss benefits of knowledge sharing, and vision to ensure knowledge initiatives re adopted by the organization. Responsible for ensuring relevant info to all personnel, implementing knowledge sharing strategy, championing cross-organizational communities, establishing incentive program for knowledge sharing and re-use, defining roles, skill-sets, and opportunities for knowledge workers, and facilitating training and education.
Knowledge Manager (KM)	Works with CKO to implement initiatives; manages knowledge efforts; looks across processes to capture tacit and explicit knowledge, balancing technology, information, processes, and individual and organizational learning within a culture of shared values to ensure sustainable competitive advantage.
Knowledge Systems Engineer (KSE)	Turns knowledge movement ideas into workable solutions by engineering appropriate sharing Internet/intranet sites, rules- based systems, portals, databases, etc. Requires intimate knowledge of systems, architectures, technologies, standards and protocols. Ensures performance is optimized through utilization of tools and systems thinking applications.

Knowledge Process Manager (KPM)	Focuses on knowledge and content integration processes; manages the efforts of the KTE, KRE, and KLE (see below). Develops process models for optimal organizational effectiveness.
-Knowledge Transfer Engineer (KTE)	Captures and codifies tacit knowledge, making it available for re-use; connects people to one another to enable the transfer of tacit knowledge.
-Knowledge Research Engineer (KRE)	Creates explicit knowledge from available resources and integrates content in systems into easily accessible knowledge for decision-makers.
Knowledge Life-Cycle Engineer (KLE)	Applies the rules and procedures that ensure the appropriate refresh and currency of information in a knowledge system; determines information birth and death for the KCO.
Knowledge Community Leader (KCL)	Facilitates communities of practice across organizations to foster innovation, improved performance and collaboration; requires facilitation skills to ensure change initiatives are supported.
Intellectual Capital Manager (ICM)	Develops the enterprise workforce; ensures the human capital aspects of a KCO are fully integrated; uses knowledge to increase the performance of the organization, the learning of the organization, and identifies gaps in knowledge competencies.
Performance Measurement Engineer (PME)	Measures and assesses the KCO model implementation and architecture. Performs analyses, develops a predictive model, shows potential impact of change, and provides implications for validation of KCO model.
Knowledge Assurance Manager (KAM)	Ensures the assimilation of information and knowledge is protected from unauthorized access and/or disclosure.
Knowledge Assistant (KA)	Understands organizational information needs; assists in data gathering activities; uses expert multimedia skills and web tools to prepare and distribute organizational products/communications; analyzes and improves organizational workflow and communications.

Note that the DON, which includes both the uniform Navy and Marine Corps as well as the civilian workforce, employs more than 800,000 people with 1.2 million contractors. Thus, it was not unreasonable to carefully think through the necessary roles to ensure the organization took full advantage of the knowledge movement. In the uniform side of the organization, the focus on knowledge was as a collateral duty, with the Knowledge Manager filling a connecting, integrating, and championing role. As was written in the May 2005 issue of *InsideKnowledge* in the cover story following a case study of the DON titled "The Art of War: Empowering Front-line Decision-making":

> *This month's cover story details what can confidently be described as the most comprehensive and far-reaching knowledge management initiative ever attempted anywhere in the world ... KM has ... become a fundamental aspect of the way the US Department of the Navy operates ... From the highest to the lowest ranks, from the corridors of Washington, DC to the front line of military engagement, there is a prevailing understanding that knowledge, and by extension knowledge management, is everyone's business.*[367]

This was researched and written eight years into implementation, and by this time significant shifts had occurred. The initial Chief Knowledge Officer champion – who had committed to a three-year leadership change approach – had retired and, by agreement and intent, the position was not filled. Her retirement, in fact, was what had driven the case study by *InsideKnowledge*, who had written a few months earlier on the impact of the loss of the World Bank CKO and the subsequent decline of their knowledge program. Assuredly the same thing was happening in the DON. It was not. Why?

The above quote captures the essence of the "why". Recall the strategy approach on the "growth and sharing of knowledge" conveyed in Figure 8-5 earlier in this chapter. Going into implementation of knowledge management to achieve a knowledge centric organization, the 300+ community of practice previously introduced, which represented various commands and functional areas across the US and several members from commands around the world, recognized that *knowledge was everyone's responsibility*. Unless they are engaged or committed, you cannot ORDER someone to learn, nor can you ORDER someone to give you a creative idea. Try it: "We want you to come up with a new idea RIGHT NOW that is implementable and going to lead to a competitive advantage for your organization." This is why the individual change strategy near the end of Chapter 10 (Prepare) is so critical. The most effective change occurs when people understand the change, believe in it, feel good about it, take ownership of it, and have the knowledge *and* confidence to change.

Knowledge Roles

Knowledge is everyone's business. Thus, regardless of the title on the organization chart, every member of the organization has a responsibility toward knowledge-based development or creating a knowledge-centric organization. What does this look like to support reblooming the knowledge movement? Table 8-2 below provides a baseline for potential choices.

Table 8-2. Knowledge roles and functions for Reblooming Knowledge.

Organizational Role	Knowledge Roles and Functions
Chief Executive Officer	Formulates and leads the knowledge vision, purpose, roles, and strategy.
Knowledge and Innovation Champion (KIC)* *The KIC is a 6-month rotating position held by a mid-level manager or above who has been identified as an	Serves as advisor and special assistant to the CEO, representing the CEO in knowledge strategies and initiatives, including facilitating corporate-level meetings and events focused on creating and sharing knowledge, and facilitating creativity and innovation. Shares latest related information in the field; coordinates efforts with IT and IM support leaders to sustain a knowledge focus; facilitates organization-wide learning experiences; and supports communities of interest, practice and learning.

integrator and who has proven experience and success in the knowledge field.	Leads special knowledge and innovation-related projects in support of the organization's mission and vision.
Vice Presidents	Identify and manage knowledge activities in their departments.
Board Members	Vote on major knowledge movement decisions in the Strategic Plan and priorities in the Innovative Creativity Scenario Plan.
Shareholders	Submit ideas about the knowledge movement in the Strategic Plan and priorities in the Innovative Creativity Scenario Plan.
Chief Information Officer (CIO)	Creates and maintains the organizations knowledge-centric IT infrastructure.
Chief Technology Officer (CTO)	Identifies, plans, and builds KCO tools required by the business plan.
Chief Learning Officer (CLO)	As a member of Human Resources, works with KIC to plan and support knowledge-related learning objectives.
Chief Finance Officer (CFO)	Assist managers, VPs, KIC, and the CEO with reporting of financial information related to becoming a KCO.
Chief Innovative Creativity Officer (CIC)	Working with the KIC, the Chief Innovative Creativity Officer facilitates, supports, and reports major IC initiatives and events.
Managers	Facilitate knowledge-related activities on daily basis. Periodically provides info related to KCO activities. Responsible for facilitating knowledge sharing.
Team and Project Leads	Facilitate knowledge-related activities on daily basis. Periodically provides info related to KCO activities. Responsible for facilitating knowledge sharing.
All Employees	Provide daily "front-line" vigilance for Knowledge-related activities, needs, and potentials in their areas of focus. Responsible for networking and knowledge sharing in their specialty domain of knowledge.

Knowledge centricity – supporting the right to learn and facilitating the creative mind – is fundamental to the democratic approach in organizations and essential to innovation, the life's blood of today's organization. As we've moved away from the bureaucratic nature of organizations where knowledge was used as a control mechanism, we've discovered that diversity and differing knowledge perspectives generate greater creativity in problem-solving and offer a wider expanse of options in decision-making. We also recognize that with knowledge comes responsibility; with the recognition of – and the "knowing" of how to resolve or take advantage of – an issue or opportunity comes the responsibility to share that knowing and act on that knowledge.

NURTURE AN INNOVATION CULTURE

KM strategies often require a change in culture – a change that both leadership and employees must actively support. Culture has been described as how the work gets done, expected behaviors, the amount of freedom given workers, the accepted or expected formal and informal relationships among workers, and even as a way of life or as a set of norms in the workplace.[368] As workers go about their daily business of communicating, solving problems, taking action, and reacting to information from others, they modify their own behavior and perception of the work environment until things "settle down" into a normal and expected way of getting the job done. Over time, the entire organization achieves a consistent way of working together to meet the needs of internal and external customers; although each knowledge worker has their own unique way of behaving, their behavior still falls within cultural expectations. A set of beliefs, feelings, expectations, and norms develops in employees that provide comfort and stability, allowing them to work with less anxiety and uncertainty. Everyone understands how, when, and with whom they should interact, how to treat each other, and how they are supposed to act as they get their job accomplished. As this atmosphere is created, with its behavior patterns and unstated assumptions, the organization's culture is created. Thus, developing over time from all of the interactions among the workforce, modulated by a myriad of events and situations both internal and external to the firm, culture includes unstated assumptions about people, relationships, and knowledge.

Thus culture is a global property of organizations and because it emerges out of the interactions, it is emergent – it cannot be traced back to any single cause or individual. New employees may have problems accepting an organization's culture, particularly if it is significantly different from their previous organization. New employees can either adapt to their new organization, get the organization to change, or leave. If they stay and do not adapt to the new culture, they will live under continuous stress. As a global phenomenon of the organization, culture plays a strong role in influencing what people should and should not do, how they see themselves and their role in the organization, and how motivated and loyal they are to the organization.

Since it is an emergent phenomenon resulting from the interactions of many different things, an environment that supports a knowledge centric culture and knowledge sharing can be nurtured. For example, a knowledge-sharing culture might emerge from (1) the clear linking between sharing knowledge and accomplishing the mission/vision of the organization, (2) the expectation of knowledge sharing and the example set by senior leadership, (3) the underlying recognition that knowledge sharing is the right thing to do and will benefit workers and their organization, (4) the alignment of organizational rewards and recognition programs with knowledge sharing, and (5) an organizational structure and technology infrastructure to facilitate knowledge sharing.

The **first step** in creating a shift in culture begins at the top of the organization, with senior leadership's awareness of the need for change. This necessitates a thorough review and reflection by all senior managers of their beliefs, assumptions, feelings, and expectations of the environment, their workforce, and their own roles and responsibilities. At a minimum, this will lead to intensive questioning of differing perceptions of reality, which will most likely result in double loop learning coupled with a deeper understanding of themselves – individually and as a leadership team – and the creation of a shared understanding of the current and anticipated environment. Most likely, this will also lead to a discussion of the history, strengths, weaknesses, opportunities, and threats of the organization, its culture, and how the work gets done.

The **second step** is to take a closer look at the environment, including (1) developing a description of the current and expected external environment and its impact on the organization's operations; and (2) preparing a strategy for surviving and growing in the anticipated environment. In a changing environment, this means that planning is for learning, becoming prepared, and the leveraging of knowledge. Local informed and aligned action coupled with quick feedback that drives any necessary changes are the keys to sustaining survival fitness in unpredictable situations. In Chapter 9 on Readiness – a critical part of the planning process – we have included a section that suggests key organizational sustainability factors in terms of adaptability, resilience, alignment, robustness and quick response.

Senior leadership must recognize that for change to be successful they, individually and as a group, will have to change their own thinking, perspectives and behavior. Although their actions alone cannot create the desired culture, those actions can easily derail any new culture formation. For example, after the desired workforce attributes are identified, every leader and manager throughout the organization will have to understand, accept, and live those attributes if they expect the workforce to do so. Further, senior leadership may have to review and revise the organization's structure as well as modulating the culture because structure can support or hinder cultural needs.

A **third step** is to identify the major characteristics of the desired culture. For a knowledge-sharing culture, these characteristics might look something like the following:

- *Flow*—Knowledge workers share information and thereby move knowledge throughout the organization.
- *Collaboration*—Workers work together in teams and small groups to leverage the knowledge and actions of everyone.
- *Creativity*—Workers have learning conversations, dialogues, open disagreement, throw out ideas, and try new approaches to their tasks.

Intelligent and prudent risk is honored. Note that innovation cannot occur without knowledge and creativity.

- *Empowerment*—Knowledge workers have the freedom (and support) to get their work done, understand the context of their work, and are aware of the boundaries of their action space.
- *Communication and networking*—Employees have open communication and there is wide networking throughout the organization and with external stakeholders.
- *Adaptability*—Employees continuously learn, change, and adapt to new circumstances and challenges, with encouragement and support from leaders and managers.
- *Action orientation*—Everyone has the knowledge and motivation to take action, observe the results, get feedback, and adjust their behavior as needed.

Note that a knowledge culture is inclusive of what has recently been called out as a "data culture", that is, with data freely accessible to the organization, with complete empowerment of the business user. Historically, IT has out of necessity had control over data systems. Technology has sufficiently advanced where that is no longer necessary or desirable, yet, somewhat like knowledge, there is data hoarding still occurring. No doubt this is largely due to the recognition that if you control the data and information management in an organization, you have control of business management in the firm.

There are several approaches to ensuring the best data is available and accessible. These include (1) conducting an inventory of structured data sources as part of the organizational knowledge audit; (2) developing a governance structure that includes data discovery and hygiene to ensure usable and comprehensive data; and (3) ensuring the application of policies and ground rules for data use and sharing. In promoting the use of their software, Scott Woestman, vice president for public sector sales at Alation, says that their system uses metadata to automate and empower people such that they no longer need to focus on 80% data gathering and 20% analysis, but can reverse that time-driven structure so the focus is on critical outcomes. Since knowledge emerges from information, and information comes from data, it just makes good sense to ensure complete empowerment of the business user in terms of data availability and accessibility.

A **fourth step** is to determine what knowledge, personal attributes, and behaviors employees need to create and implement as they perform their daily work. A sample of individual characteristics that make knowledge workers successful are: trust and trusting, self-confidence and a strong (not big) ego, integrity, the motivation and skill to apply their knowledge to new situations, social skills, self-discipline (managing self), and leadership potential.

Knowledge workers also need to be articulate, continuous learners, and team players.

A **fifth step** is to select a set of actions that create and reinforce behavior through the multiple and myriad interactions occurring as the work gets done. The intent is for these actions to move the organization toward the desired knowledge-sharing culture. In other words, the day-to-day work of knowledge workers will create customs, norms, and behaviors that help get the job done and are comfortable to the workers. *These norms should be close to the desired cultural characteristics developed in the third step.* The knowledge worker characteristics suggested above are needed to enable workers to create these cultural characteristics. Since cultural characteristics cannot be created through policy, rules, or managerial control, it is knowledge worker characteristics, skills, and behaviors that have to be nurtured and reinforced. See the discussion on becoming a change agent in Chapter 10.

The type of culture that supports an organization co-evolving in a complex, uncertain and changing environment is predicated on the following assumptions:

- Organizations will increasingly be faced with rapid change, uncertainty, nonlinearity, complexity, and anxiety.

- The future is unknowable (to regard as true beyond doubt) but not unfathomable (to penetrate to the meaning or nature of; to comprehend).[369]

- Individual actions make *the* difference.

- All individuals are creative, and can learn and develop knowledge.

- Knowledge workers want to perform and contribute to an organization they respect.

- No one individual possesses the information or knowledge to understand complex situations.

- Knowledge can be leveraged through strategy, structure, and collaboration.

- Trust, mutual respect, fairness, and collaboration are critical for leveraging knowledge.

- To survive, the organization must support all of its knowledge workers. Learning, making mistakes, and changing behavior are survival and success necessities.

- Strong control is a myth, influence is possible, and dialogue is essential.

As an example of change actions to create a knowledge-sharing culture to nurture innovation, consider the need for the culture to have the characteristic of flow to facilitate workers communicating and networking with each other. A major determinant of effective communication and knowledge sharing (the sharing of understanding and meaning, not just the transfer of information) is the degree of trust throughout the workforce as a whole, and particularly of the organization's leadership. The importance of trust will come up again and again in the discussion of the current environment. If knowledge workers trust each other and their leaders, they are much more apt to help each other and communicate openly. The question then becomes: What actions would build and improve interpersonal trust throughout the organization? Those actions might include organization-wide leadership discussions on the importance of sharing information and the responsibilities that go with that sharing. For example, De Furia describes these responsibilities as sharing relevant information, reducing controls, allowing for mutual influence, clarifying mutual expectations, and meeting expectations.[370] See Chapter 12 for a deeper treatment of trust.

As the business world more fully embraced the knowledge movement, in their best-practice report on *Creating a Knowledge-Sharing Culture*, the American Productivity and Quality Center (APQC), a leader in the implementation of knowledge management, identified ten key findings in best practice knowledge-centric organizations:

1. Best-practice organizations share knowledge to solve practical business problems or achieve specific business results.
2. At best-practice organizations people can see the connection between sharing knowledge and the business purpose – and this level of understanding is increasing.
3. Knowledge sharing is tightly linked to a core cultural value of the organization. Sharing knowledge simply enables people to pursue that value more fully.
4. The style of each knowledge-sharing approach closely matches the style of the organizations as a whole.
5. At best-practice organizations, there is strong management and peer pressure for people to help each other, collaborate, and share their knowledge. People who do not share are ignored, fail to be promoted, or are "siloed".
6. Best-practice organizations integrate knowledge sharing with people's work by holding visible knowledge-sharing events and/or embedding knowledge sharing in routine work processes.
7. The level of management support for knowledge sharing is commensurate with the scale of the overall knowledge-sharing effort.
8. Best-practice organizations enable informal networks without formalizing them.

9. Human networks, whether formal or informal, have a facilitator who "owns" the network and actively ensures that people participate.

10. Best-practice organizations see the need to align reward and recognition with knowledge sharing.

There are many ways to facilitate knowledge sharing. For example, Texas Instruments, named one of the "World's Most Ethical Companies" early in its KM implementation, held a Best Practices Celebration and Sharing Day. The day was culminated with an awards ceremony for those organizations that had most successfully shared best practices and knowledge, and produced the best results. This commitment to best practices and the sharing of those best practices, which continues today, is to "adopting and applying best practices and processes to respect human rights within our company". As they write in the first paragraph of the TI Supplier Code of Conduct, and live:

At Texas Instruments (TI), we are determined to do business the right way and build a stronger company for the long term. For decades, we've run our business and invested in our people and communities with three overarching ambitions in mind. First, we will act like owners who will own the company for decades. Second, we will adapt and succeed in a world that is ever-changing. And third, we will be a company that we're personally proud to be a part of and would want as our neighbor.[371]

The core values of being trustworthy, inclusive, innovative, competitive and results-oriented support this code. See the section on knowledge sharing in Chapter 12.

Since with knowledge comes responsibility, and change is everybody's responsibility, a unique approach identified by Dr. Joyce Avedisian in igniting what she calls a Kingdom Innovation Culture is the cultivation of culture heroes. These are employees whose heart, mindset, and behavior reflect company values and behaviors.[372] Culture heroes are intentionally developed. For example, the CEO and founder of Turbocam sponsored such a program focused on character and values as well as skills, engaged through mentored learning communities of current and emerging leaders discussing real-time business transactions and relationships. The primary question was: "How do I apply company values and principles to this situation?" In support of this program, and setting the foundation for the larger organization, everyone received "character first training" during which each month a different company leader presented a new character trait. Then, the following month, the supervisor of each team led discussion on how this character trait had been applied in their day-to-day work with customers and fellow employees.[373]

To create a culture of innovation, TATA Power in India has developed an aggressive program through Human Resources intervention. In addition to developing a Leadership Competency Model and Productivity framework for resource optimization, and talent funding for growth businesses, specific programs include: (1) *Entrepreneurship in Residence*, which provides support for intrapreneurs to actualize their business ideas through startups incubated within the organization, providing access to funding, technical networks, mentorship and expert guidance; (2) *mY Coach*, which is a transformational journey with a certified coach aimed at self-awareness, reflection, change, and development; and (3) *Future Skills Academies*, which are certification tracks to develop future skills such as data analytics and digital, project management, sales, and customer centricity. They also have an award-winning digital learning platform called *Gyankosh,* a Tier Leadership Development program for feeding the leadership pipeline, *Talent NXT* for fast-tracked career development of high potential employees, and *Yes iTrain* for leveraging the tacit knowledge of internal SMEs.[374]

As can be seen, to create an innovation culture many changes are needed at the same time and many people at several levels should be involved, i.e., creating or changing a culture requires parallel changes applied consistently and cohesively over time. Remember, we are after organization resonance and coherence, a working together to efficiently and effectively achieve organizational goals. A reminder ... you cannot just tell knowledge workers to share knowledge and come up with a new idea, and providing only technology and information solutions is never sufficient. These approaches may yield short-term responses but are unlikely to provide the long-term cultural changes intended.

While providing the structures and artifacts that make it easier for knowledge workers to obtain and share information and knowledge helps encourage this behavior, any reasons for not sharing need to be surfaced and the context changed within which they get their work done. For example, trust needs to emerge from daily interactions and become *the way things are*.

Knowledge Ignorance & Anti-Intellectualism

Knowledge as the capacity to take effective action includes an understanding or awareness of information, facts, or skills acquired through education and experience. Adversely, ignorance is the lack of knowledge or information about a particular subject or topic. It can be intentional or unintentional and can lead to misinformation. See the lengthy discussion in Chapter 3 on misinformation and disinformation. Intentional knowledge ignorance deserves to be and is unacceptable in a knowledge organization.

Stephen R. Covey, recipient of ten honorary doctorate degrees, wrote his original PhD on an analysis of self-help books and became regarded internationally for his insights into "the habits of highly successful people". In his book *The 8ᵗʰ Habit: From Effectiveness to Greatness* Covey makes this poignant note of caution:

> *As your knowledge increases, what happens to your ignorance? It obviously becomes larger, or at least your awareness of your ignorance becomes larger. So, the more you know the more you realize you don't know. What if you were trying to serve purposes greater than your knowledge—greater than your comfort zone? This would create a genuine humility and a desire to draw upon help from others—from a partnership or team. Successfully working with others makes one's knowledge and abilities productive and necessitates the creation of a complementary team of people who possess knowledge and abilities that can compensate for and make irrelevant one's individual ignorance and weaknesses.*[375]

Not to overstate this issue of ignorance, Peter Burke, emeritus professor of cultural history at the University of Cambridge and author of *What is the History of Knowledge* joins in on the subject of *ignorances* with a full volume titled just that, *Ignorance: A Global History,* wherein he catalogs major categories of ignorance over time and provides a glossary of over 50 types of ignorances! Furthermore, so that we might not become complacent with incorrect information and knowledge, half of his book draws attention to the "Consequences of Ignorances". He begins his final chapter, "Conclusions: New Knowledge and New Ignorance", with a pithy quote from C.S. Lewis: *"Perhaps every new learning makes room for itself by creating a new ignorance."* Burke's final conclusion serves well to reflect his balance of polarities; for example, academia vs. ignorance. He writes *"We should always think twice before describing any individual, culture or period as ignorant, since there is simply too much to know – an old complaint but one that has become more and more justified in our time."* Then, he closes with Mark Twain, *"We are all ignorant, just about different things. The trouble is that those with power often lack the knowledges they need, while those who possess those knowledges lack power."*[376]

Karl Abrecht, internationally regarded management consultant whose "Brain Power Course" is the basis of an American Management Association training seminar, sees other issues at play. He cautions with an important insight about the brain's pattern-creation and pattern-recognizing capacities. As he says in his book *The Power of Minds at Work: Organizational Intelligence in Action,* there is a *pattern paradox* which addresses how *"Organizations are both empowered and imprisoned by the patterns that govern their operation."* In his discussion of the positive and negative nature of mental pattern formations of both its workforce and leadership, he offers this strategic observation:

> *A highly-structured, stable, rule-based, perfective organization can be either collectively stupid or collectively intelligent, depending on how*

successful it is at mobilizing its collective brain power and achieving its mission. Some kinds of music are best played by a symphony orchestra and others by a jazz combo. The potential for stupidity is not understanding which is which.[377]

After further describing this quandary, he reports that in some cases of corporate pattern rigidity, he says that this is what Swedish managers refer to in American management methods as "the systematic stupefication of the worker."[378]

Anti-intellectualism is the rejection of, or actual hostility towards, intellectual pursuits, education, and knowledge. It can manifest in beliefs that practical skills and experience are more valuable than academic knowledge or that experts are not trustworthy. These beliefs can lead to a devaluation of critical thinking and reasoning along with the promotion of simplistic or dogmatic beliefs.

Historically, the term "philistinism" has been used to represent anti-intellectualism, a social attitude that both undervalues and despises art, beauty, spirituality, and intellect, the very elements that connect the hearts and minds of humanity. The pursuit of wealth is also suggested as a companion of anti-intellectualism, with individuals who have these collective traits called Philistines. This has been recognized for a while. For example, in 1869 when Matthew Arnold wrote about the importance of culture, which "helps us, by means of its spiritual standard of perfection, to regard wealth as but machinery, to really perceive and feel that it is so", he certainly could never have imagined the culture of connection and the flows of knowledge that were to occur during the next century. However, he went on to say that if it weren't for the purging effect of culture on the human mind, the whole world – both present and future – would "inevitably belong to the Philistines, people who believe most that our greatness and welfare are proved by our being very rich, and who most give their lives and thoughts to becoming rich."

The social attitude of anti-intellectualism can dampen an organization's effectiveness in the knowledge economy. Learning, whether through academic channels or experience, is critical to organizations, and regardless of how it is obtained represent knowledge as the capacity to take effective action. The valuing of a skill set versus intellectual ability is highly dependent on the purpose and product of the organization, with both necessary, but at different levels of intensity at different times. Recall that knowledge is relative, that is, context-sensitive and situation-dependent. Thus, even across one organization, one skill set would be required in the packing department that is quite different than that in production, or finance, or design. For organizations that deliver knowledge as its product, the social attitude of anti-intellectualism is unacceptable.

THINK SYSTEMS: A Reminder

As introduced in Chapter 2, every organization – and every individual within that organization – is a complex adaptive system co-evolving with its environment. A system is a group of elements or objects, the relationships among them, their attributes, and some boundary that allows one to distinguish whether an element is inside or outside the system. Complex systems consist of a large number of interrelated elements (parts) that may or may not have nonlinear relationships, feedback loops, and dynamic uncertainties very difficult to understand and predict. A complex adaptive system (CAS) co-evolves with the environment through adaptation, the process by which a system improves its ability to survive and grow through internal adjustments. Adaptation may be responsive, internally adjusting to external forces, or it may be proactive, internally changing so that it can influence the external environment.

What we struggle to achieve is to become *intelligent* complex adaptive systems, organizations where the decisions that are made every day at every level help the organization achieve its mission. A top-level systems perspective encourages individual managers and teams to develop and implement balanced decisions that *optimize the entire system instead of any one part of the system.*

Systems thinking provides an approach for managing complicated situations by helping decision-makers recognize and understand cause-and-effect relationships among organizational parameters. For example, identifying the boundaries of a problem or issue helps focus corrective actions, while understanding the connections among parts of the system indicates that multiple actions are required to correct a situation. As the environment becomes more uncertain and systems become more complex, it is also important to understand complexity thinking; for example, the property of emergence, and approaches to influencing a CAS such as absorption, amplification, boundary management, sense and respond, seeding, simplification, structural adaptation, and trial and error. Chapter 19 provides a depth treatment of systems and complexity thinking.

An example of a systems approach is that used by Natural Resources Canada, a leading government organization for shaping the contributions of natural resources (energy, forest, minerals, and metals) to the Canadian economy, society and environment. Analyzing behaviors in response to component interactions, feedback, and delays led to identification of four different what they referred to as "types" of knowledge services (content, products, services, and solutions) as part of a closed-loop, continuous knowledge cycle. A total of nine stages were identified in the knowledge services system. The first five (generate, transform, manage, use internally, transfer) are internal to the organization, and the last four (add value, use professionally, use personally, and evaluate) are external. Each of these nine stages includes a framework of *who* is working on *what* and *why*. A example of a knowledge service would be (content) spatial climate change information, (product) map of climate change impacts, (service) respond to queries about climate change, and solution (mitigation and adaptation strategy). A value-chain approach was used to identify the sequence of steps that defined the value of content, with a knowledge market defined as an interacting and functioning group of related knowledge services value chains. Noting that this process enabled a wider transfer to external customers, there were five major conclusions:

1. The knowledge services model provides an adequate framework to support measurement and subsequent management of knowledge services as a system.
2. Knowledge markets are richer and more complex than they are described by other provider/user models.
3. Knowledge markets have neither beginning nor end. Agents embed, advance or extract value in a continuous cycle of intellectual property transactions.
4. Knowledge service value chains have nine stages (as called out above).
5. Evaluating both post-production system performance and pre-production market needs is necessary for both supply and demand approaches to knowledge markets.

In terms of implementing a knowledge initiative or strategy, by understanding the interrelationships of, for example, a technology system storing guidance documents (information) and an expert who has a reputation for trouble-shooting (knowledge), both can be used to achieve optimum performance. For periodic issues handled in a repeatable manner, the technology system can support a training requirement to spread this ability across the organization or stakeholder groups. However, when situations arise that have different parameters than previously experienced, an expert with the appropriate knowledge needs to be consulted. Where does this expertise reside? Has this situation occurred previously somewhere in the organization? If the organization has an Artificial Intelligence component, has the latest information been fed into the system such that it can handle future potential issues in this domain? By developing a virtual expertise locator along with an understanding of the organization's AI contingent, it becomes every employee's responsibility to keep updated and connected to contextual examples. Even with an organization that is geographically dispersed, anyone can have quick access to the knowledge that is needed.

The U.S. Forest Service Nature Watch Program, which has been in existence more than 30 years, takes a systems approach by expanding beyond watchable wildlife to embrace viewing and learning opportunities focused on fish and aquatic ecosystems, and native plants and wildflowers. Further, programs are designed for children K-6, adult wildlife enthusiasts, hikers, photographers, anglers and hunters. The virtual system has five elements:

1. *Where to NatureWatch* allows the user to search for places to view wildlife, fish, and wildflowers, while providing a complete description of the sites, with maps and photographs.
2. The *Photo Library;* contains thousands of copyright free photographs available to the public.
3. *Live Video Cams* such as the ever popular Eagle Cam, receives over tens of thousands of hits daily. Through the wonders of modern technology, NatureWatch can share real-time the behavior of bald eagles and salmon that make their home in America's National Forests.
4. *Educational Programs and Festivals* which are hosted by the Forest Service allow for a wonderful opportunity to increase public awareness and involvement each year.
5. *Resources for Teachers, Kids and Planners* provide excellent educational materials for future generations to experience the wonders of nature, be responsible for their actions, and become advocates of proper and ethical behavior.

In March 2023 the U.S. National Science Foundation (NSF) launched a funding call for Proto-OKN (Building the Protype Open Knowledge Network), a $20 million initiative to build the prototype version of an integrated data and knowledge infrastructure that is an open knowledge network. This will be publicly accessible with interconnected sets of data repositories and associated knowledge graphs, enabling Artificial Intelligence-based solutions across a broad set of societal challenges in healthcare, space, criminal justice, climate change and other fields. As NSF Director Sethuraman Panchanathan forwards, this vision of an open network harnesses vast amounts of data generated in every sphere of life. "The open knowledge network will transform the nation's ability to unlock insights from data and transform these data into useful, actionable information and knowledge crucial to address challenges for a more efficient and equitable future."[379]

The intent of providing these examples is to ensure that when implementing a knowledge strategy or initiative you fully explore the opportunities offered through that strategy or initiative for both internal and external stakeholders. We live in a knowledge-live world, knowledge expands when it is shared, and with knowledge comes the responsibility for sharing.

CHAPTER 9
ASSESS READINESS

Readiness –as part of planning – is a large topic, so we have dedicated a whole chapter to it. We first look at readiness from the viewpoint of preparing for the unknown, in which knowledge accessibility and knowledge flows play a large role. We then specifically look at an organization's readiness to implement a knowledge strategy or initiative, and include a readiness assessment instrument.

READINESS FOR THE UNKNOWN

As forces build in today's world, we recognize those forces in terms of accelerating Change, rising Uncertainty, increasing Complexity, and the emergence of Anxiety as we attempt to mitigate those forces. In other words, the world is CUCA! Another well-known descriptive acronym coming out of the military is VUCA, standing for volatility, uncertainty, complexity, and ambiguity. Either way, we're in a world of extremes in every dimension of our existence; but what the heck, we're not so inherently simple ourselves. How do we ever make sense of using the 86 billion neurons in our neocortex?

With the growing 21st Century deluge of innovation and change, organizational resilience may only be sustained by a clear regard for knowledge readiness. For the success of the firm, there is no safe option for a secondary level of attention to a knowledge strategy. While knowledge readiness may be scaled down to leaner approaches, it cannot be shelved or placed on hold. The absence of a prevalent, prevailing, and passionate engagement in knowledge development is a road to failure. The commitment to a knowledge-based culture must be embedded in the DNA of the firm, in the mind-set of leadership and management, and in the productivity of all employees. Increasingly, a hallmark of the democratization of the organization is characterized by a collaborative voice of shared attention and engagement to knowledge readiness by all.

We would note that, in some cases, knowledge readiness may be overshadowed by the business success of the organization. There is a business management axiom that points to this phenomenon – *Remember, it's what you do best that may work against you!* The recent bankruptcy and closing of the Bed, Bath, and Beyond enterprise is a tragic example of this. As they successfully built hundreds of well-designed stores stocked to the ceilings, they became short-sighted on customer brand preferences and, more importantly, the expansion of eCommerce. In their case, interventions with a knowledge focus would have not been their saving grace. They truly required an embedded knowledge readiness strategy over a minimum of three years or more to enable them to make the necessary process and infrastructure investments and shift in their business model. As we watched bankruptcy fire sales empty their shelves and their doors forever close, we couldn't help but wonder how many of their employees knew in good time what could rally the enterprise. To help with constrained circumstances such as in a smaller firm or during an economic recession, we provide a Lean KR Readiness Startup Plan in Section IV.

Five critical characteristics need to be embedded into organizations for long-term sustainability. To be effective, each of these characteristics touches all four of the organizational processes (decision-making, creativity, problem-solving, and implementation), demanding empowered and fully participative employees at the point of action where and when issues and challenges emerge. In terms of readiness, discussed below are the importance of adaptability, resilience, alignment, robustness, and quick response. All five of these contribute to an organization's agility.

Adaptability

The need for, and importance of, the ability of an organization to adapt in today's environment has never been greater. In this environment as mission responsibilities and needs and expectations increase, the rate of change, level of uncertainty and complexity and scope of responsibilities make it imperative that adaptability be a major strength for sustained performance. Adaption means internally changing structure to a new form that support successful implementation in meeting major changes in the environment. Organic systems continuously change themselves either internally, their boundaries, or even the context within which they exist in order to survive within their surroundings, which are composed of other organic complex adaptive systems. New skill sets coupled with a deep understanding of complex adaptive systems are essential to recognizing and understanding the unpredictability of environmental challenges and opportunities. Surface knowledge is not sufficient to recognize and interpret the patterns and emergent characteristics.

Challenges are easier to recognize than opportunities. This is because challenges are happening to you, pushing you to seek solutions, while opportunities – which should be prime time front and center – are generally pursued as an extracurricular activity. A remarkable way to rapidly flesh out RKM opportunities is the Leap Frog Challenge – *You can't get there from here, but you can get here from there!* Adaptability is much easier when you can clearly see where you are headed and how you will achieve that end state. Here it is worth noting that one's ability to see ahead is a strong indicator of the level of leadership one can function in.

The theoretical formulation and research of the Leap Frog Challenge is well developed by Elliott Jaques[380]. So, how far into the future can you leap? Please note if you are doing this for your organization it is best to convene an assorted group of three to five leaders to have the capability for a good gaze into the future – five to ten years out. As the group envisions a desired future capacity of knowledge performance in the firm, and the related business value, the task is then to back plan milestones, etc. for how to incrementally and successfully maintain adaptability by keeping a clear view of the future. A well-conducted Leap Frog Challenge has the potential to produce a paradigm shift for both the knowledge functions and the primary business activities of the firm.

For large organizations, continuous structural change may have to be a way of life. An example is balancing classic centralization versus flexibility and decentralization to ensure the capacity to adapt in a relatively short time. Creativity, innovation, experimentation and a willingness to accept mistakes and take reasonable risks are essential. Structural change is not possible if the organization has developed a highly efficient, rigid, and control-oriented structure. Consider the structure of an organization; for example, its technology systems and physical equipment have been created to support the services as they meet anticipated or surprise challenges. If the mission changes drastically and perhaps rapidly, these physical structures may lose some of their support potency. So, what characteristics does an organization need to be able to change and adapt to new mission scenarios or collateral responsibilities? Structures take time to create and are not easily modified, yet the organization must be capable of changing its internal structure and routine ways of doing business to meet these responsibilities.

Even the best technology, if it is not designed for modular improvements or easy replacement of outdated capacities, can slow down adaptation to meet new demands. If doctrine, decision processes or practices become so strongly implanted that they cannot be challenged and modified to meet uncertainties or new mission responsibility, adaptation will be slow or impossible. To minimize the danger of this several things should be kept in mind: the organization's leadership management and workforce should be cognizant of, and sensitive to the potential for significant mission changes and the increasing uncertainty and complexity of the environment. To build this sensitivity the decisions and practices during routine operations could include consideration to structural and operational adaptations that would be need to meet specific scenarios. Thus, scenario planning becomes an important competency for the organization.

Many organizations have a natural tendency toward stability and equilibrium. To prevent this, management and the daily practices of the workforce can embrace a culture that is conducive to change. (See the discussion of systems and complexity in Chapter 19 and the discussion of culture in Chapter 7.) This requires a continuous recognition and willingness to find new ways of working together and/or changing the structure. These could include working with other organizations, or countries, upgrading technology, creating expert systems to be able to access specialized knowledge when needed, and perhaps modifying decision chains and creating emergency response teams as needed. In Chapter 14 when discussing Relationship Network Management, there is a discussion of the "mesh", which prepares organizations for emergency response scenarios. Examples of structural adaptation could also include financial and material support groups, procurement processes and human resource processes and policies. These may have to move away (at least temporarily) from their usual checks and balances, and shift their thinking and actions to focus on expediting specific needs to meet emergency requirements. Sometimes these new requirements become permanent and the adaptation becomes a new level of organizational performance.

Adaptability is often difficult because of the natural tendency to revert back to what worked in the past that appears similar to the new challenge. The risk is always higher when facing an unknown or new challenge. This can create a tendency to take the safest approach by making decisions from the past. Unfortunately, where new problems are encountered new solutions must be created, which often requires new and specialized expertise. Individuals who have the expertise should be identified relatively quickly and brought together to leverage their knowledge to enhance decision-making and implementation actions.[381]

Resilience

Resilience is the capacity to recover quickly from a shock or surprise and resume original performance. For example, in industry a key supplier may have had a manufacturing plant damaged by an earthquake in a foreign country. Or a competitor could have taken an unanticipated move and eliminated half of an organization's customer sales. From a military viewpoint a potential protagonist may have demonstrated significantly more strength than anticipated, and exposed a vulnerability in your own forces. The challenge is to develop the capacity to recover from some high impact disruption. One way to think about resilience can be taken from the material sciences and represents the ability of a material to recover its original shape following a deformation. From an organizational viewpoint, resilience addresses the ability to return to normal performance in a short time following some high impact/low probability disruption.[382]

Retired Navy Rear Adm. John Polowczyk, executive director of Ernst & Young who led the White House supply chain task force in the first year of the pandemic, says that resiliency equals visibility plus agility (R=V+A). As he explains:

The beginning piece here is end-to-end visibility as a way to monitor the risk of your supply chain. The old adage you have to be able to see a supply chain to manage it. Understanding that the ability to do what if scenarios, the ability to have some artificial intelligence and forecasting in there is a central piece of it. People are also taking a step back and saying, 'what does my supply chain look like? How do I make it an agile network?' The lesson learned from the pandemic, those linear systems really broke.[383]

When an organization is harmed by an external event, it must have the capacity to pull resources (people, knowledge, relationships, networks and vision) together quickly and take action. Decision chains have to move fast, teams need to coalesce quickly, and all parties need to create a common understanding of the situation, its nature and danger to the organization. This may not happen without conscious leadership forethought and preparation, which is sometimes referred to as designed for dexterity. As part of their sustainability strategy, Singapore Armed Forces transfers experience and knowledge through stories with full leadership participation. Used formally and informally – as part of the teaching and training processes, as well as being shared in the mess halls – stories represent an efficient, pleasant, and effective way to transfer core values, experiences, and knowledge.

External disturbances may come from a complex environment which makes it difficult to understand the source, the situation, and its behavior. Under these conditions, it is important that the organization have some level of knowledge in dealing with external complex adaptive systems. Chapter 19 is a discussion of systems and complexity thinking.

Between September 2009 and January 2010, the IBM Institute for business value and IBM strategy and change interviewed 1,541 CEOs, general managers and senior public-sector leaders, who represented different sizes of organizations in sixty countries and thirty-three industries. The title of the resulting publication was "Capitalizing on Complexity". The Chairman, President and Chief Executive Officer of IBM Corporation was interviewed and offered that,

What we heard through the course of these in-depth discussions… is that events, threats and opportunities aren't just coming at us faster or with less predictability; they are converging and influencing each other to create entirely unique situations. These first-of-the-kind developments require unprecedented degrees of creativity – which has become a more important leadership quality than attributes like management discipline, rigor or operational acumen.[384]

More than ten years later how true these words ring. In the executive summary, the IBM publication provided a number of ideas and conclusions that are relevant to many organizations today. Although the focus was on private industry, the below conclusions are also relevant to government and military organizations as well as not-for-profits.

- "Today's complexity is only expected to rise, and more than half of CEOs doubt their ability to manage it."

- "Creativity is the most important leadership quality, according to CEOs."

- "Most successful organizations co-create products and services with customers, and integrate customers into core processes."

- "Better performers manage complexity on behalf of their organizations, customers and partners."

How can organizations capitalize on complexity? The study concluded that the effects of rising complexity call for CEOs and their teams to "lead with bold creativity, connect with customers in imaginative ways, and design their operations for speed and flexibility to position their organizations for 21st century success."[385]

To summarize, in building a resilient organization, develop creative leadership, build operational dexterity and flexibility, and create and maintain close relationships with other key organizations, individuals, and perhaps nations.

Alignment

The meaning of alignment has several interpretations that will be addressed in this foundational concept. First, alignment has often been considered as the process of continually assuring that the activities of employees are supporting the organization's vision and purpose. It is sometimes viewed as the capacity of an organization to maintain its organizational cohesion and worker empowerment at the same time. The goal is to ensure that all individuals in the organization are working toward the same vision, mission and purpose. This may be challenging where, in the same organization, some leaders are still espousing bureaucratic control-oriented while others recognize the high value of fostering empowerment and collaboration. It is also a challenge considering some departments such as finance must be meticulous in their processes and actions whereas others such as research departments need to be more empowered, and free for creative and innovative thinking.

Second, looking and learning from the military perspective, the challenge of alignment is to ensure personnel are aware and have a good understanding of the "commander's intent" and of their own level of empowerment and knowledge in any given situation. An understanding of this term is in the foreword to *Warfighting, the U.S. Marine Corps Book of Strategy* in which General Gray, a former commandant of the U.S. Marine Corps, writes: "You will notice that this book does not contain specific techniques and procedures for conduct. Rather it provides broad guidance in the form of concepts and values. It requires judgment in application."[386] The general's comment is appropriate for any organization whose employees have to live with both controlling and empowering leadership. Meaning that both employees and their leaders need to use good judgment in applying organizational guidance built on a deep understanding of the vision, mission, purpose, and values of the organization.

In a CUCA environment, organizations not only have to anticipate and understand uncertainty and surprise, they also have to focus energy and talents to respond to events that call for structural or cultural adaptation. Creating alignment requires taking a broad look at the organization, seeing it as a complex adaptive system. For example, ensuring that there is clear and consistent communication to employees about the vision, mission and purpose of the organization – what is referred to as a clear line of sight – helps them understand how their specific work focus supports their organization. This is what provides a framework within which they can make decisions and take actions in times of emergency. Effective communication (the sharing of understanding, **not** the transfer of information) also encourages employees to collaborate and share their activities with others, which enables support when it is quickly needed while simultaneously opening the door for mutual trust and effective teamwork.

Alignment exists when people, strategy, processes, structure and leadership are moving in the same direction. Ideally the organization is self-aligning and has created a self-sustaining culture where leadership is distributed, with energy and thought throughout the organization resulting in a power and focus that can significantly raise the performance.

When emergencies occur, this increased performance can greatly enhance the organization's response. As turbulence rises, alignment can support the flexibility and adaptability needed to withstand disruptions. Alignment also encourages a culture of collaboration, spirit, and shared purpose by raising all employees' sensitivity and perspective to the organizational level, which may be well above their individual work-related actions. When this occurs, individuals become more aware of how their actions and responsibilities help achieve organizational goals.

Effective alignment requires balancing to achieve cohesion within the organization, while at the same time encouraging quick responsiveness and empowered decisions at the levels needed to meet challenges, which may require the organization to adapt, and to be resilient, robust and respond quickly. Effective alignment also requires a flow of knowledge across the organization to ensure rapid and clear understanding of environmental challenges and the need for specific actions to meet those challenges. All of these characteristics take time, energy, and funding and represent an investment to ensure long-term survival and mission success in a rapidly changing, uncertain and complex world. Such a knowledge organization is the ICAS model introduced in Chapter 1.

Another interpretation of alignment is offered by Labovitz and Rozanski.[387] They suggest that it is the alignment between people, customers, strategy and processes that, taken together, create a self-aligning and self-sustaining culture that distributes leadership and energy throughout the organization, unleashing organizational power.

In summary, there are two major factors in creating alignment. The first is getting everyone heading in the same direction with a clear understanding of their personal role in achieving the organization's common purpose. The second is to make sure that the integration and synergy of resources, networks and systems are there to support employees. Such alignment provides managers at all levels of the system with the ability to:

- Rapidly deploy a coherent strategy;
- Focus on specific aspects of the environment;
- Develop top-quality, empowered people; and
- Continuously improve supporting processes and structures.

Robustness

Robustness is the ability to respond to a wide range of mission requirements. It can also be considered as a capacity to withstand a broad range of perturbations or disturbances from the external environment. In either case, it means that the organization can't focus on one specific competency but rather must look at its overall vision and scope of interactions with the environment, and identify access to potentially needed competencies. It can then consider creating capabilities that cover the full range of responsibilities, and where possible, train personnel or develop partnering agreements that provide access to potentially needed competencies.

To become robust, an organization should carefully survey its potential environment and its scope of responsibilities within that environment. A classic approach is that of scenario development which identifies a broad range of potential scenarios that might occur in the future. These scenarios are then developed, studied and used to identify the competencies and capabilities within the organization needed to provide effective responses.

Scenario planning is a tool for future thinking. As seen in humans, higher order consciousness includes the ability to build past and future scenarios, and planning – related to forecasting and predicting the future – is an interactive part of consciousness. It may be surprising when we say that management is all about the future. Decisions are made based on expected outcomes, that is, things that will happen in the future. Thus, all management decisions are based on improving future organizational performance.[388]

Scenarios were introduced in the 1950's by Herman Kahn as a form of story that serve as planning tools, providing a structured process for consciously thinking about – and planning for – the longer-term future. It was first used in military war games in the 1960's, with a focus on the "predict and control" approach. Later, the emphasis shifted to analyze "cause and effect" relationships. As a foresight methodology, scenario planning is used to consider possible, plausible, probable and preferable outcomes. Possible outcomes (what might happen) are based on future knowledge; plausible outcomes (what could happen) are based on current knowledge; probable outcomes (what will most likely happen) are based on current trends; and preferable outcomes (what you want to happen) are based on value judgments.[389] See the tool in Section IV on scenario building.

Since scenarios are always "best guesses" because of the variability and complexity of the external environment and the difficulty of anticipating the future, the organization takes on various risks of error. Looking within, it becomes important to build an internal capacity development and be able to apply effective knowledge to respond to these external scenarios.

Robustness may require a number of individuals with deep knowledge and strong experience in dealing with "on the edge" challenges. These capabilities may drain resources and talent while at the same time providing insurance against surprises. As well as providing robustness, they are also providing capabilities that contribute to other sustainability characteristics such as adaptability, quick response, resilience, and perhaps alignment.

The decision to create a robust organization carries a cost in terms of training, learning, facilities, and culture building. Both individual and organizational learning become important for out-of-scope events or threats. Recognizing that time and energy are needed to develop and maintain the capacity to deal with these out-of-scope events, organizations may build these efforts directly into their normal training and learning processes. These costs can be considered as the price of sustainability to maintain performance under the conditions of uncertainty and complexity in today's environment.

Another approach to maintain robustness is to develop alliances or connections with individual experts outside the organization who are available to deal with certain external scenarios. These individuals would be on-call and available when needed. Teams of such experts could be involved in practice sessions and learn to work together in simulated exercises. This would enhance their capacity to respond quickly to unanticipated incidents. An example is the "mesh", which is discussed in Chapter 14 on Relationship Network Management.

As stated above, many of the internal characteristics needed to be resilient are similar to those needed for robustness. The major difference is that being a robust organization can deal with a wide range of unanticipated challenges. Resilience refers to a strong threat or shock whereas robustness addresses the scope and variety of the threat or shock rather than its intensity. Teams, social networking, integrated competencies and effective management actions to all support a resilient organization. Organizations in today's world facing the uncertainties created by increasing change and complexity must consciously decide and make decisions on the balance they need between resilience (sustainable effectiveness) and loss of efficiency (increased learning and preparation costs).

Quick Response

Sometimes events happen that may require very quick reaction before they become dangerous. Thus, an organization needs to be able to respond rapidly and effectively when external or internal challenges arise. Quick response, the core characteristic of agility, may not allow time for the classic decision chain or senior leaders to necessarily become involved. Often it relies on people who are on the scene, recognize the issues, and can take immediate action. Here is where core values, recognition of mission and purpose, and trust and empowerment become very valuable. When people know the core values of the organization and they are empowered to act, they can respond in a manner consistent with what they believe the organization would do. For this to occur quickly there must be a mutual trust between the organization, its leadership and the individual workers. This takes time, and some form of democratic leadership (see Chapter 1).

When rapid responses are needed, many parts of the organization may have to work together to take the necessary actions. For example, manpower, supplies and even funds may have to be allocated quickly without the usual red tape, checks, and balances. Thus, people must be capable of recognizing the relevance and importance of taking quick action for the good of the organization and must feel they have the freedom and the responsibility to protect the interests of the organization to ensure its purpose and mission are fulfilled. An organization with such a cooperative and trusting workforce and culture does not occur naturally. It can only be developed carefully and slowly by leaders and managers through their actions, staff meetings, stories, dialogue and learning sessions.

Organizations that react quickly and successfully to surprise events or threats would have characteristics such as:

- A strong, rapid, and flexible decision chain;
- A workforce with the experience, knowledge and empowerment to know what to do, and will coalesce quickly to take effective actions;
- Teams, social networks and communities of practice that leverage knowledge and focus the results for rapid action;
- Employees with a common understanding of their organization's culture, vision and purpose;
- The organization's culture is one of learning, collaborating and taking action;
- The organization has previously recognized the importance of being prepared and has identified and practiced responding to surprises;
- Leadership, management and the workforce are aware, and have some level of understanding the consequences of external and internal complexity; and
- Collaborative relationships with suppliers, other agencies/countries who would provide assistance in handling shocks or disruptions.

And then there's the innovative mindset.

Jack be Nimble, Jack be Quick

In an article titled "Innovation Power: Why Technology Will Define the future of Geopolitics" which ran in the March/April 2023 edition of *Foreign Affairs*, Eric Schmidt, the former CEO and Chair of Google, points out why Ukraine did NOT fall within one or two weeks as was estimated by the U.S. Intelligence community and most other nations around the world. Quite simply, Ukraine had the technology and innovation advantage. First, they immediately uploaded critical data up to the cloud to prevent loss. Then, they repurposed their e-government mobile application Diia to become an open-source intelligence collection platform. This meant that citizens could upload photos and videos of enemy locations and movements. Then, with the infrastructure for communications in danger, they turned to SpaceX Starlink satellites. Then, they quickly converted to drones to intercept drones. As Schmidt says, "In the cat-and-mouse game of innovation, Ukraine simply proved nimbler."[390] This was innovation power, the ability to invent, adopt, and adapt, which is the power that will determine success in both conflict and competition.

In warfare there is no question of the immediacy of response. However, in the organizational setting when responding to a crisis it is critical to give enough time to the decision-making process considering potential risks and potential outcomes of response actions to ensure that the best decision is made. In other words, there is an "optimum response time" which is different for each crisis, and both reacting too slowly or too quickly carry potential risks.

READINESS FOR A KNOWLEDGE STRATEGY

For the Organization to be ready to successfully implement a knowledge strategy, it should have certain characteristics and basic capabilities in place. Leadership, management, culture, and structure all play a role in the success of a knowledge strategy or initiative. While this instrument has been developed to assist in determining the Organizations' readiness for implementation of a knowledge strategy, the final judgment, of course, lies with the individual manager based on their experience and knowledge of their organization. They are the experts who know the need for the intended strategy or initiative, the stakeholder environment, and their organization's ability to learn and change.

Further, this instrument largely assumes that technology is in place or has been planned that will support the chosen knowledge strategy. Whatever level of technology support is needed, it is important to ensure that the technology is selected and implemented in a manner which is cohesive with organization needs and resource as well as employee acceptance. Information is the foundation of knowledge, and its accessibility and ease of use is critical for success of any knowledge strategy in today's technologically advanced environment.

Introduction to the Instrument

This assessment instrument takes 10-15 minutes to fill out, and is designed to help answer the question: **Is my organization ready to implement a knowledge strategy?** In the context of this assessment, a knowledge strategy is a program implemented throughout the entire organization or any of its sub-organizations (departments, etc.). A strategy consists of multiple knowledge initiatives.

For example, building an innovation culture, while requiring strong technology support beginning with the infrastructure for collaborative platforms and programs, would need to include all the elements of knowledge sharing – inclusive of strategies and structures for networking and communication and participation and collaboration among employees with strong leadership support. Further, collaborative innovation with clients and other stakeholders, which is becoming commonplace, adds considerable value. Blockchain, internet of things (IoT) and Artificial Intelligence could be used to connect diverse talent communities, and human-to-human contact could be ensured through locally-hosted knowledge fairs and knowledge cafes. Implementing creative space – both cyber and physical – might include hackathons, makeathons, ideathons, and several kinds of innovation jams, all supported by mind labs and idea challenges. Information on all of these concepts is widely available on the internet.

There are 40 questions in the instrument divided into five categories, each pertaining to a specific aspect of the organization. EACH QUESTION MUST BE ANSWERED. Each statement or question asks for a response on a five-point Likert scale in one of the following ways: 1/very low, 2/low, 3/medium, 4/high, and 5/very high.

For example, consider the first statement: "A knowledge strategy's contribution to the current performance of my organization would be ..." If implementing a knowledge strategy is already supported by leadership such that the value of your planned strategy is recognized and supported by the workforce, and if knowledge sharing is an accepted part the organizational culture, then you would select a 4/high or 5/very high. If the value of knowledge is understood but the strategy is unclear, or there is perhaps an uncertainty about the efficacy of a knowledge strategy even though the planned strategy seems to makes sense, you might answer 3/medium, indicating the recognition of some value accompanied by uncertainty regarding how well or how easily your employees will support such an endeavor.

It is assumed that you already have in hand a knowledge strategy that you are considering implementing. If you do *not* have a strategy in mind, then you may wish to read the subsection on Developing a Strategy in the Planning stage of the process (see Chapter 7), where short descriptions of several knowledge strategies are provided for your consideration.

Because each organization's sub-organizations (departments, branches, etc.) are unique and possesses a wide variety of characteristics – complete with their own history – this instrument must be used in concert with informed reflective thought to determine readiness. What this assessment process does is provide key questions and aspects of your organization for you to think about and reflect on before implementing a knowledge strategy. From your answers to these questions – and your reflection on what you know about your organization – you will be able to make a more informed decision on whether to proceed with implementation of your intended strategy, or whether you need to take some preparatory steps prior to implementation.

The Readiness/Success Assessment Instrument

While a description of the implications of item scoring is provided following the instrument and as Appendix D, it is strongly recommended that you do not review this material until *after* you have answered the items in the Readiness Assessment Instrument. Following completion of the instrument, there is information in Appendix D on how to complete a Readiness Assessment Scoring Sheet that provides a discussion of the implications of the item scores resulting from your specific responses.

The Questions

	VERY LOW	LOW	MED	HIGH	VERY HIGH

GENERAL QUESTIONS

	VERY LOW	LOW	MED	HIGH	VERY HIGH
Q1: A knowledge strategy's contribution to the current performance of my organization would be	1	2	3	4	5
Q2: A knowledge strategy's contribution to sustainable performance of my organization would be	1	2	3	4	5
Q3: The level of credibility of the business case for a knowledge strategy is	1	2	3	4	5
Q4: Support of the management group that oversees a knowledge strategy is	1	2	3	4	5
Q5: The level of financial resources available is	1	2	3	4	5
Q6: The availability of qualified people to implement the knowledge strategy is	1	2	3	4	5
Q7: The amount of time available for employees to implement a knowledge strategy is	1	2	3	4	5

LEADERSHIP (General Manager and Direct Reports)

	VERY LOW	LOW	MED	HIGH	VERY HIGH
Q8: Leadership's level of personal interest In the knowledge strategy would be	1	2	3	4	5
Q9: Leadership's ability to work well together in support of a knowledge strategy would be	1	2	3	4	5
Q10: The leadership team's expectation of achieving the intended results of a knowledge strategy would be	1	2	3	4	5
Q11: The leadership team's willingness to to reward employees who contribute to the knowledge strategy is	1	2	3	4	5

	VERY LOW	LOW	MED	HIGH	VERY HIGH
Q12: The leadership style in my organization is [very control oriented (1), in between (2-4) or very collaborative oriented (5)] ...	1	2	3	4	5
Q13: The level of leadership involvement with the workforce [as described by "management walking around"] is	1	2	3	4	5
Q14: In my organization leadership's acceptance of change is	1	2	3	4	5
Q15: Leadership's understanding of a knowledge strategy and its usefulness is	1	2	3	4	5

MANAGEMENT

Q16: The level of communication among organizational departments & branches is	1	2	3	4	5
Q17: The level of management's empowerment of the workforce is	1	2	3	4	5
Q18: The use of teams or groups to accomplish specific objectives within this organization is	1	2	3	4	5
Q19: Managers' willingness to accept and implement new initiatives is	1	2	3	4	5
Q20: The level of support for knowledge sharing through organizational structure is	1	2	3	4	5
Q21: The consistency of management direction and organizational goals is	1	2	3	4	5
Q22: The effectiveness of the HR Department's support of employee training and development is	1	2	3	4	5

CULTURE

Q23: The willingness of employees to accept and take advantage of change is	1	2	3	4	5
Q24: The level of trust among organizational employees is	1	2	3	4	5
Q25: The capacity of employees to tackle and take a flexible approach to problems is	1	2	3	4	5

	VERY LOW	LOW	MED	HIGH	VERY HIGH
Q26: The energy level and spirit of the workforce in my organization is	1	2	3	4	5
Q27: The percentage of workers who learn fast enough to keep up with change is	1	2	3	4	5
Q28: The level of networking and communication among organizational workers is	1	2	3	4	5
Q29: The percentage of employees who understand the vision of this organization is	1	2	3	4	5
Q30: The percentage of employees empowered to do their job with minimal direction is	1	2	3	4	5
Q31: For the critical processes of the organization, workforce discipline is	1	2	3	4	5
Q32: The level of trust between employees and managers is	1	2	3	4	5
Q33: The level of employee training, learning, and development in this organization is	1	2	3	4	5
Q34: The percentage of employees that think In terms of systems and how their work affects other employee efforts and the mission of the organization, is	1	2	3	4	5

ALIGNMENT

	VERY LOW	LOW	MED	HIGH	VERY HIGH
Q35: How well will the strategic business plan support the knowledge strategy?	1	2	3	4	5
Q36: How well will the operational plan support the knowledge strategy?	1	2	3	4	5
Q37: How well will the capital improvement plan support implementation of a knowledge strategy?	1	2	3	4	5
Q38: How well will the organization's Information technology master plan support implementation of a knowledge strategy?	1	2	3	4	5
Q39: How well will your information Technology department support Implementation of a knowledge strategy?	1	2	3	4	5
Q40: The competency and skill sets of this organization's employees are	1	2	3	4	5

Individual Readiness Assessment/Success Interpretations

It is suggested that you may want several managers in the organization to take the readiness assessment instrument, then use a team dialogue approach to arrive at a common understanding of the organization's readiness to implement a knowledge strategy.

There are several indicators that will aid your discussion. First is the **total score,** which will fall somewhere between 40 and 200, and is determined by adding all the levels of responses across the instrument. This is a general guideline; while it is one indicator, it is not sufficient to determine your organization's readiness to implement a knowledge strategy. Other factors that may play a significant role in that determination include the specific strategy being considered; the history, culture, size, vision and current situation of your organization; and the external environment (customers, government regulations, local communities, neighborhoods, Unions, political issues, etc.) within which the organization operates.

Here is a general description of what your total score represents:

(a) If your total score is 140 or greater, your organization should be ready to successfully implement a knowledge strategy.

(b) If your total score is between 130 and 140, you may consider implementing your knowledge strategy, but you may have some assessment items that need to be fixed as part of that strategy.

(c) If your total score is between 110 and 130, you may have to delay implementation of the full knowledge strategy and instead select one or more initiatives for implementation while fixing or upgrading those specific low-scored items needed for full KM strategy success.

(d) If your total score is under 110, low-scored items (levels 1 or 2) should be addressed and mitigated prior to implementing a knowledge strategy. Comments specific to each question at the level 1 and 2 are included in Appendix D.

As a second indicator, create a simple bar chart to map out the **items scored at each of the five levels** of the Likert scale. Color the bars representing "1" and "2" responses red, the bar representing "3" responses yellow, and the two bars representing "4" and "5" responses green. This will clearly show the items at levels 1, 2 and 3 that suggest additional reflection, and the items at levels 4 and 5 that will help in developing and successfully implementing your strategy.

This chart can be viewed from two perspectives. First, the number of items scored for a given level indicates their potential contribution to *assisting* in the implementation of a knowledge strategy. Second, the stop-light colors clearly support your analysis, with green (levels 4 and 5) indicating those items fully supporting implementation of a knowledge strategy; with yellow (level 3) indicating a mid-level assessment for those items and that some caution should be maintained relative to their ability to support implementation of a knowledge strategy; and red (levels 1 and 2) indicating that these items provide a low or minimum contribution to a knowledge strategy. The two red columns also indicate that the items represented *may need to be corrected prior to initiating a knowledge strategy.* For example, if you have two or three assessment items scored at a 1 or 2 level that are relevant to your specific strategy, yet all other items were scored at level 3 or higher, you will need to decide whether it is best to (a) delay starting the strategy until these low-scored items are corrected, or (b) start the strategy and improve these low-scored areas early during strategy implementation. A third option would be to modify the knowledge strategy to reduce the impact of the low-scored items. A large number of low-scored items relevant to a knowledge strategy may also drive the decision *not* to implement that specific strategy at this time.

A third step is to individually look at all of the specific items shown in Appendix D which were scored at levels 1 and 2. Next to each of the Question numbers and the level it was scored (for example, Q1-2, Q1-1) is a short discussion of that specific item. The intent is to provide information and suggestions to help you interpret the importance of each item to your knowledge strategy, the external environment, and the internal nature of your organization. These paragraphs will also direct you to related discussions in this book.

When reflecting on the results of this instrument, a team dialogue approach will be useful in order to arrive at a common understanding of the organization's readiness to implement your selected knowledge strategy. In concluding your analysis, consider the four areas below:

1. The total score and the above discussion;
2. The appropriateness of your specific strategy;
3. The impact of items scored at a level 1, 2, or 3 on your knowledge strategy; and
4. The impact of the external environment on the knowledge strategy VERSUS the impact of the knowledge strategy on the organization and stakeholders.

Then, use your judgment to determine the readiness of your organization to implement a specific knowledge strategy.

THE KM CAPABILITY ASSESSMENT TOOL (KM CAT)

The American Productivity & Quality Center (APQC) offers an assessment tool that looks at everything from strategy to funding and governance, process and approaches, technologies, and the sophistication of your measures. The details of your organization are assessed against APQC's Levels of Maturity, which is a five-step KM program maturity model developed through years of experience. It can be submitted online through a relatively simple process at https://zurl.co./8Rg92. You are provided a maturity rating in 12 component areas such as measurement, change management, IT, etc., with "more meaningful, actionable content that will support your continued journey toward knowledge management excellence and business impact." For additional information contact kmcat@apqc.org

USING KPIs TO EVALUATE THE ORGANIZATION

In his book *Story Thinking*, John Lewis says that one way to view organizations is to say that *some* are learning organizations and *some* are not. However, he contends that all humans are learners and indeed, as forwarded in Chapter 2, they are intelligent complex adaptive learning systems. Then Lewis adds that some "may have to overcome learning disabilities"; thus, all organizations are learning organizations, "with some having more learning disabilities than others".[391]

From that perspective, cultural Key Performance Indicators (KPIs) can be used to assess an effective learning organization. Figure 9-1 is an example assessment, showing the relationship between the phases of the model and the cultural key performance indicators. Story Thinking is introduced in Chapter 8.

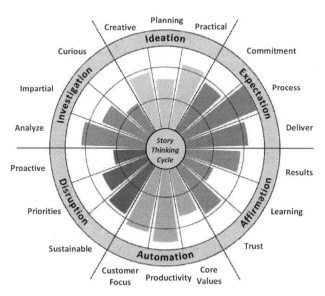

Figure 9-1. Story Thinking for Organizational Evaluation (used with permission).

TRANSITIONING FROM PLANNING TO PREPARING

Planning-Preparing-Executing-Sustaining is a continuous transaction between individuals, the organization, stakeholders, and the environment. While steps of the process often overlap, there are also specific transition phases occurring in concert with the shifts from step to step that smooth the transition. As feedback occurs and new ideas, approaches or directions emerge, the cycle begins again in a continuous loop of change and transformation. Key Elements of the transition phase from Planning to Preparing are Training and Learning and Full Spectrum Frames of Reference (with a focus on Knowledge Capacities).

Training and Learning

You will discover that training and learning is a part of every transition phase. As the organization better understands the potential offered by a knowledge strategy, which occurs when moving through the phases, questions arise and new ideas emerge which can make the strategy more effective. Thus, learning – and training when this learning needs to be shared in support of developing new skillsets and mindsets – will undoubtedly be of benefit to the organization and the success of the strategy.

In this still-early transition phase, it is critical for planners, developers, participants, and supporters to look at the strategy or initiative from a systems perspective. Thus, the knowledge competencies of **systems thinking and complexity thinking** are critical capabilities. A discussion of systems and complexity thinking is Chapter 19. Successfully implementing a bounded initiative or an overarching strategy – or anything in between – requires an understanding of the relationship of the strategy or initiative to the organization, the vision and mission, and the expectation of implementation results. Further, implementation always requires an understanding of available manpower and other resources, and relationships to other priorities. Since most organizations today operate in a changing and uncertain environment, it is also important to *understand the commander's intent*, that is, the rules and guidelines, and what is intended by leadership in the execution of those rules and guidelines. All of this understanding builds on a foundational understanding of systems, complexity, change management, knowledge, and information as well as internal processes and the culture of the organization.

Now is the time to ensure and reinforce the knowledge competencies of planning and synthesizing across the organization, which are both an important part of the human past, present and future skill set. While there is much written and available on these important competencies, these are briefly discussed below along with the importance of intention and attention.

Planning

Planning is forethought – a mental activity focused on achieving a specific goal. From the neuroscience perspective, we now understand that in developing our individual internal model of the external world, the cortical columns in the neocortex develop reference frames and track locations which allow us to plan and create movements.[392] When we expand consciousness, we expand our ability to see patterns and to develop good predictive success, and help others do the same. Thus planning, related to forecasting and predicting the future, brings the three parts of time together (past-present-future) and is an interactive part of consciousness. As a property of intelligent activity, planning always has a purpose, and includes formulating, evaluating, selecting, and sequencing thoughts to move toward a desired goal. From the instant those thoughts regarding what is planned emerge, we are on the path of creation. As Mulford describes:

> *When we form a plan for any business, any invention, any undertaking, we are making something of that unseen element, our thought, as real, though unseen, as any machine of iron or wood. That plan or thought begins, as soon as made, to draw to itself, in more unseen elements, power to carry itself out, power to materialize itself in physical or visible substance.*[393]

In the Industrial Age, plans became the mechanism to create the conditions (resources and events in time and space) to maximize the likelihood of future success. As Alberts and Hayes assert, there was the general faith that a systematic approach consisting of decomposition, specialization and optimization of components would handle even the really challenging problems.[394] Building on this approach, military planning included five elements: missions, assets, boundaries, schedules, and contingencies. While in a steady environment this approach worked most of the time, it became problematic in more dynamic environments.

While planning was centralized, there was also the acknowledgement that in a changing, uncertain and complex environment, execution must be decentralized, where "the flexibility and innovation necessary for accomplishing the mission typically resided with those implementing the plans much more than with those developing them".[395] In the knowledge field this is called decisions made at the point of action. Through cultivating deliberate acts and movement, you increasingly lay a solid foundation of courage, both moral and physical; thus, for the military deliberate planning was the process to achieve force synchronization.

Planning is a learning process which includes two parts: the creation of myths about social realities and the process of emergence.[396] For an expansion of our planning capability, we look to the ICALS (the Intelligent Complex Adaptive

Learning System that is the human) model introduced in Chapter 2. The mode of social engagement recognizes the global connectivity of people and the need for interoperability in the strategic planning approach, which brings an emergent quality into the process. Built on decentralized execution, as introduced above, an example of this is the *power to the edge* approach adopted by the U.S. Department of Defense in response to accelerating change and increased volatility.[397] This approach moves toward the metaphor of evolution in support of continuing innovation, concluding that organizations need to experiment rather than following the older concepts of planning. As Alberts and Hayes describe, "various kinds of experimentation activities ... need to be orchestrated as part of the concept-based experimentation campaign to conceive, refine, and fully mature innovation".[398] Thus, the planning process needs to move away from a centralized, top-down, engineered process to, "... a process that works bottom-up; one that creates fertility, seeds ideas, nurtures them, selects the most promising, weeds out the losers, and fertilizes the winners".[399]

See the tool on Scenario Planning in Section IV. While mental thinking can potentially prepare people for future events, it is recognized that there is no linear extrapolation into the future in a changing, uncertain and complex environment. This is why, although a good preparation point, *specific scenarios* of interest, largely scripted, cannot provide sufficient freedom to produce the high level of innovation that is needed. However, the experimentation and power to the edge approach advocated does not take into account the power of thought and the power of intention.

Intention and Attention

Before the turn of the century, Portante and Tarro argued that attention had become the scarce resource of the information economy.[400] As the information age exploded and the availability and accessibility of that information increased, the gap between the attention of individuals and organizations and the information that needs to be attended to has widened. Davenport and Beck describe attention as a slippery intangible asset, and begin their book, *The Attention Economy*, with a focus on the current attention deficit,[401] which has continued to accelerate since its original publication. For example, they describe an organization's attention deficit in terms of organizational ADD. The symptoms are the increased likelihood of missing key information needed for decision; diminished time for reflection on anything but simple information transactions such as e-mail; difficulty holding others' attention; and a decreased ability to focus when necessary.[402] This work includes an in-depth treatment of attention and approaches for improvement. A fascinating finding is the recognition that time management and attention management are *not* linked.

Stress plays a large role in arousal and attention. Surprisingly, this can be negative or positive. Stress actually focuses attention, and when there are moderate levels of arousal neural plasticity is initiated and maximum learning occurs. Yet if stress is too high, it may result in intense fear and the inability to act.

Attention is a driver of planning, and planning helps clarify and solidify intention. See Figure 9-2. Planning uses patterns from the past to predict the future, and intention is all about the future.

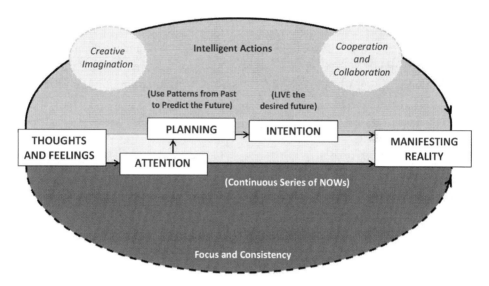

Figure 9-2. Attention drives planning, and planning helps clarify intention.

As early as the hunter-gatherer, we see the beginnings of structure and dedicated efforts to meet objectives through intention, planned action, and individual roles. Intention is the source with which we are doing something, the act or instance of mentally and emotionally setting a specific course of action or result, a determination to act in some specific way. Consciousness itself can be described as the "energized pool of intent from which all human experience springs".[403]

Searle believes that people have *mental states*, some conscious and some unconscious, which are intrinsically intentional. From this viewpoint, these are *subjective* states that are biologically based, that is, both caused by the operation of the brain and realized in the structure of the brain. Thus, intentionality is not a description of action, rather it is in the *structure of action*. We look to Searle's theory of intentionality for a baseline definition: "Intentionality is the property of many mental states and events by which they are directed at or about or of objects and states of affairs in the world".[404]

Thus, if you set an intention, it is an intention to do something. However, states such as those represented by beliefs, fears, hopes, and desires insinuate intention, and they are about something. The relationship of intent and action has two schools of thought. The ideomotor model of human actions contends that human intentions are the starting point of the actions associated with those intention.[405] Conversely, the sensory-motor model of human actions identifies sensory stimulation as the origination of actions.

In the organizational setting related to planning, we defer to the concept of *deliberate intention*, that is, choice at the conscious level which, once direction is set, is supported at the unconscious level as we act on that intent. Attention and intention are interrelated, and both are necessary to balance current priorities with future opportunities. Your thoughts and actions gravitate toward what you pay attention to; and what you intend requires your attention, and both can be the result of conscious choice.

Synthesis

Synthesis – the human ability to knit together information from disparate sources into a coherent whole – is an important human capability, both in the past and as humanity shifts into an unknown future. It could arguably be said that synthesis is a necessary skill for living. Nobel prize-winning physicist Murray Gell-Mann believes that the mind most at a premium in the 21st century is the mind that can synthesize well.[406] Gardner agrees. As he contends:

> *The ability to knit together information from disparate sources into a coherent whole is vital today. The amount of accumulated knowledge is reportedly doubling every two or three years (wisdom presumably accrues more slowly!), sources of information are vast and disparate, and individuals crave coherence and integration.[407]*

There are literally thousands – and probably more – approaches to synthesis. While certainly some level of synthesis skills are innate, early development and expansion of this skill set comes with doing book reviews, identifying plots, describing characters, linking character traits and actions to the purpose you think the author is trying to convey, and so on, looking for relationships, solving word problems, identifying themes, considering cause and effect, and exploring structure and message. During research studies, to interpret meaning in qualitative approaches, researchers search for themes and descriptions, often winnowing through large amounts of data for what is most important to their research. Experts in many fields "chunk" ideas and concepts, creating understanding through the development of significant patterns useful for solving problems and anticipating future behavior within their area of focus.

For example, a study of chess players showed that master players—or experts—examined the chessboard patterns over and over again, studying them, looking at nuances, trying small changes to perturb the outcome (sense and response), generally "playing with" and studying these *patterns*.[408] In other words, they used long-term working memory, pattern recognition and chunking rather than logic as a means of understanding and decision-making. See the tool in Section IV on "Pattern Thinking".

An important insight is the recognition that *when facing complex problems which do not allow reasoning or cause and effect analysis because of their complexity, the solution will most likely lie in synthesis*, studying patterns and chunking those patterns—organizing at several levels—to enable a tacit capacity to anticipate and develop solutions. This was demonstrated in the movie *A Beautiful Mind* staring Russell Crowe as a brilliant mathematician on the brink of international acclaim who becomes entangled in a mysterious conspiracy.

In today's global world where we have recognized the power of social interaction, synthesis is taking on an expanded meaning to include bringing people together to share and integrate their thoughts, honoring individuation as value to collective collaboration. No doubt several new treatments of this human capability will appear in books over the next few years.

Full Spectrum Frames of Reference

To gain a full perspective of any strategy, initiative, issues, or opportunities, it is necessary to look through different points of reference, through a variety of lenses. This is the role of **Knowledge Capacities**, which are sets of ideas and ways of acting that are more general in nature than competencies, more core to a way of thinking and being, that change our reference points and provide different ways for us to perceive and operate in the world around us. An in-depth discussion of Knowledge Capacities along with examples are provided in Chapter 16.

For example, *Shifting Frames of Reference* as a Knowledge Capacity – which is introduced in detail in Chapter 16 – is the ability to see/perceive situations and their context through different lenses; for example, understanding a military organization from the viewpoints of its officers, enlisted, citizen soldiers, and civilian white-and-blue-collar workers. The ability to shift frames of reference is enhanced by a diversity of experiences available to networked and interactive knowledge workers. Individuals who are subjected to a wide range of ideas and perspectives through social media are going to be much more attuned to difference, while at the same time becoming involved through dialogue.

This participation with lots of people and interaction with differences helps develop a healthy self-image, and comfortable connections with different situations and people, which builds a feeling of "capability." Through these interactions, knowledge workers are actively doing things which in and of themselves demonstrate their capability of interacting with the world. Through this broad set of reference experiences individuals can identify those disciplines or dimensions which they are excited about and capable and competent to develop and grow from, resulting in better decisions and choices that match their personal needs. Shifting frames of reference from individual perspectives to the perspective of teams, systems, and organizations is essential to develop multi-perspectives and understand complex organizations in support of effective decision-making.

CHAPTER 10
PREPARE

REVISIT VALUES (219) ... SET OBJECTIVES (224) ... CONNECT THE DOTS (224) ... Knowledge Mapping (225) ... Knowledge Audit (226) ... Knowledge Voids (229) ... Knowledge Flows (232) ... Social Network Analysis (234) ... Interweaving Strategies (234) ... PROVIDE A MEANING FRAMEWORK (235) ... Artificial Intelligence and Meaningful Work (236) ... BUILD THE FOUNDATION (238) ... Taxonomy and Ontology (238) ... GROW A KNOWLEDGE NETWORK (239) ... Relationship Network Management (240) ... Customer Intimacy (241) ... BECOME A CHANGE AGENT (242) ... TRANSITIONING FROM PREPARING TO IMPLEMENTING (245) ... Releasing the Old Culture (246) ... Social Networking (246) ... Training and Learning (247) ... *Reflective Listening and Otherness (247) ... Humility (249) ... Presencing (252)*

After completion of the planning stage of a knowledge strategy or initiative, attention should be focused on preparing for implementation. Although a necessary first step, a plan cannot succeed just because someone orders it to be done (is that phrase beginning to sound familiar?) Knowledge is tied to taking effective action. Careful consideration needs to be given to the current state of the organization or team, its culture, workload, competencies, and outside demands on its time. It is also useful to get key workers engaged early so that the purpose, nature and value of the project is made visible in a way that gives the organization time to digest and understand its goals and impacts.

REVISIT VALUES

Although the value of knowledge is in its application, with knowledge comes responsibility. When preparing to implement a knowledge strategy, it is a good idea to revisit the organization's values and ensure that these values are understood and attended to throughout the organization. Indeed, organizational values are an expression of the philosophy of the firm and serve to unify the workforce and speak to the customers.

As a noun, values have two dimensions (1) that which is highly regarded, and (2) that which is perceived as worthy or desirable. As with all knowledge, values are relative, that is, context-sensitive and situation-dependent.[409] Thus, values can be considered as a preference, that is, "A value can be described as a preference, multiplied by its priority".[410] Values provide guidelines around what is important and not important and how to get things done to meet performance objectives and scope within the environment. Shared values means that the personal values of knowledge workers and leaders are congruent with each other and within their organization's values. This is foundational to a coherent organization. Shared values provide a common context for understanding and interpreting the rapid proliferation of information from the environment and using that information to make quality decisions and take effective action. Beyond representing the heart, mind, and soul of the organization, they have an impact on what the firm envisions. As the values encourage performance to excel, they provide visibility of what the firm strives to achieve. From that vantage point, there is a tendency, an inclination, to consider: What else are we capable of creating?

Consistent with Knowledge (Informing) and Knowledge (Proceeding) (see Chapter 4), there is both an *information* (or content) part of values, and a *process* or *action* part of values, that is, Values (Informing) and Values (Proceeding). Values (Informing) relates to that which is highly regarded, perceived as worthy or desirable, and Values (Proceeding) is the way values are put together and acted upon in a specific situation or context.

Values begin as principles, a rule or standard considered good behavior.[411] As these principles are repeatedly expressed (acted upon) by an individual or across an organization, they become embedded behaviors, both considered the norm and expected. For example, the principles of freedom, equality, human dignity, tolerance, and the celebration of diversity have a long and storied history in the United States.[412] Although today these are recognized as values core to a democratic approach, Knowledge (Informing), there is still disagreement among the political infrastructure when translating them into action, Knowledge (Proceeding). Knowledge (Informing) appears to be the higher-order pattern, that is, less susceptible to change.

Values are the major determinant of what an organization holds to *be* of value.[413] Everything that is important to the organization – mission, purpose, vision – fall within the organization's cone of values, whether authentic and expressed or emerging as a form of culture. See Figure 10-1.

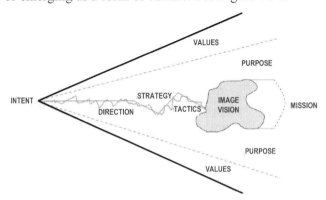

Figure 10-1: Values shape the organizational purpose, vision, mission, strategy, goals, tactics, and future[414].

When these values are understood, there is a framework from which to value direction, strategy, and tactics as well as new ideas. As Sullivan says, "Once the firm's values are known, it becomes possible to know how a firm should value an item",[415] or action.

Core values, what is actually and authentically believed and valued, provide one frame of reference for looking at organizational values. They are considered Values (Informing), and may be deeply embedded over time, that is, considered deep knowledge. What is core is fundamental, overarching or underlying all other values. They may be so deeply held that they will seldom, if ever, be changed or compromised.[416] Thus, the core values of an organization – closely related to an organization's identity – are that set of values that the organization upholds above others, and provide the roots of a strong value set. As Bennet and Bennet state:

Since values are central to our mental models, behaviors, and understanding of any situation, it is imperative that the organization has a strong value set that is understood and internalized by its employees. This ensures consistency of decisions, helps build a strong identity and culture, presents a positive image to the rest of the world, and directly impacts the everyday actions of knowledge workers.[417]

The source of core values may stem from an existing set of standards acknowledged by a group as authoritative such as the Bible, Koran, or U.S. Constitution. For example, the Chairman of the R.W. Beckett Corporation, one of the world's leading manufacturers of heating systems, and his senior leadership team identified three core values based on biblical roots: integrity, excellence, and a profound respect for the individual.[418]

Another frame of reference for exploring organizational values is as a way of perceiving, thinking and acting which pragmatically responds to the changing environment. These are Values (Proceeding), *operational rather than fundamental*, and most likely at the surface or shallow level, but still consistent with the individual's or organization's core values held at the deep level. From an organizational viewpoint, operational values can be distinguished from fundamental values as those that change along with new ideas.

When most people talk about values, they mean the big immutable ones such as honesty and integrity. But there are many other values that leaders not only can but should periodically update and change. These are "operational values," the ones that relate directly to an organization's business or its marketplace ... So when the marketplace changes, they develop new values along with new ideas.[419]

While fundamental and operational values may both be based on learning processes repeated over time which become embedded in the mind/brain, fundamental values are held at a deeper level, thereby rendering them less context-sensitive and situation-dependent. While core values of an organization often come from the fundamental values of the owners or leaders, fundamental values tend to be learned patterns stemming from deeply engrained learning during the formative developmental process of the individual, similar experiences repeated over and over again, or emerging through a highly emotionally charged transformative experience. For example, founders of companies who have strong religious beliefs frequently have personal spiritual values which undergird the fundamental organizational values they select. The values of ServiceMaster Industries which derive from the religious beliefs of the founder are: *To honor God in all we do; To help people develop; To pursue excellence; and To grow profitably.*

ServiceMaster defines the first two values *as end values,* and the second two as *means values.* The underlying belief is that by serving the customer with excellence and growing profitably, people will become more capable people and God will be honored. "It is not just what we are doing, but what we are *becoming* in the process that gives us our distinct value and is uniquely human."[420] In our model, the first two are clearly Values (Informing), and when the second two are perceived as the process to achieve the first two, they would be considered Values (Proceeding). In this respect, the second two values (more operational in nature) may be considered a subset of the first two values (more fundamental in nature).

Aligning values across the organization enables knowledge workers, individually and in teams, to solve problems, make decisions, and take actions which drive accomplishment of the mission, strategy, and goals of the organization in an integrated and coordinated way, while at the same time being responsive to change. "Shared values are the internal compasses that enable people to act both independently and interdependently."[421] See the Strategic Alignment tool in Section IV.

The knowledge worker's personal values, *which are also likely to represent generational values,* also exercise tremendous influence over his/her decisions regarding how to solve a problem and take the best action in a situation. To the extent that these values are consistent with organizational values, the knowledge worker is internally motivated to act in accordance with them. When there is an inconsistency, actions may undermine organization values and create inefficiencies by making decisions which are at cross purposes with the organization.

To empower knowledge workers and increase their capability and capacity to take effective action, part of the leader's role is to select and position operational values that are both consistent with the organization's core values and consistent with knowledge worker personal/generational values. For example, a potential checklist for leaders might include:

- Align organizational values with your personal values.

- Determine those values that are fundament to you and core to the organization.

- Define organization purpose, vision, mission, strategy, and goals based on core values.

- Clearly, consistently, and repeatedly communicate these core values in words and actions.

- Decide whether to deliberately choose operational values or let them evolve, based on shared learning, validation and consensus of what works and doesn't work.

- Decide whether or not to prioritize values and whether to differentiate 'means' and 'ends' values.

- Build the values into the organization infrastructure and policies including the compensation and evaluation system, recruiting, training and development, and the decision-making process.

- Ensure that organization values and the personal values of knowledge workers are congruent.

There must also be alignment of espoused values and personal values. When the espoused values of leaders are not aligned with their personal values and how they make decisions and act, the leaders undermine their credibility as well as the capacity and capability of knowledge workers to make the right decisions and take effective actions, particularly in a complex and uncertain environment where decisions must be made at the point of action.

There are many studies that demonstrate the benefit of aligned values to organizational success. For example, Ulrich and Lake posit that building organization capability for competitive advantage in a complex and uncertain environment can only occur as a result of a *shared mindset*. "If shared mindsets exist, the employees within an organization and the stakeholders outside it experience strategic unity ..."[422] While acknowledging the many studies confirming that values are critical for success, *specific values* were not found to be critical in fostering an adaptive, high-performance, innovative culture. As Collins and Porras confirm,

Although certain themes show up in a number of visionary companies (such as contribution, integrity, respect for the individual employee, service to the customer, being on the creative, or cutting edge, or responsibility to the community), no single item shows up consistently across all the visionary companies.[423]

The Value Infusion Methodology, which is a tool in Section IV, uses stories captured from senior leaders in the organization and storytelling to infuse organizational values throughout the organization.

SET OBJECTIVES

The project requirements must be made explicit for all personnel involved in the project. Project objectives are often defined in terms of being SMART: Specific, Measurable, Attainable, Realistic (and Relevant) and Time-based. While this approach works well for complicated systems such as building information systems or developing knowledge desk guides – an information resource specifically tied to job activity – parts of SMART may have to be modified in a knowledge project where the desired outcome is an emergent phenomenon of a large complex system (a community or team). See Chapter 19 on systems and complexity thinking.

Closely linked to setting objectives are setting targets and developing milestones. **Setting targets** creates direction and opportunities for high performance. These targets are sometimes referred to as "stretch" goals. They are challenging, but not so challenging that they are viewed as non-achievable. **Developing milestones** helps evaluate performance by comparing planned results at a point in time to actual results. Milestones are usually significant events in the project, such as completion of on-time deliverables or successful completion of phases of the project. Milestone deviations should be monitored and carefully managed throughout the life of the project. For example, there is little point of being informed of a major cost overrun at the end of a project, or of ignoring a counter intuitive result that creates unintended and harmful consequences to the project outcome. While knowledge projects are usually aimed at long-term results and may be difficult to evaluate in the short-term, activity toward the anticipated outcome and emergent indicators can be reviewed and assessed.

CONNECT THE DOTS

Any forward movement requires both a starting point and a direction in which to move. A good way to understand the knowledge currently available in the organization is through conducting a knowledge audit and creating a knowledge map. Knowledge mapping is a fundamental step in any knowledge management initiative and the first step in a knowledge audit.

Knowledge Mapping

There are many approaches to knowledge mapping, which is the process of locating important knowledge within the organization and then publishing a list or picture that shows users where to find that knowledge, connecting people to information and data repositories (whether in hard copy or virtual format), and serving as an inventory of what knowledge exists in the organization and where it may be found. The term "knowledge directories" has also been used to describe knowledge maps that serve the purpose of showing users where to obtain knowledge or expertise on specific subject matter. These directories may refer to people with expertise (an Expertise Locator), documentation libraries, process descriptions, suppliers, firm policies, methodologies, and so on.

Zack focuses on *strategic knowledge mapping*. This approach maps the firm's knowledge along two dimensions: the degree to which it supports the firm's strategy, and its quality relative to competing firms.[424] There are three focus areas in strategic knowledge mapping:

1. What the organization needs to know to execute its strategy.

2. What the organization does know.

3. What the organization's partners (or competitors) know.

In responding to each area, knowledge can be classified according to whether it is core, advanced, or innovative. Core knowledge represents the basic knowledge required to operate in the industry. Advanced knowledge differentiates a firm, enabling it to compete in a changing world and remain viable. Innovative knowledge is unique and enables a firm to significantly differentiate itself as a knowledge leader, with the potential for changing the industry in fundamental ways.

Once an organization has decided on the strategic direction for its future, it can identify the knowledge required to reach that goal. This assessment can then be compared to the organization's knowledge map to see where the gaps arise. Benchmarking, benchlearning, and mapping other organization's knowledge (who do similar work) can also provide key insights into filling those gaps as well as the feasibility and cost effectiveness of obtaining required or desired knowledge. Strategic knowledge mapping enables an organization to identify and act upon its knowledge strengths, weaknesses, opportunities, and threats (similar to a typical SWOT analysis).

As an example of knowledge mapping, Microsoft used the following process to improve the matching of employees to jobs and work teams:

1. Develop the structure of knowledge competency types/levels;

2. Define the knowledge required for particular jobs;

3. Rate employee performance in particular jobs by knowledge competencies;

4. Implement knowledge competencies in an online system; and

5. Link the knowledge model to training programs.

It is important to recognize that a knowledge map represents a point in time. Knowledge mapping is an ongoing quest within an organization (including its supply chain and customers) to help (1) discover the location, ownership, value and use of knowledge artifacts (information that has helped create knowledge in the past); (2) learn the roles and expertise of people; (3) identify constraints to the flow of knowledge; and (4) highlight opportunities to leverage existing knowledge.

Knowledge Audit

The knowledge audit is a first and critical step prior to launching any knowledge strategy in an organization.[425] It is critical to understand what an organization "knows", what knowledge an organization needs, and to strategically choose how to handle any identified gap. Further, since intellectual capital is within the heads of employees, it is critical to know exactly where that knowledge resides, who are the experts in domains of knowledge critical to the organization, and how the knowledge moves from where it resides to where it is needed.

Thus, a knowledge audit moves beyond identifying and mapping information and knowledge sources (location, access, availability, currency, validity, context) to evaluating the state of an organization's technology, how well the organization's processes support knowledge sharing, how knowledge flows through the organization, and the work styles, culture, and morale of the people within the organization. The best audits are highly context-sensitive and situation-dependent to the organization, capturing not only important key knowledge but *why* it is important.

As introduced above, the knowledge audit begins with knowledge mapping. This information is then used to design a KM system. For example, information that is used by a large number of employees would become part of a web-based application widely available to multiple employees. As a second example, communities of practice might be implemented to help mitigate identified knowledge gaps within a specific area or practice, mobilizing knowledge from one source of expertise in the organization to a larger team of employees who can use that knowledge to improve efficiency and effectiveness.

The Federal Transit Administration (FTA) is one of ten model administrations within the U.S. Department of Transportation and is tasked with administering federal fundings to support locally planned, constructed, and operated public transportation systems throughout the country. These systems include buses, subways, light rail, commuter rail, streetcars, monorail, passenger ferry boats, inclined railways, and people movers. For FTA, KM is a systematic means of capturing, organizing, retrieving, sharing and generating organizational knowledge. For FTA – an organization committed to stop reinventing the wheel – their focus is on PEOPLE and PROCESSES by which those people do their work, with technology as an enabler. To develop a knowledge strategy, FTA began with the organizational purpose, citing the founding documents (laws, charter, etc.), then completed a knowledge audit to identify knowledge strengths and needs, frankly stating what was good and could be improved, speaking in the business terms of the organization. Hand-in-hand with the vision, mission, goals, and objectives, a marketing plan was developed. As FTA states, "Yes—you do have to have one!" A basic is knowing the elevator pitch(es) and being ready to adapt it(them) depending on the audience. A lesson learned is to define knowledge strategies in terms that resonate with the organizational jargon and use words that can be understood by your husband, wife, significant other, mom, or dad. FTA's marketing plan encourages the telling of stories. While today their transit knowledge portal offering extensive knowledge resources for employees and stakeholders alike has become an integral part of the organization, they effectively continue the next steps expressed at the beginning of their journey: "Market, market, market … communicate, update, celebrate."

Tiwana offers a six-step process for the multidisciplinary group of people who make up the audit team to document knowledge assets.[426]

1. *Define the goals*. This includes the targeting of specific goals or knowledge and identifying any constraints.

2. *Determine the ideal*. It is not necessary for this to be extremely detailed.

3. *Select the method to use*. Use a method with which your organization is comfortable. For example, a virtual survey process is a good starting point for a geographically dispersed organization, but not effective for groups of employees who do not regularly use computers.

4. *Perform the audit and document assets*. This becomes an internal benchmarking product that can later be used to evaluate the effectiveness of knowledge management initiatives. It also serves as the source for developing a knowledge map for use across the organization.

5. *Track knowledge growth over time*. As the ideal defined in (2) above changes, so too do knowledge needs of the organization. Periodic knowledge audits help identify the direction the organization is heading over time and provide an opportunity for strategic shifts.

6. *Determine your organization's strategic position within its technology framework*. The knowledge audit surfaces information that can populate

information systems, helping to clarify the directions in which knowledge management and information technology should and should not focus.

It is critical to have a consistent framework to assess the knowledge assets that are discovered during the knowledge audit. While the knowledge discovery process selected in (3) and performed in (4) above often uses surveys and interviews, it may also include focus groups or Delphi studies, formal and informal reports, and exploration of databases, employee skills, the sharing of best practices, and core competencies which can provide indicators of knowledge robustness.

What is learned from the knowledge audit can now be compared to what knowledge is needed to identify knowledge gaps. These gaps could be related to current knowledge, or potential gaps as identified employees move toward retirement or as demands of the environment change.

While MITRE Corporation developed an early prototype of a knowledge system in 1994, it was near the turn of the century before they performed a knowledge audit, primarily to measure the Return on Investment (ROI) of the system and determine if changes were needed to better meet the needs of employees, and therefore customers. One of the soft benefits measured by the knowledge audit was the increase in their knowledge base. The MITRE Corporation is a private, not-for-profit organization chartered to work in the public interest partnering with the government in systems engineering and advanced technology to address issues of critical national importance. MITRE serves as the government's architect for information advantage, a trusted agent to ensure the information superiority of their sponsors. This role encompasses a wide-ranging set of responsibilities, including translating needs into requirements, defining capabilities sufficiently to enable contractor development, conducting evaluations and cost/capability tradeoffs, and prioritizing requirements. From these early beginnings, MITRE has developed platforms which are sets of integrated technologies, domain knowledge, and expertise combined to rapidly build impactful strategies.

Today their knowledge program is embedded throughout the organization. For example, the 2018 Federal CISCO Summit noted the lack of a specialized skill mix to interpret cyber-knowledge, combined knowledge of big data analytics/business intelligence, which became a focus area for MITRE. In late 2022, the Crown Jewels Analysis for Industrial Control Systems became a reality. This process provides "a repeatable approach to capturing knowledge from organizational subject matter experts, documenting known dependencies, and prioritizing assets based on their criticality to mission".[427] Also in 2018, MITRE proposed a logic model for managing open innovation competitions which can serve as a guide for planning, implementation and evaluation of prize competitions or challenges. Open Innovation competitions – event intermediation (as described below) – are a way to engage with external sources of knowledge such as individual entrepreneurs, students, experts, small firms, etc.

A recent book, *Principles of Knowledge Auditing: Foundations for KM Implementation* by Patrick Lambe, integrates theory and practice to provide a pragmatic approach for knowledge auditing. This comprehensive treatment covering the role and nature of knowledge audits looks through the lens of information, communications, and knowledge management, identifying ambiguities as well as providing guiding principles for practitioners. A successful knowledge audit approach developed by WB Lee with The Hong Kong Polytechnic University is included as a tool in Section IV.

Knowledge Voids

A knowledge void, or knowledge gap, is an identified area where little or nothing is known. Because of their direct link, the concept of knowledge voids is largely based on the absence of related data and information in an organization. As a general approach, once identified (perhaps through the knowledge audit process), a first step is to have knowledge workers who are content creators work with search engines to fill those voids with quality content, which works well for surface knowledge needs and, with intelligent searching and integrating skills, may suffice for shallow knowledge needs. However, when deep knowledge is required, it is necessary to seek out an expert in that knowledge domain.

There are a number of popular databases and platforms that can help identify knowledge gaps and voids. For example, one widely used database is Google's Knowledge Graph, a structured database that connects different entities and concepts which can provide valuable insights into relationships among various topics and can be used to identify gaps in information. Other platforms and databases would include Wikipedia (a free only encyclopedia covering a wide range of topics), ResearchGate (primarily uploaded scientific research), Scopus (a bibliographic database covering a wide range of scientific disciplines), and Microsoft Academic (access to academic articles and papers). The latter example, Microsoft Academic, uses AI and machine learning techniques to identify entities, relationships, and trends across various disciplines.

That said, all knowledge voids (KVs) are not the same. The table below breaks KVs into 12 categories. For clarity of understanding, we have included a brief description and related remarks or examples.

Table 10-1. Taxonomy of Knowledge Voids. [Adapted from the congregated model developed by Col. Kenneth Parker Thompson.[428]]

Type (Category)	Description	Remarks or Examples
Complexity Driven KVs	Information that is difficult to understand because of its esoteric nature outside of one's area of specialization.	Technical data, legal or policy details, international or economic aspects of multifaceted or multidisciplinary subjects that take years to learn.
Politically Motivated KVs	Knowledge is available but it is untapped or unused because of other agenda-driven priorities.	Policies directed toward specific action to optimize a particular political or policy agenda without pressure from constituency. This happens frequently with the current environment and worldwide and countrywide political agendas.
Interest Driven KVs	Knowledge deficiencies caused by focusing on one knowledge domain at the expense of other domains. Also includes KVs due to lack of interest.	National security or foreign policy community focused on security or foreign policy threats versus economic or competitiveness aspects. Includes information domains of no personal or professional interest. Can also be caused by organizational missions focused on specific knowledge domains to the exclusion of other domains.
Information Glut KVs	An overabundance of data and information on a specific topic or in a specific field such that it is impossible to learn it all or even to determine what part of the knowledge spectrum is important.	Multidimensionality of organizational or international issues – can be related to technical, legal, economic or policy issues. Overwhelming amount of data and information on a specific subject of interest. Extremely broad and complex knowledge areas or issues.
Low Competency KVs	Lack of mental capacity, experience, or specialized training to acquire a specific knowledge set.	"Over one's head." Personnel turnover resulting in placement of a new hire at the bottom front end of the learning curve in a complex, high-technology or deep knowledge area.

Restricted/ Unavailable Info KVs	Information only accessible to designated, authorized individuals, or information not readily available in libraries, on the Internet, or via other sources.	Unavailable information due to classification. USG: Restricted/classified info. Industry: Proprietary information. Foreign: Inaccessible or unavailable information in English, even via the Internet.
Avoidance/ Convenience/ Deliberate KVs	Refusal to accept or assimilate new information or knowledge because it "clutters my brain", is perceived to be not useful, or conflicts with personal viewpoints.	Similar to politically driven KVs above. Fear of exposure to new knowledge because it might alter perspectives, opinions or beliefs. Knowledge avoided or ignored since one doesn't want change. Different from Cognitive Rigidity KVs (which is where avoidance isn't sought but if evidence or fact is presented, it is rejected outright).
Culturally Induced KVs	A "dumbing down". Societal emphasis on divergent pursuits. Death among general populace of SME competence.	Entertainment; the glamorization of sports; various TV shows and movies, magazines, novels, or other knowledge products with minimal content. Educational programs focused on non-technical curriculum, with no opportunities for marginalized sectors of the population to participate in engineering or science education.
Priority Driven KVs	Time deficit; too busy focusing on other interests or organizational mission.	Acknowledging the need for new knowledge without having the time to do so. Demanding work schedules or knowledge acquisition workloads. Attending educational classes in another field.
Cognitive Rigidity KVs	Absolute refusal to learn, acquire, or assimilate new knowledge that would threaten preconceived notions and beliefs.	Closed mindedness. "I disagree no matter how many facts or persuasive arguments." Symptoms are statements like "It doesn't matter what you say." Or "It won't change my mind!"

Language Barrier KVs	Foreign language information needing translation.	Existing laws, regulations, policies, marketing plans, technical data, etc. are not readable due to being in a foreign language.
Combination KVs	KVs which combine one or more other categorical KVs, which is the most often occurrence.	Due to multiple causative factors, these are the most difficult KVs to eliminate.

Low Competency KVs, Avoidance/Convenience/Deliberate KVs, and Cognitive Rigidity KVs can be a direct result of knowledge ignorance and anti-intellectualism. Knowledge ignorance is the lack of information or knowledge, a condition of being uneducated or uninformed. Ignorance is the lack of a tool – knowledge – which uses the natural potential offered by the human mind. While not necessarily historically true, for a healthy individual in an information-rich and connected global world, existing in a culture of connection, ignorance is a choice. (See the discussion on Knowledge Ignorance & Anti-Intellectualism in Chapter 8.)

When discussing anti-intellectualism earlier, we introduced Matthew Arnold, who saw culture as having a purging effect on the human mind, and saying that without it the world would inevitably belong to the Philistines, with the term philistinism referring to anti-intellectualism, a social attitude that undervalues intellect. There is no question that in today's world, the Philistines are still in our midst – with many holding positions of power at the very core of our organizations. In many organizations, knowledge workers have an upfront view of sectarianism, Philistinism and avariciousness, and the resulting diminished integrity coupled to the lowering of consciousness. However, there *is* hope in Arnold's assertion that there is a purging effect of culture on the human mind, and if this is so, it is the culture of connection, the reblooming of the knowledge movement with the refocus on creativity and innovation, that is moving us into a new and better world. In terms of organizational direction shifts, while uncertainty can punctuate knowledge voids in an organization, good communication and open knowledge flows can help mitigate this.

Knowledge Flows

Having needed information available is not enough. People have to know about it in order to use it. The flow of data, information, and knowledge across the organization enables effective decision-making and facilitates the connections and continuity that maintain mission unity and organizational coherence. Flow, moving across networks of systems and people, is the catalyst for creativity and innovation. Note that the flow of "knowledge" is in reality the flow of data and information with enough context and understanding built around the data and information – and the sensemaking capability developed within the user – such that the user can effectively re-create (and use) the desired knowledge.

The flow of data, information and knowledge is facilitated through teams and communities, and can be accelerated through event intermediation. Teams, small groups, task forces, etc. accomplish specific objectives while concomitantly sharing data, information, and knowledge with other people who may come from diverse parts of the organization. Communities of practice or interest, knowledge portals, and knowledge repositories also facilitate the sharing of information and knowledge. Managers are often unaware that the greatest benefit from a team's effort is the long-term payoff in future collaboration among team members. An organization that deliberately nurtures flows will factor this payoff into team formation and team member selection.

Event intermediation is not a new idea. All too often employees work and strive to create change with only slightly visible results. Then, when some event occurs which connects all this prior activity, the understanding of change value jumps to a new strata of recognition, and the entire plane of behavior shifts upward to a new starting point. This pattern recurs again and again throughout history. The organization can orchestrate such events, formally and informally, as both change and knowledge sharing become a way of life. (See Knowledge Sharing in Chapter 12.)

An example of event intermediation used in the DON is the knowledge fair. A "fair" is a gathering of people to display or trade produce or other goods, to parade or display animals, and often to enjoy associated (carnival) or (funfair) entertainment. They can also serve as important showcases. Such was the case with the DON. In support of an aggressive knowledge strategy, the first knowledge fair occurred in the late summer of 2000, an enterprise-wide event focused on knowledge sharing. Over seventy-five knowledge-focused projects representing Defense organizations around the world and owned by DON were exhibited. A key word here is "owned", that is, this was an "internal sales event" with a zero purchase price to share what had been and was being learned such that the receiver could learn and apply this knowledge.

The event was co-hosted by the Under Secretary of the Navy, the Vice Chief of Naval Operations, and the Assistant Commandant of the Marine Corps. Over 3,000 visitors created a continuous flow of energy throughout the day, with a groundswell of exchange and sharing. Senior leaders were captured on video talking about their specific organization's accomplishments in KM, and these videos along with videos related to all 75 knowledge projects – with detail sheets, contact points, and software included – were disseminated to DON commands around the world. The opening ceremony, briefings and demonstrations were attended by thousands of interested and enthusiastic people, with the only entry requirement a Department of Defense employee or contractor badge. During the course of the day, entertaining and educational events occurred. For example, to illustrate the difficulty of transferring tacit knowledge, a magician was engaged to teach several magic tricks. To help understand the potential (and issues) offered through eBusiness, a virtual bidding process was staged with Abe Lincoln and a well-known gangster among the participant bidders.

To facilitate sharing and learning, and support both individual and team successes, the first knowledge sharing awards were presented by the Under Secretary of the Navy to seven outstanding projects, with both the teams, their immediate supervisor, and the command leader attending. Awards were given for the leading knowledge portal concept, the outstanding knowledge expert system, and the outstanding collaborative knowledge sharing approach. A second set of knowledge sharing awards was presented in San Diego the following November at the DON's Connecting Technology (CT) Symposium. The rapidly increasing number of projects and programs recommended for these awards was indicative of the massive cultural change engendered by this budding knowledge movement. Event Intermediation is a tool in Section IV.

Social Network Analysis

A method for assessing the effective flow of information through communication and collaboration is social network analysis. Interviews and surveys are used to ask such questions as: From whom do you seek work-related information? Is this person accessible to you? Does this person respond in time to help resolve your problem? To whom do you give work-related information? From the answers to these and similar questions a map is created that connects people who receive information with people who provide the information. This process allows the organization to assess its ability to create and share knowledge through connections, and identifies areas to improve these abilities. For example, a map resulting from social network analysis identifies those who are central to the knowledge sharing process. Then the following questions need to be considered: Should this individual be rewarded for the important role they are playing as a connector **OR** is this individual hoarding information and bottlenecking knowledge sharing and creation? What happens if this individual leaves? There are several software programs supporting social network analysis.

Interweaving Strategies

Another process of connecting the dots is that of identifying strategies and initiatives underway or recently completed that are similar or related to the knowledge strategies and initiatives proposed. Because knowledge is at the core of determining what individuals and organizations do and how they do it – and because there are many committed people that are already moving in similar directions (no matter what expression they use to describe it, i.e., knowledge management, process mapping, improved communication), the organization can gain greater advantage by the linking and melding of related strategies and initiatives. **Leveraging is a goal of knowledge sharing.** The similarities and differences of various strategies and initiatives – and how they complement each other – should be identified to ensure optimum leveraging of all activities underway.

PROVIDE A MEANING FRAMEWORK

As organizations have bounced through financial crises, increasing climate calamities, wars, and a pandemic, people increasingly search for meaning and purpose in their lives, and their work and productivity play a large role in that search. And in that search, we begin to recognize that nothing is arbitrary. As LeShan forwards, "Everything has meaning and is charged with implications and power."[429]

"Meaningful work" is the individual perception that work has worth and significance, or a higher purpose.[430] As knowledge, the construction of meaning is relative, highly individualized and subjective, using our creative juices to move us toward the reality we desire. It is also an intimidating responsibility,[431] for WE are the determinants of meaning.

> *Events are events, and meanings are thoughts. Nothing has any meaning save the **meaning you give it**. And the meaning you give to things does not derive from any event, circumstance, conditions, or situation exterior to yourself. The Giving of Meaning is entirely an internal process. **Entirely**.*[432]

Let's dig a bit deeper. The amount of meaning in life is directly related to an individual's level of consciousness. Primary consciousness is the ability to construct a mental scene, but with limited semantic or symbolic capability and no true language. An incoming scene, say an image, is immediately (within fractions of a second) evaluated by the brain's value systems and, through the interaction of the memory system with its previous experiences and the incoming signal, *a meaning is associated with the perception.* We never just see some "thing". The mind automatically mixes the external scenes with our own history, feelings and goals (in an associative patterning process) to give it context and meaning. In other words, meaning is created out of external events and signals *complexed with internal resources.* The way this occurs in the information processing system that is the human body is presented in Chapter 13, "Knowledge: A Life Property Revealed by The Informational Model of Living Systems".

As can be seen in this short treatment, while meaning IS determined by the individual affected by that individual's experiences, values, beliefs, etc., it is also set up by the circumstances occurring in the environment. In a 2021 research study from Pew research,[433] which included 19,000 participants from 17 advanced economies, "occupation and career" was the second most important source of meaning, second only to "family and children". It would appear that organizations are strongly looked to in order to meet this growing need.

When an organization provides opportunities for meaningful work, they are not only supporting positive work outcomes,[434] but also facilitating human well-being and flourishing.[435] One approach which amplifies the meaning of work is mindfulness training. For example, in a study in Thailand, there were 248 participants who engaged in mindful meditation courses and a control group of 315 who did not. Significantly higher levels of work engagement and a greater sense of "work spirituality" were found in those who participated in the meditation courses.[436] Mindfulness is discussed in more detail under "Self-Transcendence" in Chapter 11.

In his 2023 book, *The Meaningful Leader*, de Sousa asks: What is it that people want from work? He then quotes Leo Rosten, humorist and screenwriter, who answers: "The purpose of life is not to be happy at all. It is to be useful, to be honorable. It is to be compassionate. It is to matter, to have it make some difference that you lived".[437] In Chapter 15, de Sousa explores "How Leaders Inspire Action through Meaningful Knowledge".

Artificial Intelligence and Meaningful Work

"Meaningful work" has been defined by the Office of Management and Budget as work that is "purposeful, well-planned and optimized for in-person collaboration", although clearly what that actually looks like is highly dependent on who is doing it. For example, for the National Agricultural Statistics Service (NASS) in the Department of Agriculture, that means a focused balance on organizational health and performance.[438] However, in 2018, the World Economic Forum forwarded that as AI moved into the workplace – taking over things historically requiring human intelligence such as reasoning, planning, problem-solving, and even learning from experience[439] – it will influence "how" work is experienced and the meaningfulness of that work.[440] Otherwise, our world of meaning is changing.

While technology advancements since the first industrial revolution have historically changed meaningful work opportunities by what is done and how work is done, Bankins and Formosa contend that AI's "unique features and uses also generate new and conflicting implications for meaningful work."[441] While some organizations are excited by AI's potential, others voice fear. Clearly, there is the potential of AI to both enhance and dimmish the meaningful work experience, which is highly dependent on the implementation choices made by organizations.[442]

To outline the nature and ethical importance of meaningful work, Bankins and Formosa explored the three paths of AI deployment: replacement, creating new forms of human work, and augmenting/ assisting workers across five dimensions, which combine the job characteristics model by Hackman and Oldham[443] and the more holistic model by Lips-Wiersman and Morris.[444] From this emerged the dimensions which they labeled: *task integrity* (the range of tasks an individual does), *skill cultivation and use* (ability to use a range of work skills), *task significance* (visibility of work benefits and contributions to others), *autonomy* (self-determination of work approaches and freedom from surveillance and monitoring), and *belongingness* (generating meaning through sense of unity with others).[445] Note the close association of these five dimensions with the democratic elements and characteristics synthesized from the what's and how's of early philosophers (see Chapter 1). For ethical implications the researchers drew on the AI4People ethical framework and, specifically, its five principles of beneficence, non-maleficence, autonomy, justice, and explicability.[446]

As a short summary, in terms of the beneficence principle, there were significant benefits from AI in terms of the amplification of worker skills so employees can undertake more complex tasks and use higher-order thinking and analysis skills. There was also a higher task significance and autonomy as potentially generating new connections with others which contribute to belongingness. In terms of the non-maleficence principles, two paths were identified that generate the greatest risk of harm: the replacement of some tasks, and what the researchers call 'minding the machine' work, fragmented work. In terms of the autonomy principle, dependent on how AI is deployed in an organization, autonomy could be supported with AI by freeing up workers for more valued tasks. In terms of the justice principle, the impact of AI on meaningful work was dependent on the distribution of the benefits and burdens of AI. However, there is already "evidence that such benefits are disproportionately allocated to already privileged workforces (i.e., higher-skilled and higher-paid workers)." While the 'minding the machine' path went to lower-paid and lower-skilled workers.[447]

In terms of the explicability principle, which includes transparency, where AI plays a role right alongside employees where they are both reliant on, and accountable for the system, it is critical that the chains of accountability are clear in order to support the meaningfulness of work. An overall finding of this research, as noted several times above, is that "the implications of its deployment are strongly driven by what work remains for humans, which is something that organizations can directly influence and decide."[448] It is strongly suggested that organizations bringing in or expanding current AI systems fully read this critical research study by Bankins and Formosa to help ensure successful use of these systems in terms of employee – and organizational – wellbeing and flourishing.

BUILD THE FOUNDATION

Whether residing on the Internet, an organizational Intranet, or in the Cloud, the document repository is the place where much of the information available to organization decision-makers resides. Since the flow of information is the life blood of the organization, it is vital to ensure an integrated, connected, well-organized, and easily searchable information system that supports access to information when it is needed. The Knowledge Base roadmap – a tool provided in Section IV – provides one framework for building the knowledge base in a specific area of knowledge (for a specific community).

Taxonomy and Ontology

Development of a taxonomy and ontology help ensure a common language and understanding across the organization while also supporting ease of access to needed information. The knowledge taxonomy is a structured set of names and descriptions agreed-upon by the organization. When there is a systematic process to collect, store, and share core organizational knowledge that knowledge can be managed and used as a valuable organizational asset to greatly improve productivity and effectiveness. It can be a large challenge to effectively organize large amounts of related but disjointed information and product an accurate, trustworthy, and accurate set of knowledge. Add to this the requirement for context, which means connecting information to how it has been effectively used in the past as knowledge.

The knowledge taxonomy is built on a knowledge ontology, a conceptual framework that expresses a classification schema. An ontology specifies primary concepts in a specific domain of knowledge, and the relationships among those concepts. Ontologies are highly context-sensitive and situation-dependent in terms of ensuring a single shared conceptual understanding across the organization, which can be described as a "unifying map" of concepts and relationships. An ontology can be represented graphically or as structured text, and can be either human-centric or machine readable.

A taxonomy is a classification scheme that is used to categorize sets of information. Within organizational domains of knowledge, this represents a vocabulary of terms that have been agreed-upon and used by employees working within that domain. Generally, they have a hierarchical structure, much like libraries. To classify a framework, there must be a defined framework. For example, the Standard Subject Identification Code (SSIC), which includes records management, is used by some public and private organizations. A second example is the Library of Congress Classification (LOCC) system which uses a general purpose approach, with major headings such as philosophy, psychology, religion, history, and fine arts. Other systems might be more focused on technical issues such as aviation, chemistry, and electrotechnology, dependent on the focus of the business at hand.

There are many texts available that provide in-depth information on developing ontologies and taxonomies. For example, in a paper supporting development of a taxonomy for the DON, Malafsky and Newman offered a five-step process for developing the taxonomy and ontology in parallel.[449]

1. *Define your scope*. The first question to ask is: What purpose will the combined ontology and taxonomy serve? Answering this question sets bounds on the effort, helps identify primary domains and perspectives, and identifies the specific business activities that will use the ontologies and taxonomies, linking them directly to the mission of the organization.

2. *Check for existing ontologies and taxonomies*. There are industry standards in play in many fields of work. Using these as applicable not only eliminates what may be an extensive development effort but provides a consistent language and interface.

3. *Identify important terms*. Start with identifying key terms for knowledge that support specific business activities of the organization. These can generally be found in corporate policy or operational instructions.

4. *Define the class hierarchy*. Working from the top-down and the bottom-up, identify the most important concepts first, then generalize and specialize them, bringing in the clusters of related concepts (subclass groupings) to place under higher-order concepts.

5. *Define class properties*. Properties refers to the types of information that distinguish one from the other. For example, intrinsic properties are what is essential to a thing, which would lose its identity when the property changes. Extrinsic properties are the things around each type of information. A part could be either physical or abstract, and a relationship would be among members of a class and with other items.

GROW A KNOWLEDGE NETWORK

The knowledge network is the weaving together of people, whether through teams, communities, knowledge neighborhoods, one-on-one relationships, or through the variety of approaches to virtual social networking. As an example, a network which was developed to address environmental and economic justice issues in the U.S. is the Indigenous Environment Network (IEN). IEN's activities include building the capacity of Indigenous communities and tribal governments to develop mechanisms that protect sacred sites, land, water, air, natural resources, health of both the people and all living things, and to build economically sustainable communities. Their activities are accomplished by maintaining an informational clearinghouse, sharing of information, organizing campaigns, direct actions and public awareness, and building the capacity of community and tribes. IEN convenes local, regional, and national meetings on environmental and economic justice issues, and provides support, resources and referral to Indigenous communities and youth throughout North America. They have also built a viable network of community affiliates and partners, both indigenous and non-indigenous, to facilitate the protection and rebuilding of environmental and cultural resources worldwide.

A model to consider is collaborative entanglement, where individuals and groups continuously interact, create or identify new information and knowledge from incoming information. These interactions include emotions, dialogue, logic and even debate. An example is the innovation network set up by the Tata Power Company Limited in India, who, in addition to hosting events and a myriad of systems connecting internal teams, encourages innovators and idea generators to reach out to other technology companies, research organizations, and academic institutions "to synergize with them and develop solutions complementing their competencies with long-term partnerships."[450]

The active relationship networks that crisscross organizations increase awareness, provide redundancies, and affect organizational responsiveness in terms of agility and flexibility. An organization can react faster when information around key areas of concern is flowing freely. An active relationship network also provides a monitoring and scanning system for problems and opportunities. It is easy to see how important everyday conversations can become to both individuals and their organizations. The good news is that *each individual manages their own relationship network* of people. If an individual's networking is effective—based on interdependency, trust, a common framework, openness, the flow of information and knowledge, and equitability—that individual's decisions will be more effective.

Relationship Network Management

RNM, which focused on fully using and increasing the social capital of an organization, emerged in the U.S. Department of the Navy at the turn of the century. The relationship network is a matrix of people that consists of the sum of a individuals' relationships – whose individuals with whom the individual interacts, or has interacted with in the past, and with whom there is a connection or significant association which will continue into the future. This matrix is both horizontal, in terms of colleagues and peers, and vertical, in terms of bosses and mentors and employees and mentees. RNM occurs when we recognize the potential of these relationships and *consciously and intelligently engage them* to share information and knowledge and to learn, creating and sustaining a conscious give and take movement, or flow, across our personal and professional relationship network.

Our everyday relationships are important. It is impossible for a single individual to know everything. While our knowledge systems provide better information in terms of quality and currency, it is difficult to capture the context of this information without interjecting the human factor. In short, information (and information technology) is necessary but not sufficient to create knowledge.

Further, conversations we have had in the past are often stored in the unconscious, especially if this is a topic of interest or connected to strong emotion, and emerge later when it is triggered by a related thought or conversation. As an example, a conversation you may have had last year with a domain expert but had forgotten may come to mind when a related emergency in your organization occurs. You may not remember how you acquired the knowledge, but you have a sense of "knowing" and may even remember the why along with the what. This is the value of exposing yourself to conversations and presentations related to your work area of focus and interest.

The basic tenets of RNM are interdependency, trust, common framework, openness, flow and equitability. None of these can be controlled or ordered to happen, but arise from the sequence of interactions among the individuals involved and depend upon each person's perception and feelings about the other. Good relationships emerge from a history of interactions, and as such they must be nurtured and protected to be sustained.

The good news is that your relationship network can be managed by you. Recognizing the power of knowledge flows, RNM – the subject of Chapter 14 in Section III – is an empowering approach that makes sense for every organization.

Customer Intimacy

This is not new, but well worth a short discussion. Customer intimacy goes beyond customer service and satisfaction. While the customer-centric focus is on understanding the customer such that the customer's needs are fully met – including designing or customizing products and services to meet those needs – customer intimacy goes even further. As the word "intimacy" suggests, there is a condition of being personal and private in a trusting relationship. Existing in a co-evolving state, there is an element of empathy that emerges which supports the co-creation of innovative solutions to even perhaps recognized but unvoiced customer wants and needs.

Senivongse uses the approach of Jobs-to-be-Done coupled with Design Thinking to support customer intimacy. Jobs-to-be-Done identifies new market opportunities through focusing on underserved or unmet customer demands considered through functional, emotional, and social dimensions. "By considering all of these dimensions of consumer wants, businesses can develop goods and services that give a more holistic answer to the Jobs-to-be-Done, resulting in increased customer satisfaction and loyalty."[451]

This process can begin with a "journey map", getting inside the mind of your customer from the perspective of what they are attempting to do. Creative thinkers use ideation, intuition and judgment to surface ideas, and brainstorming to reach consensus. Ideation surfaces possibilities, which is the starting point for the process. See the discussion of Design Thinking in Chapter 8.

BECOME A CHANGE AGENT

Everyone working in their organization to improve the way it achieves its mission can be considered – and is – a change agent. Since knowledge and knowledge sharing is at the core of every individual's contribution to the mission of the organization, implementation of a knowledge strategy or initiative is no exception. Further, *an individual or organization cannot change in a vacuum*. This means that as changes occurs within an organization, other parts of the organization and, indeed, the many partners who are organizational stakeholders need to be changing as well. This is why transparency, participation, and collaboration are so important to any change effort. This also means that as the environment continues to change and the state-of-the-art changes, or another part of the organization or an external organization discovers a better way of doing things, *you and your organization must be willing to consider, evaluate, and, as appropriate, adapt and embrace these changes*. See the discussion of readiness in the first half of Chapter 9.

While the easiest approach might be to order change to occur – and this has certainly been tried in many organizations in the past – this does not work for long if at all. In order for organizations to change, people must change themselves. Change comes from within. For most people to willingly change, they must move through the following cognitive processes which can be considered impact factors:[452] Awareness (aware of the needed action)

- Understanding (understand its meaning and the expected result)
- Believing (believe that the action is real and will work)
- Feeling good (feel good about taking the action)
- Ownership (feel a personal responsibility for taking action)
- Empowerment (feel they have the knowledge, freedom, and courage to take action)
- Impact (know that taking this action will make a difference)

While this process sounds difficult (and often it is), it can also occur within an instant. For example, if you are a firefighter and there is a shift in wind, there is no doubt you will move through this process in seconds and immediately take action.

From the individual perspective, the impact factors can be looked at as moving through objective, relational, subjective and experiential phases, with each phase related to the specific approaches of instructing, teaching, coaching and mentoring, respectively. From the viewpoint of the individual, or learner, they first hear it (learning outside-in), then bring it into themselves, acting and creating (learning inside-out). An example of the first is listening to lectures; an example of the latter is involvement in simulations. Examples of these phases related to learning approaches are in Figure 10-2.

This model can also be used to assess effectiveness of a change strategy. When assessing impact factors from the viewpoint of a new initiative or process, common activities that a change management program might include are:

1. **Build Infrastructure** to serve as foundation to the program. Infrastructure is the core foundation of the system of implementation. It may include the IT systems that accommodate the program, a space to collaborate on the program, the acquiring of tools to support the program, or even the building of capabilities of staffs to charter the program.

2. **Get management buy-in** and sponsor the program. Management acts as the role model and as the change ambassador.

3. **Training**. Staff must be trained to ride the wave of change. No matter whether the system is easy or complex, training is always a crucial part.

4. **Communication**. Continuously delivering the message to make sure the program is heard, the message is clear, and to ensure understanding.

5. **Promote & Reward**. This creates recognition and brings value to individuals.

6. **Embed practice into process**. This part is very crucial to make it stick.

7. **Provide and benchmark result/value return**. Benchmarking with an easy-to-understand target with comparison of others in the same industry will boost awareness and understanding.

--- *Optional* ----

8. **Build a Knowledge Performance Index** (KPI)

9. **Shared team status**. This creates a "you are one of us" unity culture.

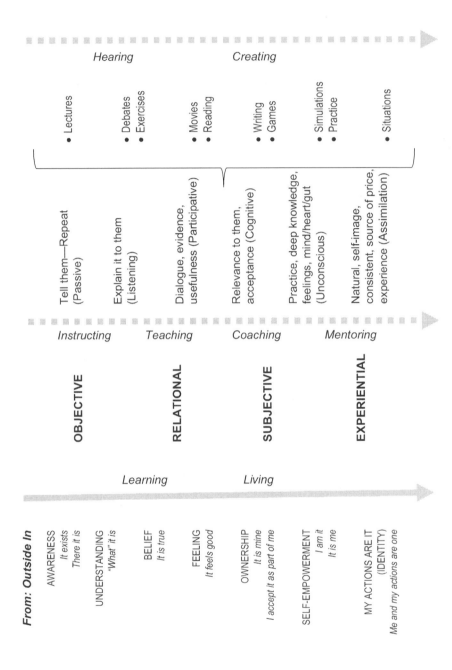

Figure 23. The Expanded Individual Change Model.

When these activities are assessed as a unit, they impact all six areas; however, no single activity can make this impact. See Table 10-2. In this example, activities 1-7 have covered all aspects of the factors. Hence, activities 8 and 9 are optional.

Table 10-2. Frame of reference for change program activities to assess whether personal action learning will take place at every level of the model.

#	Activity	A	U	B	F	O	E
1	Building Infrastructure		X				
2	Management Sponsorship and Support	X	X	X			
3	Training	X	X	X			
4	Communication	X	X				
5	Promotion and Reward	X	X		X		
6	Embedded into process					X	X
7	Benchmark and Result	X	X		X		
8	KPI enforcement	X				X	X
9	Shared team status				X	X	

In any change strategy, the challenge of management and leadership becomes that of communicating and collaborating with the organization's knowledge workers to create an environment, and an understanding on the part of their workforce, that these change factors are worthy of their consideration, acceptance and personal attention and actions. When this happens, change will come from a knowledgeable, motivated and supportive workforce.

An approach that *can* work, and work well, is to let knowledge workers take the lead in selecting, creating and determining the changes needed throughout the organization. This empowerment and trust will then unleash the energy, knowledge and creativity of the workforce and, above all, they will have ownership. Through this approach, without realizing it, they will most often create their own personal acceptance of each of the seven change factors in the personal action learning change model. Paraphrasing Lao Tzu's description of the true leader, *Of a good leader, when his work is done, his aim fulfilled, they will say: We did it ourselves.*

As indeed, they did.

TRANSITIONING FROM PREPARING TO IMPLEMENTING

Remember, **Planning-Preparing-Implementing-Sustaining** is a continuous transaction between individuals, the organization, stakeholders, and the environment. While steps of the process often overlap, there are also specific transition phases occurring in concert with the shifts from step to step that smooth the transition. As feedback occurs and new ideas, approaches or directions emerge, the cycle begins again in a continuous loop of change and transformation. Key Elements of the transition phase from Preparing to Implementing are: Releasing the Culture, Social Networking, and Training and Learning, with a focus on the knowledge competencies of "Humility" and "Otherness".

Releasing the Old Culture

During any change effort it is critical to, as forwarded by a senior admiral in the DON, "nurture our people". While certainly desirable, this means more than training on systems and expanding capabilities. It includes seeding and growing a culture of continuous learning, cultivating an innovative and collaborative mindset, and infusing thinking and acting into "our DNA". To execute effectively requires a culture that builds and releases energy and spirit throughout the work force.

Learning is a dynamic process that manifests itself in the continually changing nature of organizations, exemplified by innovation, collaboration, and culture shifts – especially during times of change, uncertainty and external challenge. When the organization learns, it generates a social synergy that creates a global knowledge, adding value to the organization's knowledge workers and to its overall performance. When such a capability becomes embedded within the culture, the organization may have what is called a core competency. The knowledge behind a core competency is built up over time through experiences and successes, resting as much in the relationships and spirit among knowledge workers as in the sum of each worker's knowledge.

While nurturing an innovation culture begins in the planning phase, it is important to revisit this as the organization moves into the implementation phase, with particular focus on ensuring the "letting go" of old paradigms and behaviors that applied to old ways of doing business but are not supportive of the Knowledge Reblooming movement, that is, the free flow and sharing of ideas built on a foundation of transparency, trust and truth; the valuing of freedom, learning, creativity and innovation; and the movement toward organizational resonance and coherence through networking and communicating, participating and collaborating, leading and visioning, and seeking purpose and meaning.

Leadership can help build a supportive, dynamic learning culture. In the phase between preparing and implementing, the leadership of the organization has a large role to play both in the example they set and the decisions they make. See Chapter 15 on how leaders inspire action through meaningful knowledge.

Social Networking

People are in continuous, two-way interaction with those around them. In today's connected global environment, the Net Generation and following generations are growing up with virtual conversations part of their everyday life.

Social networking helps build the important networking needed to support the "infusion of thinking and integrated action." As a strategy or initiative moves into the execution phase, the excitement of sharing new experiences and successes can facilitate successful implementation.

The implications of social interactions (conversation and dialogues) across an expanded global network (capacity) are that, when needed, knowledge workers will have the ability to develop context and generate ideas around specific issues at hand (capability). Creativity and innovation thrive on different ideas and ways of looking at things, and flourish from connecting different streams of thought. Thus, social networking offers the opportunity for the increase of creativity and innovation in a culturally-diverse organization.

Training and Learning

As the organization transitions from preparing to implementing, this is a good time to address any issues that have emerged during the earlier phases and ensure that they have been mitigated or resolved. ASK: Have any weaknesses or gaps been identified in knowledge competencies needed to support successful implementation?

As AI merges into the workplace, it is critical for humans to recognize that the idea of "smart" is quantity-based, and of course, it would be impossible for any human to outdo a smart machine if the knowledge standard was in terms of quantity.[453] Thus, the value of humans is not in *how much* you know but in the *quality* of what you know, and that quality has to do with thinking, learning, and how you emotionally engage with others. Hess and Ludwig refer to this quality as the "NewSmart", which leads them to what they call the Smart Machine Age (SMA) skills of critical thinking, innovative thinking, creativity, and high emotional engagement with others. Three supportive knowledge competencies are "Reflective Listening", "Otherness", "Humility", and "Presencing".

Reflective Listening and Otherness

Hess and Ludwig identify four necessary behaviors to excel at SMA skills: Quieting Ego, Managing Self (one's thinking and emotions), Reflective Listening, and Otherness (emotionally connecting and relating to others). These behaviors require shifting our current mental models focused on ego and self to a model which acknowledges our limitations and honors the experiences and learning of others.

Listening to employees is at the very core of an employee-first culture, where everyone is working together toward a similar goal and therefore has the responsibility – and is encouraged – to offer suggestions or identify problems, with leadership expected to publicly address any concerns in a timely manner. When NASA topped the Partnership for Public Service "Best Places to Work" large agency rankings for the 11th year in a row, Robert "Bob" Gibbs, associate administrator of the Mission Support Directorate, was asked their secret. Gibbs' answer was both simple and complex. After cracking a few jokes about getting astronauts and going to the moon, he stated quite simply, "It's about listening to your employees. It's about caring about what they have to say." As he described, it's having an honest conversation. It's being willing to say "I don't know. We don't have an answer for that yet, but we're working on it. And it's about being accountable for answering the questions that are asked. As Gibbs travels around the country, he spends time with employee resource group, hearing what they've got to say, "hearing from as many perspectives as we possibly can. It's beyond argument that a diversity of experience and a diversity of thought leads to a better team that solves hard problems, which is kind of what we do."[454]

Reflective listening involves more than hearing; it is a sensing greater than sound, a neurological cognitive process involving stimuli received by the auditory system. The linguist Roland Barthes distinguished the difference between hearing and listening when he said: "Hearing is a physiological phenomenon; listening is a psychological act." What this means is that there is a choice involved in listening in terms of the listener choosing to interpret sound waves to potentially create understanding and meaning.[455] There are three levels of listening: alerting, deciphering and understanding. Alerting is picking up on environmental sound cues. Deciphering is relating the sound cues to meaning. Understanding is focused on the impact of the sound on another person.

Active listening is intentionally focusing on who is speaking in order to take full advantage of verbal and non-verbal cues. As introduced in Chapter 2, reflective observation is one of the five modes of the ICALS experiential learning model, which is considered a transformation via intention with sub-elements related to understanding, meaning, truth and how things happen, intuition, integration, and looking for unity. Similarly, reflective listening, a communication technique, is a focus on understanding what is being said, with the listener "reflecting back" as accurately as possible the speaker's ideas.

The "what is being said" is more than the words, including tone and non-verbals (see the discussion of context in Chapter 12). The two primary techniques connected to reflective listening are paraphrasing and mirroring. Paraphrasing means that the listener provides back their understanding through their own words to reflect what was said. Mirroring is just that, repeating back word for word what was said, which does not necessarily convey an understanding of what was said, although this response can be followed by further exchange to ensure understanding.

There are many reasons reflective listening is important. First, when something is shared, by voicing that sharing the individual is clarifying their own personal understanding and learning/practicing how to deliver that understanding in a clear and precise way. Further, the very act of sharing knowledge and ensuring the understanding associated with that knowledge helps develop positive relationships among the individuals engaged in the sharing. This process also helps confirm the accuracy of understanding both in terms of the individual doing the sharing, and the individual(s) receiving the sharing. As can be seen, reflective listening is an important part of effective knowledge sharing.

From the viewpoint of sociology and, specifically, the study of social identities, the concepts of *otherness* has very much to do with recognition that we are social beings. Recognition of otherness is a philosophical, cognitive, psychological and social process which relates to how a group defines itself, both creating an identity and differentiating from other groups. For example, if a community is focused on customer service, that means it is not focused on design of nuclear fusion. Thus, identity and otherness are related, providing context.

This is a critically important concept to understand as we integrate AI into the workplace, identifying the relationship between machine and human. See the Human-Machine Decision Analytics Tool in Section IV.

Humility

The rapid development of the human intellect has forever changed the focus of work and play. In this context, we have introduced three forces into our world: (1) the ever-increasing necessity of learning for our survival; (2) the expansion of ego and arrogance due to mental acceleration; and (3) the emergence of technological advancements, which are replacing people in the workplace. All three of those forces are directly related to the need for, and significance of, choosing humility.

Focused from the individual viewpoint, humility is having an accurate view of yourself, neither too high nor too low. This would include knowing your strengths and abilities as well as your weaknesses and limitations, and being honest about them to yourself and others.[456] Focused from the collective viewpoint – the interpersonal level – humility is being other-oriented, focused beyond self. This would include development of empathy, knowing the needs and wants of others, and taking those into consideration in your decisions and actions. Humility is directly linked to experiential learning through social engagement and, specifically, to having an open mind, a willingness to listen and learn, and *creating resonance with people and ideas*, along with organizational coherence the focal point of the Reblooming Knowledge model.

There are multiple descriptive terms, states, or characteristics for humility, and various other states or characteristics that are considered as counter to humility. To get a grasp on these perceived differences, major texts (in terms of leading authors in their field) in the areas of philosophy, religion, psychology and leadership were researched to look at the contrasts of opposites in terms of humility. This resulted in Table 10-3 below.

Table 10-3. A contrast of opposites to deepen understanding of humility.

	Characteristics compatible with humility	Characteristics counter to humility
1	Willing to listen; Good listener; Honor and seek truth; Unnecessary to receive rewards for right actions	On broadcast; Talking too much; Voicing/pushing preferences or opinions when not asked; Bragging; Boasting; Using attention-getting tactics; Ostentatious
2	Receptive to difference and new ways of thinking; Having a teachable spirit	Arrogant; "What I have to say is more important"; Inflated view of importance, gifts and abilities; "I'm better than others"; Unteachable
3	Honor others; Serve others; Focus on others in service; Others over self	Selfishly ambitious; Greedy; Lack of service; Serve me; Meet my needs
4	Seek input and perspectives of others; Seek and follow good counsel; Thankful to others for criticism and reproof; Quickness in admitting you are wrong; Repenting wrong actions	Defensive of criticism; Devastated or angered by criticism; Dismiss instruction or correction
5	Honest/open about who you are and areas you need growth; Awareness of faults; Openly address faults; No need to elevate self; Seeing yourself and others as equals; Seeking to build others up; Minimizing other's wrong doings/shortcomings	Perfectionism; Hide faults; Minimizing own short-comings; Lack of admitting when you are wrong; Defensive; Blame-shifting; Being deceitful by covering up faults and mistakes
6	Gladly submissive and obedient to those in authority	Resisting authority or being disrespectful; Leveling of those in authority; Demeaning; Being sarcastic, hurtful or degrading
7	Gentle and patient; Gratitude; Thankful and grateful to Life; Genuinely glad for others	Scornful; Angry; Contemptuous; Impatient or irritable; Jealous or envious; Lack of compassion
8	Accurate view of your gifts and abilities	Victim complex; Poor me; Focus on lack of gifts and abilities; Complaining; Consumed by what others think of you
9	Possessing close relationships; Recognize value in others; Willingness to ask forgiveness; Talking about others only good or for their good	Not having close relationships; Passing judgment; Using others; Ignoring others; Talking negative about others; Gossiping; Lack of forgiveness
10	Strong, yet flexible	Willful; Stubborn
11	Theocentric; Recognition of being part of larger ecosystem; Realizing higher power	Anthropocentric; Exalts self; or "He is here for me"

In their book, *Humility is the New Smart: Rethinking Human Excellence in the Smart Machine Age* – which we recommend strongly, Hess and Ludwig see humility as a mindset that "results in not being so self-centered, ego-defensive, self-enhancing, self-promotional, and closed-minded – all of which the science of learning and cognition show inhibit excellence at higher-order thinking and emotionally engaging with others."[457]

Through the latter half of 2018 and continuing into 2019, as visitors moved through the Inn at Mountain Quest from around the world, we collected survey data on some pretty deep questions having to do with the current state of the world. Several of the questions had to do with humility. Moving into 2020 – before the pandemic stopped the flow of international visitors – there were 176 responders, with 12.5 percent of those born outside the United States. Of these responders, 58% were female and 42% male, and the 12.5 percent born outside the country came from Brazil, Canada, China, Ecuador, Germany, India, Ireland, Mexico, Poland, Romania, Thailand, the UK and Wales. Further, when asked about their heritage, responders offered combinations of the following: African, American Indian, Arabic, Asian, Austrian, Belgian, Black Hawk, British Isles, Cherokee, Czechoslovakian, Dutch, English, Finish, French, German, Greek, Hungarian, Irish, Italian, Japanese, Jewish, Latvian, Nordic, Norwegian, Polish, Portuguese, Scandinavian, Scottish, Sicilian, Slovakian, Spanish, Swedish, Ukrainian, and Welsh. Only two answered "American". Ages, which were distributed, ranged from under 17 to over 65, and professions ran the gamut from blue collar workers to white collar, with lots of wonderful diversity that would be difficult to fall into either of those categories, and there were students, business owners and retired people.

Why this distribution was shared is because of the remarkable results. In this international eclectic group, **more than 95% said they believed that humility is valuable when engaging others**. And they had more to say as well. For example, 27% of responders agreed that humility is letting things be new in each moment, opening the self to others' thoughts and ideas, and providing an opportunity for listening, reflecting, learning and expanding. As one said quite simply, "I believe humility is an essential characteristic for communication and idea-sharing." Regarding listening, another stated, "One has to set aside what one is thinking in order to truly listen and engage with others." Another noted that, "If one is to truly engage with another, being humble is crucial to forming a true connection." Five percent of the responders focused on this connection in various ways, many tied directly to open and free communication. This was spoken about in terms of humility helping others feel more comfortable, allowing others to open up, providing a non-threatening environment, engaging as equals, leaving social ranks and status aside, and eliminating judgment. And yet another said, "Humility allows for a deeper connection and understanding between individuals for it allows only selfless conversation to follow." Twelve percent said there is a strong connection between humility and respect. This "honor others" was further described by one responder in this way, "Respect and embracing others' beliefs and valued knowledge expands our own contextual understanding and can better the whole of humanity. Love and kindness are more easily embraced by others if we walk on the same level."

A few years ago, Gary Vaynerchuk, who calls himself an investor and serial entrepreneur, wrote a fascinating blog on confidence and humility. He is the CEO of a full-service advertising agency that serves Fortune 100 clients AND the chairman of a modern-day media and communications holding company. Vaynerchuk says he tries to get himself into a place where he simultaneously knows he's great and knows he's insignificant. This is consistent with the neuroscience viewpoint recognizing that our mind/brain is magnificent and where all the action in the world begins, yet when each of us is perceived as a separate entity it is easy to feel insignificant. Regarding confidence and humility, Vaynerchuk adds, "It's incredibly important to know when to turn on your confidence, especially when people push against you, and when people are razzing you, trolling you or doubting you, and I think it's equally important to know when to deploy your humility when people say that 'you're the best' or you are a marketing genius or the best business person or anything of that nature." See the tool in Section IV on humility.[458]

Presencing

Presencing, a core capacity needed to access the field of the future directly related to the power of intent, is consciously participating in a larger field for change through a "letting come" mode. As Senge and his colleagues describe:

> Genuine visions arise from crystallizing a larger intent, focusing the energy and sense of purposefulness that come from presencing ... Crystallizing intent requires being open to the larger intention and imaginatively translating the intuitions that arise into concrete images and visions that guide action.[459]

For Senge, intent is based on purpose, the reason for an individual or an organization to exist, that is, asking: Why are we here?[460] Thus, change is purposeful, and at the very core of change is learning, learning to do new things and learning to do things for a different reason.[461] Presencing is a core capability of the future, a way to access the living fields that connect us and that which is seeking to emerge, which is consistent with the quantum field as a probability field containing all possibilities (see Chapter 3).

Senge and his colleagues introduce seven capacities that are foundational to see, sense, and realize new possibilities: suspending, redirecting, letting go, letting come, crystalizing, prototyping and institutionalizing.[462] Each of these capacities enables various activities which serve as a gateway to the next capacity. This theory, which has become more popularly known as the *Theory of U*, was introduced by Scharmer – what he calls the "social technology of presencing" – which forwards that the awareness, attention and consciousness of people in a social system determine the quality of the system.[463] He says that we each have a blind spot that can keep us from being *present*, with presence necessary for profound systemic changes.

The idea of "letting come" is the process of *allowing*, whose importance cannot be overemphasized. As the adage goes, we are often our own worst enemies. As we realize the power of the mind/brain in terms of thought and feelings in the process of co-creating, we do not want to interject barriers to our desired progress forward. Similar to humility, presencing opens us to receiving and learning. "Over time, your appreciation for the question will become equivalent to your appreciation for the answer, and your appreciation for the problem will become equivalent to your appreciation for the solution. And in your newfound ease with what-is, you will find yourself in the state of allowing what you truly desire."[464] Despite this focus on self, presencing is not an individual concept, but rather considers the individual as a living system that is part of the whole. In other words, there is a sense of social identity present, which means consciously showing up, being aware of our inner connections to others and to the larger field (see Chapter 3).

CHAPTER 11

IMPLEMENT

Start-up of the knowledge strategy usually means the beginning of execution or implementation of the project plan. If the planning has been thorough, the project team is in place and networks have been identified or established. Now is the time to set in motion project activities such as allocating resources, contract administration, distributing information, and communicating the project plan to stakeholders. Simultaneously, the project team must be managed, motivated, informed, encouraged, empowered, and supported. If understood and engaged, collaborative entanglement can be your greatest asset for success.

After start-up, the project moves into an expansion and growth phase where the processes and approaches needed to sustain the project are established, and implementation gets underway. The following areas are important to consider during the implementation phase: leadership commitment visibility, leading and managing, resonance and coherence, the four organizational processes, communities, knowledge networks, and knowledge capture, leveraging, mobilization, and productivity as well as governance. Each of these areas are briefly discussed below.

LEADERSHIP COMMITMENT VISIBILITY

While success of any new strategy or initiative thrives on leadership commitment, this can only occur when that commitment is recognized throughout the organization. For years the approach to this was "walk-around, talk-around" leadership. However, in today's environment with geographically-dispersed organizations, virtual work, and a learned affinity for social networking, the effectiveness of this approach has diminished. One colleague brought this up in a conversation, quite proud of the fact that he texted his employees regularly. Aware that he has an organization of around 1200 people, we couldn't help but ask what happened when they texted back. He smiled and responded, "I have a team working on that. Currently they are answering for me, but soon I'll have an AI program up that will do most of the work." Somehow we wonder, does that really communicate leadership commitment?

One approach we used in the DON was pass-it-down training, where, when new strategies and initiatives were being embraced, each level of the organization would train the level directly below. In the hierarchical military structure with a direct chain of command this works well. And what we teach, we learn. This can, of course, be loosely applied to other structures. In another instance, the primary leader and second in command in an organization of about 200 people held ten weekly sessions of 20 people each to directly convey an important change in salaries and reward structures. That topic was absolutely essential to engage direct communication from senior leadership and offer the opportunity for questions. With larger organizations, the idea of a town hall is still quite viable, perhaps with a virtual Q&A opportunity. Back when phones were primary and we were moving toward simplified acquisition procedures, we set up a phone panel with six senior leaders who took calls for several hours. Today that approach could be done through social media. Virtual has provided the means to connect large numbers around the world, although the one-on-one interaction becomes much fuzzier. Clearly, knowledge intermediaries learned in the topic at hand would have to be involved.

Now, this doesn't mean that guidance documents are taboo, although distributed virtually, and leadership periodically popping into a community or team meeting, whether virtual or physical, will help spread the word across the organization. The primary consideration here is transparency, however that can be best accomplished in your organization.

LEADING AND MANAGING

With the emergence of knowledge leadership over the past several decades, new relationships between leaders, followers, and knowledge have developed. In the bureaucratic-prone past, knowledge was often held tightly at the higher levels of an organization and used to maintain control. Today, knowledge that is essential to the success of the organization resides in people at all levels of the organization. Further, since knowledge and knowledge needs shift and change in response to new demands and ideas from the environment, *no single individual or group of individuals can have all the knowledge necessary to run the organization.*

This new world necessitates a shift in authority from upper and middle management and leadership to the workforce, which essentially means that management and leadership give employees more freedom while still maintaining responsibility – something that can be difficult for some line managers and supervisors to do! Yet, for leaders and the organization to take advantage of worker's knowledge and experience for organizational improvement – including problem solving, decision-making and innovation – the context, direction and authority to make local decisions needs to reside at the point of action where the best knowledge resides. And individual and organizational learning programs need to exist that ensure knowledge workers possess that point-of-action knowledge.

Thus, the role of leaders is that of a gardener or forester. Leaders are available for advice; for integrating the efforts of knowledge workers; for nurturing an atmosphere of trust, collaboration, confidence and integrity; for listening and being a sounding board; for making relevant learning available; and for overriding knowledge workers (*only*) *when they believe that a fatal mistake is about to be made*. Mistakes will happen. They are an imminent part of living in a turbulent environment, and having the freedom to make mistakes is both the price for creativity, agility, learning, and optimum complexity as well as an opportunity to learn. What is most important is that knowledge workers learn from all mistakes so that mistakes are *not* repeated. Leaders recognize that there are some areas, and times, when workers must follow exact procedures such that deviating from the rules cannot be allowed. A clear example is safety procedures in high-risk areas. Thus, modern leaders have to work with their organizations under both conditions, perhaps simultaneously encouraging new ideas and exploration to improve efficiency or effectiveness in one area of the organization and utilizing specific processes and tight management in another. See Chapter 1 on forms of democratic leadership and Chapter 15 on "How Leaders Inspire Action through Meaningful Knowledge".

Leadership Effectiveness

Whether emerging from an individual's natural tendencies and experiences or learned and earned, the role of a "leader" is expansive and expanding. Unbelievably, the undoubtedly incomplete lists of characteristics in the multiple focus areas inherent in leadership effectiveness in Figure 11-1 below are all touched in some way by today's effective and collective leadership! And whether in a leadership role or not, this is a good set of characteristics to suggest learning opportunities for professionals in the business world.

Figure 11-1 is expanded from a model developed for the U.S. Department of the Navy's Career Path Guide as the technology explosion demanded expanding skills and the CIO shop was caught up in a war for talent. Note the consistency with both the Reblooming Knowledge model and the characteristics supporting the democratization of organizations while simultaneously touching the areas of importance learned experientially by effective organizations. However, it would be quite difficult, if not impossible, to have all the elements of Figure 11-1 integrated into one functional leader. Nonetheless, what an outcome to strive toward!

Figure 11-1. Focus areas and characteristics supporting leadership effectiveness.

Looking through the lens of more generic leadership attributes which have surfaced repeatedly throughout development of effective democratic leadership approaches (see Chapter 1), Story Thinking, developed by John Lewis and introduced in Chapter 8, can be used as a tool for leadership assessment and development. Recall that the Story Thinking cycle moves from automation to disruption to investigation to ideation to expectation to affirmation and back into automation.[465] See Figure 11-2.

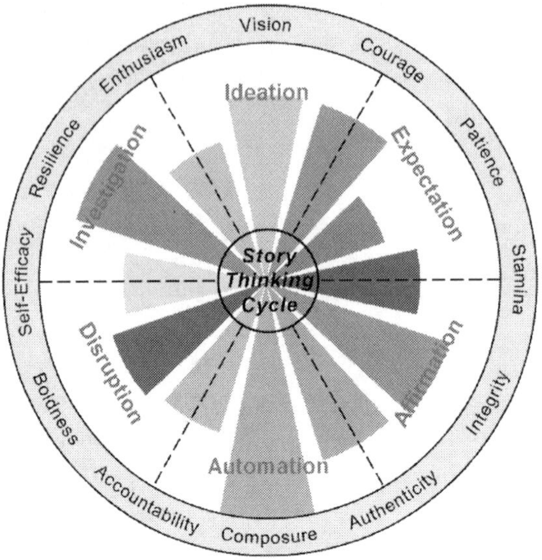

Figure 11-2. Story Thinking leadership assessment and development (used with permission).

Self-Transcendence

Self-transcendence is the expansion of consciousness, which can be considered a character trait where personal concerns are transcended such that an individual is able to perceive, for example, that problems and challenges are a small part of a larger whole, and act accordingly. In the workplace, this can be likened to Maslow's idea of self-actualization, which he considered the pinnacle of human development and, as such, is situated at the top of his Hierarchy of Needs. Of transcendence, Maslow says,

> *Transcendence refers to the very highest and most inclusive or holistic levels of human consciousness, behaving and relating, as ends rather than means, to oneself, to significant others, to human beings in general, to other species, to nature, and to the cosmos.*"[466]

Self-transcendence enables recognition of the multidimensionality of self, moving beyond perceived limits, inwardly through introspection and outwardly by reaching out to others. Reed adds that this multidimensionality is also temporal "whereby past and future are integrated into the present", and "with dimension beyond the typically discernible world". [467] See the companion book, *Unleashing the Human Mind: A Consilience Approach to Managing Self* and its Field Guide.

The most important factor to achieve self-transcendence is an awareness and openness to the idea in an energetically entangled universe. In Chapter 3 we introduced the idea of an informed universe with a two-way information exchange continuously underway with all living forms, and in Chapter 13 guest author Florin Gaiseanu, a solid-state physicist, offers the informational model of living systems. Not only do the fundaments of the functioning of our informational system assure body maintenance and species continuity, but this system connects the environment external/internal world, with specific cognitive centers for connection with this reality. We are active participants in this exchange. Self-transcendence opens the door to a larger awareness of that exchange, a greater connectedness with our environment, encouraging a sense of "wholeness". From Reed's viewpoint, as well as those of Viktor Frankl and Abraham Maslow, this natural (and desired) state is a developmental imperative "which people must reach in order to be fulfilled and to have a sense of purpose".[468] For intense examples, read the work of Viktor Frankl, who found higher purpose while in a World War II concentration camp and was able to set aside his own needs and interests in order to see the larger picture and his place in it.

According to Wong, there are four characteristics that help identify the condition of self-transcendence.[469] These are (1) A shift from the focus on self (selfishness and egotism) to a focus on others; (2) A shift in values from extrinsic motivation (external rewards) to intrinsic motivation (with the activity itself a reward); (3) An increase in moral concern, an intensive focus on doing what is right; and (4) Higher-order emotions such as awe, amazement, a feeling of being uplifted.

Inspired by Buddhism, and approaching self-transcendence with an open heart and mind, Flood proposes five creative approaches toward self-transcendence.[470] These are (1) meditation, (2) expanding your awareness and *empowering yourself with knowledge and wisdom*, (3) eliminating fear in your journey toward insight, (4) discovering the personal spiritual techniques that bring you closer to your higher purpose, and (5) raising your vibration, that is, living in a positive, transcendence-conducive environment. Some simple suggestions include (1) enter the "theta" state between being asleep and awake (meditation, prayer, hemispheric synchronization, etc.); (2) engage in meditation and mindful activities (listening, waking, eating); (3) get creative and try new experiences; (4) journal, putting your thoughts on paper to separate them from yourself; (5) commune with nature; (6) give yourself reflection time, and dive into your deepest parts; and (7) practice excellence, do everything that you do well.[471]

A one-dimensional Self-Transcendence Scale (SSTS) consisting of 15 items adapted from the DRLA (Developmental Resources of Later Adulthood) scale was developed by Pamela Reed in 1986.[472] The 15 items, which represent characteristics of a mature life, are scored from 1-4, with 1 the lowest possible level of self-transcendence, and 4 the highest possible level. Representative items include being involved with others and your community when possible, the ability to adjust well to changes in physical abilities, the ability to move beyond things which once seemed important, and letting others help when it is needed. This instrument has been validated in measuring self-transcendence.[473]

Empowerment

While the topic of empowerment has been scattered throughout Section II because of its critical importance in a turbulent business environment, this has largely been in the context of senior management or leadership in an organization giving decision authority in their work areas to lower-level employees or teams. However, empowerment also means individuals becoming stronger and more confident, that is, self-empowerment. This is the empowerment that is part of the individual change model AUBFOE detailed near the end of Chapter 10.

In terms of the first definition, empowerment can be a touchy subject in organizations who attempt to use it within a classical hierarchical bureaucratic company. At the turn of the century, de Geus said, "When push comes to shove, most managers will choose control. In fact, it is emotionally difficult, in most companies, even to relax the emphasis on control. Managers who are doers, accustomed to getting things done, will tend to trust themselves more than anybody else". [474] Whether in our personal or professional lives, I imagine all of us have felt that way at times. Yet, as complexity increases, and a volatile and uncertain business environment changes the rules of competitiveness and sustainability, control is impossible. You are probably familiar with the African proverb that "it takes a village to raise a child", meaning to provide a safe, healthy environment where a child can flourish. Well, in today's world, we can say in good faith that "it takes a team to run an organization, and a community to sustain it". While the value of teams and communities has been organizationally proven for a number of years, never was the authenticity of these relationships more critical to the life of an organization. And at the very core of both teams and communities is knowledge.

Recall what AUBFOE stands for: awareness, understanding, belief, feeling good, ownership, and empowerment. In other words, in order to change and act on that change, I need to be aware of what change is needed, understand what it means and why it is important, believe it is true, feel good about it, and accept that this is something that I need to do. And all of that can be true, but if I do not have the knowledge of *how* to change – or the confidence to act on that knowledge – then I will not – cannot – change. Thus, knowledge is at the very core of self-empowerment. Even if the chain of command "empowers" me to decide and act, if I do not have the knowledge of how to act, I cannot act.

Freedom and empowerment within a coherent team or community environment enables (1) people to cooperate together to solve problems through rational means with mutual respect and good will; (2) people dialoguing to ensure responsible decisions to common problems; and (3) people evaluating each other's assertions based on reason and evidence free of coercive influences. Note that these three descriptions – introduced in Chapter 1 – emerge from the descriptions from historical philosophers focused on the idea of democratic governance.

RESONANCE AND COHERENCE

Organizational resonance and coherence are at the core of the Knowledge Reblooming Movement. They were introduced in the Preface, more fully explicated in Chapter 7, and are mentioned and connected throughout Section II. These concepts are placed here as a reminder of the qualities we are seeking during implementation.

Briefly, resonance is knowledge sharing where individuals build upon the knowledge of others, greatly enhancing and expanding the growth of knowledge across the organization; and it is the consistency of values and beliefs with actions, both from the individual and organizational viewpoints; and it is a shared state of affective attunement, a vibrational entrainment that opens the door to learning and the triggering of new ideas, which was introduced with the flourishing of innovation in Chapter 6. Coherence is a wholeness of the organization, with synergy occurring such that the organization is greater than the sum of all of its stakeholders; and it is a clarity of thought and speech and emotional composure, with people heading the same direction toward a joint vision, a connectedness of choices.

Resonance and coherence are emergent characteristics, emergent from the learning offered throughout Section II that is congruent with your organization's vision, mission, goals, and values; emergent from the vast amount of knowledge available from the knowledge workers across the organization; emergent from the collaborative styles of your leaders and their desire for the greater good; and emergent from the democratization of your organization which enables freedom of thought, expression, association, simultaneously embracing self-development and self-organization with individual responsibility. All of this flourishing in your organization's field of trust, truth, and transparency.

Building a Deeper Understanding of Resonance

The term "resonance" originates from the Latin *re-sonare* which means to *resound*, a special relationship between two vibrating bodies (thoughts) whereby when one vibrates the other in turn vibrates. An example can be found in tuning forks, where if you strike one the other is stimulated to vibrate at its own frequency. Note that this is NOT mechanical; the two tuning forks are not physically connected to each other. Further, it is important to note that the responding tuning fork vibrates *at its own frequency*, with its own voice, and as the response is made, the original tuning fork also increases its amplitude, mutually reinforcing each other. This example distinguishes resonance in terms of *synchronous resonance* and *responsive resonance*,[475] both requiring a medium (resonant space) to allow but not compel this resonance to occur, which is the phenomenon of mutually "affecting and being affected", which builds on the physics concept of oscillation.[476]

While it would be easy to focus on resonance as a strictly *relational* concept, and certainly it is, however, as Rosa points out, it also describes a "mode of being-in-the-world, i.e., a specific way in which subject and world come into relation with each other … mutually affect[ing] each other in such a way that they can be understood as *responding to each* other, at the same time each *speaking with its own voice*."[477] Thus, this is not an echo, not a repetition, but a vibration speaking with its own voice. This is an important aspect of resonance as we reflect on its meaning in sharing knowledge and interacting with others in the organization.

Perhaps Gerhard Stumm and Alfred Pritz in their *Dictionary of Psychotherapy* offer a solid way to perceive resonance:

> *The concept of resonance, derived from physics, is (1) metaphorically the basic affective state of a healthy person who is authentically in sync with him- or herself in as many aspects of his or her personality as possible and (2) descriptive of a phenomenon in which multiple people are in sync with each other, primarily nonverbally. It is assumed that the more a person exists in resonance with him- or herself, the more the same effect is induced in other people, in terms of both their own resonant state and how they resonate with others. A state of resonance is defined by a high level of congruence between thought and feeling.*[478]

Note that while there is an emotional component to resonance – as there is to all thought – this does not mean that resonance is a purely affective state, which would also be limiting since as part of the sociology of human relationships resonance very much engages thought … and values. Rosa contends that resonant experiences are tied to the affirming of strong evaluations, that is, resonance occurs when people come into contact with an independent source of value that is something which concerns them in some way. This is what Helmuth Plessner called an "attuned appeal", an immediate intense relationship resulting from an inner attunement or internal appeal to that thought, person, or situation with which we have contact.[479]

We defer to the in-depth work of Harmut Rosa on *Resonance: A Sociology of Our Relationship to the World*, to provide a summary of what we have discovered about resonance. Because the focus of the Knowledge Reblooming movement is at the organizational level, we ask that as you read these four points you substitute the word "work" for "world".

> *Resonance is a kind of relationship to the world, formed through af←fect and e→motion, intrinsic interest, and perceived self-efficacy, in which subject and world are mutually affected and transformed.*

> *Resonance is not an echo, but a responsive relationship, requiring that both sides speak with their own voice. This is only possible where strong evaluations are affected ....*

> *Resonant relationships require that both subject and world be sufficiently "closed" or self-consistent so as to each speak in their own voice, while also remaining open enough to be affected or reached by each other.*

> *Resonance is not an emotional state, but a mode of relation that is neutral with respect to emotional content. This is why we can love sad stories.*[480]

In Rosa's deep research, she also finds value in understanding forms of alienation, an out-of-tune chord, a repulse, which is the opposite of a positive resonance. This negative resonance occurs when the subject is not touched, even potentially injured, "does not vibrate, but seeks to protect itself by dampening and closing itself off".[481] We have seen this phenomenon occur in organizations.

Before moving from this subject – and noting that resonance and coherence are what we seek in reblooming the knowledge movement – it is important to recognize that resonance is a "basic human capacity and need", with (1) "human subjectivity and social intersubjectivity basically develop[ed] via the establishment of fundamental resonant relationships", and (2) "human beings are essentially shaped by their longing for resonant relationships", with human desire interpreted as a desire for resonance.[482] Resonance is therefore the measure of a successful life.

The organizational setting can serve as a space of materially mediated resonance (a focus on the thing itself, that is, the craftsmanship of what is being created), both positive and negative in nature. Positive resonance occurs when experiencing self-efficacy through action. Negative resonance can be in response to fear or the pressure of competition. Relating to the world through work is not a new concept and has been touched in the anthropology of labor from Marx to Sennet – including in the work of Arendt, Sohn-Rethel, and Tomasello – as work forming "the constitutive basis for human sociality and thus for social conditions and relations".[483]

Regardless of the focus of a job, there are standards for the required activity, standards which imply doing the job well. Alasdair MacIntyre says that there is a *standard of excellence* for every activity, and self-efficacy occurs when we come close to achieving that standard.[484] And Sennett emphasizes that the "desire to do a job well for its own sake" is "an enduring, basic human impulse".[485]

Resonance not only occurs with others with whom we work, but also between what we are doing (whether that is with hands or head) and what is being produced. For example, Robert "Bob" Gibbs, associate administrator for the Mission Support Directorate at NASA – which in 2023 topped the Partnership for Public Service "Best Places to Work" large agency rankings for the 11th year in a row – says this is due to a very strong cultural foundation where "you have leaders that care about their people and people that care about the mission."[486] This is the idea of meaningful knowledge. By acquiring and practicing a skill (whether through thought or physical effort) we are affecting materials that are being transformed, material that is being responsive (when we are successful). We feel connected and discover meaning. (See Chapter 15 on "How Leaders Inspire Action through Meaningful Knowledge".)

This begs our reflection on the potential relationship of the human and Artificial Intelligence. As we interact in this sphere, the "voice" that is responding to our interaction is based on literally millions of discovery points, both emerging from the thought of people who have previously interacted with the system and networked information systems around the world, which are continuously being accessed and synthesized to provide responses to those people. Certainly, the "voice" that comes from the AI system is unique to that AI system. Reflect: Does this interaction produce resonance?

Building a Deeper Understanding of Coherence

Because words ground thoughts, innovative ideas often require a refinement or clarity of word meanings, or a new appreciation for old words. A profound scientific perspective emerging in the 20th century is that the universe is wholly, and enduringly, interconnected and coherent.[487] In other words,

Complex living systems, including human beings, are composed of numerous dynamic, inter-connected networks of biological structures and processes. Coherence implies order, structure, harmony and alignment within and amongst systems – whether in atoms, organisms, social groups, planets or galaxies. Thus, every whole has a relationship with and is a part of a greater whole, which is again part of something greater. In this context, nothing can be considered as separate, alone or lacking relationships.[488]

This connection based on quantum theory was introduced in Chapter 3 and again in Chapter 13, which presents the informational model of living systems.

From the perspective of science, coherence has been previously introduced as representing the degree of synchronization between coupling oscillating systems, which offers the potential for these systems, when operating at the same basic frequency, to become phase or frequency locked.[489] This cross-coherence is similar to what happens among photons in a laser. In physiology, this is what occurs when respiration and heart rhythms, operating at the same frequency, become entrained.

As with resonance, this does NOT mean that all the parts are acting in the same way at the same time. Our organizations, and the people who make up those organizations, are complex adaptive systems (see Chapter 2). Of the 73 known octaves in the electro-magnetic spectrum, complex activity in globally coherent systems has been identified in more than two thirds of that spectrum. As McCraty & Children observe:

It can appear at one level of scale that a given system is operating autonomously, yet it is perfectly coordinated within the whole. In living systems, there are micro-level systems, molecular machines, protons and electrons, organs and glands each functioning autonomously, doing very different things at different rates, yet all working together in a complex harmoniously coordinated and synchronized manner.[490]

From an organizational management perspective, this is the "connected of choices" where different decisions are made at different parts of the organization based on focus, context, capabilities, etc., which may appear unconnected, and even conflicting, but head the organization in the same direction, that is, to achieve the collective purpose and vision. The bottom line is that the clarity of thought, speech, and emotional composure that are qualities of a coherent organization provide a whole that is greater than the sum of the parts in support of sustainability and growth.

Stankosky points out that "Coherence is the important concept that provides the force multiplier effect that many organizations often dream about, let alone achieve."[491] So, how do we achieve coherence in our organizations? Clearly it starts with a value proposition, the clarity and unifying forces of the organizational mission and vision. When the U.S. was founded, the Declaration of Independence served as a rallying point to support the freedoms so important to the sustainability of organizations in today's environment. And there is no question that values and leadership play strong roles in setting and supporting the course of an organization. And when employees resonate with those values, then there is the presencing of self emerging in their everyday work efforts.[492]

So, we can look to the inner petals of the Reblooming Knowledge model to at a high-level provide the "how" ... coherence emerges through leading and visioning, networking and communicating, participating and collaborating, and seeking purpose and meaning, all grounded through truth, trust and transparency as we engage learning, freedom of thought, creativity, and innovation.

Work Engagement

A widely accepted definition of "work engagement", which has been a topic of study over several decades, is "a positive, fulfilling, work-related state of mind that is characterized by vigor, dedication, and absorption".[493] Those three concepts are powerful characteristics that positively impact the workplace. For example, vigor (which relates to high levels of energy) supports dedication which is further facilitated through absorption (a complete immersion in work activities), collectively resulting in better in-role task performance[494] and better financial results.[495]

Annually Gallop publishes a work engagement report based on a global-wide study of thousands of people. Similar to our description above, work engagement is determined by the levels of energy, dedication, absorption and professional efficacy people report in their jobs.[496] The depressing 2022 figures no doubt reflect the pandemic, with only 21% of employees saying they were engaged, 60% disengaged (emotionally detached), and 19% miserable (actively disengaged, or quiet quitting).[497]

Various studies have shown relationships between work engagement and working conditions, personal characteristics, and behavioral strategies;[498] physical, psychological, social and organizational job resources,[499] specifically job resources fulfilling the basic human needs for relatedness, competence, and autonomy;[500] personal resources related to beliefs and perceived control of their environment;[501] and the important role played by leadership, which affects all of the above. As forwarded in Chapter 15 by our special contributor Milton de Sousa, meaningful leadership plays a significant role in employee engagement. Note the importance of the amount of perceived control over the environment, that is, the amount of perceived freedom of thought, expression, association, and action, particularly in terms of job design and job resources.[502]

A recent research finding is recognition of the fluctuation across time and situations. This is not surprising. Work engagement is relative, very related to KNOWLEDGE (what is known, what is available, etc.), which is, as we are repeatedly reminded, situation-dependent and context-sensitive. And remember, people are complex adaptive systems, changing every instant of life, affected by their thoughts, feelings, and beliefs beyond the physical stress or entropy amassed.

Quiet Quitting

A worrisome trend that seemed to gain momentum during the pandemic is quiet quitting, a disengagement – the opposite of work engagement – when an employee does the minimum effort required, reflecting unhappiness with the job, and often behavior emerging as a result of stress or burnout.

In the direct sense of the term, this can also lead to an employee becoming unproductive, showing up late, taking more time off, and, eventually, just not showing up at all without any notice or explanation. Since the employee may not have previously expressed their dissatisfaction with their job or communicated any issues they are facing, there may not be any warning signs prior to this behavior, and therefore no opportunities to help mitigate it. Nonetheless, this can be costly for employers in terms of increased turnover and decreased productivity.

There are, however, sensible organizational behaviors that help keep employees engaged. These include having regular check-ins with employees, creating an open and supportive work environment, providing opportunities for growth and development, recognizing and rewarding productivity and good work, and addressing issues promptly.

THE FOUR ORGANIZATIONAL PROCESSES

In every organization there are four processes that are used continuously, although they are often used unconsciously, and are invisible or merged together depending on the problem and experience of the individual(s) involved. Together, these four processes – creativity, problem-solving, decision-making and implementation – constitute the procedures for ensuring all aspects of a situation are taken into account. Knowledge is at the heart of all four of these processes, and undoubtedly all four will play a role in planning, preparing for, executing and sustaining knowledge strategies and initiatives.

Creativity

Creativity is both an art and a science. It is the emergence of new or original patterns, which may be ideas, concepts, or actions – *the ability to perceive new relationships and new possibilities.*

The creative process is typically thought about as having four stages.

- *Stage one* is the problem, situation, or opportunity identification where a thorough discussion of the issues and objectives occurs among interested/responsible organizational employees to ensure common understanding of the desired outcome.

- *Stage two* is gathering relevant information, and particularly knowledge, needed to focus potential new ideas and to provide stimulation for idea generation.
- *Stage three* is the actual generation of ideas via self-reflection and comprehension, brainstorming, or some other technique. This is a divergent process. Generative AI supports this process by identifying associations among diverse concepts and drawing ideas from those associations.[503]
- *Stage four* is the discussion, evaluation and prioritization of ideas to determine which ones are the best. This is a convergent process.

Each of these stages is built upon collaboration and interactions among individuals and the exchange of ideas.

Creativity is part of the learning process. Each assumption may lead to an entirely different set of ideas that are acceptable for consideration. A useful technique to aid thinking out of the box is to first surface the basic assumptions of individuals and teams that may underlie an initial response, then change that set of assumptions and follow the consequences. This frees up the mind to generate more and different ideas. Tools that support the creative process include conversations that matter (see Section IV), concept mapping, and brain writing.

An approach to studying the changing times and the content and context of a situation for which you seek a solution is to identify patterns of change and the underlying principles or environmental drivers that are generating the change, unpredictability and with apparent complexity. Much of this kind of knowledge resides in your unconscious, particularly if you have previously and deliberately looked for these characteristics. Thus, you may not be consciously aware of them but your unconscious can, and often will, be aware of them as you observe and study a situation, creating knowledge in the form of understanding. See the tool in Section IV on Pattern Thinking.

Innovative Creativity

Innovative Creativity is purposefully engaging your creativity with innovation in mind. This means preparing yourself in a specific field through education and experience; developing the capability of identifying patterns and relationships related to that field; thinking in whole thought (lower mental thought, or logic, *and* higher mental thought, or concepts); paying attention to your emotions and intuitive nudges; and stretching your thought through interacting with diverse groups.

In their book *Innovative Creativity: Creating with Innovation in Mind*, Bennet and Shelley say that creativity is an aspect of consciousness and is part of everyone's birthright, but what we do with it is a choice. There are two paths, inspiration and technique, both offering the potential of innovation, with

Innovative Creativity sitting at the nexus of these paths, a point of creative tension. The text includes specific approaches and techniques to achieving Innovation Creativity.[504]

Problem-Solving

Problem-solving is one of the most important processes in the organization. Specific democratic elements identified in Chapter 1 relating to problem-solving are cooperation, critical inquiry, rational consensus; and specific characteristics are rationality, mutual respect, good will, inquisitive mind, and openness to criticism and improvement.

Taking inputs from the creative process as needed, the problem-solving process provides the links between ideas, problems, and decisions. The output of the problem-solving team or community is a solution set of alternatives that provide ways to achieve a desired situation or problem solution. In essence, this is group knowledging, that is, collectively seeking knowledge to address a specific issue at hand.

There is no one process for solving problems, and rarely is there a single solution. There are, however, different levels of problems and their associated techniques that improve a team's ability to develop solution alternatives. For example, for even relatively simple situations, it may be difficult to separate the problem from its symptoms. Under such circumstances, the Japanese *five whys* approach can very effectively and quickly home in on the problem. This approach means asking the question "why?" and when answered, asking "why?" of the answer, continuing to dig down in this manner five levels.

When people, organizations, and complex relationships exist, it is often impossible to identify causes. Before a team can solve a problem, it must first agree on exactly *what* the problem is, and *why* it is a problem. Since for most complex problems there is rarely enough right information or time to construct a definitive, clean solution, finding solutions to complex problems becomes a creative act.

For example, a problem can be viewed as an *undesirable situation*. Ideally, its solution then becomes a new, desirable situation. This process of finding ways to change an undesirable situation into a desirable one is a creative part of problem-solving, or the process of gap analysis. However, for the most complex problems it will likely be impossible to "change the situation." What is more likely is a solution that includes influencing the problem and changing/adapting the team's actions to accommodate a mutual adjustment in the relationships between the team and its environment. For ideas of different ways to look at problems or issues, see Chapter 16 on Knowledge Capacities.

Problem-solving can also be used to find and take advantage of opportunities, with an opportunity defined as a desired situation that is different from the current state of affairs. From a classical view, *the more options available to solve a problem, the better the final solution*. This simple heuristic drives the organization to share large problems and issues widely, and to welcome the thinking and passion of those who contribute critical thinking and creative ideas. Dorothy Leonard-Barton suggests selecting people to participate on problem-solving teams "*because* their ideas, biases, personalities, values, and skills conflict – not in spite of their differences. Why? Because an effective guard against people considering only a few problem-solving alternatives or, worse, framing problems so that they can be solved only with familiar solutions is to involve a variety of people, with their diverse signature skills, in the task."[505]

For the most complex problems there is never enough of the right information or time to provide a definitive, clean solution. Since finding solutions to complex problems is a creative act, experience, intuition, reflection, and dialogue among all problem-solvers will usually produce a set of sensible alternatives based on the group's collective judgment and *comfort level*.

Collaborative problem solving is an approach for solving relevant, day-to-day problems as well as creating and sharing knowledge about good practices, and The World Café is a process for building knowledge about a focused need or opportunity. Collaborative Problem Solving is detailed in Section IV. Information on the World Café can be found on the internet. Other problem-solving tools include dialogue, causal loop diagrams, and force field analysis.

Sleeping on a question – a particularly powerful way to access tacit knowledge – can yield an answer the next morning. Tell yourself, as you fall asleep at night, to work on a problem or question. The next morning when you wake up, but before you get up, lie in bed and ask the same question, listening patiently to your own, quiet, passive thoughts. Frequently, but not always, the answer will appear, although it must be written down quickly before it is lost from the conscious mind. This process becomes even more effective when the conscious mind has been primed. For example, early in the evening, prior to going to bed, take a focused period of time to "brainstorm" with yourself, asking yourself a lot of questions *related* to the task at hand. Even if you don't think you know the answers, reflect carefully on the questions and be patient. This is the process of active reflection.

Another aspect of this approach is useful when a group or team is tackling a difficult problem. It has been found that the answers from the team can be improved if, rather than acting on quick responses, the team sleeps on the problem and the following morning reviews the answers they have come up with. What happens is that while you sleep your unconscious mind is processing the information taken in that day, keeping the valuable information and discarding that which doesn't make sense. It is also connecting with previous learning and working on solutions to issues or problems that have come up during the previous day. When the team gets back together the next day, there will be new ideas and thoughts, and a clearer vision of the best way ahead.

Decision-Making

Decision-making refers to the selection of one or more alternatives generated by the problem-solving process. Some key points to note concerning decisions are:

1. *No decision* is a decision.
2. All complex decisions involve *values and judgments*.
3. No one can *predict* the future.
4. Every decision is a *guess* about the future.
5. The quality of a decision *cannot* be measured solely by its outcome.

In Chapter 2, people were described as intelligent complex adaptive learning systems (ICALS), and the knowledge organization as an intelligent complex adaptive system (ICAS). In the complex and uncertain environment of today, it is paramount that complex adaptive behaviors in organizations be understood and that leaders and managers be familiar with how to influence them. For this reason, we take a few minutes to review some of the basics in this regard. When dealing with complex systems and complex problems the decision process often requires a commitment to *embark on a journey toward an uncertain future*, creating a set of iterative actions whose consequences will cause a move from the current situation (A) *toward* a desired future situation (B) (see Figure 11-3).

Since there is no direct cause-and-effect relationship that is traceable from the decision to the desired future state, the journey may require extensive preparation; for example, consider the Lewis and Clark expedition. The decision strategy must have the capacity and internal support mechanisms needed for an implementation journey that cannot be predetermined. The decision-making journey itself, then, could be thought of in terms of complexity, with the system (and situation) having the capability to change abruptly as it adapts to external environments. In turn, the success of the organization's ability to change and adapt will be highly dependent on the self-organization and robustness of the adaptive elements built into the decision strategy. The preparation process includes: understanding the domain of interest as well as possible; recognizing the level of uncertainty, surprise potential and nature of the landscape; preparing for the journey in terms of resources, flexibility, partners, expectations, goal shifting, etc.; making sure that individuals carrying out the decision strategy are ready (i.e., sustainability criteria are met); and ensuring that all relevant alternatives have been considered.

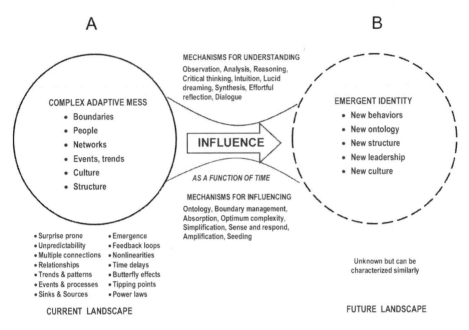

Figure 11-3. In a CAM, the decision strategy is most likely a sequence of actions to move from situation A toward situation B.

Many of the issues facing organizations in today's environment can be considered complex adaptive messes (CAMs), which are difficult to make sense of. An example would be professionals considering a road to build which deals with a complex and ill-defined situation in which geographic, topological, financial, economic, and political issues are all entangled. This means that influencing any one of those areas may well initiate an unpredictable response from another area.

It is important to note that the knowledge required to understand a system increases as you move toward more complex systems. Further, there is an exponential rise in the amount of sharing in order to create the needed knowledge. See Figure 11-4.

Armed with the realization that all of the information and knowledge gathered to this point lays the groundwork for understanding a CAM, the decision-maker then observes, studies, reflects, experiments, and uses intuition to develop a "feeling" for the key relationships and patterns of behavior within the system. Considering *why* and *how* something happens, not just *what* and *when*, the decision-maker looks for the structural sources (and the relationships among those structural sources) of multiple actions, interactions, events, and patterns. Trial-and-error perturbations coupled with effortful reflection over time will often provide a deeper knowledge and understanding of how the CAM functions and what it takes to resolve problems. In addition, where possible, talking with people in the system about how the work *really* gets done and who influences what goes on, asking questions and dialoguing to discover their insights, can provide an invaluable sensing capability. The decision-maker is learning how to *feel* the system's pulse through close attention, listening, experience and reflection. This feel for the system is essential since analysis and logic produce useful answers only if their assumptions are correct, and if all material causal relationships can be taken into account – an almost impossible task in a complex system. In a CAM, understanding its non-adaptive behavior is inadequate. The ladder of inference, with detail available on the internet, is one approach for checking assumptions related to the decision-making process.

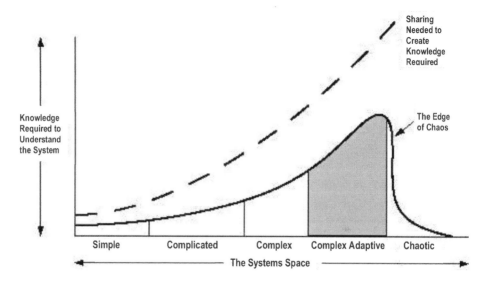

Figure 11-4. The knowledge required and sharing needed to acquire that knowledge across the systems space.

Clearly, an important consideration when dealing with complex systems is the ability to make maximum use of your past experience and cognitive capabilities. As introduced above, this means using your unconscious mind (with its memory and associative processing power) to help understand CAMs. For example, we all know much more than we think we know. We are often asked a question that we answer, and yet we didn't realize we knew the answer before the question was asked. We spend our lives soaking up data and information, creating knowledge, and, through our experiences, internal thinking, and contemplation we develop understanding, insights and feelings about things of which we are often unaware. A common way that is described is that "we don't know what we know."

If it is determined that a team should make a decision, by what process will the decision be made? What is the type and degree of *team* interaction needed during decision-making discussions? Will the decision require creative thinking, analysis and logic, intuition, and/or judgment? Do all team members need to be present? Should outside experts participate in the process? Is facilitation needed? Finally, what is the sequence of thinking (and feeling) that the team will go through to arrive at the decision? Whether a task team, project team, or interdisciplinary team, figuring out these answers as a team can help support success.

Part of the decision strategy is in preparing the team to react quickly to surprises. Quick reactions on the part of the team in dealing with surprises or unknown, even unanticipated, opportunities can make a huge difference in the success of the effort. The ability to react quickly does not come automatically. It must be *deliberately infused* into the solution set and *supported* by managers and leaders such that the team has the experience, freedom, responsibility and accountability that allows them to react quickly to externally created opportunities and threats. This means, for example, that *self-organization and empowerment* are likely to be important factors in the solution team's success. These attributes are supported through open communication so that team members who face a problem at the point of action understand the decision direction and intent, and have the ability and freedom to talk to anyone within the problem domain – and perhaps even external to that domain when needed – to quickly access information and expertise to assist in handling surprise events or opportunities.

In Figure 11-3, the mechanisms for influencing complex situations are drawn from complexity theory. Each of the following will be discussed briefly below: ontology, structural adaptation, boundary management, absorption, optimum complexity, simplification, sense and respond, amplification, and seeding.

Ontology. The ontology of the decision process represents the schema or set of characteristics and conditions surrounding the decision strategy that potentially have an important influence on the desired outcome. To the extent that these factors may be identified, they can then be prioritized, rated for significance, visualized through graphics and used to help develop the optimum decision strategy. For example, if an organization is unable to perform well in a rapidly changing, uncertain environment its senior leadership may decide that the Intelligent Complex Adaptive System (ICAS) organizational model may be the best solution. If so, the ontology would consist of the eight emergent characteristics of the ICAS model, namely: organizational intelligence, unity, shared purpose, optimum complexity, selectivity, knowledge centricity, permeable boundaries, flow and multidimensionality. The decision strategy would then be to change the current organization to encompass these eight emergent characteristics – ranked and weighted by their importance to the specific products, markets, mission, etc. of the organization – by building a set of actions that would move the organization toward the desired state.

Structural Adaptation. When the complex situation/problem lies within the decision-makers' own organization, special considerations come into play. It may become necessary to view the problem as part of the organization in the sense that both "systems" are complex and interconnected. As Stacey and colleagues describe, "Thinking in terms of interconnections and the consequent awareness of causal links that are distant in space and time alerts managers to the unintended and unexpected consequences of their action."[506] In other words, the organization may be *part of the problem* and any successful solution would include changes both inside the "problem" as well as in the surrounding organization. In a sense we have two coupled complex systems that are connected such that any change in one is likely to affect the other. Since such structural coupling or adaptation is common, the decision strategy may be to use this coupling to pull the problem situation along in the desired direction. In general, structural adaptation is a good way to influence complex organizations, although exactly where it will end up cannot be predicted.[507]

Boundary Management. Boundary management is a technique for influencing complex situations by controlling/influencing their boundary. For example, if a vendor is providing medium quality products to a manufacturing plant, the buyer may change the boundary conditions (purchase price, delivery schedule, quantity, etc.) to press the vendor to improve quality, forcing the problem into the vendor's system. Changing the information, funding, people, material, or knowledge that goes into or out of a complex situation will impact its internal operation and behavior. An example is using the external media as a vehicle for effectively communicating the importance of internal organizational messages. Such indirect actions may prove more effective than direct intervention. Complex system behavior is usually very sensitive to its boundary conditions because that is where the energy comes from that keeps it alive and in disequilibrium.

Absorption. Absorption is the action to bring the complex situation into a larger complex system so that the two slowly intermix, thereby resolving the original problem by dissolving the problem system. This may happen during a merger or takeover. A related approach is for two organizations to swap people such that each learns from the other and brings back ideas, processes and insights. In this way, workers in a "problem" environment can experience and learn from a "desirable" environment.

Optimum Complexity. Another approach to dealing with a complex problem is through embracing complexity. Consider the creation of optimum complexity as a tactic for the decision-maker. Ross Ashby's law of requisite variety states that for one organization or system to influence or control another, the variety of the first organization must be at least as great as , if not greater than, the variety of the controlled organization.[508] This comes from Cybernetics, and is more of a rule than a law, but very useful when dealing with complex problems. What it means is that your decision strategy should have more options available than the CAM you are dealing with. By building more complexity into the decision strategy – finding more alternatives for actions, pivot points, feedback networks, etc. – you are better able to deal with the unpredictable responses that may arise during implementation.[509] But beware, too much complexity can have the opposite result, driving the organization into chaos.

Simplification. Simplification reduces our own uncertainty, makes decisions easier, and allows logical explanations of those decisions. Simplicity captivates the mind; complexity confuses and forces us to use intuition and judgment, both difficult to explain to others. As humans, we tend to continuously simplify to avoid being overwhelmed, to hide confusion, and to become focused and efficient. In a simple, predictable world this is rational and generally works well. It is easy to ignore many incoming signals when we know they are not important. Unfortunately, in a complex situation and environment this approach can become dangerous, perhaps even disastrous. As Murray Gell-Mann states:

> *One of the most important characteristics of complex non-linear systems is that they cannot, in general, be successfully analyzed by determining in advance a set of properties or aspects that are studied separately and then combining those partial approaches in an attempt to form a picture of the whole. Instead, it is necessary to look at the whole system, even if that means taking a crude look, and then allowing possible simplifications to emerge from the work.[510]*

Where complexity lives, it is hard to separate the unimportant from the critical information, events, or signals. The question becomes one of what aspects of this complex situation can be simplified, and how does that simplification benefit the overall solution set?

Sense and Respond. Sense and respond is another strategy to deal with CAMs. This is a testing approach where the problem is observed, then perturbed, and the response studied, beginning a learning process that helps the decision-maker better understand the behavior of the CAM. Using a variety of sensing and perturbations provides the opportunity to dig into the nature of the situation/problem before taking strong action. This tactic is often used by new managers and senior executives, who wait, watch, and test the organization before starting any change management actions.

Amplification. Closely coupled to the sense and respond approach is that of amplification, used where the problem is very complex and the situation's response is unknown. This is the evolutionary approach where a variety of actions are simultaneously tried to determine which ones succeed. The successful actions are then used over and over again in similar situations (the process of amplification) as long as they yield the desired results. When actions fail, they are discarded and new actions are tried; time is unlikely to help failed actions succeed because of the unpredictability of the future. Many trial actions will have a short half-life. Note that this is not blind trial-and-error experimentation since decision-maker learning occurs continuously during the process and judgment, experience, and deep knowledge can create understanding and knowing that result in more effective actions. In other words, sense and respond, trial and error, and amplification used both as part of a decision strategy and learning tools – coupled with knowledge of complex systems, the use of teams, and the deliberate development of intuition – suggest valuable approaches for dealing with complex systems.

Seeding. Seeding is a process of nurturing emergence. Since emergent properties arise out of multiple nonlinear interactions among agents of the system (people), it is rarely possible to design a set of actions that will result in the desired solution. However, such actions may influence the system such that the desired emergent properties, outcomes, or something close to them, will emerge. *Emergence is not random.* It is the result of the interaction of a variety of elements and, if the exact emergent property cannot be predetermined, such as a specific culture, it may still be possible to create a culture that is acceptable – or perhaps better – than the one believed to be needed. If the right *set of actions* is found that results in the CAM moving in the right (desired) direction, then the situation might be guided to the intended outcome. Such a journey is the decision strategy.

The Challenge. The typical or traditional language of decisions implies a causal and deterministic connection between the decision and the end goal, whereas with complex systems there may be no predictable end goal and no direct causal connection that works. However, we have forwarded that one may be able to construct a decision strategy that guides problem resolution through a *sequence of decisions and actions* leading toward an acceptable solution. Such a plan might include (or anticipate) one or more of the approaches described above. While each of these has their own causal impact, the complexity of the system prohibits predicting their paths. Relative to stable pattern formats, i.e., emergent phenomena, though one cannot identify the sources of its creation, nevertheless *everything is exactly as it should be*, that is, emerging from what has happened in the past. Hindsight is 20/20; foresight is closer to 400/400.

By studying specific complex adaptive systems, we seek to create an intuitive and unconscious capacity to understand their behavior and meaning. We know that systems are often combinations of simple, complicated and complex segments, which knowing provides both advantages and disadvantages. While the simple and complicated aspects can be dealt with via normal decision processes, their success can lead decision-makers to assume that the same approach applies to complex situations. And, of course, complexity and complicated parts of the system are frequently intermixed.

Since rational decision-making can be developed and has a historic precedence, most individuals rely on logic with its supporting data and information to make and defend their decisions, even if problems are complex. In fact, it seems probable that most rational decisions that fail do so because they have not accounted for the complexity of the problem. And, of course, some rational decisions have turned out to be right not because they were logically accurate but because of the complexity of the problem. Certainly, understanding complexity is a starting point for developing a strategy that maximizes the outcome of decisions in a complex environment. And, as the environment becomes more complex, decision-makers at the point of action (residing at all levels throughout the organization) must increasingly rely on their intuition and judgment.

A positive aspect of a team's failure to achieve desired goals are the incremental benefits gained along the way. For example, project bonding can become a strong force for knowledge sharing and future knowledge productivity. Further, while deviation does not necessarily achieve the intended outcome, secondary outcomes may prove to be invaluable. For example, while the Edsel was not as successful as hoped, it led to what eventually became the Ford mustang, which is still in demand in today's market.

Implementation

Implementation is the act of taking good decisions and turning them into actions and changes that solve problems, satisfy customers, take advantage of new opportunities, and enhance the value added of the organization. Implementation is the most situation-dependent of the major processes. The details of the actions required to achieve the desired results cannot be generalized. However, there are a few overarching points to remember.

Here are three: (1) When individuals who have responsibility for implementation understand and agree on the problem and are aligned with the decision, implementation becomes much more effective. (2) Ultimately, implementation is built on relationships and an understanding of the objectives and the environment. (3) Efficiency and clarity of communication, coupled with openness and a sincere concern to share understanding and gain participation of all stakeholders, helps ensure success and find the best solution.

COMMUNITIES[511]

In the knowledge movement, formation of communities of practice (COPs) are core structures for continuous knowledge sharing across functional areas in an organization. Emerging out of the work by Etienne Wenger, the community of practice (CoP) is comprised of a network of people who work (practice) in a common field with similar goals and purpose. Let's explore the concepts of community and practice a bit deeper.

Community: In pursuing their interest in a domain, members engage in joint activities and discussions, help each other, and share information. That is how they form a community around their domain of focus and build relationships. Having the same job or the same title does not make for a community of practice unless members interact and learn together. The claims processors in a large insurance company or the students in American high schools may have much in common, but unless they interact, they do not form a community of practice. The Impressionists, for instance, used to meet in cafes and studios to discuss the style of painting they were inventing together. These interactions were essential to making them a community of practice even though they usually painted alone.

The practice: A community of practice is not merely a community of interest – people who like certain kinds of movies, for instance. Members of a community of practice develop a shared repertoire of resources: experiences, stories, tools, and ways of addressing recurring problems – in short, a shared practice. This takes time, and trust built over time. A good conversation with a stranger on an airplane may give you all sorts of interesting insights, but it does not in itself make for a community of practice. The development of a shared practice may be more or less self-conscious. The "windshield wipers" community of practice at an auto manufacturer makes a concerted effort to collect and document the tricks and lessons they have learned into a knowledge base. By contrast, nurses who meet regularly for lunch in a hospital cafeteria may not realize that their lunch discussions are one of their main sources of knowledge about how to care for patients, even though in the course of all these conversations, they have developed a set of stories and cases that become a shared repertoire for them to think about and discuss new cases.

To differentiate, a community of interest is a community of people who are interested in a specific domain of knowledge and either (or both) want to learn more, or have information to share. Comprised of a network of individuals who have a common interest in an area of knowledge, a CoI communicates virtually to share and learn from each other's experiences, insights, good practices, and lessons learned. A CoI is primarily a community of learners who exchange ideas, develop relationships and work towards furthering their knowledge, and perhaps the application of that knowledge, in their area of interest.

Communities of practice serve many different purposes and come in many different flavors. For example, some are informal and some are highly structured. All communities have some degree of boundary and criteria for membership, but some have more formal boundaries and specific membership criteria. Some communities are focused on building explicit collections of reusable knowledge assets, and other communities of practice are more focused on providing forums in which ideas and problems can be shared and discussed.

Coming out of the work of the American Productivity and Quality Center (APQC), four primary strategic intents for communities were identified and validated. These are: Helping Communities, Best-Practice Communities, Knowledge-Sharing Communities, and Innovation Communities. While there is generally a primary type that can be related to a specific community, most communities serve more than one purpose.

Helping Communities provide a forum for community members to help each other solve every-day work problems. This is really a function of all communities, but this type of community emphasizes *connecting* people across teams and organizational boundaries, and *creating* people-to-people connections. *Best Practice Communities* develop and disseminate best practices, guidelines and procedures for their members to apply. These communities use specific processes to validate the effectiveness and benefit of new practices. *Knowledge Stewarding Communities* organize, manage, and steward a body of knowledge from which community members can draw. These communities are distinguished from best practice communities in that they focus on *all* types of content, not just best practices, and they organize, upgrade and distribute the day-to-day knowledge their members use. These communities might also conduct research to discover new knowledge. *Innovation Communities* create breakthrough ideas, knowledge, and practices. While almost all communities have innovation as an objective, communities with innovation as their primary intent spend more effort intentionally connecting people who have different perspectives and perhaps represent different organizations.

The CoP operates on the basis of joint interest, spontaneous interaction, and mutual development. Beyond strategic intent, successful communities of practice are organized around the needs of their members and, as such, exhibit a wide range of sizes, structures, and means of communication. However, even with this diversity, effective communities share common characteristics that generally include voluntary participation, a common interest or goal, a common means to stay connected, a willingness to share knowledge They are facilitated not dominated, and have management support not control. Each of these is briefly explicated below.

- *Voluntary participation* – Members choose to participate due to the "value added" in performing their jobs, the excitement of building new ideas, and the satisfaction of relationships. Communities complement existing functions and organizational structures; they do not create additional ones.

- *Common interest or goal* – Communities are organized around topics that are important and meaningful to their membership. The focus often evolves as issues and opportunities emerge across the organization and enterprise.

- *Common means to stay connected* – Communities stay in frequent contact using technology like Web forums, email, wikis, and list servers and/or more traditional approaches like face-to-face meetings and teleconferences. Virtual connectivity offers the opportunity to build time for community participation around other work requirements.

- *Willingness to share knowledge* – Members are willing and able to share what they know, respond to requests, and collectively solve problems. They build trusting relationships. See the in-depth discussion of Trust in Chapter 12. Also, trust is one of the tenets of Relationship Network Management (Chapter 14).

- *Facilitated, not dominated* – Successful facilitators focus on recruiting and engaging members, not dictating content.

- *Management support, not control* – Management provides tools and a supportive environment that includes giving employees the time to participate, and recognizing those who demonstrate an exemplary attitude toward community and sharing. Communities set their own agendas, aligned with the enterprise or organizational mission, and based on the needs of members as they perform their jobs.

A CoP communicates virtually to share and learn from other experiences, insights, good practices and lessons learned. Since CoPs are defined by knowledge within a specific domain, they align the organization around competencies without reverting to functional structures. Membership therefore implies a minimum level of knowledge of that domain – a shared competence that distinguishes members from other people. As community members interact and new knowledge emerges, the agenda of the CoP evolves.

While communities are supported by technology and are largely virtual, their social dynamic plays a much larger role than technology. They are managed by making connections, dialoguing and building relationships based on trust and mutual interests. The focus is on value added, mutual exchange, sharing and continuous learning.

CoP members are often brainstorming and seeking solutions to specific issues and problems forwarded by community members, which is by definition the process of knowledging, with CoPs often acting as part of a knowledging network. When this occurs, there is a sense of urgency that stimulates the exchange and surfaces new ideas. Thus, participation in and reliance on CoPs increases over time, with CoPs often becoming the primary source of learning and knowledge – and a continuing source of energy – for community members.

Quick Start. As a "Quick Start" for communities, the DON provided a roadmap for community start-up from concept to reality. The steps of the Quick Start process as outcomes are as follows:

- Community identity, including name, knowledge domain, type of community, and organizational fit;
- The CoP's value, including purpose and how the CoP will help with the organization's mission and goals, and generally how the CoP will meet member needs;
- Initial direction for community type and organization fit;
- A clear understanding of the community roles and responsibilities;
- A Core Group planning meeting;
- An Initial Community Workshop;
- A foundation for community activities;
- An approach for establishing a collaborative work environment;
- Assessment of community progress; and
- Initial input to a Community Experience Locator.

Benefits of COPs to the organization include accelerating the use of good practices, access to just-in-time expertise, and knowledge sharing; leveraging capabilities for virtual work, access to just-in-time expertise, and confidence for risk management; and increasing access to resources, transfer of lessons learned, and flexibility of work groups. Benefits that accrue to the individual include accelerating (nearly instantly for CoP members) the transfer of know-how from other members, the capacity for ubiquitous collaboration between members and in the organization generally, and a virtual creative problem-solving environment; leveraging (can be cutting edge) opportunities for change and growth, the capacity for knowing, and professional experiences and commitments; and increasing information and knowledge competencies, just-in-time learning, and professional enjoyment.

COP Development Model

The DoN model, developed with David Sibbet, Grove Consultants, introduces seven stages of CoP development: (1) Initiate, (2) Connect, (3) Share know-how, (4) Build trust, (5) Collaborate, (6) Create knowledge, and (7) Sustain. Each stage is discussed in terms of what helps success and what hinders success along the path of developing an effective CoP. The stages are not necessarily sequential; they can occur simultaneously and/or in parallel, primarily due to the periodic infusion of new members into the community. This continual expansion of membership is a characteristic of communities, along with variability intensity of participation and involvement.

Despite the continuous fluctuations in participation, there is still a general sense of community development along the path described in the development model. The brief explication of each stage included below begins with characteristics that help success and those that hinder success.

(1) Initiate. *Help success:* Open leadership, compelling need, clear domain, and CoP type identified. *Hinder success:* Desire to control, preconceptions, and unreal expectations.

During Stage 1 activities, an individual or a group has a driving need or passion that prompts initiation of a community. This may be an individual employee who sees the potential value in increasing collaboration across the organization within a given professional domain. Or it could be a group of managers who see the need for fostering greater availability of expertise in a specific technical domain. Or perhaps the vision is to expand the knowledge of a small group of experts who currently experience little or no networking.

Clearly, capturing the idea and making it clear and feasible requires open leadership that appreciates the domain of expertise which has been identified and accepts the compelling need for an increased level of that expertise. Why is it important to engage in this endeavor? Someone also needs to determine the type of community of practice that will be most suitable to this expressed need (see earlier discussion).

Tip: Management must resist the tendency for over-control. Incorrect preconceptions and unrealistic expectations will hinder the germination of the community. It is important for organizational leadership to give those who have the vision and the capacity to launch this opportunity the latitude to make it happen.

(2) Connect. *Help success:* CoP veteran practitioners, interest in networking, appetite for learning, and mutual respect. *Hinder success:* No place to engage, conflicting demands, and non-supportive organization.

Stage 2 is about creating a new tapestry of like minds. Who is out there who can be engaged? Given a core group, CoP practitioners can help with finding and involving new members to expand that group to reach across the organization (and beyond?). Membership grows as individuals who have a desire to learn and mutual interest link with other professionals who share the same interests.

Tip: Special attention must be given to ensure appropriate resources are provided for interacting. These resources include space for face-to-face meetings, or networking and Internet capabilities for virtual interaction. If the organization is not supportive, networking and membership development will be slow and elusive. With support, connecting will not only tend to self-perpetuate; it will also create momentum for other community activities.

(3) Share Know-How. *Help success*: Benefits clear, common language, processes and tools. *Hinder success:* Lack of openness, expertise gaps, and no time to participate.

Stage 3 occurs when "light bulbs go on around the community" and people begin to realize the value of finding answers to key questions. What information and knowledge is most needed in the community practice, the shared assets of the community? The pay-offs start to become clearer, and the documents, tools, processes, and common language are all regarded as "shared community practice." The community is very sensitive at this juncture to any indications of lack of openness to sharing, expertise gaps in the community, and lack of time to adequately invest in the community.

(4) Build Trust. *Help success*: Helpful relationships, shared values, and vigorous commitment. *Hinder success*: Self-serving orientation, skepticism, and levying demands.

Stage 4 is a launching point for exploring and expansion. How can trust in the community support effective interaction? There are many ways. Trust nurtures bonding, and helpful relationships become commonplace. As recognition of shared values and shared motivation emerges, the commitment to community gains enthusiasm and members enjoy the community as a new resource for their professional interests and needs.

Hopefully, any members who are characteristically self-serving or skeptical do not hinder the community at this pivotal point. The levying of demands early in development, including those from sources internal to the CoP, can restrict healthy community dynamics. In Peter Drucker's words, organizations can either force compliance or build commitment.[512] Commitment cannot exist without trust, and commitment needs to be a key ingredient of communities. In today's knowledge environment, forced compliance as a management work philosophy is no longer good enough.

Workers must be committed, and organizations must foster trust to gain commitment. High trust engenders creativity, collaboration, innovation, connections, sharing, and openness. On the other hand, low trust engenders hoarding, skepticism, vested interests, self-serving orientation, employee dissatisfaction and distrust. Thus, the importance of trust within an organization becomes critical. Trust is a foundation for social capital, and, as such, is a key ingredient in holding networks and communities together.[513] The ability to garner trust is tied directly to the social capital and performance of the organization. Trust cannot be mandated, but can be fostered via the actions of leaders, and the culture of organizations.

Leadership trustworthiness is characterized by fair and consistent behavior that is reliable and reasonable. Organizational openness (transparency) encourages effective communications, policies, values and principles. Also, trust begets trust and assumes that employees are conscientious, committed, and capable. Conversely, untrustworthy and controlling behaviors in an organization tend to be secretive, deceptive, biased, and lack openness. This requires excessive monitoring and is focused on restrictive enforcement of rules.

Research on the relationship of trust and knowledge sharing by a leading researcher[514] focused on three questions about the kinds of trust that matter. First, in what sort of knowledge exchange does trust matter? Second, what kind of trust matters? Third, given the answers to the above, what are the predictors of trust? In 2001 the Institute for Knowledge Management under the auspices of IBM and led by Larry Prusak, drafted a Trust Model (see Figure 11-5 below) which provides some a framework for addressing these questions. Note that the number of trust builders in the model reflects the breadth of their considerations.

The building of trust – at the core of community development – is the midpoint in the Development Model, serving as a turning point for increased knowledge sharing and higher value community activities. As community members increase their knowledge and turn to more creative activities, they eventually begin to question the ongoing need for this community. This is where shifts begin to occur. Has the community served its purpose? Are the members still interested in participating? Do members want to continue with a different focus?

As noted earlier, trust is discussed in detail in Chapter 12 (Sustain), as previously noted, is one of the five basic tenets in Relationship Network Management (Chapter 14).

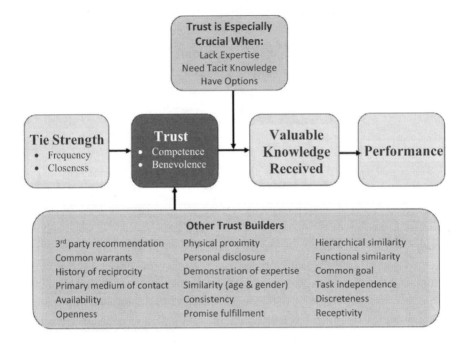

Figure 11-5. The draft Trust Model introduced in the IKM.

(5) Collaborate. *Help success*: Joint interest, enjoying synergy, and ready access. *Hinder success*: Hoarding, becoming too formal, and a non-collaborative environment.

Stage 5 involves a totally new level of collaboration. Where are the places in the organization that the community members can really make a difference? Members are discovering newly found joint interests and enjoying the synergy of interacting with ready access, when and where needed.

At this stage the community needs to watch out for extremes, both hoarding and becoming too formal with its new activities. (See the discussion on knowledge hiding in Chapter 12). If the organization's environment is non-collaborative, barriers will arise at the organization, workgroup, and individual level.

(6) Create Knowledge. *Help success*: Co-creative mindset, imagination, and dynamic interaction. *Hinder success*: Vested interests, fear of innovation, and rigid boundaries.

Stage 6 engages people beyond basic knowledge sharing. There is a clear sense of moving beyond normal capacity. With a sense of flowing forward, members are asking, "What can we create?" New ideas are popping up, and innovative possibilities are coming out of very vibrant interactions.

Margaret Boden says there are two types of creative thought: P-creative (psychological, personal) and H-creative, historical. P-creative ideas are fundamentally new to the individual mind. H-creative ideas are historically grounded, but fundamentally new to the whole of recorded human history. Observably, the H-creative ideas, which by definition are also P-creative, are the ones that are socially recognized as creative. But P-creative ideas are possible in every human being; these are the ideas that promote innovation and move the organization forward to dramatically improved results. (While creativity is addressed throughout this book, there is a focused discussion in Chapter 11.)

Hopefully, there will be no restrictions placed on the new capacity of the CoP. If people fear innovation and hesitate to span boundaries, the value of the community will be heavily curtailed.

(7) Sustain. *Help success*: Supportive climate, acknowledgement, continuing need, and continuous learning. Hinder success: Dwindling participation, and disconnect among participants.

Stage 7 is a crossroad of sorts. What does the community want to do? If the degree of involvement has tapered off, is there capacity for renewal at a new level of engagement? A supportive climate, proper acknowledgements, and clear opportunities for continued learning accompanied by a clear need will inspire an evolution in activity. While the flow of people in and out of communities can facilitate creation of new ideas and the spreading of knowledge across the enterprise, when too many members shift their attention, or when many people change their employment, the options for renewal may be restricted.

This can offer a turning point in the community's activities. The CoP now has the opportunity to recreate itself at a new level of engagement, or to appropriately disband in a way that honors the life of the community and effectively transfers its knowledge assets.

Collaboration Overload

Collaborative overload is a response to the collaborative intensity of work accompanying the knowledge economy. The trend for matrix organizations, the recognition of the value-added of teamwork, and the learning offered through communities moved organizations into a collaborative mode, necessary for successfully navigating the complexity and uncertainty of today's work environment. Yet when collaboration is the default mode and employees are constantly bombarded with emails, messages, meetings and requests for input from multiple sources, collaboration overload can lead to decreased productivity and job satisfaction, with employees having little control over their work and struggling to effectively manage their time. This, of course, can also lead to a lower quality of work as well as burnout.

In his book *Beyond Collaboration Overload*, Cross says the problem is the dysfunctional forms of collaboration which are a default mode for "most" of us. He sets forth three strategies for achieving what he refers to as essential collaboration. These are: "Tapping broad networks early in the life of each new project …, becoming an energizer to stimulate a flow of great ideas and great people toward you, and engaging in targeted collaborative renewal activities to build greater physical and mental well-being."[515] He provides practical approaches to achieve these strategies.

Ways collaboration overload can be addressed include prioritizing communication channels (identifying the most effect channels for different types of messages), setting boundaries (turning off notifications during non-work and designating time for uninterrupted work), streamlining communication (using project management tools or collaboration platforms to consolidate messages and tasks), and providing training and support (for managing time and communication).

KNOWLEDGING NETWORKS

Knowledging – seeking specific knowledge to address an issue or problem – was introduced in Chapter 4. Recall that knowledge (the capacity to take effective action) is relative, that is, situation-dependent and context sensitive. Think about your life at home or work and you will be able to identify conscious events of knowledging throughout your day.

Knowledging does not happen in isolation. We seek knowledge from many different places, sometimes directly from others, and sometimes in resources prepared by others. While a CoP or CoI can serve as a source for knowledging, the focus of a community is on a domain of knowledge, while the focus of knowledging is on a specific issue or problem, which may or may not be tied to a specific domain of knowledge. Thus, the knowledging network – which is primarily informal – is perhaps a trusted group of friends and colleagues, or even strangers related to the business at hand accessed on the internet as you search for solutions to an issue. And when another issue emerges, the knowledging network may be comprised of entirely different people with very different expertise.

As can be seen, the knowledging network is as large as necessary to address a current issue, and when a solution is found, the network ceases to be of any value to the knowledger, who has moved on to other emerging issues presented in life. As AI moves into larger roles in the organization, clearly it will play a large role in the knowledging network.

This brings up the issue of trust – trust of information and trust of people – which is extensively addressed in Chapter 3.

KNOWLEDGE CAPTURE

What we refer to as knowledge capture is actually the capturing of information that can then be used by decision-makers to create knowledge. Information can be captured in many ways. Surface knowledge is easily captured (see Chapter 4). For example, every time knowledge workers develop white papers, research papers and reports they are capturing their knowledge in the form of information which can be easily understood. This is much more difficult for tacit knowledge. A discussion of tacit knowledge (that which cannot be made explicit) is in Chapter 4.

A large part of how well information is understood is based on context and a common language. Documents that are stored in information systems with contact information for the originators, and connected to similar and complementary information that can help build a deeper appreciation of when and how to use this information in future situations, offer an increased potential for shared understanding.

A simple approach to capturing lessons learned that emerged early in the knowledge movement is after action reviews. These are real-time communication vehicles that share understanding across the implementation team while also serving as lessons learned for those who later read them, and as assessment instruments for those who later analyze them. After action reviews are held immediately after an event has occurred while the details are still fresh in the minds of participants. The actual outcome of the event is compared with the intended outcome to discover what went right and why, and what went wrong and why in a candid, open discussion. There must be sufficient detail and clarity to ensure everyone understands what did and did not occur (and why) so that lessons can be understood and applied to future actions. A Facilitated Learning Analysis is focused on the same four questions used in an AAR: What did we intend to do? What actually occurred? What went well, and why? What can be improved, and how? The intent is to capitalize on the shared experience of participants. As an example, DaimlerChrysler fostered communities of practice called "tech clubs" to reunite designers and engineers with peers from other platform groups. Each community was charged with codifying its knowledge. Part of this process was to maintain EBOK (the Engineering Book of Knowledge), a knowledge repository of process good practices and technical "know-how."

Many organizations also hold pre-event (before) and during-event reviews. The pre-action review brings an implementation team together to focus on the direction ahead, how progress will be assessed, and sharing lessons from previous projects or related events. The during-action review provides the opportunity to assess progress and adjust actions underway accordingly. Other tools would include peer-to-peer and the peer view process. An approach that can be used as part of during and after action reviews is the continuous improvement review (CIR), which is included in Section IV.

It may be useful to explore other modes of knowledge capture which organizations have found useful. The learning history is a structured process for gathering information related to a project, mission or initiative. It is a retrospective history of significant events in an organization's recent past described in the voices of people who took part in those events. Researched through a series of debriefings or reflective interviews, the learning history uses feedback from employees at all levels to help an organization evaluate its progress and provide information for future decisions. A similar approach based on storytelling is the use of oral histories.

The knowledge desk guide is a document residing on the desk (or virtually within the system supporting that desk) that contains the specific information needed to successfully accomplish the job of the individual who works from that desk. Each desk guide is updated annually, as changes occur, or as an individual is preparing to leave a position to support ease of job transition. The knowledge desk guide can also serve as a resource for temporary employees and development of an expertise locator.

A variation of the knowledge desk guide focused at the career level is the leave a legacy approach developed by the US Department of the Army. Maj. Ryan Kenny, a Signal Corps officer stationed in Hawaii, feels that leaders should consider the legacy they are leaving throughout their career. He has developed five legacy principles to guide the leave a legacy approach: (1) Discipline your leadership energy (prioritizing and resisting distractions); (2) Understand operational factors (deliberate choices in terms of time, space, and force), which include learning, staying focused and transitioning; (3) Schedule your priorities (what matters to you most and avoid the rest); (4) Keep your eye on the prize by deploying trust and encouraging "satisficing"; and (5) Nest for success, keeping your ear open to shifting priorities.[516]

The exit interview uses the interviewing process to capture the knowledge of individuals who are leaving an organization. While interviews with highly knowledgeable employees will generally prove valuable at some level, the capture of "knowledge" from departing individuals requires a systems approach. For example, thinking ahead, setting up shadowing opportunities, mentoring programs and apprenticeships, and six months before retirement ensuring participation in communities, setting up blogs, and holding lunchtime exchanges. For posterity, in addition to the capture of information in context, explicit capture can include video clips, community dialogues, and the sharing of stories. An agreement can also be arranged for employees with unique expertise and proven decision-making skills in a critical domain of knowledge to continue a few hours a week for a number of months, perhaps serving as the expert in a virtual community setting or knowledging network for a period of time after retirement.

Absorptive Capacity

In a highly dynamic, turbulent, and competitive market, a firm must be able to absorb new knowledge quickly and effectively. For example, an influential factor that determines the trustworthiness of IT companies is their ability to rapidly respond to their customers with the latest technologies.

Absorptive capacity is the ability of an organization to acquire and rapidly apply new knowledge, skills, and technologies from external sources to improve both performance and competitiveness. This would include the abilities to identify and evaluate new information, integrate it with existing knowledge and organizational processes, and apply it to solve internal issues or create and offer new products and services. The concept was introduced by Cohen and Levinthal,[517] who forwarded that organizations with a high level of absorptive capacity would likely be more innovative and successful.

Absorptive capacity is particularly important to small firms who do not have R&D budgets but are dependent on emerging technologies from larger firms. It can be increased through fostering a culture of learning and innovation, encouraging knowledge sharing within the organization, and developing partnerships and collaborations with external organizations. See Chapter 17 in Section III on "Absorptive Capacity 3.0".

Knowledge Elicitation

Knowledge Elicitation – as part of knowledge engineering which includes eliciting, representing and processing – is the specific process of extracting knowledge from domain experts for a knowledge base. As can be expected, this methodology is shifting as that knowledge base is hosted by an Artificial Intelligence component.

Traditionally, and KM has now been around long enough to reflect on "traditional" approaches, knowledge elicitation has had two foci, explicit and tacit knowledge,[518] or, in the DON model, surface, shallow and deep knowledge (see Chapter 4), which require different techniques to extract and systemize for organizational use. Once "knowledge", or what can be called "knowledge artifacts" (that is, information that has previously been successfully used to take effective action) is explicit it can be stored as information connected to enough context to make it understandable and potentially valuable in future situations.

Using the DON framework, surface knowledge, which answers the question of what, when, where and who, is easily captured and generally accessible and understood. Surface knowledge can be stored in books and computers and easily memorized, although it is also prone to a short shelf life in a shifting and changing work environment. Shallow knowledge is information plus some understanding, meaning and sense-making. To understand is to make some level of meaning, with meaning typically relating to an individual or organization and implying some level of action. *To make meaning requires context*, enough so that the knowledge maker can identify cohesion and integration of the information in a manner that makes sense. This can be created via logic, analysis, observation, reflection, and even – to some extent – prediction. In an organizational setting, shallow knowledge emerges (and expands) through interactions as employees move through the processes and practices of the organization. Thus, shallow knowledge is largely the realm of social knowledge.

Deep knowledge is developing understanding and meaning, integrating it, and shifting those patterns to a different frame of reference as the context and situation shift. The source of deep knowledge lies in creativity, intuition, forecasting experience, pattern recognition, and the use of theories. In short, this is realm of the expert, whose unconscious has learned to detect patterns and evaluate their importance in anticipating the behavior of situations that are too complex for the conscious mind to understand. During the lengthy period of practice needed to develop deep knowledge, the expert has developed an internal theory that guides their Knowledge (Proceeding), supporting their unique decision-making capability.

And here is the challenge to knowledge elicitation. Two tools are provided as examples of this process, both of which are included in Section IV. The first is called "Engaging Tacit Knowledge" and proposes a four-prong action model for greater access to an individual's tacit knowledge. The second is called "Group Reflection and Inquiry Protocol" (GRIP) which provides a group setting for extracting judgmental knowledge through storytelling and sensemaking.

As AI is becoming more prevalent, it is critical to have "experts" join in the exchange, that is, ensuring the domain expertise in an organization is fed into the AI system. This can be done by consistent conversations – question and answer sessions and the sharing of stories – between experts and the primary organizational AI system, all supported by the feed-in of and connection with surface and shallow knowledges that have been previously elicited. Advanced AI is designed on the functioning of the human mind/brain. Thus, it just makes sense that all we have learned to date (and continue to learn) about the intelligent complex adaptive learning system which is the human (see Chapter 2) can provide us insights into how to head our focused organizational AI system in the needed direction. This approach offers the opportunity to integrate the diverse expertise across the organization while simultaneously encouraging continuing deep dives from the human perspective in specific domains. In short, having the advantage of both the trees and the forest as we move into an uncertain future.

Knowledge Curation

The idea – and recognized importance – of curation has been around for centuries, and is well-used in connection with museums and other collections of important historic artifacts. However, in the 80's and 90's as data became more largely available, the idea of data curation appeared, shifting the focus from "things" or items in a collection or exhibition to data, information, and knowledge. At the data level, the focus is on the annotation, publication, and presentation of data to ensure that over time it is preserved for reuse. As we moved into the era of big data, curation of data became more significant as high volume and complex data systems emerged. Early examples include the Linguistic Data Consortium (a repository for linguistic data dating back to 1992) and the Sloan Digital Sky Survey (which began surveying the night sky in 2000). DataNet, a research program of the U.S. National Science foundation Office of Cyberinfrastructure, funded various data management project in the sciences, including DataONE (Data Observation Network for Earth), which helps the environment science community preserve and share data.

Recognizing the need for organizations to not only get useful insights faster, but to ensure a high level of fidelity and accuracy, IBM is blending foundational AI models and pretraining them on specific sets of data inclusive of an organization's curated data. In this way, the AI system is fine-tuned to better serve the organization in which it is embedded. Further, AI responses are now more trackable, that is, there is a wider opportunity to see why a particular solution is generated for a specific situation, which helps build trust in the system's response.

Knowledge curators play a significant role in organizing, evaluating, and maintaining an organization's knowledge assets to ensure easy accessibility to valuable and relevant information. Tasks might include categorizing information, creating and/or managing databases or knowledge repositories, developing taxonomies and ontologies, and/or implementing effective search and retrieval systems. In short, in a virtual world doing many of the historical jobs of a librarian. A knowledge curator might also participate with subject matter experts and other stakeholders to help identify critical knowledge areas and potential gaps or inefficiencies in those areas. By curating and organizing knowledge resources, they help maximize the value of the organization's intellectual capital, enabling employees to access the right information at the right time.

The knowledge team at George Washington University presents a straightforward four-step approach: (1) Perform an initial knowledge curation assessment (know you level of curation maturity and identify your starting point); (2) Knowledge capture and transfer (identify the knowledge to be curated, the human and automated sources of knowledge, the human and automated recipients of knowledge, the format for the knowledge, how the knowledge should be organized, and primary knowledge capture and transfer modalities); (3) Design the infrastructure (knowledge systems architecture, and tools land platforms); and (4) Formulate the governance model. That governance model has seven facets: (1) roles and responsibilities, (2) competencies, (3) knowledge assurance, (4) performance monitoring and adjustment, (5) training, (6) evangelizing/socializing, (7) reward/recognition systems.

KNOWLEDGE LEVERAGING

Best practices and lessons learned have no intrinsic value. Their benefits come from ensuring that they are effectively transferred and applied. However, recognizing that knowledge is relative, how do we make use of these practices in different situations?

Knowledge leveraging starts with good information (see Chapter 3). The harvesting of information that can create the knowledge needed to make the best decisions is achieved through good information systems, the flow of information and knowledge across the organization, and the decision-makers' knowledge and competency. Good information systems are systems and processes that ensure the quality, value, relevancy, integrity, currency and credibility of information and the ability to access what is needed. The flow of information and knowledge across an organization is enabled by the interactions among people, whether that is through formal work structures, teams and communities (addressed at length above), relationship networks (see Chapter 14), and casual conversations and discussions (see the discussion of knowledge sharing in Chapter 12).

But knowledge leveraging is even more. From his days in the military setting, Stankosky builds on the Force-Multiple Effect when talking about leveraging. He asks, so what if 1 + 1 = 2? He sees compounding as a very powerful financial concept, that is, focusing on how to *multiply knowledge assets* much like compound interest. As he says, "The beauty of knowledge assets are their intangibility, knowing no boundaries, [they] are limitless, and do not pollute. The management challenge is how to create an environment to leverage all the assets – both internally and externally."[519] Competitive advantage requires exponential growth. He suggests several approaches to multiply knowledge assets. First is good Business Intelligence – collecting data, information, and knowledge that can impact your organization to mitigate risk and improve decision-making. Second is innovation. While benchmarking is certainly a good learning tool, Stankosky pushed his students to go after "best-practices-to-be", looking to the future, not the past, leveraging knowledge assets to provide a unique window into the future. As he concludes: "Imagination is greater than knowledge".[520] And indeed, it is.

KNOWLEDGE MOBILIZATION (KMb)

Knowledge mobilization is the process of creating value through the creation, assimilation, leveraging, sharing and application of focused knowledge to a bounded community. This means that there is specific knowledge and a specific community and this specific knowledge is to be mobilized such that future decisions and consequent actions taken by community members are effective and sustainable. Thus, KMb is a process for moving specific knowledge to action (and value) in a bounded situation or location. Thinking in terms of *specific* knowledge (bounding this knowledge) and *specific* people who need that knowledge in *specific* situations helps produce an effective, targeted strategy for mobilization. This is the idea of chunking in order to achieve the successful embedding of knowledge in the target community. *Chunking* is the bringing together of several areas of knowledge in a manner that creates a more powerful set of related, integrated knowledges applicable to a predetermined need.

Activities that support KMb roughly fall into three categories: events occurring at a specific point in time (point events); meta-tools; and sustainability (Figure 11-6). Point events are product-based and are situation dependent and context sensitive. Research, products, and decisions are point events since they occur at a point of time within an identified framework. Examples would be research findings, reports and studies, fact sheets, policy and direction, and books and articles. Events might also include knowledge fairs, town halls, symposia, and conferences. The value of point events is generally understood by those who have engaged in knowledge transfer.

KMb meta-tools reflect set design philosophy, a robust capability in that they can be used in different situations and contexts. Different tools can be used individually or in varying combinations to achieve the desired results. This "set design" approach was introduced in the automobile industry in the 1980's by requiring subsystem contractors to design their subsystems with significant flexibility to adjust their parameters. For example, a manufacturer might make tradeoffs within certain bounds such as designing an item so that it could be used within flexible parameters such as smaller but heavier, or with less power but greater volume. Eventually set design led to open systems design. The concept as used here represents a process in which KMb tools are designed with the flexibility to respond to different situations as they unfold.

Meta-tools are process accelerators that are repeatable, scalable and robust. Examples would be good practices and best practice patterning (observing the patterns emerging from multiple applications of a best practice in different situations or different best practices in the same situation), andragogy-pedagogy and curriculum for classes, or a model for the transfer of research language. Integrative competencies could also be considered meta-tools (examples are systems thinking, complexity thinking, risk management, information literacy, relationship network management, knowledge management). Recognition and awards programs can also be considered meta-tools. In general, meta-tools are multidimensional and designed for multiuse, to be used in different ways in different situations.

Sustainability of KMb is based on developing a living network focused on connectivity and open resources, information flows, and the sharing of understanding through trusted relationships. Technology-based examples would be interactive learning environments and web-conferencing. With acknowledgement of boundaries, AI would be included as a sustainability tool. Teams, communities, internships, mentoring, job shadowing, and processes for the continuous sharing of information resources might also be considered sustainability processes.

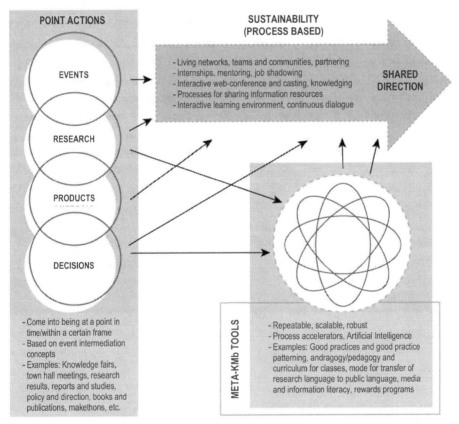

Figure 11-6. Knowledge Mobilization program activity.

It is always appropriate to note that any model is an artificial construct, yet models provide a vehicle for focusing on, understanding, and sharing concepts. Considerable overlaps in the KMb activities model will occur. For example, while development of a technology system might be considered a point event, the use of that system would be considered either a meta-tool (for example, a process for extracting research summaries) or a sustainability factor (an on-going community of practice support system). Likewise, point events develop resources for sustainability systems, and meta-tools may be technology-enabled for wide dissemination, ease of use, and continuous availability (becoming sustainability tools). What is important is to ensure that the value of all three activity areas is understood and engaged as appropriate to a specific knowledge mobilization need. The Bennet's book titled *Knowledge Mobilization in the Social Sciences and Humanities: Moving from Research to Action* developed in cooperation with the Social Sciences and Humanities Research Council of Canada contains multiple appendices full of point action, meta-tool, and sustainability examples.[521]

An example of knowledge mobilization is included in the discussion of knowledge types at the end of Chapter 4.

KNOWLEDGE PRODUCTIVITY

Knowledge productivity has been a dynamic element of human labor since the beginning of humanity. Across the centuries and around the world, the drive to make work easier and more productive by thinking smarter has blazed a wide trail of progress for the improvement of work. Results have been more than flashes of brilliance by gifted individuals. Progress has come in large measure by incremental gains, achieved with persistent thinking by shared minds seeking better ways to work.

Along the way, the myth that "productivity doesn't benefit workers" emerged, which originated from economists Thomas Piketty and Emanuel Suez, who forwarded that between 1979 and 2014 the real income growth in the U.S. declined by 8 percent while simultaneously labor productivity more than doubled. However, measuring real income, wage growth, and productivity is difficult and full of assumptions. When the internationally agreed-upon Canberra method is applied, the results are quite different. And there are other differences. Many studies measure only wage growth, not total compensation growth (which includes health care and retirement benefits). And some include only non-supervisory workers, dropping out millions of middle-wage supervisory workers. Further, all monetary measures over time need to be deflated to account for inflation; so it matters HOW productivity is measured. And, finally, over the last several decades government statistics have overstated productivity because of the methods used to measure the output of the computer sector. Looking at this from the bottom line, if indeed productivity was growing more than wages, then we would see profits growing dramatically, both of which have more or less kept pace.[522]

Now, in our times, the nature of knowledge productivity has been formalized and labeled – and is infinitely more complex – and seeks knowledge advancement more earnestly than ever. We need to employ it wisely because the next big leap in knowledge productivity, which is already in process, is immense. If we use knowledge well now, we will be ready for the next level.

Looking to the middle of the last century right after WWII, expectations and hopes were rising with the preservation of democracy and freedom. In the U.S., and in many other nations around the world, there was a formidable drive for learning how to do new things for one's livelihood. This soon led to excitement for discovering what could be created in this new information-rich environment, the Post-Industrial Era which came to be viewed as the Information Age. How did we shift from an Agricultural Economy to an Industrial Economy to an Information Economy, then to the current Knowledge Economy in one century with a depression decade and a World War in the middle for hard lessons? The emergence of Knowledge Economy indicators has been well documented in the extensive research and writings of the eminent economist Fritz Machlup. One of his landmark works, *The Production and Distribution of Knowledge in the United States*, details the nature of this emergence throughout the U.S. workforce. Machlup's research estimated that as of 1962 knowledge sector industries added up to nearly 30% of the gross national product.[523]

In concert with Machlup's early unveiling of the Knowledge Economy, Peter Drucker also laid out the economic patterns that were unfolding. Both saw the new economic catalyst of knowledge and innovation as a basic dynamic. Since Peter Drucker was widely regarded as the Father of Modern Management, when he labeled the modern workforce as *knowledge workers* there was global acceptance. Furthermore, in his book, *Post-Capitalist Society,* the final section titled *Knowledge* focused on the productivity of knowledge. He concluded with this pronouncement: "The only thing that increasingly will matter in national as in international economics is management's performance in making knowledge productive."[524]

The complexities of these shifts and how they challenged the prevailing culture were expressly addressed in Alvin Toffler's internationally regarded book *Future Shock,*[525] which has been translated into over 20 languages and published in over 50 countries. The concept of future shock caused by rapid economic change was clearly compared to the culture shock experience of transitioning from a familiar culture to a markedly different culture. We are experiencing that trauma now. Effective adaptation of knowledge productivity measures embolden this shift and enable the next shift, which will unfold by mid-century.

As the Knowledge Economy began to flourish, it gathered momentum from the accelerating pace of concurrent innovations in communication, transportation, and computer science. At the same time, informal and formal education, including advanced degrees, raced to keep up with the rising tide of learning needs. Endless advances in data and information performance along with volume also dominated the new economy. At the center of all this, in many ways knowledge itself was becoming the currency of the Knowledge Economy. This trend parallels the attention to intellectual capital concepts and measurements. Nevertheless, it is held here that valuing knowledge as an economic medium of exchange not only holds economic prominence; it is also likely to radically alter how knowledge is created and valued, how it flows, and how it is used during the 21st Century.

Given the accumulating value and the speed of change gathering in the Knowledge Economy, which is still underway, what can we expect when we turn to knowledge productivity? Simply defined at this juncture, *knowledge productivity is an organization's effective and efficient use of knowledge to achieve its goals and objectives.* This would include creation, acquisition, curating, sharing, using, leveraging, mobilizing, and mitigating knowledge risks.

Knowledge productivity strategies such as creating knowledge repositories, encouraging knowledge sharing and collaboration, and investing in training and development programs that promote continuous learning, leverage knowledge productivity. Technologies can also be used to facilitate sharing and collaboration and expand access to information and expertise, with astonishing capabilities in AI and Quantum unlocking our future. By effectively managing knowledge assets, organizations empower the ability to innovate, adapt to change, and achieve strategic objectives. To that end, we must individually have knowledge about how AI works. Moreover, we must contemplate how it can be developed to serve us at the next level of human economic, intellectual, organizational, social, and cultural endeavor.

As can be seen, knowledge productivity has the capacity to change dramatically against the quantity, quality, speed, prominence, and results of modern knowledge capacities. **The role of knowledge has now become a strategic element of human industry**; we could even say it plays a dominant role in our current and future history. Therefore, *What* is the nature of knowledge? and *What* is its potential? These are indeed questions related to why this book was written. In fact, the importance of this subject and the complexity of it are driving knowledge productivity and our lives in new ways. While knowledge management laid the groundwork, we are just at the beginning of the knowledge movement.

Future knowledge productivity, again with knowledge as "currency", may well comprise a "Knowledge Value System" including "banking" and "investment services". Furthermore, we are beginning to envision types of knowledge systems that are so different and powerful that some may function significantly without human participation. We might venture that the expansion of knowledge in human work is building to a crescendo of vibrant activity, in fact it may be leading to a level of bifurcation or state change in the human condition where services, growth, and needs are met in unprecedented ways. While we offer some potential insights in this volume, another book is warranted as a harbinger of the future. But for now, let's reflect: *How is knowledge rising in the Knowledge Economy and the Knowledge Age? Can you envision a Knowledge Culture? What is your personal model of knowledge productivity for yourself and what is at the heart of your personal model? And how does AI fit into this picture?*

KNOWLEDGE GOVERNANCE

Governance is about authority, decision-making, and accountability. Knowledge Governance includes the formal and information rules of how knowledge is handled in the organization, including the "management" activities related to creating, sharing, networking, organizing, storing, mobilizing, using, embedding, absorbing, and other "ing" words that relate to knowledge, inclusive of individual and organization learning as well as improvement processes relating to explicit and tacit knowledge. Wow, what a mouthful! Basically, it is the traditional idea of having a formal structure to ensure knowledge processes are managed throughout the organization, with someone or some part of the organization formally responsible and accountable to see that happens, and to integrate all of this with the information technology that supports it, the data assurance necessary for good information, the information management necessary for good knowledge, the integrative competencies necessary for leaders effectively using that knowledge, and the continuous validating in terms of value, relevancy, currency and credibility to ensure the availability and accessibility of the best knowledge in domains of interest to the organization. Of course, a good part of all that is what we have defined in the past as knowledge management.

Yet clearly governance is inclusive of MORE than management. In a paper titled "Distinguishing Governance from Management", Bader proposed seven guiding questions that determine what falls under governance. These address whether or not the issue/problem is about the future, whether it is mission critical or core to the organization, whether it has a big-picture scope, whether it is a high-level policy, whether it is an ethical issue, whether it requires oversight intervention, and whether it requires the highest level (CEO and Board) attention.[526] While this is a good set to reflect upon, and is focused on higher-level issues rather than the day-to-day issues that must be resolved at the point of action, all of these are equally important to the organization, as Bennet and Bennet posited when structuring the Intelligent Complex Adaptive System (ICAS) model for organizations of the future (see Chapter 2).

In short, knowledge governance is a job that no single person or part of the organization can accomplish ... that is, a job that needs to be spread throughout the organization, with accountability for the ownership of key knowledge areas where they reside in the organization, with monitoring and measuring of the application of knowledge at the point of action where its sharing and use occurs, and with everyone aware of, concerned with, and applying good knowledge practices in support of decision-making and innovation. And while a good Human Resources department will offer training resources, it is each employees responsibility to ensure they understand corporate expectations in this regard, and know HOW to ensure they meet those expectations. In short, **knowledge is everybody's business**.

When implementing Knowledge Management in the U.S. Department of the Navy (DON), we tied KM into the Chief Information Officer functions, with the Chief Knowledge Officer double-hatted as the Deputy CIO for Enterprise Integration. Thus, under the Office of the Secretary, they had the authority, decision-making, and accountability at the highest levels, yet this position and the supporting team was in the role of *leading and supporting* the organization as a *change agent* focused on the implementation of knowledge management, collaborating with IT and HR while simultaneously coordinating with (and learning from) a 300-strong community of practice who were the true knowledge leaders distributed around the world touching every functional area of the DON.

In 2002 based on the "strength of its knowledge management strategy and program", the DON was the first public sector organization to receive the Northern American MAKE (Most Admired Knowledge Enterprise) award, specifically noted for the leadership of its knowledge-based programs and initiatives, and its emphasis on organizational learning. While receipt of this visible recognition provided external validation of the effectiveness of the extensive program underway in the DON, the benefit to the Navy and Marine Corps had already been recognized and acknowledged at the highest levels of the organization. As the Secretary of the Navy wrote about the Chief Knowledge Officer later that year, her innovative enterprise knowledge technology and information management efforts had "transformed the DON as it entered into the 21st century", reducing costs, increasing operational effectiveness, and improving the quality of life for Sailors, Marines and civilians. In 2005, *Inside Knowledge* investigated the state of KM in the DON expecting to see a decline since there was no longer a CKO at the top of the organization. The resulting story titled "The Art of War: Empowering Front-Line Decision Making" was also featured in the editor's notes as he said,

> *This month's cover story details what can confidently be described as the most comprehensive and far-reaching knowledge-management initiative ever attempted anywhere in the world ... KM has ... become a fundamental*

aspect of the way the US Department of the Navy operates ... From the highest to the lowest ranks, from the corridors of Washington, DC to the

front line of military engagement, there is a prevailing understanding that knowledge, and by extension knowledge management, is everyone's business.[527]

And there it is. **Knowledge is everyone's business**. Note that this was not a one-time finding. In 2001, Larry Prusak, then-executive director of IBM's Institute for Knowledge Management in Cambridge, Massachusetts, wrote "The Navy has gone full speed ahead in adapting knowledge practices and processes. There is no company in the world anywhere near it in scope ... and it's a very balanced endeavor. They are talking about people, technology, and social relationships that make things work." That same year *Computer World* wrote in an article titled "Charting a Knowledge Management Course" that "The military's knowledge management programs are so comprehensive in fact that the private sector can learn much from them, from more effective ways to apply IT to new ways of teaching."

While this certainly started with a clear knowledge governance approach at the highest level of the organization, there was a three-year plan to embed KM throughout the organization at every level. In the course of this plan, every element in the current criteria for the MIKE (Most Innovative Knowledge Enterprise) award was addressed and aggressively pursued. Those criteria can be accessed at https//www.globalmikeaward.com. Knowledge is everybody's business.

Throughout Section II, there are short discussions on various aspects of knowledge governance, including potential roles and structures in Chapter 8, knowledge competencies in Chapter 12, and some sample tools in Section IV. All of these have a part to play in an overall knowledge strategy. Yes, knowledge governance is important, but perhaps not sufficient as it is historically perceived.

TRANSITIONING FROM IMPLEMENTING TO SUSTAINING

As noted previously, but as a reminder, **Planning-Preparing-Implementing-Sustaining** is a continuous transaction between individuals, the organization, stakeholders, and the environment. While steps of the process often overlap, there are also specific transition phases occurring in concert with the shifts from step to step that smooth the transition. As feedback occurs and new ideas, approaches or directions emerge, the cycle begins again in a continuous loop of change and transformation. Key Elements of the transition phase from Preparing to Implementing are Co-Evolving with the Environment and Training and Learning with a focus on Pattern Thinking and Managing Self.

Co-Evolving with the Environment

To sustain high performance, most organizations have to co-evolve with, rather than try to dominate, their environment. Co-evolving requires continuous training and learning and an openness and willingness to try new ideas (see the tool "Humility as a Choice" in Section IV). This means there is an element of risk that must be accepted and supported for long-term gain. It is important to make course adjustments as strategies and initiatives are implemented, and be willing to shift or modify a well-laid plan as internal and external perturbations occur.

Take a few minutes to review the readiness elements in Chapter 9: adaptability, resilience, alignment, robustness, and quick response, and look at "Jack be Nimble, Jack be Quick". As no doubt you have experienced in the current competitive environment, sustainability continues to rely on the organization's ability to be adaptable, resilient, aligned, robust and to respond quickly. All of these contribute to the organization's future success.

Training and Learning

In a changing and uncertain environment, an organization is considered healthy when it has the internal capacity and capability to deal with this new reality over time. Sustainability requires continuous training and education, the measurement of performance, and long-term consistency of direction of the organization. While the organizational sustainability factors are critical, individual competencies are also important to enable wise decision-making at all levels. One of the most important – if not the most important – individual knowledge competency in a shifting world space is managing self. Below, we first address the important competency of pattern thinking, which enables seeing the larger picture, and then introduce managing self as a competency.

Pattern Thinking

More and more organizational science has developed an understanding of pattern thinking. Whether in scenario planning or on the competitive battlefront of business, identifying and understanding emerging patterns and the entanglement among those patterns can determine the best decisions and actions. The same is true for information superiority, whether connected to warfare or business strategies. Identifying and studying unfolding patterns related to the content and context of an implementation situation enables informed decision-making. Through observation and feedback (the sense and response mode of complexity thinking), clear patterns will begin to emerge that identify strengths and weaknesses in the implementation process. Most often, the earlier these are identified, the easier it is to make a course correction.

Pattern Thinking is not primarily thinking *through* patterns, although over time this will occur, rather it is looking for patterns in the outside world and bringing them into your conscious awareness. The intent of Pattern Thinking is to let the pattern emerge as a mode of understanding a situation, purposefully thinking about external patterns in order to understand, solve problems, create new ideas, and improve the capacity to forecast the outcomes of decisions. Thinking *about* patterns is different than thinking *with* patterns. If you start with a specific pattern in mind, no doubt you will find it, to the exclusion of other significant patterns that may be occurring. However, using archetypes can also stimulate recognition; for example, reflect on the value of the archetypes used in Peter Senge's Systems Thinking, which is based on matching a recurring set of relationships (archetypes) to a situation at hand. While this force-fitting helps facilitate an understanding of causal relationships in simple and complicated situations, complexity infers the inability to understand simple cause-and-effect relationships due to the large number of unpredictable relationships and nonlinearity. Still, once you have used the Systems Thinking models a number of times, you begin to think systems and discover systems patterns beyond the archetypes.

Pattern Thinking utilizes both systems thinking and complexity thinking. From the neuroscience perspective, Pattern Thinking involves mental exercise that stimulates the brain. The best mental exercise is new learning in multiple areas of the brain, acquiring new knowledge and doing things you've never done before. Looking at things differently, making new connections, seeing new relationships, and bringing patterns into your conscious stream of thought does just that. (See Chapter 16 on Knowledge Capacities.) When addressing a difficult situation where there are not a clear cause-and effect relationships, individuals who are continuous learners, regardless of their focus of learning or areas of passion, will often see patterns that suggest decision directions. Once in the middle of a situation comprised of networks of relationships, even the most rigorous focus and attention to detail may not present solutions. However, this type of rigor does supply your unconscious with additional patterns to complex with all your past experiences and education. While immediate answers may not be available, this process accelerates unconscious learning (the unconscious can detect patterns that the conscious mind cannot), thus increasing the potential for intuitive insights. See Chapter 19 on systems and complexity thinking.

Managing Self

While clearly it would be impossible to cover the topic of "managing self" in a few paragraphs since we are all aware that humans are complex adaptive systems (see Chapter 2), and hopefully *intelligent* complex adaptive systems, we still intend to direct your attention toward this critical knowledge competency. And the first point IS to acknowledge that we are complex adaptive systems, which means that we are changing every minute of our lives, and that as our large number of interrelated parts interact there is the quality of emergence occurring, allowing us to adapt to changing inner and outer environments. This also means that we are operating at some level of disequilibrium – which is necessary for adapting but which can contribute to unpredictable behavior! (Now you have something to blame that unpredictable behavior on!)

A second point is that we have an inner and outer self, a consciousness and an unconsciousness, both powerful forces but *not always in sync*. Within each of us, embedded across cortical columns in the neocortex, is a personal ever-changing representation of the world. The neocortex is the organ of intelligence, which receives input from movement, generates behaviors, and predicts the future. Reference frames within the cortical columns enable the ability to perceive shape, changes, and locations relative to each other, providing the flexibility to process and navigate a changing, uncertain and complex environment.

A third point is that we individually and collectively are on a learning journey which encompasses the physical, mental, emotional, and spiritual domains, what is described as the Intelligent Social Change Journey.[528] And each of us is all those things – physical, mental, emotional and spiritual – and they cannot be separated out. We have learned this lesson through the progression of our organizations. Not too many years ago in the world of business, assembly line workers were asked to just do certain physical tasks, repeatedly and well. They were paid for the physical actions of their bodies and hands, often without knowledge of what happened next or how the work they did related to the whole. This "management" knowledge was held closely by the supervisor or the manager or the owner, and served as a source of power. This is where the concept of "knowledge is power" emerged.

Then, businesses began to realize that good ideas could emerge from people throughout the workplace, and as these ideas added to the bottom line, the power of mental thought in terms of new products and processes came to the fore. The focus of work began to shift from the product of the physical body to the product of the mental plane, with physical strength still retaining a place of honor. This mental focus flourished in the bedrock of bureaucracy, where knowledge continued to be held close since position and remuneration were highly dependent on that knowledge, i.e., knowledge as power. The self that was valued, then, was determined in a dualistic fashion, that is, the capabilities of this physical body versus the capabilities of others; the knowledge of this manager versus the illiteracy of others. Intelligence was determined by an IQ test, and competition moved to the front line, determining success in sports, education and business, and creating winners and losers.

It wasn't until the latter part of the 20th century that it was generally recognized that emotional intelligence had a great deal to do with success. As previously believed, emotions could *not* be left at the door when entering the workplace. Discernment and discretion (D^2) – judgment and decision – engage emotions and feelings, whether occurring with conscious awareness or being processed in the unconscious. Thus, the emergence of Emotional Intelligence along with the physical and mental, but for goodness sakes leave your spirituality and religious beliefs at the door! They don't belong in the workplace! Only, as we moved toward the 21st century, we began to realize that basic spiritual and religious grounding play a very large role in values, beliefs, and ethics that are core to an employee's – and the organization's – success! Table 11-1 details this journey.

Table 11-1. Workplace progression expanding through IQ, EQ and SQ.

In addition to physical activity, recognition of power in, need for, and potential value to the organization of worker's:

Thinking Capabilities (Mental body)	Emotions & Feelings (Emotional body)	Values & Meaning (Spiritual body)

1970	1980-2010→	1998→	2012→
Beginning of post-bureaucratic era. (More benign and malleable structure.)	Rise of Information and Knowledge Organization (Full employee involvement)	Emotional Intelligence (Can effectively manage ourselves and relationships.)	Spiritual Intelligence (Grounding for values, virtue, and morality. Ability to behave with wisdom and compassion.)
Building on new theories such as Theories X, Y and Z, charismatic and Transformational Leadership, General Systems Theory and Organizational Linking Pins, Tayloristic time and motion mgmt. and participative mgmt. bring in worker responsibility and empowerment. Language of innovation in and out of the spotlight.	Technological advancements and virtual connectivity on a global scale enabled increased communication, collaboration and networking, both virtual and real. Wide knowledge creation, sharing and application. Increased economic affluence of the worker in developed countries coupled with increased education level.	Focused on learning more about ourselves and others: self-awareness; social awareness and social skills. EI recognized as a basic requirement for effective use of the intellect. Recognition that emotions/feelings are necessary part of judging and decision-making.	Spiritual is standing in relationship to another based on matters of the soul, the animating principle of human life in terms of thought and action focused on its moral aspects, the emotional part of human nature, and higher development of the mental faculties. Pertains to the intellect and the ability to think abstractly or profoundly and to the sensitivity of the mind beyond material things.

We had finally recognized that people are complex adaptive systems, and, as noted above, that the entangled physical, mental, emotional, and spiritual systems *cannot be separated from each other*. Reality System Theory says just that, taking a holistic approach to management and leadership in organizations, comingling the dynamically interacting influences of the intellectual, emotional and spiritual. Reality System Theory specifically focuses on how this comingling *energizes* organizational culture, thereby improving individual, team and organizational performance. As Stebbins describes, "The human reality is a dynamic holistic system subject to the continuous ebb and flow of intellectual, emotional, and spiritual influences."[529]

Reality System Theory looks through the lens of Quantum physics, building on Heisenberg's uncertainty principle[530] and the contextualism of the Quantum field.[531] The now-classic uncertainty principle refers to the particle/wave fluctuation and contextualism refers to context sensitivity, that is, change as a function of surroundings. Of contextualism, Wilber reminds us that, "Meaning is context-dependent, and contexts are boundless."[532]

Humans are integral parts of a larger whole, part of a holistic human potentially capable of intelligent decisions and actions. As Zohar and Marshall quote, "Neither IQ nor EQ [nor SQ], separately or in combination, is enough to explain the full complexity of human intelligence nor the vast richness of the human soul and imagination."[533]

Thus, as can be seen, managing self is a lifetime occupation, but one which can have rich rewards for the individual and any organization of which they are a part. While there are many good books, and more emerging, on aspects of managing self, we humbly recommend *Unleashing the Human Mind: A Consilience Approach to Managing Self* for deep seekers of knowledge. This book – to which both authors contributed – is grounded in the Intelligent Complex Adaptive Learning System (ICALS) theory based on over a decade of researching experiential learning through the expanding lens of neuroscience. The ICALS theory was introduced in Chapter 2.

CHAPTER 12

SUSTAIN

SELF LEADERSHIP (308) ... Mindfulness (309) ... NURTURING ORGANIZATIONAL HEALTH (311) ... The Microstress Effect (312) ... KNOWLEDGE COMPETENCIES (313) ... KNOWLEDGE EMBEDDING (313) ... KNOWLEDGE SHARING (315) ... Context (315) ... Memes (317) ... Knowledge Hiding (318) ... TRUST (319) ... Transparency (323) ... Perception Management (324) ... EVALUATING AND MEASURING (325) ... Measuring with the MIKE (326) ... RECOGNITION AND REWARDS (327) ... CONTINUOUS LEARNING (328) ... Consciousness Expanding (329) ... CHANGE AS A CONSTANT (330) ... MOVING TOWARD WISDOM (332) ... Defining Wisdom (333) ... The Wisdom Model (336)

The strategy or initiative is underway. While your measures have been determined early in the Planning stage, now is where they will tell the story. Thus, a discussion of measures is included below. A classic and continuing challenge to managers is to follow through on a strategy, program or project. Too often they start with a big bang and gradually fade into the distance as other demands (and perhaps opposition) slow down momentum. Understandably, from experiences like these, many workers take a cautious or even cynical view of new efforts to "improve" the organization. This makes it even more important that any new program or strategy is designed to be sustainable for as long as it contributes to the health and performance of the organization.

The responsibility for success is that of every employee in the organization. By now it may be clear that a knowledge strategy is not "done to" but "done with". In a highly-dynamic operational environment with increasingly complex workloads and less time to manage, direct, and develop subordinates, [534] a higher value is placed on self-learning,[535] soft skills,[536] and self-leadership.[537]

SELF-LEADERSHIP

Self-leadership is on the spectrum that moves from external management towards self-management, with employees at all levels of the organization becoming over time more dependent on intrinsic incentives. Self-leadership is built on the premise that ultimately human composures are controlled by internal forces. As Manz says, it is a process which assumes a "comprehensive self-influence perspective" that concerns "leading oneself toward performance of naturally motivating tasks as well as managing oneself to do work that must be done but is not naturally motivating".[538] We begin to see why managing self is such an important competency personally and professionally. Self-leadership has many work-related benefits. For example, it has been found to have positive impacts on productivity, quality of work, self-efficacy, job satisfaction, and career success; and dampening impacts on absenteeism, turnover, stress, and anxiety.[539]

There are three distinct strategies for operationalizing Self-leadership: a behavior-focus (BF), natural rewards (NR), and constructive self-thought (CST).[540] BF raises self-awareness to encourage desirable behaviors and discourage undesirable behaviors. For example, strategies include self-goal setting, self-cueing, self-observation, and self-reward and self-punishment. NR concerns the creation of situations where motivations and rewards stem from inherently enjoyable task activities. This might mean including enjoyable features specifically, or redirecting attention from unpleasant job aspects to rewarding ones. CST pertains to positive habitual thinking, which improves efficacy perceptions and, subsequently, performance. This requires identification of dysfunctional thoughts and replacing them with constructive assumptions and beliefs, engaging a mental imagery visualizing successful task completion prior to engagement, or it might take the form of a constructive internal dialogue towards a positive disposition.

With self-leadership a highly desirable 21st Century work competency, there is a need to foster and nurture this capacity with employees, which is a dual-held responsibility of the organization and the individual.[541] The good news is that self-leadership can be learned,[542] and its contribution to the organization is considerable.

Mindfulness

Mindfulness can be described as non-judgmental awareness and attention occurring in the instant at hand on thoughts, feelings and emotions;[543] the learning to change perspectives,[544] with open interpretation of objects rather than seeing them as fixed; and the ability to switch attention between events with unbiased thoughts.[545]

Both focused on self-regulation, self-leadership and mindfulness are linked. Self-leadership engages future-oriented strategies towards an internal drive for positive outcomes, and mindfulness focuses on the self in the present context, with self-awareness of personal values towards authenticity[546] and attention to the moment[547] both sitting at that nexus.

Self-leadership is very much concerned with a "way of being" focused on personal development of the self, with this development involving the cultivation of present awareness and mental models[548] integrated with a sense of identity[549] stemming from beliefs, values and abilities.[550] Learning how to anchor one's self in the present and aligning with appropriate goals and momentary sensations[551] can be drawn upon as an awareness-expanding process to develop leadership capacity in people.[552]

In a 2022 research study of non-managerial employees, Worawichayavongsa and Bennet[553] found that mindfulness practice induces engagement in a comprehensive breadth of self-leadership strategies. Participants reported improvement in the areas of personal, individual work, and working with others. In the "personal" areas, they reported greater emotional control (53%), more self-compassion (38%) and self-control (9%); a greater feeling of being supported (43%), self-worth (19%), purpose (19%), and professional image (19%); increased job satisfaction (56%) and positive emotion (35%); and greater attention to detail (37%), higher awareness (27%) and self-reflection (27%), and a higher level of alertness (9%). As an example of a summary comment from one participant: *When I am working now, I have a clear sense of why I am doing this job and how it is important to* [the organization]. *Before, I had no idea really why I was doing many things I was doing.*

In the "individual work" areas, when looking at self-initiated behaviors, participants reported greater independence (42%), involvement (17%), engagement (13%), proactiveness (6%), problem-solving (8%), self-motivation (6%), organizational comfort (4%), and critical thinking (4%). They also reported an improvement in positive attitude (46%), the ability to embrace change (25%), as well as being committed (16%) and motivated (13%). There was also an increase in ownership (53%), professional capacity (29%) and confidence (18%) as well as learning (75%) career focus (19%), and the recognition that helping leads to more work (6%), although there was no indication of whether that was positive or negative. Re their perceived work performance, they reported an increase in quality output (46%), an increase in effectiveness (27%), and an increase in productivity (20%). The bottom line is summed up in this participant's statement: *I have been seeing that the work I produce is much more professional and of a higher standard ... I get more done and do it better.*

In the areas of working with others regarding relationships, participants reported better interactions (36%), improved relationship building (22%), trust and support (10%), team spirit (8%), knowledge transfer (7%), and better conflict resolution (7%). They also felt they had improved perspective taking (67%), were able to take a systems view (18%), and increased empathy (15%). And from one participant: *I know things that others can learn from and I have been teaching some of my younger colleagues how to do their job better ... it feels really nice to share what I know because I have realized I get pleasure out of passing on what I know so they can become better at their job.*

While this is only a short summary of the results, it is clear that mindfulness practice appears to be a promising professional development route to nurture self-leadership.

NURTURING ORGANIZATIONAL HEALTH

To be sustainable, a program has to validate its contribution to the vision and mission. But that is not enough. The program needs to be able to co-evolve with its environment, adapting to the changing needs of the organization and its stakeholders. A major contribution offered by implementation of a knowledge strategy is its ability to help the entire organization adapt and maintain sustainable high performance by nurturing organizational health.

Organizational health is the capacity to maintain high performance in a changing, uncertain, complex and anxiety-producing environment. An organization is considered healthy when it has the internal capacity and capability to deal with this new reality *over time*, i.e., sustainability. Sustaining high performance in a dynamic and uncertain environment is a significant challenge. All contributing to agility, eight factors that significantly influence the capacity of organizations to sustain high performance in such an environment are provided below with descriptions.

- ❖ **Continuous learning** (workers and organizations always gaining knowledge and adapting behavior)
- ❖ **Quick response** (the organization is capable of reacting/responding quickly when needed)
- ❖ **Robustness** (the capacity to operate in a broad range of environments)
- ❖ **Resiliency** (the ability to recover from shocks or setbacks and resume its original performance)
- ❖ **Flexibility** (capable of being changed, or flexed, susceptible to influence or persuasion, tractable)
- ❖ **Adaptability** (the ability to change to fit a specific need or situation; an alteration or adjustment in structure or habits)
- ❖ **Stakeholder satisfaction** (providing value that satisfies stakeholders— customers, governance boards, regulatory agencies, local communities and employees)
- ❖ **Alignment** (the capacity of an organization to simultaneously maintain organizational cohesion and worker empowerment).

In a 2005 MQI research study involving participants from 24 U.S. government organizations, 200 senior executives surveyed felt that stakeholder satisfaction, resilience, and robustness were strengths of their organizations. On the other hand, alignment, adaptability, quick response, and flexibility were seen as organizational capabilities that were below average. This meant that their organizations were controlling without good cohesion, structurally difficult to change, and perhaps slow to respond and not very flexible – characteristics typical of a bureaucracy. Rightfully so, there was significant concern expressed regarding the government's ability to deal with an environment that is rapidly becoming more dynamic, uncertain and complex.

This has become even more difficult today in an economically fluctuating, politically divisive, environmentally challenging, and pandemic stricken worldscape, regardless of the knowledge domain of focus. Certainly not for lack of trying, small and large organizations are closing their doors while others need to completely rethink the way they do work. The foundational concepts of Adaptability, Resilience, Alignment, Robustness, and Quick Response are detailed in-depth in the first half of Chapter 8 on Readiness.

When an organization recognizes the value knowledge and knowledge sharing contribute to organizational sustainability – a focus on the value of people, their learning, and their interactions – they begin building the foundation for sustainability. In a coherent organization, when the organization is aligned with its mission while focused on stakeholder satisfaction, then the best knowledge can be made available to decision-makers every day at all levels of the organization.

The Microstress Effect

Cross and Dillon's new book on the *Microstress Effect* is an eye-opener – or perhaps we should say a mind-opener. They forward that a hidden epidemic has infiltrated our organizations with invisible and devastating effects. While we might immediately credit this to demanding work and anxiety emerging from the confluence of internal and external problems and challenges, this is not the case. Surprisingly, microstress "embeds itself in our minds and accumulates daily, one microstress on top of the other" with a debilitating long-term impact.[554] Their finding is that this stress, which is "baked into our lives", largely comes from colleagues, friends, and family!

In the workplace, microstresses drain personal capacity (examples include misalignment of priorities, others' unreliability and unpredictable behavior, or volume of collaborative demands), deplete emotional reserves (confrontational conversations, mistrust, political maneuvering), and challenge your identity (pressure to pursue goals inconsistent with your values, attacks on self-confidence, or disruptions to your network).[555] This, of course, goes two ways. Whether realized or not, through behaviors such as second-guessing your team or offering help beyond your capabilities you can cause others microstress.

The authors suggest developing a "resilience network", which they see as essential to coping with microstress.[556] This is a network where you can have authentic, revitalizing conversations with others. In Chapter 14 six basic tenets for building a successful relationship network are forwarded. As noted, these are interdependency, trust, common framework, openness, flow, and equitability. This chapter on Relationship Network Management is worth reading.

KNOWLEDGE COMPETENCIES

In the transitioning phrases from **Planning** to **Preparing** to **Implementing** to **Sustaining** we have included short segments on various knowledge competencies, touching briefly on Planning, Intention and Attention, Synthesis, Reflective Listening and Otherness, Humility, Presencing, and Managing Self. Other knowledge competencies are mentioned throughout Section II. An important organization competency for small knowledge organizations who do not have R&D capability is absorptive capacity, which is briefly introduced in Chapter 11 and detailed by an international expert in Chapter 17.

In the competitive landscape of today's business environment, knowledge competencies can be the determinant of organizational success. Yet the competencies needed in each organization to a large extent are relative to the organization, and if not fully understood, benchmarked, and assessed can become a failure point for the organization. Competencies – the skills, personal traits, and behaviors contributing to exceptional performance[557] – include both technical skills and the personal qualities related to high performance.

Senivongse contends that since competency inherently resides at the individual level and each person plays a role in the organization, that effectively managing individual competency is a critical initial step towards securing a sustainable competitive advantage for the organization. He forwards that to proactively manage competencies requires collaborative efforts between leaders and the HR department and involves three key activities: (1) identifying specific competencies needed for each occupational role, (2) using assessment tests to evaluate the presence of these competencies, and (3) establishing a correlation between individual competencies and performance indicators in order to judge effectiveness.[558] In short, in a knowledge organization, competency management is essential.

KNOWLEDGE EMBEDDING

All the steps taken in the start-up and the growth and expansion phase ensure project expectations are firmly in place during the sustainability phase. The implementation team understands expectations and is a cohesive, connected body, empowered and making decisions at the points of action. The ultimate goal is for the implementation team to *move into a supporting role* as the strategy or initiative becomes embedded in the everyday life of the organization.

There are various ways to facilitate this embedding. For example, storytelling is a powerful tool for sustaining change. Throughout history stories – accounts or recitals of an event or series of events which may be real or fictional – have shared a unique relationship with mankind. Stories are knowledge, a breathing example of the "what" and "why" of our experiences, and our knowledge of the world is more or less equivalent to our experiences.

Storytelling has been used in American Indian communities from their early beginnings to recount the history of the people, tell where they came from, educate children about cultural morals and values, and explain the supernatural and peculiar aspects of animals and the environment. The construction of fictional examples (or of true experiences) to illustrate a point can be used to effectively transfer knowledge. When well-constructed, stories can convey a high level of complex meaning and values. There are many excellent books available on the power of story in organizations.

A variety of story forms exist naturally throughout every organization, including scenarios – the articulation of possible future states, constructed within the imaginative limits of the author, and anecdotes – brief sequences captured in the field or arising from brainstorming sessions. While scenarios provide awareness of alternatives, they can also be used as planning tools for possible future situations. Anecdotes can be used to reinforce positive behavior; leaders can seek out and disseminate true anecdotes that embody the values desired in the organization. Healthy organizations are filled with anecdotes.

For example, Singapore Armed Forces (SAF) using story and storytelling as a form of knowledge sharing to inculcate organizational core values. Stories were collected from 25 senior leaders (admirals and generals) and 8 officers who had been involved in SAF foreign operations related to humanitarian or peacekeeping assignment were interviewed. These stories generally fell into three categories: (1) stories of which leaders were a part or that had impacted their lives as remembered by them; (2) views, opinions and feelings about specific core values, specifically those values in the context of a military career; and (3) personal journeys, those situations in their careers and lives about which leaders have passion. Themes emerged which helped understand and define what those core values meant to SAF leadership. See the tool titled Value Infusion Methodology in Section IV.

The second part of the project was operationalizing the stories and the values they convey. This might begin with a train-the-trainers workshop to embed the stories throughout other training and educational opportunities in the organization. Initial workshops for employees would cover the telling, analysis, interpretation, and meaning of the values as they relate to the performance and reputation of the organization. The role of each value in support of organizational performance would be addressed, and open discussions give everyone the opportunity to participate. Working in small groups, each group would consider a story and its value(s) with regard to their personal values, identifying and discussing different perspectives and feelings. During the course, participants are encouraged to write and tell their own stories, and provided tools to help them capture, sculpt and tell their stories.

Another popular approach is the creation of a virtual storyteller who is available to tell the stories in the story repository in response to specific related questions. And in today's world, let's bring in AI as an element of our storyteller, based on the stories collected from organizational leaders, of course. A contest might be regularly held where the best stories contributed by employees become part of the story repertoire of the virtual storyteller. Another approach would be creation of a knowledge fair with stories and storytelling a key focus area. As can be seen, the story repository as a knowledge sharing approach has a high potential for use as a resource for infusing organizational core and operational values in both new and long-term employees.

KNOWLEDGE SHARING

Knowledge sharing is not merely a transfer of information; it is bringing people together to interact and exchange different experiences and develop shared understanding and create a coherent organization. Any time two or more employees talk – and listen to each other – dialogue is occurring. Through dialogue an individual's context can be conveyed, allowing each participant to gain the explicit knowledge shared by the other and to create new knowledge through a mutual learning process. For example, mentoring – a relationship between an experienced leader and a younger professional in a related field – can facilitate the sharing of context that supports development of shallow and deep knowledge.

While knowledge sharing is referenced throughout this book, we specifically explore knowledge sharing below in terms of context, memes, and knowledge hiding.

Context

Context is an important concept in the knowledge movement. While not everyone recognizes that Einstein's "relativity" applies to our everyday world, all knowledge – whether your personal knowledge or anyone else's – is context sensitive and situation dependent. This means something that works in one situation may not work in what is perceived as a similar situation. In *The Course of Knowledge: A 21st Century Theory*, there are eight avenues of context identified beginning with information (the content) and ending with the overarching pattern context. See Figure 12-1.

Knowledge is one of those rare things you can give away and still have. As introduced earlier, in the past, knowledge was used in organizations to control others and maintain power. Today, "knowledge hoarders"—still operating on the bureaucratic meme that knowledge is power – have limited value to their organizations and often create cultural barriers to learning. Clearly, it is best to develop and share as much knowledge as possible so that others can act

PATTERNS IN TERMS OF CONTEXT

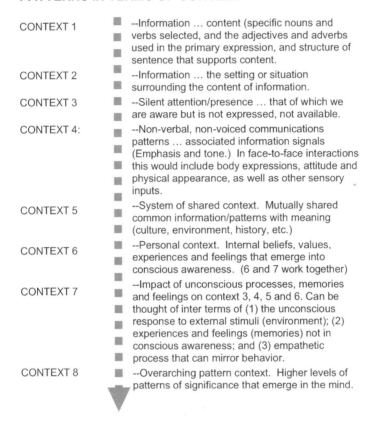

CONTEXT 1 — --Information … content (specific nouns and verbs selected, and the adjectives and adverbs used in the primary expression, and structure of sentence that supports content.

CONTEXT 2 — --Information … the setting or situation surrounding the content of information.

CONTEXT 3 — --Silent attention/presence … that of which we are aware but is not expressed, not available.

CONTEXT 4: — --Non-verbal, non-voiced communications patterns … associated information signals (Emphasis and tone.) In face-to-face interactions this would include body expressions, attitude and physical appearance, as well as other sensory inputs.

CONTEXT 5 — --System of shared context. Mutually shared common information/patterns with meaning (culture, environment, history, etc.)

CONTEXT 6 — --Personal context. Internal beliefs, values, experiences and feelings that emerge into conscious awareness. (6 and 7 work together)

CONTEXT 7 — --Impact of unconscious processes, memories and feelings on context 3, 4, 5 and 6. Can be thought of inter terms of (1) the unconscious response to external stimuli (environment); (2) experiences and feelings (memories) not in conscious awareness; and (3) empathetic process that can mirror behavior.

CONTEXT 8 — --Overarching pattern context. Higher levels of patterns of significance that emerge in the mind.

Figure 12-1. Descriptions of the avenues of context. The higher the number of related (relevant) patterns, the greater resonance between the source and perceiver and the increased sharing of understanding.

independently and develop their own internal, and situation-driven, behavior. Knowledge begets knowledge. Through reciprocal sharing, creativity and innovation spring into being.

While a necessary first step, simply having access to information that has successfully been used as knowledge in the past (knowledge artefacts) does not constitute sharing. For example, many organizations make information available through technology systems, but fail to incorporate knowledge maps or expertise guides for users so they can find what they need, have a deeper understanding of the context of what they find, and put it to effective use. Yet, knowledge sharing and the movement of knowledge throughout the organization has become a strategic necessity to survival. The knowledge, skills, and ideas that need to be connected expand beyond corporate and industry boundaries, with collaborative innovation with clients and other stakeholders becoming common place. As Lee discovered when evaluating the Most Innovative Knowledge

Enterprises, networks form the backbone for an organizational knowledge chain to tap into community resources needed to run their businesses, and organizations are reaching out to the general public through Web 2.0, mobile Apps and mainstream social media.[559]

Open communications across an organization play a large role in facilitating knowledge sharing, and cyber space events such as hackathons, makeathons, ideathons and innovation jams can be both fun and productive. In addition to interactions through teams, communities and meetings, good practices, lessons learned, discussion forums, and anecdotal circles still prove useful, especially for new employees, and can be supported through regular communications vehicles, whether virtual or face-too-face, some of which can be made available to stakeholders. Specific ways to engage stakeholders include community meetings, focus groups and town halls, all of which can be facilitated virtually, as well portals, a customer-oriented product data center, Wiki libraries, and mobile phone Apps.

Ideally, knowledge sharing supported by truth, trust, and transparency emerges as part of the culture. Some examples that facilitate knowledge sharing include the support and use of teams and communities as part of the everyday work process, the example of openness and integrity set by senior leadership; and a recognition program that rewards knowledge sharing. An APQC (American Productivity & Quality Center) report on "Creating a Knowledge-Sharing Culture" stated that "there is no one right set of motivators to encourage people to share insights and build on the ideas of others." While indeed this is true, what draws people to share knowledge in a specific setting is alignment with the current culture and a practical purpose to share.

Memes

As introduced previously, a meme is an idea, behavior pattern, or piece of information that is passed on, again and again, through the process of imitation such that it takes on a life of its own.[560] Memes may or may not reflect the original intent of an idea. They act as replicators of information (that may become knowledge) as they spread throughout groups of people.

The role that memes play in learning, the creation of knowledge, comes from their capability to be retained in memory because of their sound and perceived meaning. Of course, learning only occurs if their meaning and relevance is understood by individuals within the group. This means that for memes to spread they need to relate to the culture, attitude, expectations and interest of a group.

Learning can be greatly enhanced by the effective choice and use of memes throughout the communication process. Because they are symbolic, people using similar memes, together with common syntax and semantics, can understand each other much more effectively and rapidly, thereby more easily creating social networks which facilitate the transmission of information and the creation of knowledge. Memes become strong (more memorable) when they are delivered in connection with an emotional event that engages the feelings of the listener/participant. A well-known example of a meme is the U.S. Army's slogan for many years: *Be all you can be!*

In the DON we used this understanding to communicate concepts that were critical to the Department. For example, to promote creativity and innovation in the Acquisition cycle we developed a program called "Change through Exchange" which quickly spread across the Acquisition Workforce, where it originated. A strategy was developed and a stand-down day designated to start the behavior change necessary for implementation. One over-arching event that day was an opening ceremony with representations from various commands (enough to fill an auditorium), an introduction by the Undersecretary, who, since it occurred on St. Patrick's Day was bagpiped down the center aisle up to the stage. Each participant had a "dance card" which had to be filled by the end of the two-hour event. In between each speaker (who were command representatives sharing an innovative idea that was adding value) were 15-minute breaks where, to fill their dance card, participants had to connect with someone new in the auditorium and share an innovative idea related to the Acquisition process (and that's a big "A", which means multi-million dollar and up platforms such as ships and weapons) from their command. It proved amazingly successful, with commands setting up their own "Change through Exchange" follow-on events.

Knowledge Hiding

As the necessity for knowledge sharing in organizations became more fully recognized, along with that recognition came awareness of knowledge withholding, hoarding, and hiding as non-sharing behaviors.[561] As Yang, Ribiére and Bennet convey – based on the findings of dozens of organizational research studies from 2014 through 2019 – this behavior

> … not only results in harmed interpersonal relationships, reduced individual creative performance, and decreased innovative work behavior, but also jeopardizes team viability, team creativity, and project team performance, while encouraging organizational deviance.[562]

In her focused research on this topic, doctoral candidate Kaiyu Yang, studying at IKI-SEA Bangkok University, forwards that organizational culture plays a prominent role in mitigating knowledge hiding since employees generally tend to comply with organizational norms and expectations. Her research has shown that building a positive and open environment leads to collaboration and knowledge sharing, which helps remove the organizational foundation of knowledge hiding, thus limiting it.

However, because of the amount of effort and length of time required to change a culture, Yang says that "developing and promoting prosocial leadership styles is a more maneuverable strategy."[563] This would be utilizing leadership style as a management intervention to deter employee knowledge hiding. In this regard, role modeling as well as transformation, empathic, altruistic, ethical and individual-focused empowering leadership styles have all been found to help mitigate knowledge hiding behavior.

Another mitigating approach is task design, ensuring that members involved in the same task depend on others' work to accomplish their work. This interdependency opens lines of communication and knowledge sharing on a daily basis. This is explained by social exchange theory,[564] which posits that interpersonal relationships are based on a cost-benefit calculation, and thus prosocial activities generate favor in return and mistreatments generate retaliation. When knowledge sharing is an indispensable part of an employees work the undesirability of knowledge hiding is strengthened throughout the task process.

Yang further forwards that human resource management needs to get involved when knowledge hiding behavior is identified in an employee. Since this behavior has been identified with the dark triad – Machiavellianism, narcissism, and psychopathy – she suggests that a "personality traits test can be used as an important reference for management when deploying individual employees for particular job tasks",[565] thus avoiding assigning an employee with this behavior to project tasks requiring abundant and fluent knowledge exchange among task members.

TRUST

Trust is critical to a coherent organization. As a foundational quality of the Knowledge Reblooming Movement – along with truth and transparency – it is a major determinant of effective communication and knowledge sharing in an organization as a whole, and particularly of the organization's leadership. If knowledge workers trust each other and their leaders, they are much more apt to help each other and communicate more openly. The question then becomes: What actions would build and improve interpersonal trust throughout the organization?

As De Furia notes,

Interpersonal trust is present in a situation in which one individual places his or her interests under the control of another individual, with the expectation of gaining a desired outcome for which the potential negative consequences of violated trust are greater than the value of the potential desired outcome.[566]

For me to share my knowledge with you, I must believe that you will not misuse that knowledge, will not use that knowledge against me, and that if I need some knowledge from you, you will reciprocate. If I do not believe all of these things, then why should I share my knowledge? Note that feelings about a person may have nothing to do with trust. Trust is a cumulative belief that another individual because of my perception of who they are – or by virtue of their position in the company – will live up to our expectations, i.e., trust takes time to create, but can be lost in a single event. (See the deeper discussion of trust built on ideas rather than relationships in Chapter 3, and Chapter 14 on Relationship Network Management.)

De Furia proposes five behaviors that help build trust: sharing relevant information, reducing controls, allowing for mutual influence, clarifying mutual expectations, and meeting expectations.[567] Now we are in a position to set up actions and encourage behavior throughout the organization that will lead to interpersonal trust. We can explain the importance of sharing information and the responsibilities that go with that sharing, with leaders discussing these responsibilities in the teams and communities and over the networks of the organization. Information and knowledge sharing can also be made a part of the organization's performance appraisal system. On a one-to-one basis, collaborative leaders can work with team members who provide extraneous, irrelevant, or confusing information and explain how these traits make them appear untrustworthy.

Looking from another viewpoint, it maybe be beneficial to think of trust in terms of a surety spectrum with four main categories: Direct Knowledge, Direct Trust, Deferred Trust, and Faith Trust.[568]

Direct Knowledge is knowing that we know our own observations and conclusions, and can therefore base future decisions on what we currently know. To prove our direct knowledge, we may be asked to "verify" what we know by showing examples, research, etc. While this type of knowing provides us with a feeling of deep surety, the "grounding" that it provides from past experiences may also keep us from taking new/future ground.

Direct Trust is knowing that we trust our own observations and conclusions, and can therefore base future decisions on what we currently and directly trust. This type of trust simply projects our current direct knowledge into the future as expectations of continuity. This continuity can be linear or non-linear, and applied to situations or ourselves. When we describe our trust towards future expectations, as it relates to our own abilities, we usually use the term "self-efficacy" to describe this concept.

Deferred Trust is knowing that we trust someone else, based on "credibility," which is simply the quality we use to determine if they are believable or worthy of trust. This quality we use can vary widely between people and circumstances. For example, some may deem others credible based on the *authority* of the position they hold, while others may only deem them credible after reviewing the authorization process which was used to place them into authority. Note that the initiative to overthrow monarchies was through this lens, since "birthright" became a questionable authorization process. Given the need to be clear about the exact ways that we trust in others, the term *vericate* is increasingly used to specify certain qualities of trust. Just as the term "verify" places specific qualifications for how we reference direct knowledge, the term "vericate" places specific qualifications for how we reference deferred trust. To vericate means that you are relying on someone's socially recognized experience and expertise in a specific area, not just their authority or ungrounded opinion.

Faith Trust is knowing that we trust in a general outcome based on *our perceived nature of the Universe*. For example, we may be called a *pessimist* if we believe in Murphy's law, which states that "if anything can go wrong it will go wrong." Or we may be called an *optimist* if we believe that "the cup is half full, not half empty" and that things have a way of working out. How much does our perceived nature of the Universe influence future events? From a psychological viewpoint, the study of self-talk and affirmations looks at the impact these beliefs have on our confidence, which can directly affect our approach and expectations. From a neuroscience viewpoint, we know that our thoughts and feelings influence the structure of the brain, and the structure of the brain influences our thoughts. But the more-interesting study of Quantum reality looks at the impact these beliefs have on connected consciousness, which can directly affect the situation and outcome. A tool titled "Trust Mapping" in Section IV provides a way to visualize trust for each key activity within an organization.

For the organization to gain the trust of its employees, all leaders, managers, and influential workers have to be trustworthy and sensitive to their words and deeds *as seen* by the workforce. For example, senior manager's statements concerning the organization's direction, objectives, and vision should be cohesive and consistent, supporting a coherent organization. While differences among senior personnel are often a good thing, workers may interpret those differences to be deceit, defection, or distrust. From an overall organization's view, all communication should be open, honest, and thorough so that context and understanding are shared by all parties. (See the short discussion on transparency below.) This is not an easy thing to accomplish, yet it is essential for flexibility, collaboration, innovation, and fitness for survival.

Managers and team leaders can facilitate staff meeting dialogues on the importance of trust and, asking for employee ideas, discuss factors involved in creating and maintaining trust. They can point out daily examples of the need and benefit to individuals and the organization of working together and sharing knowledge, answering WIIFM (what's in it for me) questions in real time. To show that they trust their workers, managers can reduce their own controls by giving more freedom to their workers, letting them self-organize when and where it makes sense, and bringing them into relevant decisions, sharing the context and consequences. This is of immediate importance to an innovation culture because local self-organization, decision-authority at the point of action, and team leveraging of knowledge for innovation all call for increased worker participation, authority, and accountability.

By giving up control, managers and team leaders model the trust behavior they want others to exhibit. Clarifying mutual expectations is basically open, honest communication on what each person expects of the others and prevents misunderstandings that can quickly be misinterpreted as a failure of trust by either party. When all parties meet other's expectations over time, trust, collaboration, and camaraderie build up in teams, networks, and organizations. Because of the importance of collaboration and knowledge sharing to innovation, the level and importance of trust needs to be a continuous item for discussion throughout the organization, at least until it is firmly embedded in the culture. On the down side, if individuals clearly prove that they are untrustworthy and beyond redemption, they cannot remain in the organization. As harsh as this may seem, organizational survival and health cannot tolerate wounds or possible cancers within its body.

An interesting side anecdote from Covey and Merrill described leading organizations as asking their employees the simple direct question in a formal 360-degree feedback process: "Do you trust your boss?" As they explain, "These companies have learned that the answer to this one question is more predictive of team and organizational performance than any other question they might ask."[569]

Finally, trust is as much a communication problem as an attitudinal problem. Often people do not have the communication skills to clearly signal their intentions or expectations. Good communication skills and the ability to clearly communicate intent are essential for each and every knowledge worker.

We have dwelt on trust because it is a foundation for leveraging knowledge for innovation, and because it is so fragile. De Furia offers five "facts" about trust that provide the context for our concern: (1) low trust drives out high trust unless behaviors are corrected, (2) building trust is a slow process, (3) trust can be destroyed by a single event, (4) trust is destroyed by a win-lose mentality, and (5) groups [and organizations] with low intermember trust can be so unsuccessful as to self-destruct. See also the discussion of trust in relation to communities in Chapter 11.

Transparency

Transparency – together with truth and trust the foundation of the Reblooming Knowledge Movement – is a companion necessity to trust. Self-directed organizations, where equality and fairness are a requirement, demand transparency. In 2016, The Engagement Institute, a part of The Conference Board, which believes in and develops innovative approaches that make you think-and-act-differently, identified the most valued qualities of engaging leaders as trust and integrity. In a research study by Dirks and Ferring examining 106 studies with over 27,000 people, job satisfaction and higher commitment to an organization was directly linked to trust of leaders.[570] And the one characteristic that keeps coming to the fore when examining leadership trust is transparency.

An example is Futurice, which is a digital innovation and engineering company originally out of Finland. The company is very much focused on helping organizations become more capable for the future, which transformation touches cultures, digital strategies, and "turning technology into business". While autonomy can make it difficult to share, especially in a rapidly growing organization, Futurice introduced Artificial Intelligence approaches to mapping experience, knowledge and competencies, that is, creating a knowledge map of who knows what. A special search engine was developed which draws from discussion, meetings, documents, calendars, and incoming information to data systems to, over time, track both development and implementation of new ideas. Jack Welch is quoted as saying, "Trust happens when leaders are transparent", which means being open and honest, which in turn builds relationships and respect.

Open Science and Open Data are not new, although increasingly repositories and publisher websites are becoming the most widely accessible in terms of research data, both preserving and making it usable for decades to come. Open data significantly increases the integrity of research as well as supporting transparency and reproducibility. Examples include ResearchGate.edu and Academia.edu which have global connectivity. Open Source publishing, generally requiring author fees, also provides wide access to current research.

CERN, the European Organization for Nuclear Research, which is the world's largest laboratory for particle physics, has implemented an open-access policy since 2014. Demonstrating its commitment to open science, more than 95% of its published research is freely accessible to the public. Dr. Kamran Naim, the Head of Open Science at CERN, forwards that openness alone is not sufficient, that for meaningful openness additional preservation activities are crucial. He specifically points out the vital role that persistent identifiers and comprehensive metadata play in making complex experimental data accessible, which, to ensure quality, needs to occur from the beginning of its availability. Thus, it is necessary to (1) implement consistent and realistic policies that promote effective data management, (2) invest in people, data experts and storage in order to manage data efficiently and make it more easily accessible, and (3) collaborate in releasing scientific data to enable drawing conclusions and benefits across the scientific community.[571]

Catherine Ellwood, a consultant at the Myers-Briggs Company who says that transparency is contagious, that is, transparency begets transparency, forwards six steps on the journey to transparency. Those are: consistency, shared reasoning, being open and receptive to feedback, communicating openly, spreading the word, and recognizing the limits of transparency. That last would involve the intelligent and necessary balancing that needs to occur between transparency and confidential or sensitive information.

We would add humility to this list. From an individual perspective, humility is having an accurate view of yourself, neither too high nor too low (strengths and abilities as well as weaknesses and limitations) and being honest about this to yourself and others. From a collective viewpoint, this means being other-oriented, focused beyond self, such that you are open to others ideas, taking those into consideration in your decisions and actions. As can be seen, humility supports consistency, shared reasoning and being open and receptive to feedback. See the discussion on Humility at the end of Chapter 10 and the tool "Humility as a Choice" in Section IV.

Perception Management

While transparency goes a long way to managing trust and truth, with information overload and the vast amount of misinformation and disinformation floating through public media, a course correction may be necessary to clarify reality, first ensuring that the "reality" YOU perceive is the "reality" that is. Truth and trust cannot be over-emphasized. However, in the current landscape, perception management can play an important role in organizational sustainability and has increasingly become an essential part of a successful business strategy to shape and sustain organizational reputation.

Perception – the human ability to become aware of (see, hear, feel) something through the senses – is what is felt *by* a particular person or group as well as what is felt *about* a particular person, situation, event, or organization based on stimuli that has been received. While that stimuli can be the result of a personal experience, it is often the result of media coverage, which can be either favorable or negative. Thus, perception management itself is both an art and a science, which engaged the "how" to create a favorable impression of an organization to its stakeholders, prospective and existing employees, and potential customers.

While perception management does, both internally and externally, affect people's thoughts and opinions, the intent is to communicate and ensure the organization's alignment with its values. It also serves as a tool to develop an understanding of how an organization is perceived, which provides the opportunity to choose to create a positive and engaging environment in the workplace, directly impacting employee engagement, satisfaction, and retention as well as affecting the culture and knowledge productivity.

There are a number of strategies for managing perceptions. Transparency, open communications, and creating a positive organizational culture based on truth and trust is a good starting place. Ensuring leadership consistency with intention is essential. A hiring strategy based on not only skills but fit with the organizational values and culture can help ensure alignment and facilitate the resonance and coherence required for creativity, innovation, and sustainability. Monitoring and immediately addressing any negative perceptions is also important, which can be done through periodical stakeholder surveys, focus groups, or through other feedback mechanisms such as communities, help desks, or social media.

There are excellent examples of companies that are succeeding in perception management. For example, Peleton, which started in 2012 as a cycling shop, and is now described as the "Netflix for fitness", mission statement is to help people become the best versions of themselves. They have created a culture of inclusion and collaboration, providing both an enriching work experience and encouraging employees to take ownership of their roles.

EVALUATING AND MEASURING

Linking knowledge and action provides a foundation for measuring knowledge effectiveness. Knowledge itself is neither true nor false, and its value in terms of good or poor is difficult to measure other than by the outcomes of actions based on that knowledge. Good knowledge would have a high probability of producing the desired (anticipated) outcome, and poor knowledge would have a low probability of producing the expected result. For complex situations the quality of knowledge (from good to poor) may be hard to estimate before the action is taken because of the system's unpredictability. After the outcome has occurred, it may be possible to assess the quality of knowledge by comparing the actual outcome to the expected outcome; although it is also possible that there may not be a direct observable causal relationship between a decision made/action taken and the results of that action. As noted previously, to change a complex system generally involves a decision set implemented over time.

While there is a need to measure expenses, schedules, scope, and quality, there are also subjective measures for things like the team's relationship with stakeholders, knowledge sharing, innovative ideas emerging, etc. Any measure is appropriate if it helps ensure the project is on track with its strategic intent.

When picking metrics, *ensure that you are measuring for the future*. Since what gets measured is what gets attention, it is important to think forward to the desired end state and identify performance measures that move beyond specific goals to serving as part of the implementation change strategy. The knowledge centric organization model designed by the Department of the Navy uses three types of metrics to assess different levels of KM impact, namely outcome (enterprise or overall value), output (project or task), and system (technology tools).

The perspectives of the customer, department, organization, and individual are critical to the project's success and, as appropriate, need to be incorporated into its evolution. The implication for organizational metrics is that it is important to identify who is likely to use the performance measurement information. Potential users include strategic decision makers, special project decision makers, funding and approval stakeholders, other government agencies involved in approval or regulation, or customers. Measures should be in terms that are familiar to the stakeholders. There is no one "right" set of measures, and most initiatives will require a combination of measurement types and classes to reflect the overall mission and strategy of the organization, and effectively communicate with key individuals.

Measuring with the MIKE

In Chapter 6, we introduce the use of the MIKE (Most Innovative Knowledge Enterprise) international award as a diagnostic tool for assessing and improving practices in enterprises, as a basis for international benchmarking studies, and as a vehicle providing a context-rich data pool for guiding innovation research. As introduced, the MIKE framework for judging effective innovation is focused on human capital (leadership and knowledge workers), relation capital (networks and user needs), and structural capital (culture, creative space, systems/practices, and products/services).

Instead of comparing output, the MIKE is focused on intellectual capital related to the practices most impactful to the organization, those that can sustain systematic innovation. Examples of that output in each of the eight areas are included in Chapter 6. The use of this instrument as an assessment tool enables an organization to look at their practices in comparison to what is going on in leading innovative organizations around the world. By benchmarking these organizations, or through deeper research into their practices, new ideas in terms of innovation designs, processes and practices can emerge.

RECOGNITION AND REWARDS

There are many reasons it is a good idea to have a formal recognition and reward policy for improvements and innovations. Certainly these can prove strong incentives for improved knowledge productivity and innovation, directly affecting the bottom line of a company. But there are other pragmatic reasons as well. For example, TATA Power Ltd. in India has a Reward & Recognition Policy for Improvement & Innovation across TATA Power and subsidiaries. The policy is focused on the following three goals:

- To promote the culture of Excellence & Innovation by recognizing employees, teams for their contribution to continuous improvements in the organization.
- To capture & share organization-wide improvements and innovations.
- To identify & share best processes & practices across the organization.[572]

In this journey, TATA Power has received external validation through Excellence Awards in the areas of continuous improvement and process management, and knowledge management; and Power Innovista Awards in the areas of Implemented Innovation, Dare to Try, Piloted Technologies, Design Honor, and Sustainability Impact Innovation.

Recognition and rewards range from informal to formal, focused at the individual or team level, and originated from peers to project or senior leadership, and can be presented annually or when a special contributing circumstance demands immediate recognition. As some examples, a "Knowledge in Action Award" is given to individuals who leverage the organization's knowledge infrastructure, knowledge assets, expertise directory or good practices to deliver meaningful value to their project or business unit or other stakeholders. A "Not Invented Here Award (But I Did It Anyway)" promotes desired behaviors. A "Shared Knowledge Award" (certificates, coins, small statues) for the shared knowledge voted by organizational members to be the most helpful to the organization is a powerful support for knowledge sharing. Peer recognition (a simple thank-you phone call) and nomination for awards by peers can be especially valued. An example is a team of individuals contributing lessons learned on a particular project, which is referred to as a peer view, with a second team utilizing these lessons on a similar or related project, resulting in improved decision-making capability and improved results. The second team then nominates the first team for some kind of reward and recognition based on these results.

And, of course, it is important to recognize creativity and innovation. One organization with which we worked annually gave the "[organization name] Outstanding Creativity" award to the team that came up with the most creative ideas for improving the organization and facilitating new products. And when a new product came to market, every individual who had contributed to the learning stream (which was captured virtually in community conversations and team notes) earned a dinner for two at a local high-end restaurant.

An unusual award was an "Emergent Success" award for creating a successful innovation from hard-won lessons learned, that is, turning failure into success, which acknowledges leadership understanding of the value of failure, and their commitment to learning.

CONTINUOUS LEARNING

If there was one single core competency of an organization that could be culled out from others to ensure success, it is learning. Learning is the process that creates knowledge and, in doing so, also creates new meaning from experience and new capabilities for action. Strangely enough, while learning is critical to the life of individual employees as well as every organization, few people have ever focused on learning how to learn, which is a Knowledge Capacity (see Chapter 16).

To become a knowledge organization means to become a learning organization. To put learning in perspective, consider several closely related concepts: training, education, and what might be called acquiring deep knowledge. All of these are forms of learning, each emphasizing a different goal with varying processes used for each. **Training** deals with developing skills and abilities that do not require abstract concepts or a great deal of experience. Training usually has a narrow focus, and results that achieve a specific situational capability. **Education** is usually thought of as a process of learning *about* things that provide the learner with a broad, balanced perspective on the world and the ability to understand and deal with many areas of life. **Deep learning** refers to the acquisition and understanding of highly abstract and complex concepts, systems and information, that is, grasping the underlying patterns. For example, a deep knowledge of calculus would be the ability to solve calculus problems which would include understanding the foundations of the theory, its limitations, and domain of application. Deep knowledge is created by study, reflection, assimilation, practice, problem-solving, and "living with the subject." See the discussion of levels of knowledge in Chapter 4.

Most people learn best by doing. Action learning is a task-oriented group process that is useful for approaching narrowly focused issues. Today, individual and group learning can be facilitated through the use of technology in so many ways, although face-to-face learning, when possible, through retreats, brown bag lunches, speaker series, and workshops are still intricate to a successful organization.

Continuous learning (the continuous creation of new ideas and knowledge) and the ability to effectively (and often quickly) act on those ideas is paramount in any organization engaged in knowledge work. Continuous learning is a daily routine for knowledge workers as new challenges require new ideas, solutions and approaches.

Consciousness Expanding

Through neuroscience research, we now know that thoughts change the structure of the brain, and brain structure influences the creation of new thoughts. This means that the accelerated mental development – as evidenced through expansive technological achievements such as AI – is producing a higher level of mental thought. There are two levels of mental thought: logic, built on cause and effect (lower mental thought), and concepts that emerge from logic patterns (higher mental thought).

Logic uses the past-present, in that order, with a primary focus on the past, and if you put everything together it supports itself, consistent with experience and with no conflicting information coming in through the senses. Lower mental thought begins with examples from experience, bringing cause-and-effect examples together that result in new information in the form of patterns. When those patterns are recognized, an individual has moved into the higher mental thought of conceptual thinking. From this viewpoint, we are looking for logical examples that demonstrate the concepts and the relationships among concepts that are emerging in the mind. As we discover examples that lie outside of a concept, the concept is no longer true and must be shifted to include these new examples, ever asking *Why?* and expanding our level of truth as well as our consciousness. Thus, it can be recognized that thought at the conceptual level vibrates at a higher frequency than thought at the cause-and-effect related logical level.

This very much applies to innovation. Quite literally, a mind that is capable of creative thought (conceptual thinking) and applying that creative thought (moving the concept down to the logical thinking frame) is a mind thinking in "whole thought" that is expanding consciousness, with consciousness defined as a process, a sequential set of ideas, thoughts, images, feelings and perceptions and an understanding of the connections and relationships among them. And, as introduced above, as the mind expands so too does the structure of the brain, enabling ever higher-level thought. Thus, *creativity and innovation are themselves continuous learning experiences* which are in service to both the individual and the organization.

CHANGE AS A CONSTANT

Consistent with the conversation in Chapter 10 on becoming a change agent, change does not just happen. Assuming cohesive thinking and compatibility between the organization's needs and the change initiative, introduction of a new organizational initiative (I_1) requires setting a clear intention, and follow-on consistent and continuous energetic attention and focus at all levels of the organization. Over time, this pressure will result in recognition of the value of the change initiative by the organization. It is at the point of value recognition that the organization's Proactive Forerunners – explorers, learners, and ingratiators – embrace the initiative and begin implementation.

If the Proactive Forerunners appear to be successful with I_1, implementation of the initiative quickly cascades down through the ranks of the Doubting Thomases – those adverse to change, "wait and see" people. The greater the appearance of I_1 success by the Proactive Forerunners, the faster change cascades through the Doubting Thomases. Then, the hard work resumes. Again, consistent and continuous attention and focus, with the additive of pressure and providing working examples in the organization, continues. And slowly, slowly the top layer of resisters opens up. How long and how far down into the resister layer the system can continue is highly dependent on the thickness of the resistor level and the resources of the change effort. For at some point behind I_1's introduction, and prior to system value recognition, I_2 has been introduced and is requiring the same consistent and continuous attention and focus across the organization to enable success. Then, near the value recognition point of I_1 , and while I_2 is still in need of consistent and continuous attention, focus and pressure at the resistor's level, I_3 has been introduced into the organization. As demonstrated in Figure 12-2, to achieve change as a constant (continuous change acceleration), value recognition points are built on overlapping change efforts. In our example, note that I2 requires a second push before it is fully picked up by the Proactive Forerunners, but when it is picked up that extra energy (time and effort) propels it further through the ranks of the resistors. In the example at hand upon which these patterns are based, this was because the Proactive Forerunners were still busy with I_1 and not yet into the pattern of change as a constant. Note also that different change initiatives (for a total of 24, all of which were a part of a larger change strategy) during the time span of assessment did not all show the same level of receptivity from the Doubting Thomases and, of course, Resistors. For the Doubting Thomases, this was largely related to the difficulty of implementation in terms of immediacy of results. For the Resistors, it was based on a conscious choice to not spend the extra time and energy to bring them fully on board.

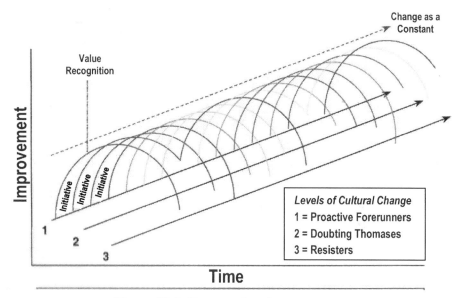

Figure 12-2. Patterns for change as a constant.

Here is where the intelligent learning system comes into play, built on open feedback loops. It is best explained by example. When the DoD Secretary mandated the use of Integrated Product Teams (IPTs), within 48 hours DoD teams of every type began calling themselves IPTs, while struggling to figure out exactly what IPTs were. Within a couple of weeks of announcement of that policy, the DoN Acquisition Reform Office virtually posted *draft* IPT guidelines. During the following two weeks more than 600 emails, phone calls and personal dialogues ensued across the staff asking: "When will the final guidelines be issued?" Approximately six weeks into the change process a second *draft* version was posted virtually (complete with feedback and the learning that had surfaced). Over the following two weeks a flurry of questions ensued, but this time those questions numbered in the dozens instead of the hundreds. Three months into the change process you began to see programs differentiating between IPTs and other types of teams. When a third, updated *draft* set of guidelines was posted, the two dozen responses to that posting were focused more on how to improve the guidelines rather than asking "When do the final ones come out?" These response patterns, observed over a three-year period, could eventually be granulated down to sub-elements of the organization, each of which had a different culture and a different receptivity rhythm.

The response patterns demonstrated that initiatives too closely introduced failed to work through the organization. This, of course, is partially due to the reduction of consistent and continuous attention and focus (energy), which is difficult to sustain when multiple initiatives are simultaneously introduced. Conversely, if too much time elapsed between change initiatives, the initial buildup to the point of value recognition became slower and more difficult for follow-on initiatives. It was as if the organization had settled into a lower level of receptivity. It was repeatedly noted that as change behavior becomes embedded in an organization, is understood, connected with a repeatable process, and accepted as an organizational "norm", the organization once again becomes static, and slower to respond to change. See Figure 12-3.

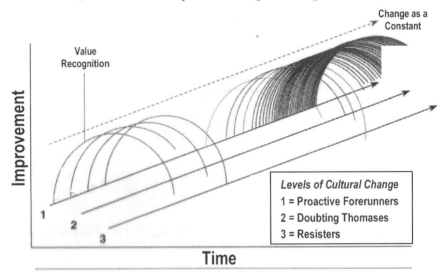

Figure 12-3. Gaps in patterns for change as a constant.

Once intention is set, change requires aggressiveness in terms of continuous and consistent energy, attention, and focus. This implies the power of energy directed into action. The transformation of any idea into realization is the result of this creative focused energy. The organization is a living system. (See Chapter 13 on the Informational Model for Living Systems.)

MOVING TOWARD WISDOM

The highest part of mental thought is wisdom, yet it is something *more* than mental thought. Representing completeness and wholeness of thought, wisdom is universally a somewhat lofty consideration. The more we seek it, the more we understand that it comes through experiencing and learning, and brings with it the desire to learn more. It also comes with an ever-deepening connection to others.

Wisdom occurs when activity matches the choices that are made and structured concepts are intelligently acted upon, thus *directly connecting wisdom to intelligent action*. Action, based on knowledge, occurs in our perceived physical reality, in our everyday personal and professional lives. *Intelligent* activity represents a state of interaction where intent, purpose, direction, values and expected outcomes are aligned, clearly understood and communicated among all parties, reflecting wisdom and achieving a higher truth.[573] "Knowledge can be by education, but wisdom, which is indispensable to true culture, can be secured only through experience and by men and women who are innately intelligent. Such a people are able to learn from experience; they may become truly wise."[574] Thus, a discussion of wisdom is a discussion of intelligent activity, which is a good place to end this section as we focus on sustainability.

Defining Wisdom

A rich diversity of definitions and descriptions of wisdom abound, all aiding in our understanding. Focusing on work occurring around the beginning of this century, Csikszentmihalyi and Nakamura, educators who collaborated to write about the role of emotions in the development of wisdom, described wisdom as referring to two distinct phenomena.[575] The first was the *content* of wisdom (information) and the second an individual's *capacity to think or act* wisely.

Focusing on the content of wisdom, Clayton and Birren, early explorers into wisdom psychology, said that individuals perceived wisdom differently when socio-demographic variables were changed, that is, as we now recognize about knowledge, *they considered wisdom as context-sensitive and situation dependent*.[576] This is consistent with the position that wisdom is grounded in life's rich experiences.[577] However, wisdom moves above and beyond specific circumstances as patterns develop. Wisdom "therefore is developed through the process of aging ... [and] seems to consist of the ability to move away from absolute truths, to be reflective to make sound judgments related to our daily existence, whatever our circumstances."[578]

A large number of writers have considered wisdom as a part of intelligence.[579] Baltes and Smith go on to say that wisdom is "a highly developed body of factual and procedural knowledge and judgment dealing with what we call the 'fundamental pragmatics of life'."[580]

In contrast, from qualitative research with Buddhist monks, clinical psychologist Heidi Levitt said that the monks tended toward a spiritual definition and believed that all people were capable of wisdom, regardless of their intellect.[581] From a similar persuasion, Chögyam Trumpa, a Buddhist meditation master who coined the term "crazy wisdom", sees wisdom as a state of consciousness with the qualities of *spaciousness, friendliness, warmth, softness and joy.*[582] Similarly, Woodman and Dickson see wisdom as the state of consciousness that *allows the spiritual Self to be active.*[583] Again, tying wisdom directly to action.

Wisdom also appears to have an affective (emotional) component.[584] The neurobiological roots of this were confirmed by Sherman, who discovered that some brain-damaged patients who lacked wisdom also lacked the evaluative affects used to choose a course of action (make a decision),[585] in which emotions have a role to play. Clearly, these researchers have all given a great deal of thought to the subject of wisdom. These are all captured in the endnotes and bibliography should you wish to explore them further.

Some core words associated with wisdom that appear throughout the literature include: *understanding, empathy, knowledge, knows self, living in balance,* and *systemic thinking.*[586] Macdonald – who is a social experimenter, inventor, engineer, ecologist, philosopher and independent scholar – describes this systemic thinking as "*acting with the well-being of the whole in mind.*"[587] This is the concept of the greater good.

Further, it has been pointed out that wisdom is at home in several levels of the hierarchy of complexity, with the understanding that "a phenomenon at each level of the hierarchy can be enhanced by relating it to its neighboring levels."[588] Another researcher explains that the levels of a hierarchy are interrelated via feedback loops, and that increased understanding results from following these feedback loops from one level to another and back again.[589]

Similarly, artist Joan Erikson says that a sense of the complexity of living is an attribute of wisdom. In a rather wordy, but interesting, description, Erikson says that a wise person embraces the

> ... *sense of the complexity of living, of relationships, of all negotiations. There is certainly no immediate, discernible, and absolute right and wrong, just as light and dark are separated by innumerable shadings ... [the] interweaving of time and space, light and dark, and the complexity of human nature suggests that ... this wholeness of perception to be given partially and realized, must of necessity be made up of a merging of the sensual, the logical, and the aesthetic perceptions of the individual.*[590]

As can be noted in this brief treatment, the concept of wisdom is clearly related to knowledge – in particular, to tacit knowledge – and has also been related to the phenomenon of consciousness. It is connected with systemic, hierarchical thinking, and the complexity of human nature has been brought into the discussion. Further, wisdom appears to deal with the cognitive and emotional, personal and social, as well as the moral and spiritual aspects of life.

Costa sums this all up in his book *Working Wisdom*: "Wisdom is the combination of knowledge and experience, but it is more than just the sum of these parts. Wisdom involves the mind and the heart, logic and intuition, left brain and right brain, but it is more than either reason, or creativity, or both. Wisdom involves a sense of balance, an equilibrium derived from a strong, pervasive *moral* conviction ... the conviction and guidance provided by the obligations that flow from a profound sense of interdependence. In essence, wisdom grows through the learning of more knowledge, and the practiced experience of day-to-day life – both filtered through a code of moral conviction."[591]

And, again, we reiterate its connection to action. As Sternberg describes, "Wisdom is not just a way of thinking about things; it is a way of doing things. If people wish to be wise, they have to act wisely, not just think wisely. We all can do this. Whether we do it is our choice."[592]

Intelligent activity is continuously being created by people as, from one thought to the next, there is mental integrity, a consistency in the truth of thought. Recall that intelligent activity is described as *a state of interaction where intent, purpose, direction, values and expected outcomes are aligned, clearly understood and communicated among all parties, reflecting wisdom and achieving a higher truth*. Thus, intelligence is not about who will benefit; it is what you do in interacting with others so they can do the same with others, building consciousness and freedom in those with whom we interact.[593]

Psychologist Robert Sternberg says that intelligence without wisdom has not served the world well. He gives examples of cruel despots and greedy business tycoons who are quite intelligent and successful at the expense of others. This example points out that intelligence alone does not infer wisdom. Thus, Sternberg developed a balance theory. As he describes: "I view wisdom as the value-laden application of tacit knowledge not only for one's own benefit (as can be the case with successful intelligence) but also for the benefit of others, in order to attain a common good. The wise person realizes that what matters is not just knowledge, or the intellectual skills one applies to this knowledge, but how the knowledge is used [emphasis added]."[594] Again, we see the **connection of wisdom to the concept of the greater good**. This insinuates the counterbalance necessary when developing the mental faculties, and is consistent with the usage of wisdom in the definition of intelligent activity.

This *filtering through a code of moral conviction* is critical. Knowledge acted upon without the actor taking responsibility for its use can be dangerous for both the actor and those affected by the action. In short, *knowledge has to be used wisely*. A counterbalance is necessary to move into wisdom, that is, taking responsibility for our knowledge. This is consistent with Sternberg's conviction that: "The wise person realizes that what matters is not just knowledge, or the intellectual skills one applies to this knowledge, but how the knowledge is used."[595]

The Wisdom Model

Let's see if we can develop a conceptual model based on this learning. As forwarded above, the integration and balance of development of our mental faculties and deepening connections with others emerges as wisdom and manifests as intelligent activity. Thus, the model is going to have two paths moving toward wisdom. The first is that of knowledge. While not a part of a linear continuum, the concept of wisdom is clearly related to knowledge. More importantly, wisdom is not in isolation; it indeed appears to deal with the cognitive and emotional, personal and social, as well as the moral aspects of life, very much based on the interconnectedness of people, which represents the second path. For a deeper treatment of these concepts tied to the Intelligent Social Change Journey, which is the developmental journey of the human through life, see *The Profundity and Bifurcation of Change Part IV: Co-Creating the Future*,[596] and/or *Possibilities that are YOU! Volume 15: Seeking Wisdom*.[597]

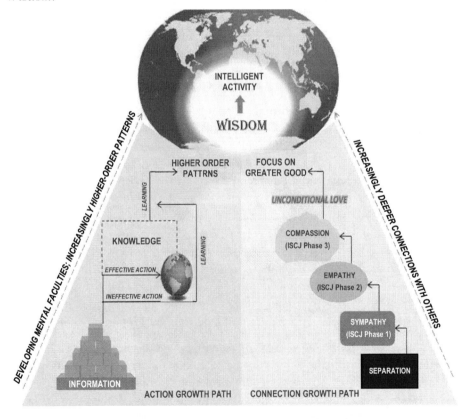

Figure 12-4. The integration and balance of development of our mental faculties and deepening connections with others emerges as wisdom and manifests as intelligent activity.

Development of wisdom can be escalated when an individual chooses to engage in mental discipline. What does this mean in practical terms? While during the course of life an intuitive flash can occur to pretty much anyone, disciplined preparation is required in order to interact with others and bring that idea into service, what could be defined in the business world as innovation.

Mental discipline is advantageous for *all* domains of knowledge. For example, an athlete requires disciplined preparation of the body accompanied by a harmonious consciousness (disciplined preparation of the mind) to perform well. Physical actions are repeated over and over again to embed them in the very fabric of our bodies such that they become an unconscious response to self (embodied tacit knowledge). See the companion book to Knowledge Reblooming: *Innovative Creativity: Creating with Innovation in Mind.*[598]

Since mental is of, or having to do with, the mind, mental discipline as applied to the self is in terms of self-control, self-mastery, self-governance, self-direction and self-reliance, all connected with self-knowledge. For example, planning is a tool for preparation of the mind. It involves recognition of past patterns, a higher level of truth, the ability to have more effectiveness and accuracy in our living, and increased intelligence in our actions. Then, consistency is necessary such that wisdom is intelligently applied wherever it can be used, where it can be of service. See *Unleashing the Human Mind: A Consilience Approach to Managing Self.*[599]

And now we are beginning to understand that "something more" that early thought leaders recognized in the knowledge movement, and that academics and philosophers recognize as part of wisdom. In these times of extremes, we are asked "to distinguish what is important from what is not, what has meaning from what has not".[600] As Dolphijn so aptly says, "The micropolitics of that which matters have a lot to say to us, in times where we humans are more and more confronted with responsibilities for which we need to think beyond the human."[601] With knowledge comes responsibility.

"That which matters" concerns employees at every level. For example, de Sousa says there is a growing concern for the climate which is already having a significant effect on both employment and consumer behavior.[602] In a recent study by Deloitte, 64% of participants said they seriously considered a potential employer's commitment to meet energy transition goals when deciding whether to work for them.[603] In another study focused on Millennials, two-thirds of employees said that if they lacked a sense of fulfilment in their work or a lack of purpose beyond financial results, they would leave their jobs.[604]

In Chapter 13, Florin Gaiseanu presents the informational model of living systems, affirming that knowledge is the key to living life and moving toward wisdom. In Chapter 15, Milton de Sousa talks about the power of meaningful knowledge to engage people. In Chapter 18, Francisco Javier Carrillo forward that knowledge-based value generation offers the opportunity to restore a balance with the natural world as well as maintaining an open door to a framework for human improvement. Emerging from information and knowledge – flourishing with freedom of thought – this is the action growth path toward wisdom. Now it is up to us, in our everyday lives, in our organizations, to marry this new awareness, this new understanding, with the connection growth path in our organizations, that is, collectively collaborating to move toward wisdom to achieve a greater good.

SECTION III
SPECIAL TOPICS

Knowledge is always partial and incomplete. How could it be otherwise? We ARE complex adaptive systems – hopefully intelligent ones – continuously adapting and growing to address emerging external and internal opportunities and challenges. So, when we set our intent in a specific knowledge domain and then keep our attention on that domain in terms of thinking and acting and learning, wonderful ideas emerge, and then those new ideas set the stage for even larger ideas, and so forth!

This chapter is full of ideas emerging from thought leaders writing in their areas of passion, some ideas which you have no doubt thought about, only perhaps from a different perspective, and some which may be new to you, and all of which are worth reflection.

In Chapter 13 we begin with a deep-dive into the **informational model of living systems**. We are information systems And, in the words of Dr. Florin Gaiseanu, knowledge – the effective application of information – is an attribute of life, in which we seek and find ourselves, a goal and at the same time a dream, an aspiration, an endless path building the pyramid to wisdom, a road in steps paved with promises and hesitations, but also with successes, and which makes us feel the pulse of life and trust in what it can offer us.

Chapter 14 delves into the value of social engagement, recognizing that the conversations we have today drive the decisions that we make tomorrow. And WE have the power to manage those conversations through **Relationship Network Management**, a core competency supporting future sustainability of ourselves and our organizations. The six basic tenets of RNM are discussed which enable an organization to successfully take collaborative, cohesive action. These are interdependency, trust, common framework, openness and flow.

Chapter 15 focuses on effective leaders and how – as meaning creators, storytellers, enablers, and mentors – they inspire action. In this chapter (and reflecting de Sousa's new book on *Meaningful Leadership*), Milton de Sousa and his colleague Pedro Brito explore the sense-making process that integrates prior and new knowledge to form **meaningful knowledge**. The authors illustrate how leaders promote the acquisition of meaningful knowledge through a mindset of awareness, service motivation, and commitment to transform.

Chapter 16 forwards that in today's changing, uncertain, and complex environment where surprises emerge and must be quickly handled, that capacity is more important than capability. In this context, a variety of **Knowledge Capacities** are explored which can shape and influence our future thinking and behaviors. Knowledge Capacities are sets of ideas and ways of acting that change our reference points, providing different ways for us to perceive and operate in the world around us. Examples include comprehending diversity, learning how to learn, orchestrating drive, refocusing, reversal, shifting frames of reference, and symbolic representation.

Chapter 17 connects **absorptive capacity** to what has been gleaned from years of research and experience in organizational learning and the learning organization. Absorptive capacity, an organization's ability to effectively acquire and utilize external knowledge, is crucial to the ability to adapt to change, increase competitive advantage, and foster innovation. In this chapter, Dr. Chulatep Senivongse introduces Absorptive Capacity 3.0, developing a model to re-conceptualize absorptive capacity, and then provides a case study to demonstrate the effectiveness of this new thinking and doing.

Chapter 18 focused on **Knowledge Management and Knowledge-Based Development** for human flourishing. Dr. Francisco Javier Carrillo moves our thinking from the more abstract arena of a conceptual framework into the more pragmatic one of applied processes with international project examples. In the current geological age in which man is the dominant influence on the environment, Carrillo calls for the urgent reinvention of Knowledge for the Anthropocene and for each of us to fully engage our knowledge to become the best we can be.

CHAPTER 13

KNOWLEDGE: A LIFE PROPERTY REVEALED BY THE INFORMATIONAL MODEL OF LIVING SYSTEMS

Florin Gaiseanu

Professor, Science of Information and Technology, Bucharest (Romania) and Barcelona (Spain)

ABSTRACT

From the time they start rummaging through the secrets of life and up to the age of senescence, people ask themselves what it consists of, and where is the most valid value they need to fulfill their dreams and achieve the wisdom and peace that it confers. And the answer is so simple, but at the same time so complicated: knowledge. It is simple as contained in a single word, but not as simple in the penetration of its meaning, and the continuous march towards wisdom. In the present chapter, we learn that knowledge is actually a native attribute of life, in which we seek and find ourselves, a goal and at the same time a dream, an aspiration, an endless path building the pyramid to wisdom, a road in steps paved with promises and hesitations, but also with successes, and which makes us feel the pulse of life and trust in what it can offer us. It is up to each of us to recognize this enchanted key, and to use it with ingenuousness and cleverness to unlock the secrets of life and what it can offer us in abundance: wisdom and its achievements. And to use it with ingenuousness and cleverness, that means to choose – to choose right.

Key Words: knowledge, life, information, info-structuration/functioning, mind and consciousness, learning/education, compatibility, decision/attitude, practical method, wisdom.

WHAT THIS CHAPTER IS FOR…AN INTRODUCTION

In every moment of life, even in this one, we are on a journey of knowledging, asking ourselves questions and looking for answers, even without realizing it: Is it good? It's not good? What to do? How to do it? We measure time with the clock; when we wake up, we ask ourselves where we are and what we start the day with, then how to accomplish everything we set out to do in the necessary time, how to solve our duties for others and then our own needs. Everything "flows" between questions and answers, between Yes or No choices, everything flows and "drains" between momentary choices, which in fact lead our lives, without even understanding it. Is this a way of choosing a chain of elementary YES/NO decisions? A kind of Bit-like informational chain? YES, it is![605] Is this the best way to spend life, without stopping and taking a deep breath to ask ourselves if we are not chained/leashed in our own mental chains,[606] and to ask ourselves a big question: How can we organize ourselves better to live easier and better? Reblooming Knowledge, this is the right time and place to explore the best answer to this question!

Information. we are talking about information in this century of informational civilization,[607] when all the means at our disposal are, or are about to become, informational,[608] when life itself pulsates with information. Information marks our rhythm,[609] the rhythm of others, and the rhythm of the whole society![610] It makes the questions and answers move more frequently and faster, so as to develop the information itself! And we pulse together with it. ARE WE KEEPING THIS RHYTHM UP? DO we KNOW how to orient ourselves in life?

But this question contains in itself an implicit answer: TO KNOW – KNOWLEDGE! Knowledge? What is this? I believed that I understood it! Did you indeed? So, let's start going through the pages of this chapter, and see what we know and maybe what we don't know, about KNOWLEDGE, what this concept has to do with INFORMATION[611] and how we can learn to use it.

This chapter is, however, not a large peroration on how to do something or not. Children often give up listening to their parents' advice because they become too repetitive and therefore boring for them, and the part of pleading and real argumentation is missing. Other times, they already consider themselves capable enough to use their own mind to discover the meaning they have to choose. Therefore, this chapter aims to present the essential, but well-chosen and well deepened, showing in fact how life works, both on an organic and mental level, in which everyone can discover their ideal and the way of initiation, if of course they dedicate themselves to carefully following the background of the problem and its effects. Also, this chapter is not here to provide a recipe for happiness. This chapter reveals for the first time in our living world, the wonderful musical organ in seven registers at our disposal and their functioning, so that each of us can discover his/her *own* score that can be interpreted on this natural organ to obtain the most wonderful music, that which is optimal and adequate for one's own life, and which constitutes the endless source of contentment and wisdom for new conquests on the path of knowledge.

In the first section, this chapter refers therefore in a direct and suggestive way to the fundaments of the functioning of our informational system, which assures the body maintenance, its evolution and species continuity, and shows how we connect the environment external/internal world, pointing to the cognitive centers for connection with this reality. The second section is dedicated to understanding their functioning and application in life, each of us getting the possibility to choose what is good, suitable and adaptable to his/her style and aspirations. However, although short, this chapter is dense on information, so maybe it is better for each of us to read it with enough attention for better understanding, and to appeal to the cited references for more details. And along this incursion, always welcome, is meditation, a useful halt in the course of any journey of knowledge, not only to take a deep breath before the next stage to be conquered, but also to make the necessary mental connections on the stage already passed, for info-selection and integration. This exercise is also welcome for dealing with any problem in life as it will appear implicitly from going through the pages of this chapter.

AN ESSENTIAL QUESTION: HOW RUNS OUR LIFE AND ORGANISM?

Something maybe novel, or even strange, but not less true: our organism, we ourselves, function as informational "devices".[612] Yes, this could seem to be a sensational affirmation, and more than that, maybe a little bit "cruel"! How could be this real? But YES, this is true: not in the sense of actual devices, because the mechanisms of informational processes are different, and our devices are still not sentient/"sentimental" machines, but in the strict informational sense, the fundamental functioning is similar! Nature "invented" already – by its own means – its own informational systems: life, living specimens, and humans at a top of the most developed living being from the informational point of view, on the complexity organization/evolutionary scale.[613]

Knowledge of Matter: Programmed Processes in the Human Organism

Who we actually are? We are living organisms connected first of all to matter, necessary to provide us the adequate nutrients (foods, air water) – the life "fuel" for energetic consumption, which serve to all components of the organism, composed by many billions of cells (about 3.7×10^{13} cells or more[614] – the minimal units of our organism – to fulfill their tasks. But it is just as important to realize/know that we are connected to information, otherwise we would not be able to perceive the environment, to react, therefore to decide, and to feel what the received information makes us feel. We are therefore matter-related informational structures, which operate with information, so we are informational systems.[615]

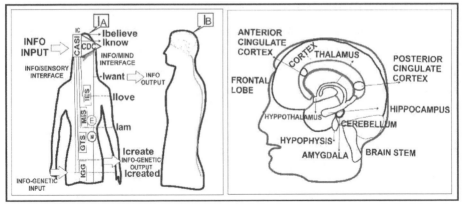

Figure 13-1. The informational systems of the human organism (left side), the correlation with the brain (right side) and the body (left side), and their projection in consciousness (left side of the figure). The arrows indicate the information transmission.

To grow/develop and maintain the body, our informational system must operate with matter: the foods are converted not only in energy (E) in our body (Figure 13-1 left side), used for the movement of the motor elements (M) (stomach, heart, muscles) and for chemical reactions (the excess is eliminated outside to maintain the corporal temperature nearly the same), but also the body itself extracts the necessary micro-material components for its maintenance and growth. This task is complied by the metabolic system, which "knows" what kind of components are necessary and where these should be transported and collocated. That means this system is driven by informational processes, otherwise everything should become chaos. The metabolic system is driven therefore by what we can call the maintenance informational system (MIS),[616] which possesses the "knowledge" of what kind of matter/material foods the body should receive from the outside and how should it be used. So, our body is an intelligent – even if this system is a silent – and very diligent collaborator that disposes of "knowledge" – a natively inherited knowledge, because this works automatically, without any additional intervention.

But from where comes such an intelligent diligence which we dispose of? From the body itself: from the incredible well-clever library of data, transferred from one generation to another, which is the genome – a collection of genetic "knowledge" located in the nucleus of each cell of the body … the same for the entire body! So, our body is endowed with "knowledge" coming from genes and inherited from our parents. A beautiful inheritance … life from life … beautiful continuity of life … and beautiful continuity of "knowledge" – the basic, initial unit of life (the fertilized "zipped"-like egg or zygote) of the body building, the "hardware" of our future informational system, the "software" which processes information resulting from the connection with the environmental reality.

We will refer therefore to this system as an *Info-Genetic Generator* (IGG), because this is able to drive the growth and development of our body according to our age along all of life.[617] But how does IGG process information, and how is the body built up by this informational process? IGG "knows" to extract/copy the necessary information from the deoxyribonucleic acid (DNA) by means of the messenger ribonucleic acid (mRNA), which copies with an incredible precision some sequences from DNA genes, just it is necessary, by a transcription process, and transfers them to the transport tRNA in ribosomes, some organelles of the cell. Then, together with amino acids (20 types in the human body – 11 fabricated and 9 ingested), the IGG "knows" exactly the necessary type in the necessary combination to form in the cytoplasm of the cell the necessary proteins, the bricks of the body.[618] And why is this an informational process? Because the gigantic DNA molecule is formed on the basis of only 4 types of nucleotides – "letters" of the DNA "alphabet" – adenine (A), thiamine (T), guanine (G) and cytosine (C), but with a very high number of combinations of such sequential structures, transcribed as "messages" by mRNA, which transmits/translates (=>) it to tRNA and then to protein, combined in a mixed "language" with amino acids. The proteins play various roles in the body, as body structuration or informational agents, transmitting information between various parts of the body, as matter-related information, or as surface receptors on the cell membrane, each of them specific to receive/accept only the right info-agent, with complementary YES/NO-type structure.

However, the body structuration doesn't stop with such processes: the body itself, by specialized organs, assures also the info-genetic preparation and transmission for the creation of the new generation, so a *Genetic Transmission System* (GTS) could be defined, complying with this function. At the cellular level, such a process is initiated and fulfilled by the replication process, which consists in the splitting of the DNA informational molecule in two strands of carbon atoms together with the corresponding nucleotides components and the reformation of each strand into full DNA molecules for the building of a new genome of a new cell. This is a "knowhow"/knowledge transfer from one individual to another. Info-Genetic processes are also automatic, based on the same genetic "knowledge", inherited from parents, and w a beautiful and priceless source of "knowledge"/acknowledge they are.

These are intrinsic/matter-related automatic "knowledge"/informational processes, consciously non-detected/non-realized. Thus, they are a "knowledge" of the "life matter", not of the mind. We can define therefore the *Programmed*

Informational System (PIS) with **PIS = MIS+GTS+IGG**, which works for us "blindly", but precisely. Physics/chemical/mathematic/biologic laws establish/act as operators of these informational processes, information intervening as their result.[619] Information is therefore, in a much larger sense, a result of the actuation of such laws for the organization – configuration/reconfiguration of matter – in informational systems, which thus are able to absorb, transmit/transfer and release information, just as the living systems are, assuring the body development/maintenance/transgenerational continuity transfer of information, assisted/supported by the tireless activity of PIS.

As can be seen, matter can contain and process information, not only the mind! Matter contains "knowledge", not only people and living organisms! This is an important feature of reality; an amazing and wonderful discovery! So, the difference between matter and mind already seems not so distinct as our predecessors/philosophers believed, who treated the mind-matter relation as an unsolvable problem.[620] We are kneaded from a "knowing" matter, otherwise we would not be what we are! **Knowledge and information are a universal property of the living world,**[621] and not only the "living" world.[622] And there is something more to observe: in order that a message to be rightly understood by a receiver, the source of information and the receiver need to be compatible with one another. The protein receives the "message" from the DNA sequence through the chain mRNA/tRNA by compatibility, they are able to "understand" each other because the "codified" message of DNA sequence is rightly "decoded"/understood by each component of this informational chain. This is also a wonderful property of the living systems – the ability to communicate fluently between their components of the large family of organic (carbon-based) structures, creating "living matter".[623] The essential characteristic of such components and of the codifying/decoding process consists in their structure complementarity, accepting (YES) or not (NO) to form composing/"computing" structures, similar to a binary YES/NO Bit-type informational system.[624]

Knowledge by the Mind: The Informational System of the Human Body

Another category of informational processes assures the connection with the informational environment, as a source of information, detected/perceived by our main senses/sensors of information – sight, hearing, touch, taste, and smell – and also with the internal informational sources detecting the state of the body – pain, hunger, thirst, and other sensations and impulses. And also, feelings: love, fear and all the intermediary subdivisions, interpreted as GOOD (acceptable – YES) or BAD (rejectable – NO) categories. The perceived information is processed by the short-time memory in real time, allowing the interpretation of reality, analyzed/compared with the already existing information in long-term memory, which acts as a reference/decision criterion. Therefore, it can be defined as a *Center of Acquisition and Storing of Information* (CASI), supporting the process of info-acquisition by sensors and the storing of information, a *Center of Decision and Command* (CDC), elaborating the decisions, which are then sent to the voluntarily executing elements (muscles), and an *Info-Emotional System* (IES), which manages emotions and moods. These components engage the organism in informational processes of adaptation for optimal decision-making in function of the external/internal circumstances. Thus, an *Operative Informational System* (OIS) can be defined as **OIS = CASI+CDC+IES**, which operates information (context-sensitive and situation-dependent) according to the circumstances.

The brain is the general manager of all these operations (Figure 1, right side). MIS manages the metabolic processes and is supported mainly by the brain stem, which coordinates the vital functions of the organism; it is connected with the main organs of digestion and the solar plexus – the second "brain" of the body. GTS and IGG manage the sexual and body development/defense (immunity) functions, respectively, and are supported by the hypophysis-hypothalamus axis.[625] Emotions are managed by the limbic system (amygdala, hypothalamus, hippocampus – shared with memory), situated in a superior position in the brain and connected with the heart, the info-sensitive motor organ for feeding nutrients, hormones and immune (white) cells the body through the blood stream, especially the zones stimulated by emotions, which activate spontaneous reactions. The amygdala is the alarm component, showing the importance, which the organism confers to danger situations. The activity of the CDC is supported by the prefrontal cortex for judgement and the two cortex hemispheres, connected with the vocal system, as the main info-output expression of decisions. The activity of CASI is supported by the prefrontal cortex for current informational running of the transposed reality in the mind – the personal/virtual/interpreted world; by the hippocampus for long range memory; and by the thalamus – a hub in the middle of brain essential for integration and (re)distribution of information, supporting consciousness together with the cortex,[626] the cerebellum for memory of the motor abilities, and the network red of external and internal sensors.[627]

Vision is the most developed human sense, and for it is allocated more than half of the cortex, showing that the connection with the external reality is a high-cost informational process, supported especially by the superior zones of the brain. An interesting feature of the economic development/functions of the brain is that the imagery circuitry used by the brain is the same when information is provided by the direct exploration, or recalled from memory. This shows that the human can explore his own virtual reality – composed by the accumulated experience and expressed as language – by means of his "mind eye", referred also to as the prefrontal cortex, where actually the "mass-media" reality is projected in real time, much like on a "movie screen". We may discover therefore that we are a beautiful creation of nature, functioning and activating like an informational mass-media system, living our own reality, as each of us succeeds in capturing and interpreting life through our own judgement tool and judgement criteria. Therefore, the projection of reality in the mind creates our personal (virtual) reality, expressed as "Self", an "I" composed by the contributing activity of each component of our informational system as follows: CASI is detected as memory, and interpreted as *Iknow*, CDC as *Iwant* (decision), IES as *Ilove* (emotions), MIS as *Iam* (self-image, vivacity/power, health), GTS as *Icreate* (biological creation/reproduction), and IGG as *Icreated* (biological creation of Self and evolution cycle).

However, something more should be added to our informational system: the "competence" component – the info-"decoder"/"warner" of our received information, which compares incoming information with the trusted experience previously gained/acquired, and notifies the disagreement, an 'out of order', or out of the domain of "competence"/regular experience. Such function is complied by the *Info-Connection* (IC) system, which marks the limits of competence of our knowledge according to our precious experience, warning when exceeding those attributions. This system informs on the outside information from the current experience and that which is accepted already as reliable information, maintaining thus the integrity/security of the existing informational domain. This is actually the domain of personal mental comfort and habits, inherited and acquired during the first years of life in family and living community, forming the personal mentality, a strong/powerful founder of the domain of the decision criteria, which determines the acceptance (YES) or rejection (NO) of external information, with direct effects on the judgement of reality and the compatibility question, and so too on social relations, planning projects, adaptation and orientation/navigation at the border between certainty and uncertainty during the exploration of reality.[628] This activity is supported in the brain by the anterior cingulate cortex (ACC), driving the warning[629] and posterior cingulate cortex (PCC), driving the scrutinizing of future and daydreaming projects.[630] Therefore, IC is actually represented in the mind as *Ibelieve*, defending the "territory" of firm information considered reliable and fully acceptable for wellbeing and trust.

Therefore, the Informational System of the Human Body (ISHB) can be defined as:

ISHB = CASI + CDC + IES + MIS + GTS + IGG + IC   (1)

As a consequence of the functionality of ISHB and the mind operability with information, the activity of each component of ISHB is projected as cognitive centers in our kind. Therefore, the Self – "I", can be defined as the sum of all these contributing components described above, according to the expression:

$$I = Iknow + Iwant + Ilove + Iam + Icreate + Icreated + Ibelieve \quad (2)$$

With each of them intervening when it is the case, and with the intensity depending on conjuncture and/or the state of the body.

FROM KNOWLEDGE TO WISDOM: A WAY TO FULFILL LIFE DREAMS/ASPIRATIONS

The knowledge of the informational system of the human body and how this is reflected in mind can be used as a great tool for driving personal and professional life, which cannot remain at the mercy of momentary random events.

What Are the Mind and Consciousness and How They Work

Once we understand how the human organism works, we can learn further how to use this wonderful native system, ready to learn for us, and ready to learn what we ask it to learn for its and our benefit. Looking to relation (2) above, we can discover that living matter is able/disposed not only of its own knowledge, but also is able to create knowledge. How? By learning – Yes, by learning! What was defined earlier as CASI is in fact the seat of learning, the base that ensures the data field with which the organism is born, as well as the one in which new data are acquired from the interaction with reality, and with which the decision center CDC operates. CDC searches for the data which are needed to be used at a certain moment, and processes them as a database to prepare a new judgment and a new decision, which also can be transmitted to CASI. During the first months even years of life, the brain is reorganized rapidly, eliminating many (inutile) connections and forming others, as a function of new acquired data from the interaction with family and environment.[631] So, the children learn, learn from interaction with reality by info-connection with the senses to environment (at info/sensory interface), and learn the meaning of this reality by interpretation of what they perceive (info/mind interface – Figure 1, left side), expressible by language.[632] The learning process doesn't ever stop; the human is actually a LEARNING SYSTEM, accumulating permanent KNOWLEDGE, and/or reformulating/adapting it to a new reality as is the case, in interaction with environment and with him/her own world representation.

Mind operates therefore with "pure"/conceptual information, with language and symbols, recognizing the perceived reality as per comparison with already acquired/learned concepts on it, an associative patterning process.[633] Mind is also a creation of body matter, which supports such activity. For this, the body itself creates/builds the necessary circuits, transduces the informational signals from sensors into specific signals, translating them from cell to cell of the nervous system to the central (CASI ⇔ CDC) processor, and transducing them "back" into "mass-media"-like signals/information on the prefrontal cortex, this time together with the associated/corresponding significance. Mind operates thus in two steps – feeding (reception) and recognition of information.[634] Mind is therefore an operative, actually a CDC/CASI system capable of allowing the access to stored/momentary external registered or internal (recalled) information. Consciousness, expressed by the cognition centers in relation (2), is a representation of reality, as transposed in mind and judged by Self with judgment criteria according to previous experience, so $I_A=/=I_B$ (A and B distinct persons), as is shown in the schematic representation in Figure 1, left side.

The operational tandem (*Iknow* ⇔ *Iwant*), assisted by *Ilove*/*Ibelieve* as pre-decisional/impulsive factors, is fundamental for the connection with reality and the decisional act for adaptation. Decision is an analytical comparative process with respect to the accumulated experience – *Iknow*, choosing between elementary YES/NO steps during a decisional processing chain, going to a final firm decision, which can be stored in CASI and becomes a further decisional criterion (Gaiseanu 2018b; 2020c). Knowledge is therefore a crucial foundation for attitude (Gaiseanu, 2020b), which is the output expression of the reaction to information. Therefore, if attitude is only the result of an immediate (native) response, without the intervention of judgement (CDC), this is an impulsive reaction, not always or perhaps never recommendable. A judicious attitude is the contribution of all other cognitive centers, or a part of them, depending on the situation.

Reblooming Knowledge: A Guide for Optimal Decision and Attitude

How does the cognitive center contribute to attitude? This is an important question, which determines the decisional process, so the knowledge of their contribution allows a better "driving management" of decisions in any situation.

Iknow is submitted to permanent training and goals; even without a specifically established target, the native tendency of our organism is to learn by the direct interaction with the neighboring environment (experiential learning). This is a natural consequence of the connection of OIS + IC with reality. Actually, IC is a part of OIS, which acts automatically during this connection, warning or predisposing to daydreaming on this reality. Such connection allows us to orient and decide on current daily activities. However, such an operative manner is subjected to arbitrary reactions, especially coming from the instinctual/native impulses. What we have to learn from this kind of behavior is not always good since this does not take into account the consequences. Judicious involvement into a certain situation should consider all or most of the factors and personages taking part in that scenario, and choose between possible variants as a function of consequences. In any case, consideration of the rules/laws of life and of society are obligatory.

A real objective/goal in life which allows the Self to mobilize and drive the resources of the organism to a fulfillment is certainly the major proposed accomplishment for a successful trajectory in life – whether this refers to the high preparation and education during childhood, youth or maturity for a suitable carrier; to formation of a family; to education of children; to promotion on the professional scale; or to creational and scientific activities.[635] The enlargement of the *horizon of knowledge* offers the possibilities to choose among more options. A minor/restricted number of options reduces the decision to an impulsive one: the lesser the knowledge, the more restricted the number of options for an appropriate choice

The creation of models worth following in life and the creative imagination play defining roles in drawing a goal and the path to follow to achieve it, especially for young people. Parents (*Icreate*) are the first model that children have and that they can follow. Therefore, parents not only have the duty to choose a worthy path to follow for themselves (*Iam*), but also for their children (*Icreated*). An ideal in life can constitute a guiding beacon to reach it, and which -- no matter what may seem difficult for oneself and for others – cannot stop the advancement towards it. The ideal enlivens, mobilizes energy, engages confidence in one's own forces and in obtaining the result, and therefore maximizes the chances of success. The mass media, as an illustration of a virtual reality, plays an extremely important role in this regard. The exacerbation of violence, as well as extreme sensations, sexuality or perversion in all their aspects, can only fuel curiosity and even the temptation to imitation of young generations in which the level of maturity of brain development in its normal phase (25 years) has not reached its peak.[636] Therefore, the connection to healthy information sources – as well as healthy food – ensures mental health, just as material healthy foods ensure body health.

Not all the events saved in our memory are worth keeping. If we want to maintain our balance and mental health, we must take care of the quality of the thoughts and memories planted in the memory, and which, like in a real garden, accompany, take root and flourish the mind and soul, or, on the contrary, whose growth suffocates and destroys or poisons the true blooming garden of thoughts and the feelings born from them, turning the garden not only into a desolate desert, but even into a place of lost hopes and despair. Hell and heaven are actually part of the concepts that humans created precisely to describe two very different faces of reality, or imaginary reality. In order to distinguish well between YES and NO in every step of choice we make, and in every stone we let sit in the edifice of the foundation of our inner garden, we must first of all know that *the value of any thing is that which we ourselves attribute to it*. If we give attention and importance to minor things, they will grow in our memory like a plant that covers the life of all the others previously planted with care. The distinction between major and minor is primarily marked by what is attached to a goal or not. The distinction between positive (acceptable) and negative (rejectable) is fundamental for the garden from which we expect to pick the flowers of joy and the fruits of success. Whining and negativism must disappear not only from the momentary behavior, but also from the language and the way of thinking. The exhortation 'YES, WE CAN', can achieve success, triumphing not only in politics but also in any other sector of life, including, and perhaps especially, in private life. Fortifying positive thinking and eliminating negative thoughts of helplessness and fear is the first decision that must be taken by each of those who want to embark on the path of rebirth and tending the mental garden of thoughts. Thoughts awaken feelings, making newly planted seedlings bloom or wither.

That is why the inner monologue should be applied in the form of daily reflection/meditation in order to discover and eliminate or stop the virusing of our inner garden in time. Our informational field (CASI) is also that of the soul, and thoughts (concepts - information) are accompanied by feelings (IES) whether we follow this or not. The call of memories awakens in the soul the echo of feelings too, with their film unfolding simultaneously, because CASI in its long-term form shares the hippocampus with the IES, the domain of emotions in the limbic system.

Repetition deepens/strengthens learning. Even schoolchildren know this simple fact, but most people tend to forget or neglect it. Sustained repetition over time – or living with great intensity of some events – means it is more and more imprinted in the body's informational system. Through epigenetic mechanisms, this process leads to the adoption of new traits in the cells,[637] which the informational system assumes as if they had forever been its own. These traits can even be passed on genetically. So, the importance of paying attention to what we think increases accordingly. The repetition of negative thoughts attracts negativity and poisons positive thinking, pro-life, and pro constructive activity. Repetition expands what we think; this is how the living organism works. And if we know this, let's start paying attention to what we think, to the sources of information, and to the credit they deserve. Consolidating positive thinking strengthens mental health and the road to success, and is in favor of achieving the proposed objectives, which should not be forgotten on any occasion.

The frequent encounter with nature is always a rebirth, a reblooming. The comparison of the domain of thoughts and the soul with a blooming garden is not accidental. Nature is the mother of the creation of living organisms and is part of ourselves; we are ourselves in another form. We are born, grow and green/bloom in life as a blessed tree, fruitful in what it gives to others. It is the very fruit of life, as it is built. It is her joy to be generous and to offer herself through the creation of new lives. We are born through its eternal mechanisms, we feed on organic matter, not only from a material point of view, but also mentally and spiritually. Scientists still wonder if plants are intelligent or not, taking into account that they do not have a nervous system. But the nervous system is not the only system that supports intelligence, even if it is evident in humans and in animals. Bacteria do as much harm as we can see they do precisely because they have learned to "orientate" in the world and their lives, and that behavior makes scientists attribute an intelligence quotient to them. (Gaiseanu, 2023c,d) And as regards plants, it is perhaps enough to ask ourselves: if they are not intelligent, in their own system of course and in interaction with the environment in which they live, how is it possible that they have developed in the course of evolution such a splendid representation and diversity of flowers and perfumes, if not to attract insects for pollination, then to stimulate/ensure the creation of life! And why do we believe in their beauty and how it attracts us? How do we already "know" that they are beautiful? Because there is a knowledge of life. And a common origin. And because there is this compatibility of life with life, of course, as commented on above. And even if in fact this compatibility also has a dramatic component, that of devouring between the various categories of living things.

Iwant represents sometimes a desire, sometimes a confirmation, another time a decision, and sometimes a command; a large range and variety of nuances involves this I 'want'. As long as we are aware, broad conversations with ourselves take place in mind, and there are many other real or imaginary interlocutors alongside us who occupy the scenario of the conversation, often an extension of some facts or situations that happened during the day or on other occasions. These inner monologues/dialogues are actually decision analyses. However, too long monologues are tiring, they prone to sleep because nothing new appears as something interesting, but worse, they can predispose to depression, intolerance, aggression and reckless acts if they revolve in the same circle of ideas. The effect of reporting through epigenetic mechanisms strengthens the conclusions, even if they are affected by the lack of information, and therefore by a correct interpretation. This point is particularly important in making a decision. Widening the area of information completes the picture of the whole and brings new arguments into the analysis. Sometimes, sharing justice among all, or neutrality, is the right decision/attitude in a dispute and a good way out of critical/tense situations. The one-sided view on a subject is not enough, and it is always altered by referring to an inherently limited baggage of information. Treating the same subject from several perspectives always adds value to the analysis, which supports the value of knowledge capacities. In a subject in which several people are engaged, giving a space to understand the behavior of others is not only welcome, but absolutely necessary. Following the reasons that lead to a certain type of behavior on the part of other people can reveal new arguments for adjusting the initial decision and adapting it to the new reality.

Therefore, the system of judgment is and must always be dynamic, in rhythm with reality.[638] Acceptance is again a good and wise measure in the face of the "crude" reality. Our system of values –and therefore of decision criteria – must be permanently reformed, bringing new data/information into the circle/center of the debate. Relinquishing the obsolete criteria and granting the credit necessary for new criteria (Ibelieve) is a reforming process that is both welcome and necessary. Keeping up with the changes in this era of unprecedented information development changes people's mentalities and their way of thinking on the fly, making them more flexible and observant than occasional decision-makers. A correct decision requires evaluation time, and thus a quick decision is not always correct, and *intelligence is not necessarily demonstrated by the speed of the decision but rather by its depth*, i.e., thinking harder, not faster.[639]

For some, *Iwant* represents a way of authoritarian command, more and more resentful in today's society, which is more and more democratic and informational. This archaic and tribal way of backward and casual voluntarism, still practiced in the family not only by men but also by women in some societies or communities where the leading role of the home by women ends up subordinating the whole family, if not always directly especially through manipulations, is curiously still present. Probably born from the need for defense in the far past, and for confinement sometimes originating from religious concepts or community mentality, it has become inadequate today when the sources of information are, or should be, available to everyone, and to which women just as well as men can connect and manifest their creative qualities not only in the biological field but also in the mental field for the benefit of the family and the whole society.

On the other hand, the group generalized stigmatization of men for the so-called "macho" behavior still practiced in some societies, does not have the mission/effect of solving the problem of incongruity/discordance between the sexes in some particular cases, but only leads to the opening of a new front of discord and inequality in society.[640] The decent, reasoned/reasonable fight for a cause cannot become an excuse or a motivation for inciting hatred, let alone hatred between the sexes, to the extent that it manifests itself by going out into the street with a raised fist, which is practiced by some feminist organizations. Justice is not done with the fist, only with the law. This is valid for any other manifestation or behavior of this kind, regardless of the nature of the motivation. The right to dignity should be respected regardless of gender, race or religion; it is a right of people and humanity, and not only of some groups, which dedicate themselves to this way of behavior. And in this case, as in many similar ones, information and education – so therefore knowledge – have a special and decisive role. The practice of offense cannot lead to social harmony, and education and respect in the family is the duty of all its members, regardless of gender. Provocation is also a stigmatizable behavior. Addiction to drink, drugs and antisocial behavior deepens and ruins any kind of relationship, not only that between sexes, and the obligation to be submitted to a periodic mental medical examination or, in occasional circumstances, institutionalized, regardless of gender or other characteristics.[641]

Own mentality (marking *Iwant* and also *Ibelieve*), becoming group mentality increases the tendency towards action/aggression with each member of the group feeling more encouraged to practice it.[642] Manipulation of information, modification of its meaning, lies, disinformation and instigation are weapons as provocative and repugnant as aggression itself, although more invisible, but for this very reason even more dangerous. Reason can triumph in these cases, standing over primary impulses and giving way to civilized access to dialogue and negotiation, or to compliance with rules. The best outcome of any negotiation is the one in which each of the parties is advantaged in one way or another. The promotion and practice of the intolerant, aggressive mentality[643] – through info-diversionist, terrifying, provocative, threatening manifestations on behalf of those who present themselves as the loudest, the most intelligent, or anything else – demonstrate the lack of culture, education and therefore *sufficient knowledge* to cross in silence and peace prejudices, incompatibilities, incompressibility, or dissatisfactions of any kind and nature. The due attention to knowledge brings such behaviors closer to the level of wisdom, suitable for any situation.

These paragraphs have been presented as examples. As long as we are aware, broad conversations such as these take place within ourselves and we have many other real or imaginary interlocutors alongside us who occupy the scenario of the conversation, often, as mentioned above, as an extension of some facts or situations that happened during the day or on other occasions. As we need to be fully aware, imagination and creative imagination[644] are forms of anticipation and are stimulated by knowledge, and at the same time they can stimulate/enlarge knowledge (*Iknow*). Imagination allows a "talk" with Self or others within the inner world, by using of the vehicles of words, images, sounds (so conceptual information), on the wings of fantasy, sometimes during daydreaming process,[645] and is a form to scrutinize the border between reality/certainty and uncertainty, welcome and practiced in science, arts and other creative activities, but also for personal use and planning of future. When the thoughts are expressed by words, these words become very powerful tools.[646] Once they are pronounced, they touch not only the target they are directed towards, but also, as a fully engaged information system, yourself. Before influencing someone else, they touch your Self, with their verbal utterance and reception amplifying this effect several times over. Therefore, the careful choice of vocabulary is not only a problem of social ethics, but also of one's own mental health and that of those around the speaker. The attitude expressed in words is therefore an instrument of great strength, and its employment in favor of the treated subject is beneficial as long as it is used with prudence, understanding, and respect for oneself and for all other interlocutors.

Asking someone what he/she cannot give is a delusion, and the relationship in question is doomed to failure. Compatibility in a relationship is not a sterile concept invented by scholars and experts. It is a strict reality, invented by the very nature that created us. Indeed, the IC center helps us understand this: it warns us on compatibility in social relations,[647] and is a worthy seeker/warner on the border between certainty and uncertainty, with qualities of premonitions, inspiration, and revelation in art and scientific investigation, always tailored on a platform of good knowledge and high training in the field but also functioning in the current life of each one of us. It is therefore useful to take into account the opinion of this center, and to look deeper for the source/reason of this warning because appearances are sometimes deceiving. A "first impression" is also a result of the activity of this center. The first impression is a quick x-ray of the mind on a subject or person based on the integrated level of previous knowledge, and so it is good to be taken into account. Fighting against a first impression can become an endless road, but above all without results, which leads not only to failure, but also to disappointment, if this fight involves a major change of one's own Self or of the other.

The compatibility of partners (*Ibelieve*) is revealed from an informational point of view by the ease with which each decodes/understands the thinking and reasoning of the other, because they are found in the common or corresponding level of training and life experience/culture in the way of looking at/judging life. In the business partnership, friendship, professional relationships, and especially in matrimonial ones, compatibility is one of the most important values to sustain the relationship, or that which can put it in danger. Struggling with oneself to modify one's thinking criteria, when necessary, is not an easy process to achieve. It requires time and effort of understanding and training. But if the change refers to the entire way of looking at life – along with mentality, traditions, and culture – then it is even more difficult, and the achievement of a "forced" compatibility in this way is always subject to doubt, or even failure.

The importance of the way of thinking and choosing between "healthy and unhealthy" thoughts is also depicted by the signals/silent voice coming from predecessors through the *Icreated* center. This center highlights the inherited qualities, predispositions, abilities and talents of each one, already practiced by the ancestors and transmitted inter-genetically. Ensuring a healthy way of thinking means taking over thoughts beneficial to body health and mental health and eliminating/avoiding/ignoring those with adverse effects. Life is therefore an endless series of YES/NO choices, in favor or to the detriment of the health of the whole body and its functioning. Listening to the internal voice, which means a certain kind of activity or thinking, is fundamental for the future development of children, and therefore discovering it as early as possible and cultivating it is beneficial for the development of the capacities to express later, for their value. Predispositions/talents/skills are already an invaluable preliminary gain genetically inherited from parents or grandparents, and their inclusion in the development/learning circuit of this endowment of knowledge makes the performances of those gifted in a certain field much easier to recognize in society. Searching for and finding a job and an activity suitable for these characteristics makes the yield increase and the support effort lower. The educational and guidance role of parents and teachers is equally important in encouraging this trajectory. The "nature" (native endowment) vs. "nurture" (training/learning/knowledge) dilemma is very easily solvable, knowing the composition and mode of operation of the informational system of the human body.[648] Genetic endowment offers a starting level that favors the holder, and helps him in training and finding/practicing a professional career.

Feelings (*Ilove*) make people human. They make them to feel touch/melt, to desire and love. Love is the most precious feeling, which unites people, binds the family, parents and children in a unique and peerless relationship. The feeling of protection is part of the same category. Children feel the need to protect weaker beings like them, to take care of them and defend them; this feeling is innate. Animals know it and practice it to the same extent. The feeling of love is genetic when it is related to the formation and care of the family, but it can refer to loved ones as part of sociability, or to the dear places of childhood, special landscapes, nature and its beauties, and art – painting, music, sculpture, literature, architecture, or any natural or human representation that delights the senses and makes them manifest intensely. Beauty is therefore the essential attribute that evokes positive emotions,[649] and emotions inspire action.[650] The job you do can be beautiful, as much loved as anything else. *Beauty is therefore an attribute that everyone assigns according to the qualities they consider special*. The formation of these attributes is also the privilege of the genetic voice (*Icreated*), and as previously noted also of training in the first years of life. The openness to the beauty of life and the world is the contribution of parents too, facilitating contact and connections to known and recognized sources of beauty, and transmitting them to children, making their internal strings vibrate and their vocation to listen and practice beauty. Love unites and elevates, hate separates and divides. Love is a universal characteristic of the living world, both through the need for reproduction (*Icreate*) and for unity and defense, practiced in family and community. As a social being, the human needs to socialize, to enrich his/her own knowledge from the experience of others, and to share/confess his/her own experience to others. Confession is part of the procedures for "detoxification"/purification of the tension created by stagnant or unresolved problems and thoughts, dissatisfaction or disillusionment, and is a means of release from their pressing/pressure. But confession itself does not solve the problems, and sometimes it even complicates them, if the interlocutor is not "comparable" to suggest or offer solutions. One's own judgment and the call to widen the horizon of knowledge with new data is the savior.

A Practical Method to Evaluate Own Attitude and Make a Right Decision

To elaborate a decision, expressible by attitude, *Iwant* "consults" the other cognitive centers, or anyway, these other centers send signals to it.[651] *Iknow* is the first which signals whether the approached issue is on the data field "map" and how much of it is really known. *Ilove* signals about feelings; *Iam* about momentary necessities or power/health over the medium/long range; *Icreate* about the specific impulses (if any), depending on the nature of goal; *Icreated* provides the internal/inherited "voice"; and *Ibelieve* does the evaluation comparatively with the already "known". *Iwant* is also in doubt whether the attitude should really express the real desire, or better, an "elaborated"/diplomatic response. Therefore, attitude is actually a function of all these centers.

If the external expression is taken into account, the attitude can be measured in Bits.[652] According to the above discussion, attitude A is a function of the information of each contributing center, so this can be expressed as:

A = function of (Iknow, Iwant, Ilove, Iam, Icreate, Icreated, Ibelieve)   (3)

which can be actually expressible by a sum like the relation (2) shows, because A is actually the expression of "I" – the Self. In other words, A in a self-analysis emphasizes actually the own Self

At any given A is working, that is, as long as we are connected to the environment, whether internal or external. A is therefore a dynamic function, and in any moment the contribution of each center could be different in intensity, and a value may be positive (YES – pro-acceptance), negative (NO – pro-rejection) and even zero (neutrality or inactivity). If it is considered the contribution of each center to the total quantity **Ao (t)** in Bits (or arbitrary units), then this can be evaluated by ourselves; for instance, in a scale of ten units, and the sum will give the total quantity. The fraction of each contribution, which is the result of ourselves evaluation, would be expressed respectively as A(Iknow)/Ao (with values always positive or zero – the last one corresponding to 'I don't know'), A(Iwant)/Ao (desire), A(Ilove)/Ao (inspired feelings),

A(Iam)/Ao (power of execution), A(Icreate)/Ao (sociability), A(Icreated)/Ao (predisposition/ abilities), A(Ibelieve)/Ao (trust), and the sum should be a value within the range [-1,1], with the extreme values included. These fractions can be furthermore expressed in prevents by multiplication with 100, and in this way a comparative proportion of the participation of all components to the final attitude is obtained.

Iknow represents the knowledge already acquired, so will always get a positive or zero value, the last one corresponding with 'I don't know' (nothing) on the involved issue. The rest of the contributions could be assigned with fractional positive or negative values. As a note, we have to observe that if a value of a certain component is 1 or -1, because of the normalized operation described above the rest should be zero , restraining the maximum range of variation in the specified interval only.

This result inspires/constitutes a method to personally fine the chance of success in the engagement in an important project. For the obtainment of a job, for instance, of a project or of something similar, the contribution of Iknow should be the most important, but the contribution of Ilove is also important because it indicates if you really like what you have to do.

The state of body power (*Iam*) in the long term is a priority reason to think on the practical possibility of fulfillment with duties and responsibilities, especially if the job requires physical effort or intellectual effort exceeding personal capabilities.

The promotion of personal abilities (*Icreated*) is recommendable, because as it was shown above, the level of the initial start point is favorable, based on the endowed capabilities, predispositions and abilities, if these exist.

Ibelieve is also an important counselor, because the trust in what we have to do fully engages even the hidden resources of the organism. Trust is the beacon of light that illuminates consciousness and directs it towards fulfillment of the objective, its polar star which always remains lit in the dark sky of the future. Even in momenta without too many experiences and visible chances, this center should remain alive and bright. If not, this is a serious alarm signal.

Ilove is a measure of the goodwill/"feel for it" towards the goal. The question of whether the objective is really desired or not, and if the proposed project ignites/invigorates the soul and wings the creative imagination is particularly important for embarking on a new path. Full participation with the soul in an activity not only leads to effective results in achieving it, but also brings immediate soul satisfaction with each step on the path to success.

Icreate is a measure of sociability and shows the availability/facility to work within – or with a team – as a Self-driving worker.

Finally, calculating the average value of A as a sum of fractional contributions divided by 7 (the number of contributions), the obtained value should be interpreted as following:

(i) if this is positive and higher than 50%, then a pro-active attitude is obtained, favorable of the proposed project;

(ii) a positive value, but less than 50%, shows a pro-active attitude, but no so successful results may be obtained;

(iii)a value zero shows inactivity, so no implication;

(iv)the negative values indicate the rejection of the project.

So, evaluating the participation of each center at the attitude level required by a certain job/project/issue, we can find/evaluate finally the degree of comfortable/conformance or compatibility with it by a pro-active acceptance, or rejection.

CHAPTER THOUGHTS – AS CONCLUSIONS

As you will note, values, beliefs, experiences, and culture – along with all the diversity and complexity of being human – are all related with the informational model of living systems, and over the years this model has shifted and changed as more learning has been developed as more learning has surfaced,[653] proving itself a living model, able to describe the dynamic running/'alive' life, in various hypostases. It is from this viewpoint that the following simple yet profound learning points have emerged along this journey, which can perhaps be of service to you, dear reader, as distinguished/proposed reflection topics.

- Meditate on the running of life; assume the reality, and also its beauty.
- Be aware of the charm of life and let yourself be engulfed by it.
- Visualize your cognitive centers and try to discover the qualities of each of them.
- Contemplate on your most important project and discover the contributions which you added during the day to it and the successful results.
- Contemplate if your decisions were GOOD or BAD, and revise the actions as needed before you apply them.
- Ask yourself if you have sufficient knowledge on a topic you analyze and, if necessary, add more information to your knowledge, even though this seems to be a time and energy cost. Prevention is better than unsuccessful/regretful action.
- Don't be passionate and don't criticize, rather try to understand and help: the poisoned arrows will hit yourself.

- Be a friend with knowledge and try to enlarge it on every subject converging with your project and purposes.

- Discover the beauty everywhere, enjoy it in peace, and ignore what you don't like.

- Use your knowledge only for GOOD purposes and don't hurt anyone.

- Respect you and anyone around; peace is the best gift given us by nature and life.

- Be the friend of a chosen/distinguished vocabulary of respect, appreciation and understanding in any and all situations.

- Learn to defend yourself with conviction, but with elegancy.

- As much as it is possible, be the decider of your life yourself.

- Let yourself be carried away by beautiful dreams, as if they would become real.

- Enjoy the small successes and give yourself a reward, as small it may be. Small steps lead to the big successes.

- Don't stop dreaming, even if sometimes things are not exactly as you would like them to be.

- Live in the present and future. Living in the past makes the present worse and ruins the future.

- Don't be upset on the world and life; they move forward no matter with what attitude you address them.

- Knowledge is the mother of wisdom.

About the Author

Dr. Florin Gaiseanu, Professor, Science and Technology of Information Bucharest (Romania) and Barcelona (Spain)
https://independent.academia.edu/fg140/CurriculumVitae

Dr. Florin Gaiseanu, PhD in Solid State Physics since 1984 from the Physics Faculty, University of Bucharest, is a Principal Senior Researcher (Professor) from Bucharest (Romania) and Barcelona (Spain). Born in a family of professors in a city (historical capital) near Bucharest, he was since 1971 an active scientist, principal researcher in the former Research Institute of Semiconductor Components (ICCE) - Institute of Microsystem Technology (IMT) in Bucharest, in the National Center of Microelectronics in Barcelona and other companies of similar field. He is the author of 14 patents and about 200 published scientific articles in national and especially in international Journals like *Proceedings of the Romanian Academy, Series A* (2013), *Annals of the Academy of Romanian Scientists, Series on Science and Technology of Information* (2017), in the *Journal of the Electrochemical Society, NeuroQuantology, Consciousness and Life Physics, Astrophysics and Cosmology Journal, EC Psychology and Psychiatry Journal, Gerontology and Geriatrics Studies, Philosophy Study*

Journal, Archives in Neurology and Neuroscience, Archives in Biomedical Engineering and Biotechnology. He was member of the Electrochemical Society, member of the Conference Committee and Chairman of the International Semiconductor Conference (CAS - Romania) and in the Micromachining and Microfabrication International Conference in USA. He is the author of the book *Physics of Consciousness and Life: Informational Model of Consciousness – Information in Neurosciences, Biocomputers and Biosystems,* of three chapters of books published in USA by IGI Global, *and* Honor Member of the Editorial Board of the *NeuroQuantology* and *International J. of Neuropsychology and Behavioural Sciences,* member of the *Journal Information Science and Systems Science* of the international Science Research Association, of the *Archives of Biomedical Engineering and Biotechnology, J. of Philosophy Study* (USA) and *American Journal of Psychiatry and Neuroscience (2018-2022).*

Acknowledgments

To Prof. Dr. Alex Bennet, a great Editor, life visionary and friend, for kind invitation and editorial support.

To Academician Florin Gheorghe Filip, for kind attention and support on this special matter.

To Adrian Gaiseanu, for continuous attention and support in life, and to Ana-Maria Gaiseanu, our beautiful flower of life.

To Adrian Gaiseanu and his family, and to Ana-Maria Gaiseanu and her family, with love and proudness for their high qualities, merits and their results.

To my family, for which I dedicated my feelings, my thoughts and my best deeds, every time.

To all those who marked out my life with thoughts, gestures, beautiful and good deeds, known or unknown.

In the memory of my loved parents Professors Emanoil and Florica Gaiseanu, who planted in my life only beautiful and priceless feelings and values, of my brother Professor Constantin Gaiseanu, and of the other members of my family, who marked positively my existence.

Chapter 14
Relationship Network Management

Although successful organizations have always recognized the importance of relationships, it was through the Total Quality Leadership focus on teams and the Knowledge Management focus on communities that the value of social capital was finally tied to the bottom line: sustainable competitive advantage for industry and sustainable high performance for government. Cohen and Prusak define social capital as "the stock of active connections among people: the trust, mutual understanding, and shared values and behaviors that bind the members of human networks and communities and make cooperative action possible."[654] Building on this definition, the social capital of an organization is the total value of all personal and professional intra-organizational relationships, and the personal and professional relationships among employees and other individuals external to the organization. And it is even more. Looking from a broader perspective, we would include the relationships between the organization and other organizations, particular among partners and competitors in the knowledge domain of focus, as well as the relationship between the organization and its environment. While all relationships are important in terms of potential value, it is critical to consider and actively manage these latter relationships.

INTRODUCING THE RELATIONSHIP NETWORK

Relationship Network Management (RNM) focuses on fully using and increasing the social capital of an organization. We begin this discussion focusing on the connections among people managed from the perspective of the individual employee. In this context, the relationship network is a matrix of people that consists of the sum of a knowledge worker's relationships – those individuals with whom the knowledge worker interacts, or has interacted with in the past, and with whom there is a connection or significant association which will continue into the future. This matrix is both horizontal, in terms of colleagues and peers, and vertical, in terms of bosses and mentors, employees and mentees. RNM occurs when we recognize the potential of these relationships and *consciously and intelligently engage them* to share information and knowledge and to learn, creating and sustaining a conscious give and take movement, or flow, across our personal and professional relationship network.

Organizational structures as depicted on organizational charts, teams, and communities are units for managing relationships, with teams and communities a central and fundamental element of organizational design. Teams and communities have the ability to integrate and enhance cross-functional knowledge and cross-organizational perspectives to provide faster and more effective decision-making, problem solving, innovation, and implementation of organizational strategies and initiatives. The use of teams and communities in organizations can be likened to the industrial revolution, when the assembly line replaced the craft shops where craftsmen individually made the whole product. The assembly line sped up production by moving the products around and having different elements of the products added by different individuals in order to more efficiently achieve the whole. Each individual, then, became highly efficient as part of the process. On the negative side, this process reduced the amount of learning each individual achieved, limiting their growth and ability to contribute, and removing ownership of the whole product.

Today, where we have achieved a high degree of specialization in our career fields, teams and communities move information around much like the assembly line, with individuals adding their experience and perspective. The difference is that teams and communities provide a way to *integrate individual pockets of knowledge.* As information flows among members of a team or community, the individual has not lost it. Rather, an individual's knowledge is increased as each member contributes to, and gains from, the flow of thoughts, bringing diverse thoughts into resonance and spreading ownership among all members of the team or community and, by design, across the organization.

Why is Relationship Network Management Important?

As we become a global world and the amount of information available increases, decisions have become increasingly more complex while simultaneously needing to be made faster to ensure sustainable competitive advantage and sustainable high performance. It is impossible for a single individual to know everything. While our knowledge systems provide better information in terms of quality and currency – with active available chatbots now joining that mix – it is difficult to capture the context of this information without interjecting the human factor. In short, information (and information technology) is necessary but not sufficient to create knowledge.

How are most good decisions really made? The decision-maker pulls together all the information readily available on the subject, considers (either consciously or unconsciously) their own personal experience, and then, if their own experience is insufficient in the area of the decision, consults a trusted source. This consulting of a trusted source of information is the process of verification, where a decision is grounded by the explicit knowledge of another. *An active relationship network provides a source for getting one or more opinions in a trusted environment*, whether it is achieved through consulting a boss or employee, a mentor or mentee, or a knowledgeable member of a team or community.

Active relationship networks crisscrossing the organization increase organizational awareness, reduce redundancies, and, in turn, *affect organizational responsiveness in terms of agility and flexibility*. An organization can react faster when information around key areas of concern is flowing freely. For example, the concept of the "mesh" (described below) emerged in response to the events of September 11, 2002. And with the spread of disinformation, misinformation and propaganda in today's environment, it is important to find someone to converse with who you trust.

An active relationship network provides a *monitoring and scanning system* for problems and opportunities. If a line of thinking gets off track, it is easy to correct the course through an open dialogue, where individuals share their thoughts and stories in a comfortable and trusted environment. Simultaneously, an increase in the exchange of ideas resulting from Relationship Network Management also *increases the number of new ideas*. Creativity is an attribute that resides in all individuals. The more an individual learns and understands, the more opportunity to build on that learning and understanding. Note that the concept of "learning" includes the attribute of openness. Creativity can be limited by rigidity or the belief that there is only one answer to every question.

Another benefit is that of ownership. When a group of individuals contribute to a decision there is *broader ownership* of that decision, providing a number of people who are already committed to it. This commitment is particularly significant when decisions require broad support in order to be successfully implemented.

On the individual side, the networks we belong to help define who we are, contributing to our self-confidence, purpose, identity and morale. Affiliation with a team or community that is actively contributing to the organization, and is recognized for its contributions, can produce a high degree of *collegial synergy and self-satisfaction*.

Relationships are ultimately about people and the way they interact with each other over long periods of time. Ironically, the fundamental principle of success in relationships parallels Sun Tzu's fundamental principle of success in warfare, i.e., know thyself, know thy enemy (the other), and know the situation. Principles of Relationship Network Management start with the individual (know thyself): what the individual brings to a relationship in terms of values, ability to communicate, expertise and experience, and willingness to share and learn. Second, the culture of an organization and the environment in terms of place and time (the situation) significantly impact relationship building and sustaining. For example, are people promoted for their personal knowledge, or for their ability to share and problem solve in a team environment, creating systems solutions instead of individual solutions. Third, what do others (the other) bring to the relationship in terms of values, ability to communicate, expertise and experience, and willingness to share and learn.

Basic Tenets of RNM

Taking the above into account, there are six basic tenets that successful Relationship Network Management is built upon. These will be discussed in terms of: interdependency, trust, common framework, openness, flow, and equitability. Collectively, these key success factors support the team's, community's or organization's ability to successfully take collaborative, cohesive action.

Interdependency. Interdependency is a state of mutual reliance, confidence and trust. It connotes a two-way relationship, with both parties taking responsibility for nurturing and sustaining the relationship. Each party depends on the other for their own success.

Trust. Trust is based on integrity and consistency over time, saying what you mean, and following through on what you say. Trust is directly tied to individual and organizational value sets and is measured by proven behavior. As the old adage says, "To be trusted one must be trustworthy." Respect and reputation also contribute to the perception of trust across teams, communities and organizations. Trust takes time to build, yet can be lost in a second. In the Reblooming Knowledge, transparency, truth and trust form the outer petals, and an organization that embodies these values is more likely to build strong relationships with stakeholders and achieve long-term success.

Common Framework. In this context, there must be a common framework upon which the exchange of information can lead to the creation of knowledge. This framework could include a common language (cultural, functional, organizational); common stories; shared values (the ground truth); shared moral standards; or a shared vision and mission. This is not to say that ALL of these need to be in place. Diversity of ideas and thinking styles can add value in a trusting environment where differences are clearly and openly discussed.

Openness. Openness is directly related to trust and a willingness to share. Without initial trust, it is difficult to have openness; yet openness contributes to the spread of trust and cooperation. When the organization rewards knowledge sharing, it is easier to be open with our thoughts and ideas. Nonetheless, recognition that (1) in today's environment it is important to stay at the front of ideas, not to hold on to the old ones, and (2) value is in how these ideas are used, moving knowledge professionals from the concept of "knowledge is power" to "knowledge shared is power squared."

Flow. A relationship cannot exist without interactions, without the flow of information and knowledge. The flow of data, information and knowledge moves around in the networks of systems and people, is shared through knowledging, team interactions, communities and events, and is facilitated through knowledge repositories and portals. This free flow is mutually dependent on both the individual and the organization. It is each individual's responsibility to assure she has what she needs when she needs it to make the best decisions (in alignment with the strategy and vision of the organization). This flow is both horizontal and vertical, and includes the continuous, rapid two-way communication between key components of the organization and top-level decision-makers that is essential to mission success, all part of an individual's relationship network. See the discussion of knowledge flows in Chapter 10 under "Connecting the Dots".

Equitability. An equitable relationship is one that is characterized by fairness and reasonableness. When used in law, the concept includes the application of the dictates of conscience or the principles of natural justice. The intent of an equitable relationship is that both sides get something out of the relationship. In reality this is often additive, with both sides often gaining more than either contributes, since relationships produce synergy and ideas shared beget new ideas.

None of these six tenets – interdependency, trust, common framework, openness, flow, and equitability – can be controlled or ordered to happen. They all arise from the sequence of interactions among the individuals involved and depend upon each person's perception and feelings about the others. Effective relationships evolve over time and are created by interacting, testing, questioning, and carefully building a grounded, experientially-based, image of and belief about the other person. Good relationships emerge from a history of interactions, and as such they must be nurtured and protected to be sustained. This is discussed further below.

GUIDELINES FOR MANAGING

How do you manage relationships? The individual's ability to manage their relationship network is based on (1) recognizing the value of relationship networks; (2) identifying their personal network of relationships; (3) consciously choosing to develop and actively sustain those relationships through continuing interactions; and (4) staying open to sharing and learning through their relationship network. Each of these will be briefly discussed below.

Recognize the Value of Relationship Networks

We have talked above about the value of using relationship networks, of knowing our own value and limitations, and of valuing the expertise and "know how" of others.

Interestingly, these concepts are consistent with the definition of humility which, from the individual viewpoint, is having an accurate view of yourself, neither too high nor too low. This would include knowing your strengths and abilities as well as your weaknesses and limitations, and being honest about them to yourself and others. From the collective viewpoint – the interpersonal level – humility is being other-oriented, focused beyond self. This would include development of empathy, knowing the needs and wants of others, and taking those into consideration in your decisions and actions. This attitude opens the door to learning as well as the potential for greater creativity and innovation. Considering humility as a learning tool is included in Section IV.

In the day-to-day world, as we interact face-to-face and virtually with others, moving in and out of meetings and teleconferences, it is easy to take all these interactions for granted. *Yet these interactions are the way we do business and from which we are learning, often unconsciously.* The nature of these interactions determines the type and value of the relationships that exist. Generally, how we value an interaction is directly proportional to our short-term decision-making process driven by need, situation and time. However, every interaction causes information to be embedded in our subconscious, information that emerges as it is needed, often without reference to where it was obtained.

Most organizations of today operate with permeable and porous boundaries. As organizations move into and function in a more complex environment, management concepts that developed with the bureaucratic model, so successful in the past, lose their effectiveness. Over the long term, knowledge cannot be controlled, and people cannot be controlled. As information moves in, around and out of organizations, and as people move in, around and out of organizations, it is difficult to identify the origin of a new idea. Indeed, ideas are the product of multiple processing in terms of people and time. Ideas beget ideas, and grow and mature through interactions with others and over time.

The bottom line is that our interactions with others affect the way we think, feel and make decisions, over both the short and long-term. When we recognize that *how* we interact is more important than *how often* we interact, we begin to realize the importance of building relationship networks and choosing our interactions carefully.

When an idea's time has come – that is, there is some need or opportunity that presents itself which triggers the idea – it is often simultaneously emerging, in different contexts, around the world. Thus, what is important to competitive advantage is how effectively and how quickly ideas are applied in context, which can be more effectively accomplished with people working together.

Identify Your Personal Network of Relationships

The first step in managing your relationship network is awareness of who is (or should be) in your network. This will take time to build, since our networks encompass past and present relationships, are not instantly available in our conscious mind, and are subject to continuous change. Developing a simple relationship network chart is a good start. The chart begins with an individual's name and organizational affiliation, followed by the length of relationship (how long you have interacted with this individual). The information entered in the next six columns is based on your experience with this individual and personal judgment. For each individual, team, or community, the column headings in Table 14-1 are: (a) name and relationship; (b) length of relationship; (c) related expertise and knowledge; (d) access; (e) openness to sharing; (f) follow-through; (g) your feelings; (h) your contribution; and, in the final column, NOTES AND ACTIONS. Column "h" is critical to consider because it is important to recognize that we do not necessarily enter into relationships strictly because of what we get out of them. Humans are social animals … interactions are an integral part of our life activity and growth. For those who love people, connection can be its own reward.

Here's the process for using the RNM table:

Step 1: On a separate sheet of paper list the critical knowledge and skill areas which are needed to achieve your goals and create innovative solutions. Remember, while most likely your professional goals center around a specific domain of knowledge, integrative skills such as systems thinking, decision-making, leadership, risk management, and even having a trusted "sounding board", are also necessary. Put that list aside, adding to it when you think of additional items that should be on it.

Step 2: Fill out columns a and b (listing the individuals with whom you interact and the groups in which you participate). Examples of "Relationship" would be: friend, colleague, mentor, manager, etc.

Step 3: Assess columns c through h in terms of a strength scale from 1-10, with 1 being weak and 10 being strong. "Your Feelings" would be rated in terms of respect, trustworthiness and ability to interact. "Contribution" refers to the level or value of knowledge you contribute to the relationship. Positive learning relationships would be those rated above the midpoint (5).

Step 4: Under "NOTES AND ACTIONS" write anything that comes to mind which you think may be important to the relationship; for example, "Need to interact more often."

Step 5: From this simple chart, assess your gaps, that is, circle any number less than 5, and – comparing your RNM table with the critical knowledge and skill areas developed in Step 1, determine the relationships that need to be expanded or relationships that need to be added to ensure interaction with those who have the expertise you require. For example, if your numbers are low and a specific individual or team is important to accomplishing your goals, then actions must be taken to build/expand that relationship and increase the assessment numbers. (This may be a good time to review the RNM key success factors discussed above.)

Step 6: Add the actions you plan to take under "NOTES AND ACTIONS". If gaps are noted, consider how best to fill those gaps – perhaps joining a community, attending a seminar, or taking a night class – and consider letting go or curtailing any relationships have no internal or external value on either side of the relationship

Recalling that successful Relationship Network Management requires two-way responsibility, fill out a chart on yourself from the perspective of individuals in your network. Periodically repeating this process can serve as a check to ensure your contributions to others in your relationship network.

Table 14-1. The Relationship Network Management Assessment Chart.

a. Name and Relationship	b. Length of Relationship	c. Related Expertise and Kn	d. Access	e. Willingness to share	f. Follow-through	g. Your Feelings	h. Your con-tribution	NOTES AND ACTIONS

At the organizational level, **Social Network Analysis** (SNA) is a process for mapping the relationships among people, teams, or across organizations, which can help you better understand the people with whom you interact in an organization. SNA is particularly effective in assessing the flow of information through communication and collaboration. It also identifies people who are central (overly central?) and peripheral (under-utilized?) to an organization. The extent to which a group is connected, or the extent to which it is split into sub-groups, can be an indicator of a problem, difficulty, or strength in moving information from one area of the organization to another. willingness

The process of SNA begins by collecting data through interviews or surveys. Examples of questions asked would be:

- From whom do you seek work-related information?
- To whom do you give work-related information?
- When you need information or advice, is this person accessible to you?
- When you need information or advice, does this person respond within a sufficient amount of time to help you solve your problem?
- How frequently have you received work-related information from this person in the past month?

From the answers to these questions a map is created that connects people who receive information with people who have provided that information. Arrowheads indicate the direction of that relationship. There are several software products available to do SNA mapping such that it is not a difficult or time-consuming process. The survey is done on-line, and simple screen-oriented interfaces allow the user to drag nodes with the mouse and click to add new modes. Each node is assigned a number of attributes, which are highlighted using color and shape. There are also several tools for automatic layout of the network. Once the mapping is complete, analysis of this structure of connections can provide information on relationships that facilitate or impede work, offering intervention opportunities.

Actively Develop and Sustain Relationships

Understanding the makeup and nature of our relationship network provides the opportunity to assess its strengths and weaknesses. Consider these questions:

- Do you have active exchanges with individuals who are knowledgeable in your area of work?
- Do you belong to a team or community that is accessible and available when you have a problem to solve?
- Do you share your ideas, learnings and successes with other members of your organization?

- Do you have a support network that helps enable thoughtful reflection?

It is imperative in this age of ever-increasing information and complexity that every knowledge worker has access to a trusted network of thought leaders in their area of concern. If your personal relationship network is not robust enough to serve your knowledge and decision-making needs, it is your responsibility to develop a relationship network that is. With communities emerging across organizations and social networking around the world, there is ample opportunity to develop collegial exchanges with knowledgeable coworkers and experts in government and industry alike.

Somewhat more difficult is sustaining the relationship network. It is easy to dialogue on an issue when we are on the hook to make the best possible decision, which is the process of knowledging. It is more difficult to take the time to respond to others who are working toward making the best possible decision, and it is even more difficult to take the time to dialogue when there is no immediate decision to be made. However, this is often when the greatest headway can be made, i.e., when an innovative idea emerges, because we are not focused on one issue, on one decision, but open to exploring.

Relationships of any nature need to be nurtured. What exactly that entails is relationship-dependent. For example, a problem-solving team that convenes once a month will expect participation at least once a month. An active community may encourage weekly interactions. A dialogue on a critical issue that is time sensitive may require three or four exchanges in a single day, with a follow-up in a week or so, then fall off to "keeping in touch" every month or six weeks until another critical issue arises. The nature of nurturing is to support, to care for, and sustentation, the maintenance of being and activity.

The quality of both intellectual and emotional exchange is of primary consideration. When connecting virtually, there is an entirely new set of communication rules. In a networked world, communicating virtually is an essential integrative competency – and supports all other integrative competencies. With Generation Z, most parents would say this comes naturally, that the issue is to get them to interact with others face-to-face!

On the negative side, the very characteristics of relationship networks that make them cohesive, effective partners for decision-makers can become a problem if they become closed, dominated, controlled, or corrupt. Take for example the emotion and temper that may emerge during a football game when two colleagues are rooting for different teams. A mutual love of football can bring people together, while passion and loyalty to different teams may pull them apart. This is happening around the world in the political arena. In organizational terms, in a relationship network it is critical to have different thinking, which promotes creativity, yet essential to have agreement on the mission of the team or organization, and always to have and exhibit respect for the other person.

A second issue that has emerged is Collaboration Overload, which can lead to decreased productivity and job satisfaction with employees having little control over their work and struggling to effectively manage their time. This, of course, can also lead to a lower quality of work as burnout. An excellent book titled *Beyond Collaboration Overload* by Robert Cross offers strategies for mitigating collaboration overload. These are briefly address in the Chapter 11 discussion of communities.

Stay Open to Sharing and Learning

Receptivity to new ideas is critical. Your personal receptivity is affected by a combination of internal and external information and current beliefs, all of which are subject to continuous examination and update. All incoming information is colored by an individual's current beliefs and feelings. This means that incoming information, whether originating from the external environment or within the unconscious mind of the individual, is under continuous examination and, as a result, the individual's beliefs themselves are also subject to continuous reexamination. This powerful process goes on at various levels within all learning individuals.

A first step to receptivity is gaining attention. As the environment bombards the senses, attention itself rapidly becomes a scarce resource. Since the perceived trustworthiness of information is highly dependent on the sender, information from a network built on strong, trusting relationships has high value, and is more apt to gain attention. A second step to receptivity is listening. "Listening" is far more than an aural sense; it is the mental act of engaging and reflecting on incoming information and is highly dependent on the perceived value of that information. The sub-text of incoming information is in the form of questions being answered by the subconscious. *Is the sender trustworthy? Is the information I am receiving worth my time to think about?* There is a depth treatment of misinformation, disinformation and propaganda in Chapter 3.

When the answers to these questions are positive, a transformation occurs as we move from listening to thinking and understanding, considering the information, its context (our context) and meaning, driving the question: *What does this information mean to me?* Our understanding relates to what we already know. We build relationships with not only people, but with things and situations and ideas, and these relationships are largely based on patterns from the past, what we have learned and what we have experienced as well as the beliefs and values that have emerged from our learning and experiencing. **There is no separate entity called "understanding".** Understanding is a state of mind related to some situation, problem or set of concepts in context. Remember, all knowledge is relative. Our understanding – filtered through our own consciousness in light of what we know and believe – is ever changing and unique to each interaction. In dynamic relationship networks, where a dialogue pursues, different forms and perspectives of the information emerge that facilitate a shared understanding and new, innovative ideas.

REFLECTIVE QUESTIONS

The questions below are provided as tools to guide your individual thinking patterns as you digest the concept of Relationship Network Management and make sense of it in terms of how it can personally benefit you. It is important to realize that **the conversations you have today, whether you consciously remember them or not, will drive the decisions you make tomorrow**. When you expose yourself to a diversity of thought and the opportunity to dialogue with true and trusted resources, you are filling your internal reservoir in support of future decision-making, creativity and innovation.

There is no right or wrong answer for these questions; there are only *your* answers as they relate to your personal network or situation.

- Am I viewing my relationships differently after thinking about the concepts introduced in Relationship Network Management?
- Does my current relationship network provide all the resources I need to do my job well?
- Do I invest the time needed to build new relationships and sustain old ones?
- What is the role of emotions in Relationship Network Management?
- Do I follow through on commitments I make to others?
- What actions can I take to improve my relationship network?

VIRTUAL RELATIONSHIPS

While each individual has the opportunity to build and fully utilize their personal relationship network, in today's challenging environment they also daily engage in social networking and larger virtual communities such as the mesh which offer opportunities to expand their relationship network. However, in these virtual settings, a shift has occurred where there is less focus – or none – on relationships among people but increased on focus of *relationships among ideas*. We will first briefly touch on communities, which in today's environment have become primarily virtual, using the emerging idea of the mesh and recognizing the importance of idea resonance (see Chapter 3).

Communities of Practice, Interest, and Learning

Communities came into focus in the second round of Knowledge Management as a new management approach. They recognize the power of diversity of thought in stimulating new thought and, while perhaps at the time of their emergence not in conscious awareness, that (1) physical mechanisms have developed in our brain to enable us to learn through social interactions, (2) social relationships build and shape the brain, with social bonding a significant source of brain stimulation, (3) the brain actually needs to seek out an affectively attuned other for learning, which contributes to the evolution and sculpting of the brain, (4) cognitive mimicry transfers active behavior and other cultural norms, and (5) mirror neurons, facilitating neural resonance between observed actions and executing actions, can enable the rapid transfer of tacit knowledge, by-passing cognition.[655]

Teams and communities where people are focused, working together in a specific domain of knowledge or on a specific issue or problem, are powerful vehicles to facilitate the flow of information and knowledge in organizations, and to facilitate the building of relationship networks. A Community of Practice (CoP) is a group of people who have a common work focus, or practice, and engage in a deliberate process of collective sharing and learning. Over time, the dialogue that develops across a community builds bonds, and in a healthy community fosters trust among the participants. Etienne Wenger, co-author of the term "community of practice", states there are three fundamental elements that shape a community of practice. The community must (1) have a shared interest in a topic; (2) interact and build relationships; and (3) share and develop knowledge. All of this is done in order to contribute to the success of the mission of the organization. Communities of interest are groups of people who have a common interest and engage in a conscious process to share what they know and learn more about their area of common interest. The use of teams and communities was a comfortable fit for the Department of the Navy (DON), whose sailors on a ship and whose ships in a Battle Group operate with the same interdependencies that develop in teams and communities.

Effective communities are built on relationships. The DON CoP Development Model published by the DON Chief Information Officer in a practitioner's guide entitled *Cport: Building Communities of Practice, Creating Value Through Knowledge Communities*, introduces seven stages of CoP development: (1) conceiving and catalyzing; (2) connecting people; (3) sharing know-how; (4) building trust; (5) collaborating; (6) creating knowledge; and (7) continuation-renewal.[656] These same stages are critical in developing relationships, whether in a team or community, across an organization, or in an individual's personal life. In thinking about managing the relationship network, an individual consciously chooses those relationships to sustain – and develops the new relationships necessary to expand – their ability to solve problems and make decisions. (See a detailed discussion of communities of practice in Chapter 11.)

The Mesh

The concept of the *Mesh* builds on a network of interconnected communities of practice across the Federal, State and local governments. This example is built around homeland security. Key functional/organizational representatives retain interaction within their organizational frame, but expand their direct interaction cross-organizational and cross-functional to focus on specific pre-identified event/idea response *as the need arises*. Much like the early FEMA (Federal Emergency Management Agency) model, which in the US deteriorated when resources were redirected after 9/11, when an emergency arises, the experts come together from across government while continuing to link back to senior leadership in their home organizations, serving as conduits to pull/push expertise in terms of information, people, and other resources needed to build a response approach. This self-organizing, focused team is hosted – facilitated and supported – by, for example, Homeland Security. When a response is developed, an emergency addressed, and a long-time, follow-up home is found in the appropriate government agency, community members fall back into their parent organizations, while retaining the flow of ideas and thought (a trusted relationship) through the continuing virtual community linked to the implementing agency. A visualization of the Mesh concept is Figure 14-1.

Clearly, trust cannot happen in the instant without considerable pre-planning. As has been said above and will be discussed further below, relationships and trust are built over time. The "mesh" is pre-thought as an element of scenario planning, and then specific skill points (with specific people with special expertise in appropriate partnering organizations connected to those skill points) are designated as a virtual community, interacting quarterly (practice sessions) to ensure a common understanding of responsibilities and actions should the scenario play out in real life. Note that while this design emerged as a government model that could also reach into industry expertise as needed in response to emergent disasters, it is also applicable to surprises occurring in private industry. Few organizations can internally sustain all the expertise that may be required in a changing, uncertain and complex environment. Thus, relationships among organizations – partners and competitors alike – need to be considered in light of possible and probable future scenarios.

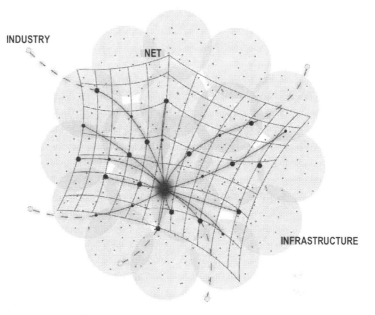

Figure 14-1. A Model of the Mesh.

The Knowledging Network

The "knowledging network" is centered around the idea of knowledging, which is purposefully seeking a solution or opportunity, *a conscious learning choice in a specific situation and context,* virtually reaching out to others who have expertise that may help. While potentially sustaining its existence for a long period of time, the knowledging network is most often informal and emerging out of a need for a solution to a particular problem or issue. When the problem goes away, the network fades, with members of the network potentially engaged when a different situational issue arises.

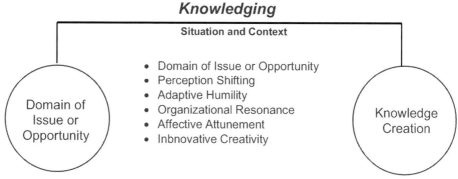

Figure 14-2. Knowledging, the focused link between expertise and knowledge creation, situation dependent and context sensitive.

Recall that knowledge is the capacity to take effective action in a specific situation and context; thus, "knowledging" is the process of seeking knowledge for a specific situation in a specific context. While learning, the creation of knowledge, is the outcome of knowledging, they are very different terms since knowledging is purposefully – formally or informally, externally or internally – seeking knowledge (the capacity to take effective action) specific to an issue at hand. In other words, a community is focused around a domain of knowledge and certainly can address issues in that domain, while the knowledging network is focused around a specific issue in a specific context, perhaps a problem that needs resolving NOW. Thus, the six capabilities supporting knowledging relate to the specificity of focus. *Environmental awareness* is the ability to identify and understand the situation at hand and the context in which that situation is occurring in addition to, as noted above, the ability to scan the environment and identify the environmental opportunity space to consider the best solution, ensuring conscious exposure to related issues, challenges, and ideas.

Perception shifting is the ability to look at the situation at hand or domain of focus from different perspectives. Examples of this are provided in Chapter 16 on Knowledge Capacities. *Adaptive humility* is a necessary ability which does not only entail listening to and considering others' ideas, but the ability to connect those ideas to information gleaned from environmental awareness and perception shifting as well as adapt those ideas to the situation at hand.

Organizational resonance is a necessity – a recurring realization – and it is one of the overarching goals of Reblooming Knowledge. Within the organization, this reiterates the need for a "connectedness of choices" between the knowledger (the individual who is knowledging) and organizational values, beliefs, and actions. As introduced in the Preface and detailed in Chapter 4, this is a knowledge exchange that represents the shared state of *affective attunement*, the vibrational entrainment that opens the door to learning, deeper and easier knowledge sharing, and, collectively, the triggering of new ideas. To this group of abilities, we add *innovative creativity*, which is purposefully engaging your creativity with innovation in mind (see Chapter 10) or the companion book *Innovative Creativity: Creating with Innovation in Mind* by Bennet and Shelley.[657]

AI AS PART OF YOUR RELATIONSHIP NETWORK

In today's technology environment, where we are every day changing the face of work and life, AI is rapidly becoming an integral part of our future. This occurrence is not random. As each of us has observed – and many have been drawn into – there are battles underway that fragment our society, pitting one person against another, one community against another, one nation against another. The very sanctity of human life is diminishing, giving way to rife and hate against others who are born into different circumstances or make different life choices than our own. And in the midst of all of this noise – financial and banking crises, weather disasters linked to climate change, the war in Ukraine, social crises, and on and on – Artificial Intelligence (AI) has become available widely to all those who choose to engage. While all the daily distractions of a world in chaos keep us from exploring the larger picture of the impact of AI on humanity, we are at a crossroads.

How will we choose to use this technology? There are so many amazing ways. For example, handling the virtual help desk in an organization, linking the knowledger (seeker of information specific to a situation and context) to all available materials in organizational databases, and other people who have expertise in the area of interest, adding the context of how it has been used in the past. Or, perhaps confirming the ways we're looking at a problem. In Chapter 7, ChatGPT joined the authors to help validate the Reblooming Knowledge model and the value of its elements to the organization. And while what is being forwarded is certainly a synthetization of input from the initial developers and the learning that has occurred during tens of millions of interactions with other people, remember that each human is unique, that *you* are unique, and while ChatGPT can provide and connect ideas, it cannot "know" what is best for you and your organization in terms of the human dynamics at play and internal desires of participating humans. Although admittedly we are heading into the unknown, we are part of an exciting era in human history filled with potential. We do not KNOW the full potential of AI. But then, neither do we know the full potential of the human mind/brain, which, even as AI, is continuously evolving and expanding. While we encourage you to bring AI into your relationship network, we simultaneously encourage you to remember that YOU have agency, it is important that your thoughts and feelings (intuition) guide your decision-making, and for you to remember that YOU are the decision-maker.

In a recent court filing, an attorney licensed in New York for over three decades filed a brief with supporting cases that appeared to be bogus judicial decisions with bogus quotes and internal citations. The attorney was ordered by the judge to show cause why he shouldn't be sanctioned for the use of a false and fraudulent notarization. The attorney had used ChatGPT as a legal research source, and, when asked about each case, ChatGPT "doubled down" that each was a "real case", providing the reputable legal research databases where each appeared.

There are various possibilities contributing to ChatGPT's failure. First, ChatGPT does not have human "judgment", that is, it is unable to tell a made-up example case, perhaps available as a training tool, from a legitimate "real" case. Since there is much fiction available on the internet and throughout various databases – along with misinformation and disinformation (see Chapter 3) – this contributes to the data being combined and synthesized along with "real" data. Further, the search criteria must be exact. We all have seen what happens when you change one letter of the search criteria! What you are searching for is unfindable. Further, ChatGPT does not have the capability of fully understanding context, associations certainly, yes, but the context of the human related to choice and judgment (which are both driven by emotions and preferences) is not available to ChatGPT, or, as some AI champions would say, at least not yet. Purpose and direction related to choice and judgment emerge from the "old brain" where emotional tags are placed on incoming information and are fed to the neocortex, which, with its matrix of cortical columns, is the seat of human intelligence. *No thought or decision is separate from its thinker and decision-maker.*

AI has the capability of augmenting the human in so many ways, and intelligently embracing that contribution is both exciting and rewarding. However, in that embrace we must not give up our freedom of thought, the gift of humanity. AI is not a replacement for the human mind. Nor is AI a replacement for human interaction, even if that interaction is largely virtual in nature.

VALUE ADDED AND MOEs

Looking back one hundred years from now, people will see the beginnings of a new age of connecting: people working together in fascinating ways, augmented through technology, forming relationship networks and communities across time and distance to organize and create. All of this taking place in a new space, the global space enabled by technologies not even conceived at this time, transpiring at the new speed, the speed of thought. People working intelligently – with other people and AI – with a synergy of knowledge interaction never dreamed possible.

As introduced and discussed above, Relationship Network Management contributes the following value to an individual and organization:

- Provides a vehicle for targeting and managing the sharing of knowledge and taking actions.
- Enhances the transfer of tacit knowledge.
- Facilitates knowledge flow throughout the organization.
- Increases the number and diversity of new ideas available.
- Provides a source for decision-makers to get a second opinion in a trusted environment.
- Improves organizational responsiveness in terms of agility and flexibility.

- Provides a monitoring and scanning system.
- Contributes broader ownership of decisions and decision implementation.
- Provides a sense of control over and participation in self-learning.
- Produces collegial synergy and self-satisfaction.

What is significant about thinking about purposeful connection and interaction is that the individual is clearly in charge of their own relationship network, yet the effectiveness of the collective networking of individuals directly impacts the effectiveness of the organization.

Chapter 15
How Leaders Inspire Action through Meaningful Knowledge

Milton de Sousa
Nova School of Business & Economics, Portugal

Pedro Brito
Nova School of Business & Economics, Portugal

ABSTRACT

As meaning creators, effective leaders enable knowledge acquisition to inspire action among followers. In this article I explore how that takes place through a sense-making process that integrates prior and new knowledge to form meaningful knowledge. That is, knowledge that is coherent, purposeful, and significant. I make use of the new model of meaningful leadership to illustrate how leaders promote the acquisition of meaningful knowledge through a mindset of awareness, service motivation and commitment to transform, and the roles of storyteller, enabler of action and mentor.

Keywords: Meaningfulness, Meaningful Leadership, Meaningful Knowledge, Knowledge Acquisition, Sense-Making

INTRODUCTION

Imagine you have just been appointed as manager of a relatively large department. You come from another company. Even from another country. You may have worked in the same industry for many years but, apart from that, everything is new. During your job interviews, you realize that people seem to have lost their sense of shared identity. There are many concerns about new and disruptive competitors that pose many threats to the long-term survival of the company. You conclude that the department needs a new and inspiring vision and a course of action to help people reconnect and contribute to the survival of the company. There is a townhall meeting planned two months after you start where you will be holding a speech to the whole department. This is a unique opportunity to set the tone of your tenure and announce your ambition. Your goal is threefold. First, you want to get people excited about the future, and how they can make a difference to the company. Second, you want them to be able to retain the main strategic guidelines of your plan, as a compass for future decisions. Third, you aim to create an environment where people can fulfil their personal ambitions and dreams. In essence you want to inspire action. How would you prepare that speech? Reflect on this question for a while. Take some notes.

When leaders want to convey their message, like in the scenario above, in essence they want to promote effective knowledge acquisition. Knowledge is a measure of a potential for action. As such, an effective message will be one that invites people to act given their understanding and adoption of the leader's purpose and strategy. I offer that the more meaningful leaders are in their capacity to transmit the knowledge of their ambitions while considering the prior knowledge of their followers, the more they will be able to inspire action. Let us explore these ideas.

MEANINGFULNESS

Baumeister[658] defined meaning as mental representations among things, events, and relationships. Following Baumeister's concept, meaning, in life, work and other contexts, is like the meaning of a sentence, namely: (1) its parts need to fit together into a coherent pattern, (2) it needs to be understood by others, (3) it fits into a broader context and (4) it invokes implicit assumptions shared by other members of the culture. He continues by arguing that meaninglessness, like a meaningless sentence, shares common features of disconnected chaos, internal contradiction, or failure to fit context.[659]

Batista and Almond defended that meaning needs to be defined from a relativistic point of view.[660] It follows that the process of creating meaning can be seen as a sense-making process in search of coherence at the personal level, which "involves the ongoing retrospective development of plausible images that rationalize what people are doing."[661] As such, meaning is an ever-evolving image, continuously under construction internally as our social contexts demand us to re-evaluate our choices and assumptions.

It is also relevant to highlight the distinction between meaning and meaningfulness.[662] Meaning is the sense that we make of something, while meaningfulness implies a personal sense of relevance. Based on the extensive empirical work of Michael Steger and colleagues,[663] we can establish that meaningfulness requires significance, purpose, and coherence. In a short summary, significance is about the personal relevance and value we attribute to something, be it a speech, our work or even life in general. Purpose revolves around having a compelling ambition for the future, which can involve personal achievements or contributing to others. Coherence is about the personal logical sense that we experience in the context we find ourselves in. As Paul Wong explains, these three components involve different mental processes towards meaningfulness, namely affective (significance), motivational (purpose), and cognitive (coherence).[664]

Meaningfulness and Knowledge Acquisition

The relationship between meaningfulness and knowledge has been explored before. For instance, a study published in the pharmaceutical industry establishes that work meaningfulness moderates the relationship between social capital and knowledge sharing, which then stimulates creativity.[665] In other words, meaningful work amplifies the effect of the social ties in an organization towards greater creativity. Likewise, work meaningfulness moderates the relationship between a person's positive core self-evaluation, which includes self-esteem, generalized self-efficacy, locus of control, and emotional stability[666] and its effect on creativity through knowledge sharing.[667] The more confident we are about ourselves, the more knowledge we share, which leads to greater creativity. This causal chain is stronger when our work is meaningful. But how does this relationship between meaningfulness and knowledge take place in more general terms?

Knowledge acquisition can be understood at two levels of cognition: remembering and applying.[668] Remembering includes recognizing and recalling the new knowledge, either verbatim or by paraphrasing. Applying involves identifying or producing new instances of that knowledge in the context of the knower. So, in the case of the story above, as a manager you would want the people in your department to be able to remember your strategic guidelines. They should be able to at least paraphrase what your strategy is, as close as possible to what you intended. Simultaneously, people should be able to enact those strategic guidelines in their context. In other words, they should be able to apply the knowledge of the new strategy by identifying how it can be of use and by producing relevant and consistent actions in their specific work situation. For example, if your strategic guidelines would involve eliminating products that damage the environment above a certain threshold, a product manager should be able to identify within his or her portfolio which products need to be eliminated and why. Or, if the strategy calls for greater collaboration with external partners in open innovation, that same product manager should be able to identify and select which partners to work with for his or her product line.

This importance of meaningfulness for knowledge acquisition, organization, and retrieval has been advanced already in the 1960s by Ausubel.[669] In essence, what Ausubel concluded was that when new knowledge is meaningful, we learn better. It follows that acquiring new knowledge, like a new strategy in our example, only becomes meaningful when people can relate it to prior knowledge,[670] as they make sense of the new knowledge concomitantly with frames of reference previously assimilated. Prior knowledge can rely on past experiences, models, or analogies. Charles Reigeluth suggests seven specific types of prior knowledge, including arbitrary knowledge (mnemonics or heuristics), superordinate knowledge (concepts preceding the new knowledge), coordinate knowledge (structures and frameworks), subordinate knowledge (types and categories), experiential knowledge (instances and examples), analogic knowledge (metaphors and analogies), and cognitive strategies (rules and steps to process the new knowledge).[671]

To summarize, using the articulation of meaningfulness introduced above, we can offer that when knowledge is meaningful, we perceive it as significant, purposeful, and coherent. That is, it is relevant, guides future action, and makes logical sense. In addition, new knowledge can only become meaningful when it intersects with prior knowledge. It is that prior knowledge that will help make sense of the new knowledge as significant, purposeful, and coherent. This convolution between new and prior knowledge happens in the intersection between the inner world of the transmitter and the inner world of the receiver. In a speech there is a one-way communication between transmitter and receiver, but in a conversation there is a continuous exchange of roles between transmitter(s) and receiver(s). Regardless, effective knowledge acquisition requires that both parties acknowledge and willingly integrate each other's new knowledge with their prior knowledge. Said differently, knowledge becomes meaningful through a shared sense-making process between transmitter(s) and receiver(s), which facilitates its gradual acquisition into future prior knowledge. The diagram below depicts the process of knowledge acquisition and the role of meaningful knowledge as explained above.

Now that we understand how meaningfulness contributes to knowledge acquisition, we can start answering the questions posed with our initial challenge. Before we do that though, I provide a brief introduction to the new concept of meaningful leadership.

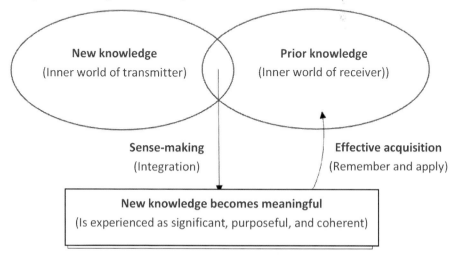

Figure 15-1: The process of knowledge acquisition through meaningfulness

MEANINGFUL LEADERSHIP

The importance of meaning in leadership has recently received some attention among the organizational scholarship community. For example, Daan van Knippenberg provides a rationale for meaning-based leadership to sustain purpose-driven organizations.[672] Based on a qualitative study, Frémeaux and Pavageau further advance how meaningful leaders operate.[673] I offer a model of meaningful leadership based on the leader's capacity to positively influence others through a compelling significant, purposeful, and coherent organizational narrative.[674] At the same time, meaningful leaders enable action within that larger narrative, and mentor people to craft their work in meaningful ways. The figure below further depicts the mindset and main roles of meaningful leadership.

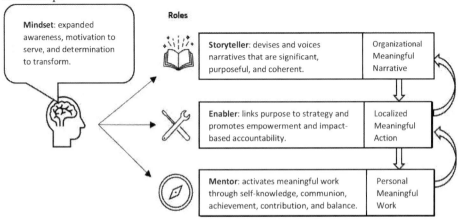

Figure 15-2: The integrated meaningful leadership model and its roles.[675]

The mindset of meaningful leaders starts with an expanded awareness of the environment and one's role in it as a change agent towards impact. This is about developing what Robert Kegan called a self-authoring and self-transcending mind.[676] From this expanded awareness, compassion for others can unfold, which is translated into a motivation to serve people to be at their very best. This is inspired by the notion of servant leadership,[677] in which the leader enables people to grow and further develop themselves. Such focus promotes meaning. Finally, meaningful leaders have a mindset of transformation, showing determination to mobilize the organization towards greater impact, and indeed be of service to others.

Based on this mindset, meaningful leaders embrace three main roles. The first one is as a storyteller of organizational narratives that promote significance, purpose, and coherence. As storytellers, meaningful leaders know how to activate these three processes by appealing to the values and shared identity of the organization, promoting a future-oriented purpose that excites people, and creating coherence between the two.

The second role of meaningful leaders is to enable action, mainly at the team level, which is the main driver of change in organizations.[678] The purpose set in the meaningful organizational narrative needs to be applied at the point of action. This requires translating the overall purpose into the specific context of each team. On the other hand, meaningful leaders empower and hold teams accountable for both the outputs (production) and outcomes (the actual impact on others) of their work.

Finally, as mentors (the third role), meaningful leaders help people craft meaningful work at a personal level. This can be achieved by promoting a healthy balance between being and doing, while integrating the self and others[679] in what I call the paths of self-knowledge (being with self), communion (being with others), achievement (doing for self), and contribution (doing for others). As mentors, meaningful leaders share their own personal stories, while practicing active listening and humble inquiry[680] to help people realize and craft meaningful work in their own context.

INSPIRING ACTION THROUGH MEANINGFUL KNOWLEDGE

When considering the role of meaningfulness for knowledge acquisition and the model of meaningful leadership we just explored, some important conclusions can be established. First, leaders should be mindful of the importance of understanding, respecting and actively integrating the prior knowledge of those they try to influence through their actions. This is true for all three roles. As storytellers, leaders should have a profound knowledge of the reality of those they try to inspire. Only then will their narratives become meaningful for those listening based on their own images and experience of the organization (prior knowledge). With this regard, storytelling is equally about listening. A good story is one that can be retold by the listener in their own way. Regarding the second role, enabling action involves translating the broader and more generic stories into practices and processes that people can relate to in their work reality (prior knowledge). Not being able to do that will limit the potential of the story as a guide for concrete action. It becomes void of practical relevance. Finally, as mentors, leaders should always operate with the other in mind. The personal stories and examples of the leader are only means to the end of helping the other grow. A mentor that just tells based on his or her experience becomes prescriptive and limited in the capacity to raise awareness and self-development in those they are helping. The aspirations, needs, experiences, challenges, and strengths (prior knowledge) of the mentee are critical for the new knowledge transmitted by the mentor to be significant, purposeful, and coherent (i.e., to become meaningful).

For a leader to learn about the prior knowledge of the people in the organization, the meaningful mindset explained above will be important, especially the motivation to serve. Leaders should realize the importance of serving people so that they, "while being served, become healthier, wiser, freer, more autonomous, more likely themselves to become servants."[681] At the same time, as put by philosopher Joan Tronto, caring requires paying attention, taking responsibility, competence, and being responsive to the specific condition of those we aim to help.[682] Responsiveness is the exercise of learning about the prior knowledge of the other. This is an exercise of cognitive empathy[683] that involves asking and listening humbly.[684] Such responsiveness can only be of use though, through motivational empathy, as an act of conscious compassion[685] which strongly relates to the serving mindset. Based on these reflections we can establish some guidelines to answer the questions of the hypothetical case presented initially.

First, a powerful and inspiring story should be anchored in the values and history of the organization, making it meaningful for the audience through significance (affective) and resonant coherence (cognitive). Reminding and activating the deeply ingrained foundational prior knowledge is essential to arouse an emotional connection to the place, promoting a shared identity and strengthening the organizational culture. It is a paradox that to promote progress, leaders often need to reconnect and heighten the roots of the organization. This is because behind the history of any organization there is likely a story of ambition and determination of the founders. This sets the stage to promote a purpose, the dimension of meaningfulness, that mobilizes people towards an aspirational future. In that sense, the past becomes an anchor of prior knowledge that enables people to realize how they can move towards the future. The past leaders and their examples (prior knowledge) become models to assimilate and integrate a future oriented purpose.

Second, when leaders communicate their views, they should come prepared with many hours of listening to a wide range of people from different areas. Holding conversations that revolve around their views of the organization and their work, without pre-judgements, to learn about the reality of the organization as seen from the field. This exercise will be important not only to measure the overall sentiment, but also to collect concrete stories and examples that can be used to anchor the leader's narrative in a way that makes sense to those listening. Likewise, attentive listening will be useful to incorporate the language, analogies, mental models, and metaphors of the audience to create more resonance and establish relatable parallels with the leader's narrative. When this is done effectively, from the perspective of the listener, the leader becomes "one of us". The additional advantage is that reflecting the listening into the narrative will add to the perception of procedural and relational justice, which has been shown to contribute towards greater commitment.[686] By listening attentively, leaders can integrate prior knowledge more effectively and speak to the audience in their own terms, which will invite aligned action.

Finally, leadership narratives should set the background for people to express themselves and realize their potential. Based on a deeper insight into the individual stories of team members (the more personal prior knowledge), leaders can add and contribute to their needs and aspirations through their own knowledge. As such, a meaningful leader communicates in ways that invite people to be at their best and perceive the organization as a vehicle of personal growth, while creating the space for dialogue to establish a meaningful relationship with followers.

Let us now conclude. Through this chapter, I aimed to establish how meaningfulness contributes significantly to knowledge acquisition. Knowledge becomes meaningful, and therefore more easily acquired, when it is significant, purposeful, and coherent. This happens through an effective process of sense-making between transmitter and receiver that integrates prior knowledge and further facilitates remembering and applying the new knowledge. Meaningful leaders are aware of this process. They actively learn about the prior knowledge of those they serve, integrating it in their narratives to convey knowledge that is meaningful and inspires action.

About the Authors

Milton de Sousa is Associate Professor at the Nova School of Business and Economics in Portugal. His research interests revolve around different forms of human-centric leadership, including servant and meaning-based leadership. He works closely with many multinational organizations, offering learning and development solutions to equip leaders with the competencies necessary to promote agility, innovation, sustainability, and people-centric practices that promote meaningful work. Milton has a degree in Engineering from the University of Porto, an MBA from the University of Bradford and a PhD from the Rotterdam School of Management, Erasmus University.

Pedro Brito is currently serving as Associate Dean at the Nova School of Business & Economics, overseeing Executive Education, and spearheading the Corporate Engagement Strategy. In that quality he works with many senior executives designing and offering learning & development solutions. Prior to joining Nova SBE, Pedro worked in the HR Consulting Business at Mercer as Country Business Leader. This followed from the acquisition of Jason Associates, a successful leadership development consultancy firm that he founded in 2004. Before that, Pedro worked as Business Manager at Michael Page and as consultant at Arthur Andersen. He is a member of the CPOs (Chief Portuguese Officers), and a certified coach, with a post-grad in people management and a bachelor's in organizational technology. His research and teaching interests focus on mentoring.

Chapter 16
Knowledge Capacities

In a changing, uncertain and complex environment where surprises emerge and must be quickly handled, capacity is more important than capability. This is especially true for sustainability over time. When you plan an outdoor event, you create an alternate plan for inclement weather. When you're raising a family, you try to put aside a bit for kid's learning experiences such as a school visit to the museum. When you study a domain of knowledge in college, you learn the theory right alongside pragmatic applications. This is why the case study approach was successful for so many years in higher education.

One of the authors' spouses, who taught nuclear physics for the U.S. Department of the Navy, recalls a story about a time when, in response to needed budget cuts, classes dealing with theoretical physics were on the chopping block. A short scenario quickly demonstrated the need for theory. Imagine a nuclear submarine with a full crew on board, deep under the North pole when the reactor fails. While there are a large number of possibilities for failure, this particular situation was not in the textbooks; it had never happened before. Do you want a nuclear officer well-trained in pragmatic responses, or do you need someone who also has the capacity to explore and understand the theory and deep relationships within the core which could have caused this failure? Both theory (capacity) and practice (pragmatic actions) are important and necessary in a CUCA[687] environment.

As is clear in this example, knowledge itself is a capacity. Knowledge is defined as the capacity (potential or actual) to take effective action. Capacity is the ability to receive, hold or absorb, a *potential for accomplishment.* Thus, to think-know is a multi-asset, using knowledge from the past focused in the present offering potential for the future. Each learning experience builds on its predecessor by broadening the sources of knowledge creation and the capacity to create knowledge in different ways. For example, as an individual engages in more and more conversations across the Internet in search of meaning, thought connections across disciplines occur, causing an expansion of shallow knowledge. Knowledge begets knowledge. In a global interactive environment, the more that is understood, the more that *can* be created and understood.

We create knowledge every single day of our lives, with this knowledge serving the self and others with whom we interact as a bounding off point to bisociate ideas and trigger new thoughts. Expansion of shallow knowledge (the realm of social knowledge) is an area of strength for the Net Generation.

Through continuous connectivity and engagement in conversation and dialogue (a search for meaning), NetGeners have grown up with and developed a wide array of shallow knowledge. This knowledge (as a potential or actual capacity) prepares individuals for a changing and uncertain future by expanding areas of thought and conversation beyond a bounded or limited functional and operational area of focus, supporting collaboration and knowledge sharing, primarily through social media. Thus, new areas of interest are discovered, ideas expanded, and judgment and decisions made from a broader scale.

Capability is a subset of capacity, that is, a specific ability – a capacity to be used, treated or developed for a *specific purpose*. Take the simple analogy of a bucket (capacity) which sits in the locker of a speedboat among various ropes and floats until needed for bailing water or holding your daily catch (capabilities).

Our thoughts affect our mind and body. We now know that thoughts and feelings can nurture, develop and change the infrastructure of the mind/brain/body system. In short, thoughts in the mind are patterns of neuronal firings, which in turn can change the physical structure of the brain. Simultaneously, the emotional tags connected to those thoughts affect the release of chemicals, which impact the neuronal junctions (synapses), which influence thoughts. As understood more fully over the last decade, this is at the core of the mind/brain/body system. Eric Kandel,[688] who won the Nobel Prize in 2000, showed that when even simple information came into the brain it created a physical alteration of the *structure of neurons* that participate in the process. Thus, we are all continuously altering the patterns and structure of the connections in our brains. As introduced above, the conclusion is significant: thoughts change the physiological structure of our brains, with this plasticity resulting from the connection between the mind (patterns in the brain) and the physical world (atoms and molecules of the brain).

Thus, we have the capacity – which can become a learned capability – to shape and influence our future thinking and behaviors through current thoughts and behaviors. Certainly, competencies and learning skills participate in this process. However, more often than not, we repeat over and over again the *way* we perceive the changes around us, exploring those changes through our mental models or from comfortable reference points. When this occurs, the things around us are perceived and fixed from those reference points. For example, when you stand under a star-lit night sky, *you* are the center of the Universe in terms of the point of reference, with the magnificence of your surroundings seen from – in comparison with the Universe – the viewpoint of the tiny spec of life that is you.

Knowledge Capacities are sets of ideas and ways of acting that are more general in nature than competencies, more core to a *way* of thinking and being, that change our reference points and specifically support building capacity for sustainability in a changing, uncertain and complex environment. *They provide different ways for us to perceive and operate in the world around us.* The analogy here would be the building of an expanded infrastructure of sorts relating to the mind/brain (information, knowledge and the structure and connection strengths of neurons within the brain).

The building and expansion of relationship networks, the widening of interests and knowledge, and the opening of possibilities – undergirded by continuous change and uncertainty – all contribute to removing limits, real and perceived as well as self-imposed. These connections can open the door for new ways of thinking and acting upon the world that are participative and collaborative. As situations become more complex, the nature of learning, knowledge and action shifts. *Building knowledge capacity lays the groundwork for better understanding those shifts.*

Exploring Knowledge Capacities

Knowledge Capacities are developed from combining senses while co-evolving with a changing, uncertain and complex environment, complementing six different ways that humans operate in the world. These mental changes are described in terms of (1) looking and seeing, (2) feeling and touching, (3) perceiving and representing, (4) knowing and sensing, (5) hearing and listening, and (6) acting and being. Each of these sets has two concepts introduced because, while they are related, there is clarity added by coupling the concepts. Each area is briefly addressed below. See Figure 16-1.

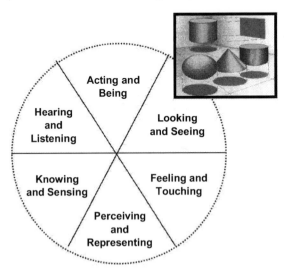

Figure 16-1. Ways humans operate in the world.

With our compliments (and apologies) to *Encarta World English Dictionary*,[689] we attach specific meanings to these six ways humans operate in the world, meanings that suggest ways of observing and processing the events that occur in our lives. Knowledge Capacities are all about expanding the way we see those events in order to raise our awareness and, in the case of problem solving and decision-making, offering new ideas and a larger set of potential solutions.

Looking and Seeing: To direct attention toward something in order to consider it; to have a clear understanding of something. (*Examples*: Shifting Frames of Reference, Reversal)

Feeling and Touching: The sensation felt when touching something; to have an effect or influence on somebody or something; to consider the response of others being touched. (*Example*: Emotional Intelligence) A great deal has been written on Emotional Intelligence, beginning with the excellent treatment by Daniel Goleman in a book by that name.[690]

Perceiving and Representing: To acquire information about the surrounding environment or situation; mentally interpreting information; an impression or attitude; ability to notice or discern. (*Examples*: Learning How to Learn, Refocusing, Comprehending Diversity and Symbolic Representation)

Knowing and Sensing: Showing intelligence; understanding something intuitively; detecting and identifying a change in something. (*Example*: Engaging Tacit Knowledge) Engaging Tacit Knowledge is included as a tool in Section IV.

Hearing and Listening: To be informed of something, especially being told about it; making a conscious effort to hear, to concentrate on somebody or something; to pay attention and take it into account. (*Example*: Active Listening) Active reflective listening is discussed at the end of Chapter 10 as part of "Training and Learning".

Acting and Being: to do something to change a situation; to serve a particular purpose; to provide information (identity, nature, attributes, position or value); to have presence, to live; to happen or take place; to have a particular quality or attribute. (*Examples*: Orchestrating Drive, Instinctual Harnessing)

We briefly introduce some of the Knowledge Capacities cited above as examples. These include:

Comprehending Diversity (perceiving and representing);

Learning How to Learn (perceiving and representing);

Orchestrating Drive (acting and being);

Refocusing (perceiving and representing);

Reversal (seeing and looking);

Shifting Frames of Reference (seeing and looking); and

Symbolic Representation (perceiving and representing).

While this set is certainly not complete, an no doubt you can add some personal examples, it provides a good starting point.

 Comprehending Diversity (perceiving and representing)

From an internal perspective, quick responses require a *diversity* of responses from which to draw. Since there is not much time to effectively respond in a CUCA environment, and yet essential that the best response is engaged, it makes sense to explore and develop a variety of potential responses prior to their need. An example is the use of scenario building, a foresight methodology that has been well-developed and tested in government, business and education. Scenarios are a form of story that can be used to consider possible, plausible, probable and preferable outcomes. Possible outcomes (what might happen) are based on future knowledge; plausible outcomes (what could happen) are based on current knowledge; probable outcomes (what will most likely happen) are based on current trends; and preferable outcomes (what you want to happen) are based on value judgments. For a well-connected knowledge worker, building scenarios can be both fruitful and fun. When facing surprises, scenarios can help in understanding new situations, or at least foster a faster response by comparing the surprise with a related scenario.

From an external perspective, Comprehending Diversity means developing a competency in identifying and comprehending a wide variety of situations. For example, if you know nothing about complexity you won't be able to differentiate a complex system from a complicated system, each of which requires different sets of decisions and actions to achieve goals.

A first step is to recognize what you are looking at: the existence of diversity, the situation, and its context. Key questions: Is it diverse? Does it have many aspects that are in play or that may come into play? A second step is to comprehend it. *Vericate*, that is, consult a trusted ally, someone who understands the systems at play. Develop knowledge about a situation to *comprehend it within the context of the situation*. That means engaging social knowledge, people who are in the midst of related or similar situations. Move through the knowledge chain to develop knowledge about the diversity of this specific situation, that is, awareness, understanding, meaning, insight, intuition, judgment, creativity, and anticipating the outcome of your decisions and actions.

Learning How to Learn (perceiving and representing)

Every individual is unique. Each person has a unique DNA, unique early development history, and adult life experiences and challenges different from all other humans. This uniqueness means that each of us learns differently and, to maximize that learning, we must understand ourselves, how we think and feel about specific subjects and situations, and how we best learn. For example, people who are more visual learners would prefer learning through books, movies or databases; those who are more auditory would prefer learning through stories and dialogue; those who are kinesthetic would prefer learning through hands-on approaches such as role-playing.

A first step is to observe ourselves as we learn and assess our efficacy in different learning situations, noting what works well and what doesn't work well. We can also try adding different techniques that aid learning such as journaling, creating songs and stories, or asking others (and ourselves) key questions, then trying to answer those questions, recognizing the importance of emotions and repetitiveness in remembering and understanding. For skills that require body movements, then similar body movements must be included in the learning process. For skills that require mental agility, then mental games or simulations might be involved. In other words, the best way to learn is to understand your preferences and ensure that the learning process is consistent with the skill or knowledge you want to learn.

Undoubtedly, *the most important factor in learning is the desire to learn*, to understand the meaning, ramifications and potential impact of ideas, situations or events.[691] In the present and future CUCA world (increasing change, uncertainty and complexity and the resulting anxiety), learning – that is, the creation and application of knowledge, the capacity to take effective action – is no longer just an advantage. It is a necessity. Because of their uniqueness, each knowledge worker must learn how they learn best.

There is a relationship between your own learning style preferences and the way you share. Effective facilitation and communication requires tailoring learning techniques to the preferred learning styles of your target audience. Applying multiple learning and communication styles enables you to reach target audiences with multiple preferences. Further, exposing multiple learning styles to the larger audience helps expand individual learning capacities, enriching the personal learning experience.

Orchestrating Drive (acting and being)

There are many wives' tales and beliefs about our personal energy. One is that we just have so much in a life, and we just sit down and die when it is spent.

Another says the more you give away the more you have. Regardless of whether we refer to this energy as spark, subtle energy (metaphysics); prana (Hindu), chi (Chinese), libido (Freud), orgon energy (Reich); or any other of the numerous other descriptive terms, every individual possesses a life force or, as described by Henri Bergson, a French philosopher, the élan vital, a source of efficient causation and evolution in nature.[692] What we have learned about this energy – both by observation, and confirmed more recently through neuroscience findings – is its relationship to feelings. As Candace Pert, a research professor of physiology and biophysics at Georgetown University Medical Center, describes, "… this mysterious energy is actually the free-flow of information carried by the biochemicals of emotion, the neuropeptides and their receptors".[693]

While the expression of any strong emotion requires an energy output, the expression of negative emotions generally represents an expenditure of energy, and the expression of positive emotions represents a generator of energy. For example, consider the crowds following a close-tied football game. While all may be physically tired from the experience, those who supported the loosing team are generally depressed and drag home with low energy, while those who supported the winning team are generally buoyant, and may well go out and celebrate.

By understanding – and using – the emotions as a personal guidance system and motivator, knowledge workers can orchestrate their energy output. For example, by interacting, working with, and writing about ideas that have personal resonance, a knowledge worker is generating energy while expending energy, thus extending their ability to contribute and influence.

Refocusing (perceiving and representing)

While Refocusing can have many contexts, it is uniquely tied to perceiving and representing in terms of meaning, that is, what is important. It considers the impact of an action on humans, and the social change brought about by that impact. While some impacts can be directly attributed to identifiable refocusing, many are indirect, and therefore it may be difficult to identify specific causal relationships between actions and impacts, although over time these may become clearer. For example, when Xerox moved their purpose from selling copy machines (an output) to intelligent copying solutions (an outcome), the focus was changed from the economics of sales to the satisfaction of the customer, which over time clearly elevated their sales. When this refocusing occurs from output to outcome in terms of impact, it is necessary to develop an understanding of the customer, an empathy, a connection.

Indirect impacts emerging from refocusing may have to do with the personal development of individuals in a stakeholder group, or the building of relationships across communities. Therefore, focal points for assessment of impact may be individual or collective as well as offering potential evidence of larger cultural and social change. For participating individuals, a significant outcome may be the amount and nature of learning that has occurred, unintended shifts in their frame of reference, and behavior changes, many of which would be reflected in decisions made or actions taken. In a collective shift such as that made by Xerox, another outcome may be a pattern of learning across all participants (employees), resulting in a visible collective behavior and cultural change.

The importance of a focus on impact measures (both in terms of outcome and sustainability) cannot be overemphasized. This means thinking long-term, making decisions. and taking actions based on a human-centered design focus. Human-centred design is introduced in Chapter 8.

 ### Reversal (looking and seeing)

One of the fun ways to shift our frame of reference is Reversal, that is, the ability to see/perceive situations and their context by turning something inside out, or upside down, generally reversing the order of things, whether front and back, or top and bottom, or side to side. There are lots of ways to think about this. For example, during the big Acquisition Reform movement in the U.S. Department of the Navy, part of which was the shift to performance-based standards, there was the need to eliminate thousands of standards that had crept over the years into various contracting vehicles. Given one year and a pot of money to accomplish this task, the DON began down the same path as the other services, holding mini-trials with each standard the defendant, where, one-by-one, it had to be "proved" that a standard was *not* needed. This task was an impossible one; there was always a contractor or contracting officer who felt that each standard was absolutely essential. As the weeks went by and maybe 5 or 6 standards had been eliminated out of several thousand needing to be addressed, it was clear this approach was doomed to failure. A different approach was needed. Embracing the Knowledge Capacity of Reversal, *all* of the standards were eliminated, and mini-trials were held for those around which contractors and contracting officers had enough energy to bring back to the board and prove the need for their reinstatement. This was a game changer; when all was said and done, a couple of hundred standards were important enough to invest the energy necessary to have them reinstated.

 ### Shifting Frames of Reference (looking and seeing)

When we find ourselves in confusing situations, ambiguities, or paradoxes where we don't know or understand what's happening, it is wise to recognize the limited mental capacity of a single viewpoint or frame of reference. Confusion, paradoxes, and riddles are not made by external reality or the situation; they are created by our own limitations in thinking, language, and perspective or viewpoint.

The patterns in the mind have strong associations built up through both experience and the developmental structure of the brain. For example, as children we learn to recognize the visual image of a "dog" and with experience associate that visual image with the word "dog". As our experience grows, we identify and learn to recognize attributes of the visual image of "dog" such as large, small, black, brown, head, tail, poodle, Akita, etc. The way we store those in the brain are as associations with the pattern known to us personally as "dog", perhaps connected to the particular characteristics of a beloved childhood pet or with the negative experience of a dog bite. Thus, when we think of dog, we immediately associate other attributes to that thought.

Shifting Frames of Reference is the ability to see/perceive situations and their context through different lenses, not through our limited experiences and perceptions; for example, understanding an organization from the viewpoints of its executives, workforce, customers, banker, etc. The ability to shift frames of reference is enhanced by a diversity of experiences available to networked and interactive knowledge workers. Even with the strong presence of their own experiences and perceptions, individuals who are subjected to a wide range of ideas and perspectives through social media are going to be much more attuned to difference, while at the same time becoming involved through dialogue. This participation with lots of people and interaction with differences helps develop a healthy self-image, and comfortable connections with different situations and people that build a feeling of "capability." Through these interactions, knowledge workers are actively doing things, which in and of themselves demonstrate their capability of interacting with the world. This broad set of reference experiences individuals can identify those disciplines or dimensions they are excited about, and are capable and competent to develop and grow from. This process can result in better decisions and choices that match both personal and professional needs.

Frames of reference can be both expanding (as introduced above), and focusing and/or limiting, allowing the individual to go deeper in a bounded direction. Learning to consciously shift our frames of reference offers the self the opportunity to take a multidimensional approach in exploring the world around us. As introduced above, one approach is by looking at an issue from the viewpoint of different stakeholders. For example, if you are looking at an organization problem, you might ask the following questions: How do our customers see this problem? How do other employees see this problem? How does senior management see this problem? How would the bank see this problem? As another example, when exploring a systems issue you might look at it from the inside out as well as the outside in, and then try to understand how you might see it differently from looking at it from the boundaries. Another example is learning to debate both sides of an issue. Still another approach is to look at an issue first as simple, then as complicated, then as complex, and then as chaotic, each yielding a different potential decision set. A unique capability that develops as the self becomes proficient at shifting frames of reference is the ability to extend our visual and auditory sensing perception capabilities by analogy to other dimensions. For example, having the ability to "see" and "hear" some point in the future that is the result of a decision that is made today.

An excellent example of shifting frames of reference is the use of Dihedral Group Theory. Thought processes of entrepreneurs like Steve Jobs follow six distinct shifts in perspective which directly correspond to the six permutations of what is known in mathematics as a Dihedral (3) Group. Each of the six models changes the relationship of subject/verb/object, offering the opportunity to discover hidden connections and unique insights, giving rise to faster innovation and potentially more significant breakthroughs.[694] This meaning-making approach also helps individuals understand their personal focus, that is, where their awareness is centered, which is generally initially labeled as "subject".

Mathematician Tom McCabe's legendary work on algorithm complexity has led to an even more impactful mathematical breakthrough. He has discovered a connection between mathematical group theory and consciousness, directly connecting the mathematical group Dihedral order 6 with different perspectives of our thoughts.[695]

Symbolic Representation (perceiving and representing)

Representations in terms of words and visuals are the tools of trade for facilitating common understanding. The mind/brain does not store exact replicas of past events or memories. Rather, it stores invariant representations that color the meaning or essence of incoming information.[696] There is a hierarchy of information where hierarchy represents "an order of some complexity, in which the elements are distributed along the gradient of importance."[697] This hierarchy of information is analogous to the physical design of the neocortex, "a sheet of cells the size of a dinner napkin as thick as six business cards, where the connections between various regions give the whole thing a hierarchical structure."[698] There are six layers of hierarchical patterns in the architecture of the cortex. While only documented for the sense of vision, it appears that the patterns at the lowest level of the cortex are fast changing and spatially specific (highly situation dependent and context sensitive) while the patterns at the highest level are slow changing and spatially invariant.[699] For example, values, theories, beliefs and assumptions created (over and over again) through past learning processes represent a higher level of invariant form, one that does not easily change, compared to lower-level patterns.

Thus, once learned, the mind/brain can quickly associate with symbols, which can represent large amounts of context yet be immediately understood and interpreted. For example, a cross or menorah carries with it all the myths it represents. "It is an outward sign of an inward belief."[700]

Symbols are everywhere we look. Mathematics is built on hypotheses, that is, patterns, assumptions, and relationships. Letters represent sounds, notes represent tones, pictures represent thoughts and beliefs, shapes of signs on the highway represent the context of rules, and so on. We use symbols to organize our thoughts. For example, in human face-to-face interactions it has long been recognized that non-verbals and voicing (tone, emphasis) can play a larger role in communication than the words that are being exchanged. New patterns are emerging in social media that represent and convey these aspects of communication, helping provide the context and "feeling" for what is being said. In electronic communication, these symbols, or emogi, are small icons used to express a concept or emotion. For example, whether on Twitter or eMail, ":)" immediately conveys a smiley face, so much so that when these keystrokes are entered in MSWord followed by a space, they are immediately translated into ☺. As social media has matured, these symbols have become patterns of patterns, well understood by practicing social networkers and quickly conveying the message they are sending.

Patterns are symbols. (Pattern Thinking is provided as a tool in Section IV.) For example, over time patterns represent trends, cycles, spikes, curves, sinks, sources, and so on. Forecasters use scenario planning to set up patterns, create self-consistent patterns over time, and look at what happens. Scenario development can be used to create applicable knowledge by starting with the recent past and developing several possible scenarios for the future. (Scenario Building is also a tool in Section IV.) Here you may have to identify trends by averaging over time, considering the most desirable, acceptable, and least desirable possible outcomes. Knowledge can be developed from creating, studying and playing with the possible results of these scenarios. Other ways to think about forecasting is in terms of laying out a trail (a pattern) with milestones (symbols), and, of course, through dynamic modeling.

There is an important role that symmetry and parsimony play in patterns and in the physical world. Symmetry is the exact correspondence of form on opposite sides of a centerline or point. Parsimony is the principle of least action or energy and conservation. Nature is fond of doing things in the most economical and efficient way. Since symbols are short forms of larger patterns, they help facilitate thinking about symmetry, and can help us recognize simpler solutions to issues and situations.

A Working Knowledge Capacity Example: *Instinctual Harnessing*

To facilitate a deeper understanding of the nature of Knowledge Capacities, we focus on a single example, what can be described as Instinctual Harnessing (acting and being), as supported and described in the work of Arthur Shelley in *The Organizational Zoo: A Survival Guide to Work Place Behavior.*

Shelley begins his book with the appropriate dedication:

To all who have been preyed upon and survived: May your experiences continue to make you stronger, wiser and better at reading the behaviors of those above you in the food chain, and ... To those about to begin your career safari: Prepare well! Invest time with positive creatures and ensure conflicts happen in your territory on your terms.[701]

And so, the building of capacity begins, the capacity to observe the characteristics and behaviors of the creatures in your personal "organizational zoo" and to build self-awareness of your own characteristics and behaviors. Because it provides a removed perspective, it is possible to dissociate from personal feelings and more objectively (and metaphorically) view the organization as a collection of creatures interacting in, and with, their environment.

Shelley (2007, p. xiii) determined that perhaps human thinking, feeling, and acting had not evolved as far as we could and would like to, and that we could learn from how nature responds. As he describes:

There are many lessons that we could learn from nature, which could apply very well to the business world. The natural balance that exists in nature is something rarely achieved in human systems ... nature usually rebalances herself. It is only when humans interfere that nature loses control and falls out of balance. Could we learn from nature how to better manage our systems?[702]

From this starting point, the model expanded to (1) figure out who's who in the zoo, and (2) determine what to fight for and what to concede. Figuring out who *we* are in the zoo in a given situation provides us a sense of belonging, an identity in relationship to the others (in terms of attributes or characteristics) we see in the zoo. As Shelley points out, identities and classification schemes represent patterns we put people in to make our lives easier. The mind is continuously – mostly unconsciously – organizing and classifying people, and then using this schema for unconscious profile matching and passing judgment. And sometimes we are right and sometimes we are wrong. However, "having better defined character profiles and a wider set of profiles helps us to understand others more and interact better with them."[703]

Developing the capacity of Instinctual Harnessing goes beyond just knowing the capabilities, tendencies and behaviors of the characters in your zoo. It helps you understand moods, inconsistencies and vagaries, know their strengths and weakness, and know how to manage through these. It assists you in constructing strategies, relieving some of the stress by making this a game, and it assists in your personal development and the development of others.

In the traditional zoo, when in a survival mode, the characteristics that emerge in the zoo animals include aggression, leadership (lion style), hiding and/or camouflage, assertiveness, ubiquity, dependencies, endurance, and accountability. When your zoo is flourishing, techniques that are employed include leadership (eagle style), motivation, maturity, productivity, pro-activity, collaboration, networking, control, and awareness.

Shelley points out that there is a growing shift toward communities, which form a very different type of zoo. These tend to be more knowledge focused creatures who genuinely like helping others. As Shelley describes:

The community is more of a well-balanced environment, maybe more like an open plains Zoo, but with no boundaries at all. Creatures can come and graze as they desire and interact as they please. They can come as often as they like and leave whenever they want, most unlike the corporate Zoo. Community Zoos satisfy the mind and spirit ...[704].

Each zoo character – ordered from "a" to "z" – has a profile that includes characteristics, some behaviors relating to the character, the meaning of success to the character and a list of attributes often applied to the character and attributes not often applied to the character. There are many ways to use these profiles, including workshop games not requiring any special tools or preparation, enabling learning in a fun atmosphere, and include creature introduction, an attribute ice breaker, network diversity analysis, and business partner (or competitor) analysis. Metaphoric representation of behaviors provides a safe language for behavior conversations.

As the value of Instinctual Harnessing as a learning tool and management aide has become more widely recognized and used, Shelley has collected data and developed new approaches to use this Knowledge Capacity as an individual or as a group or organizational exercise. See www.organizationalzoo.com Built on this learning, we offer the tool Focused Trait Transference as an example of a Knowledge Capacity.

TOOL: FOCUSED TRAIT TRANSFERENCE

This short process provides a focal point for looking at specific animal traits that correlate to human traits, helping us to understand ourselves and others. Note that the human is a complex adaptive system with incredible diversity and individuation. In the list below we have identified and described seven diverse animals with the hopes that each individual will be able to identify with at least one attribute from each animal. Then, understanding the set as a whole and how they work together begins to honor the complexity of the human.

STEP 1: Make a copy of the list below of the seven different animals with short descriptions of traits that they represent. Read the descriptions for each animal. Because these are animals most likely familiar to you, perhaps you are aware of additional traits. Add these to the list.

STEP 2: Reflect carefully on the traits for each animal. *Ask*: Are these traits that I see in the people around me? Are any of these traits that I have or exhibit to others? Highlight the traits for each animal that you see in yourself.

STEP 3: Bring all the traits that you see in yourself together as a set. Identify the strength of each trait in terms of their value to you. *Ask*: Which ones are the strongest? How do these traits work together? How have these traits been valuable in the past?

How do these traits impact my interactions with others? How do these traits impact my work? How can I use these traits to my benefit and the benefit of others with whom I interact? *or* How can I change these traits to add more benefit to myself and others?

STEP 4: Consider the value of this exercise. *Ask*: What have I learned about myself and my interactions with others?

THE LIST*

(1) *Elephants.* Symbolically, elephants represent *strength and power*, especially power of the libido. Their strong sense of smell represents higher forms of discrimination leading to *wisdom*. Elephants also show *great affection and loyalty* to each other and their families. In their behaviors are the ideals of true societies.

(2) *Mountain gorillas.* Mountain gorillas, *strong and powerful*, are generally *gentle and shy*. They are *highly social* and live in relatively *stable, cohesive groups*, with long-term bonds developing between the males and females. The dominant males mitigates conflicts within the group and protects the group from external threats.

(3) *House cats.* The cat represents the attribute of *independence* and a wide variety of traits such as *curiosity, cleverness,* unpredictability, unsociability and

healing. Because they can see in the dark, they are often associated with mystery and magic. Shelley attributes the following to cats: individualist, agile, aloof, self-interested, vain, selfish, frustrating, and arrogant.

(4) *Songbirds.* This group of perching birds (*Passeriformes*) includes over 4,000 species of birds found around the world, all equipped with vocal organs that produce a diverse and elaborate bird song. Both physical and spiritual, sound is an expression of energy. For example, the canary reflects the *awakening* and stimulation of the throat and heart, which gives increased *ability to feel and to express feelings*. Since the power of voice, music and sound is within you, what you say and the way you say it will be keenly felt by others.

(5) *Horses.* Key concepts connected to the horse are travel, *freedom* and *power*. The horse's energy is expansive, historically serving people in agriculture, recreation, war and travel, enabling people to explore the world and discover freedom from historical constraints. They signify the *power* and *movement* contributed to the rise of civilization, and have been poetically connected with the wind and foam of the sea.

(6) *Dogs.* The two words that immediately come to mind for dogs are *faithfulness* and *protection*. Other terms associated with the dog include companionship, nurturing and caring and guardianship. Shelley says that dogs, a highly versatile and enthusiastic group of creatures, are loyal followers, not leaders, with the behavior highly dependent upon their master (leader) and their environment. He attributes the following to dogs: *loyal, trusting,* energetic, *enthusiastic,* boisterous, gullible, reliable, predictable, *happy, playful,* protective (when directed), and trustworthy (mainly).

(7) *Rabbits.* Connected to fertility and new life and imbued with *ambition, finesse and virtue,* the rabbit brings with it the *sensitive* and *artistic* powers of the moon. Moving in hops and leaps, it is fleet of foot and active both day and night. Although associated with fear by some, the rabbit has wonderful defenses, clever at doubling back and making quick and rapid turns.

*These characteristics and short descriptions are pulled from T. Andrew's *Animal Speak: The Spiritual & Magical Powers of Creatures Great & Small* and A. Shelley's *Organization Zoo: A Survival Guide to Workplace Behavior.*

Why Is *Instinctual Harnessing* Effective as a Knowledge Capacity?

Whether our beliefs lean toward creation or evolution – or both or neither – there is general recognition that humans and animals share many attributes. From the creation viewpoint, we can approach this relationship metaphorically. From the evolutionary viewpoint, Homo sapiens and Homo sapiens sapiens are classified as a branch of the Hominini, a taxonomical tribe belonging to the family of great apes.[705] Gifted with larger and more complex brains, this tribe is characterized by erect posture, bipedal locomotion and manual dexterity.[706]

Common attributes found in humans and animals include culture, emotions, language, humor, tool use, memory, self-awareness, intelligence, farming and building. For example, animals that pass the self-awareness test include great apes, some gibbons, elephants, magpies and some whales. As another example, Mulcahy (2012) says the greatest builders are Nigerian termites. They build

> ... *fantastically huge mounds with internal ventilation, heating, and cooling systems through specially designed tunnels so that the termites living inside enjoy a pleasant climate at all times. they even have self-contained nurseries, gardens, cellars, chimneys, expressways, and sanitation systems.*[707]

A common attribute in both animals and humans is the concept of instinct. What is instinct? Merriam-Webster sees instinct as a way of behaving, thinking or feeling that is not learned; a natural desire or tendency that makes you want to act in a particular way; something you know without learning it or thinking about it; a natural ability. Instinct is a complete pattern of behavior that is given to animals. Sheldrake's hypothesis of formative creation proposes that memory is inherent in nature,[708] suggesting that all natural things inherit a collective memory from previous populations of similar natural things. This would explain the passing down of instinct within an animal group from one generation to the next. Sheldrake describes this process as morphic resonance.

Identifying animal characteristics and behaviors that metaphorically parallel human characteristics and behaviors provides the opportunity to separate emotional baggage from past experiences. This past experience may have been with that individual or others perceived as similar with the focus on the good or bad characteristic, or good or bad behaviors, rather than a specific individual's actions. This separation, or looking from the outside in, provides the opportunity for mental engagement at least partially disconnected from specific past events and the emotions and feelings connected to those events.

Further, as a set and considering the diversity of attributes, there is the opportunity for learning through different frames of reference. While the attributes to each animal are rather succinct and somewhat related, the attributes of humans can be collectively pulled from *all of these animals* and combined to produce unique and individuated results. For example, diversity coupled with individuation provides tremendous flexibility, potentially resulting in the bisociation of often unassociated attributes and leading to expanded creativity. When directed outwards and through cooperation and collaboration with others, learning and creativity lead to expanded self-awareness and consciousness.

Chapter 17

Absorptive Capacity 3.0: Emerging from Organizational Learning and The Learning Organization

Chulatep Senivongse, Ph.D.

Institute for Knowledge and Innovation, Bangkok University

ABSTRACT

This study examines the interrelationship of Absorptive Capacity, Organizational Learning, and the Learning Organization. Absorptive capacity refers to an organization's ability to effectively acquire and utilize external knowledge. Organizational learning focuses on collective learning processes, while the Learning Organization fosters a culture of continuous learning at all levels. There is a triangular relationship between these concepts. Absorptive capacity serves as a vital component within the Learning Organization, facilitating knowledge acquisition and integration. Organizational learning enhances absorptive capacity through collective learning, and the Learning Organization provides an environment for its development. Understanding these connections is crucial for organizations aiming to improve learning capabilities, adapt to change, increase competitive advantage, and foster innovation. This understanding leads to the re-definition and reconceptualized of the theoretical construct of absorptive capacity.

Keywords: Absorptive Capacity; Organizational Learning; Learning Organization; Sing-Loop Learning; Double-Loop Learning; Reflexive Learning

INTRODUCTION

In today's rapidly changing and competitive business environment, organizations face the challenge of staying adaptive, innovative, and continuously learning. To meet this challenge, several interrelated concepts have emerged that shed light on how organizations acquire, assimilate, and utilize knowledge effectively. Among these concepts are absorptive capacity, organizational learning, and the Learning Organization.

Absorptive capacity refers to an organization's ability to identify, acquire, assimilate, and exploit external knowledge to improve its performance and foster innovation.[709] It encompasses the processes and capabilities that enable organizations to effectively access, understand, and integrate new knowledge into their existing knowledge base and practices. Absorptive capacity acts as a foundation for organizational learning[710] and plays a crucial role in enabling organizations to adapt to changes, leverage external knowledge sources, and enhance their competitive advantage.[711]

Organizational learning goes beyond individual learning, emphasizing the collective learning within an organization.[712] It encompasses the acquisition, interpretation, and integration of knowledge at both the individual and collective levels.[713] Organizational learning involves the continuous improvement of organizational processes, systems, and routines based on insights gained from individual and collective experiences.[714] It focuses on process, routines, past history, and guided behavior of individuals in the organization.[715]

The Learning Organization represents an organizational model characterized by a culture, systems, and practices that actively support and promote learning at all levels.[716] A Learning Organization emphasizes the importance of creating a shared vision, fostering a culture of inquiry and experimentation, and enabling continuous learning and adaptation. It involves building a learning infrastructure, encouraging collaboration, and promoting systems thinking to understand and navigate complex dynamics.[717]

These three concepts – absorptive capacity, organizational learning, and the Learning Organization – form a triangular relationship that mutually reinforces and supports each other. Absorptive capacity serves as a vital component within the Learning Organization, enabling the organization to effectively acquire and integrate external knowledge. At the same time, organizational learning provides the mechanisms and processes for individuals and groups to learn collectively, contributing to the development of absorptive capacity. The Learning Organization, with its emphasis on a culture of learning and continuous improvement, creates an environment that nurtures absorptive capacity and facilitates organizational learning.

Understanding and leveraging this triangular relationship can help organizations enhance their learning capabilities, adapt to change, and drive innovation in today's dynamic and competitive business landscape.

ABSORPTIVE CAPACITY IN THE ORGANIZATION

As introduced above, absorptive capacity refers to an organization's ability to identify, acquire, assimilate, transform, and utilize external knowledge or information to improve its performance.[718] This includes the organization's capability to acquire new external knowledge, understand its significance, and integrate it into existing knowledge and practices. The concept was introduced by Cohen and Levinthal to explain why some firms are more successful than others in terms of innovation and knowledge utilization.[719]

Absorptive capacity consists of four key dimensions:[720]

Acquisition – The organization's ability to access and obtain new knowledge from external sources, such as research institutions, customers, competitors, or partners;

Assimilation – The process of understanding and comprehending the acquired knowledge, connecting it to existing knowledge structures within the organization;

Transformation – The ability to modify and reconfigure existing knowledge and routines to accommodate the newly acquired knowledge; and

Exploitation – The organization's capability to apply the integrated knowledge to enhance its performance, develop new products or services, or gain a competitive advantage.

Conceptualizing absorptive capacity, Cohen and Levinthal grounded the concept of absorptive capacity in 1990, with the original version of absorptive capacity consisting of the three sub-processes of acquisition, assimilation, and exploitation. Absorptive capacity was thus positioned to be the firm's capability to absorb and utilize knowledge from external sources, with the assimilation process the spreading and learning of the new knowledge across the entire organization. New knowledge is then combined with existing knowledge, ready to be utilized to create competitive advantage. This is Absorptive Capacity 1.0.

The first reconceptualization occurred in 2002 from Zahra and George. Embracing the Resource Based View (RBV), they pointed to absorptive capacity as a firm's *dynamic capabilities*. In this version of absorptive capacity, two major reifications are imposed. First, another sub-process of transformation is included in the model. Absorption is not just considered the wide-spreading of new knowledge, but requires some reconfiguration of the firm's resources and facilities to accommodate the change. Second, acquisition and assimilation are grouped and called Potential Absorptive Capacity (PACAP); and transformation and exploitation are grouped and called Realization Absorptive Capacity (RACAP). This separates the ability to identify the values from the implementation ability. Organizing absorptive capacity in this manner treats organizational knowledge as a firm's resource. This can be considered Absorptive Capacity 2.0.

The second reconceptualization occurred in 2007. Todorova and Durisin argued that the grouping of absorptive capacity into PACAP and RACAP had introduced ambiguities, reducing flexibility in responding to the externality. Following Zahra and George's construct means knowledge absorption requires the reconfiguration of a firm's resources, and thus the grouping is not valid. Another limitation is that the knowledge flow from acquisition to exploitation does not occur in a sequential linear function, with some interchanges of the flow between the assimilation and transformation sub-processes. To correct these limitations, Todorova and Durisin suggested that the construct should contain four sub-processes of acquisition, assimilation, transformation, and exploitation, without the groupings, enabling the flow path to be acquisition-assimilation-exploitation, or acquisition-transformation-exploitation, or acquisition-assimilation-transformation-exploitation, or even acquisition-transformation-assimilation-exploitation. They also suggested that there is a pre-acquisition process, namely *value realization,* that occurs before the actual starting of acquisition and the feedback loop process to reflect the learning result. This can be called Absorptive Capacity 2.5.

By continuously improving its absorptive capacity, an organization can stay responsive to changes in its environment, adapt to new technologies, and foster innovation.[721] Figure 1 shows the evolution of Absorptive Capacity. We will build on this learning to enable the full potential of absorptive capacity in the current environment.

The original intention of the absorptive capacity concept is to look at the entirety of organizational learning across the vertical span. Learning starts at the micro (individual) level and escalates up the organizational tiers from micro to meso (team, unit, or department) and then to the macro (organization) level. PACAP occurs at the individual level as the individual activity, and PACAP is the capability at the organizational level.

However, absorptive capacity does occur at different levels of the firm.[722] The assimilation sub-process is where the combination of existing knowledge and the new external knowledge occur. In some organizations in a rapid moving industry where instant responding to the incurred external knowledge incremental is common, these events trigger a firm to absorb the new knowledge and instantly apply that knowledge in responding to customer demands.[723] In this scenario, where high agility is required, the absorptive capacity process is triggered at the individual level only.

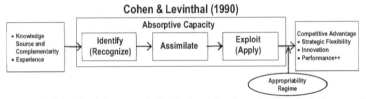

Absorptive Capacity is the ability of a firm to recognize the value of new information, assimilate it, and apply it to commercial ends.

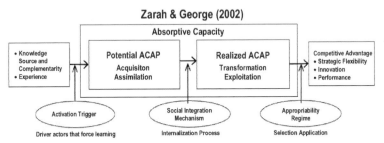

Absorptive Capacity (ACAP) is a dynamic capability pertaining to knowledge creation and utilization that enhances a firm's ability to gain and sustain a competitive advantage.

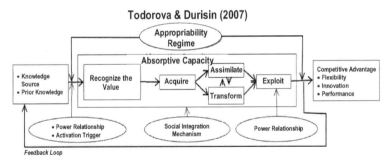

Absorptive Capacity is the ability of firms to identify, acquire, assimilate, transform and exploit new external knowledge to create competitive advantage.

Figure 17-1: The Evolution of Absorptive Capacity.

ORGANIZATIONAL LEARNING

> *Individual learning is a necessary but insufficient condition for organizational learning.* (Chris Argyris)

As previously introduced, organizational learning is the process of acquiring, creating, interpreting, and applying knowledge to improve performance and adapt to a changing environment.[724] It is more than just an individual's learning; rather a collective of individual learning in combination with organization memory[725] to create organizational knowledge.[726]

Single-loop and Double-loop Learning

Argyris[727] coined the terms single-loop and double-loop learning to distinguish the learning methods in the fields of organizational learning and knowledge management. Recognizing organizational learning as "a process of detecting and correcting errors",[728] when an error is detected from a common organization operational procedure, the error is examined, the cause and solution are defined to fix the problem, and the operational process and routines continue to proceed. This learning of identifying and fixing error is called single-loop learning.

In organizations that only adopt single-loop learning, organization members are commonly the professionals in the field doing what they routinely do. Excellence in operation is their ultimate target, and they are almost always successful, with rare "failing" experiences. Thus, learning from failure is not common for them. When the single-loop learning strategy goes wrong, these professionals tend to blame other causes or anyone else who may have caused it, but not themselves.[729] Since the ability to learn has been switched off, learning rarely occurs in this situation.

Double-loop learning is a form of learning that goes beyond merely adapting to existing situations. It involves challenging the cause of the problem, a reasoning of how things happened and whether there is a better way to do things.[730] In double-loop learning, the underlying assumptions, values, and mental models that shape an organization's actions and decisions are questioned.

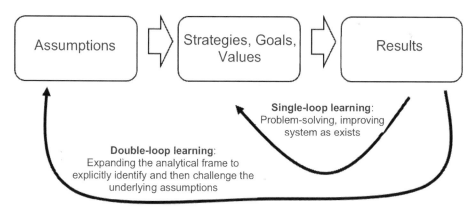

Figure 17-2: Single-loop and Double-loop Learning

In single-loop learning, the organization focuses on action of the routine incremental under the existing mental model frameworks, norms, cultures, policies, and rules.[731] Engaging in double-loop learning, organizations can uncover and address the root causes of problems, question the effectiveness of existing practices, and explore new possibilities and paradigms, open to changing the mental model frameworks, cultures, norms, routines, procedures, and rules.[732] Organization members combine the mastery of new technical methods to the existing knowledge. Success comes from the team of professionals working together, accommodated by the interpersonal relationships of the stakeholders. As can be seen, double-loop learning encourages a more critical and innovative approach to problem-solving and decision-making.

Triple-loop Learning

It has been questioned whether triple-loop learning exists as an extension to double-loop learning. Argyris mentioned in his work that triple-loop learning *should* exist from the action of feedbacking and as a change mechanism for the individual. Tosey et al. think that triple-loop learning must go deeper than that and involve the questioning and challenging of underlying assumptions, processes, and the systems that initiate those assumptions.[733] In this way, the idea of triple-loop learning is to examine the underlying values, norms, and beliefs that shape those mental models; reflecting on the very nature of the learning process itself and the systemic structures that influence it.

Triple-loop learning takes the inquiry one step further from double-loop learning and questions the processes, systems, and values that underpin the assumptions and mental models. It explores the broader context and asks why certain assumptions and values are in place and how they influence learning and decision-making processes within the organization. It aims to identify and transform the deep-seated structures that perpetuate certain patterns of thinking and behavior. Triple-loop learning is a process of learning that transforms the core beliefs and spin offs to something radically new.[734] This learning can lead to groundbreaking innovation that fosters a new set of mental models, culture, norms, strategies, processes, procedures, and policies.

In comparison, single-loop learning is a process to correct the problems to keep the current system going; second-loop learning is a more complex step to question and change the normal routine and re-introduce a new and improve process; and triple-loop learning involves some shift in regime.[735] While there is a thinking paradigm shift when moving from single-loop to double-loop learning, moving from double-loop to triple-loop learning requires a shift of business regime. A new way of doing business or pivoting the business objective is a common phenomenon at this level, with whole processes and facilities needing to be reconfigured and transformed. Figure 17-3 denotes the differences among these three.

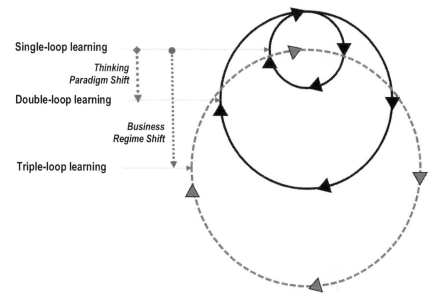

Single-loop learning

Thinking
Paradigm Shift

Double-loop learning

Business
Regime Shift

Triple-loop learning

Figure 17-3: Triple-loop Learning (adopted from Tosey et al.[736])

Conceptualizations of triple-loop learning have diverse origins. For example, Argyris defines triple-loop learning as the learning from reflection,[737] which McClory et al. define it as the learning through ethos.[738] Kwon and Nicolaides state that it is from the byproduct of regulations[739] (equal opportunity act., workplace diversity act., and equal learning and development act.) that govern the workplace environment. Bennet et al. see it as a complete change in terms of our system of beliefs and values.[740]

Bennet et al. build a learning model starting at "Learning 0", which represents the status quo, a behavioral response to a specific situation, and extending through Learning IV. Learning 1 (single-loop learning, first order change) is a stimulus-response conditioning including simple skills such as walking, eating, driving and working. These basic skills are pattern forming, becoming habits occurring through repetitiveness without conceptualizing the content, with no question of reality. Learning II (deuteron or double-loop learning or second order change), based on mental constructions that depend on a sense of reality, includes creation or change of context inclusive of new images or concepts, shifting the understanding of, and connections among, existing concepts such that meaning may be interpreted. Learning III (triple-loop learning or third order change) is considered thinking beyond current logic, changing our system of beliefs and values such that there are different sets of alternatives from which choices can be made. Expanding further, Bennet et al. identify Learning IV as revolutionary change, getting outside the system to look at the larger system of systems, awakening to something completely new, different, unique and transformative. This is at the quantum level, tapping into the larger mind of which the individual mind is a sub-system. An example of Learning IV is Buddha's use of intuitional thought to understand others, using this ability to think in greater and greater ways to help people cooperate, share together, and think at a higher level.[741]

Reflexive Learning

Expanding on triple-loop learning as learning from reflection, Cotter and Cullen say that reflection and reflexive learning – two concepts often confused but which they see as quite different – are widely used in relation to management learning.[742]

Reflection is a "process of making connections and constructing an understanding of situation by testing 'intuitive' understandings of experienced phenomena".[743] Reflexive means a complex thought process system comprised of experiences of contradictions, doubts, dilemmas, and possibilities.[744] It also involves the sociological aspect of critical reflection, knowledge, interaction, and engagement with others.[745] In other words, reflection is the mirroring of the image of things, events, or phenomena, while reflexive is the *thought process* of mirroring such phenomena.

One of the five modes in the experiential learning model is reflective observation.[746] After information is taken in through concrete experience, it is reflected upon to *make sense* of the experience. This is an integration process which may take some length of time to see the full meaning of the experience, a search for unity, an image that fits all of our experiences.[747]

Reflexive learning is a learning from embodied knowledge in the dialogical reflection.[748] Its principle is to help a learner navigate the world from learning through experience[749] and its purpose is to delineate and improve problem-solving.[750] Thus, reflexive learning engages with social skills, communication skills, and the knowledge construction process.

Parker et al. indicate that there are three types of reflexivity.[751] First is self-reflexivity, the learner capability to realize his own action of what goes wrong. This type of reflexivity relies on the cognitive power of the learner to recall the past action, analyze through the problem, understand the cause, and establish new knowledge from the existing knowledge stock to reach a counteraction to remedy the fault. Second is critical-reflexivity, which involves dialoguing. The learner needs social capability and communication skills with the understanding of an organization's policies on allowable and prohibitive corrective actions. Third is radical-reflexivity, which roams around the sociological relationship with embodied knowledge in the process to the realization of values and actions. Radical-reflexivity deals with the existing theory of practice which leads to the construct of a new theory to practice with radical change.

Radical-reflexivity enhances the ecocentric view of organizational operandi,[752] allowing recognition of business responsibilities and the impact of business practices. It also offers the potential for exploring underlying assumptions which may discourse some actions. This type of reflexivity requires mental model and system thinking capabilities. (See Chapter 19 on systems and complexity thinking.)

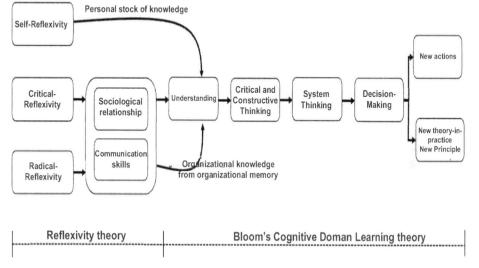

Figure 17-4: Reflexive-learning Process showing the learning process constructed in the cognitive space of a learner. (Adapted from Allen et al.[753] and Bloom[754] with the three types of reflexivity treated as the source of information.)

THE LEARNING ORGANIZATION

The organizations that will truly excel in the future will be the organizations that discover how to tap people's commitment and capacity to learn at all levels in an organization. (Peter Senge)

Senge coined the term "Learning Organization" and defines it as an "organization where people continually expand their capacity to create the results, they truly desire, where new expansive patterns of thinking are nurtured, where collective aspiration is set free, and where people are continually learning how to learn together."[755] With this definition, the learning organization is about the organization that facilitates and accommodates its members to seize the opportunity in learning to improve organizational performance.

According to Garvin et al., the learning organization needs to have these three building blocks: (1) A supportive Learning Environment – psychological safety, appreciation of differences, openness to new idea, blameless society, and allow time of reflection; (2) Concreate Learning Processes and Practices – experimenting, information collection, information analysis, education and training, and information transfer; and (3) Leadership Reinforced Learning – a dialoguing process between leader and subordinates with encouragement to learn.[756]

For an organization to become a learning organization, individual learning is deemed essential.[757] Senge indicates the five principles for every organization member as necessary competency traits: (1) Personal Mastery – each individual must learn to become expert in the field he is responsible for; (2) Mental Models – the thought process of understanding the ecological system of the organization; (3) Shared Vision – each individual must abide by the organizational goals, values, and mission that drive to long-term high performance; (4) Team Learning – individuals as members of working teams interconnect with conversational dialogue and learn to think together and discover the new insight from the interaction; and (5) Systems Thinking – individuals understand that every functioning part of the system influence one another, and the impact to one sub-system will influence other sub-systems in consequences.[758]

When an organization becomes a learning organization is when the following characteristic traits manifest. First, there is a learning culture.[759]. Second, there is supportive leadership and a culture that respects individuals, supporting their development and encouraging them to speak freely and honestly.[760] Third, individuals in the organization perform critical thinking, problem-solving, and feedbacking in the process of learning.[761] Fourth, there is openness to ideas from the outside.[762] Fifth, there is high autonomy and accountability with freedom to learn and make decisions versus a bureaucratic hierarchy. Sixth, there is performance improvement with consistency and sustainability.[763]

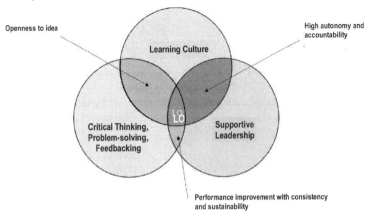

Figure 17-5: Characteristic Traits of the Learning Organization (LO).

TRIAGONAL RELATIONSHIPS OF ABSORPTIVE CAPACITY, ORGANIZATIONAL LEARNING, AND THE LEARNING ORGANIZATION

This section defines the relationship among, and clarifies the evolution of ,the organizational knowledge creation paradigm.

Organizational Learning and the Learning Organization

Sometimes Organizational Learning and the Learning Organization are related concepts and used interchangeably,[764] but they differ in their focus and scope. Organizational learning deals with the *process of learning*, involving the cognitive inception and processing of incoming information. The Learning Organization is focused on the *outcome of organizational learning*. It is the practical part of implementing processes of organizational learning to create the learning organization.

Organizational learning starts with individual learning, then escalates to the collective level, organizational level, and inter-organization level. Organizational learning is more involved with academic research,[765] while the learning organization focuses more effort on the behavior that drives the organization to cultivate values using knowledge in the domain of the practitioner.[766]

According to Odor, the processes of organizational learning are knowledge acquisition, knowledge sharing, knowledge interpretation, and knowledge utilization.[767] The Learning Organization is the organization with skills in crafting knowledge, acquiring and transforming knowledge, and modifying the behaviors of organizational members to drive organizational performance. Figure 17-6 clarifies the relationship between the organizational learning and the Learning Organization.

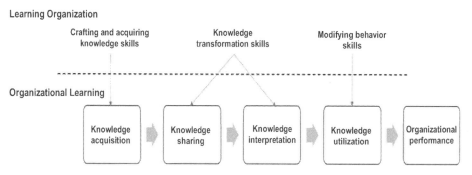

Figure 17-6: Relationship of Organizational Learning and Learning Organization (Adapted from Odor.[768])

Absorptive Capacity and Organizational Learning

Absorptive Capacity and organizational learning are both learning processes in the organization, with both concepts tightly referred to the same perspective of the learning process. The delineation of the relationship between the two is rarely articulated.[769]

There are a few major differences. The first is the unit level of study. Organizational learning is involved with learning at all levels from individual to collective (groups, teams, communities) to organization-wide,[770] while absorptive capacity is specifically focused at the organizational level of learning.[771] According to Nonaka and Takeuchi,[772] the creation of organizational knowledge starts from individual learning assisted with the sociological process among organizational members and then spurred up to become organizational knowledge, sharing space and support from management.[773] However, the studies from Cohen and Levinthal;[774] Lewin et al.;[775] and Zahra and George[776] confirm that absorptive capacity at the individual level does exist but only to support the three processes of identification, acquisition, and assimilation.[777] The study from Senivongse et al. expands this to say that the exploitation process is also accommodated at the individual level.[778] Thus, from these findings, absorptive capacity has the recursive property[779] of generating at the individual level and rising to the organizational level.

The second difference lies in the context of learning. Learning occurring in an organization is abided in the organizational context.[780] The articulation of knowledge from individual to the organizational level is differentiated by the difficulties of knowledge transfer and the absorption mechanism in each organization. This organization capability that determines the efficacy of knowledge absorption is governed by the individual's behavioral factors, such as the five principles of Senge. Sun and Scott demonstrate that to escalate the knowledge from the individual up to the organization level, there are some other factors that accommodate the transformation, including the intrapersonal nature of individuals and interpersonal relationships among peers, the structure and culture, and the social dimension.[781] While absorptive capacity only mentions the necessity of having socialization,[782] these other factors must be incorporated into the process of absorptive capacity development.

The third difference is the involvement of a mental framework. Absorptive capacity ignores the sociological aspects such as intuition, interpretation, institution, and integration that are required for knowledge creation. These aspects result in the altering of individual behavior and are inscribed into organization systems, processes, and practices, which are the many types of organizational memory.[783]

The fourth difference is the use of diverse terminologies to explain the same things.[784] To compare and conclude that organizational learning, the learning organization, and absorptive capacity all lead to the same principle and deliver the same objective, all these terminologies must then be clarified.

The fifth difference is the process path of learning. Organizational learning follows three paths of triple-loop learning, with each loop identifying the different types of learning phenomena. In contrast, absorptive capacity only learns through the process of assimilation and transformation. To compare the learning model, absorptive capacity has to clarify and incorporate the learning process to match the three learning instances.

Figure 17-7 denotes how absorptive capacity and learning organization concepts are grounded. Absorptive capacity is originally intended to be the vertical learning process, while organizational learning is intended for the learning in a horizontal manner.

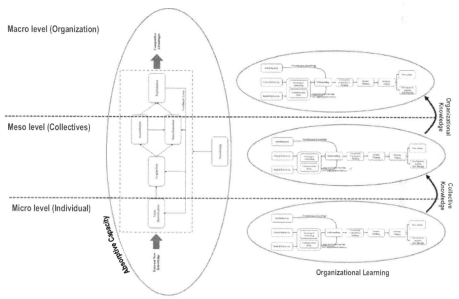

Figure 17-7: Original Placeholder in the Organization of Absorptive Capacity and Learning Organization

ABSORPTIVE CAPACITY RE-CONCEPTUALIZED

To integrate all the organizational learning theories, absorptive capacity needs to be reified. First is to bring triple-loop learning into the absorptive capacity construct. From both the Zahra and George and the Todorova and Durisin constructs, there has been a falsely defined sub-process of transformation. In their term, transformation represents the process for an organization to "understand the situations and ideas, which are perceived as incompatible with the current cognitive frames of reference through a process of bisociation."[785]

This definition fits second-loop learning where there is a paradigm shift challenging the way to operate. This sub-process should be re-named to Re-configuration.

Apart from renaming a sub-process, another sub-process should be added. This sub-process is the actual process of transformation. Transformation is the process for an organization to impose changes in the key business structures, establish new management practices, and govern the transfers through the change complexity.[786]. This sub-process follows the third-loop learning path as transformation requires a shift in the managerial regime of the company.

The third component is the revision of supporting elements. The Todorova and Durisin's model indicates the three elements of appropriability – a combination of means to protect knowledge and the return of investments made on innovation.[787] This is the ability to foresee the values the new knowledge brings to the organization to improve performance; social integration – the ability of the organization members to enable the widespread adoption of knowledge through process of socialization; and power relations – the ability to influence the valuing and exploitation of new knowledge.[788] In addition to these three factors, additional characteristic traits of the Learning Organization are to be integrated into the model, which includes mental models, personal mastery, shared vision, team learning, and systems thinking.

The fourth component is the revisit of the feedback loop. The feedback loop, by definition, is the only activity to share information of what happen when executing absorptive capacity. This loop is very important as a learning source from the internal organization. The learning from historical phenomena fits with reflexive learning. By re-naming the feedback loop to reflexive learning, this also requires a change of absorptive capacity definition.

Figure 17-8 reflects the new theoretical construct of absorptive capacity. With the new construct, absorptive capacity can be re-defined as follows: "The firm's ability to realize the values, acquire, combine, re-configure, transform, exploit, and re-learn through reflexive-learning the implementation of new knowledge to improve the firm performance and increase the competitive advantage."

Applying the Model

Value Realization begins with value identification, triggering and recognizing the potential of new knowledge to business, analyzing it, and making the decision to absorb it. Triggering generally comes from customers, which can be in the form of expressed needs and wants, or specific to a new capability or product out on the market. Keeping the purpose of the organization in mind, the value of potential new knowledge can be assessed through an information analysis which identifies both the strategic opportunity and constraints associated with the new knowledge. Source trustworthiness is vital for reliability and value realization.[789] It is critical for the decision-maker to have the technical knowledge as well as the context of the organization, that is, a depth understanding of the organization's values, vision and strategies, and need for change.[790] This process requires a capability to explore for information, understand the context, judgment, and decision-making.

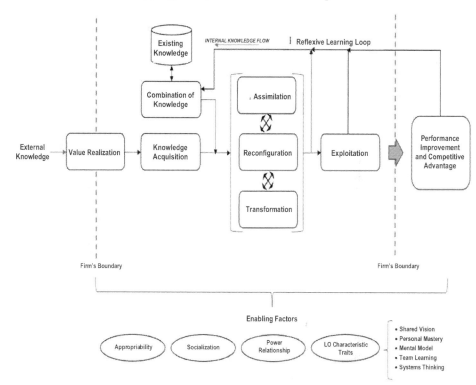

Figure 17-8: Absorptive Capacity 3.0 Reconceptualization

Knowledge Acquisition, the process to incept external knowledge is focused on intensity (seeing the necessity of having new knowledge), speed (how fast adoption can occur), and direction (the path to accommodate implementation of external knowledge into the firm).[791] As the knowledge crosses the physical boundary of the company, the process of assimilation involves a multidisciplinary inception team,[792] that is, working with members from multiple teams. The inception team organizes (who is to perform what) and schedules the sharing, sets up the lab and prototype as necessary, and ensures questions have answers before going out and seeing customers. This process requires interpersonal management skills, functional knowledge of related fields, social capability, individual self-organization, project management skills, leadership skills, and communication skills.[793]

Prior knowledge plays an important role in *Knowledge Assimilation*, easing the absorption, integration, patterning, and conceptualizing necessary to integrate new knowledge into the existing organizational knowledge structure.[794] In an open-space office where conversations are easily heard, and in a technology-savvy organization who engages "social media" and free and open virtual interaction, assimilation can happen rapidly. The process of assimilation requires individual analysis, synthesis, interpretation, comprehension, learning, and understanding ability.[795] *Reconfiguration* was introduced above. As single-loop learning migrates into double-loop learning, updating occurs and the sharing of knowledge and practices spans both internal and external persons based on the coverage of the business network. Note that throughout the process there is reflecting, updating, and replicating of knowledge and practices. Creativity and innovation lead *Transformation*, the process of knowledge creation,[796] which involves problem-solving and combined knowledge internalization. A key enabler is effort intensity, which enforces entrepreneurial action and the recognition of business opportunity.[797]

Exploitation is where combined knowledge is applied[798] and operationalized,[799] with the outcome a new product or service[800] aimed at competitive advantage. Some companies are involved in the transferring of knowledge to customers, business partners, suppliers, or educating the whole market. Market knowledge is a key success enabler, with the decision-maker understanding customer dynamics and the firm's strategy. Necessary skills include analytic capability, market testing, and conceptual thinking.[801]

The enabling factor of *Socialization* is the key component that enhances collaboration of both external and internal parties,[802] strengthening the relationships among internal knowledge transferers and recipients as well as the external knowledge sender and internal knowledge receivers. It eases coordination for resource configuration and operational process integration, and improves the relationship between the organization and its customers, which sets the foundation for future technical support.

Recognize that feedback – the reflexive learning loop – plays a crucial role in enabling individuals to learn and adjust, ensuring they are on the right path and enhancing the firm's agility and adaptability in an uncertain product development environment.

Absorptive Capacity 3.0 and the Firm's Strategy

Strategy refers to the set of activities a firm undertakes to establish a distinct competitive position and deliver better, more cost-effective, or faster offerings to customers compared to its competitors.[803] This entails creating new strategic positions by aligning with customer needs, improving accessibility for customers, and offering a diverse range of products or services. The definition further narrows down strategic options into three categories:[804]

- Pioneering something new,
- Leveraging existing strengths and capabilities, and
- Capitalizing on emerging opportunities opportunistically.

These perspectives serve as a foundation for formulating a firm's strategy in the context of market competition. By adopting a 2×2 matrix to map out the future direction of the firm, we can gain a clearer understanding of the specific type of strategy the firm should adopt.

If firms are content with their current market position and performance, the most suitable strategy for them is Operational Excellence (OE). This strategy revolves around maintaining and enhancing the firm's existing capabilities, where they outperform their competitors and enjoy a certain degree of monopoly in the market. Firms pursuing the OE strategy strive for best practices in standard operating procedures, employing activities such as Total Quality Management, benchmarking, time-based competition, outsourcing, reengineering, and change management.

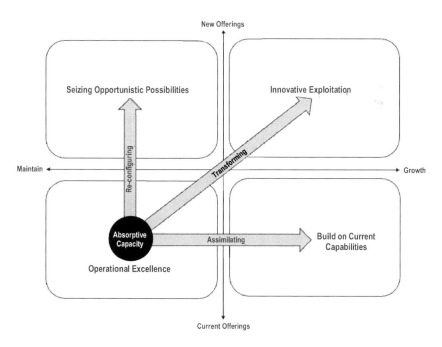

Figure 17-9: 2×2 Strategy Matrix based on Market Competition Position

On the other hand, if a firm aims to improve its current market position, it must adopt the Build on Current Capabilities strategy. This involves offering better value in terms of price and performance to customers, thereby attracting and retaining them in preference to competitors. Effective marketing activities can also play a role in raising awareness and capturing a larger market share. This requires the assimilation process of absorptive capacity to expand and enhance the current capability in offering the product or service that can better serve the needs of the existing customers.

For firms looking to seize opportunistic possibilities, the strategy involves sensing emerging opportunities and adjusting current capabilities to capitalize on them. This requires continuous improvement of products and processes to create new and improved customer experiences, leading to an expansion of the existing market. This approach, in turn, requires the process of re-configuring the absorptive capacity by modifying the current process, policy, procedure, and capture of new product or service offerings to the market.

The last strategy, Innovative Exploitation, centers on exploring new products and services. Recognizing the inevitability of innovation, firms pursuing this strategy focus on introducing novel solutions to address new problems and needs in the market. Cultivating an innovative culture and fostering personnel capabilities are critical elements in this category. This involves new thinking and a new business model in marketing the new product or service. This business regime shift is the transformation process of absorptive capacity.

ABSORPTIVE CAPACITY 3.0: ENHANCING ORGANIZATIONAL RESILIENCE (A Case Study)

Muangthong Telecom Co., Ltd. is a telecom network laying and construction company operating in Thailand. This case explores how Muangthong Telecom utilized Absorptive Capacity 3.0 to adapt and thrive in a dynamic and evolving industry. The company has undergone three distinct business pivots. Each pivot was driven by external and internal triggers, necessitating changes in the organization's strategies, capabilities, and workforce. This study analyzes the three assimilation loops, which encompassed changes in project execution methods, technological shifts, and strategic transformations, underscoring the importance of absorptive capacity in fostering organizational survivability and competitive capability.

Company Background

Thongchart Karbkaew established Muangthong Telecom in 2010 as a telecommunication cable-laying company. As a former corporate network engineer for Ericson, Karbkaew recognized an opportunity in telecom network construction with the growing demand for internet services. The company was originally a sub-contractor to primarily serve True Corporation, a prominent mobile telephone network and internet service provider in Thailand.

The first era of network cabling was based on the hybrid fiber-coaxial cable, which is known as DOCSIS (a.k.a. FTTC: fiber-to-the-curve). DOCSIS is an economical solution to the house-hold, with fiber cable at the core and the coaxial cable to the residence. DOCSIS is a good solution for rapid expansion due to its ease of installation and maintenance. However, some drawbacks with DOCSIS were recognized as customers started to complain about the quality and stability of their Internet connection.

The First Loop – Assimilation: Task-Based Completion Method

The surge in demand for network expansion created installation capacity limitations. Muangthong Telecom had 30 installation teams simultaneously handling 30 installations. To overcome this challenge, and inspired by the production line model, Karbkaew adopted a task-based completion approach. He combined all the teams, then divided them into separate functional teams according to project tasks with each functional team handling each task. By coordinating theses functional teams efficiently, the company doubled productivity, accelerating project completion.

In the assimilation loop, a key observation is that the only change was in operating procedure and technique while exploiting the same set of knowledge and skills.

The Second Loop - Re-configuration: Technological Shift to FTTH

A few years later, True Corporation decided to transition from a hybrid fiber-coaxial network (DOCSIS) to an all-fiber-to-the-home (FTTH) technology due to continuing customer complaints about service instability. Muangthong Telecom had to adapt to the technological shift, requiring investments in new tools and skills. The company facilitated knowledge transfer through on-the-job training, ensuring a seamless transition to the new technology. To finance the project, a unique financial model based on factoring was adopted, allowing Muangthong Telecom to secure the necessary funds for equipment purchases.

The major characteristics of the re-configuring loop was extensive change in the set of knowledge and skills. This involves changes in many major parts of the organization, including re-structuring and additional investment in uplifting the competency of the company.

The Third Loop - Transformation: Embracing the Solar Photovoltaic Market

As the telecom cabling market approached maturity, Muangthong Telecom faced declining project opportunities. To respond to the changing business landscape, Karbkaew seized the emerging market of Solar Photovoltaic. This transformation necessitated a fundamental shift in the organization's skills, knowledge base, and partnerships.

External Training in electrical system wiring and equipment installation was provided, and certifications for skilled electricians were obtained. The company diversified its workforce, recruited new personnel, and established relationships with new suppliers to venture into the individual household market. This represents a change in the model of doing business, moving from being a sub-contractor to a big organization, into an offensive, self-driven customer reach.

CONCLUSION

The triagonal relationships among absorptive capacity, organizational learning, and the Learning Organization highlight the interconnectedness and mutual reinforcement of these concepts in the context of organizational learning and knowledge management. This study has revealed that absorptive capacity plays a crucial role as a component within the Learning Organization, enabling organizations to effectively acquire, assimilate, and exploit external knowledge. Organizational learning, in turn, contributes to the development of absorptive capacity by fostering collective learning and knowledge integration. The Learning Organization, with its focus on creating a culture and infrastructure that supports learning, provides an environment where absorptive capacity and organizational learning can thrive.

By understanding and leveraging these triagonal relationships, organizations can enhance their learning capabilities, adapt to change, and drive innovation. By strengthening absorptive capacity, organizations can effectively acquire and utilize external knowledge to fuel their learning processes. Organizational learning mechanisms, such as shared learning and feedback loops, contribute to the development and enhancement of absorptive capacity. The Learning Organization, with its emphasis on a culture of learning, provides the necessary framework and systems to facilitate organizational learning and the integration of absorptive capacity.

The exploration of interconnectedness of the three concepts reflects the need to reconceptualize the construct of absorptive capacity. The reconceptualization integrates the three concepts and accommodates all the enabling elements that foster the development of the organization's absorptive capacity. The new construct better serves the organizational learning ability that leads to the improvement of performance, enhances the competitive advantage, and fosters innovation. The new construct includes the capability to pivot into a new business regime.

In conclusion, organizations that prioritize and cultivate absorptive capacity within the context of organizational learning and the Learning Organization are well-positioned to thrive in dynamic and competitive environments. By actively acquiring and integrating external knowledge, fostering collective learning, and promoting a culture of continuous improvement, organizations can enhance their agility, adaptability, and innovation capabilities. The interplay of absorptive capacity, organizational learning, and the Learning Organization serves as a powerful framework for organizations seeking to navigate the complexities of the modern business landscape and achieve sustainable success.

Chapter 18

Knowledge Management and Knowledge-Based Development for Human Flourishing[805]

Francisco Javier Carrillo[806]

President of the World Capital Institute and Emeritus Professor of Knowledge Based Development at Tecnológico de Monterrey, Mexico

ABSTRACT

This chapter attempts to revitalize the original Knowledge Management (KM) value drive for organizations and project it onto the social significance of Knowledge-Based Development (KBD). While there has been an impressive development and growth in technical capabilities to handle data and information at both the organizational and social levels, the sense of purpose conveyed by clear strategic imperatives is often missing. This situation characterizes the zeitgeist in many organizations and societies today. Enter the Climate Emergency and the urgency for being able to reset priorities and enable actionable knowledge becomes prominent.

The chapter moves from the more abstract arena of a conceptual framework into the more pragmatic one of applied processes and international projects examples. A value-centered epistemology provides the basis for an operational KM model, while a Capital System method allows organizations and communities, both large and small, to set up shared preferences and focus action. Furthermore, in the aftermath of the Post-Development era, KBD offers a workable integration of Beyond-Growth Economics and the Environmental Justice dimension of Social Ecological Economics. Such integration serves as the basis for an urgent reinvention of Knowledge for the Anthropocene, the current geological age in which man is the dominant influence on the environment.

Keywords: knowledge event, knowledge object, knowledge agent, knowledge context, alignment, capital systems, knowledge management, knowledge-based development, knowledge-based value creation, knowledge markets, KM generations, capital cities, Anthropocene

KNOWLEDGE-BASED VALUE CREATION

In understanding the rise of knowledge societies, economic theory confronts two major challenges. The first is a characterization of *knowledge-based*, while the second is an understanding of the underlying value dynamics.[807] This section attempts to frame these two issues. Notwithstanding the abundant literature, the closest consensus regarding the knowledge economy is the recognition of an unprecedented increase in the importance of intangible capital in post-industrial societies and the positive effects it has on productivity.[808] It appears that we have failed to develop a formalized and well-supported theory.

In order to put some key developments in perspective, it is useful to examine three successive approaches or *generations* that have been used since 2000 in understanding what knowledge-based means.[809] Each of these three generations is distinguished by the progressive addition of three necessary and sufficient conditions for the emergence of knowledge:

- *First generation*: an object-centered infrastructure for increasing the stock of knowledge, aiming at higher returns through digital-intensive production.

- *Second generation*: a platform to facilitate knowledge flows based on object-plus-agents, aimed at developing human capital and facilitating knowledge transfer.

- *Third generation*: a strategy for balancing traditional and intangible capital aiming at total system well-being by aligning object-plus-agent-plus-context.

The first view, or the instrumental view, remains the dominant logic and is applied mainly to development planning.[810] In contrast, the incremental approach has gained popularity among government agencies, social policies, and place-based development since it establishes a connection between economic growth and human capital.[811] As for the third view, the disruptive view, it is still marginal since it involves a qualitative change in economic culture that might be prompted by the emergency conditions resulting from the Anthropocene.[812]

To transition from the first or second view to the third, it is necessary to modify the boundaries, elements, and rules of economics as a formal system. In other words, it implies that there are qualitatively different possible outcomes (for example, the knowledge items are non-rival and non-excludable, meaning that accessing an item and consuming it by one agent does not prevent other agents from simultaneously accessing and consuming the item), which is illustrated by the acknowledgement of open access and public knowledge goods. To recognize the sociobehavioral economic base, one must shift from a functional level of physical reality to a symbolic level of reality. It is important to note that value production goes beyond the physical transformation of matter and energy and includes both semiotic and axiological components as well. The relationship between knowledge and value needs to be re-evaluated to accommodate this transition (Table 1).

Rather than simply providing us with sensory or instrumental records, material objects form the basis of human experience through their representations and interpretations. In order to maintain their interdeterminacy and functional continuity, the underlying phenomenology shifts the emphasis from things-in-themselves[813] to second order learned objects. As a result of this behavioral transposition, an association of values is formed that provides the basis for economics, and an association of meanings is formed that provides the basis for semiotics:[814] sensemaking generates value. This shift in explanation appears to be elusive, as can be seen from the gradual transition between the second and third generations. This chapter will explore several perspectives on the third-generation explanation of knowledge-based.

To begin with, some initial considerations could assist in framing this issue. As long as there are biophysical limits to industrial production, the knowledge economy and society are concerned with the viability of human civilization.[815] It entails the ability to achieve a balance between handling of energy and matter, and the sustainability of life.[816] Moreover, it is consistent with the axiological tenets of "social ecological economics".[817] This implies that democratic agreements can be reached regarding a manageable set of collective preferences.[818] Hence, the term "knowledge-based" refers to a broader axiological order that emphasizes intangible values in addition to material and financial ones.

Based on the third or disruptive view of knowledge, the context dimension offers economic relevance (value) and cultural significance (meaning). Throughout this chapter, the concept of knowledge is explored as a connection between an object, an agent, and a context, allowing for justified beliefs to be formed and effective action to be taken. Based on concepts such as *phronesis*, *Lebenswelt* (lifeworld) and *savoir*, such an exploration has led to the more recent conceptions of *vernacular knowledge* and *actionable knowledge*. Knowledge-based capital incorporates value dimensions that have been excluded from traditional economics and institutions.[819] The degree of human consciousness and evolution determines when civilization and knowledge are mutually redefined.[820]

A qualitative gap between the natural principles describing the behavior of objects, the natural principles describing the behavior of ideas and emotions, and the subsequent impact that such difference makes on social and economic possibilities is assumed by the dominant logic. In the same way that human activity concerning matter and energy is bounded by time and space constraints, so are the social norms that govern their production, distribution, and ownership, which result in property law.

Material value is determined by the dynamics of the physical world, including the inevitability of entropy.[821] Economic theories, accounting systems, management practices, and policy decisions have been greatly influenced by physical realities until recently, although materiality has been fully recognized. Moreover, knowledge-based realities have existed since the dawn of human history – that is, since the origin of distinctively "human" psychological phenomena.[822]

Frederick Soddy, the 1921 Nobel laureate in chemistry, provided an insightful analysis of the interaction among knowledge-based and material-based economic production. Thus, he presented an integrated naturalistic view, which could act as a lemma for social ecological economics: "The principles and ethics of human law and convention must not run counter to those of thermodynamics."[823] The interplay between knowledge-based and material-based value creation may be best explained by a three-phase interdependence between physical capital, monetary capital, and intellectual capital (IC), to be synthesized by a holistic theory of value.[824]

Despite the widespread presence of knowledge-based realities, they have not been accorded an economic status equivalent to that of material and monetary units, remaining anathematized as "intangible". This is reflected in most methods used to measure intellectual or knowledge-based capital. Hubbard shows how measuring the value of knowledge is at the core of the current trap regarding the nature and significance of measures in our lives in his defacing of "the illusion of intangibles".[825] Several studies have explored how much the ability to comprehend and capture collective value will constrain the development of knowledge societies.[826]

In many ways, money is as evanescent as software or technical procedures, except that it has always been at the center of economic activity and the development of Western culture.[827] As Michael Reiss summarizes the enshrinement of the golden calf, "It is not much of an exaggeration to say that the history of economics has been a history of mankind's attempts, and mostly dismal failures, at establishing and sustaining a stable monetary system."[828] It is still the economic base of physical assets and monetary assets which dominates the world of economics and management. Physical and monetary dimensions remain the limits to social language and, according to Wittgenstein's criterion, the limits to the world – of economics, accountancy, and administration.[829]

For alternative paradigms to flourish, the limitations of current paradigms must continue to be challenged by realizations outside and contradictions within. Knowledge-based economics, management, and politics are becoming increasingly possible as behavioral and knowledge-based realities become more widely recognized and accepted.

In contrast to physical production, human creation is based on ideas and emotions that possess a dynamic of their own. The knowledge economy, however, lacks a formal theory. The knowledge-based theory of the firm, which is applied at an organizational level, and the knowledge-based theory of the society, which is applied at a societal level, are far from being formalized.

Several studies have contributed to the substantiation of the need, identification of features, and formulation of specifications at both an organizational level[830] and societal level;[831] however, a formal theory of knowledge-based value production has not yet been developed. When counterexamples contradict prevailing explanations, boundary cases escape dominant theories, or alternative conjectures are recognized, Kuhnian paradigm shifts occur. Even though there is no formal theory of knowledge-based value production, several distinctive characteristics have been identified. Table 18-1 summarizes some of the most prominent attributes of knowledge-based value creation.

Table 18-1. Attributes of knowledge-based value creation.

Non-rivalry	Possession and use of a knowledge item by an agent does not consume it and therefore does not prevent possession and use of the same item by another agent
Non-excludability	Access to a knowledge item by an agent does not prevent access by another agent
Non-scarcity	A knowledge item can be replicated indefinitely at no extra cost
Non-decrementality	The rent value of successive knowledge units x_i x_{ii}, ..., x_n, may increase, rather than diminish as a function of iterations of the production cycle
Capital / labor convertibility	Labor and capital can be partially and mutually convertible
Ubiquity	A knowledge item can be simultaneously available to anyone, anywhere
Time and context dependency	A knowledge item can decrease in value as a function of time and sometimes may become obsolete soon after it is being released
Connectivity	The sum value of a network increases as the square of the number of members
Intangibility	The exchange value of a knowledge-intensive entity can (largely) surpass that of its book value
Externalities	Unintended consequences, positive or negative, can (largely) surpass the value of producing a knowledge item

AN ECONOMY OF WHAT MATTERS

Human social life can have a different economic dimension from what we experience today. This has been, can be, and must be the case. Throughout human history, it has been different for most human civilizations, where diverse economic cultures[832] have been documented by economic anthropology.[833] Since it has been different in the past, it may be different in the future. It will be different because the Holocene is over and as we enter the Anthropocene, the *Goldilocks economy*[834] in an extended sense of prevailing life-sustaining conditions is bound to be severely disrupted. The terms of relationship with the planet are bound to change.

Excruciating conditions caused by global heating and extreme weather events, disruption of food production, breakdown of global supply chains, states failures, competition for fresh water and other critical goods, multiplication of climate refugees, etc., will only get worse as the state of the biosphere continues to deteriorate. Only by devising and implementing a basic global economic culture that enables a viable transition might humankind have a chance of overcoming this critical hour. A test of this magnitude will undoubtedly force all living beings to contemplate what is truly important in life. If there will be an economics for humanity and the planet, it shall be an *economy of what matters*.

Ernst F. Schumacher, argued in his influential 1973 book *Small Is Beautiful: A Study of Economics as if People Mattered* that a human-scale economy should be pursued, and argued against solely using new technologies for the purpose of resolving mounting world problems, such as the depletion of natural resources and pollution of the environment. He included within that book a famous chapter entitled "Buddhist Economics" in which he characterized the concept as follows: "But Buddhism is 'The Middle Way' and therefore in no way antagonistic to physical well-being. It is not wealth that stands in the way of liberation but the attachment to wealth; not the enjoyment of pleasurable things but the craving for them. The keynote of Buddhist economics, therefore, is simplicity and non-violence. From an economist's point of view, the marvel of the Buddhist way of life is the utter rationality of its pattern – amazingly small means leading to extraordinarily satisfactory results. For the modern economist this is very difficult to understand."[835]

According to André Gorz, the modern economic mindset is a manifestation of ontological distraction comparable to the current wizards of artificial intelligence: "But they have never asked themselves the central question about the ability to define the problems that were to be solved; to distinguish what is important from what is not, what has meaning from what has not; to choose, define and pursue a goal, to modify it in the light of unforeseen events; and, more fundamentally, the question of the reasons and criteria on the basis of which the goals, problems and solutions are chosen."[836]

Dolphijn invites us to revisit subjectivity and materiality, "Starting from 'that which matters' (in the double sense of the word), New Materialism frees itself from the ruins of modernity and, with the arts, can show us the world we have been blind to for so long. The micropolitics of that which matters have a lot to say to us, in times where we humans are more and more confronted with responsibilities for which we need to think beyond the human."[837] In broadening the analysis to cultural subjectivity (i.e., humanity as historic agent of anthropogenic climate change), Smil makes a clear indictment of our current materiality:

> *At the most fundamental level, the question is about the very nature of modern economies. All but a tiny minority of economists (those of ecological persuasion) see the constant expansion of output as the fundamental goal. And not just any expansion: economies should preferably grow at annual rates in excess of 2%, better 3%. This is the only model, the only paradigm, and the only precept, as the economists in command of modern societies cannot envisage a system that would deliberately grow at a minimum rate, even less so one that would experience zero growth, and the idea of a carefully managed decline appears to them to be outright unimaginable. The pursuit of endless growth, is, obviously, an unsustainable strategy.*[838]

Thus, we come full circle to the beginning: "We need a new theory of value if we are to face an even bigger threat" suggests Ian Gough's opening statement to the essential question of this chapter: "In times of climate breakdown, how do we value what matters?"[839] Against the backdrop of social and economic disruption, the COVID-19 pandemic "has begun to question the nature of economic value. We can discuss again 'valuing what matters'. Yet a much, much greater crisis is now walking towards us – that of climate and ecological breakdown. What are the lessons we can learn from the above? … And one aspect of the economy thrown into revolutionary relief is the nature of economic value – what activities have value, are essential or critical to survival, prosperity and justice in some way, and what are wasteful or destructive?"[840]

Thus, it is evident that a completely different mode of thinking and acting is required in the economic sphere of culture – namely, a cultural paradigm of post-Holocene climate crisis management of priorities. Whether or not professional economists are willing to participate in this endeavor is not the crucial issue. The hope is that they will do so; however, it would not matter much if they do not since they have not done so thus far. Moreover, this is not even a matter of economic theory, institutions, or practices in the current state. Whatever it may be called, whether it is considered "economic" in any sense is irrelevant. Ultimately, what matters is finding an alternative way of thinking and doing that contributes towards coordinating the implementation and pursuit of priorities within the global context of the Anthropocene. We can come up with an alternative that stops pretending that we are progressing while it drives us closer and closer to self-annihilation: economics as if what matters mattered, redefining economics in terms of Polanyi's substantive concept: economics is the way society meets the needs of its members.

Several authors[841] have documented techniques that enable organizations. "finding ways to make the invisible value of things which are essential to quality of life visible and measurable, in short – valuing what matters."[842] It is also suggested that deliberative multiple criteria analyses can be used to develop socioeconomic-ecological indicators, according to Roman and Thiry, the aim being "not so much to create a certain final set of technical indicators, as it is to engage a range of stakeholders in society in discussions about what it is that we value."[843] In parallel, a wide array of alternative economic thinking and doing has been condensed under the umbrella term of *knowledge markets*.[844]

THE TRIADIC MODEL OF KM

Knowledge Events

Studies of the evolution of KM paradigms reveals several *generations*,[845] as discussed below (Table 4). The approach undertaken in this chapter is based on *Third-generation* KM.[846] Based on this KM perspective, a knowledge event may be defined as a discrete phenomenon resulting from the alignment of three necessary and sufficient conditions, namely *a knowledge object*, a *knowledge agent*, and a *knowledge context*, as shown in Figure 1. In light of the interplay between these concepts, the alignment of relevant parameters has become a fourth, integrative concept that is increasingly recognized. At the organizational level, alignment has traditionally been viewed in terms of a correspondence between a firm's resources and structure, and its identity and intelligence, respectively.[847] Bosua and Venkitachalam apply this concept to KM, as "a continuous process of refinement that comprises the fit and linkage between an organizational KM strategy emphasis and associated KM processes".[848] Within the framework presented in this chapter, alignment is defined as the degree of correspondence among the relevant attributes of knowledge objects, agents, and contexts. Alignment can be seen as analogous to the concept of molecular folding or intramolecular self-assembly. Anfinsen's principle may be paraphrased by stating that the three-dimensional structure of knowledge events is wholly and uniquely determined by the attributes of an object–agent–context alignment.[849]

Knowledge

The concept of knowledge can be viewed from two perspectives: either as content that must be acted upon or as a value-creating event.[850] Identifying the conditions that result in knowing is a key task in the latter sense. In this context, a knowledge event occurs when the attributes of an object, an agent, and a context correspond with each other. As a result of these conditions, knowledge becomes an emergent integration.[851] Whenever these three factors are aligned effectively and mutually, knowledge occurs.

Therefore, KM seeks to align knowledge objects, agents, and contexts.[852] Similarly, the occurrence of fire (chemical chain reaction) also requires a convergence of heat, oxygen, and flammable material (reactants) in an appropriate proportion,[853] just as knowledge requires all three elements – object, agent and context – to converge in adequate parameters.[854] While aggregating objects, agents, and contexts increases the likelihood of knowledge occurring, it is not sufficient to do so, just as storing combustible materials in non-insulated spaces increases the risk of fire but does not necessarily start it. For a fire to be intentionally started, flammable materials, oxygen, and heat must be available in an adequate combination. By appropriately adjusting temperatures, oxygenation, and flammability, fire management can be achieved. The prevention and suppression of fires is achieved by excluding or removing any of these factors. Likewise, KM facilitates alignment among knowledge objects, agents, and contexts by identifying their relevant dimensions and enabling their correspondence.[855]

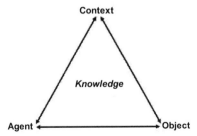

Figure 18-1. Elements of a knowledge event.

Knowledge Object

In first-generation KM,[856] knowledge objects were understood in terms of instructional design: as units of subject matter content.[857] Therefore, in the composite term KM, knowledge is associated with content and management is associated with handling content structures such as databases, repositories, libraries, archives, and taxonomies. The object-centered knowledge management (KM) approach is based on variations of the knowledge lifecycle:[858] the operations on knowledge reifications that correspond to inventory management in industrial settings (e.g., identify, categorize, store, retrieve, distribute and use). So, first-generation KM, or content-based KM, resonates with the industrial mindset since it aims to collect and store knowledge.[859] The recent boom of AI-based KM applications has brought a renewed emphasis on content.[860]

In contrast to object-centered knowledge management, which assumes that the known can be separated from the knower, critical theory[861] asserts that knowledge is always constructed by an agent, so it is possible to understand and manage them only interdependently. A dualism arises only when agents and knowledge objects are regarded as independent entities. Once the dichotomy between knowledge object and human action has been challenged, knowledge "takes on a political dimension rendering it neither neutral nor value-free."[862] As a consequence, knowledge becomes "an organized combination of data, assimilated with a set of rules, procedures and operations learnt through experience and practice."[863] We are left with information or data in the absence of meaning. Consequently, the distinction between information and knowledge is determined by the perspective of the user. Insofar knowledge is contextually dependent, meanings are formed in accordance with a particular worldview.[864]

In KM theories, object, agent, and context are often recognized as interdependent. Knowledge objects are those that are explicitly or tacitly constructed by agents, either as representations (e.g., texts and images), experiences (e.g., memories), or socialization (e.g., discourses). Knowledge objects are value-laden, meaningful portions of engaged actors' perceived reality at any given time, usually in the form of a content vehicle (e.g., sound in digital files, ideas in printed text, and perceptions on sensory paths). If a knowledge object has attributes that a knowledge agent can interpret within a certain context, the two are aligned.

To maximize the value of all other elements within the organization or community, managing the object element requires creating an optimal array of conditions and resources – for instance, clear instructions, sufficient bandwidth, current software versions and accessible databases are attributes of knowledge objects that should be aligned. For KM to be effective, it must ensure that all relevant knowledge objects are defined by attributes corresponding with agent competencies within the appropriate organizational context.

Accordingly, a knowledge object implies a knowledge agent. A purpose of knowledge management is to determine and develop the appropriate attributes of the object and agent in relation to one another. An effective collaborative management platform, for example, must consider in its design the competencies and motivations of its users.

Knowledge Agent

The critical role of agency can be seen in several prominent KM categories, including knower, agent, and human capital.[865] The concept of the knowing agent is one in constant evolution; it tends to express situated and social action. In a similar way to knowledge objects being defined as functions of knowledge agents, agency implies that "there can be no separation either between individual and social knowledge, or between knowledge and action."[866]

According to first-generation knowledge management, the design of repositories must incorporate motivation, user-friendliness, and collaboration just as much as content structure and consistency; otherwise, intended users will not be engaged or interested.[867] Agent management evolved from object management. The management of agents is characterized by exchange-intensive processes such as organizational learning, value practices, and competency development. Thus, second-generation KM has placed a strong emphasis on knowledge flow and transfer.[868]

A knowledge management perspective views agents as performing the knowledge act. The term knowledge agent refers to anyone who participates in knowledge events, either independently or collectively. A key aspect of managing agents is developing the value-generating capabilities of individual agents, teams, and organizations. Second-generation knowledge management involves agent-centered approaches.

In spite of the fact that agent-object interactions may occur, they are insufficient to spark knowledge. It is imperative that engaged actors understand the specifics of the situation and act accordingly. Knowledge management attempts to integrate the range of agents' potential actions, the properties of objects, and the context in which they are meaningful.[869] As a result of ubiquitous learning and knowledge transfer, performance management increases agent alignment. Training programs can be enhanced by reducing the time needed by personnel to engage in new processes. In this way, agent capital refers to demonstrated or potential capacity to act.

The concept of knowledge agency is closely related to that of human capital.[870] The focus of this perspective is on knowledge sharing as well as team-based organizational design.[871] Open innovation is promoted by interaction with external actors, as indicated by Saenz and Perez-Bouvier.[872] In summary, agent actions are determined by situational variables and by each other, so there is no agency apart from its context.

Knowledge Context

In spite of the complexity and difficulty of assessing the role of context in knowledge events, it has been extensively discussed in the literature, focusing primarily on the interaction between theory and practice as well as the epistemological foundations of knowledge events.[873] Based on the view that knowledge objects are constructed through situated practice, the notion of knowledge context has come to be increasingly important in a newer KM generation.[874] Insofar as meanings are related to particular paradigms, Bhatt stresses the context-dependent nature of knowledge.[875] The *ba* concept was introduced in 1995 by Nonaka and Takeuchi to explain situational knowledge-transfer variables.[876] Similarly, John Dewey distinguished context from *situation*, which has a temporal component – meaning "all those moments in which interaction between a living being and its environment takes effect in the form of a reciprocal action."[877] Thus, it is similar to Jacob Kantor's *interbehavioral field* as a unit of analysis, which was in turn influenced by Dewey.[878]

An important challenge in knowledge management is creating an environment conducive to sharing knowledge.[879] One of the earliest approaches has been to attribute meaning to experience or sensemaking.[880] Several studies have been conducted on sensemaking both at the individual and organizational level.[881] As individuals and groups interact with each other, and organizations determine context interpretation, identity has been suggested as a key dimension of sensemaking. Hence, identity management can facilitate knowledge-sharing through sensemaking in KM. The continuous interplay between stimulus discrimination and generalization is at the heart of behavior analysis. Throughout her work, Donna Haraway stressed the importance of placing each knowledge event in its corresponding material context. According to her, "the only way to find a larger vision is to be somewhere in particular."[882] By situating, we contextualize and the ability to move along perspectives (levels of analysis and synthesis) leads to the recovery of the continuum.[883]

The context in which content is embedded has semantic and economic significance from a knowledge management perspective.[884] In a political economy, this concept is similar to Hay's notion of context: "the setting within which social, political, and economic events take place and acquire meaning."[885]

Knowledge context is defined here as the set of circumstances that provide direction and choice capacity for matching meaningful agent-object transactions among potentially infinite possibilities. As a result of the referential character of the context, relativism is overcome by providing a preference criterion.[886]

KM involves the management of knowledge objects and agents, as well as the management of context. Incorporating this strategic level of intervention enables the development of a third-generation approach to knowledge management.[887] As relevant objects are aligned by capable agents in meaningful contexts, knowledge is generated, and value is created.

Table 18-2. Definition and alignment of key KM concepts.

Key KM concept	Definition	Process capacity	Alignment
Knowledge Object	Explicit or tacit associations abducted from real objects by knowledge agents	Perceivable and accessible	No object without agent
Knowledge Agent	Individuals or groups carrying out the knowledge act	Competent and engaged	No agency without context
Knowledge context	Circumstances providing semantic and economic significance to object–agent associations.	Meaningful and valuable	No context without alignment

Alignment

According to Bhatt, knowledge cannot be managed merely through the analysis of processes and technologies separately.[888] Thus, strategic alignment becomes an essential part of KM.[889] Management literature emphasizes the primacy of alignment,[890] as well as the concept's complexities and difficulties of measuring it.[891] In essence, KM is the alignment of knowledge object, agent, and context.[892] As outlined above, this is accomplished by identifying, measuring, and designing the correspondence between the attributes of objects, agents, and contexts.

The following is an example of an agent-object transaction. Consider a graphic designer selecting a series of illustrations that must be framed in a relevant context (such as a new service launch) for the specific object-agent-context convergence to make sense, become a knowledge event and acquire economic significance (Table 2). Removing the process capacity of any element will result in the dilution of meaning and value, for it will no longer be knowledge and will become useless.

Value realization will be impaired unless a competent knowledge agent is provided with appropriate contextual clues to interpret the knowledge object.[893] In this regard, alignment represents the next challenge. Which conditions enable an object-agent-context set to align and emergence of knowledge to occur? Despite having defined the object concept (as constructed by agents) and described the agent concept (as socially situated), the notion of context needs to be clarified.

First, a clear KM strategy is required by the *tacit* nature of critical knowledge, particularly in complex environments such as personalized service settings.[894] The role of tacit knowledge in strategic alignment is stressed by Saint-Onge.[895] In terms of KM, this issue has remained a significant concern.

Secondly, contextual sensemaking is intrinsically *social*. While du Toit claimed that knowledge emerges from social sensemaking,[896] Dulipovici and Robey argued that KM-based alignment is shaped by the interaction between and within groups.[897]

Thirdly, knowledge contexts can be enabled through a value balance that includes *shared culture* and *incentive distributions*.[898] As Bontis and Fitz-Enz assert, knowledge-sharing relies on value alignment,[899] which is a key goal of managerial leadership.

A fourth factor that contributes to KM is the formalization of strategic alignment through measurement and reporting of intellectual capital (IC).[900] It may be necessary to provide effective performance feedback in order to obtain effective alignment.[901]

The conceptual framework outlined here proposes that by drawing on those four key concepts from KM discussed above, knowledge generation and value co-creation in particular, might be leveraged by identifying the need for objects to be relevant, agents to be capable and contexts to be meaningful.

CAPITAL SYSTEMS

The conventional Intellectual Capital (IC) model consists of three distinct categories: human, structural, and relational.[902] Such categories correspond with an inductive phase in the configuration of an IC taxonomy.[903] The Capital Systems Model aims at capturing a set of value dimensions that is complete and consistent as well as practical. Therefore, the taxonomy should consist of a handful of proto categories, cover all scenarios, and ensure that none contradict each other. A further requirement is that all empirically documented subcategories can be hierarchically nestled within previously established categories. By meeting these requirements, all possible instances should be included, in addition to identifying general attributes as well as specific ones distinguishing each category. To the extent that capital systems reflect actual communities, they are meaningful.[904] Capital Systems can serve as the base for 'an economy of what matters'.[905]

To sum up, the set of attributes of a capital system:

i. Constitute a homogeneous value whole. A capital system denotes a culture.

ii. Cannot be reduced to any of its constituent parts (financial capital cannot express the whole). And,

iii. Is interchangeable with others through correspondence rules, while every capital expresses a value dimension of its own.

Accordingly, *a capital system* can be defined as *a universe of collective preference orders within a human activity structure*. This definition includes all elements that stakeholders recognize as valuable at all levels of analysis: individual, organizational, social, and global. Each category is further subdivided into distinct value functions. According to the direction in which they operate on the system, each holds either a negative (liability) or a positive (asset) sign. Table 3 includes definitions for major capital orders.

Table 18-3. A taxonomy of capital.

Capital System Universe of value orders of collective preference	Metacapital *Multiplicative (divisive)*	Referential *Structure:* rules of belonging	**Identity** Auto-significance	Capacity to differentiate value elements belonging into the system and to consequently adjusting action
			Intelligence Also-significance	Capacity to identify significant agents and events in the system and responding accordingly
		Articulating *Function:* rules of relationship	*Monetary* Exchange	Capacity to represent and exchange value elements
			Relational Bonding	Capacity to establish and develop bonds with significant others
	Productive *Additive (subtractive)*		**Input**	Natural services, cultural heritage, and exogenous value
			Agential	Capacity to perform value-increasing actions
			Instrumental	Capacity to leverage the performance of value-increasing actions
			Output	Cumulative addition to or subtraction from a system

The following assumptions summarize the rationale for a capital system based on the former analysis:

i.   All value systems are based on production functions. In this way, they convey the system's ability to achieve and maintain value balance.

ii. In all production functions, an input, an agent, an instrument, and a product are required. These are productive capitals. Productive capitals are required by all forms of value systems.

iii. Throughout history, meta-capitals have been developed to enhance the value-generating capabilities of productive capitals. Currency enabled productive capitals to be represented and exchanged, thus increasing their spatial and temporal accessibility.

iv. Knowledge-based production involves two major forms of meta-capital. By providing focus, reference meta-capital multiplies the effectiveness and efficiency of the system, reducing error through increasingly precise internal and external feedback. It includes identity and intelligence capitals. Through articulating meta-capital, the system becomes more productive by providing cohesion, thereby reducing transaction costs and redundancies. It includes relational and financial capital.

Any given entity's value blueprint is represented by accurately and consistently capturing its capital system, i.e., its ideal state (homeostasis in living systems). Such an ideal state is one in which each of the value elements is present in just the right proportion to achieve full balance and continuously adjust it. Therefore, value systems are unique, just like personalities and cultures. As a result, capital systems are as diverse as the multiplicity of systems that can be described in a single way. This would apply to every individual, organization, and society. In focusing on meta-productive values, we begin to realize that there is no single form of value that holds primacy: it is the degree of equilibrium of all value elements (whatever their relative weights) that becomes an ideal value system.

KM PROCESSES AND APPLICATIONS

Knowledge-based Value Systems Processes

By operationalizing KM into measurement-driven definitions, KM becomes actionable. Literature reviews have documented the diversity of KM processes.[906] Nevertheless, few processes stand up to scrutiny when drawn as operational definitions. Pragmatist epistemology, a systems perspective, and a confluence of the sciences of knowledge provide the foundation for the KM model and processes outlined here. By integrating state-of-the-art inputs from evolutionary biology, neurology, behavioral, and social sciences, knowledge can be understood as an emergent property arising from the three necessary and sufficient conditions reviewed above: an object, an agent, and a context. In order for a knowledge event to occur, these three elements must satisfy the following attributes: objects must be perceptible, subjects must be responsive, and contexts must be distinct. Thus, KM involves identifying the key elements in an expected knowledge outcome and creating the conditions to connect them. Therefore, three generations have been evident in the literature in the evolution of KM and KBD, depending on what knowledge components are addressed, what management actions are taken and, accordingly, how KM concepts are constructed.[907] The following table summarizes the key understandings about knowledge and management that led to the respective first-, second-, and third-generation concepts.

Table 18-4. Three KM generations.

Concept	Generation		
	1st Generation: Object-centered	**2nd Generation** Agent-centered	**3rd Generation:** Context-centered
Knowledge	Information content	Flow capacity	Value alignment
Management	Accumulate and retain stock	Facilitate and increase circulation	Dynamically adjust to sustain balance
KM	KM is a **technique** to secure knowledge possession	KM is a **platform** to maximize knowledge flow	KM is a **strategy** to facilitate value alignment and balance

Corresponding to a third-generation KM and KBD paradigm, the knowledge-based value systems approach,[908] is especially amenable to process operationalization since it is explicitly based on the three elements of a knowledge event. Therefore, it is comprised by three blocks of processes dealing with objects (instrumental capital), agents (human capital) and context (capital systems). The core KM processes following from this model are described on Table 18-5.

In addition to private companies in The Americas, public administration organizations around the world have applied this model. In most cases, it has been used as a benchmark resource for urban KBD, that is, for Knowledge Cities.[909] This model is the basis for the MAKCi Awards (Most Admired Knowledge Cities), held annually since 2007.[910] So far, more than 100 cities around the world have used this model. In addition, a variety of direct applications to regional development and policy analysis have been documented at the city and municipal levels, including Brazil[911]; Chile[912]; Colombia[913]; El Salvador[914]; India[915]; Peru[916]; Spain[917]; the United Kingdom[918]; and other countries.

Table 18-5. Third-generation KM processes.

Process Group	Process	Capital	Dominant Dimension
Capital Systems Management	KM Strategy	All	All
	Reference Capital	Identify Capital	Context
		Intelligence Capital	
	Articulating Capital	Financial Capital	
		Relational Capital	
Human Capital Management	Competencies System	Agent Capital	Subject
	Value Practices		
	Organizational Learning		
Instrumental Capital Management	Organizational Memory	Instrumental Capital	Object
	ITC Tools for KM		
	KM Methods and Techniques		

Each of the three major processes will be described next in terms of the expected outcomes. Operationalization is a key leverage to KM process instrumentation, whether for integrating KM into software development standards[919] or for knowledge cities benchmarking.[920] In each of the following tables, the outcomes for one of the three major sets of processes are summarized.

A value alignment assurance is provided to an organization by the capital system management group of processes.[921] It implies the identification, systematization, and further development of the organization's capital universe.[922] This group of processes focuses on three aspects: KBD strategy, referential capitals, and articulating capitals. The outcomes listed in Table 18-6 should be achieved by an organization that implements this group of processes effectively.

Table 18-6. Outcomes of capital systems management processes.

Process	Outcomes
KBD Strategy	1. A set of variables and strategic indicators to determine the state of each capital in the capital system is defined and calculated. 2. An Integrated Value Report – IVR – to understand and visualize the relationships between all capitals in the organization is built from the former set of variables and indictors. 3. Capital development gaps are identified through the IVR. 4. Objectives and actions to diminish or close those gaps are defined and implemented. 5. The KBD implementation strategy is evaluated and adjusted.
Referential Capitals	1. Endogenous referents (distinctiveness, congruence, continuity, affiliation, resilience and renewal) that constitute identity capital are identified and measured. 2. Exogenous referents (relevant objects and events in the environment) that constitute intelligence capital are identified and measured. 3. The organization value alignment framework is built based on endogenous and exogenous referents. 4. Criteria to assess value elements in the organization identity and intelligence capitals regarding the reference framework, are defined. 5. The value alignment framework is evaluated and adjusted through improvement actions or radical transformations.
Articulating Capitals	1. Monetary representations of value elements in the capital systems are defined. 2. The structure of relationships with significant agents in the environment is identified in the capital system. 3. The reference framework for capital system value exchanges is built upon monetary representations and structure of relationships. 4. Criteria to assess value elements in the organization financial and relational capitals regarding the reference framework, are defined. 5. The value alignment framework is evaluated and adjusted through improvement actions or radical transformations.

Agent capital is managed through the second group of processes. Human capital management processes focus on developing learning capabilities at three levels: the individual, the team, and the organization.[923] Competency systems are mainly used for designing and implementing individual learning strategies. Value practices management becomes critical at the team level. As concerns the whole organization, organizational learning management is involved.[924] Table 18-7 summarizes the results of an organization that effectively implements processes in this group.

Table 18-7. Outcomes from human capital management process.

Process	Outcomes
Competency Systems	1. Necessary competencies for adding value within the organization capital system framework are identified. 2. Identified competencies are functionally mapped and documented under an organizational norm or standard establishing the competency profiles of roles undertaken by employees. 3. The individual competency level is diagnosed using as a reference the competency profiles and the organizational standard. 4. Learning programs for individual competency development are designed and implemented 5. Individual competencies are evaluated and certified using as a reference the competency profiles and the organizational standard.
Value Practices	1. The universe of organizational practices adding value to the capital system is identified and categorized. 2. Value practices are specified in terms of operational action attributes and their correspondence with the organization value framework. 3. Specified value practices are benchmarked against external and internal referents to identify gaps, decide improvements and determine their strategic value. 4. Value practices are optimized and standardized to be replicated across organizational units. 5. New businesses are developed throughout the replication of value practices in other contexts.
Organizational Learning	1. Learning culture and paradigms in the organization are identified and characterized. 2. Organizational learning processes are assessed in both value alignment and implementation terms. 3. Organizational learning processes are re-designed to ensure value alignment and effective implementation. 4. Learning motivation and incentive elements are identified and leveraged. 5. Learning facilitation elements are deployed.

Processes that manage knowledge-based value production make up the third group. These involve organizational memory management processes, digital infrastructures such as big data, AI applications and analytic capabilities, as well as the management of tools and techniques for KM.[925] As a result of effectively implementing processes in this group, an organization should be able to achieve the outcomes outlined in Table 18-8.

Table 18-8. Outcomes from instrumental capital management processes.

Process	Outcomes
Organizational Memory	1. Knowledge to be integrated into the organizational memory is selected according to relative value criteria in the organization's capital system. 2. Selected knowledge is codified using appropriate collection and elicitation methods, as well as adequate representation and documentation techniques. 3. Codified knowledge is organized, classified and stored in organizational repositories. 4. Knowledge is accessed in an ubiquitous organizational memory through agile and appealing search and retrieval tools. 5. Knowledge stored in organizational memory is evaluated to determine its value for the capital system.
IT tools for KM	1. IT support needs for KM model processes are identified. 2. Functional and non-functional characteristics of IT tools are specified. 3. IT tools satisfying former specs are acquired or developed. 4. IT tools are deployed within the organization digital infrastructure and are used to perform KM processes. 5. IT tools are evaluated to determine their effectiveness and value regarding the capital system and to undertake improvement actions.
KM methods and techniques	1. Needs for methods and techniques for furthering KM processes are identified. 2. Methods and techniques satisfying the former needs are selected. 3. Selected methods and techniques are documented and stored as part of the organizational memory. 4. Methods and technique are applied in performing KM processes. 5. Methods and techniques are evaluated to determine their effectiveness and value regarding the capital system and to undertake improvement actions.

On the basis of these three processes and outcomes, a KM intervention strategy can be developed. A sample of about 100 consultancy and assessment projects carried out using this approach between 1993 and 2018 can be found in

Table 18-9. Each of these projects is grouped according to its process focus: capital system (strategy), human capital, or instrumental capital. Cities and countries of consulting are indicated for international projects.

Table 18-9. Sample of KM&IC contracts at CKS, 1992-2017.

KM strategy and capital system development	1. World Bank Program for the Development of the National Research Center Network SEP-CONACyT as Knowledge Research Centers (1997-1998). 2. Aeroméxico Strategic KM System, (2000-2003). 3. 'Caldas -Coffee Knowledge Axis' Strategy, (Manizales, Colombia, 2006, 2008, 2013). 4. Corporate KM Strategy at: EDS, (1995 - 2000), Empresas Polar (Caracas y Valencia, Venezuela, 1996-2000), GAMESA (2001), PEMEX-PEP (2002-2003 and 2012-2013), Volkswagen (2002), CEMEX (2004 - 2005), PROLEC (2005 - 2015), Federal Electricity Commission -CFE (2006 - 2007), GESEM (2008), AHMSA (2009 - 2010). 5. Most Admired Knowledge City Awards -MAKCi, 2007-2020. 6. Knowledge City strategies for: Monterrey (México), Arequipa (Perú), Caxias do DSul and Bento Gonçalves (Brazil), Legazpi (Spain), Bogotá and Manizales (Colombia) 7. CEMEX-TEC Research Chair, 2006-2014
Human capital development	1. National Competency System Strategy -CONOCER (1998), John Deere (1998-1999). 2. Value Practices at ADIAT (2004 – 2005), LAMOSA (2007), XIGNUX (2009-2010). 3. Bancomer University (1990-1992), PEMEX Technical and Managerial Capabilites (1992-2014), Cuauhtémoc-Moctezuma Brewery Supervisors (1994), Banorte Personnel Development (1994 – 1996), TV Azteca Production Capacities (1997-1998), State of Guanajuato HighSchool Level System (2000). 4. 'Human Capital in Mexico for NAFTA' study for Mexican Academy of Sciences 5. Corporate University processes for Motorola University, Chicago, US. 6. 'A Research Company' Program for VITRO (1996-1999) 7. Assessment Centre for Medicine Faculty Training, UANL (1998) 8. Diagnostic study on labour demand in ITC in the States of Mexico, Nuevo Leon, Jalisco and Distrito Federal (2013)
Instrumental capital development	1. Organizational Digital Memory for MABE (Querétaro, 2008 – 2009), and Liverpool Stores (2008). 2. Virtual Reality Applications for IBM Training (El Salto, Jalisco, 1996-1997), Ministry of Develoment-Spain (Madrid, 1997), Museum of Monterrey (1997). 3. Alliances with TRO (Florida, EUA, 1994-1996) y MFR (Houston, EUA 1997-2012) 4. R&D Expert Knowledge Identification and Representation at EFFEM (2005 – 2006). 5. Instrumental Capital Platform, Sekurus/E-NEXOR (2001)

KNOWLEDGE-BASED HUMAN FLOURISHING IN THE ANTHROPOCENE

The last two decades of the 20th Century saw the convergence of opposite drives in the global ethos nourishing the prospects of continued improvement for humanity. On the one hand, KM, KBD, and the whole concept of a knowledge economy or an "economy of abundance",[926] seemed to open unprecedented paths for social value creation. In parallel, approaches to development intending to circumvent the social costs of a narrow focus on economic growth and GDP – such as *Quality of Life*[927], *Human Development*[928]; *Subjective Well-Being*[929]; *Sustainable Development*[930]; and *Discretionary Time*[931].[932] On the whole, these trends shared an optimistic perspective on human progress. KBD offered the possibility to integrate the best of these human improvement dimensions beyond the realm of economic growth.[933]

On the other hand, the very idea of development as a post-WWII re-enactment of modernity soon exhibited its constraints and became increasingly scrutinized.[934] Postmodern worldviews became pervasive in the Global North, while the Global South reacted to the neo-colonial realities of the post-war world order. As the 20th Century was closing to an end, the inability of the established world order to address the basic rights and needs for most of the world's population became evident. By 1992, the first edition of *The Development Dictionary* was declaring its death "The time is ripe to write its obituary."[935] Gilbert Rist, the prominent historian, wrote as an epitaph: "Development…is like a dead star whose light can still be seen even though it went out for ever long ago."[936] Esteva suggested only a retrospective view of the idea of development had any significance: "Only an archaeological gaze could give us proper accounts of the ruins left by development."[937] Brinkeroff[938] was lapidary: "Development is dead".[939]

In a post-development age, the illusion of a global progress path that was actually deepening inequalities and cancelling the future of most peoples on Earth, had vanished by the turn of the millennium.[940] A grim reality became increasingly apparent instead: human impact on the planet's climate and ecosystems – largely due to industrialized nations – has been of such magnitude that it can characterize a new geological epoch: the Anthropocene.

Coming to terms with the cumulative consequences of human action on the Biosphere – the externalities dismissed by economics – implied *reversing* the path of progress: "[e]verything happens as if the Global – what modernity has supposed to deliver on the surface of the planet – is entering into conflict with what Chakrabarty calls "the planetary" – that is, the same planet once dreamed of, except now it appears concrete, material, reacting to human actions, and above all, limiting global development."[941]

Two recent movements carry on this line of explanation and praxis. *Social Ecological Economics* (SEE) explicitly addresses the sociological and political bases of economic activity, as well as the biophysical bases.[942] Given the material impossibility of an infinite expansion of the economy, *Degrowth* looks at alternative terms of relation with the planet that while operating within planetary boundaries best serve socio-economic and climate justice.[943]

There are two cultural drivers that contribute to the distinct possibilities of future knowledge-based social value: (1) an effective decoupling between environment and knowledge-based productivity; and (2) an unprecedented path to social improvement on a rational and political basis. The first could be pursued through the combination of quantitative degrowth strategies in the realm of material-based production and consumption as well as qualitative growth strategies in the realm of knowledge-based production, where continuous improvements would result from systematically asking: how to achieve better (net future value) with less (material input)? The second would be a radical shift away from material growth and capital accumulation towards social development and planetary value balance.[944]

In his characterization of *non-rivalry*, David Foray stresses the characteristic that often underlies the notion of the knowledge economy as an *economy of abundance*: "This is where knowledge differs from situations in which positive externalities are limited. As a resource, knowledge can be characterized by its inexhaustibility. Why? Because…economic agents are no rival users of a resource when that resource is knowledge… The use of existing knowledge by an additional agent does not imply the production of an additional copy of that knowledge. The author does not have to produce an additional unit of knowledge every time its use is extended."[945] In addition to the attributes discussed above, knowledge-based production has additional attributes that allow value output to be multiplied with a given amount of physical input (Table 1).

Due to its independency from the biophysical constraints of raw materials as the foundation of the economy,[946] knowledge capital has the potential for sustaining a qualitative development over a quantitative one. Although human improvement still requires a material basis, this burden does not necessarily have to be placed on material expansion. This condition underlies the concept of 'economy of abundance' mentioned earlier. In fact, the Economics Nobel laureate Edmund Phelps provides an alternative account of the economic surge of modernity as *mass flourishing*,[947] i.e., a widespread experience of generalized actual and potential improvement.

Through his *theory of resonance*, Hartmut Rosa proposes an approach to indefinite improvement that does not depend upon or require resources. As part of his critical approach to individual fulfillment, he challenges the dominant perspective based on the requirement for acquiring the necessary developmental resources.[948]

As paradoxical as it may seem, the dual challenge of decoupling value from material wealth and overcoming assumptions of resource-based approaches to social improvement opens the door to KBD for continuous social improvement. According to the P2P Foundation, knowledge-based value generation would decrease resource demand and, thus, decrease scarcity, while increasing net social capitalization.[949]It is difficult to see any alternative to addressing these two simultaneous and ineluctable challenges: first, managing a progressive degrowth to restore a balance with the natural world until a steady state is achieved; second, maintaining a door open to a framework for human improvement. In essence, KBD is a sensible and viable alternative to resetting humanity's relationship to the Biosphere without sacrificing its pursuit of the highest levels of human flourishing. As we face the existential challenges for the Anthropocene, we need not renounce to being the best we can be.

SECTION IV
A COMPENDIUM OF TOOLS

Through the years, many tried and true "management" tools were recognized as knowledge tools. Little wonder, for while the business focus and value of knowledge had not yet been voiced, it was always there as creative minds learned, and then acted on that learning. However, with the refocusing on the value of intellectual capital, small shifts began to occur in the way these tools were thought about and applied. We slowly moved into a more connected and collaborative world, even as the hiccups of control and power continued to ferociously play out in an unprecedented world drama.

Throughout this text we have referenced systems and complexity. For example, the environment in which we and our organizations live is described as having accelerating change, rising uncertainty and increasing complexity. In Chapter 2 we touch lightly on systems and complexity thinking, introducing the human as an ICALS (intelligent complex adaptive learning system), and our organizations as an ICAS (intelligent complex adaptive system). In Chapter 5 – when sharing the 2004 research study that engaged dozens of Knowledge Management thought leaders – we recognize that the field itself is a complex adaptive system with many possibilities and opportunities. At the end of Chapter 8, which touches aspects of the planning process, we caution "THINK SYSTEMS". In Chapter 11 in a discussion of decision-making, various ways to influence a complex adaptive system are introduced. Clearly, the importance of understanding systems and complexity cannot be overstated.

Recall that knowledge is not only context-sensitive and situation-dependent, but always partial and incomplete. Learning is never done, and what we perceive we know in our specific space at any given point in time is continuously changing, shifting and/or expanding at other points of the space/time continuum. Thus, it is important to recognize that a knowledge tool(s) do not provide a "silver bullet" approach, but rather are part of a larger systems approach. It is within this context that Chapter 19 – the first chapter in this final section of the book – is "Systems and Complexity Thinking", and every knowledger, whether familiar with the topic or not, is encouraged to read this. As a long-time colleague recently reminded, systems and complexity thinking provide a framework, or lens, through which all tools should be operationally evaluated. So often we have a tendency to grab ahold of something that has worked and think everything will fall into place, which seldomly occurs. As we embrace new ways of thinking and doing, it is critical to think systemically.

In Chapter 20, we include 29 representative people-focused tools that are either unique, particularly pertinent to this book, can serve as examples, or are favorites of the authors and contributors. These are listed at the beginning of the chapter.

Of course, there are in our rapidly advancing technological world, many technology tools that support the knowledge movement. We briefly explore a few examples below that ChatGPT, our Chapter 7 contributor, joined us in pointing out, with the first tool being itself.

Artificial Intelligence (AI) Chatbots: AI-powered chatbots help organizations by providing instant responses and solutions to frequently asked questions. These chatbots can access and retrieve information from various knowledge bases, helping employees and customers get the information they need quickly.

Augmented Reality (AR): Technically, AR is reality with a digital layer. Of specific focus as we moved through the pandemic is new emerging technology which provides an increased sense of presence and cohesion among distributed team members. AR is already providing significant contributions to training (bringing people from around the world into the same space), crisis management (strategizing crisis response tactics, exploring options, and ensuring consistent thinking and doing), and collaboration (blending the physical and digital worlds). At youtube.com hear "What is AR, XR, MR, VR? | Spatial computing".

Semantic search engines: Traditional keyword-based search engines can sometimes deliver irrelevant or incomplete results. Semantic search engines use natural language processing and machine learning algorithms to understand the context and meaning of queries, leading to more accurate search results.

Collaboration platforms: Collaboration platforms such as Microsoft Teams, Slack, and Google Workspace have become popular for knowledge management. These platforms provide shared spaces where employees can collaborate, create, and access knowledge resources, including documents, wikis, and discussions, fostering a culture of knowledge sharing within organizations.

Knowledge wikis: Wiki-based knowledge systems like Confluence and Notion allow organizations to create and maintain a centralized knowledge base. Employees can collaboratively contribute, edit, and organize information, making it easier for them to access and share knowledge across the organization.

Data analytics tools: Data analytics tools help organizations analyze and make sense of large amounts of data to identify patterns, trends, and insights. These tools enable organizations to extract knowledge from their data, uncover hidden information, and make data-driven decisions.

Social learning platforms: Social learning platforms, such as Learning Management Systems (LMS) and online forums, facilitate knowledge sharing and learning among employees. These platforms allow employees to share their expertise, ask questions, and engage in discussions, fostering a culture of continuous learning and knowledge transfer.

This is just a representative set. As technology continues to advance and the knowledge movement continues to evolve, new tools and technologies are continuously emerging to help organizations effectively capture, share, and utilize their knowledge assets.

Chapter 21 provides a Knowledge Tool Matrix, which suggests additional tools, with information regarding their use easily available on the internet or through your AI partner.

CHAPTER 19

SYSTEMS AND COMPLEXITY THINKING

Dr. David H. Bennet, Mountain Quest Institute, USA

THINKING ABOUT SYSTEMS

Introduction to Systems Thinking

Systems thinking is a conceptual framework, or body of knowledge and tools, that has been developed over the past 70 years to clarify the structure of systems and their patterns of change to enable a better understanding of their behavior and solve problems more effectively. The term is often used to describe a new way of interpreting the world and our place in it. This new way of thinking began in the late 1950s and was originally known as General Systems Theory (GST). A seminal book published by the biologist Ludwig von Bertalanffy in 1968 introduced theoretical and methodological reorientations of systems thinking as they could be applied to the physical, biological and social sciences.[950]

General systems theorists studied many types of systems in search of their underlying principles of operation. In the mid-seventies, Weinberg and Sutherland wrote basic texts that introduced students to general systems and systems analysis, respectively.[951] Other aspects of systems theory included management systems, hierarchies, world systems and even social systems and the quality of life.[952] While only moderately successful, they were able to identify many insights and observations that help to recognize major system parameters and understand overall system behaviors. For an excellent review of holistic thinking of some of the greatest systems thinkers of the time, see Koestler and Smythies book *Beyond Reductionism: New Perspectives in the Life Sciences.*[953]

A significant methodology for understanding systems was provided by J. W. Forrester[954] at MIT through his System Dynamics modeling approach. He was able to analyze systems by identifying their influence elements and modeling their feedback loops and time delays on early computers to simulate a system's behavior. Forrester's work has been built upon by many workers in the systems dynamics field until today it is used extensively in business and academia.[955] Since these early years, with the advancement of computer power and software program sophistication, great improvements in modeling systems and using the models to aid teams in understanding and solving complicated organizational problems have yielded highly effective results.[956] This is also a venue where Artificial Intelligence is a significant additive.

Miller's work in the late seventies provided an extensive analysis of living systems in terms of the overall systems perspective, hierarchies and system interfaces and structures.[957] In early 1991, MIT's Peter Senge published his seminal book *The Fifth Discipline* that made systems thinking, as a conceptual approach, a popular subject with managers throughout the world.[958] Senge's approach, formally called "Systems Thinking", is still widely used in management and organizations to visually and qualitatively understand how system elements interact and affect each other and to provide a comprehensive perspective of the role of work in organizations. It is a conceptual process of analyzing organizations using what are called system archetypes – 12 patterns of relationships that occur over and over in organizations – which provide individuals with a powerful conceptual and problem-solving tool. See, for example, Kim's *Systems Thinking Tools* or Anderson and Johnson's *Systems Thinking Basics*.[959] In addition, O'Connor and McDermott's book provides many specific examples of systems properties such as emergent phenomena, feedback loops, system metaphors, causal loop analysis and mental models.[960] With the increasing interest in and explosion of information several books have addressed information from a systems perspective.[961] Laszlo's book entitled *The Systems View of the World* was the first to introduce a modern systems perspective,[962] and the relatively new fields of ecology and biocosmology both wholeheartedly embraced the systems perspective, with considerable gain in understanding how those systems work.[963] The relationship between social analysis and systems is addressed in Luhmann's book *Social Systems*.[964] Many current books continue to build on these themes.

Two final comments are noteworthy. Physics, historically a reductionist science, has become more of a systems science as it moved into the domains of particle physics, field theory, quantum mechanics, and cosmology.[965] An interesting use of systems thinking at the intersection of physics and Buddhism is provided in *The Quantum and the Lotus* by Ricard and Thuan.[966] Applying systems thinking to thought, the physicist David Bohm explores ways in which thought actively assists in forming our perceptions, sense of meaning and daily actions.[967] The extent of penetration of systems thinking into modern areas of thinking can best be appreciated by noticing how often its methods and perspective are used without ever mentioning the words systems or systems thinking.

As professionals and knowledge workers, we all strive to become knowledgeable and competent in specific fields of inquiry to better meet our responsibilities. In schooling, training, and on-the-job experience we typically concentrate on fulfilling the immediate task, seeing the world as a never-ending sequence of problems and challenges that demand immediate attention and resolution. Understanding these tasks as elements or parts of systems that are holistic entities containing elements, relationships and feedback loops suggests a better way to view our work and its place in the world. First, it helps broaden one's perspective, to see our work fitting into a larger scheme and purpose. Second, we learn to understand and appreciate what systems are and how they work. Third, we have some tools that help us model systems to better understand the key forces and the effect of major relationships within the system. It has often been said that everything is a system and that all systems are connected, it is only a matter of *how closely* they are connected. With a new way of perceiving the world comes a new way of talking about it. While the language of systems thinking uses many familiar words, they have new meanings. Definition of terms is a good place to start a deeper discussion.

Definition of Terms

System: A system is a group of elements or objects, their attributes, the relationships among them, and some boundary that allows one to distinguish whether an element is inside or outside the system. Elements may be almost anything: parts of a TV set, computers in a network, people in an organization, neurons in a brain, patterns in a mind, ideas in a system of thought, etc. The *number of elements and their relationships to each other* are very important in determining system behavior. The following are all systems because they have many parts and relationships: automobiles, ER teams in a hospital, cities, organizations, pipes on a submarine, ant colonies, and individuals. We often find systems within systems within systems. This can easily be seen when reflecting on the typical organization—department—division—branch—section—individual hierarchy. Some modern organizations are also structured to have teams within teams within teams. The ICAS (intelligent complex adaptive system) model introduced in Chapter 2 of this book has a graphical example of this approach. Systems can evolve in time and they can change size and space, and processes are often seen as systems moving through time. So, along with the experts, we can now agree that "everything is a system" and the specific system you are looking at just depends on where you define the boundaries and from which perspective you are looking.

System Boundaries: All systems have boundaries that separate them in some way from the environment or other systems. Organizations have people and facilities that are in the organization (internal stakeholders) and there are external stakeholders and customers that are outside the organization. Typically, lines of authority, policies, technology, and many processes and functions lie within the organization, but not always. The boundary may be highly permeable and porous, or have a low leakage. Completely closed systems are rare; gas in a closed bottle would be an example. Completely open systems are just as rare because then there may be no way to define the system. There are degrees of openness in systems, some have boundaries that are very open to interaction with the outside world, others very controlling, with news agencies an example of the former and the Berlin Wall an example of the latter.

Environment: The region outside the boundary of a system is referred to as its environment. Since the environment may also be considered as a system, it is sometimes referred to as the supra-system. All open systems have inputs and outputs consisting of material, energy, and/or information. In Chapter 3 we gained the understanding that, just as energy and matter, energy and information are interconvertible, that is, they can be exchanged one for the other, and energy can be converted into either information *or* matter. In essence, whether information or matter or both, systems transform their inputs into outputs that satisfy internal purpose and environmental needs.

Inputs and outputs: Every system has inputs (energy, information, people, or material) from the environment and provides outputs (energy, information, people, or material) to its environment. As noted, to continue existing, organizations, particularly companies, must transform their inputs into outputs that add value to their environment. Without this value added, no company can stay in business and no government organization can justify its existence. In our world of information and knowledge, many organizations add value through the creation or leveraging of information and knowledge. Life forms – which are information processing systems as described in detail in Chapter 13 – are both open and closed systems. They are open in that they take in energy and information and extrude energy. They are closed systems in that they maintain internal patterns of organization that create their identity and implement their replication capability.[968]

Feedback and regulation: Systems, particularly organizations, contain many elements with causal relationships within them. Some of these may be positive, reinforcing feedback loops, and some will be negative, balancing feedback loops. Such feedback loops are needed to perform their mission during stable times and provide internal change and adaptation during times of change. Positive feedback loops create new ideas, products, and energy to try new ways of getting the job done – all needed during times of uncertainty and change. Sometimes, of course, positive loops can lead to disasters, such as when large funds are invested in new technology without a full understanding of the limitations of that technology. Often the idea of having the latest and greatest technology, the wonderful promises of venders, and the need to improve organizational performance form a positive, reinforcing loop that can be very costly to an organization.

Purpose: There are two uses/meanings of the idea of purpose in systems theory. The first is the stated intention of the organization, its official goal or purpose. For technology systems, purpose would be the use of the system intended by the system designers. The second interpretation of purpose is the set of interactions between the system and its environment. In other words, what the system does through its interaction with the environment, not necessarily what is officially stated or is intended to do. When a system has a mission or purpose, the individuals within that system work to adjust their relationships and individual actions so that the sum of those actions achieves the desired purpose.

Structure: As noted earlier, systems that survive over time usually have some form of hierarchical structure. The reason that hierarchies and systems within systems are so prevalent is that systems, with their boundaries, are more stable than groups of elements without boundaries. This is because subsystems within a hierarchy tend to be more stable and able to withstand shocks from outside. Even if a subsystem fails, the rest of the system may maintain its integrity, permitting the entire organization to survive. The Noble Laureate Herbert Simon demonstrates this in his famous parable of the watchmakers.[969]

As the story goes, two watchmakers, Hora and Tempus, both manufactured very fine watches, were highly regarded, and had phone orders and visitors to their workspaces throughout the day. However, Hora prospered while Tempus became poorer and poorer (finally losing his shop). While the watches both had the same level of complexity, about 1,000 parts each, the difference was in their approach to creating the watches. Tempus constructed his watches such that his work fell to pieces every time he had to answer the phone. Hora designed his watches so that he could put together subassemblies of about ten elements each, so that when he had to put down a partly assembled watch to answer the phone, he lost only a small part of his effort. The implication for biological forms, and organizations as living systems, is that "the time required for the evolution of a complex form from simple elements depends critically on the numbers and distribution of potential intermediate stable forms." This is a hierarchy of potential stable "subassemblies," what Simon says is "nothing more than survival of the fittest – that is, of the stable."[970]

This said, there are also detrimental side effects of too strict a hierarchy. Flexibility, adaptation, empowerment of individuals, creativity and innovation are all essential when the external environment is rapidly changing and threatens or offers opportunities to the system. Most organizations today have structures that combine hierarchies and teams, self-organizing groups and somewhat flexible structures

Equifinality: A system that tends to reach the same final state almost independent of its initial starting point is called an equifinal system. Most systems are not equifinal, although all living systems age and eventually dissolve. A common example would be highly successful organizations that become so self-centered, complacent, and perhaps arrogant that they refuse to listen and change, resulting in decline or dissolution.

While there are other concepts and terms used in systems thinking, these are addressed in the second half of this paper that deals with a subset of systems – complex adaptive systems, which include organizations (as intelligent complex adaptive systems) (ICAS) and people (as intelligent complex adaptive learning systems) (ICALS), both with knowledge at the core of their existence.

Useful Principles

In the following we consider some useful principles for thinking about systems and applying systems theory. These principles, or rules, are primarily applicable to living systems such as organizations and should be considered more like guidelines that are useful but not always appropriate for a given situation.

Principle 1: Structure is a key to system behavior

In addition to observing and reacting to events and patterns in the system, a useful insight and understanding of how organizations as systems behave is found in their structure. The nature of the elements of a system and their function is derived from their position in the whole and their behavior is influenced by the whole-to-part relation. In other words, recognize that relationships and structure play a large role in driving individual and team behavior, that is, there causal interactions. Thus, while it is normal to watch for and react to events that impact our organization, we should be wary of reacting to events without being conscious of the context and subsystem within which these events occur. We often react to singular events when it is the patterns of events that are more important. When we observe patterns of events, we should look at the underlying structure of the system for root causes and possible leverage points for problem resolution. Systems thinking would suggest that when we understand the structure of a system, we are in a much better position to understand and predict the behavior of the individual elements (people) and their relationships, and can therefore make better decisions and take more effective actions. Also, recognizing the importance of structure, we are less tempted to make one change to fix a problem, since the complex set of relationships will often require multiple changes to have a lasting result.

Principle 2: Systems that survive tend to become more complex.

This usually is a result of the system's response to and defense against the external environment becoming more complex. When this happens, the immediate reaction is to simplify the system, whereas in fact the best action may be to take advantage of the environment's increased complexity. For example, if you normally receive 30 e-mails a day and you start getting 300, the natural reaction would be to quickly scan and ignore all but 30. You have simplified your own system at the risk of overlooking something that might be very important. Another approach is to assign another person the responsibility for reviewing and responding to the e-mails. This has increased the complexity of your system (you and now the other person) but it also has given you more options and possibilities for expanding business, etc. While this is a simple explanation, it can be extrapolated to more complex situations.

There is some danger in oversimplifying organizational complexity. For instance, it is easy to assume that people will work harder if they are paid more salary. With the modern workforce, individual needs vary drastically and are usually quite complex. Often it is the challenge of contributing to a worthwhile cause and of working with others whom they respect and can learn from that motivates them. These drivers – worthy cause, respect and learning, etc. – frequently come from the entire system, that is, they are a result of the culture, the structure, and the individuals involved and they cannot be decreed by any single manager. An understanding of the organization as a system of relationships and patterns helps managers to recognize that they do not control the system, but rather must learn how to nurture and influence the organization to achieve desired ends. This is why many organizations today thrive operating through collaborative leadership, leaders who work with and nurture teams and colleagues rather than managing through command and control. In the final analysis, complexity drives more complexity, which results in an exponential rise in overall complexity in many advanced systems. There are, of course some simple, stable, living systems that have withstood millions of years in an increasingly complex environment.[971]

Principle 3: Boundaries can be barriers.

It generally takes more energy and time to send information or products through a boundary than within the system. Most organizations require some form of approval for formal letters, products, etc. that go out of the firm to another organization. In a dynamic environment, such policies can slow down the organization's reaction time. While open-door policies, empowerment, communities of practices, partnering, social networking, knowledging networks, etc. are opening organizational boundaries, boundary protection is a natural phenomenon of systems and as such must be recognized and managed carefully. Many world class organizations maintain their self-identity while minimizing boundary protection by combining a shared vision and purpose with trust, knowledge sharing, learning, empowerment, and self-organizing teams. All of these give knowledge workers at the boundary the *freedom and competency* to make good decisions both internally as well as through the organization's boundary. For a more detailed discussion of this balance see *Organizational Survival in the New World: The Intelligent Complex Adaptive System* by Alex and David Bennet.[972]

Principle 4: Systems can have many structures.

Systems often exist within systems, and each level usually has a different purpose or objective. Given the hierarchical structure of most organizations, senior leaders select and integrate the information and knowledge needed to make decisions that optimize the right system-level objectives. By recognizing the long-term consequences of those decisions, they can optimize the desired results over time. This is the classical control-type of management. However, system structures can vary from pure hierarchical to flat to matrix to networks to any combination of these. The optimum structure will depend upon the nature of the system and especially the nature of its environment, particularly concerning the rate of change, predictability and complexity of that environment.

Principle 5: Be extra careful when intervening in a system, especially organizations.

To minimize the unintended consequences of intervening in a system, consider the impact of second-order and long-term effects and the power of the systems internal (and informal) networks. Where organizations are concerned, a common rule of management is to *do no harm*. This means thinking about the possible consequences of decisions from a systems perspective, not only first-order effects but second and third order effects as well. Here is where knowledge of key causal paths, feedback loops, and how the organization will react to the decision implementation become significant. A corollary is to *beware of unintended consequences*. Here again systems thinking helps in recognizing potential results of actions and decisions. Sometimes small changes can create big results caused by leveraging phenomenon or positive feedback loops, and more often seemingly big changes have very little impact on organizational performance due to damping or negative feedback loops. It is helpful to separate the formal rules, policies, and directives of the organization from how the work really gets done. The work usually gets done through the informal network, giving it a vital role in determining the organization's performance. This informal system should always be taken into account when making changes within the organization.

In both living and non-living systems there often exist many fine, overlaying (sometimes invisible) networks that serve as mechanisms for integrating the system's behavior. These networks can be highly influential. Examples would be gravity's influence in a galaxy and reentrant connections in the human brain.[973]

Applying Systems Thinking

Since everything can be viewed as a system, it would seem that systems thinking would apply everywhere. While this may be true, it does not always prove productive to do so. For example, if your objective is to focus and produce a product and not be concerned with broader implications, this may not be the time for systems thinking, particularly if your processes are efficient and have six sigma quality. A good time for systems thinking would be when there is concern that workers are working independently when they should be communicating their actions to others. Or when things become uncertain, people become protective and parochial, and no one knows what to do. When any of these things happens, a shift to a higher perspective can illuminate and clarify the real problems and open the window of perception to allow new solutions to emerge. Here is where understanding the structure, relationships, boundaries, and informal networks of your organization pay off. The more you can get others to see and understand their organization and their own work as a system the easier it will be to talk about and resolve systemic issues and problems.

When communicating your thinking to others, make sure they understand the language of systems thinking. It is often difficult to grasp the meaning and insights gained without some familiarity with the systems approach. Do not confuse systems thinking with systems engineering or systems analysis. These latter two are well-defined disciplines that are very effective in their domain of applicability; however, they are very different from the systems thinking addressed here.

One very effective way for groups to apply systems thinking to their workplace is to get the participants to write down and agree on the mission, vision, and purpose of their organization. Then, prepare a high-level diagram of the organization, showing boundaries, inputs, outputs, internal structure, and key processes. Next, identify the environment together with its major characteristics that impact the organization. Be sure to include all significant stakeholders and external threats and constraints, going as deep or shallow as desired. At this point, get the group to ask questions about the networks and relationships that exist in the organization, discussing the current structure, the relationships that should exist, and finding the key factors that make the organization successful. The diagram mentioned above will be useful for locating problems and helping to identify the causes of those problems. An important benefit will be the group's agreement on what the organization is, what its environment is like, and the common language they have developed to communicate with. This will then serve as a common artifact for discussion, problem identification, idea generation, and even decision-making.

Individuals can also move through this same process to create a systems view of their own part of the organization and their local work environment. You can use your own part of the organization as a tool for explaining and understanding organizations as systems. For example, take your own division, or a division you are extremely familiar with, and prepare a system drawing showing inputs, outputs, boundaries, structure, any emergent properties, stakeholders, key relationships, and major dependencies. Now, draw the environment and highlight the key characteristics of it that impact your division's success. After describing its purpose or mission, try to trace the relationship of your past week's activities to that purpose or mission. How many other people were involved in using or contributing to your own activities? Identify the people who get the most work done and their relationships to each other and others in the organization. Why are they so productive? How much networking do they do? Remember the last time someone suggested a new idea at a staff meeting. What was the reaction of the group (or of the boss)? Did the reaction spur more ideas and exploration of how the idea could be used? In other words, was it a positive reinforcing feedback loop, or did the response stifle the idea without further thought, signifying a negative feedback loop? Such observations tell a lot about the strength, character, and probably the future of the organization.

Advantages of Systems Thinking

Below are listed some advantages of systems thinking (ST):

- ST expands an individual's critical thinking skills and provides a framework for observing, analyzing and understanding situations, organizations, and systems in general.

- ST helps identify parameters that play a crucial role in system performance. These parameters can be used as guides for taking corrective action in a given situation.

- Adopting a top-level systems perspective encourages individual managers and teams to develop and implement balanced decisions that optimize the entire system (or subsystem) instead of the more common sub-optimization action that so often occurs.

- ST can provide a basis for filtering information applicable for a subsystem while keeping the total system in balance. It can also help set relative priorities in an organization by offering an objective and agreed-upon framework for discussion, interpretation, decision-making and action.

- When applied to specific problems, Senge's Systems Thinking offers causal loop analysis to bring out the major causes and identify their relationships, thereby making possible solutions visible. It provides a set of twelve archetypes (recurring patterns of relationships) that help understand human behavior and organizational issues.

- ST expands individuals' thinking skills and changes their perception and interpretation of the world around them. Systems thinking enables a clearer perception of the patterns of change and the structure of systems to better comprehend their behavior and improve corrective actions.

- Using computerized model building, ST allows an in-depth model of organizations to be developed which can serve as a representation of organizational behavior. ST, when combined with computer modeling and group dialogue allows organizational leaders to define problems, test ideas, build consensus, anticipate possible reaction to decisions, and identify opportunities for growth.

- ST allows the creation and implementation of complicated systems that can operate successfully in real time application. Even information and knowledge systems can be developed in support of their supra-systems. One of the most famous examples is the information system developed by the British in 1938 that prevented Hitler from conquering Britian. Known as the Battle of Britian, an outclassed and outnumbered British air force made it so difficult for the German Luftwaffe that Hitler ended operation sea lion and turned his attention to Russia. A key factor in winning was the outstanding information system created, without computers, to manage the information needed by the RAF pilots. The importance of the system was highlighted by Sir Winston Churchill's remark after the war that: "Never have so few done so much for so many." For a lucid description of this famous conflict see Checkland and Holwell's book *It's Alive*[974] (or check with your latest AI system).

- ST suggests the usefulness of using metaphors and analogies for observing, interpreting, and responding to system-level problems through the areas of commonality of all systems from physical to biological to social to psychological to organizational. Today, metaphors and analogies are used from neuroscience, complexity theory, biological organisms, and psychology to find new ways of viewing and managing organizations.

To briefly summarize, we have tried to demonstrate the scope and power of thinking in terms of systems. After seventy years of growth and application, systems thinking is still at the forefront of human endeavors and has expanded into the physical sciences and almost all others areas of inquiry. With computers and learning tools such as dialogue and group analysis, systems thinking offers a powerful way of understanding and working with systems. Complex systems and complex adaptive systems, specifically, are addressed in the next section.

THINKING ABOUT COMPLEXITY

Introduction to Complexity Thinking

While complexity theory has been studied in the sciences for four decades, it's only since the turn of the century that it has been expanded to apply what has been learned to organizational and management issues. But do not be misled; complexity is still a young field searching for laws, rules, and principles that can be used to build a structure and a discipline. Even the definition of complexity is not widely agreed upon. Nevertheless, most organizations today can be considered as some form of a complex adaptive system (hopefully intelligent) and, as such, complexity theory provides useful metaphors, analogies, and insights into their operation.

To survive the increasing complexity emerging throughout the world, most organizations have to become more knowledgeable and complex. A number of organizations today are consciously trying to become complex adaptive (which include agility, resilience, alignment, robustness, and quick response) so they can survive and grow in their increasingly complex environment.[975] The Intelligent Complex Adaptive System (ICAS) model introduced in Chapter 2, operating at the leading edge of the age of complexity, served, and still serves, as a prototype organization of increasing knowledge and complexity.[976]

Some basic concepts, definitions, ideas, strategies, and examples of complexity as they apply to present-day problems and organizational challenges are considered in this paper. For those who have not tuned into complexity thinking, my objective is to make the reader aware of what complexity is and why it is important. In addition, we will explore ideas and principles that can help knowledge workers recognize, assess, understand, and interact with complex organizations. Right up front, let's agree that there are no cookbook solutions; every complex situation is unique, context dependent, and by their very nature difficult to understand. Although there are no "laws" of complexity theory, there are guidelines and principles that, when coupled with the right questions and perspective, may lead to insights, understanding, and solutions.

Lest we think that complexity is a fad, note that both evolution in general and human history in particular have repeatedly shown that systems that survive over time do so by becoming more and more complex. The problems of dealing with complexity are both formidable and long term, and are challenging enterprises, companies, government organizations, teams, and most professionals and knowledge workers now, and will do so for many years to come. In simple terms, complexity describes a system or organization that has so many parts (people) and relationships that it is not possible to take into account all of the causal relations underlying its behavior. Earlier in this paper, we discussed Forrester's System Dynamics with its causal relationships; in complex systems it is often not possible to clarify, or even identify, the specific causal phenomena. Understanding organizations, their environment, or even individual work tasks becomes increasingly difficult as situations and issues become highly dynamic, less predictable, more confusing, and often paradoxical. And surprises seem to increase exponentially with expanding time horizons and increasing complexity.

The word "complexity" often comes up when people are discussing the problems and challenges of today's fast paced, day-to-day activities. Our daily work may present us with hundreds or even a thousand e-mails a day, 10 action items to be done "now," a decision needed when no one knows whether a right decision even exists (much less what that decision should be), or our bosses insisting on solutions where no solutions seem possible. Many of today's problems are what Russell Ackoff terms "messes."[977] A mess is a situation where you know there is a problem but you don't know what that problem is. Some examples of messes that have occurred throughout industry and government are:

- Poor communication throughout most organizations.
- Isolation of individual departments within organizations—stovepipes.
- Cultures that perpetuate processes and beliefs rather than adapt to changing needs—
- Organizational defense patterns.[978]
- Retirees and departing employees who take critical knowledge with them—the brain- drain.
- The demands of the new economy, technology, and workforce versus the inertia and resistance to change of many organizations.
- Rapidly changing leadership that prevents long-term consistent organizational improvements to meet ever-changing market needs.
- Emphasis on efficiency, productivity, and working harder and longer instead of working smarter and more effectively to achieve sustainable competitive advantage.

Just as being able to recognize, understand, and think about systems has become a hallmark of many of today's successful professionals, being able to recognize, understand, and deal with complexity is the challenge of the immediate future. Let's dig deeper.

Advantages of Complexity Thinking

Complexity theory is still in fairly early stages of growth, using biological metaphors and insights from computer modeling which suggest new ways of seeing organizations that provide insights into why they operate as they do and how they can improve performance in complex environments. Complexity thinking suggests that leaders and knowledge workers should take a new perspective on their organizations, develop new competencies, and take different actions to create and maintain high-performing organizations.

Although all organizations are complex and adaptive to some degree or they wouldn't still be in existence, complexity thinking applies particularly to those firms that are living at the leading edge of change and must deal with an increasingly complex environment. These organizations have to manage their own internal complexity while concomitantly coexisting with an increasingly messy and complex environment. Within this context, what value can complexity thinking add to organizational performance and survival?

Since complexity thinking offers a different perspective or way of looking at organizations, its largest contribution is found in the new questions it raises and the possibilities they create. Recall Einstein's famous quote, *"The significant problems we face cannot be solved at the same level of thinking we were at when we created them."*[979]

Some of the ways complexity thinking (CT) helps leaders, knowledge workers, and organizations are called out below.

For organizations,

- CT increases awareness and understanding of the importance and necessity of facing the oncoming problems of uncertainty, rapid change, and complexity.
- Events, patterns, and structure are better understood in terms that make decisions more effective.
- CT provides a rationale and a path to building a flexible and adaptive organization better able to achieve sustainable high performance in a complex environment.
- CT suggests an entirely new set of questions relative to organizational problems and management issues.
- CT improves organizational performance by suggesting a balanced approach to the efficiency/effectiveness problem.

For leaders and managers,

- CT provides a broad context within which leaders and managers can understand and improve decisions relative to organizational strategies and performance improvement.
- The value of structure and relationships is made visible and gives managers more options and ideas for reorganizing and solving problems.
- CT encourages leaders to rethink and consider other options to their past approaches to organizational structure and leadership and management.
- Leaders better understand the importance and advantage of empowerment and self-organization.

For knowledge workers,

- CT provides an understanding of complexity and techniques to deal with complex problems.
- CT makes visible the value of divergent thinking and the need to create new ideas and options for action.
- CT puts complex adaptive systems in perspective relative to chaos and complex systems and explains the need for KM, knowledge leveraging, and learning.

Complexity Thinking as an Integrative Competency

NOTE: This discussion supports the decision model and mechanisms for influencing complex situations provided under "Decision-Making" in Chapter 11. Those mechanisms are not repeated here.

Complex systems are different from simple or complicated systems. Complex systems are difficult to predict and control, and continuously change and interact with their environment. These changes occur over time, are often unpredictable, and are heavily driven by relationships and distributed autonomy. The bottom line is that to understand and deal with such systems requires new ways of thinking and new competencies. Integrative competencies bring cohesion into critical areas that are needed by workers who live in the middle of complexity or perhaps, using the popular quip, "near the edge of chaos."

One such competency is the capacity to think about complexity, complex systems, and their own complex organization in a way that creates insights and understanding of how these systems work and respond to their environments. Complexity thinking is a shift in the way we understand our world and how we relate to it. It changes the context within which learning occurs by encouraging us to observe differently and perceive intrinsically by combining rational thought with intuitive understanding, judgment, and experience. In a way, we could group this as a Knowledge Capacity as well as a competency. (See Chapter 16 on Knowledge Capacities.)

As the world careens through the age of complexity, our primary resource is the personal ability to comprehend complex phenomena and devise organizations and strategies for dealing with the uncertainty, nonlinearity, and rapid change that are ubiquitous in our working lives. Just as we learn to understand and deal with simple systems through rational thinking, complexity thinking helps us to understand complex systems and, in doing so, increases our capacity to solve problems, make decisions, and take effective actions to improve organizational performance. When dealing with complex situations we need to ask better questions, look for different things, and take multiple perspectives before forming conclusions and taking action.

An apt metaphor would be that organizations living in a world of countless factors and innumerable forces are slowly becoming immersed in a "fog of complexity." We can only lift this fog through collaboration, information, learning, knowing, knowledge, networking, creating resonance and coherence in our organizations, and applying a good understanding of systems and complexity. While each one of these alone can contribute to our performance, taken together they offer an integrative and synergistic capacity for dealing with complexity; thus, the rationale for the development of systems and complexity thinking as an integrative competency.

At the forefront of organizational actions, complexity thinking makes use of specific ways of understanding the world around us. These skills and cognitive approaches are called integrative competencies because of their capacity to integrate or align one's knowledge and actions with the surrounding context in the work place. Examples of other integrative competencies that work with complexity thinking are briefly described as follows. Information literacy (see Chapter 3) represents the competency to efficiently locate and validate information needed to solve complex problems. Relationship network management (see Chapter 14) provides a platform for interactions that helps leverage knowledge needed to perceive, interpret, and act effectively in complex situations. The systems thinking competency is essential for recognizing and understanding systems, clearly a prerequisite for complexity thinking. Knowledge management (see Chapter 4 as an introduction) provides ways to create, store, share, leverage, and apply the knowledge so essential for handling complex issues. The knowing competency (a core topic in the companion book, *Innovative Creativity: Creating with Innovation in Mind* by Alex Bennet and Arthur Shelley, addresses the application of intuition and judgment utilizing experience to better understand situations and how to deal with them. The learning competency (see the Chapter 2 discussion of the human as an intelligent complex adaptive system, and the training and learning section at the end of Chapters 9, 10, and 11) helps each of us *learn how to learn* (addressed as a Knowledge Capacity in Chapter 16) and supports the need for lifelong learning – the secret of keeping up with change and staying open to the growth of complexity and the changing nature of the working environment. Thus, assuming that the hallmark of organizations is the set of actions they take to meet mission responsibilities, complexity thinking is directly in the line of action, and uses all of the integrative competencies mentioned above to help decide what action will work best.

Definition of Terms

Much like systems thinking 40 years age, scholars, researchers, and practitioners have developed a common language to talk about complexity, combining new words with new interpretations of well-known words. For purposes of this discussion consider the following definitions.

Context. By context is meant the set of circumstances or facts that surround a particular situation, the totality of features having relevance to the causation, meaning, or effect of an event or situation.

Patterns. Sets of elements (people, events, objects), their attributes and their relationships in space and time that are stable or slow to change over time.

Patterns are usually observed within some situation or background, i.e., there is some context associated with the pattern.

Complexity. Conceptually, complexity is the condition of a system, situation, or organization that is integrated with some degree of order but has too many elements, attributes and relationships to understand in simple analytic or logical ways. Examples are a team of people, an individual, a city, and an ant colony.

Adaptation. Adaptation is the process by which an organization improves its ability to survive and grow through internal adjustments. Adaptation may be responsive, internally adjusting to external forces, or it may be proactive, internally changing so that it can influence the external environment.

Chaos. Chaos is the condition of a system exhibiting disorganized behavior with little or no predictability; a system that appears to behave randomly, with little or no underlying coherence in its local interactions. Typically, chaos is a state of bounded instability, where high nonlinear feedback exists but is not so high as to create explosions. Examples are turbulent streams, the weather, a sand pile, some organizations.

Internal Complexity. The complexity of a system that exists within the system. It is measured by its variety, the number of possible states that the system can have. A state is a specific configuration of the system. An organization of high variety has a large number of options and choices of actions it can take to adjust itself internally or when responding to or influencing its environment. If its variety becomes too high, the organization may become chaotic, with no coherence of thought or action. Thus, in the intelligent complex adaptive system (ICAS) model of the knowledge organization, one of the necessary emergent characteristics is "optimum complexity", which will be different for different organizations, and different for the same organization at different times as it progresses through issues and challenges.

Agent. In the literature the term refers to a semi-autonomous decision-making unit of a complex system that determines its own behavior within general guidelines. We consider individuals to be the agents in complex adaptive organizations. Other examples of agents would be ants in an ant colony, individuals, or groups in organizations, and cities in a metropolitan area.

Emergence. Emergence is a term representing a global property of a complex system (organization) that results from the interactions and relationships among its agents (people), and between the agents and their environment. Emergent characteristics represent stable patterns recognizable in an organization that are qualitative and often exert a strong influence back on the individual agents and their relationships. While they are recognizable, it is difficult if not impossible to trace a cause-and-effect origins. Examples are culture, team spirit, trust, consciousness, laughter, and individual emotions.

Nonlinearity. A system possesses nonlinearity when actions within the system generate responses that are not proportional to the action. A small action may generate a very large outcome – or a large action may have very little effect on the system. Examples are: a program office with a budget squeeze eliminates travel budgets causing increases in contractor costs due to lack of program office oversight; a key individual leaves the organization, resulting in many future, expensive mistakes; a new leader comes in and redirects programs, thus raising costs and slowing down past investments; an influential low-level employee supports a management change effort and by doing so significantly moves the entire organization towards a better future; a butterfly flaps its wings in South America and causes a severe snowstorm in New York (a well-known story from chaos theory).

Self-organization. A complex system in which the agents (individuals) have a high degree of freedom to organize themselves to better achieve their local objectives. They also determine how to accomplish their objectives. Most complex systems found in nature are self-organizing, though human organizations are often the exception due to a human tendency to control. Current organizations exhibit a range of self-organization, from little or no control at the top to autocratic leadership. Self-organization provides the organization with robustness and resiliency. According to Wheatley, "Prigogine's work [on the evolution of dynamic systems] demonstrated that disequilibrium is the necessary condition for a system's growth. He named these systems dissipative structures … they dissipate or give up their form in order to recreate themselves into new forms. Faced with increasing levels of disturbance, these systems possess the innate ability to reorganize themselves to deal with the new information. For this reason, they are called self-organizing systems. They are adaptive and resilient rather than rigid and stable."[980]

System Types in Terms of Complexity

Systems range on a continuum from simple to chaotic, with complicated, complex and complex adaptive systems in between. There is increasing complexity as you move along the continuum from simple to chaotic systems. See Table 19-1. Recognize that these categories are a convenience of language. Nature does not separate systems into different types. So the description of each type represents an ideal state to facilitate differentiation.

Table 19-1. System types in terms of complexity.

1. Simple	2. Complicated	3. Complex	4. Complex Adaptive	5. Chaotic
Little change over time Few elements Simple relationships Non-organic No emergent properties	Large number of interrelated parts Connections between parts are fixed Non-organic Whole equal to sum of its parts No emergent properties	Large number of interrelated parts Nonlinear relationships and feedback loops Emergent properties different than sum of parts May be organic or non-organic	Large number of semi-autonomous agents that interact Co-evolves with environment through adaptation Varying levels of self-organization Partially ordered systems that evolve over time Operates in perpetual disequilibrium Observable aggregate behavior Creates new emergent properties	Large number of parts that interact Behavior independent of environment Minimal coherence Emergent behavior dependent on chance
Knowable and predictable patterns of behavior	Knowable and predictable patterns of behavior	Patterns of behavior difficult to understand and predict	Patterns of behavior may be unknowable but possibly not unfathomable	Random patterns of behavior

Simple systems remain the same or change very little over time. There is very little or no change in the elements, relationships, or their attributes. They have few states, are typically non-organic and exhibit predictable behavior. Examples are an air conditioning system, a light switch, and a calculator.

Complicated systems contain a large number of interrelated parts and the connections between the parts are fixed. They are non-organic systems in which the whole is equal to the sum of its parts; that is, they do not create emergent properties. Examples are a Boeing 777, an automobile, a computer, and an electrical power system.

Complex systems, as distinguished from complicated systems, while consisting of a large number of interrelated elements, have nonlinear relationships, feedback loops, and dynamic uncertainties very difficult to understand and predict. Complex systems have the ability to create global emergent properties that come from their elements and interactions yet these characteristics cannot be traced back to the connections because of the nonlinearity and unpredictability of the elements and relationships. These emergent properties make the whole of the system very different than just the sum of the parts. Examples of complex systems include organizations (with culture being an emergent property), teams (with *esprit-de-corps* being an emergent property) and a dialogue relationship between two knowledge workers (with an increase in knowledge and understanding being an emergent result).

As introduced above, a CAS contain many agents (people) that interact with each other who, in organizations, are semi-autonomous and have varying levels of self-organization. They operate and direct their own behavior based on rules and a common vision of the organization's direction, working in small groups to take advantage of the local knowledge and experience of coworkers. The aggregate behavior of all knowledge workers is a top-level characteristic commonly referred to as organizational performance. The interactions that create this performance are numerous, complex, and often nonlinear, making it impossible to derive global behavior from local actions.

In complex adaptive organizations where the attributes, experiences, attitudes, personalities, and goals of leaders and knowledge workers significantly impact their relationships with each other, the global emergent characteristics such as trust, flow, intelligent behavior, etc. will arise if – and only if – many employees work together to create them. The variety and diversity of individuals also contributes to the creation and characteristics of the aggregate behavior. If one person leaves, a complex adaptive organization can immediately reorganize to fill the vacuum and the firm internally adapts to its new structure, often including some stress and learning. As people move in and out of the organization, its global behavior may shift and change, adapting to its new internal structure as well as its external environment. This continuous flexing of complex adaptive systems – sustaining in a condition of disequilibrium – keeps them alive and gives them the capacity to quickly change pace and redirect focus.

Many modern organizations work in a dynamic, uncertain, and complex environment and to survive they must continually reinvent themselves, create, and act on new ideas and knowledge, innovate, and take risks. They tend to operate (or oscillate) between stability and chaos. It is that narrow region just before chaos in which creativity, dialogue, and innovation serve to accelerate learning and facilitate adaptation. *Complex adaptive systems have the best chance of surviving in environments of rapid change, high uncertainty, and increasing complexity.* They have the potential to create new emergent properties that provide the intelligent behavior to adapt to such environments. Examples of successful complex adaptive organizations can be seen in successful start-up companies, surviving Internet businesses, and government organizations that have recently changed policies, created teams and are empowering employees.

In review, complex adaptive systems are partially ordered systems that unfold and evolve through time. They are mostly self-organizing, learning, and adaptive. To survive they are always creating new ideas, scanning the environment, trying new approaches, observing the results, and changing the way they operate. As previously noted, to continuously adapt they must operate in perpetual disequilibrium, which results in some unpredictable behavior. Having nonlinear relationships, complex adaptive systems create global properties that are called emergent because they seem to emerge from the multitude of elements and their relationships. They typically cannot be understood through analysis and logic because of the large number of elements and relationships. Examples are life, ecosystems, economies, organizations, and cultures.[981]

It is not just the number of agents involved that creates complexity. For example, a closed bottle full of oxygen contains billions and billions of oxygen molecules but their interactions are simple and predictable in principle, and the system is not complex – it is complicated. Although its agents (molecules) are independent, they cannot take individual actions and make decisions, and the interaction of the molecules will not create an emergent property.

On the other hand, two individuals interacting to solve a problem may exhibit a high variety of behavior and thoughts during their conversation. This variety will depend, among other things, on how they feel about each other as well as their own experience and need to solve the problem. In solving their problem, they will have created an emergent phenomenon – the solution – something that came into being from the two individuals *and* their interactions and is different and better than either one could have developed alone. Neither person alone knew the solution, so the solution is more than what each person could have developed independently. Clearly this is a complex adaptive system, yet there are only two agents. When two people share their information and knowledge, more knowledge is created, but only if their relationship is up to the task.

Chaotic systems, or more to the point, chaotic organizations, rarely survive because they are unpredictable and independent of their environment. They are complex organizations that have *lost much of their coherence* and can no longer function through communication and collaboration of people. Perhaps this discussion helps us understand the importance of coherence in an organization! In a chaotic system, there is often continual disagreement, poor communication, infighting, and a lack of leadership. Sometimes the chaos can be hard to observe. As Stacey has pointed out, "... chaos is a state of limited or bounded instability ... Chaotic behavior is random and hence unpredictable at the specific or individual level ... The particular behavior that emerges is highly sensitive to small changes and therefore depends to some extent upon chance."[982] For example, chaos may exist when firms are going bankrupt or undergoing a merger, when standing down a government office, or when an organization suffers from a repeated change of divergent leadership over a short time. More subtle forms may occur when managers create and use conflict to meet their own agendas, or where small changes escalate and become reinforcing loops, creating a great deal of conflict and misunderstanding.

Figure 19-1 below, entitled The Systems Space, shows the five categories of systems laid out roughly in terms of their difficulty of understanding and predictability. The curve provides a nominal indication of the knowledge required to understand each type of system. In fact, highly complex systems may never be understood by humans; that remains to be seen as research continues to hunt for theories, laws, and underlying principles that would help explain their behavior. The dashed curve at the top demonstrates that the required knowledge increases as you move toward more complex systems.

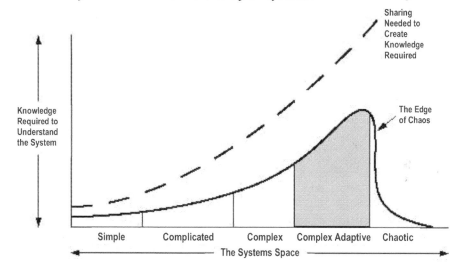

Figure 19-1: The Systems Space

Example: Complexity and the Art of War

With the current state of the world, perhaps this is a good example to use. Warfare has long been recognized as a complex activity. Military experts from Sun Tzu to Carl von Clausewitz to General A. M. Gray, former Commandant of the U.S. Marine Corps, have written on the complex nature of war. The well-known metaphor "the fog of war" is famous for its descriptive accuracy of the friction, uncertainty, fluidity, volatility, and disorder of battles. Von Clausewitz noted that: "Everything in war is simple, but the simplest thing is difficult. The difficulties accumulate and end by producing a kind of friction that is inconceivable unless one has experienced war."[983]

General Gray, in his foreword to the U.S. Marine Corps Book of Strategy entitled *Warfighting*, wrote: "You will notice that this book does not contain specific techniques and procedures for conduct. Rather, it provides broad guidance in the form of concepts and values. It requires judgment in application."[984] What better advice could a CEO or senior government executive give to their people as their organization enters the twenty-first century of uncertainty and complexity? This is the underlying premise of "commander's intent", which requires a deeper understand than an order, rule, or regulation.

Below are additional phrases from the Marine Corps book that will ring familiar when considering complex adaptive organizations. They are listed to highlight the similarity between two very different worlds – warfare and business – yet with the commonality of operating in an uncertain, rapidly changing, complex environment.

- "In an environment of friction, uncertainty, and fluidity, war gravitates naturally toward disorder."

- "As the situation changes continuously, we are forced to improvise again and again until finally our actions have little, if any, resemblance to the original scheme."

- "War is shaped by human nature and is subject to the complexities, inconsistencies, and peculiarities which characterize human behavior."

- "… command must be decentralized. That is, subordinate commanders must make decisions on their own initiative, based on their understanding of their senior's intent, rather than passing information up the chain of command and waiting for the decision to be passed down."

- "In practical terms this means that we must not strive for certainty before we act for in so doing, we will surrender the initiative and pass up opportunities. We must not try to maintain positive control over subordinates since this will necessarily slow our tempo and inhibit initiative."

These comments are enough to suggest the complexities of warfare and, as we will see below, many of these same ideas are useful in working and leading complex adaptive organizations.

Guiding Principles

The following principles are presented to give the reader a flavor of the nature and behavior of complex systems. Each must be treated as a rule-of-thumb that may or may not apply in any given situation.

Guiding Principle 1. The future is truly unknowable and therefore we must learn to live and deal with uncertainty, surprise, paradox, and complexity. It may, however be fathomable in the sense of being able to comprehend certain probable future scenarios or trends.[985]

Guiding Principle 2. Over time complexity increases in complex adaptive systems. Complex adaptive systems evolve and survive by learning, adapting, and influencing their environment, thereby increasing their own complexity. As a general rule, complexity begets complexity as systems strive for survival and growth through learning and adaptation with their concomitant increase in internal complexity.[986] Although, as new generations emerge, remember that they enter what older generations consider complexity, and as such they perceive this as the "norm", that is, it garners a "simplicity of normalcy" in their perception.

Guiding Principle 3. Complex systems generate emergent characteristics through the rich and myriad relationships and interactions among their agents. These emergent properties may be volatile and hard to control because a few agents can make changes that may propagate through the structure via nonlinear reinforcing or damping feedback loops. Relatively stable emergent patterns such as cultures may also arise. One way to influence complex systems is to create, nurture, and modify their emergent phenomena by dealing with their structures, relationships and second order causal factors.[987] (Ways to influence complex adaptive systems are presented in the "Decision-Making" section of Chapter 11.)

Guiding Principle 4. Complex adaptive systems cannot be controlled; they can only be nurtured. Control stifles creativity, minimizes interactions, and only works under stable situations. It is not possible to control a worker's thinking, feelings, creativity, trust, spirit, or enthusiasm.[988]

Guiding Principle 5. When two complex adaptive systems are interacting, the one with the greatest variety will usually dominate. However, too much variety may lead to chaos.[989] This supports the concept of "optimum complexity", which is one of eight emergent characteristics in the ICAS model of a knowledge organization (see Chapter 2).

Guiding Principle 6. Diversity, innovation, selection, interaction, and self-organization are critical for the successful evolution and adaptation of complex systems.[990]

Guiding Principle 7. Complex adaptive systems cannot be highly efficient and survive in a complex, dynamic environment. High efficiency leaves no room for creativity, learning, exploration or surge energy in response to threats. A certain level of noise is needed to maintain the system's ability to learn, change, and adapt since learning requires some level of error and instability.[991]

Guiding Principle 8. Effective structures are essential to a complex adaptive system that can survive in a complex environment. Structures influence relationships. Relationships drive interactions, patterns and actions. Actions create events. Events cause external changes that feed back to the originating complex adaptive system structures. This is how organizations and their environment co-evolve, with each affecting the other, resulting in iterative and recursive changes in both systems.[992]

Guiding Principle 9. Self-organization encourages a diversity of patterns to develop, optimizing the interactions among people and creating more options for action, thereby supporting flexibility and adaptability.[993]

Thoughts on Dealing with Complex Adaptive Organizations

The following ideas are provided to suggest ways of looking, thinking, and evaluating complex adaptive systems that will help decision-makers understand and deal with the uncertainty and complexity in their milieu. They are heuristic and suggestive in nature rather than definitive. The following ideas and considerations also suggest an approach for applying complexity thinking to complex organizations or problems. The following are not meant to be applied sequentially; as always, context is king.

- Understand the complex adaptive organization of concern.
- Review its history and context.
- Look for the emergent characteristics of the organization.
- Analyze the organizations networks, their functions and sources of influence.
- Use more nurturing than control when intervening.
- Use all available mental resources in trying to understand the organization.
- Beware simplicity, organizational complexity may be immune to single and/or simple actions.
- Self-organize your own learning. Let the complexity lead your path to its comprehension.
- Expect mistakes, sense and response, feedback and learning may be the best approach.

These ideas are explicated below.

1. Understand the complex adaptive organization of concern.

Observe, study, reflect, and use your intuition to develop a "feeling" for the key relationships and patterns of behavior in the system. Think how and why something happened, not just what and when. Look for the structural sources of actions, events, and patterns. Talk to people in the system about how the work really gets done and who influences what goes on, asking questions and dialoguing with others. Learning to feel the organization's pulse comes only through close attention, listening, experience, and reflection. Trial-and-error and living with the organization over time can develop a deep knowledge and understanding of how the organization functions and what it takes to correct problems. Unfortunately, we frequently tend to simplify by finding what we believe is "the cause" of events or patterns and taking action to correct that cause. While sometimes this is right, often the action does not change the organization and the problem resurfaces at another location or time or in another way. The typical solution to a bad event is to create a policy that prohibits that event in the future. Over time this approach results in so many (often conflicting) policies and rules that the only way that work gets done is by ignoring or working around them.

Remember that analysis and logic produce useful answers *only if their assumptions are correct, and if every material causal relationship can be taken into account* – a difficult task at best in an organization. When in a position to manage or impact an organization that operates in a dynamic, complex environment, do not try to control its operation, rather nurture the people, networks, relationships, and processes. This approach encourages people to think for themselves, feel empowered, and create solutions at the local level. Encourage many simultaneous small changes if needed; just be sure that the organization knows where it is going and people know what values are important.

2. Review its history and context.

History gives us a perspective on the past and on possibilities and probabilities for the future. It can provide context and highlight major forces that have influenced the complex organization in the past. Patterns are usually easier to identify in history than in the present, and they may extend into the future. The present context illuminates what the present situation looks like and what forces are currently in play, and context may indicate emergent characteristics that will extend into the future. Each of these perspectives provides insights into the workings of the organization and why it behaves as it does.

3. Look for the emergent characteristics of the organization.

Emergent properties are meaningful, qualitative, global, and can be very informative. To find out what integrates and creates these emergent characteristics, reflect on the systems behavior, history, patterns, and flows. Patterns are composed of relatively stable sets of relationships and events that occur throughout the organization. Look for the properties created from the interrelation of all of the parts – the networks, teams, structure, hierarchy technology, and individuals. These properties can rarely be reduced to single causes and therefore must be observed and understood as broad, qualitative phenomena. Their source may be a particularly creative team, a disgruntled employee who is successfully spreading rumors and discontent, or from nowhere that can be identified. Some events result from single causes and others come from multiple sequential or simultaneous causes throughout the organization. Try to understand how and why the event happened, any related patterns, and what structural aspects could be involved. Ask yourself the following: Am I looking at the problem or a broader situation? At a symptom, a cause, or a complex causal network that spreads throughout the organization? Is the formal or informal structure of the organization causing this property? What can be controlled? What can be influenced? What desired behavior can be nurtured to emerge?

4. Analyze the organization's networks, functions, and sources of influence.

Knowledge is created and embedded in individuals and their relationships. Networks – formal, informal, social, and technological – leverage the creation, sharing, and application of the ideas and knowledge of individuals and their relationships. Observe and study the networks in your organization. These networks, as an important part of the overall structure, play a significant role in creating the organization's culture and other emergent properties of the organization. In addition, they can create ideas and new ways of getting the work done, thereby increasing the variety within the organization. Study your own internal networks and those in the external world; they have a significant influence on the complexity of both the organization and its environment.

5. Use more nurturing than control when intervening.

Considering the management of a complex adaptive system operating in a complex environment, no one is in control in the sense of setting goals *and* making employees follow a specific regime to achieve those goals. While leadership can set the goals, direction, vision, and structural form of the organization, it is the knowledge workers and their relationships that primarily drive how the work gets done and often even what gets done. What leaders and managers can do is make decisions and establish relationships that open the organization to change, and then guide and nurture that change to keep it moving in the desired direction. In complex adaptive organizations it is essential to bring employees into the decision-making process *whenever possible*. This gives them a context for their own work, adds value to the decision quality, and aids employees in better understanding and supporting implementation because of their involvement and ownership. It also encourages more ideas and options for actions to respond to external demands. See Chapter 15, "How Leaders Inspire Action through Meaningful Knowledge".

In most organizations today, the certainties of command and control are myths. To the extent that current organizations are complex and adaptive, they exhibit various degrees of unpredictability and no one fully understands, nor can predict, their behavior. This observation says much about the future of autocratic leadership and the importance of nurturing and collaborative leadership, democratic leadership, and of the positive effects of the growth and empowerment of employees. Leaders do not understand complex systems any more than workers, but if the environment is open and conducive to collaboration and inquiry, solutions can be found through leveraging the knowledge of the right people, wherever they are in the organization. This is not to imply that hierarchical structures will go away, nor that they should. Chains of command, responsibility, and accountability are needed in all organizations; they just play a different role in complex adaptive systems. The hierarchy maintains the administrative oversight and its communication channels help ensure the *coherence of direction* of the subunits. It also supplies resources and knowledge support where needed. What it cannot do is dictate local tactics, schedules, and responses. By setting basic rules of operation and guidelines for decisions, leaders can free workers at the lower levels to empower and figure out for themselves how to work together and achieve their goals. Such freedom is, of course, situational and dependent on the task, the environment, and the individuals and their managers.

6. Use all available mental resources in trying to understand the organization.

In complex systems there may be times when a small number of dominant causes drive the system. Under these circumstances logic and analysis can be used to identify, study, and understand how the system works. Causal feedback loops can be described and modeled to predict the system's behavior. MIT's systems thinking and J. W. Forrester's system dynamics are representative of this approach. Unfortunately, as introduced earlier, we are often unable to trace the cause-and-effect paths within the system because they are too numerous, nonlinear, and have too many connections. These complex systems unfold and evolve through multiple interactions and feedback loops; there is no small number of causes behind their movement. Because of this fundamental behavior, we cannot understand them by using logic, analysis, and the reductionist approach. Under these situations, complex systems can only be understood by holistic thinking.

Experts who understand certain complex systems use their experience, intuition, and judgment to solve problems. They know, but are often unable to explain how they know. When dealing with complexity, we need to actively learn from experience, deliberately develop our intuition, build our judgment, and play with the system in our minds and especially in-group dialogues. It is through these activities that our experience and intuition become capable of recognizing the unfolding of patterns and the flow of activities in the complex system or situation. Such recognition leads to intuitive understanding and a sense of what the primary drivers are in the system. Sometimes a combination of analysis and educated intuition work best. For example, with practice a leader may learn to "sense" how well the structure, culture, processes, and customer relationships are going. To resolve problems or make changes in their organization, they can combine a systematic analysis with their intuition and emotion by looking for leverage points, patterns, and key relationships in all of the following: structure, culture, processes, customers, technology and knowledge systems, leadership, management, and knowledge workers. Asking how one feels about an event, pattern, or situation provides another perspective with attendant insights. In summary, complex systems can best be understood holistically; they take on a life of their own and often a speed of their own. To be prepared to deal with complexity, we need to develop and use all of our mental capabilities: logic, analysis, intuition, judgment, and emotion. The key to living with a complex adaptive organization is learning and knowledge, everything else is guesswork.

7. Beware simplicity; organizational complexity may be immune to single and/or simple actions.

Simplification reduces our own uncertainty, makes decisions appear easier, and allows logical explanations of those decisions. Simplicity captivates the mind; complexity confuses and forces the use of intuition and judgment, both difficult to explain to others. We continuously simplify to avoid being overwhelmed, to hide confusion, and to become focused and efficient. In a simple, predictable world this is rational and generally works well. It is easy to ignore many incoming signals, knowing that they are not important to our work. Unfortunately, in a complex world this can become dangerous, and even disastrous. Where complexity lives, it is hard to separate the unimportant from the critical information, events, or signals. It is under these latter conditions that teams, networking, contingency planning, experience, and deep knowledge become so essential. The hardest thing of all is for a leader to admit, "I don't understand this and need help in making this decision." Sometimes the hardest way is the only way!

8. Self-organize your own learning. Let the organization's complexity lead your path to its comprehension.

Accept full responsibility for your own learning and use problems and complex organizations as opportunities to learn how you learn and improve your judgment and intuition. Develop your listening capacity by thinking about the above ideas and practice in all conversations. (See the discussion of reflective listening under "Training and Learning" at the end of Chapter 10.) Enter into dialogues more often than discussions. Spend time reflecting, asking yourself difficult questions, and deliberately shifting your perspective on topics of importance. Always strive for insight, understanding, and balanced decisions. Let the complex adaptive organization drive your learning path. It may lead the way better than you can. With complexity, logic and rational thought have their place and their limitations. Do not hesitate to ask unreasonable or irrational questions, make guesses, and speculate with metaphors when trying to comprehend a complex situation.

9. Expect mistakes; sense and response, feedback, and learning may be the best approach.

Mistakes are a necessary part of interacting with complex adaptive systems. Anyone attempting to change a complex adaptive organization from within, or trying to understand and deal with an external CAS, is bound to make mistakes during the process. Every CAS is unique and to deal effectively with them requires experience, intuition, judgment, innovation, trial-and-error, testing, and feedback. Since no one has total control in a CAS, it is not possible to completely understand and predict the behavior. Complex adaptive systems are by their very nature unpredictable – recall that they operate close to the boundary between complexity and chaos, with their behavior contingent upon a large number of semi-autonomous individuals. Thus, mistakes are to be anticipated as part of the learning, understanding, and intervention process. However, prudent risk assessment should always be considered prior to any intervention. While clearly a good risk assessment of unintended consequences is difficult for complex adaptive systems, nevertheless, the first rule of management, "do no harm," should always be considered before any significant intervention.

Where the system under study is highly complex and adaptive, it will be impossible to know how it will respond to some action. Evolutionary biology has dealt with this problem throughout the evolution of Life. It appears that the standard solution is to create a variety of actions, try them, and use feedback to find out which ones succeed. The successful actions are then used over and over in similar situations as long as they yield the desired results: survival and reproduction. When they fail, they are stopped and new actions are rewarded. It is important not to continue with an action that is not working. Time is unlikely to help the action work because in a highly complex environment the only future is the present; in a short time the environment will probably have a very different nature. This is not a pure trial-and-error procedure, since learning continuously occurs and judgment, experience, and deep knowledge may create a level of understanding that aids in moving into the future. As knowledge of the complex adaptive organization improves, better actions can be selected and used to change the system. See Axelrod and Cohen for an extensive treatment of the role of variation, interaction, and selection in dealing with external complexity by creating internal complexity within your own organization.[994]

Final Considerations

In the age of complexity and complex organizations, old assumptions and beliefs may have to give way to new ways of thinking and acting. Think about the following possibilities:

- The capacity to learn may be more important than experience.
- Leadership may be more important than the knowledge one possesses.
- Effectiveness may be more important than efficiency.
- Teams may be more effective than individuals.
- Nurturing may be more effective than controlling.
- Intuition may be more powerful than logic.
- Understanding and meaning may be more important than analysis.
- Context may be more powerful than facts.
- Patterns may be more important than events.
- Structures may be more important than patterns.
- An open and inquisitive mind may be more valuable than a brilliant one.

About the Author:

Dr. David Bennet's experience as a nuclear physicist, mathematician, engineer, educator, businessman, and neuroscientist spans many years of service in the Military, Civil Service and Private Industry, including fundamental research in underwater acoustics and teaching nuclear physics, frequent design and facilitation of organizational interventions, and serving as technical director and chief engineer of two major ACAT I DoD Acquisition programs. Prior to co-founding the Mountain Quest Institute – a research and retreat center located in the Allegheny Mountains focused on the quest for knowledge, consciousness and meaning – Dr. Bennet was CEO, then Chairman of the Board and Chief Knowledge Officer, of a professional services firm in Alexandria, Virginia. In 2004 he co-authored a new model of the firm based on research in complexity and neuroscience and incorporating networking theory and knowledge management, turning the living system metaphor into a reality for organizations. Since that time, he has co-authored dozens of journal articles, chapters and books. Dr. Bennet is a Phi Beta Kappa, Sigma Pi Sigma, and Suma Cum Laude graduate of the University of Texas, and holds degrees in Mathematics, Physics, Nuclear Physics, Liberal Arts, Human and Organizational Development, Human Development and Neuroscience. A life-long learner himself, Dr. Bennet dedicated ten years of his life exploring new developments in neuroscience and their impact on adult learning, culminating in the development of an expanded model of adult experiential learning, which provides the grounding for *Unleashing the Human Mind: A Consilience Approach to Managing Self* (2022).

CHAPTER 20
29 PEOPLE-FOCUSED TOOLS

Is "29" a magic number? No, not necessarily. It just fell out that way after we explored the context of, and internet resources related to, literally over 500 people-focused tools that have been collected working int this field through the years. What we have tried to provide here are tools that are both generic and unique, particularly pertinent to this book, can serve as examples, or are favorites of the authors and contributors.

The following tools (with page numbers following each for ease of access) are included in this chapter:

Following the name of each tool (placed in alphabetical order), we include a one-line description, and then suggest business/organizational areas it can support. A small chart then indicates the level of effort, the size of the organization, and the scope of impact. These specifically translate as follows:

Level of Effort [Low/Medium/High] = Relative amount of investment (time, people, funds) needed to implement this initiative.

Size of Organization [Small/Medium/Large/Scalable] = Indicator of relative size of the organization where this tool has been successfully applied. Small is 0-50; Medium is 50-300; Large is greater than 300 employees. Scalable means that the tool has been used successfully in organizations of all sizes.

Scope of Impact [Narrow/Medium/Wide] = Range of situations, issues, problems that this initiative has the potential to improve.

C^2 means that the initiative is highly context sensitive and situation dependent and is difficult to categorize.

We begin with the "Affinity Diagram" to trigger thought about your organization's specific knowledge needs. This is a highly-effective learning process that supports organizational sustainability.

****

 Affinity Diagram[995]

A **process** for categorizing organizational knowledge needs in a diagram format to exhibit differences and relationships.

Supports: group learning, knowledge audit, organizational sustainability

LEVEL OF EFFORT	LOW
SIZE OF ORG	SCALABLE
SCOPE OF EFFORT	WIDE

The Affinity Diagram can be used to take specific knowledge needs, group them, and create representative categories called content centers. The Affinity Diagram is a simple tool that enables the user to enter the knowledge requirements of some process, issue, or situation; gather similar requirements together into small groups; evaluate those groups; and decide on a category name for each grouping. The groups you will develop will serve as content centers for the development of communities of practice as part of the knowledge management system.

Constructing an Affinity Diagram

The most effective group to do an Affinity Diagram is one that has the necessary knowledge to uncover the various dimensions of the issue, process, etc. This works best when the group or team is accustomed to working together and there is representation from all departments involved in this area of knowledge. This enables team members to communicate clearly because of their relationship and common experiences. Personnel should be included that have valuable input and who may not have been involved in the past. Also, keep the team fluid; bringing in resource people as needed. There should be a maximum of five to six members on the team. Since the team will explore the categorization of organizational knowledge needs, it should also ensure that the team members are personally aware of user knowledge requirements.

1. Phrase the issue for discussion. The issue seems to work best when vaguely stated. For example, "What are the main communities of practice needed to help the organization become more valuable and effective?" To review, communities of practice are groups of people whose responsibilities require access to similar information. Communities are discussed in Chapter 11. Once everyone agrees on the question, place it at the top of the diagram.

2. List and Display all your knowledge requirements. To begin this exercise, refer to your knowledge requirements. All of these should be transcribed so that the team can see them clearly. Enter all the knowledge requirements onto the small note cards, one idea per card. Whenever possible the knowledge requirement should have a noun and a verb (i.e., complete status report). This tends to make the statements clearer to understand.

3. Find the First Cut Affinity. Although it is possible for one person to complete an affinity diagram, all of the benefits are lost that come from the melding of perspectives, opinions and insights. The team approach is highly recommended. Look for two cards that seem to be related in some way and group them together. Look for other cards that either are related to each other or to the original two cards that were set aside. Repeat this process until all the cards are placed in 6-10 groupings. Do not force-fit single cards into groupings in which they do not belong. These single cards ("loners") may form their own grouping or never find a "home". Encourage team members not to "contemplate" but to "react" to what they see.

Many managers would like to mentally structure all the cards like an oversized chess game. The only thing left to do is to move the pieces to their appointed spots. In an Affinity, speed rather than deliberation is the order of the day. Doing an Affinity should be a high-energy process, not a contemplative exercise. Disagreements over the placement of cards should be handled simply and undiplomatically: If you don't like where the card is, move it!

It is critical that the team allows new groupings to emerge from the chaos of the cards. For the process to work best, members should avoid sorting cards into "safe" known categories. This pigeonholing will force fit everything into existing logic, preventing breakthrough from occurring.

4. *For each grouping, create summary or header cards using consensus.* Look for a card in each grouping that captures the central idea that ties all the cards together. This is referred to as a "header" card. The header card should be typed onto the heading line. In cases where a central idea does not exist (which happens often), a header must be created. Gather each grouping together with its header at the top of the column.

The headers should be, above all, concise. They should say in one to three words the essence of each grouping. Think of it as an *idea still*. Ingredients are thrown into the hopper and distilled until the powerful stuff remains. The headers should therefore *pack a punch* that would be clear to anyone reading it. Imagine that all of the detailed cards under each header were removed; all that remained were your headers. Would someone who was not a team member understand the essence and detail of the groups you formed?

To be effective, the leader must now help clearly identify the common thread that ties all of the cards together. This is a central concept, like "budgeting". However, this is not enough. The leader must also help the team reflect on the color and texture of the common thread identified. The header can be a breakthrough idea when it reflects the individual content of the cards as well as the "spirit" of the grouping. Creating headers is an opportunity to create new twists in old topics. If the headers sound too familiar, they may deserve another look.

5. *Draw a finished affinity diagram.* Draw lines around each grouping, thereby clearly connecting all of the items with the header card. Related groupings should be placed near each other and connected by lines. Often when this is done, the user finds that another header card must be created (referred to as a "superheader") that sums up how these two groupings are related to each other. This would be placed above these two columns and also connected with lines. The final drawing can be done right on the original sheets or only when the completed diagram has been transferred to another sheet of paper. It is usually transferred because an Affinity Diagram is often shared with people outside the team for comments and changes. Remember that it is a reiterative process that should be changed until it reflects the actual situation and key factors.

When finished with these steps, several communities for the KCO should have been produced. These communities will be storage areas for the information needed to meet organizational knowledge requirements. See the tool "Knowledge Base Roadmap".

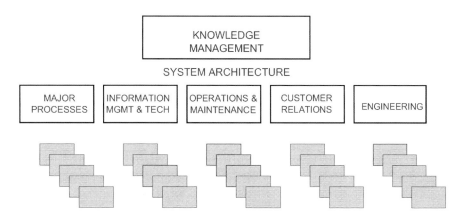

Figure 20-1. System Architecture.

Expected Outcomes: A successful diagram provides visible relationships and differences among ideas generated to address some issue or situation. The visibility aids observers in interpreting and understanding the meaning of, and patterns among, the ideas generated. The process of creating an affinity diagram represents a highly effective learning process for the group participants.

****

 Being Adaptable

Contributed by Dr. Arthur Shelley[996]

An **exercise** to facilitate individual and group behavioral change in support of organizational health and agility.

Supports: individual learning, behavioral modification, group learning, collaboration, problem solving, organizational health and agility

LEVEL OF EFFORT	LOW
SIZE OF ORG	SCALABLE
SCOPE OF EFFORT	WIDE

Choosing consciously works best when we apply all three aspects of capability – knowing, doing, and being – in the context of our situation. Knowing comes from reflecting on the knowledge available and determining what is most relevant. Doing comes from drawing on our skills and talents to determine how to act on that knowledge. Being is how we choose to interact with others in the context and spirit of the moment consistent with our inner self – beliefs, values, and virtues. Each of these three elements of capability can change in the moment in emergent and complex situations, which is why being adaptable is critical.

Since being adaptable is a significant part of sustained success and ongoing development, it draws on sensemaking, emotional intelligence, empathy and critical thinking, to make better judgements about which behaviors are best matched to your current situation, and when to shift from one situation to another. To do this, we use the Organizational Zoo metaphor. The OrgZoo is a collection of 27 common behaviors, each represented by an animal. OrgZoo activities use these fictional characters to explore human behavior objectively, cocreating a common understanding of what is possible and appropriate. Of course, with humans there are differences of opinion. OrgZoo distinguishes between the person and their behavior, allowing a neutral dialogue that builds relationships rather than damages them. Figures IV-2 provides visuals of the animals (representing behaviors) that are part of the OrgZoo teams.

Figure 20-2. (Left) The OrgZoo Basketball Team, (Middle) The OrgZoo Football Team; (Right) The OrgZoo Office Team. (Drawings by Mark Boyes.)

Inviting the critters into this exercise, the table below provides an example of where each critter's characteristics/behaviors would be helpful and unhelpful. Interestingly, although the behavior is the same, the outcome is different in different situations. In other words, we choose when specific behaviors are effective and when they are not, adapting to the situation at hand.

Step (1): Browse each critter and think about an example when you displayed this behavior when it was helpful, and another when it was unhelpful.

Step (2): Reflect on the outcomes from each and why this was the case.

Step (3): Practice each of these behaviors using safe conversations to familiarize yourself with them, aiming to build your confidence and competency to consciously choose to apply them when they are necessary to apply in your everyday life.

Table 20-1. Behaviors are context sensitive and situation dependent. The same behavior can produce different results.

Critter (Behavior)	Matched behavior (Helpful for context)	Mismatched behavior (Not helpful for context)
Ant	Getting things done when strong task orientation is required.	Focus on task completion when creativity and alternative thinking required.
Bee	Inclusive interactions and communication in collaborative team activities.	Aggressively defending the team despite them doing unhelpful activities.
Chameleon	Fitting into the current status quo to go with the flow.	Not challenging others when alternative options are better.
Dog	Supportive of the team with absolute loyalty.	Blindly following leadership into a crisis without critical thinking.
Eagle	Inspiring others as a role model for decisive action	Acting too swiftly when a considered decision may have been more constructive.
Feline	Ensuring productivity among team members.	Playing mind games to reinforce their own position in the hierarchy.
Gibbon	Leveraging humor to reduce tensions.	Not focusing on the key issues in a crisis.
Hyena	Networking with colleagues to ambush challenges through shared insights and resources.	Politicking to call on return favors that may compromise others.
Insect beneficial	Providing insights and experiences to accelerate resolutions.	Advocating for a particular option when a range of alternatives may work.
Insect pestiferous	Provide a variety of ideas from external sources.	Self-interested actions being advocated which may not be best options.
Jackal	Social care and emotional support for the group members.	Taking advantage of privileged position, often leveraging deferred power.
Kid	New creative (naïve) insights that stimulate	Offering naïve ideas that cause distractions for

Critter (Behavior)	Matched behavior (Helpful for context)	Mismatched behavior (Not helpful for context)
	creativity and innovation.	resolving a crisis.
Lion	Controlling processes and resources to ensure safety and productivity.	Leveraging position to force others to follow directives against their will.
Mouse	Engaging in productive work when focused and well managed.	Engaging in non-productive or even destructive activities when bored.
Nematode	Indulging oneself to relax when on holidays, so you return to work completely recharged and ready.	Almost any work situation — taking benefit without giving back is unforgivable and bound to destroy relationships and damage culture.
Owl	Mentoring others to become adaptable and knowledgeable.	Rarely, perhaps being too open and not pushing for mentees to act more quickly in important developmental needs.
Piranha	Aggressively tearing a problem apart to remove the issue.	Engaging in damaging gossip to undermine people
Quercus robur	Philanthropy and giving are almost always beneficial when well directed towards deserving recipients	Rarely, perhaps if too soft on some who may be taking benefit, but not fully deserving of the support.
Rattlesnake	Highlighting they are challenged by your presence by making a lot of noise about an issue (without striking).	Making a lot of noise about minor challenges.
Sloth	Waiting to allow things to settle for themselves, rather than blowing them up into big issues.	Not acting fast enough to correct situations before they become a bigger issue.
Triceratops	Stubbornly refusing the change things that should be maintained as is for good reason.	Stubbornly refusing to change to better approaches and good evidence to support the benefits.
Unicorn	Creatively offering very	Offering alternative ideas

Critter (Behavior)	Matched behavior (Helpful for context)	Mismatched behavior (Not helpful for context)
	different options without restraint.	that are totally disconnected from reality of the moment that are simply impractical.
Vulture	Finding weaknesses in the plan or system and taking out the weaker options before they become an issue.	Criticizing problems after they have happened (when perhaps they could have highlighted the risks earlier, in time for preventable actions).
Whale	Bring intellectual insights to the conversations, especially around specialist areas like technology, knowledge and science.	Sometimes too smart for their own good and beach themselves because of their certainty of being right.
X-Breed	Provide a range of perspectives into the conversation based on prior experiences and learning and recommend which they believe is best and why.	Overconfidence based on their multitalented capabilities and knowledge can lead them to make a limited decision that does not consider wider or longer-term implications.
Yak	Some of the greatest inventions come from errors, for example penicillin. Enthusiasm to act and see what happens can generate new insights.	Actions without appropriate reflection can cause a lot of unpredicted collateral damage, both in short term and longer term.
Snail Hidden background behaviors	Getting in to do the basic routine activities in background, without the need to be noticed or provided with kudos.	Background routines can become quite outdated and inefficient without regular review. Limited attention to such activities can become poor habit.

See also the related tool "Instinctual Harnessing" provided at the end of Chapter 16 on Knowledge Capacities.

Dr. Arthur Shelley is a collaborative community builder, multi-awarded learning facilitator and creative education designer with over 30 years of professional experience across the international corporate, government and tertiary education sectors. He is the author of 4 books, has worked in

Wes333aq12 countries, is a mentor in several international communities, and has supervised PhD candidates in 5 countries. He has collaborated with organisations as diverse as NASA, Cirque Du Soleil, Local and National Governments, Universities, start-ups, SMEs, and multinational corporations. https://www.linkedin.com/in/arthurshelley/ Contact him at Arthur@IntelligentAnswers.com.au

****

 ## TOOL: Collaborative Problem-Solving Forum

An **approach** for creating and sharing knowledge about good practices.

Supports: collaboration, problem solving, process improvement, workforce learning

LEVEL OF EFFORT	MEDIUM
SIZE OF ORG	SCALABLE
SCOPE OF EFFORT	WIDE

A forum is a periodic meeting or gathering for purposes of discussion, dialogue or debate. It is a means of sharing information, knowledge and research while focusing on common interests and challenges. A well-facilitated forum can be an excellent approach to creating and sharing knowledge about best practices. These forums can serve a variety of purposes such as solving relevant, day-to-day problems; building trust among community members by actually learning from and helping each other; and solving problems in a public forum thereby creating a common understanding of tools, approaches, and solutions. This is also an effective approach for groups to develop common standards and guidelines.

A five-step roadmap for problem solving as a means to generate new knowledge is provided below which can be used by an individual or a group. It is a variation on an approach commonly used for problem solving. This roadmap works well for best practices that can easily be reused; for example, methodologies, analytical models, diagnostic approaches, case studies, and benchmark data. The steps are: (1) Define a problem, (2) Conduct analysis, (3) Generate ideas, (4) Select a best practice or solution, and (5) Capture the knowledge in explicit form.

(1) Problem Exploration and Definition

Explore the problem and determine if additional information is needed. For example, members of the group may decide to observe specific practices, or research existing information on a topic. Methods to collect additional information might include conducting interviews with impacted individuals or subject matter experts. Jumping to a conclusion without understanding a problem can save time, but it can also waste time if you solve the wrong problem. Before jumping to the wrong conclusion, consider the following:

- Examine the problem from all angles. Try to see it from the perspective of different stakeholders.
- Separate fact from fiction. Perception is important, but it must be distinguished from fact.
- Identify key players affected by the problem. Who is responsible for solving the problem, and who has the authority to accept and implement a solution?
- Dissect or decompose the situation. Break the problem down into pieces.
- Develop a plan for gathering information. Use surveys, interviews, observations, brainstorm sessions, or benchmark reviews if needed.

Clearly defining a problem using clear, plain language is like having your finger on its pulse. Defining a problem is often more difficult than solving it. However, the right definition of a problem will make the solution much easier. A clear definition builds a strong foundation for subsequent fact finding, communication, and analysis. A good definition distills the situation into a brief, concise statement; provides key words to get to the bottom of the situation; states what a problem is rather than what it isn't; and states a problem in terms of needs, not solutions.

(2) Analysis

Typically, what you "see" is only the tip of the iceberg, or the *symptoms* of a problem rather than its root cause. It is important to distinguish cause from effect to ensure that you are actually solving the source of the problem, not just addressing its symptoms. Consider a medical analogy. You have many symptoms of the common cold, but you may, in fact, have a sinus infection that can only be cured with an antibiotic. While you are using over-the-counter cold medicines to alleviate your symptoms, the original infection continues to become worse. This is just what can happen in an organization. By addressing only the symptoms you miss the root cause, and the condition persists and may become worse.

Discovering the root cause of a problem can be tricky. Sound questioning techniques are a good start. Using your problem definition statement, answer the following questions.

- Why does the problem persist?
- Where did it start and where did it come from?
- What caused it in the first place?
- What changed right before it started?
- Why doesn't it resolve itself or just go away?

- Why do we keep getting pulled back into the situation?
- Why won't things improve no matter what we do?

Still not sure? Don't move to the solution phase until you are sure you have found the root cause. Test your tentative conclusion using the following indicators. Continue analysis until you can answer yes to each of these indicators.

☐ Dead end?	You ran into a dead end when you asked, "What caused the proposed root cause?"
☐ Conversation ends?	All conversation has come to a positive end.
☐ Feels good?	Everyone involved feels good, is motivated and uplifted emotionally.
☐ Agreement?	All agree it is the root cause that keeps the problem from resolving.
☐ Explains?	The root cause fully explains why the problem exists from all points of view.
☐ Beginnings known?	The earliest beginnings of the situation have been explored and are understood.
☐ Logical?	The root cause is logical, makes sense, and dispels all confusion.
☐ Controllable?	The root cause is something you can influence, control, and deal with realistically.
☐ Hope?	Finding the root cause has returned hope that something constructive can be done about the situation.
☐ Workable solution?	Suddenly workable solutions, not outrageous demands, begin to appear.
☐ Stable resolution?	A stable, long-term, once-and-for-all resolution of the situation now appears feasible.

Use of analytic techniques such as diagramming and process modeling can also be applied during the analysis stage. A few additional techniques for analyzing a problem are Napoleon (imagine you are someone else to gain new perspective), morphological analysis (systematically examine each attribute of the problem), create a deadline, or sleep on it (literally, writing the issue on a piece of paper beside your bed before going to bed, forgetting it, waking up in the morning and immediately writing down your thoughts).

(3)   Idea Generation

Once the root cause is identified, it is time to generate possible solutions. This is the time to be really creative. One useful way to generate a storm of ideas with a group is Brainstorming. But before generating ideas, try some creativity exercises. Von Oech offers some good exercises to get the creative juices flowing. For example, when generating ideas, try to avoid mental locks. The Ladder of Inference is one approach to use. The following are common mental locks and possible techniques to overcome them.

Mental Lock	Consider
□ The right answer	There is often more than one right answer.
□ That's not logical	Excessive logical thinking can short-circuit your creative process. Be curious and look for surprises.
□ Follow the rules	Challenge the rules. (dick Nicolosi, Philosopher: "Slaying sacred cows makes great steaks."
□ Be practical	Ask *what if* questions. Use them as stepping-stones.
□ Play is frivolous	Use play to fertilize your thinking. Make a game of it.
□ That's not my idea	Specialization limits you. Develop an explorer's attitude. Leave your own turf.
□ Don't be foolish	Foolish thinking can get you out of a rut.
□ Avoid ambiguity	Too much specificity can stifle your imagination.
□ To err is wrong	Don't be afraid to fail. (Grace Hopper, Inventor and naval Officer: "A ship in port is safe, but that's not what ships are built for.")
□ I'm not creative	Believe in the worth of your ideas.
□ I don't have time	You don't have time *not to*.

(4) Solution Selection

The goal at this point is to narrow the list of ideas into feasible, creative, and win-win alternatives. By using an objective, criterion-based method to select ideas, you will coincidentally make the decision-making process much easier in that you have defined the terms for reaching consensus. The process therefore becomes one that is fact-based and less emotionally charged.

Establishing objective criteria is similar to judging a sporting event. Olympic judges use consistent, objective criteria to evaluate the performance of athletes to select winners. In addition to *establishing* criteria, you may want to *prioritize* criteria. For example, some criteria may be mandatory while others are optional. Another technique is to set acceptable ranges. For example, if an idea meets less than 80 percent of the criteria, it will be removed from the running. If a clear winner does not emerge, identify the best and worst outcomes for each idea and/or the pros and cons of each idea. An additional step might be to validate the practice with stakeholders or peers.

For a final check, ask yourself the following questions:

- Is the good practice, or alternative, based upon good, sound reasoning and data?
- Were the right people involved in the problem-solving process?

Following this roadmap will serve to create new knowledge that can improve not only your own job but also the overall performance of your organization. Expected outcomes include improved problem resolution, team members learning how to solve problems, and reduced probability of generating poor quality solutions.

Other tools that can be utilized in the Collaborative Problem-Solving Forum include the causal loop diagram (a process for representing the cause-and-effect relationships among variables) and force field analysis (a mechanism for assessing and dealing with the various forces that aid or hinder the implementation of a program or project). Information on both can be easily pulled up via the internet.

****

☀-TOOL: Continuous Improvement Reviews

An **approach** or **process** that helps both individuals and the organization improve future performance by identifying and capturing lessons learned from the past.

Supports: problem solving; identifying, collecting and sharing lessons learned and good practices

LEVEL OF EFFORT	MEDIUM
SIZE OF ORG	SCALABLE
SCOPE OF EFFORT	WIDE

Continuous Improvement Reviews (CIRs) help people improve business performance by allowing them to (1) objectively and constructively learn from experience; (2) develop forward actions and recommendations to do things better the next time; and (3) allow others to reapply lessons learned to prevent reinvention and avoid mistakes.

Continuous Improvement Reviews ask individuals and teams to systematically and methodically answer five simple questions:

1. What did we intend to do?

2. What did we actually do?

3. Why were there differences?

4. What do we want to sustain?

5. What do we want to do differently?

6. CIRs are effective when:

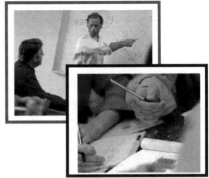

- **They are targeted at driving specific business improvements** – Since there is always room for improvement, CIRs should only be conducted when there is a specific business need.

- **Management sponsorship has been secured** – For the more complex and systemic issues, a CIR sponsor provides visible leadership by attending the wrap up meeting and validating the lessons to ensure that the learnings, forward actions and recommendations will drive targeted business results.

- **Forward actions are implemented and management recommendations are taken seriously** – CIRs are just documents if the organization does not have the discipline to reapply lessons learned and implement forward actions.

Understanding why there were differences (3 above) is very important to ensure that the individual (or teams) can determine what and how to do things differently.

Consider using a CIR when there is a clear business purpose to:

- **Capture new Learnings and Best Practices** – For example, reapply lessons to a project, team, or function when they share a common challenge such as learnings around animal models or assay development.

- **Prevent re-occurrence of an unexpected positive or negative event or issue** – For example, conduct CIRs with suppliers when they do not deliver an agreed upon service or product; unexpected toxicity issues arise; or a regulatory crisis has been successfully handled.

- **Capture innovations** – For example, conduct CIRs when performance exceeds expectations because of innovations in the science or in processes which accelerate compound development.

- **Improve a specific business process or initiative** – For example, conduct CIRs when processes are not producing the desired outcomes and need improvement, e.g., quality control, POS development, out-sourcing.

- **Improve cross-functional/cross-team/cross-site alignment and communication** – For example, conduct CIRs when a project does not move forward as anticipated due to delays in decision making, poor team communication, lack of project management, lack of alignment, etc.

- **Build into an existing activity that requires a regular debrief or presentation** – For example, conduct a CIR when a major milestone is accomplished, there is a change in development strategy, or progress is being reviewed quarterly against goals.

Seven Basic Steps

A CIR can be thought of in terms of the following seven basic steps:

STEP (1): Preparation. Prior to the CIR meeting, you will receive CIR Pre-work. Pre-work includes a draft of the meeting objectives, a project or event chronology, an assessment of the project/event outcomes and a list of "differences" issues or best practices for discussion at the meeting.

STEP (2): Ground rules. To begin the CIR, the facilitator will review the meeting ground rules and the CIR process.

STEP (3): What Did We Intend to Do? Here, the team will quickly review and obtain consensus on the project/event objectives.

STEP (4): What Did We Actually Do? Here, the team will quickly review and obtain consensus on the assessment of the project/event outcomes and/or the chronology of events. In the description of what actually happened be aware that even seemingly small things may hide root causes.

STEP (5): Why Were There Differences? Here, the team will look for the root causes for differences (issues or best practices) between the objectives and the assessment. If the process is simple this will be easy. If the process is somewhat complicated look carefully for relationships and causes that may have created the differences between the expected outcome and the actual outcome.

STEP (6): What Do We Sustain/Do Differently? Based on the conclusions drawn in Step 5, the team will develop lessons learned that will include what to keep and what to do differently. Both of these may be very important in learning from the lessons learned (LL) process.

STEP (7): Forward Actions. Finally, the team will develop forward actions and recommendations for each root cause. The focus here is to determine how we can do it "Better the Next Time." This may include not only identifying the root causes but studying them to develop an understanding of what each root cause did to change or influence the expected outcome, and how each root cause specifically created the outcome. It may happen that several root causes interacted in a way that created the unanticipated outcome.

To do it better the next time it may be necessary to identify (in addition to the root cause) the context and precise process that was used. This may be important because the LL process may be sensitive to small context changes rather than a major root cause. The conditions and context of the initial process should be carefully recorded so that they can be compared to the next application of the L2 process. This will ensure a more successful second process.

Once the cause(s) have been identified, make sure that these lessons learned are shared with others. This sharing could include how the root causes were uncovered (the investigation approach) to aid others who may be applying the same lessons learned process. Also make sure that what went well in the process is described in the lesson learned. This may be almost as important as the root cause identification.

****

 ## TOOL: Conversations that Matter

Contributed by Dr. Arthur Shelley

A **process** for facilitating co-creative conversations that matter.

Supports: planning, problem solving, knowledge sharing, group learning, creativity; innovation.

LEVEL OF EFFORT	MEDIUM
SIZE OF ORG	SCALABLE
SCOPE OF EFFORT	WIDE

A starting point to assessing our readiness to move into the future is co-creating an idea of what that future looks like. Figure 8-1 on page 170 is one of many images designed to stimulate *Conversations That Matter* around the concept of visioning the future. It is designed not to define the path, but to engage people to explore their perspectives of what the *range of paths* may be, and to share pespectives on their current point in this journey. This process occurs with the tenets of Appreciative Inquiry in mind (see Chapter 8).

It is not uncommon for people in the same organization (and even on the same team) to perceive their current position to be very different parts of this image. Experiences using this image (and others with a different focus) have demonstrated the power of exploring individually, and then in pairs or small groups, before engaging in whole group wider discussion. This maximises the range of perspectives available through divergent thinking before the convergent dialogue begins. Cycling between divergent (focusing on openly exploring and option generating) conversation and convergent interactions (focusing on merging, prioritizing and reducing ideas and concepts) enables us to optimise the outcomes. This iterative approach has been successfully adopted in several design and problem solving approaches such as Design Thinking.

The process for facilitating co-creative conversations that matter is quite simple.

STEP (1): Show the image or object in question, and …

STEP (2): *Ask* a question. The questions can be changed depending on the desired oucomes. The question can be completely open-ended, such as: "Tell me what you think about this image?" Or, it can be somewhat leading to get a different focus, such as: "Where do you think our organization fits into this image and why?"

Best results come when you ask each person to write down a few quick bullet points. (You want them to capture their initial FEELING about the question before the thinking mind begins to over analyze ... that can wait for the wider conversation.)

STEP (3): Engaging intelligent rules of etiquette for dialogue, start the wider conversation. There is an amazing set of themes that come out of such conversations. Some people inherently see the pessimistic side of their situation and highlight barriers to progress. Some do the opposite and talk of the positives, perhaps even over-estimating the quality of what is being done. Some see the component parts of the organization, while others take a more holistic or systems point of view. The key is to engage participants in exploring the reasons behind the differences to share why there are multiple perspectives. This is where the insights come from as ideas shared stimulate others to respond and new knowedge is co-created through this exchange.

The specific image itself is not the critical factor. Although Figure 1.1 has been deliberately designed to stimulate conversations around strategic leadership, knowledge and realtionships in visioning the future, it can be used for other conversations with great effect. Equally, other simpler artifacts can also trigger rich conversations. Combining a creative and out-of-context stimulant with a provocative question and open and inclusive facilitation generates optimal outcomes. All these elements leverage the diversity of views of engaged participants to create new knowledge and insights, which form the basis of new options. Synergies emerge from the connections between thoughts and ideas, and each component is critical to the richness and success of the interaction.

The key to remember about such interactions is that, as the facilitator, your aim is not to lead the participants to a predetermined outcome,but to co-create a set of options that did not exist before, and then intermix these to generate a range of options to co-create a future that does not yet exist. Now, it is time to explore the group's readiness for change.

Dr. Arthur Shelley is a collaborative community builder, multi-awarded learning facilitator and creative education designer with over 30 years of professional experience across the international corporate, government and tertiary education sectors. He is the author of 4 books, has worked in 12 countries, is a mentor in several international communities, and has supervised PhD candidates in 5 countries. He has collaborated with organisations as diverse as NASA, Cirque Du Soleil, Local and National Governments, Universities, start-ups, SMEs, and multinational corporations. https://www.linkedin.com/in/arthurshelley/ Contact him at Arthur@IntelligentAnswers.com.au

****

TOOL: Designing a Successful KM Initiative

Contributed by Dr. Michael Stankosky

A high-level **approach** for designing a successful knowledge management initiative.

Supports: planning, preparing, implementation, group learning

LEVEL OF EFFORT	MEDIUM
SIZE OF ORG	SCALABLE
SCOPE OF EFFORT	WIDE

Designing a successful KM initiative requires a systems design approach to incorporate and integrate the necessary critical elements of codification, collaboration, convergence, and coherence.

The starting point needs to be a common understanding. For purposes of this approach, we look at KM as a process for leveraging relevant knowledge resources to optimize effectiveness, efficiency, and innovation. Further, it is important to take a few minutes to review ten principles of KM as follows:

(1) Why KM? Knowledge is the raw material for producing goods and services in the 21st century.

(2) KM = strategic resource management.

(3) Name your knowledge, and it is yours to manage.

(4) If you know what and who you know, you can profit from that knowledge.

(5) Leverage knowledge by codification and collaboration.

(6) Link KM to your work.

(7) Use systems approach to engineer a KM initiative – leadership/management, organization, technology, learning.

(8) KM behaves differently than its design.

(9) Design KM from the top; build from the bottom.

(10) There is no "one size fits all" KM initiative.

This simple approach considers three aspects: input, process, and output. Strategic direction are the first inputs to consider in terms of vision/mission, goals and objectives. Once the strategic direction is clear, it is time to gather the data and information needed to support the development of knowledge, that is, the capacity to take effective action.

The process has four primary considerations: coherence, codification, convergence and collaboration. Driven by the strategic direction, coherence means implementing the business strategy throughout all layers of the enterprise. Driven by the data, information, and knowledge, codification translates into classifying, storing, retrieving, visualizing, and valuing all relevant KID (knowledge, information and data). Convergence integrates disparate functional areas, tasks, and people throughout the enterprise. Collaboration is connecting the right people with the right KID at the right time.

The output is increased efficiencies and performance, increased profits, decreased costs, and achievable metrics. See Figure IV-3 below.

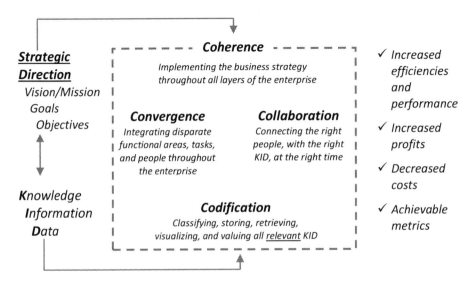

Figure 20-3. The overarching design process for a successful KM initiative.

Dr. Michael Stankosky was a Professor in Engineering Management & Systems Engineering at George Washington University (GW). He is an author, scholar, and consultant in the field of Knowledge Management (KM), General Management, Innovation, and Organizational Behavior. His latest work: *21 for 21: Leading the 21st Century Global Enterprise* has been published by the Emerald Publishing Group in April 2018. He has participated as a speaker in the Global Forum for over twenty years, on such topics as Innovation, Management, Cybersecurity, and Globalization. While on the fulltime faculty of GW, he created the 1st Masters and Doctorate for KM at a major university. These were documented in *Creating the Discipline of Knowledge Management*, and *In Search of Knowledge Management*. He also founded and directed the Institute for Knowledge & Innovation, which comprised over 80 scholars and practitioners worldwide. He is Editor Emeritus of *Vine: The Journal of Information and Knowledge Management Systems*.

****

 ## TOOL: Engaging Tacit Knowledge

A **knowledge elicitation approach** to make better use of our tacit knowledge.

Supports: collaboration, organizational learning, creativity, innovation

LEVEL OF EFFORT	CONTINUOUS
SIZE OF ORG	SCALABLE
SCOPE OF EFFORT	WIDE

Often, we do not know what we know. Tacit knowledge is that knowledge which cannot be voiced, that knowledge which is not easily conveyed to others but often serves as the origin of an intuitive nudge or "knowing" that we do not know how we know. Since tacit knowledge resides in the unconscious, Engaging Tacit Knowledge addresses the challenge of **making better use of our tacit knowledge** through creating greater connections with the unconscious, building and expanding the resources stored in the unconscious, deepening areas of resonance, and sharing tacit resources among individuals. We propose a four-fold action model with nominal curves for building what can be described as "extraordinary consciousness" within individuals. The model includes surfacing tacit knowledge, embedding tacit knowledge, sharing tacit knowledge, and inducing resonance (see Figure IV-4 below). Each of these approaches will be briefly addressed.

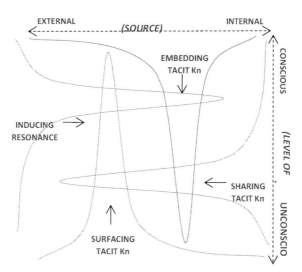

Figure 20-4. Four-prong action model for engaging tacit knowledge.

Surfacing Tacit Knowledge

The first approach is surfacing tacit knowledge. As individuals observe, experience, study and learn throughout life they generate a huge amount of information and knowledge that becomes stored in their unconscious mind. Even though an individual may have difficulty pulling it up when needed, learning how to access their unconscious – and listen to it – can become a valuable learning resource. Surfacing tacit knowledge is focused on accessing the benefit of that which is tacit by moving knowledge from the unconscious to conscious awareness. Three ways that tacit knowledge can be surfaced are through external triggering, self-collaboration, and nurturing.

As represented in Figure 1, the process of triggering is primarily externally driven with internal participation. For example, conversation, dialogue, questions, or an external situation with specific incoming information may trigger the surfacing of tacit knowledge needed to respond. The unconscious is aware of the flow of consciousness, available to affect decisions as incoming information is associated with internal information. In these cases, we would describe the knowledge surfaced from the unconscious as implicit, with externally-generated information mixing with tacit knowledge in order to create that surfaced implicit knowledge. (See the discussion on implicit knowledge in Chapter 4.) Triggering is often the phenomenon that occurs in "sink or swim" situations, where an immediate decision must be made that will have significant consequences.

Triggering can also be achieved through sound. By listening to a special song in your life, you can draw out deep feelings and memories buried in your unconscious. Sound and its relationship to humans has been studied by philosophers throughout recorded history; extensive treatments appear in the work of Plato, Kant and Nietzsche. Through the last century scientists have delved into studies focused on acoustics (the science of sound itself), psychoacoustics (the study of how our minds perceive sound) and musical psychoacoustics (the discipline that involves every aspect of musical perception and performance). Sound (as do all patterns in the mind) has the ability to change and shape the physiological structure of the brain. Neuroscience has slowly begun to recognize the capability of both internal thoughts and external incoming information (including sound) to affect the physical structure of the brain—its synaptic connection strength, its neuronal connections and the growth of additional neurons.[997]

Although collaboration is generally thought about as interactions among individuals and/or groups, there is another collaboration that is less understood. This is the process of individuals consciously collaborating with themselves. What this means is the conscious mind learning to communicate with, listen to, and trust its own unconscious. In order to build this trust, it is necessary for individuals to first recognize where their tacit knowledge is coming from. Recall that tacit knowledge is largely created from the continuous mixing of external information with internal information and stored in invariant form. This means that when you trust your unconscious you are trusting yourself, and the semantic complexing of all the experiences, learning, thoughts, and feelings throughout your life. Thus, the process of associating (learning) in your unconscious is related to life-long conscious learning experiences (see the text below on embedding tacit knowledge).

One way to collaborate with yourself is through creating an internal dialogue. For example, accepting the authenticity of and listening deeply to a continuous stream of conscious thought while following the tenets of dialogue. Those tenets would include: withholding quick judgment, not demanding quick answers, and exploring underlying assumptions,[998] *then* looking for collaborative meaning between what you consciously think and what you feel. A second approach is to ask yourself a lot of questions related to the task at hand. Even if you don't think you know the answers, reflect carefully on the questions, and be patient. Sleeping on a question will often yield an answer the following morning. Your unconscious mind processes information 24/7 and exists to help you survive. It is not a figment of your imagination, nor your enemy.

Although requiring time, openness, and commitment, there are a number of approaches readily available for those who choose to nurture their sensitivity to tacit knowledge through exploring their inner self. These include (among others) meditation, mindfulness, inner tasking, lucid dreaming, hemispheric synchronization, and flow. Other practices such as changing one's frame of reference and other Knowledge Capacities also create new ways to view problems which often lead to new creative solutions. (See Chapter 16.)

Embedding Tacit Knowledge

The second approach is embedding tacit knowledge. Although information is continuously going into our unconscious, only "significant" things (significant to the individual) stay in memory—often without our conscious awareness. Said another way, **every experience and conversation is *embedding* potential knowledge in the unconscious as it is associated with previously stored information, creating new patterns**. Thinking about embedding as a process for improving our tacit knowledge can lead to new approaches to learning, and can be considered a preparatory state for future decisions and creativity. In Figure 1, we see that embedding is both externally and internally driven, with knowledge moving from the conscious to the unconscious. Embedding knowledge in the unconscious can occur through exposure or immersion, by accident or by choice. Examples would include travel, regularly attending church on Sunday, or listening to opera and imitating what you've heard in the shower every day. Practice moves beyond exposure to include repeated participation in some skill or process, thus strengthening the patterns in the mind.

Creating tacit knowledge occurs naturally and quietly as an individual lives through diverse experiences and becomes more proficient at some activity (such as public speaking) or cognitive competency (such as problem solving). As their scope of experience widens, the number of relevant neuronal patterns increases. When an individual becomes more proficient in a specific area through effortful practice, the number of neurons needed to perform the task decreases and the remaining pattern gradually becomes embedded in the unconscious, ergo it becomes tacit knowledge. When this happens, the reasons and context within which the knowledge was created often become hidden from consciousness. Recognizing the differences among the four aspects of tacit knowledge suggests specific ways to embed knowledge. Figure 2 offers representative examples of each type of tacit knowledge (embodied, intuitive, affective, and spiritual), which are further described in Chapter 4, and suggestions for embedding each.

Embodied tacit knowledge requires new pattern embedding for change to occur. This might take the form of repetition in physical training or in mental thinking. For example, embodied tacit knowledge might be embedded through mimicry, practice, competence development or visual imagery coupled with practice. An example of this would be when an athlete training to become a pole vaulter reviews a video of his perfect pole vault to increase his athletic capability. This is a result of the fact that when the pole vaulter performs his perfect vault, the patterns going through his brain while he is doing it are the same patterns that go through his brain when he is watching himself do it. When he is watching the video, he is repeating the desired brain patterns and this repetition strengthens these patterns in unconscious memory. When "doing" the pole vault, he cannot think about his action, nor try to control them. Doing so would degrade his performance because his conscious thoughts would interfere with his tacit ability.

In the late 1990's, neuroscience research identified what are referred to as mirror neurons. As Dobb's explains,

> *These neurons are scattered throughout key parts of the brain—the premotor cortex and centers for language, empathy and pain—and fire not only as we perform a certain action, but also when we watch someone else perform that action.*[999]

When the goals of "others" in a video are understood,[1000] watching a video is a cognitive form of mimicry that transfers actions, behaviors and most likely other cultural norms. Given goal coherence, when we *see* something being enacted, our mind creates the same patterns that we would use to enact that "something" ourselves. As these patterns fade into long-term memory, they would represent tacit knowledge, both Knowledge (Informing) and Knowledge (Proceeding) (see Chapter 4). While mirror neurons are a subject of current research, it would appear that they represent a mechanism for the transfer of tacit knowledge between individuals or throughout a culture.[1001]

Figure 20-5. Embedding Tacit Knowledge.

Intuitive tacit knowledge can be nurtured and developed through exposure, learning, and practice. Intuitive tacit knowledge might be embedded through experience, contemplation, developing a case history for learning purposes, developing a sensitivity to your own intuition, and effortful practice. Effortful study moves beyond practice to include identifying challenges just beyond an individual's competence and focusing on meeting those challenges one at a time.[1002] **The way people become experts involves the chunking of ideas and concepts and creating understanding through the development of significant patterns useful for solving problems and anticipating future behavior within their area of focus.**

A study of chess players concluded that "effortful practice" was the difference between people who played chess for many years while maintaining an average skill and those who became master players in shorter periods of time. The master players, or experts, examined the chessboard patterns over and over again, studying them, looking at nuances, trying small changes to perturb the outcome (sense and response), generally "playing with" and studying these *patterns.*[1003] In other words, they use long-term working memory, pattern recognition, and chunking rather than logic as a means of understanding and decision-making. This indicates that by exerting mental effort and emotion while exploring complex situations, knowledge – such as problem-solving expertise and what some call wisdom – becomes embedded in the unconscious mind.[1004]

An important insight from this approach is the recognition that when facing complex problems which do not allow reasoning or cause-and-effect analysis because of their complexity, the solution will most likely lie in studying patterns and chunking those patterns to enable a tacit capacity to anticipate and develop solutions. This was demonstrated in the movie *A Beautiful Mind* staring Russell Crowe as a brilliant mathematician on the brink of international acclaim who becomes entangled in a mysterious conspiracy.

Affective tacit knowledge requires nurturing and the development of emotional intelligence. Affective tacit knowledge might be embedded through digging deeply into a situation – building self-awareness and developing a sensitivity to your own emotions – and having intense emotional experiences. How much of an experience is kept as tacit depends upon the mode of incoming information and the emotional tag (unconsciously) embedded with it. The stronger the emotion attached to the experience, the longer it will be remembered, and the easier it will be to recall (even when you don't want to!) Subtle patterns that occur during any experience may slip quietly into our unconscious and become affective tacit knowledge.[1005]

Spiritual tacit knowledge can be facilitated by encouraging holistic representation of the individual and respect for a higher purpose. Spiritual tacit knowledge might be embedded through dialogue, learning from practice and reflection, and developing a sensitivity to your own spirit, living with it over time and exploring your feelings regarding the larger aspects of values, purpose and meaning. Any individual or organization who demonstrates – and acts upon – their deep concerns for humanity and the planet is embedding spiritual tacit knowledge.

Sharing Tacit Knowledge

The third approach is *sharing tacit knowledge*. In our discussion above on surfacing tacit knowledge, it became clear that surfaced knowledge is new knowledge, a different shading of that which was in the unconscious. If knowledge can be described in words and visuals then this would be by definition explicit. Yet the subject of this paragraph is sharing tacit knowledge. **The key is that it is not necessary to make knowledge explicit in order to share it.**

In Figure IV-4, sharing tacit knowledge occurs both consciously and unconsciously, although the knowledge shared may remain tacit in nature. The power of this process has been recognized in organizations for years, and tapped into through the use of mentoring and shadowing programs to facilitate imitation and mimicry. More recently, it has become the focus of group learning, where communities and teams engage in dialogue focused on specific issues and, over time, develop a common frame of reference, language and understanding that can create solutions to future complex problems. These solutions may retain "tacitness" in terms of understanding the complexity of the issues where it is impossible to identify all the contributing factors much less a cause-and-effect relationship among them. Hence these solutions would not be explainable in words and visuals to individuals outside the team or community. When this occurs, the team (having arrived at the "tacit" decision) will often create a rational explanation of why the decision makes sense to communicate to outside individuals.

There is much research and literature available on knowledge sharing.

Inducing Resonance

The fourth approach toward building extraordinary consciousness is *inducing resonance*. A 2008 MQI research study found that through exposure to diverse, and specifically opposing, concepts that are well-grounded, it is possible to create a resonance within the listener's mind that amplifies the meaning of the incoming information, increasing its emotional content and receptivity. While it is words that trigger this resonance, it is the current of the search for truth flowing under that linguistically centered thought that amplifies feelings, bringing about the emergence of deeper perceptions and validating the recreation of externally-triggered knowledge in the listener.

Humans operate from a place of *yearning to know truth*. Truth – which is relative to a specific context and situation – is a living, dynamic awareness that expands our consciousness. It is the neocortex, as the organ of intelligence, that is very much concerned with updating its models of the world based on a continuous stream of incoming sensory input, ever creating new models. Connections are not fixed. As we learn, connections are strengthened; as we forget, they are weakened. Truth, trust and transparency are the outer petals of the Reblooming Knowledge Movement (RKM) model. (See Chapter 7.) Truth is also addressed in Chapter 3, and two related tools are in this section: "Truth Searching" and "Trust Mapping".

When we experience a positive reaction to someone's spoken words or written thoughts, we are experiencing a *resonance of thought*, with those ideas consistent with the rhythm of our natural frequency, that is, with our truth, beliefs and values. Through exposure to diverse, and specifically opposing, concepts that are well-grounded, it is possible to create a resonance within the receiver's mind that amplifies the meaning of the incoming information, increasing its emotional content and receptivity.

In Figure IV-4, inducing resonance is a result of external stimuli resonating with internal information to bring tacit knowledge into conscious awareness. When resonance occurs, the incoming information is consistent with the frame of reference and belief systems within the receiving individual. This resonance amplifies feelings connected to the incoming information while also validating the re-creation of this external knowledge in the receiver. Further, this process results in the amplification and transformation of internal affective, embodied, intuitive or spiritual knowledge from tacit to implicit (or explicit). Since deep knowledge is now accessible at the conscious level, this process also creates a sense of ownership within the listener. The communicators are not telling the listener what to believe; rather, when the tacit knowledge of the receiver resonates with what the communicator is saying (and how it is said), a natural reinforcement and expansion of understanding occurs *within* the listener. This accelerates the creation of deeper tacit knowledge and a stronger affection associated with this area of focus.

An approach to inducing resonance can be seen in the movie, *The Debaters*. We would even go so far as to say that the purpose of a debate is to transfer tacit knowledge. Well-researched and well-grounded external information is communicated (explicit knowledge) and tied to emotional tags (explicitly expressed). The beauty of this process is that this occurs on *both sides* of a question such that the active listener who has an interest in the area of the debate resonates with and is pulled into one side or the other. An eloquent speaker will try to speak from the audience's frame of reference to tap into related tacit knowledge. She will come across as confident, likeable and positive to transfer embodied tacit knowledge, and may well refer to higher order purpose, etc. to connect with the listener's spiritual tacit knowledge. A strong example of this occurs in the Presidential debates. This also occurs in litigation, particularly in the closing arguments, where opposing sides of an issue use emotional tags to connect to the jurors and affect their judgment.

A second approach to inducing resonance is paradoxical thinking. As we expand our understanding of the way the mind/brain works, we can now recognize that the mind is *primed to support paradoxical thinking*. A "paradox" is considered sets of inconsistent propositions with a "set" including an explicit contradiction or entailing one.[1006] Alternatively, from other viewpoint, a paradox is considered an apparently unacceptable conclusion derived by apparently acceptable reasoning from apparently acceptable premises[1007] or could be thought of as two contradictory propositions to which we are led by apparently sound arguments.[1008] This means that two "ideas" or "positions" can both be right when looked at individually, yet when looked at as a set they do not agree, that is, they can't both be right since they oppose each other.

Whether from an individual viewpoint or in a group, when coupled with humility paradoxical thinking can lead to highly creative thought. One approach to bringing paradoxical thinking into a larger context is to identify a paradox related to the specific domain of focus – when addressing an issue at hand or during a training session – and introducing that paradox in a warm-up session prior to addressing the larger issue. A second approach would be to introduce a selected (unrelated) paradox just before a meeting, then break for a few minutes, and spend 15-20 minutes at the start of the meeting soliciting thoughts from participants. Since paradoxes have been identified dating back to the early days of our Western Philosophers, and probably earlier, there are numerous texts that can serve as guides to identify paradoxes which have "taxed thinkers" from Zeno to Galileo and Lewis Carroll to Bertrand Russell."[1009] The use of paradoxical thinking helps open the door to our unconscious.

****

☀ TOOL: Event Intermediation

An **event** for which the planning process and actual event are strategically used to bring about large-scale change across an organization and its larger stakeholder group.

Supports: change management, knowledge flows, knowledge sharing, customer relations, organizational learning

LEVEL OF EFFORT	MED-HIGH
SIZE OF ORG	MED-LARGE
SCOPE OF EFFORT	WIDE

Event intermediation is the use of a planned, collaborative event to move from intention to reality. An intermediary connects knowledge seekers with knowledge sources by relating, researching, validating, reshaping, and transferring information. Planned and supported through groups, teams and communities, event intermediation is a tool for facilitating the horizontal and vertical sharing of knowledge at a point in time as part of a larger change strategy. Historically, humans work and strive to create change with only slightly visible results, then some event occurs which connects all this prior activity, and the understanding of change pushes everyone to a new strata of recognition, with the entire plain of behavior shifting upward to a new starting point. A good analogy would be the growth of bamboo. For the first four years the young bamboo plant is watered with relatively little visible evidence of growth. But during this time, out of sight, the roots are spreading, interconnecting and growing in strength. Then, during the fifth year, the bamboo plant streaks upward some 20 or more feet.

Using Appreciative Inquiry (introduced in Chapter 8) , sources within an organization are identified where desired actions are successfully occurring, and these are highlighted, widely shared and rewarded at this event. Although each of these sources may bring to the event only part of the process needed to accomplish a desired end state, collectively they provide the evidence that what is being attempted can be done, and they act as indictors of how to accomplish it, providing context to on-going activity. This is similar to the amplification and sense and response approaches in complexity thinking (see Chapter 19).

A larger event approach such as a town hall or knowledge fair provides the venue for event intermediation. An event of this nature requires wide participation of stakeholders as both presenters and participants, and coordinated, high-level planning for what must be thought of as self-organized local events. For example, in a knowledge fair this might take the form of booths where dozens of participants plan and share their stories. Unlike traditional approaches, the "booths", while supported by contracts as necessary, are hosted by employees of the company who are domain knowledge experts working with projects, systems, and innovations ALREADY OWNED OR UNDERWAY BY THE ORGANIZATION, that is, sharing what is a successful part of the organization's efforts. Simultaneously, there might be more formal presentations balanced against demonstrations on the hour, and awards programs highlighting future projectories. In a town hall format, this might mean simultaneous events such as an expert panel with an audience and live video-feed, a telethon, and a question-and-answer session being web-cast, with participants moving from one form of media to the next. Other formats include "stand-downs" or road shows, taking what is happening in the central part of the organization to distributed facilities. Stand-down is a term used in military organizations to refer to a period of time where everyone in the organization "stands-down" from their day-to-day job/requirements to focus on a significant need, event or aspect of the organization.

The event selected is then followed by development of a virtual toolkit which would include video interviews capturing the words of experts and high-level policy-makers; presentations, stories and, video clips representing each booth with points of contact; the latest research findings; dialogues from a panel discussion; resource documents; pictures of groups of people; award honorees with descriptions of their work and activity, and so forth.

Expected Outcomes include increased knowledge sharing and knowledge reuse; organization-wide change based on a large number of people having the opportunity to meet and share their interests and knowledge and to learn about knowledge initiatives being implemented by others; relationship building across the organization and larger stakeholder group; and increased resonance and coherence across the organization.

****

TOOL: Group Reflection and Inquiry Protocol (GRIP)

Contributed by Dr. WB Lee, Behavior and Knowledge Engineering Research Center, The Hong Kong Polytechnic University, Hong Kong

A **knowledge elicitation technique** for an organizational development intervention.

Supports: problem solving, business strategy formulation, group learning, knowledge capture

LEVEL OF EFFORT	MEDIUM
SIZE OF ORG	SCALABLE
SCOPE OF EFFORT	WIDE

Organizational development (OD) is the study and practice of enhancing organizational performance and effectiveness through intervention methods, bringing about changes in human processes. Examples include business process reengineering, team building, job enrichment, performance appraisal, and planning and goal setting.

Depending on the purpose for which organizational knowledge is used, it can be classified into exploitative[1010] (propositional and practical knowledge including statements, know-how and skills engaged in problem-solving activities[1011]) and judgmental[1012] (beliefs, views, opinions, and perceptions that are contextual and value dependent[1013]). While there are many knowledge engineering techniques focused on the extraction of exploitative, procedural or practical knowledge, the judgmental knowledge needed from stakeholders in order to form the basis of a diagnosis in an OD intervention can be difficult to elicit. The GRIP process is specifically focused on that gap.

Both executive-level and mid-level staff are engaged in a storytelling session and a sense-making session to attain an OD comprehensive view from varying perspectives. As sense-making devices, stories and narratives convey meaningful context to recipients,[1014] while organizations serve as interpretation systems,[1015] the process through which meaning is given in order to guide actions. The GRIP methodology embodies these theoretical concepts in a group setting, providing the context to extract judgmental knowledge. See figure below.

There are three phases in the elicitation process: (1) Unstructured narrative interviews of the top executives, (2) Sensemaking Workshop with its mid-level staff, and (3) Alignment Workshop to formulate the business strategy. Each is described below.

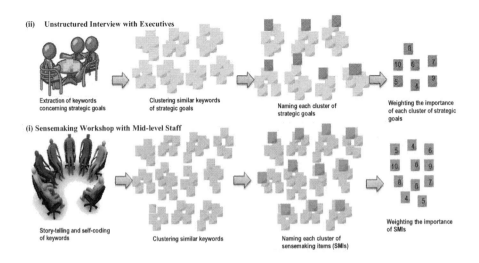

Figure 20-6. The GRIP methodology.

Unstructured Narrative Interviews with Top Executives

The starting point for the methodology is an unstructured narrative interview with executive staff with the intent of extracting both the strategic goal and vision for sustainable organizational development. Respondents are asked to share recent stories regarding organizational happenings, which trigger thoughts about how to manage in the future. As these stories are being told interviewees in the group are asked to jot down keywords related to the strategic goals on post-it notes. When the interview is concluded, these notes are examined and clustered (per similarity of meaning) by the executive staff, with names given to each cluster, which now represent major strategic goal themes. Importance weightings on a scale of 1-10 are also assigned to each cluster.

Sensemaking Workshop with Mid-Level Staff

A similar process is conducted with mid-level staff in a workshop, who are first invited to tell workplace-related stories, then to interpret those stories, writing down their views and feelings on "post-it" notes, hereafter called "Sensemaking Items" (SMIs).[1016] Sensemaking is literally gaining understanding and attributing meaning to something. SMIs are then collected and randomized on a large paper, with workshop participants moving the post-it notes around and grouping the SMIs into meaningful clusters, becoming stable after a few rounds of arbitration. The group then gives each cluster a name (hereafter called themes) representing what has emerged from the self-organization process. These too are weighted in terms of importance on a scale of 1-10.

Alignment Workshop to Formulate Business Strategy

The next step is to conduct an alignment workshop to map the major strategic goals from the executive workshop with the sensemaking items (SMIs) from the mid-level workshop. This will identify the types of operational concerns that need to be addressed to achieve the strategic goals of the company. Each strategic goal is placed in the first horizontal row of a large table (part I in Figure 20-7), and the SMIs are placed in the first vertical column of the same table (part ii in Figure 20-7). The staff then reviews the SMIs in each row to determine whether they are relevant with each strategic goal.

	Strategic Goal 1	Strategic Goal 2	......	Strategic Goal n
Sensemaking Item 1	Blocker Enabler		Blocker Enabler	
Sensemaking Item 2	Blocker Enabler	Blocker Enabler		Blocker Enabler
Sensemaking Item 3		Blocker Enabler	Blocker Enabler	
Sensemaking Item 4		Blocker Enabler	Blocker Enabler	
Sensemaking Item 5	Blocker Enabler	Blocker Enabler		
......	Blocker Enabler	Blocker Enabler		
Sensemaking Item n			Blocker Enabler	Blocker Enabler

Figure 20-7. Alignment Table.

If they think there is relevance, a sticker is placed on the box vertically under the strategic goal and horizontally beside the SMIs (part iii in Figure 20-7). Each colleague is limited to placing a maximum of three stickers in each row of SMI so as to prioritize which strategic goal each SMI is most closely aligned.

After completion of the alignment table, the facilitator sums up the number of stickers horizontally and vertically to reveal the score of correlation between strategic goals and staff concerns (part iv in Figure IV-7). The horizontal row with the highest number of stickers represents the SMI which is most relevant to the strategic goals. More resources should be invested to improve the effective functioning of this SMI so as to achieve the organization's strategic goals. The vertical column with the highest number of stickers represents the strategic goals which are most relevant to the SMIs raised by frontline staff.

This particular strategic goal attracts more operational attention and is more relevant to the concerns of colleagues. Higher synergic effects will be harvested if management can make improvements in the areas of strategic goals which also yielded support from the operational level.

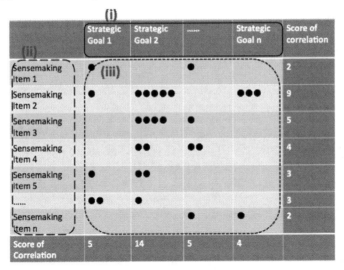

Figure 20-8. Strategic Map for Organizational Development.

The top three or four SMIs with the highest scores are then discussed by mid-level staff. The discussion topic will be (1) what blockers (inclusive of difficulties, concerns, misalignment amongst resources, etc.) colleagues have encountered in the various aspects of the SMIs, and (2) the enablers needed to ease the effect of blockers discussed in (1). Following the discussion, the blockers and enablers are placed in the boxes of the alignment table with corresponding vertical strategic goals and horizontal SMIs forming an OD strategic map. The OD strategic map (Figure 3) summarizes the blockers to be addressed and the enablers to be actioned in order to achieve the organization's strategic goals. Through such a process, participants aim to reach common understanding of their judgmental knowledge, fostering good will and consensus in pursuit of shared objectives.[1017]

Dr. Rongbin W.B. Lee is Professor Emeritus in the Department of Industrial and Systems Engineering of The Hong Kong Polytechnic University and founding Head of the Partner State Key Laboratory of the University. He had been President of the Hong Kong Chapter of the Institution of Electrical Engineer (UK) and had served as the President of the Hong Kong Association for the Advancement of Science and Technology. He was the ex-chief editor of the Journal of Information and Knowledge Management Systems (Emerald) as well as the chief editor emeritus of the International Journal of Knowledge and Systems Science (IGI Global). Prof. Lee is now the Chairman of the International Committee of the Global MIKE Award. He has published more than 250 papers in referred journals and three books. He may be contacted at wb.lee@polyu.edu.hk

****

 TOOL: Human-Machine Decision Analytics Tool

A decision tool developed by Art Murray, Applied Knowledge Sciences, Inc.

An **approach** for human-machine interaction in the decision-making process.

Supports: decision-making, organizational productivity

LEVEL OF EFFORT	HIGH
SIZE OF ORG	SCALABLE
SCOPE OF WORK	WIDE

The continued explosive growth of human knowledge, along with recent acceleration in the growth of machine knowledge, led to the current situation along with its many challenges and opportunities. (See Figure IV-9.) AI is here to stay. Machines do what they do best (computation). Humans do what they do best (intuition, creativity, foresight, insight, etc.). Together we accomplish more than either one could do by working alone. Thus, it just makes sense to explore how Organizations can best engage AI in support of their mission and vision.

We are still in the early stages of this evolutionary trajectory, which will likely take technology, the human neurophysiology, society, and even human consciousness, to ever-higher levels. Figure IV-10 on the next page shows how the human path and the machine path come together in the decision process to emerge actions/recommendations, including correcting biases and misalignment.

[See the end of the Afterword as an example of human-machine interaction, what might be called AAI, that is, Augmented Artificial Intelligence.]

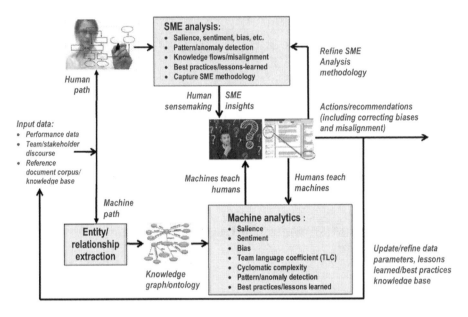

Figure 20-9. The desired Human-Machine end state.

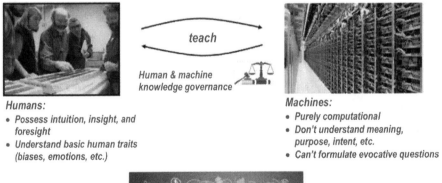

Humans:
- *Possess intuition, insight, and foresight*
- *Understand basic human traits (biases, emotions, etc.)*

Machines:
- *Purely computational*
- *Don't understand meaning, purpose, intent, etc.*
- *Can't formulate evocative questions*

More powerful together

Figure 20-10. Human-Machine Decision Analytics Tool
© 2023 Applied Knowledge Sciences, Inc.
(Permission to distribute granted, with attribution)

About Dr. Art Murray: For over 40 years, Art Murray's passion has been getting people to draw out their deeply hidden knowledge so they and others can benefit from it and grow it. He has done this for hundreds of organizations, large and small, public, private, and nonprofit, all around the world. His current focus is on building and curating digital bodies of knowledge, human and machine knowledge governance, and developing systems in which humans teach machines and machines teach humans, including a system for detecting and responding to weak signals in large, complex projects and organizations. For added insights, check out Art's books on *Human Deep Learning* and *The Enterprise of the Future*, and his bi-monthly series: "The Future of the Future" at kmworld.com. Art may be contacted at amurray@aksciences.com

****

 ## TOOL: Humility as a Choice

A truth-seeking **process** providing the opportunity for listening, reflecting, learning and expanding.

Supports: individual learning, decision-making, creativity

LEVEL OF EFFORT	LOW
SIZE OF ORG	SCALABLE
SCOPE OF EFFORT	WIDE

Simple, yet profound, the conscious choice of humility is a powerful tool for the discovery of truth. The greatest barriers to learning and change are egotism and arrogance, which are fundamental difficulties in a rapidly-developing, mentally-focused business environment. Egotism says, "I am right." When egotism advances to arrogance, it says, "I am right. You are wrong. And I don't care what you think or say." As can be seen, egotism shuts the door to learning, and arrogance ceases to listen to or consider others at all, which is necessary for the discovery of truth as well as growth and expansion of an individual or organization. Since others are irrelevant and largely non-existent, an arrogant individual often does not care what harm is inflicted on others.

Both egotism and arrogance increase the forces being produced. Conversely, humility opens the self to others' thoughts and ideas, providing an opportunity for listening, reflecting, learning and expanding, and the discovery of new truths. Humility is the choice of letting things be new in each moment.

STEP (1): To develop humility, first *open your mind* to accept that, by nature, at this point of development human beings have egos and desires, both of which can have strong emotional tags connected to them. It can be quite difficult for an individual to recognize egotism and arrogance in themselves. Remember, the personality, not the self, is often in control, so the individual may or may not be aware of their projection or position. This is potentially true of the individual with whom you are interacting, as well as yourself.

STEP (2): Second, *assume the other is right*. Set aside personal opinions and beliefs for the moment, accept what is being said, this idea or concept, and reflect on this new perspective in the search for truth. While this may prove quite difficult for an individual who is highly dependent on ego and arrogance to survive in what can be a challenging world, almost every individual has someone or something they love more than themselves. Try imagining that this new idea is coming from that someone whom you love, or emerging from something that you love. This simple trick will help increase your ability to engage humility.

STEP (3): Adopting this new idea or concept, *try to prove it is right*, pulling up as many examples as you can and testing the logic of it. If all the examples you can pull up fit this new perspective, then you have discovered a new level of truth. If the examples contradict the concept, then bring in your ideas and test the logic of those. Again, if the examples do not all fit, continue your search for a bigger concept that conveys a higher level of truth. The critical element in this learning approach is giving up your way of thinking so that you can understand thoughts different than your own, discovering new truths. You can compare the various concepts, asking which is more complete.

One issue that may emerge is the inclination for people to think how they feel first, then think about the logical part to determine truth. The "feeling" has already colored their higher conceptual thinking, which may result in it being untrue. It is necessary for us to develop a new sense of self that does not require us to be right in order to feel good about our self.

STEP (4): Once we come to a conclusion, we need to take action. It is time to affirm our incorrectness as appropriate to those with whom we have potentially lacked humility, and to *show gratitude for them sharing their thoughts with us*. Note that the expression of appreciation and gratitude reduces forces. It is not enough to say that you were wrong, *nor is that an important issue*. What *is* important is to acknowledge that someone else is right, and that you are appreciative of learning from them.

STEP (5): Finally, *ensure that your motive for adopting humility is your search for truth*. Motive eventually comes out, and the wrong motive will defeat the purpose at hand. In this search for truth, you are using mental discipline to develop greater wisdom. It is difficult to overcome the urge to "look good" and to be "righter" than others. But remember, when we are "full" there is no room for new thought. When choosing humility as part of our learning journey, we discover that it is not about being right, rather it is about the continuous search for a higher truth.

****

TOOL: Innovation Structuring Process

Contributed by Dr. Mark Boyes, Lecturer, RMIT Graduate School of Business and Law, Australia

A **process** to ensure structure for and sustainability of innovation.

Supports: planning, organizational learning, innovation

LEVEL OF EFFORT	WIDE
SIZE OF ORG	SCALABLE
SCOPE OF EFFORT	WIDE

The pursuit of innovation is often viewed as an unstructured set of unimpeded activities with little or no order or preparation needed. The truth is, innovation requires a structured process from beginning to end. To help decide the appropriate model, we first must answer some questions.

- What is our purpose/strategic objectives?

- Who are we doing this for?

- At a high-level what is the opportunity?

- What is the scope of the project?

- Who is on the team and are there any capability gaps?

- What level of investment are we considering?

- And finally, but most importantly who will realise the value?

Once these questions are suitably retorted, the choice of innovation process from the 3.7 billion Google results will depend on the situation. Whether you choose a 10 or 6-Step process – or something completely different – will depend on what is the best fit for the situation. However, the author has witnessed many teams skipping or glossing over the early steps of discovery, which leads to frustration, rework and, at times, complete failure. Regardless of the approach chosen, SUCCESS WILL LARGELY DEPEND ON ADEQUATE PREPARATION.

Applying the Process

Kicking off a project might adopt a process like this Design Thinking model from Liedtka and Ogilvie:[1018]

What is? This stage is all about discovery through research, where we develop a deep understanding of the problem we are trying to solve. This phase avoids looking too far into the future so as not to cloud the view of the current state. It is, at this point, that most initiatives are won or lost. Not until the problem is triangulated can we truly look at it with fresh eyes and generate innovative ideas.

What if? This stage is akin to brainstorming. It should be highly creative, fun, and generative, producing a mountain of ideas that can be built upon and converged into robust concepts that can be assessed, prototyped, and developed. The trick with this phase is having the right facilitation. There is no point putting the most creative people in the room without the right stimulus and method for collecting, grouping, and selecting ideas.

What wows? In this stage we test the future in the present. This is about testing and validating the key assumptions. This phase can include physical and non-physical experiments that provide feedback and data collection. For example, prototyping is a great way to show a group of customers what your solution might look like and get real-time input into the design process.

What works? Now we are at the business end of the process, separating innovation from invention. Invention is the creation of a novel idea and innovation requires the creation and realization of value. With all the lessons learned from the previous stages, we narrow our attention onto the best and most feasible idea, the idea that will create the most value with ease of implementation. A matrix like Figure supports this process.

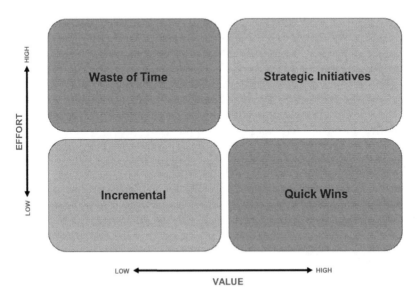

Figure 20-11: Value Effort Matrix

Non-Disruptive Design Doing

With the innovation process near to completion, an investment decision is required to build and scale the *fully researched and tested idea.* If the time is right, a "go" decision will usually lead to a program of works to design, build, test and implement the initiative. At this point we shift from **Design Thinking** to **Design Doing**. While moving beyond the theoretical aspects of design thinking can be challenging, the level of preparation required to get to this stage is vital. It reduces risks, tests assumptions, avoids misinterpreted requirements and ensures the chosen idea has every chance of creating the value that the investment case says it will.

Without a robust and suitable innovation process, it is likely the project will become a talent show, where the best ideas are pitched without robust research or deep understanding of the problem they are claiming to solve. Idea selection may come down to who is the best presenter on that day, or who has the best-looking slide deck. The well-intentioned project sub-committee, who are oblivious to the lack of preparation, select the best ideas for implementation. After the show, the project might well be on the path to failure or miss prized opportunities.

Design thinking combined with design doing aims to create meaningful and impactful solutions that address complex challenges while considering the needs and aspirations of the people who will interact with the product or service. Adding the layer of sustainable innovation ensures that the impact on the environment, industry and the economy is a positive one.

A non-disruptive approach keeps the focus on solving the problem while ensuring the solution was fit for purpose that led to the creation of value, often without the need to disrupt and kill off other companies. There are some clear examples of non-disruptive, market-creating innovations that have created immense value. For example, Micro-Finance enabled lending to lower socio-economic communities, with whom the big banks had no interest in dealing with. These innovations start where the service ends, and, in some cases, before it began. This shift in thinking from disruptive to sustainable innovation is a modern twist with a corporate responsible attitude that creates new economic activity without a path of destruction and chaos.

Non-disruptive innovation is vital for established businesses to stay relevant in their respective markets and evolve in response to emerging trends and opportunities. While it may not create the buzz and hype that we witnessed in recent times, it plays a crucial role in sustaining growth, driving progress, ensuring long-term success, and ultimately shaping the world we live in. So, next time you work on an innovation project, take some time to consider all the phases of the process, including sustainability and ensuring the world is left a better place.

Dr. Mark Boyes holds an Executive MBA (Distinction) and a PhD in Innovation. He has over 20 years of leadership experience in diverse project teams, information technology, business transformation and innovation. He has also been a Lecturer in Technology, Innovation Strategy, and Design Thinking at RMIT's Graduate School of Business and Law. Mark has co-developed several of the world's first technologies and more recently is leading multi-million-dollar and award-winning digital health projects.

****

TOOL: Interrupted Case Study

Contributed by Dr. Joyce Avedisian, Avedisian Consulting

A **real-time interactive process** to focus on specific challenges (either retrospectively or prospectively) to explore solutions.

Supports: problem solving, good practices, organizational learning, networking, lessons learned, future decision-making

LEVEL OF EFFORT	MEDIUM
SIZE OF ORG	SCALABLE
SCOPE OF EFFORT	WIDE

Case studies have been used to educate students in law, business, and medicine for decades. In the last twenty years they have been used to instruct students in the basic sciences. The strength of the method is that it presents real world problems to students with that learning occurs in context, defined as *stories with an educational message*. It is the story that provides a hook into the material and captures the interest of the audience. The method has great potential to serve as an educational model to deal with issues of importance in a diversity of organizations.

The "Interrupted Case Study" approach is specific to the organization, that is, a "story" that is specific to, and has happened, to the organization, noting that this is a "good practice" and "lessons learned" opportunity such that what is being shared offers the potential for future decision-making.

STEP (1): Discovering the Lessons

The first step is to define the learning that needs to occur, that is, the purpose and objectives of the case study, and *what* to communicate. This means defining the topic and actual challenges related to the topic which are timely and relevant in the day-to-day world of the participants. If this learning relates to a past or present decision-point in the organization, then that would be the desired case study to use.

Once the *what* is defined, the next step is to determine, with some degree of specificity, just *who* within the organization possesses the knowledge we seek. Lab workers? Middle managers? Project leaders? Senior executives? A cross-section of these people? It is important to identify all possible types of people who are involved in the story or affected by it, e.g., the key stakeholders.

STEP (2): Capturing the Lessons

Methodology: The most common methodology for capturing information for case studies is one-on-one interviews, although sometimes group interviews are conducted. The interviews should focus on identifying the major problems which the case highlights, the story surrounding those problems, and the relevant data needed for problem-solving.

It is also helpful, prior to the interviews, to do research to learn about the background of the story from documentation, reports, meeting minutes, e-mail communication, etc. What is particularly helpful is to develop a history or story line, which identifies the date the story begins and key events and turning points in the story. This sets the context in which the story and the problems and 'lessons learned' associated with it can be better understood.

Media: Interviews are usually recorded and later transcribed to capture the information verbatim. Additional media may be used such as videotaping the interviews. The primary media for case studies is a written story followed by questions related to resolving the problems presented. The written case study can be complemented and enlivened by excerpts from a videotaped or an audiotaped interview in a workshop setting. (This material also has usefulness on the web).

STEP (3): Refining the Lessons

The first part of step three in refining the lessons is to identify 1-3 major challenges based on the data collected. The case study focuses on these major challenges.

The second part of step three is to decide what type of case study format to use, based on the objectives of the case and the target audience. The method that seems most likely to be of use to Sanofi-Aventis is the Interrupted Case Study Method. In this approach the audience is presented with a short scenario with data, and a dilemma to be solved. Then, by working in small groups, the participants discuss strategies and offer tentative solutions to solve the dilemma. (*Challenge 1*) Then they are presented with additional information, leading to a second challenge question(s) (*Challenge 2*) and they evaluate the situation and decide what to do. Again, the facilitator gives more information, and again the group decides next steps (*Challenge 3*). The cycle is repeated until a final conclusion is reached. The value of this approach is that it mimics what happens in the real world when people are forced to deal with uncertainty and inadequate information and still must make decisions, which may be modified in light of further discoveries. This technique seems particularly applicable to the decision-making process that occurs as a pharmaceutical product passes through the stages in the value chain. As part of the process, principles or generalizations, based on 'lessons learned' from the Case, are extracted and can be applied in situations which the participants face. (See the flow chart below for a summary of these steps).

Dr. Clyde Herreid, a leading international expert, on the use of case studies for scientific audiences defines the elements of a good case as follows:[1019]

1. A good case tells a story
2. A good case is set in the past 5 years.
3. A good case creates empathy with the central characters.
4. A good case includes dialogue.
5. A good case is relevant to the reader.
6. A good case serves a teaching function.
7. A good case requires dilemmas to solve.
8. A good case has generality.
9. A good case is short.

The best approach is to write the case from the viewpoint of one person, and to write challenge questions at the end of each section. Herreid also explains several other issues to consider when writing a case.

1. *Target audience* – For whom is the case intended; what is their background; and why would they be interested in such an experience?
2. *Objectives* – What are the concepts that you want to focus on in the case? What is it that you wish to achieve by this particular case for this particular audience?
3. *Teaching Format* – What method is best to present the case? Should you use a discussion method, small groups, public hearing, debate, etc.?
4. *Product* – What do you wish the audience to produce as a result of this case? A report? An action plan? In other words, how will the lessons learned be demonstrated?

5. *Resources* – What are the resources the audience will need in the course of analyzing the case? Data? Reports? Lab results?

6. *Assessment* – How will you know you have accomplished your objectives?

What will the participants be able to do after the case that they could not do before? How will you communicate (share) this assessment of success to external and internal communities of interest?

There are two major ways to write a case: (1) You start with a good story. Then, you look for the principles (lessons to be learned) that will emerge from a deep understanding of the story. These principles must be embedded in the story in a way that they will be discovered, understood, and processed by the audience. And (2) You start with the principles that you wish to teach and then you look for a story or create one to teach. Whichever method you choose, you will have to do research, collect data, write the case in an engaging way, try the case out, revise and rewrite until you are satisfied with the result.

The fourth step in refining the 'Lessons Learned' is to write Case Teaching Notes composed of the following categories defined by C. Herreid.[2] An instructor can prepare any new case more rapidly, using this roadmap.

1. Case Overview and Background
2. Objectives of the Case
3. Major Issues
4. Classroom Management
   - How to run the case in the classroom
   - Pre-class assignments
   - Questions to facilitate discussion
   - Blackboard Work
   - Follow-up Assignments
5. References

STEP (4): Communicating/Applying the Lessons

There are four major ways that cases (stories) can be delivered to an audience: (1) lecture; (2) discussion, (3) small group, and (4) individual, one-on-one presentation.

All four modes of delivery are enhanced by face-to-face interaction in a workshop setting. However, when face-to-face interaction is not feasible, a workshop can be videotaped in one site and used in another site. Or, for live global participation in a workshop setting, videoconferencing or web-meeting technology such as Net Meeting can be used.

A critical factor is the facilitator(s). A good rule of thumb is to have a subject matter expert co-facilitate with a process facilitator. Together, they can ask the right challenging and provocative questions and elicit answers which foster a deep level of understanding. They also enable participants to develop and analyze their solutions so that they come up with the best possible solution. Finally, they help participants to extract 'lessons learned' in the form of principles which can be applied in other situations. The ultimate test of a good facilitator is how they foster the application of the principles by the participants in meeting scientific and business objectives.

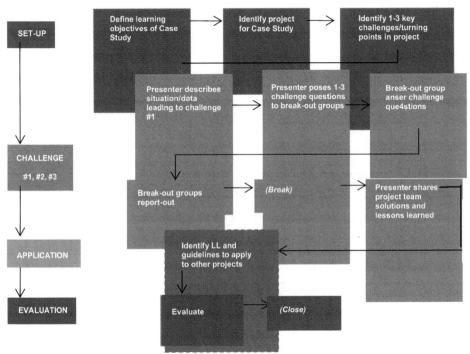

Figure 20-12. Interrupted Case Study Flow Chart.

Dr. Joyce Avedisian-Riedinger is the founder and President of Avedisian Management Consultants. She helps business leaders in all size companies build high performance, customer-focused, and innovative cultures based on values which enhance humanity. Joyce has worked with businesses in the U.S. and in Europe for over 30 years as an executive coach, consultant, and speaker. She works at the C-suite, team and organization levels. Joyce is the co-author of *Reflecting God's Character in Your Business* and *The Course of Knowledge: A 21st Century Theory*, and author of numerous articles on values. She is a lover of the arts, and wants to increasingly integrate the arts into her workshops. Joyce active engages in bicycling, hiking, and swimming. She holds a Ph.D. in Organizational Behavior.

****

TOOL: Knowledge and Innovation Management System (KIMS)

Developed and contributed by Dr. Rajat K, Baisya, President, Project and Technology Management Foundation; Chairman and Managing Director, Strategic Consulting Group Pvt Ltd., India

A **model** to assess the maturity level of innovation in your organization.

Supports: strategic planning, organizational learning, knowledge sharing, innovation, collaboration

LEVEL OF EFFORT	SCALABLE
SIZE OF ORG	SCALABLE
SCOPE OF WORK	WIDE

Industry 4.0 and the pandemic have changed business models and revenue models of many industry verticals and industry is still grappling with this challenge. New generation technologies including AI, machine learning, IoT, block chain technology, robotics, nanotechnology, genomics etc. are redefining products and services. Product life cycles are getting compressed, product failure rates are increasing, regulatory compliance requirements becoming more stringent and escalating, ESG criteria and other societal pressures are becoming key guiding criteria and, in that environment, customers are now more discerning, discriminating and demanding as they have many choices. In terms of today's fiercely competitive business environment, innovation and value creation in business is the key imperative to survive and grow.

Key tasks of organizations in this context when customer bargaining power and customer acquisition cost are high is to retain existing customers by delivering superior value in relation to their own competitive set. Becoming cost competitive and increasing the benefits in their products and services thus are no longer a choice or option, but the key imperative for survival.

In the ever-expanding global knowledge economy, organizations need to create a culture and innovation infrastructure for bold innovations and creations to routinely happen. Organizations are increasingly competing on products and services quality to meet the market demand. The focus now has to shift from incremental innovation to redefining the customers need for the future and direct organization-wide innovation program to remain aligned with the new realities. This calls for managing innovation for effectiveness. And for that, businesses need to create, collect, capture and process information for quality decisions.

Acquire new knowledge, collaborate and co-create as well as adopt new technologies.

There are many tools, frameworks, models being used by practitioners and researchers to manage these knowledge and innovation challenges. While many prove useful, it is critical to look at knowledge and innovation management as a system to link performance with the basic intrinsic strengths of the businesses at various stages of evolution taking a practitioner's perspective. This has been shown in Figure 20-13.

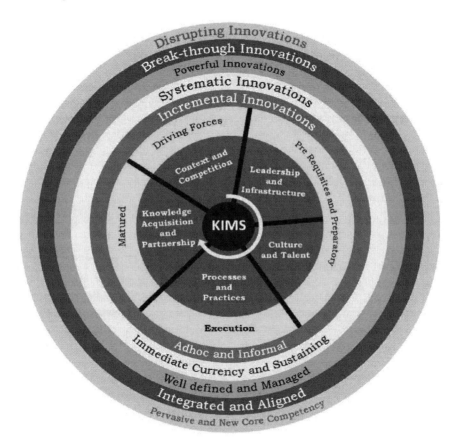

Figure 20-13. Knowledge and Innovation Management System (KIMS). (Used with permission. Copyright by Rajat K. Baisya.)

Innovation Framework

Keeping practitioners' perspectives in mind, the Innovation management framework as proposed has been designed to help businesses manage their responses to the challenges that they are facing. This helps businesses make informed decisions based on alternative scenarios and insights into potential options. The framework suggests a set of tools and practices to generate and evaluate ideas and develop products and services in line with the future needs of identified customers to remain relevant in the market.

This framework takes into consideration five basic building blocks: **context and competition, leadership and infrastructure, culture and talent, processes and practices, and knowledge acquisition and partnership.** These are the essential success criteria for any innovation to happen. The efficiency and effectiveness of these building blocks will determine the success of the initiative in any enterprise. These building blocks are not separate, but work together. For example, leaders have to nurture (and example) the basic culture and environment of trust, empathy and freedom to the talent that the leader hires, who can then add value by reducing cost and/or increasing the benefits from the products and services of the corporation through creative processes and best practices.

At the initial KIMS stage, the corporation will be showing gradual and sporadic performance which can be described as ad-hoc and informal and, with the continuous support of leadership, innovations at this level become incremental. The next level of maturity in the KIMS system is described as immediate currency and sustaining, with the expected outcome of regular and sustaining as the system moves to the next level of maturity, which is "powerful" since it is well defined and managed, giving the corporation a competitive edge in the market place. For the next two levels of KIMS maturities, the corporation needs to take a quantum jump in terms of processes, new knowledge acquisition, collaboration, and co-creation forging synergic and symbiotic alliances and partnerships. Organizations during these two phases will be in possession of unique, proprietary, and break through knowledge in their own area of business to show a new direction aligned with future customer requirements. The innovations at these stages will thus fall into the categories of break-through (radical) and disrupting innovations, helping the corporation to redefine their business models and create new products and services for which they will be the natural owners and leaders. Corporations will acquire new competencies in this context, and innovation is pervasive and fully integrated into the system, with the whole organization at this stage of maturity working together in resonance and coherence.

Innovation Maturity Model

The five stages of maturity of innovation management in the KIMS model are detailed below. The descriptions can be used to evaluate where your organization is focused in terms of innovation maturity, as well as offer ideas on how to move to the next level of maturity.

1. Ad hoc and Informal. At the ad hoc and informal level, knowledge management practices are not structured, rather sporadic and unstructured. The knowledge primarily remains as implicit or tacit knowledge within the mind of the learned and knowledgeable individuals who help the business create small incremental and gradual innovations. The overall approach to innovation is not consistent and focused on narrow organizational issues.

2. Immediate Currency and Sustaining. While business units and departments share good practices and processes, nothing has yet been standardized at the enterprise level. Selective business units, which are in focus for their importance in terms of the dependence on organizational performance, demonstrate a regular and sustained level of innovations. Systematic innovations are created at regular intervals at this level.

3. Well defined and Managed. Processes, methods and tools are all standardized and formalized across the organization. Best practices are shared, and strategies and actions are focused on business results. The organization establishes and sustains clear policies, procedures, and guidelines for knowledge management. Organizations also produces powerful (in the context of offered products and processes) and significant (in terms of level of improvement and having a novel nature to the market) innovations at this stage.

4. Integrated and Aligned. In this stage, knowledge management practices have become embedded into the organization's culture and daily operations. Knowledge sharing and collaboration are actively encouraged and supported. Continuous improvement and innovation emerging from knowledge management practices are emphasized at this level, and there is integration with other business processes and systems such as performance management, learning and development. Organizations also achieve some major and minor breakthrough innovations impacting the business in terms of competitive advantage.

5. Pervasive and New Core Competency. This level represents the highest level of knowledge and innovation management maturity. At this stage, knowledge management is fully integrated into the organization's culture, processes, and systems. Knowledge is shared across the organization and the organization continuously learns, adapts, and leverages knowledge for strategic advantage. There is a strong focus on innovation, learning, and leveraging knowledge for competitive advantage. Collaboration and co-creation are emphasized for speed of innovation, and knowledge sharing and innovation become ingrained into the organization's culture. Disruptive innovation may emerge at this stage of maturity.

The five-stage innovation maturity model is shown in Figure 20-14.

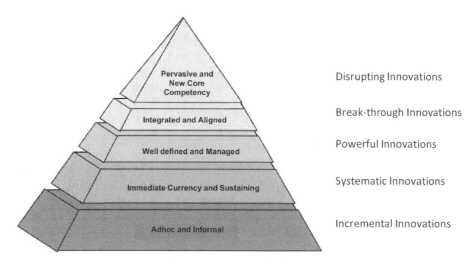

Figure 20-14. Knowledge and Innovation Management Maturity Model. (Used with permission. Copyright by Prof. Rajat K. Baisya.)

Prof Dr. Rajat K Baisya is an accomplished consultant of international repute working for global corporations with decades of leadership experience in large organizations and multinationals in a global environment. He is one of the few who has spent decades in industries like United Breweries Group and Reckitt and Colman and many more, and also served on the Board of Directors of many companies across India, then moving into academia teaching in India and Europe. Rajat Baisya is the Former Professor & Head, Department of Management Studies at Indian Institute of Technology, Delhi and he also taught in China. Currently, Rajat Baisya is the President of Project & Technology Management Foundation (www.ptmfonline.com; info@ptmfonline.com) and CEO of an online platform for consultants: www.winningsparrow.com. His current interest is in the areas of technology, and project and innovation management.

****

☀ TOOL: Knowledge Audit

Developed and contributed by Dr. W.B. Lee, Behavior and Knowledge Engineering Research Center, The Hong Kong Polytechnic University, Hong Kong

A **methodology** for discovering and mapping out an organization's knowledge assets in an open and participative manner.

Supports: organizational assessment, strategic planning, succession planning, decision-making, knowledge sharing, knowledge capture, knowledge retention, organizational learning

LEVEL OF EFFORT	HIGH
SIZE OF ORG	SCALABLE
SCOPE OF WORK	WIDE

STOCKS (Strategic Tool to Capture Critical Knowledge and Skills) – developed by the Knowledge Management Research Centre of the Hong Kong Polytechnic University – is a systematic, contextual and action-oriented, integrated knowledge audit methodology. Using input from both interactive workshops and structured questionnaires, STOCKs maps out an organization's knowledge assets in an open and participative manner. There are seven phases: (1) process prioritization and selection; (2) STOCKS form filling; (3) workflow study and STOCKS workshop; (4) knowledge inventory; (5) data analysis; (6) interviews and data validation; and (7) recommendations.

Phase 1, the selection and prioritization of critical business processes, provides the opportunity to understand the criticality of specific knowledge. All knowledge is not equal. The prioritization process is explored through two lenses: the impact on the organization if knowledge is lost, and knowledge retention. For example, if knowledge is lost it may impact supply reliability, service provision to customers, asset performance, safety, and costs. Knowledge retention issues might include a high chance of losing the expertise, which could be due to key personnel near retirement age, a limited number of employees with this specific knowledge, a high market demand for this knowledge, or a high tacit to explicit knowledge ratio. It would follow that it may be difficult to hire in the current market. Further, there would be a learning time for new employees in what may be a very complex area. Based on these criteria, critical business processes can now be prioritized.

Phase 2 is STOCKS form filling. STOCKS participants are provided with various forms about frequent use of IT tools/platforms; document flows; tacit knowledge flows (knowledge sources to knowledge suppliers, and user groups to knowledge customers); and industrial technologies. See IV-2 on the next page.

Form 1 would list IT tools and platforms available in the workplace such as intranet, internet, extranet, email, shared network drive, electronic document management system, document workflow control system, KM portal, content management in enterprise portal tool, SAP, search and retrieval (intranet and internet), bulletin board/discussion forum, wireless/mobile devices/solutions, online communities, trouble call and outage management system, geographic information system, mind/process mapping, e-learning, and then several blanks for "other".

Table 20-2. Stocks Form Filing.

Form No.	Form Name
Form 1	Information Technology Tools and Platforms
Form 2	Document Received/Retrieved
Form 3	Document Sent/Submitted/Forwarded/Uploaded/Produced
Form 4a	People You Usually Consult for Advice on Technical Tacit Knowledge
Form 4b	People You Usually Consult for Advice on Non-Technical Tacit Knowledge
Form 5a	People Who Contact You for Advice on Technical Tacit Knowledge
Form 5b	People Who Contact You for Advice on Non-Technical Tacit Knowledge
Form 6	Document and Tacit Knowledge Owned and Used by You Only
Form 7	Extra Knowledge Possessed by You Related to Your Industry but Not Used in Your Present Past
Form 8	List of Industrial Technologies/Core Competencies
Practical Hints for Describing Tacit Knowledge	

Form 2 would have columns asking for the following information about each document sent/submitted/forwarded/uploaded/produced: task number, rating on the ease of obtaining the document, rating on the importance of the document to the process, document format, and the people to whom the document was sent, or if it was for self-use.

Form 3 would have columns to describe the technical knowledge requested (experience, skills, know-how) in a key phrase, task number, rating on the importance of the knowledge, where the people are located (internal/external) and communication channel(s) used.

Forms 4a through Form 7 are self-explanatory. *Form 8* would address both existing industrial technology and desirable industrial technology. Columns requesting information regarding existing industrial technology deal with ratings on the ease to learn, time to learning, and importance.

Phase 3 is the workflow study and STOCKS workshop. Each workshop would include around 30 staff participants, with participants working on the same business process – who should come from different levels who work on the same process – clustered into one group. The objective of the workshop is for the staff inside the organization to consolidate and validate the data collected from the completed STOCK forms. The STOCK schema is prepared before conducting the workshop, containing field which include a business process, the tasks inside the process, and the related industrial technology, documents and tacit knowledge. At the beginning of the workshop, in order to control the vocabulary and taxonomy, participants agree on the terminology of the knowledge items and staff names as well as the relationship and hierarchy of such items. As a validation of inputs from STOCKS Forms, results are charted in a STOCKS Schema. The documents and tacit knowledge re related and mapped with the industrial technology. See a template for the STOCKS workshop schema below.

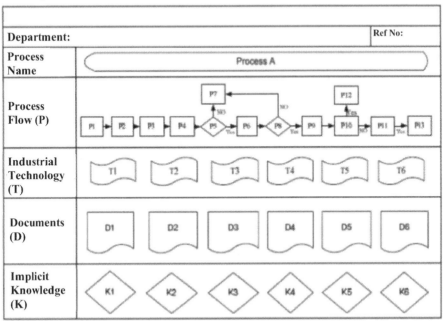

Figure 20-15. Stocks Workshop Schema Template.

Phase 4 is the knowledge inventory. After identifying the knowledge assets of the selected critical processes, explicit and tacit knowledge inventories are generated separately. A knowledge profile of major knowledge sources and types of user groups to which the knowledge is transferred are determined. See Tables 20-3 and 20-4 on the next page.

In **Phase 5** it is time to analyze the results. In addition to a stakeholder analysis, things you specifically want to look for would include: distribution of knowledge in tasks, critical knowledge workers, critical industrial technologies, mapping of knowledge with business processes and industry technology, critical tacit knowledge, and the distribution of explicit knowledge by knowledge categorization (critical, focus, abundant, normal common, working, popular). See Table 20-5, Distribution of Knowledge in Each Task; Table 20-6, Ranking on industrial technologies; Figure 20-16, Knowledge mapping – knowledge fountains; and Table 20-7, List of critical implicit (tacit) knowledge.

Table 20-3. Example of explicit knowledge inventory.

Document Name	Process(s)	Task(s)	Document Format	Where From People	Where From IT Tools / Platforms	Major Users	Score
11kV open-circuit report	Distribution	P1:System Security Assessment, P4:Develop Contingency Plan	Excel		17:DMS (Distribution Management System)	PY Hung (SOD)	5
11kV open-circuit report	Distribution	P1:System Security Assessment, P4:Develop Contingency Plan	Excel	PY Hung (SOD)	17:DMS (Distribution Management System), 28:Change From Normail (CRN) record system	TK Wong (SOD)	5
Code of Practice	Distribution	P1:System Security Assessment, P2:Outage Execution, P9:Conduct Problem Analysis / Fault Diagnosis, P10:Formula / Counter Check Restoration Strategy / Plan, P11:Implement Restoration Plan	Jpg, Word	Joe Tang (AMD)	6:電子文件管理系統 -EDMS	KO Ho (SOD)	5
Discrepancy Reports	Distribution	P3:System Monitoring / Alarm Alert	Printed, SAP	PY Hung (SOD)	9:SAP - EFMS/EWMS, 17:DMS (Distribution Management System), 28:Change From Normail (CRN) record system		5
Discrepancy Reports	Distribution	P3:System Monitoring / Alarm Alert	Printed, SAP	PY Hung (SOD)	9:SAP - EFMS/EWMS, 17:DMS (Distribution Management System), 28:Change From Normail (CRN) record system		5
Distribution System Operation Manual	Distribution	P1:System Security Assessment, P2:Outage Execution, P9:Conduct Problem Analysis / Fault Diagnosis, P10:Formula / Counter Check Restoration Strategy / Plan, P11:Implement Restoration Plan	Pdf	Joe Tang (AMD)	6:電子文件管理系統 -EDMS	KO Ho (SOD)	5
DMS picture revision record	Distribution	P13:DMS Diagram Update	Excel	WK Wong, Norris (SOD)	1:內聯網 (Internets) - 資訊中心/部門網頁, 部門分處網頁	SOD, Regions	2
DMS Pictures	Distribution	P13:DMS Diagram Update	IDES	KS Lee (SOD)	17:DMS (Distribution Management System)	WT Lau (SOD)	5
DR completion notification	Distribution	P12:Review and Cancel "System Emergency"	Email	Andy Lee (SO/PC)	4:電子郵件 (Email) - Outlook	WK Wong, Norris (SOD)	4
Engineering Instructions	Distribution	P2:Outage Execution	pdf, Word, Scanned copy	System Control Managers (SOD)	6:電子文件管理系統 -EDMS	HS Chan (SOD)	4
General fault reports	Distribution	P3:System Monitoring / Alarm Alert, P4:Develop Contingency Plan	Printed, WMS	PY Hung (SOD)	20:WMS (GFR) Work Management System	YM Yu (SOD)	5
List of HV Fault / Forced Outage (with supply interruption)	Distribution	P10:Formula / Counter Check Restoration Strategy / Plan	Printed	KC Chan Terence (SOD)	19:TCOM (Trouble Call and Outage Maintenance System)	PY Hung (SOD)	5

Table 20-4. Example of implicit (tacit) knowledge inventory.

Department	Knowledge Owner	Knowledge Item Level 1	Knowledge Item Level 2	Process(s)	Task(s)	Communcation Channel	Major Knowledge	Score
SOD	Arthur Pang (SOD)	Alarm handling	Knowledge on alarm handling in Distribution System	Distribution	P2:Outage Execution, P9:Conduct Problem Analysis / Fault Diagnosis	Face to Face, Telephone, Telephone, Email	HS Chan (SOD)	5
SOD	CF Tsui (SOD)	System security	Reconfigure the system during emergency and uniform condition, restoration after fault outage	Distribution	P1:System Security Assessment, P11:Implement Restoration Plan	Face to Face, Email, Technical Seminar	WL Fung, Ricky (SOD)	4
SOD	CH Choi (SOD)	System security	Reconfigure the system during emergency and uniform condition, restoration after fault outage	Distribution	P9:Conduct Problem Analysis / Fault Diagnosis, P10:Formula / Counter Check Restoration Strategy / Plan, P11:Implement Restoration Plan, P12:Review and Cancel "System Emergency"	Face to Face	TW Ho (SOD)	5
SOD	CK Yim (SOD)	System security	Reconfigure the system during emergency and uniform condition, restoration after fault outage	Distribution	P9:Conduct Problem Analysis / Fault Diagnosis, P10:Formula / Counter Check Restoration Strategy / Plan, P11:Implement Restoration Plan, P12:Review and Cancel "System Emergency"	Face to Face	KO Ho (SOD)	5
SOD	CW Man (SOD)	System security	Reconfigure the system during emergency and uniform condition, restoration after fault outage	Distribution	P1:System Security Assessment, P11:Implement Restoration Plan	Face to Face, Email, Technical Seminar	WL Fung, Ricky (SOD)	4
SOD	CW Man (SOD)	Power System	Design and Formulate power system configuration	Distribution	P1:System Security Assessment	Face to Face, Technical Seminar	WL Fung, Ricky (SOD)	4
SOD	Edmund Fung (SOD)	System security	Reconfigure the system during emergency and uniform condition, restoration after fault outage	Distribution	P1:System Security Assessment, P11:Implement Restoration Plan	Face to Face, Email, Technical Seminar	WL Fung, Ricky (SOD)	4
SOD	G So (SOD)	Power System	Design and Formulate power system configuration	Distribution	P1:System Security Assessment	Face to Face, Technical Seminar	WL Fung, Ricky (SOD)	4
SOD	G So (SOD)	Power System	Design and Formulate power system configuration	Distribution	P1:System Security Assessment	Face to Face, Technical Seminar	WK Wong, Norris (SOD)	4
SOD	Kevin Tang (SOD)	Knowledge on EMS (Energy Management System)	Justify EMS alarm behavior, identify faulty parts by analysis the alarms.	Distribution	P2:Outage Execution, P9:Conduct Problem Analysis / Fault Diagnosis	Face to Face, Telephone, Telephone	SC Fan (SOD)	5

Table 20-5. *Distribution of Knowledge in Each Task*

Task No.	Total No. of Explicit Knowledge Items	Total No. of Implicit Knowledge Items	Number of Knowledge Workers
P1	13	7	8
P2	15	11	9
P3	20	32	15
P4	2	5	6
P5	8	17	22
P6	3	4	10
P7	2	4	4
P8	6	3	10
P9	9	1	1
P10	2	10	7

Table 20-6. *Ranking on industrial technologies (1 means most important).*

	Industrial technology	Ranking of difficulty	Ranking of time to learn	Ranking of importance	Overall ranking
T1	Switchgear	1	1	1	1
T9	High-voltage	3	3	3	2
T10	Electrical insulation	3	8	2	3
T2	Cable technology	1	5	7	4
T4	Transformer technology	6	5	3	4
T7	Electrical power	12	1	5	7
T14	SAP/EDMS	3	3	9	6

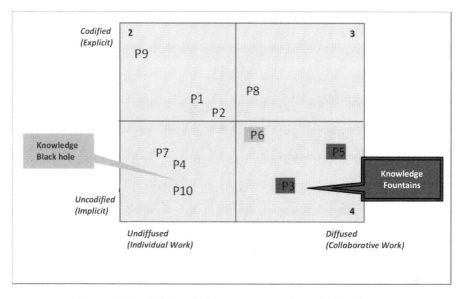

Figure 20-16. Knowledge mapping – knowledge fountains.

Table 20-7. List of critical implicit (tacit) knowledge.

	Number of users	Average score of importance	Number of related critical technologies
Approval of engineering changes in Installation and operation to suit specific site conditions	6	4.33	3
Frequent problems encountered in project implementation)	4	5.00	3
Choice of backup protection issues	3	5.00	3
Assessment of transmission plant performance and user experience maintenance problem	4	5.00	3

The distribution of knowledge is initially assigned according to the ratio of identified explicit knowledge items and the number of knowledge workers involved in knowledge. The following 2 X 2 can be filled in by task.

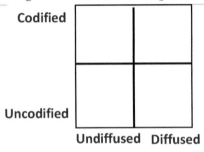

Figure 20-17. Distribution of knowledge.

The number of tacit knowledge items would be shown in terms of self-owned, shared, and number of knowledge workers. The number of explicit knowledge items would be shown in terms of common, critical, abundant, normal, and focus. Critical knowledge workers are identified, and to encourage the sharing of knowledge through linking people with people, an expertise directory is developed for critical knowledge workers.

Phase 6 consists of interviews and data validation. The interviews are focused on the use of knowledge and the knowledge need for the business processes.

The advantages of the STOCKS approach are as follows:

- It's an effective way to collect a large amount of information from staff at different levels of the organization.
- It provides a larger scale when compared with interviews, which only cover a sample size of participants.
- It reduces the number of interviews required.
- Provides collective thinking and learning.
- Generates innovative opinions/ideas through interactive face-to-face discussion.
- Encourages a better understanding of different business operation of the organization during face-to-face discussion and interaction.

There are several journal papers focused on the STOCKS approach which are available through the internet and which provide more detail.

Dr. Rongbin W.B. Lee is Professor Emeritus in the Department of Industrial and Systems Engineering of The Hong Kong Polytechnic University and founding Head of the Partner State Key Laboratory of the University. He had been President of the Hong Kong Chapter of the Institution of Electrical Engineer (UK) and had served as the President of the Hong Kong Association for the Advancement of Science and Technology. He was the ex-chief editor of the

Journal of Information and Knowledge Management Systems (Emerald) as well as the chief editor emeritus of the International Journal of Knowledge and Systems Science (IGI Global). Prof. Lee is now the Chairman of the International Committee of the Global MIKE Award. He has published more than 250 papers in referred journals and three books. He may be contacted at wb.lee@polyu.edu.hk

****

 # TOOL: Knowledge Base Roadmap

Adapted from the DON KM Toolkit

A **framework** for building the knowledge base in a specific area of knowledge.

Supports: knowledge sharing, communities of practice, knowledge reuse, knowledge capture, knowledge retention, collaboration

LEVEL OF EFFORT	C^2 Dependent
SIZE OF ORG	SCALABLE
SCOPE OF EFFORT	C^2 Dependent

The Knowledge Base roadmap provides a framework for building the knowledge base in a specific area of knowledge. A knowledge base is the collection of information, supporting context, and the individuals and groups who possess and can share and apply the knowledge necessary to ensure the performance and sustainability of the organization. It is generally focused in a specific domain of practice (thus the emergence of the term community of practice), with the knowledge base supporting an established community of practice or a group of employees working in the same functional area. While your organization may already have an information infrastructure in place, the Knowledge Base development process focuses on creating collaborative processes and information support as well for a specified area of knowledge, that is, adding the human element which – at least to date – cannot be performed by AI or quantum computing.

The Implementing Community

Development of a knowledge base is best implemented by community members practicing in that functional area, with a core group of community members involved in the entire initial process. These individuals would take on the roles of Community Leader, Coordinator, Cybrarian, and Technologist. The *Leader* provides day-to-day support while serving as an active, contributing member. The Leader strives to further the community's goals by: (1) serving as a subject matter expert; (2) coordinating with and connecting other team or community members; (3) planning, scheduling and managing activities; (4) interfacing with senior leadership; (5) representing the Knowledge Base effort at briefings; (6) recognizing contributions; and (7) tracking budget expenditures, if applicable. The *Coordinator* assists the Leader in performing the above tasks, but focuses on internal coordination rather than external relations with the organization. While *Cybrarian* is a fairly new cyber-term, it easily resonates with most people. Cybrarian conveys the notion of one who looks after the collecting and access to web-based library-type resources needed by the organization. This role can be largely done in association with AI capability. Regardless of the extent of dedicated Web support that is available to the organization, the Cybrarian will provide help with finding and connecting domain-related assistance in the Web environment, and, when working with AI, in evaluating and making decisions on located data and information, building on their expertise in the domain married to an understanding of the usage of domain knowledge in the context of the organization to relate discovery and context. This person has at his or her fingertips both internal and external sites of value. The *Technologist* watches over infrastructure support. As the Knowledge Base comes together, the Technologist ensures employees can connect and communicate through various media, providing them options and resources for collaboration. When decisions are being made regarding the infrastructure, the Technologist is available to relate technical issues to Knowledge Base requirements. This role is best filled by a person who both knows the domain and is technically savvy.

The following products are developed as part of the Knowledge Base:

1. Matrix of groupware functions that the community will focus on for its first release of the Knowledge Base

2. List of identified knowledge domain information (documents, presentations, spreadsheets, etc.) that includes specific documents

3. List of folders used for organizing domain information

4. Graphical model and supporting narrative of "AS-IS" information flows between the community of practice and stakeholder organizations

5. List of community members and the folders that they have been assigned

6. Groupware electronic repository. Information will have been migrated to the groupware application under the given folder structure.

7. List of asset rules that ensures all groupware transactions are done in a manner consistent across the community

8. Graphical model and supporting narrative of "TO-BE" information flows between the community and stakeholder organizations. This would include a list of organizational performance measures and expected efficiencies from the Knowledge Base (e.g., cycle time = 8 weeks; goal is a 2-week reduction).

The Key Tasks to develop a Knowledge Base are the following. Each key task is first introduced and then discussed in greater detail below.

1. *Requirements:* Map identified collaborative tool functions to organizational requirements to simplify deployment, narrow training scope, and ensure more efficient use of the groupware.

2. *Inventory:* Define knowledge assets in an organizational process context and identify whether they will be created by the community or borrowed from other business owners.

3. *Taxonomy:* Develop an organizational context classification structure for organizing the inventory of information. It should provide an intuitive navigation scheme for members of the community and other interested stakeholders.

4. *Flow Model:* Model AS-IS business processes based on the flow of inventory assets to and from customers. Focus on how assets are created and disseminated.

5. *Migrate:* Provide necessary technical support to migrate inventory assets that exist in legacy repositories. Inventory should be organized, classified as relevant, and mapped to a classification owner. Owners are typically subject matter experts from within the organization.

6. *Map:* Identify owners of the Inventory folders and designate life-cycle responsibility at a folders structure level.

7. *Asset Rules:* Establish organizational rules for the use of the groupware to maintain consistency while performing organizational transactions. Designate which groupware functionality will be used to process specific transactions.

8. *Transformation:* Identify, in priority order, high value/low risk business processes that provide the group with the highest value in terms of organizational performance, cycle time reduction, and total cost. Focus on measures that correlate to related performance measures.

9. *Training:* Secure computer-training facilities to allow "hands-on" training for users. Transformed processes will be simulated in a training environment for user testing and acceptance.

Each key task will be briefly addressed below.

Key Task 1: Requirements. This task is aimed at narrowing the functional scope of the selected groupware application to only those functions that enable the achievement of mission-related measures. For example, given a groupware application, conduct a functional analysis of the application. At minimum the analysis should include the function name, description and release. List all of the functions that the groupware application is capable of performing (such as, add a new document). This list should not include any extended or custom functionality. Focus on the basic functionality of the groupware.

Once a list has been prepared, convene the community members to review the list. Leaders should aim at obtaining consensus over which functions meet the general requirements of the community's needs within the first release of the Knowledge Base. Enter 1 for "release" if the community requires the function in the first release. Enter 2 or 3, respectively, if the community feels as though that particular function can be postponed for a later release. The community is expected to base its functionality decisions on lessons learned and past experiences, and the requirements of the project.

Work Product: Requirements Traceability Matrix - Excel spreadsheet containing the following elements: REQ ID, REQUIREMENT (or Function Name), DESCRIPTION, RELEASE (version of the implementation that will contain the corresponding function), NEW or EXISTING, FULL/PARTIAL, COMMENTS, DOCUMENTS

Key Task 2: Inventory. The inventory offers community members the opportunity of identifying all information associated with established organizational processes. With the help of a facilitator or community leader, convene a session of community members and conduct a brainstorming session on information that is either inputs to, or outputs of, the community's business processes.

Once the list has been developed, assign each member the responsibility of reviewing the baseline list and adding information not captured during the community session. Compile the baseline list along with the individual input from community members. This will become the baseline inventory for the community.

Work Products: Inventory List - Excel spreadsheet containing the following elements: ASSET ID#, NAME, DESCRIPTION, BEST PRACTICE, RECORDS MANAGEMENT META DATA (SSIC data)

Key Task 3: Taxonomy. The objective of taxonomy building in the community is to provide an intuitive structure for users who are interested in obtaining information from or contributing to a community's practice. Convene the community to brainstorm a list of categories based on the prepared inventory list. The objective of the taxonomy brainstorming session is to develop as complete a list as possible. Disregard the length of the list. The actual list can be finalized during a separate community session. See the discussion on

"Taxonomy" in Chapter 10. *Tip 1*: Limit the final consolidated list to ~9 categories. *Tip 2*: Limit sub categories to 3 levels.

Once the group has developed a list, distribute the list to group members and have them conduct a personal assessment of the list, asking them to add, consolidate, or recommend deletions to the list. Community leaders then consolidate the group and individual lists into a single group list. Once completed, inventory items can be assigned to their respective categories.

Work Product: Taxonomy List - Excel spreadsheet consisting of the following elements: FOLDER ID #, CATEGORY, LEVEL, OWNERS, STATUS, DESCRIPTION, and REVISION NOTES.

Key Task 4: Flow Model. The purpose of flow modeling is to graphically illustrate how inventory items are transferred between organizations as organizational transactions are conducted. The model will present a view that allows for easy identification of "As-Is" business processes. To begin, model the organizations involved in the inventory exchange as depicted below.

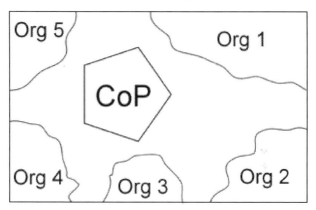

Figure 20-18. Sample Flow Model

Using the baseline inventory list, illustrate how each item travels between community and organization. In some cases, an inventory item may traverse several paths between organization and community until the business process cycle is completed.

The "As-Is" flow model is complete when each of the inventory items has been illustrated on the model.

Once the graphical model has been completed, the Leader will write a narrative that describes the path of community inventory items. The narrative should be written in terms that are easily comprehensible. Within the narrative, incorporate details that are not readily apparent within the model. Other approaches that are supportive would be developing a picture map and/or a storyboard, details of which are available on the Internet.

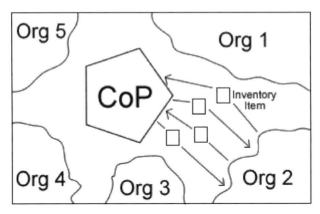

Figure 20-19. Sample Flow Model w/ Path Example

Work Product: "As-Is" model and narrative of the organizational process and the knowledge assets transacted during the identified processes. Illustration of community, stakeholders or customers and the direction flow of assets between services and customer.

Key Task 5: Map. Mapping provides a means for the community to maintain its data. Community members will be designated as the point of contact for a particular category of data within the Knowledge Base. As with any community, it is necessary for all members to participate in the maintenance and upkeep of its locale.

Mapping is a relatively quick and informal process. Convene a meeting of community members. Using the established taxonomy list, have community members volunteer for folders that fall within their area of responsibility. Record these assignments in the ASSIGNED OWNER column of the taxonomy list. Additionally, have members volunteer for folders as an alternate point of contact. Therefore, each folder will have two community members who are familiar with the folder structure, content, and access privileges granted the folder.

Work Product: See Taxonomy above. List - Excel spreadsheet of ASSET CLASSIFICATIONS and ASSIGNED OWNER.

Key Task 6: Migration. Migration of data is important to demonstrating the capabilities of the groupware application. It also provides a means of validating what has been accomplished in terms of data organization. Finally, it provides a context for discussing how inventory and taxonomy contribute to the organization's business processes.

Migration begins with validation of both Inventory and taxonomy lists. This ensures what has been gathered thus far accurately reflects the needs of the community. Convene the community and conduct a quick review of both lists. Pay particular attention to those Inventory items that (a) are not associated to an organizational process and (b) are not products of the community. Items that are not associated to an organizational process may be considered for removal. Items that are not a product of the community may exist as parts of an adjacent community. If so, eliminate redundancy by cutting out "borrowed" items.

Once the lists have been validated, begin populating the project workspace according to the taxonomy. Data can be populated manually or in batch. Tools are available for large-scale conversions.

Work Product: Tool user accounts for all core group members and operational prototype of current release of the collaborative workspace.

Key Task 7: Asset Rules. Asset Rules provide members with groupware guidelines for moving data in and out of the Knowledge Base. They also designate which groupware function will be used to support specific transactions in an organizational process. An example of an asset rule is using a compound document instead of a folder to collect and present periodic volume releases of a newsletter. In this case, two different groupware functions could be used to achieve similar results. Establishing asset rules provides a consistent means for interacting with the Knowledge Base.

Sets of asset rules exist for each organizational process supported. Regardless of the size, rules must be put in place to avoid differences in practitioner usage. While asset rules will most commonly be identified with a business process, in some cases specific documents may have an asset rule associated with them.

Begin with listing the different processes or documents that will require an asset rule. Remember, all transactions conducted within the groupware application will require a set of asset rules that provide guidance to the community members and other users as determined by the community. As a simple example, let's say a particular community maintains a community calendar within its groupware application. The document format of the calendar is a Microsoft Word file. To provide guidance to the community on the use of this document, the following asset rules have been created:

1. Calendar only maintained by assigned owner
2. Community members who need to add a date to the calendar will use the groupware's document Check-in / Check-out function

   ○

3. The community will maintain three months of its calendar. One month of past events and two months of future events

4. All community members will create a change notification on the community calendar thus allowing them to receive email notification upon calendar update

Again, a set of asset rules should be developed for each process or document involved in a community organizational transaction. Asset rules should be reviewed periodically to ensure applicability and effectiveness.

Work Product: Asset Rules - Excel spreadsheet including BUSINESS RULE NUMBER, BUSINESS RULE, DESCRIPTION, REVISION, STATUS, and COMMENTS

Key Task 8: Transformation. Transformation is key to achieving value from the Knowledge Base. The use of the Knowledge Base process implies communities will undergo a transformation in how they do business. If transformation is not achieved, the community has done nothing more than increase its burden and develop another data repository.

To transform, begin by selecting "high value/low risk" flows of inventory identified in the flow model stage. The flow selection should be based on that which the community believes would bring the highest value at the lowest risk to the community's mission, that is, the most likely to be successful with no side effects or perturbations. List and prioritize which flows will be transformed into the groupware application such that all future transactions relating to the selected process will be conducted via the groupware.

Once processes have been listed and prioritized in terms of value and risk, prepare an assessment or "gap analysis" of the "AS-IS" process and the "TO-BE" process. The analysis should include:

1. List of stakeholders who will be affected by the process change

2. Changes to the process in terms of steps required to complete the process - Are there any changes to the process? If so, document the changes.

3. Measures and metrics for assessing the value achieved by transforming the "AS-IS" process to the groupware application environment

4. Document asset rules associated to conducting the process in the "TO-BE" environment

Work Product: TO-BE model and narrative of the business processes transacted. Includes a Gap Analysis identifying changes to AS-IS model and documented asset rules.

Key Task 9: Training. Training ensures that all community members possess the necessary skills to function within the collaborative work environment. Community leaders should not assume that its members understand and can operate within the Knowledge Base without training and support.

Training in this context includes more than just application training. It includes context-based training that is rooted in business processes. That is, members are trained in both the use of the groupware application and the business processes it supports. This way, training has relevance to the community member and has immediate application.

Training can be accomplished within the community by identifying a training lead for the community. Typically, this person will possess an above average aptitude for Information Technology and has a good grasp of the business processes.

The trainer will use the Requirements Traceability Matrix (RTM) developed earlier in the process to design a course for community members. The RTM provides the basis for the training. That is, it lists what groupware topics the trainer will cover. It is up to the trainer to select the organizational context of the functional topics. The trainer should develop a group of "use" cases or scenarios that illustrates to community members how the groupware will be utilized within the community's environment. An example of a use case is: (1) update group calendar; (2) login to groupware; (3) check-out calendar; (4) add new calendar entry; and (5) check-in calendar.

There is no replacement for hands-on training. Where possible, utilize a training center to deliver training to community members. Training should be designed to be brief and specifically geared towards organizational processes. Long training sessions greater than 1.5 hours have proven to be less effective than short sessions. If training seems too long, scale back on the coverage areas. Keep it manageable, applicable, short, and enjoyable for your community members.

Expected Outcomes include (1) an established knowledge inventory and folder structure for the domain of knowledge; (2) a process for capturing documents; (3) a framework to continually improve organizational processes leveraging lessons learned and reusing best practices; (4) increased community collaboration and support; and (5) identified target efficiencies in mission related measures such as cycle time, customer service and total ownership cost.

****

TOOL: Knowledge Moments[1020]

Adapted from the DON KM Toolkit

A **frame of reference** for creating and supporting situations that connect people and knowledge.

Supports: knowledge sharing, organizational learning

LEVEL OF EFFORT	LOW
SIZE OF ORG	SCALABLE
SCOPE OF EFFORT	WIDE

An organization can be viewed as a collage of human knowledge moments. This refers to the daily experiences and interactions across the organization and among the organization and its larger stakeholder community as people read, write, converse and think during their workday—and often in reflection and mental chatter outside of the workday.

Knowledge moments happen at the intersection of people, places, processes and purpose, with every knowledge moment offering a learning experience to those involved. Since knowledge is defined as the capacity to take effective action, knowledge moments refer to exchanges that provide the potential for, or lead to, effective action. Thus, the behavior of the organization is enhanced by the result of the interaction of all decisions made and actions taken based on the knowledge moments of every individual in the organization. Similar to the butterfly concept in chaos theory, there is the potential for success or failure based on knowledge moments which cannot be specifically identified or tied directly to that success or failure.

A sustainable organization is co-evolving with its environment. Thus, the quantity and quality of both planned and spontaneous exchanges within the organization's larger stakeholder community affects both the *quality* of the organization's work products and stakeholder's *perceived quality* of the organization's work products.

This new frame of reference lays the groundwork for applying this understanding to the organization. The questions an organization must ask are:

- How can the organization increase the quantity and quality of knowledge moments for its employees?

- How can the organization increase the quantity and quality of knowledge moments with the larger stakeholder community?

****

TOOL: Lean RKM Readiness Startup Plan

A modified **start-up plan** for Knowledge Reblooming.

Supports: readiness, knowledge flows, collaboration, change, knowledge productivity, sustainability

LEVEL OF EFFORT	MEDIUM
SIZE OF ORG	SCALABLE
SCOPE OF EFFORT	SCALABLE

A modified Reblooming Knowledge Movement readiness approach may be undertaken in constrained circumstances such as by a smaller firm or during an economic recession. Please see Chapter 9 in Section II for the indispensable need for RKM readiness in 21st Century enterprises.

The Lean RKM Readiness Startup Plan below outlines readiness startup in resource limited circumstances. It is aimed at reducing initial engagement costs, eliminating barriers to entry, and dismissing procrastination tendencies. In reality, all RKM Readiness efforts should be embraced as potential ways to reduce business costs and/or generate profit. This applies to Lean RKM efforts as well. Additionally, even Lean RKM Readiness Startup efforts may create initial surprises. A rising sense of freedom and motivation can unveil early innovative results. Here is the Lean RKM Readiness Startup Plan:

Table 20-8. Lean RKM Readiness Startup Plan

Step	# Days	Who	Tasks
1	30	Sr. Exec + Other Exec	Review the firm's vision, values, mission, and business plan and select language to add from the RKM book. Reflect on customers and use language to encourage the workforce. Be modest with these initial communication changes and outline the startup schedule. Enlist help of another executive.
2	15	Sr. Exec + Other Exec	Select a RKM Readiness Team with three team members—one of the firm's leaders, one from the management/supervisor level, and one from the workforce. Provide a facilitator to help follow a process and agenda. Double the size of the team if deemed feasible for backup.
3	45	Other Exec	Develop the RKM skills of the team members by providing a RKM library, links to online resources, and basic formal RKM training.

4	30	RKM Readiness Team	Review the executive document additions and Team adds. Conduct very general assessment of RKM needs. Develop draft 3-yr RKM strategic plan with milestones. Review RKM roles and recommend one specialist from the firm to add to the team.
5	30	RKM Readiness Team, Sr. Exec & Other Exec. Exec Board	RKM Readiness Team presents firm document changes and RKM strategic plan to Exec Board for approval. Exec Board votes on 3-yr tenure of RKM Team.
6	20	Sr Exec	Communicates all new docs to the workforce, shareholders, and customers. Formally announces RKM Team. Hosts appreciation/celebration for RKM Team.

****

☀ TOOL: Option Outline

A Story Thinking tool developed by Dr. John Lewis[1021]

A **process** to view options and choices, for decision transparency, project summaries, and lessons learned.

Supports: decision-making, knowledge sharing, group learning, problem solving

LEVEL OF EFFORT	LOW
SIZE OF ORG	SCALABLE
SCOPE OF WORK	NARROW

The Option Outline is a Story Thinking tool. Building on the natural story cycle, Story Thinking uses the structure of story as an operational strategy. (See the Key Principles in Chapter 8.)

In a decision journey, the Option Outline, because of its structure, provides the opportunity to quickly capture options being considered, identify which option was chosen (listed last), and show the entire consequential thought process (via indention). This simple but effective tool uses a table-indent format. The Option Outline moves through the Story Thinking process of automation, disruption, investigation, ideation, and expectation.

The table will discuss a past or present project with sufficient complexity built from a paper draft of an Option Outline that captures the significant choices to support decision transparency and project summary. An Option Outline for "buying a car" is exampled in Table 20-9 on the next page.

1. **Automation**: "We had successful operations at work."
2. **Disruption**: "But we knew more competition was coming."
3. **Investigation**: "We discovered a new idea that we could incorporate."
4. **Ideation**: "And created a new vision."
5. **Expectation**: "Development took some time."
6. **Affirmation**: "But it all came together!"
7. **Automation**: "Now operations are even better."

There is an elegance in simplicity found only after having the knowledge of the options and choices considered and tradeoffs throughout the "story" which have been boiled down to the basics of what to do. The Option Outline offers the opportunity to do just that.

Table 20-9. Option Outline for buying a car.

Option Outline: Buying a car	
Phases	Goal: Replace old car and save money
Automation	Accept unreliable car as the status-quo
Disruption	The car will not pass inspection
Investigation	Fix the old car
Investigation	Buy a replacement car
Investigation	Get a new car
Investigation	Get a used car
Ideation	Gas car
Ideation	Electric car
Ideation	Hybrid car
Expectation	Purchase and collect data

Dr. John Lewis is a coach, educator, and consultant in leadership, innovation, and KM. John helps leaders and organizations reach their peak potential through evidence-based performance strategies. John has "Big 4" management consulting experience and was acknowledged by Gartner with an industry "Best Practice" for an innovative global KM solution. John is the author of *Story Thinking* and *The Explanation Age*, which Kirkus Reviews described as "An iconoclast's blueprint for a new era of innovation." He is an associate editor of the *Journal of Innovation Management* and holds a Doctorate in Educational Psychology.

****

 ## TOOL: Pattern Thinking

An **approach** to studying the changing times and the content and context of a situation for which you seek a solution.

Supports: change management, problem solving, creativity, forecasting

LEVEL OF EFFORT	C^2 Dependent
SIZE OF ORG	SCALABLE
SCOPE OF EFFORT	SCALABLE

This tool helps identify patterns of change and the underlying principles or environmental drivers that are generating the change, unpredictability and apparent complexity. Much of this kind of knowledge resides in your unconscious, particularly if you have previously and deliberately looked for these characteristics. Thus, you may not be consciously aware of them but your unconscious can, and often will, be aware of them as you observe and study a situation, creating knowledge in the form of understanding.

As we are exposed to more diverse and varying conditions, the brain creates new patterns and strengths of connections and thereby *changes its physiological structure*.[1022] It is also true that the structure of the brain – containing a huge number of networks of neurons – significantly influences how incoming signals representing new thoughts (patterns composed of networks of neurons) are formed. Through the process of associative patterning, these new patterns entering the brain associate or connect with patterns already in the brain.

Pattern thinking is not primarily thinking *through* patterns, although over time this will occur. Rather, it is using your inside world to *look for patterns in the outside world*, and bringing them into your conscious awareness. The intent of pattern thinking is to let the pattern emerge as a mode of understanding a situation, purposefully thinking about external patterns in order to better anticipate and respond to change, that is, to expand your understanding, solve problems, create new ideas, and improve your capacity to forecast the outcomes of decisions.

Thinking *about* patterns is different than thinking *with* patterns. If you start with a specific pattern in mind, no doubt you will find it. This is the same phenomenon that occurs when you purchase a new car and you begin seeing similar cars every time you are on the freeway, although you'd never noticed them before! However, pattern emergence can be stimulated by other patterns. For example, the systems thinking approach developed by Peter Senge is based on matching a recurring set of relationships (archetypes) to a situation at hand.[1023] While this force-fitting can certainly help facilitate an understanding of causal relationships in simple and complicated situations, it does not work well in complex relationships.

Complexity infers difficulty in understanding something due to the large number of unpredictable and nonlinear relationships. Yet, once you have used the models of complexity over and over again, you begin to think systems and *discover system patterns beyond the archetypes*. Both systems thinking and complexity thinking are forms of pattern thinking, enabling a person to build the ability to recognize, comprehend and learn how to influence complex systems, and find creative solutions to complex issues.

From the neuroscience perspective, pattern thinking involves mental exercise that stimulates the brain. The best mental exercise is new learning in multiple areas of the brain, acquiring new knowledge and doing things you've never done before.[1024] Making new connections, seeing new relationships, and bringing patterns into our conscious stream of thoughts does just that.

In early briefings on decision-making, one of the author's favorite slides included the phrase *every decision is a guess about the future*. And, as we moved past the beginning stages of KM in the U.S. Department of the Navy, it became clear that the practices considered as "best" in one part of the organization often failed in other parts of the organization, that is, it appeared that what we labeled as a "best practice" was also a guess about the future.

At that time recognition of knowledge as context sensitive and situation dependent was just emerging. Yet as more examples of application of best practices surfaced, we noted there were similarities, that *types* of things were similar, and, as more implementation examples of similar practice became available, recognizable patterns began to emerge. At this point, we purposefully looked for patterns. If we found similar patterns occurring, we could more accurately predict the outcome of our implementation process. In other words, it was no longer a random guess about the future. Lipton and Bhaerman confirm this finding when they say "If a pattern can be recognized, then the accuracy of predicting a future event is relatively high … if events are found to be random, then all predictions are essentially guesses with an accuracy based on chance."[1025] This tool is focused on tapping into the innate human ability to recognize patterns.

STEP (1) Find a place where you will not be disturbed and briefly close your eyes and take several deep breaths. Open your eyes. Then sit comfortably, ready to take notes.

STEP (2) Consider the group of things or series of incidents in which you are searching for connections. If this is a group of things, briefly write down each item's characteristics such as how it looks and what it is made of, how it is created/developed, its purpose, how it is used, etc. If this is a series of incidents, briefly write down for each incident the subject (who or what) and the very (action occurring) and any descriptive adjectives that come to mind describing the incident, the people involved, the place and timing, the outcome, and the why (if known).

STEP (3) Look across the group and consider the *differences* among the things or incidents. Note these as characteristics.

STEP (4) Look across the group and consider the *similarities* among the things or incidents. Note these as characteristics.

STEP (5) Considering both differences and similarities, identify categories into which these differences and/or similarities could fall. Keep searching until you can bring two or more characteristics of *different things or incidents* together into a category. Repeat until you have discovered all the categories that connect the things or incidents.

STEP (5) Now, look at how the categories fit together OR don't fit together. *ASK*: How do these things relate? Are these different things the same *types* of things? Are there patterns emerging? Is something missing?

STEP (7) Repeat Steps 3-6 until you are satisfied you have discovered all there is to discover. Then, go do something entirely different, perhaps play a game of golf or enjoy a pleasant meal with a friend or take a nap. In other words, let your unconscious take the lead, and be prepared to take notes when perhaps the next day some new idea regarding the group or series of incidents pops up in your head.

HINT: This process works well in a facilitated collaborative group looking from multiple frames of reference!

There is a reminder in this exercise that bears repeating. STEP (7) asked that you be prepared to take notes when new ideas pop into your head. It is important to build your personal Idea Book and, just as you deposit money in a savings account, to deposit ideas in your Idea Book. As we will repeat several times in this text: ideas beget ideas. And often a big idea arrives in small bites, little ideas that build up over time to a big idea. Looking to the future, capture those pleasant and worthwhile ideas that may come with real results in future years. Because these often arrive while you are in an expanded state of consciousness they may, like dreams, be difficult to remember when everyday responsibilities engage your attention. So, if you are serious about fully engaged your creativity capabilities, it's time for you to start your Idea Book, and have it handy as you go about everyday living.

****

TOOL: Reverse Bloom Learning Framework (RBLF)

Contributed by Dr. Arthur Shelley

An **approach** to interactive experiential learning.

Supports: group learning, creativity, problem solving, collaboration

LEVEL OF EFFORT	C² Dependent
SIZE OF ORG	SCALABLE
SCOPE OF EFFORT	SCALABLE

The Reverse Bloom Learning Framework (RBLF) is new unique approach to interactive experiential learning. Involving iterative cycles that generate options and create new opportunities, it develops capabilities across cognitive, social and practical application in real situations to address unknown challenges. This is a reversal of the order of the traditional learning approach, and covers all three learning dimensions of cognitive, psychomotor and affective. It starts with cocreation, to synthesize options for analysis and application, which triggers deeper understanding and generates new knowledge.

The RBLF approach (shown in the visual below) engages participants in experiences that stimulate cognitive, social and application aspects of learning in interactive social learning cycles. The six actions in the image below highlights the flow of how this works. With a limited exposure to some insights first, learners explore possibilities and implications of a real context through co-creative interactions (**Action 1**). This enables participants to synthesize a set of possible options for the diversity of ideas across the group (**Action 2**). These options can then be analyzed to assess implications and to deconstruct the challenge presented (**Action 3**). Once learners design or prototype some options, they apply them (**Action 4**) to understand the best possibilities for further use and development. Reflections between the learners before, during and after each action stimulates socialization of the possibilities, which further expands their understanding (**Action/Outcome 5**). This deeper and wider understanding leads to the generation of new knowledge (**Action/Outcome 6**). The generation of new knowledge and insights triggers the whole process to restart, stimulating professional processes like creativity and innovation. The experiences using RBLF develop our collaboration capabilities and grow our confidence with working in unpredictable environments. We build greater adaptability and resilience as a result.

In the RBLF approach, much of the knowledge generated is new, rather than just transfer of prior existing knowledge. Each participant contributes their own perceptions to a diverse mix of ideas and insights. This highlights why reflective conversations about their perspectives and understanding are important throughout the whole process. It enables all participants to benefit from the understanding of everyone involved, not just from their own insights. The outputs of one cycle become inputs to the next. These reflective conversations happen throughout all cycles in the process to generate not just an understanding of the original concept, but a greater set of insights and new possibilities for adaption of the concepts into other options or fields.

Figure 20-20. The RBLF cycle.

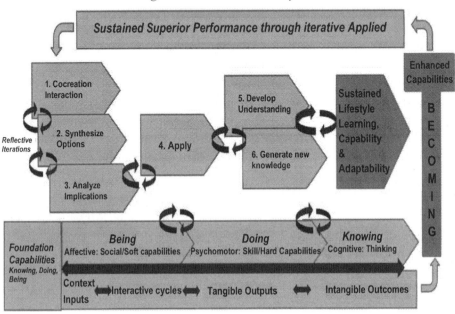

Experienced facilitators already do some of the elements described in this article. However, for the first time the Reverse Bloom Learning Framework provides an academically sound framework to describe how to practically achieve consistent high-quality outcomes. The process is described in greater detail in the open-source journal article at https://coming.gr/wp-content/uploads/2020/12/2_December2020_JEICOM_FINAL_Arthur-W-Shelley.pdf

Dr. Arthur Shelley is a collaborative community builder, multi-awarded learning facilitator and creative education designer with over 30 years of professional experience across the international corporate, government and tertiary education sectors. He is the author of 4 books, has worked in 12 countries, is a mentor in several international communities, and has supervised PhD candidates in 5 countries. He has collaborated with organisations as diverse as NASA, Cirque Du Soleil, Local and National Governments, Universities, start-ups, SMEs, and multinational corporations. https://www.linkedin.com/in/arthurshelley/ He may be contacted at Arthur@IntelligentAnswers.com.au

****

TOOL: Scenario Building

A form of story that provides a **structured process** for consciously thinking about – and planning for – the longer-term future.

Supports: decision-making, problem solving, team learning, knowledge capture

LEVEL OF EFFORT	MED
SIZE OF ORG	SCALABLE
SCOPE OF EFFORT	WIDE

Scenario Building is a creative and shared process that involves groups or teams while allowing time for reflection and creative dialogue about the current and future environment and what the organization may become. Introduced in the 1950's by Herman Kahn, scenario planning was first used in military war games in the 1960's, with a focus on the "predict and control" approach. Later, the emphasis shifted to analyze "cause and effect" relationships in order to better prepare for the future. As a foresight methodology, it is used to consider possible, plausible, probable, and preferable outcomes. Possible outcomes (what might happen) are based on future knowledge; plausible outcomes (what could happen) are based on current knowledge; probably outcomes (what will most likely happen) are based on current; and preferable outcomes (what you want to happen) are based on value judgments.[1026]

The focus on critical uncertainties necessary to move through scenario planning is often quite difficult. Wade argues that scenario planning is all about thinking the unthinkable, although in today's reality the "unthinkable" emerges in our everyday lives.[1027] Yet, simultaneously, we are moving closer to understanding the powerful impact of attention and intention and thought in the process of co-creation.[1028] Thus, an intelligent approach is necessary for effective scenario planning, that is, building scenarios that are based on facts while simultaneously ensuring the opportunities offered by every situation are creatively planned into the scenario, always ending with multiple options, multiple choices, and flexibility at the "point of action".

Ultimately, planning is about the future and, as we all have learned along the road of life, living is a continuous journey of change. There is also a moral challenge associated with planning. Planning is intended as a fundamental guideline, with the objective of planning to *maximize the options of future decision-makers*.[1029] While we cannot control the future, we can influence and nurture its unfolding, and prepare for potential opportunities. Thus, planning itself becomes a tool for change, and helping others learn how to use this tool fully – a *pass it on* strategy – becomes a powerful way to help emerge the best future. This specific process was developed for the U.S. Department of the Navy.

STEP (1): Identify a central issue or question. This step involves clarifying the strategic decisions the organization faces that are critical to the future, establishing the inter-relationship among them, and establishing a horizon time.

STEP (2): Identify the key decision factors within the immediate (micro) environment. This is generally done through brainstorming and answering a series of relevant structured questions.

STEP (3): Identify the larger drivers of the key decision factors in the macro environment (social, technological, economic, environmental and political).

STEP (4): Develop the structure for the scenario by grouping high impact/high uncertainty forces and drivers and potential responses. Wild cards, that is, low-probability, high-impact events such as a terrorist attack or disrupted water supply may be considered. Pre-thinking these events offers the opportunity to examine their implications and make better decisions should they occur. This process develops a ranking of possibilities.

STEP (5): Explore the implications of each scenario in relation to current and future strategy, and identify early indicators. This step should result in core strategies and contingency strategies. The aim is to identify strategies that are robust across all scenarios, given what is known and what might occur in the future.

STEP (6): Flesh out the details of the scenarios, creating a logical cause-and-effect flow with a timeline.

STEP (7): Refine and rewrite the scenarios to take them into a narrative form that is easily understood.

HINT: Consider the tenets of Appreciative Inquiry as you develop and refine these scenarios. (See the discussion of Appreciative Inquiry in Chapter 7.)

While these scenarios may prove useful, a significant advantage of this process is the perceptions, awareness and attitudes of the participating strategists relative to their organization, its environment and its evolution into the future. In other words, they will become much more sensitive to changes and potential risks and opportunities that may arise, and potentially more open, and responsive, to unknown and unperceived events.

✳✳✳✳✳✳✳✳✳✳✳✳✳✳✳

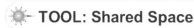 **TOOL: Shared Space**

A **concept** that promoted environments for nurturing knowledge sharing.

Supports: knowledge sharing, creativity, problem solving, collaboration

LEVEL OF EFFORT	MEDIUM
SIZE OF ORG	MED-LARGE
SCOPE OF EFFORT	WIDE

One of the impacts of our post-industrial society and an increasingly virtual workforce, is the exponential rise of the need for collaborative environments and new ways of behaving to effectively engage those environments. For example, as more and more meetings take place with larger and often geographically dispersed groups, the role of facilitators and the value of agendas with good process design were recognized. Highly specialized process design along with unique environments has been found to vastly increase creativity and significantly reduce the time required for interacting.

The idea of shared space moves far beyond the room in which those meetings are held or even a virtual meeting platform. In the paragraphs below shared space will be discussed in terms of both the physical and virtual workspace.

Schrage uses a story to build an understanding of the importance of shared space, and how it expands the space between the sender and receiver in a conversation.[1030] You are at lunch with a colleague when an idea emerges from the conversation. Pulling out a pen you quickly jot down a diagram of the idea on a napkin. Watching you closely, your colleague says "No, no that's not what I meant", takes the pen, and adds a few lines and additional context to the diagram. Now the conversation turns to exploring the meaning of the images on the napkin. If a waiter came and took the napkin away, the conversation might go away. You were talking to each other through a medium, a shared reference point (or shared space) that changed the dynamics of the conversation and served as a mutual communication and learning tool. In a research study with Singapore Armed Forces, it was discovered that the stories shared in the lunch space, which is a large covered open-air space accommodating hundreds and lined with vendors, were the primary source of understanding core values. These are stories that are regularly used by leaders and passed on to both civilian and military in their various leadership capacities.

In terms of workspace, a lot has been learned about the importance of shared space. A common example is the value of conversations that occur around the water fountain or during the coffee break. Many organizations now take this into account when designing office space. For example, centrally locating a wide staircase with highly visible seating spaces when spaces reside on two levels to facilitate interactions or Knowledge Moments (see the simple and short tool on this important concept). Nonaka and Takeuchi introduced the idea of "Ba Spaces", common seating areas or small conference areas centrally located with a pleasant and stimulating environment.[1031] The intent is to encourage people to engage in conversations in their day-to-day work environment.

Virtual Shared Space

As virtual systems have become part of daily work life, a great deal of research has gone into designing stimulating and user-friendly systems. As shared space has become available over time and distance, arriving just in time to support the need to work at home promoted by the global pandemic, the boundaries and reach of organizations has widened. This reaching out offers the opportunity for an expansion of thought built on an ecology of shared space. Some descriptive terms for this ecology include: cool, fast, free, open, global, relevant, compelling and rich.

Cool is both tangible and intangible. In the tangible sense, how does this shared space impact your senses? Is it attractive? Can you be in it with a clear sense of presence? In the intangible sense, how does it make you feel? Does it meet your needs?

Fast is critical in the ever-increasing pace of our lives. We now reach around the world in fractions of seconds to obscure sources of the latest scientific or business developments. Speed is becoming "multi-media", meaning that one media supports another. You reach for your mouse to find and send an email, 30 minutes later you're on the phone with someone you've never met, and three weeks later you've having lunch with that individual during a conference at a distant city.

Free has to do with minimizing the costs for people to engage. Nothing is free. But focusing on the cost of engagement may be a barrier to entry, whether it be time and space for a face-to-face engagement or the cost of a collaborative software environment. There are two issues addressed here. One is that inordinate costs are distracting to building relationships. The second is that costs become a hurdle for every opportunity reaching out. This design principle simply says to make the costs transparent to the individual, pursuing economies of scale and absorbing the cost at the organizational level.

Open refers to both the boundaries of the system and the expansion of thinking. An open information technology architecture is a fundamental design principle. Opening up space to colleagues definitely fosters the notion of networking. Opening up to new ideas and different ways of thinking fosters learning and innovation.

Global has to do with exploration and the emerging sense of unity as a world. In the future global may truly become the concept of shared space. But even today, no matter what our field of expertise, it is pursued in a global context with the realization that the global space has much to offer in terms of learning.

Relevant initially implies relevance to the topic of the domain and the assets of the knowledge base. Relevance is also the building of ideas as individuals, groups and the organization learn from each other.

Rich means that the space is rich in design (colors, ideas, variety, complexity) such that it stimulates all areas of the mind/brain.

Compelling starts with the stickiness of the virtual system, then moves beyond that stickiness to considering shared space in terms of its ability to attract and retain participation. Does the shared space operate in such a way as to become a key asset to participants in their day-to-day work?

Wenger describes 13 fundamental elements of community that technology can affect.[1032] These are: presence and visibility, rhythm (in terms of events and rituals that reaffirm value), variety of interactions, efficiency of involvement (must be easy), short-term value (each interaction needs to create some value), long-term value, connection to the world, personal identity, communal identity, belonging and relationship, complex boundaries (multiple levels and types of participation), evolution (maturation and integration) and active community-building.

It is also important to recognize that in many ways the resources of a shared space are to knowledge workers what tools or instruments have been in many crafts, guilds, and builders throughout history. In many instances the relationship to tools has taken on a reverence that has deep cultural or religious meaning. Such relationships complement or build upon regard for professional skills and status. Such is the transformation that occurred as knowledge workers moved from typewriter to computer to computational computing power to the computer as a communications tool to a virtual space in the 21st century "my-workspace" revolution, then extended into Wikis and Blogs, and now are reaching and discovering the benefits of human-machine partnering.

Expected Outcomes: (1) Knowledge transfer among employees; (2) Creative ideas that help the organization; (3) Improved organizational learning and communication; and (4) A sense of ownership and belonging.

****

TOOL: Strategic Alignment

Contributed by Dr. Arthur J. Murray, Applied Knowledge Sciences, Inc.[1033]

An **approach** to determining where to focus your knowledge efforts through aligning the organization's vision, mission, strategic goals, strategic objectives, master strategy, performance drivers, core capabilities, key process areas, and key enablers.

Supports: strategic decision-making, organizational agility, sustainable performance

LEVEL OF EFFORT	HIGH
SIZE OF ORG	SCALABLE
SCOPE OF WORK	WIDE

For any enterprise, achieving tight integration across internal and external components is a must. Sustained performance simply isn't possible if there are gaps between the many organizational and infrastructure elements involved. These include business models, information and knowledge flows, human capital, research and development, marketing and sales, customer support, finance and accounting, physical plant and equipment, and intellectual property protection. Indeed, all of the elements of an enterprise, which have typically operated under their own separate processes and systems, need to perform as an integrated whole. This presents a significant challenge in building an enterprise of the future.

A leader's greatest challenge is figuring out how to make strategic business decisions without restricting the organization's agility. This means maintaining close coupling up, down and across the organization. For example, if an organization chooses a product innovation strategy, it needs to first identify the key performance drivers needed to support that strategy. In the case of the *3M Company,* for example, rapid concept-to-market cycles are a key performance driver.

Next, the underlying core capabilities needed to achieve that level of performance need to be determined. These core capabilities must be woven tightly together, starting with R&D, and running through design, manufacturing, supply chain logistics, marketing, sales and support). Finally, the processes for managing the primary intellectual assets (human, social, structural and organizational) which enable rapid innovation and learning must be thoroughly understood and well-managed. Former Procter & Gamble Chairman and CEO A. G. Lafley and Rotman School of Management Dean Roger L. Martin emphasize the importance not only of alignment but prioritization by *clearly defining success, playing to your strengths* and *only where winning is possible,* and *managing what matters.*[1034]

Figure IV-20 illustrates the notion of strategic alignment, in which a strategy is developed top-down, and the execution occurs from the bottom-up. Our experience has shown that the more closely these nine layers are aligned, the better the chance of successfully planning and executing a strategy, and making rapid adjustments as conditions change. Thus, each layer needs to be addressed and considered in this context. To assist this process, a brief description of each layer follows.

Vision. As a leader, the place to start before planning any strategy is the vision for your enterprise. A vision is *a description of the future you are trying to co-create.* Some examples of vision are:

- A world shaken by radical new technologies, such as producing living organisms in the laboratory, non-invasive surgery by nanorobots, and dramatically increased lifespan through gene therapy and epigenetics.

- "No child left behind"

- Billions of people in developing countries coming online and having access to world markets.

- New breakthroughs that will provide cheap, inexhaustible supplies of energy.

Mission. Having painted the vision, your next step is to *clearly and succinctly define the impact your enterprise will have on the world.* Examples are:

- "Preserving and improving human life."[1035]

- "An astronaut walking on Mars by 2030"

- "A cure for cancer within our lifetime"

- The ability to travel anywhere on the globe in four hours or less.

Strategic Goals. Your strategic goals *capture, in a measurable way, the end results you want to deliver to your clients, and the kind of enterprise you wish to become.* On the external side, a client-centric strategic goal captures the primary benefit clients receive from doing business with you. Internal goals may be more employee- and/or stakeholder-oriented, such as being recognized as one of the "Top 50 Best Places to Work", or making the "Fast-Growth 100" list. In either case, they should answer the question, *Why would someone deal with you instead of your competitor?*

A strategic goal should be anchored around one or two key elements. It could be size, measure of quality, or strategic positioning in the marketplace, to name a few. Two well-known client-oriented examples are:

- "Delivered to your door within 30 minutes or it's free"
- "When it absolutely, positively has to be there."

Figure 20-21. Strategic flow-down from vision to key enablers.[1036]

Strategic Objectives. Once you've clearly defined your strategic goals, your strategic objectives *define how you are going to accomplish your goals.* For example, a strategic goal might be to become a billion-dollar company. In order to get there, depending upon where you're starting from, you may have to increase sales by fifty percent every year for the next seven years.

Strategic objectives and strategy are closely linked. One might drive the other and vice versa. For example, in a product-oriented strategy, a sales target of $1B might require a significant investment in R&D and marketing. Or the targeted sales growth might be achieved through acquisition.

Strategic objectives are measurable, and should stipulate a time frame. Examples are:

- Revenue growth of 50% per year over the next seven years

- Two new acquisitions per year

- Four new product innovations per year

- Become one of the "top five" in market share within five years.

Master Strategy. Your master strategy *is a clear, understandable statement of how you will align and focus your resources in order to achieve your strategic goals and objectives.* Master strategies are usually made up of one or more sub-strategies. Some master strategy examples are:

- Market domination through competitive pricing and value chain optimization

- Growth through acquisition

- Pre-eminence through world-class expertise and client education

- Gaining maximum leverage through strategic alliances.

Examples of sub-strategies which support the master strategy are: (1) Marketing: social networking and saturation advertising; (2) Sales: point-of-sale up-selling/cross-selling and competitive pricing; (3) Product innovation: planned product obsolescence in 2-year cycles; (4) Financial: leveraged buy-outs and licensing; (5) Human capital: 80 hours of specialized training annually; (6) Customer service: a real person answers the phone within two rings, 24/7/365; and (7) Quality: xix-sigma, with advancement to seven-sigma.

Performance Drivers. Your organization's performance drivers *are the primary factors that make the difference between success and failure in achieving your strategic goals and objectives.* For example, if your mission is speed-oriented, such as "absolutely, positively by 10:00 a.m." or "delivered in 30 minutes or it's free" then your performance drivers should be speed-oriented as well. In this case, the performance demands will be focused on the logistics of preparation, packaging, and delivery.

Likewise, if your primary marketing message is "if you are dissatisfied for any reason, return the product for a full refund" then your major performance drivers will be quality-oriented. A low-price strategy such as Wal-Mart's places huge performance demands on supply-chain systems. Other examples of performance drivers include consistency, efficiency, accuracy, responsiveness, cost control, reliability, availability, asset utilization, and superior technical support.

Core Capabilities. Your core capabilities are *the underlying competencies and capacities for producing the results you are promising to deliver*. We divide these into two areas: competency-focused capabilities (human and social capital) and capacity-oriented capabilities (organizational and structural capital).

Examples of human and social capital are:

- Fully certified and accredited support staff
- Fluency in the native languages of our major clients
- Personalized service
- Recognized top experts in the field.

Examples of organizational and structural capital include:

- State-of-the-art testing laboratory
- Mobile showroom
- Electronic Data Interchange (EDI) and other supply-chain infrastructure
- Just-in-time inventory system
- Fully integrated design and production facility
- 24/7/365 call center.

Key Process Areas. We've now "drilled down" far enough to reach the point at which the work is actually performed. We define *work* as the activity that needs to occur in order to produce a specific result. *Work processes* are repeatable models of that activity. The activity can be performed by humans, machines, or both. The goal is to seek the most efficient and effective aggregation of people and work processes which consistently delivers the desired results.

Examples of human and social capital-intensive work processes include: recruitment, hiring and retention; sub-contract management; relationship management; relationship network management; leadership development; and training and certification.

Examples of organizational and structural capital-intensive work processes include: proposal preparation; product life cycle management; project management; quality management; and agile development and/or manufacturing.

Key Enablers. Key enablers are *the methods, practices, and underlying technologies which support the execution of work processes in the most efficient and effective manner possible*. We define *methods* as repeatable formulas, algorithms, rules, techniques, or behaviors underlying a work process. Simply stated, the discovery of a more efficient algorithm, or a more complete set of business rules, could increase the efficiency and effectiveness of a given work process. Examples of methods include: lease vs. buy algorithms, source selection methodologies, and balanced scorecards.

A *practice* is the actual application of a work process within a given organizational context. Examples of practices include: interviewing techniques; welcoming/onboarding new employees/associates; capturing and sharing lessons learned; and guidelines for participating in a community of practice.

By technologies we mean tools, techniques and infrastructure that enable efficient and effective performance. Examples of technologies include platforms, data lakes/warehouses, virtual/augmented reality, mobility, AI/robotics, and data analytics.

About Dr. Art Murray: For over 40 years, Art Murray's passion has been getting people to draw out their deeply hidden knowledge so they and others can benefit from it and grow it. He has done this for hundreds of organizations, large and small, public, private, and nonprofit, all around the world. His current focus is on building and curating digital bodies of knowledge, human and machine knowledge governance, and developing systems in which humans teach machines and machines teach humans, including a system for detecting and responding to weak signals in large, complex projects and organizations. For added insights, check out Art's books on Human Deep Learning and The Enterprise of the Future, and his bi-monthly series: "The Future of the Future" at kmworld.com. Art may be contacted at amurray@aksciences.com

****

TOOL: Truth Searching

A **process** for searching out the level of truth in a situation at hand.

Supports: decision-making, learning, performance and sustainability, transparency

LEVEL OF EFFORT	LOW
SIZE OF ORG	SCALABLE
SCOPE OF EFFORT	C^2 Dependent

As a foundational concept in the democratic approach, the importance of truth emerges throughout this book. Truth, trust, and transparency are the outer petals of the Reblooming the Knowledge Movement (RKM) model and "The Search for Truth" is explored in Chapter 3. This tool is in support of that search. Since truth deals with what is generally believed or considered "facts" in a particular context or focused on a particular situation, the search for truth is a search for examples of the level of truth currently known. Note that truth and untruth both build in waves.

STEP (1): Clearly define the truth which you are affirming (Truth A).

STEP (2): Understand the context and/or situation clearly from which this truth is emerging (Situation/Event A). In this stage, it is important to engage both logical and conceptual thinking; logic is lower mental thinking and concepts, as patterns based on logic, are higher mental thinking.

STEP (3): Search for other situations or events that reflect similar patterns (Situations/Events B, C, etc.). For each situation or event, *ask*: Is Truth A also true in this situation or event?

STEP (4): Determine the *level of truth* of Truth A. If Truth A is true in every situation and/or event you have identified, then, for the present, you can be confident of its truth value in Situation A. If Truth A *does not* work in one or more of the events and/or situations you identified, then reconsider the value of Truth A in Situation A.

STEP (5): For any event/situation identified where Truth A does *not* work, first ensure the event/situation has a similar pattern of activity. If so, then reflect on how Truth A might be changed in order to become true in both Situation A and in this new event/situation. Continue with this process until you discover a higher level of truth that works in all of the events/situations you have identified or can identify that reflect similar patterns to Situation/Event A.

NOTE: While your personal beliefs may be difficult to circumvent, your body will often indicate that this is the case. A cognitive dissonance can occur when considering two beliefs which are in conflict with each other. To help mitigate the possibility of cognitive biases and the injection of hidden assumptions, *vericate* your findings with others in your network. *Verication* is the process of consulting a trusted ally, that is, someone with expertise in the domain of knowledge in which you are truth searching. There is considerable discovery power in engaging groups of minds in truth searching.

Note that new ideas can emerge from a negative insight, that is, recognition that the current theoretical body of knowledge is insufficient to explain a current situation. This requires discarding previous beliefs and theories in preference to a new or expanded conceptual truth. An example is Einstein's early paper on relativity, published at age 26 in 1905. In this paper Einstein had to break away from the concept of absolute space and time so that he could accept the general principles of Maxwell's equations for electromagnetism, which are the symmetries that correspond to special relativity.[1037]

See the related tool "Untruth Rhythm Disruptor".

****

TOOL: Trust Mapping

Contributed by Dr. John Lewis

A **process** to visualize trust for each key activity within an organization.

Supports: collaboration,

LEVEL OF EFFORT	Medium
SIZE OF ORG	SCALABLE
SCOPE OF EFFORT	Wide

While trust plays an important role in all interactions, in the process of sharing knowledge and co-creating it is a necessity. Yet in a CUCA environment (change, uncertainty, complexity, and anxiety) where anxiety and fear often find their way into our living space, trust can be hard to build and sustain. Instead of thinking of where we place our trust as a dichotomy (others vs ourselves), it may be more accurate to think in terms of a surety spectrum with four main categories: Direct Knowledge, Direct Trust, Deferred Trust, and Faith Trust. Before introducing the process of trust mapping, these categories (which were introduced in Chapter 12) are briefly defined below.

Direct Knowledge is knowing that we know our own observations and conclusions, and can therefore base future decisions on what we currently know. To prove our direct knowledge, we may be asked to "verify" what we know by showing examples, research, etc. While this type of knowing provides us with a feeling of deep surety, the "grounding" that it provides from past experiences may also keep us from taking new/future ground.

Direct Trust is knowing that we trust our own observations and conclusions, and can therefore base future decisions on what we currently and directly trust. This type of trust simply projects our current direct knowledge into the future as expectations of continuity. This continuity can be linear or non-linear, and applied to situations or ourselves. When we describe our trust towards future expectations, as it relates to our own abilities, we usually use the term "self-efficacy" to describe this concept.

Deferred Trust is knowing that we trust someone else, based on "credibility," which is simply the quality we use to determine if they are believable or worthy of trust. This quality we use can vary widely between people and circumstances. For example, some may deem others credible based on the *authority* of the position they hold, while others may only deem them credible after reviewing the authorization process which was used to place them into authority. Note that the initiative to overthrow monarchies was through this lens, since "birthright" became a questionable authorization process. Given the need to be clear about the exact ways that we trust in others, the term *vericate*

(Bennet & Bennet, 2004) is increasingly used to specify certain qualities of trust. Just as the term "verify" places specific qualifications for how we reference direct knowledge, the term "vericate" places specific qualifications for how we reference deferred trust. To vericate means that you are relying on someone's socially recognized experience and expertise in a specific area, not just their authority or ungrounded opinion.

Faith Trust is knowing that we trust in a general outcome based on *our perceived nature of the Universe*. For example, we may be called a *pessimist* if we believe in Murphy's law, which states that "if anything can go wrong it will go wrong." Or we may be called an *optimist* if we believe that "the cup is half full, not half empty" and that things have a way of working out. How much does our perceived nature of the Universe influence future events? From a psychological viewpoint, the study of self-talk and affirmations looks at the impact these beliefs have on our confidence, which can directly affect our approach and expectations. From a neuroscience viewpoint, we know that our thoughts and feelings influence the structure of the brain, and the structure of the brain influences our thoughts. But the more-interesting study of Quantum reality looks at the impact these beliefs have on connected consciousness, which can directly affect the situation and outcome.

The Process

In this example, David is the person overseeing the work, and in addition to assigning an owner to each change program activity, he has mapped where trust is placed.

In the example trust map that is Table 20-10, David owns activity 0 (program oversight), and he expects to rely on all four trust categories. Alex owns activity 1, and while not the expert for this specific task, does rely on self-efficacy (direct trust), verication of experts (deferred trust), and her optimistic nature (faith trust). David has assigned activity 2 to himself as he is the expert for this task and has self-efficacy given the new team and tasks. Theresa owns activity 3, and expects the task to be predictably within her current expertise. Arthur owns activity 4, and while having knowledge of the task is going to be heavily reliant on a contractor. John owns activity 5, and without specific expertise will be overseeing the results of a contractor, while relying on his optimistic nature. Alex owns activity 6, and is the known expert. Notice for activity 1 and 6, Alex has been assigned ownership of two important tasks, but instead of becoming overloaded is relying on experts for one of the activities. Theresa owns activity 7, and will be primarily trusting another department. Arthur owns activity 8, and will be primarily trusting several other department heads. John owns activity 9, and at this early point in the program is optimistic but has not yet assigned subtasks with deferred trust.

Table 20-10. Frame of reference for change program activities and trust mapping.

#	Activity	Owner	Direct Knowledge	Direct Trust	Deferred Trust	Faith Trust
0	Overseeing the Program	David	X	X	X	X
1	Building Infrastructure	Alex		X	X	X
2	Management Sponsorship	David	X	X		
3	Training	Theresa	X			
4	Communication	Arthur	X		X	
5	Promotion and Reward	John			X	X
6	Embedded into process	Alex	X	X		X
7	Benchmark and Result	Theresa			X	X
8	KPI enforcement	Arthur			X	
9	Shared team status	John				X

Discussion

In today's environment our organizations are increasingly becoming more matrixed and project-based, so instead of a hierarchy of known relationships and known capabilities, it is necessary to rely more on trust. Using a Trust Mapping tool allows us to articulate and share our status of trust along with the activities and progress. It enables us to see if we are overloading team members and encouraging them to be individual performers rather than team players and also relying on others. It allows us to see if we are outsourcing work for which we can provide coaching since we have retained a core competency, or if we are outsourcing work which will require a high level of deferred trust and faith trust. Finally, it allows us to track stretch goals for leaders to own more activities in areas where they are not direct experts.

Note that this example trust map is for David, who is overseeing the program. If the six people in our example mapped their perspective of trust in this grouping, they might get different answers, because their "knowledge" of the tasks, people and relationships will be different. As owners of specific activities complete their own trust map for specific tasks, they will capture specifics for where they are placing their trust at a deeper level. For deferred trust, additional qualities may be documented for: (1) Applicability (how a task aligns with their expertise), (2) Accountability (how they have met previous requirements), and (3) Authorization (what experience and education has defined them as an expert).

In trust mapping, when trust is strong, we get overlaying maps, which forms a strong basis of relationships. However, where trust is uneven, people can be taken advantage of. For example, if James trusts Marie, but actually Marie has portrayed herself through a mask that James has not seen through, Marie can manipulate James. For this, she does not have to trust him, just ensure that James cannot see through her mask. Whilst James' trust of Marie remains, the knowledge flows freely from him to her, which she may use appropriately (for mutual benefit) or inappropriately (to take credit for James' work, or take advantage of him). If James sees through the mask and realizes he has been inappropriately manipulated, not only does his trust diminish, but he actually builds a *distrust* for Marie. Unfortunately, there is only a two-letter difference between distrust and destruct, with the first being the precursor of the latter. From this point on, James will not view Marie neutrally, but from a negative perspective. This completely changes the relationship and effectively stops the flow of knowledge. As the old adage goes, *Trust takes forever to build and only a moment to destroy*.

Note that distrust is quite different than having no trust. Trust is directly related to the belief in someone or something in terms of truth and reliability or strength. As with truth, there are levels of trust. Distrust is generally related to a feeling rather than a belief, and has to do with doubting the truth and reliability of someone or something. It also carries with it an element of suspicion. What is fascinating is that while trust and distrust may be opposites in the world of duality within which we live, there is a neutral spot in between, where there is neither trust nor distrust. For example, this would occur when a person or product is unknown.

In exploring the relationship between trust and distrust, Lewicki et al. (1998) talk in terms of high trust and low trust, and high distrust and low distrust. High trust is characterized by hope, faith, confidence, assurance and initiative. Low trust is characterized by no hope, faith or confidence, passivity and hesitance. High distrust is characterized by fear, skepticism, cynicism, wariness and watchfulness, and vigilance. Conversely, low distrust is characterized by no fear, the absence of skepticism and cynicism, low monitoring and no vigilance.

Dr. John Lewis is a coach, educator, and consultant in leadership, innovation, and KM. John helps leaders and organizations reach their peak potential through evidence-based performance strategies. John has "Big 4" management consulting experience and was acknowledged by Gartner with an industry "Best Practice" for an innovative global KM solution. John is the author of *Story Thinking* and *The Explanation Age*, which Kirkus Reviews described as "An iconoclast's blueprint for a new era of innovation." He is an associate editor of the *Journal of Innovation Management* and holds a Doctorate in Educational Psychology.

****

TOOL: Untruth Rhythm Disruptor

A **process** to interrupt the rhythm (pattern) presented through the weaving of truths and untruths.

Supports: decision-making, learning, performance and sustainability

LEVEL OF EFFORT	C^2 Dependent
SIZE OF ORG	SCALABLE
SCOPE OF EFFORT	C^2 Dependent

Following the exploration of "The Search for Truth" in Chapter 3, there is an in-depth discussion of misinformation, disinformation and propaganda. Two primary forms of propaganda – (1) the shifting of cause and effect and (2) the strategic weaving of untruth and truth, creating layers of lies – are introduced and examples provided. A higher level of propaganda is to become creative in negative ways, that is, create a causal reality of intricately constructed lies that are hard to challenge.[1038] Objects are created to convince people that what they last heard is connected to what you are telling them, even though these may be opposites. When a mind focused on cause and effect hears one recognizable truth, they can easily connect other things told to them as true, not recognizing the lack of consistency or the contradictions that are present. Responses may follow the path of false perceptions and logic such as: "If she told the truth in the past, then this must be true.: Or, "If this was successful in the past, then it will be successful now." Or, "If he is wealthy and in a position of power, then it must be right."

A key factor in the weaving of truths and untruths is rhythm, which can lead to diminishing or destruction of the mental capabilities. Whether in a personal or professional setting, if you can recognize the rhythm and mentally disrupt it, the truth is easier to discern. Following is a process to do just that.

STEP (1): Identify any desire (feeling) you have that is related to what is being promised/said. These are not just mental ideas, but are also connected to emotions. Regardless of the level of truth, you are being offered something that you are told will be forthcoming in the future. *Tapping desire is the first beat to developing a rhythm and bringing others into that rhythm.*

NOTE: It is a good idea to understand your fixed desires, that is, those desires that come up over and over again in life (professional and personal). Do a periodic review of your desires. *Ask*: Do I really want this now, or is this a hangover from some emotionally-charged event from the past? Is this desire beneficial to me and/or others? Is this desire selfish? Is this desire worth spending my energy/thought/feelings pursuing?

STEP (2): Think about what has been promised/said in the past from this same source. Try to put this in a time sequence, that is, when was this promised/said? Create a timeline by drawing a straight line on a piece of paper, putting tick marks to indicate promises/statements with the date above each tick mark and a short description of the promise/statement below the tick mark.

HELPFUL HINT: When considered from the mental focus, when something is equally presented and balanced it connects to an event representing three parts of time (past, present, future). This means that it has a low degree of context sensitivity: it was true in the past, is true now, and will be true in the future. In a lie, *at least one part of time is imbalanced*; thus, something SOUNDS or FEELS untrue. Listen to this feeling. You must recognize untruths before you can respond to them.

STEP (3): Look for a rhythm in what is being said. As we are warned, "Don't fall into the rhythm of the lie."[1039] The goal of propaganda is not to *convince* you of truthfulness, but to *confuse*, **drawing you into the rhythm of the lie so you cannot perceive the truth.** Note that both truth and untruth build in waves.

STEP (4): Disrupt the rhythm by creating discord. This can be done by engaging in a contemplative or self-reflective session where lies can be felt and recognized. Interacting and reflecting with trusted others who are open communicators can provide valuable input to this process.

See the related tool on "Truth Searching".

****

 Value Infusion Methodology

Contributed by Drs. Alex Bennet and David Bennet, Mountain Quest Institute

A **methodology** using stories captured from senior leaders in the organization and storytelling to infuse organizational values throughout the organization.

Supports: every aspect of organizational performance

LEVEL OF EFFORT	HIGH
SIZE OF ORG	SCALABLE
SCOPE OF WORK	WIDE

"Let me tell you a story ..." is the oldest invitation in the human experience. Stories are knowledge, and our knowledge of the world is more or less equivalent to our experiences. As we become more and more conscious about our stories, and our vicarious roles as characters in those stories, we have more clarity about who we are, why we are here, and how we should act in the world.[1040] Stories can communicate values, ideas, modes of thinking, and frames of reference, and can be used as guides for actions. When used to solve difficult problems, stories can act as a substitute for experience.[1041] They capture tacit knowledge, convey feelings, and can embody and transfer knowledge;

communicate complex knowledge holistically; make information more memorable; help us relate incoming information to those experiences already in memory; and provide the context in which knowledge rises as well as the knowledge itself.

Values play a special role in human endeavors in that as they become part of the employee's belief system, significantly affect how the employee looks at, understands and supports the organization. Since values are central to our mental models, behavior and our understanding of any situation, it is imperative that the organization have a strong value set that is understood and internalized by all employees. This ensures consistency of decisions, builds a strong culture and identity, and presents a positive image to the rest of the world.

The methodology presented in this paper uses **the power of stories combined with the relevance of specific values** to build employee awareness and appreciation for the role of their values in supporting organizational performance. It is assumed that the organizational core values have been previously determined. It should be recognized that this methodology is flexible and can be adapted to each organization's specific needs. This process includes (1) engaging senior leaders on organizational values, (2) building the value stories, (3) organizing and accessing the stories, and (4) mobilizing the value stories. Each of these phases with their sub-steps are detailed below.

PHASE 1: Engaging Senior Leaders on Organizational Values

This phase includes five steps: designing the interview process, interviewing senior leaders, analyzing interview results, identifying emerging value themes, and developing communications packages.

STEP (1): **Designing the interview process** involves designing interview protocols, selecting senior leaders to be interviewed, and setting up the interviews. Senior leaders are most responsive if the process has been pre-vetted in staff meetings, is championed by a senior leader within the organization, and the interview scheduling done under the auspices of that champion.

Most of the questions are focused in areas related to the organizational values. An overview of the interview process is provided, and a starting set of questions is prepared as part of the pre-interview information packet to be sent to senior leaders prior to the interview process. The credentials of the interviewers are also included in this pre-packet.

STEP (2): **Capturing senior leader's thoughts and stories.** Senior consultants conduct the interviews, and as such they are able to create an open, give-and-take interaction that can lead to deeper responses. Since questions are primarily open-ended, the interviewers encourage senior leaders to follow their thoughts and areas of passion in responding. Throughout the open-ended questions and responses, senior leaders are asked for stories; for example:

"Could you give me an example of that?" or "Can you recall an incident where that happened?" or, more directly, "Could you tell a story about that?" The entire process is recorded. Organizations often prefer to have the tapes transcribed in-house because of the potential for difficulties resulting from cultural and functional language discrepancies. Since the interviews are conducted as non-attribution, when this is done it is paramount for this raw material to be controlled.

STEP (3): **Data reduction and analysis**. A rigorous process is undertaken to ensure effective use of interview materials. Transcripts and supporting documents are dissected into stand-alone passages (thoughts ideas, concepts, examples, stories) and clustered around emerging similarities, allowing the data to drive these groupings. These groups are then organized by second-order similarities to provide glimpses of emerging themes and allow the researchers to begin the sense-making process which will result in the communications packages. During the data reduction process of the leadership interviews, potential stories are identified and placed (with context) in separate piles related to the emerging themes.

STEP (4): **Identification of the emerging core themes**. As repeated themes emerge through the grouping and chunking process in STEP 3, they are further explored in relationship to the core values. Where there is a clear relationship to a value, this theme is linked to that value. Where the relationship is not clear, this theme will become a topic of discussion for the IPT in order to ensure the best linking possible. The themes that emerge through this process are used in three ways: (1) they are used to help understand the core values from the viewpoint of the leadership team; (2) they are integrated with the results of the core values themselves; and (3) they become part of the organizational schema for the book of stories resulting from the interviews and, potentially, for use by a virtual system storyteller available across the organizational intranet (discussed further in Phase 4).

STEP (5): **Interviews with additional leaders at all levels** of the organization who have dealt with high visibility situations that may be repeated in the future of the organization. In other words, individuals who have made decisions, taken actions, and had experiences that are important for others to understand. These interviews are focused around specific experiences and as such become a series of stories related to those experiences. While they are transcribed, they are used solely for stories and do not become part of the leadership communications packages. Specifically, these individuals are provided the emerging themes from the leadership interviews and asked for their thoughts on these themes. They are also asked how their "stories" related to these themes.

PHASE 2: Building the Value Stories.

The leadership stories gathered will generally fall into three categories: (1) stories of which leaders were a part or that had impacted their lives as remembered by them; (2) views, opinions and feelings about specific values, specifically those values in the context of their careers; and (3) personal journeys, those situations in their careers and lives about which leaders have passion. As noted above, the stories described in STEP (5) of PHASE 1 above elicited from leaders at all levels would be experiential in nature and directly related to the organization and its performance.

The potential stories identified in the data analysis process and those emerging from the interviews surrounding specific situations all undergo **story development**. This involves moving through a sculpting process which includes expanding, tightening, molding and polishing each of the stories. During this process the sculptors attempt to shape every potential story offered through the interviews. A "story" used in this context may be an account or recital of an event or series of events (real or fictional) or it may be a descriptive passage captured and sculpted in anticipation of combining additional detail from a later interview. The term "story" also includes analogies. Note that these are kept to an "optimum" length, that is, what is needed to convey the story and no more. No embellishments are added, and the tone of the story is sustained. Simultaneously, language is corrected as needed, and the "leader's intent" (commander's intent) is conveyed.

While all stories are non-attribution, some of the relationships between leadership levels and positions may be discernible, in particularly by close working colleagues. Part of the IPT's responsibility is to review the sculpted stories and mark questionable stories for further discussion.

Before release to the larger organization – but following PHASE 3 below – the stories should be provided back to the senior leaders interviewed to ensure their intent was captured and no sensitive areas have been included. It is important for leaders to note that the stories are not always related to a single source; they may be the result of combining two or three or more leadership responses that provided different details when relating similar or related stories.

PHASE 3: Organizing and Accessing the Stories.

While indexing is initially provided manually, the **multiple approaches to indexing** lay the groundwork for creating a virtual repository of organizational stories. Three indexes are developed to enable users to identify and locate stories for specific applications. Each story is assigned a label (a three-digit number with a letter preceding it) that will exist as long as the story stays viable. If the story falls out during the sculpting and approval process, that number is not reused, allowing a clear audit trail should a question be asked later about a specific story that dropped out during the process.

The first index is by specific value and value theme. The second is a description of the activity involved in the story. The third is by subject, interweaving the value themes as part of the subject index. This index would embrace special areas of focus and interest determined by the organization representatives on the IPT. For example, the first story in the Singapore Armed Forces Storybook – which has been presented at various conferences so can be shared freely – looks like this:

> S001   LOYALTY TO COUNTRY: MISSION (HUMANITARIAN)
> PROFESSIONALISM: RESPONSIBILITY/ ACCOUNTABILITY
> NAVY
> CRASH OF SILK AIR MI 185
>
> We were practicing mine detection and diffusion underwater. If we had been in Palembang on 19 December 1997, we might have heard the late-afternoon mid-air explosion of the Silk Air MI 185 flight. But within minutes, we had heard the news and were scrambling towards the helicopter deployment site. Ours was the second rescue group to arrive in Palembang, joining the Indonesian Navy which had deployed ships and divers to the area. Working together, we quickly located the crash site.
>
> What we saw was unexpected and is difficult to describe. Pieces of twisted metal and mangled passenger seats half submerged in the murky waters of the Musi River. Luggage and body parts were floating with the current. A lifejacket and teddy bear were entangled in tall grasses at the river's edge. Our teams dove into the grisly work of search and salvage, hoping beyond hope that the river-soaked teddy bear had a live owner. It didn't.
>
> We worked through the night and stayed through the Christmas holidays. Families of the victims lined the river banks, participating in religious rites, never giving up even when there was no more hope. Day after day our team worked with diligence and respect, combining sensitivity and professionalism to execute a difficult mission.

As labeled, this story relates to two core values. The first value is Loyalty to Country, with the theme related to "mission" (other themes were commitment and sacrifice) and the sub-theme "humanitarian" (with other mission sub-themes: deterrence, diplomacy, nation building, and peace keeping). The second value is Professionalism, with the theme responsibility/accountability. Other themes related to professionalism are systems perspective, learning, networking and sharing, knowledge, knowledge management, ideas, and excel/excellence. The next line says that the participants are in the Navy. The bottom line is the subject matter of the story.

The stories can also be classified according to the MQI Story Characteristics Classification Schema based on Kohlberg's Moral Development

Model and the Bennet Level of Comprehension Model. This provides a way of characterizing the potential user audiences and aligning characteristics of selected stories to those audiences. See Figure 20-22 below.

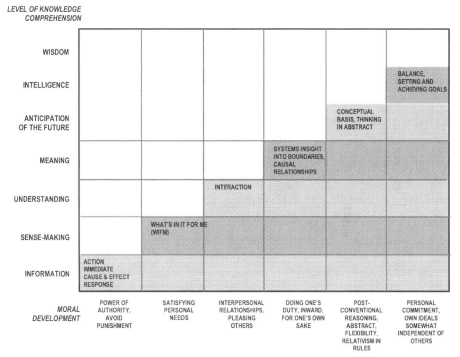

Figure 20-22. The levels of knowledge comprehension relative to Kohlberg's stages of moral development.

Note the moral development line in Kohlberg's model and the first two levels of knowledge comprehension. The characteristics at the nexus points read: action, immediate cause & effect response, and WIFM (what's in it for me). Consistent with Kohlberg's model, the entry level of the military organization is where discipline is paramount. Whether conscripts or volunteers, recruits rapidly gain large amounts of information and knowledge in an unnatural environment with new rules, restrictions, requirements, and values. The stories collected stories can be related to these nexus points and used where they can have the greatest impact from the viewpoint of volunteers and recruits in terms of moving from information to sense-making to understanding.

PHASE 4: Mobilizing the Value Stories

The final part of the methodology involves **mobilizing the stories and the values they convey**. The entire process is designed such that mobilization is the beginning of implementation of the stories and their capacity to transfer knowledge and values. While the mobilization program developed depends upon the nature and needs of the organization, it would most likely include a number of different approaches. One mobilization approach includes a workshop to prepare organizational instructors and/or trainers to work directly with employees by discussing stories, values, and their importance to the organization, which may include train-the-trainer materials. A second approach would be to organize "pass-it-down" sessions such that each level of the organization would be responsible for "training" their direct reports. While this is time consuming, the results are innumerable and long-lasting.

The workshop for employees would cover the telling, analysis, interpretation and meaning of the values as they relate to the performance and reputation of the organization. Attendees would work in small groups that allow them to discuss the stories and their values in terms of their impact on each employee as well as the organization. The role of each value in support of organizational performance would be addressed and open discussions would give everyone the opportunity to participate. Working in small groups, each group would consider a story and its value(s) with regard to their personal values, identifying and discussing different perspectives and feelings. During the course of the workshop participants would be encouraged to write and tell their own stories. They would also be provided tools to help them capture, sculpt, and tell their stories.

Another approach is the creation of a virtual storyteller who is available via the intranet or internet to tell the stories in the story repository in response to specific related questions. A contest might be regularly held where the best stories contributed by employees during training sessions become part of the story repertoire of the virtual storyteller. Another approach would be creation of a knowledge fair (event intermediation) with stories and storytelling as a key focus area. As can be seen, the story repository has a high potential for use beyond training purposes as a resource for infusing organizational values in both new and long-term employees.

****

 Writing a Good Practice

Adapted from the DON Toolkit

A **template** for capturing and clearly communicating in context a good practice.

Supports: Transfer of good practices, organizational learning, knowledge capture, collaboration

LEVEL OF EFFORT	MED
SIZE OF ORG	SCALABLE
SCOPE OF WORK	WIDE

There are 11 steps to follow to write a good practice. Specific instructions are related to each step.

Step (1): Name the good practice.

Instructions: Create a short descriptive title which enables potential users to find the general topic/theme.

Step (2): Target potential users.

Instructions: (1) Identify those individuals or teams who encounter similar situations and challenges and can use and/or benefit from this practice, including individuals, teams, functions, and business units. (2) Identify the types of situations and challenges in which this BP might be applicable.

Step (3): Identify keywords.

Instructions: (1) Brainstorm the key elements or sub-topics of the general topic. (2) Identify one or more keywords from your perspective and the perspective of potential users for the topic and subtopics. If the users were to use keywords to search for this practice, what would they be?

Table 20-11. Identify keywords.

	What we call it	What the users might call it
Overall Topic	keywords	keywords
Element 1	keywords	keywords
Element 2	keywords	keywords

Step (4): Describe the process for identifying/creating the practice.

Instructions: Describe the organizational context in which the BP was created, including: the triggering event, problem or challenge; when it was created; who created it; the data collection process; how the data was analyzed; conclusions drawn from the data; how the data were validated; where the practice has been implemented and for how long.

Step (5): Define the good practice.

Instructions: Capture the answers to the following questions: What are the objectives/deliverables? What are the process steps and tasks involved? Who is responsible for what in implementing the process? What milestone and outcome measures are associated with the practice? What tools and techniques are used?

Step (6): Specify the results:

Instructions: Answer the following questions: How is the practice efficient and effective at delivering a particular outcome when applied to a particular condition or circumstance? What is the improvement on services/products to patients, internal customers? What are the bottom-line measurable results, e.g., time and cost savings, productivity improvement, quality enhancement, other KPIs? What is the improvement in building capacity and capability from an individual, team, and/or organization level for the present and the future, e.g., skills, knowledge? How are teamwork and collaboration enhanced? Give testimonials/quotes to illustrate the benefits.

Step (7): Identify lessons learned and recommended improvements

Instructions: Answer the six questions based on the Continuous Improvement Review tool: What was intended? What actually happened? What was the gap between the intended and actual results? Why? What would you do the same? What would you do differently? What are the specific improvement recommendations going forward?

Step (8): Define the critical success factors.

Instructions: What has occurred or has to occur for this practice to continue to be successful including: leadership commitment; enrollment of people to create and sustain enthusiasm, ownership, and commitment; tools and techniques; software and/or hardware, people resource requirements such as roles, skills, etc.; performance measurement and tracking; rewards and recognition; communication including formal and informal, virtual and face-too-face; training; other (specify).

Step (9): Identify recommended vehicles for the effective transfer of this good practice.

Instructions: Identify multiple vehicles for sharing BPs which have proven to be effective and/or are recommended. The vehicles may vary based on the potential user population. Vehicles should assume that both explicit and tacit knowledge is being shared.

Table 20-12. Identify recommended vehicles for effective transfer of this good practice.

Potential User Population	Vehicles to share explicit knowledge, e.g., people to information	Vehicles to share tacit knowledge, e.g., people to people

NOTE: **Storytelling** is a powerful vehicle for the effective transfer of good practices.

Step (10): Identify point(s) of contact/subject matter expert(s).

Instructions: Identify pertinent details of point(s) of contact and subject matter expert(s). This would include name, title/position, business unit/function, location, email address, phone numbers, and areas of expertise.

Step (11): Identify links to other resources.

Instructions: Identify links (locations) to other resources such as workbooks, video clips, articles, transcripts of review meeting, web links, pictures, templates, manuals, PowerPoint slides, white papers, reports, etc.

****

CHAPTER 21
THE TOOL MATRIX

There was a time when we would have needed to develop a second (or third) book to focus on the knowledge and innovation tools that can make a difference to individuals and the organization. Today, however, that is not the case. The Knowledge Tool Matrix below is intended as a mind jogger, that is, some suggested tools – both simple and several a bit more complicated – that have worked in the immediate past and may be of service to you, the reader. And if they are of interest to you, each of these can be easily searched on the internet or inquired about through your Artificial Intelligence partner as to how to best use them.

We have included the name of the tool, a one-line description, and an idea of the areas it can support. Consistent with the earlier tools, the right-hand column provides an idea of level of effort, the size of the organization it can assist, and the scope of impact. As a reminder, these specifically translate as follows:

Level of Effort [Low/Medium/High] = Relative amount of investment (time, people, funds) needed to implement this initiative.

Size of Organization [Small/Medium/Large/Scalable] = Indicator of relative size of the organization where this tool has been successfully applied. Small is 0-50; Medium is 50-300; Large is greater than 300 employees. Scalable means that the tool has been used successfully in organizations of all sizes.

Scope of Impact [Narrow/Medium/Wide] = Range of situations, issues, problems that this initiative has the potential to improve.

C^2 means that the initiative is highly context sensitive and situation dependent and is difficult to categorize.

Those tools that have an asterisk following the name are included as examples at the beginning of this chapter.

Tool	Description	Supports	Level of Effort Size of Org Scope of Impact
Action Learning	A process involving a small group of people learning as they solve real problems.	Problem solving, individual and group learning, team collaboration	Low/Scalable/ Wide
Affinity Diagram	A process for categorizing FS knowledge needs in a diagram format to exhibit differences and relationships.	Group Learning, knowledge audit	Low/Scalable/ Narrow
After Action Review	A group process for assessing the effectiveness of events or the way situations were handled.	Knowledge sharing, learning, assessment, knowledge retention, innovation	Med/Scalable /Wide
Anecdotal Circles	A focus group when people come together to share their experiences around a specific theme. Designed to elicit people's stories (real events).	Knowledge sharing, planning, individual and organizational learning	
Appreciative Inquiry	A positive approach to accelerating receptivity to new ideas, behavior change, and the adoption of best practices.	Organizational learning, culture change	Med/Scalable /Wide
Ba Spaces	Collaborative Spaces designed into the workplace to facilitate knowledge moments	Knowledge Sharing, learning, team building, knowledge retention	Low/Scalable/ Wide
Barrier Buster	Process to identify and address policy barriers to an initiative.	Implementation, knowledge sharing, policy change	Med/Wide
Benchmarking	A process for identifying good practices in external organizations, learning from them, and adapting them to your organization.	Organizational learning, process improvement, culture change	Med/Scalable /C^2

Tool	Description	Supports	Level of Effort Size of Org Scope of Impact
Best Practices	A systematic process for transferring best practices between groups within the organization or across the enterprise.	Organization learning, operations, performance and sustainability	$C^2/C^2/C^2$
Blog	A conversational website maintained by an individual.	Knowledge sharing, learning, team building, relationship building	Low/Scalable/ Wide
Brain Writing	A process to help groups collaborate when dealing with a sensitive idea or issue.	Collaboration, problem solving, conflict, resolution, group learning	Low/Scalable /Med
Brainstorming	A process for enhancing the creation and flow of new ideas.	Innovation, consensus building, problem solving, team building, relationship building	Low/Scalable/ C^2
Bridging Generations	A program or series of actions for engaging employees who have retired or external experts who are no longer fully engaged in the workplace.	Knowledge retention, organizational performance, organizational learning, employee development	Med/Scalable /Wide
Case Study	An approach to learning and decision-making grounded by real-life situation.	Knowledge sharing, learning, assessment	Med/Scalable /C^2
Causal Loop Diagram	A process for representing the cause-and-effect relationships among variables.	Problem solving, knowledge sharing, learning	Med/Scalable /Narrow
Checklists	A document that lists various tasks that need to be accomplished.	Human factors, learning, procedural support, supports communication with the public	Low/Scalable/ C^2
Collaborative Problem-Solving Forum	An approach for creating and sharing knowledge about best practices.	Collaboration, problem solving, process improvement, workforce learning	Med/Scalable /Wide

Tool	Description	Supports	Level of Effort Size of Org Scope of Impact
Continuous Improvement Reviews (CIRs)	An approach or process that helps both individuals and the organization improve future performance by identifying and capturing lessons learned from the past.	Problem-solving, identifying, collecting and sharing lessons learned and best practices	Med/Scalable /Wide
Commitment Planning	Process for identifying the type and level of stakeholder support needed to successfully implement a decision, program, project, change initiative, and/or vision/mission	Assessment, change management, communication plan, stakeholder analysis	Med/Scalable /C²
Communications Plan	A method for linking messages to target audiences and indicating the timely communication of important information.	Knowledge sharing, learning, assessment	Low/Scalable/ C²
Community of Interest (CoI)	A group of people with a common interest, which does not necessarily relate to their day-to-day work.	Knowledge sharing, learning, knowledge retention, cross training	Med/Large/Wide
Community of Practice (CoP)	A group of individuals who work in a common area of knowledge.	Knowledge sharing, learning, knowledge retention	High/Med-Large/Wide
Concept Mapping	The technique for mapping the relationships among different concepts.	Knowledge sharing, ideas generation, learning	Low/Scalable/ Wide
Crowd Sourcing	A practice of engaging a group or "crowd" (volunteers) to obtain information for a common goal. Typically via the internet.	Open innovation, problem-solving, efficiency	Low/ Scalable/C²

Tool	Description	Supports	Level of Effort Size of Org Scope of Impact
Desk Guide	An information resource specifically tied to job activity.	Knowledge retention, new hires, job transition, knowledge sharing, resource management	Med/Scalable /Wide
Dialogue	A small group of people seeking a common understanding through a specific process of interaction that involves deep listening.	Knowledge sharing, knowledge creation, individual and organizational learning, group collaboration, creating a shared/common understanding	Low/Scalable/ Wide
Document Repositories	A technology for storing, tracking and managing formatted information objects.	Expertise location, knowledge sharing	High/Scalable /Wide
Event Intermediation	An event for which the planning process and actual event are strategically used to bring about large-scale change across an organization and its larger stakeholder group.	Change management, knowledge flows, knowledge sharing, customer relations	Med-High/Med-Large/Wide
Expertise Locator	A system for connecting knowledge seekers with knowledge holders to facilitate knowledge exchange.	Knowledge sharing, decision-making	Med/Scalable /Wide
Facilitation	A process for leading and collaboratively working with a group of individuals to achieve a specific objective by maximizing group synergy.	Knowledge sharing, problem sharing, brainstorming, leadership development	Low/Scalable/ Med
Fairs, Festivals and Celebrations	A period or program of festive activities, cultural events, or entertainment.	Knowledge sharing, individual and group learning	C^2/ Scalable/C^2

Tool	Description	Supports	Level of Effort Size of Org Scope of Impact
Force Field Analysis	A mechanism for assessing in dealing with the various forces that aid or hinder the implementation of a program or project.	Problem solving, decision support, collaboration and knowledge-sharing	Low/Scalable/ Narrow
Framework	A framework is a basic conceptual structure used to solve or address complex issues.	Organization, organizational performance, structure, problems, solutions, work styles, decision-making processes, decisions, information, knowledge, knowledge flows, flows, value systems , designs, governing bodies, issues, tools, development and deployment	Low/Scalable/ C^2
Geographic Information System (GIS)	GIS is an integrated system of computer hardware, software, and trained personnel linking topographic, demographic, organization, facility, image and other resource data that is geographically referenced.	Data modeling, topological modeling, networks, cartographic modeling, map overlay, automated cartography, geostatistics, interpolation, geocoding, reverse geocoding	Med/Scalable /Wide
Hackathons	A virtual gathering focused on a problem or improvement where ideas are exchanged until a solution is found.	Problem-solving, knowledge generation, knowledge sharing, innovation	Medium/ Scalable/ Wide
Hypothesis Testing	An approach to testing an idea or declarative statement that may or may not be true.	Knowledge generation, decision-making, implementation	Low/Wide

Tool	Description	Supports	Level of Effort Size of Org Scope of Impact
Ideathon	An intensive brainstorming event engaging people with different backgrounds, skills, and interest to address identified problem or opportunity and ideate a viable solution or action plan.	Problem solving, knowledge sharing, innovation	Medium/ Scalable/ C^2
Innovation Jam	A "massively parallel" online conference (two sessions of three days each) to (1) brainstorm for "big ideas", and (2) cluster, refine ideas and propose new business.	Brainstorming, knowledge sharing, creativity, innovation	Large/Large/ Wide
Interrupted Case Study	A real-time interactive process to focus on specific challenges (either retrospectively or prospectively) to explore solutions.	Problem-solving, best practices, networking, lessons learned	Med/Med-Larger/Wide
Interviewing	A one-on-one process for gathering first-hand information.	Knowledge sharing, knowledge retention, information gathering	Med/Scalable /C^2
Interviewing Profiling Tool	Provides pertinent questions to interview key personnel.	Learning, knowledge retention, knowledge sharing	Med/Scalable /C^2
Journey Map	A process for getting inside the mind of your customer from the perspective of what they are attempting to do.	Customer relationship management, organizational learning, strategic planning	Low/Scalable/ Potentially Wide
Key Learnings Document	Short summaries of specific actions and results in context.	Knowledge retention, knowledge sharing, learning	Med/Scalable /C^2

Tool	Description	Supports	Level of Effort Size of Org Scope of Impact
Knowledge Audit	An inquiry into what knowledge the organization has, who has it, and how it flows throughout the organization.	Strategic planning, succession planning, decision making, knowledge sharing, knowledge retention, organizational learning	High/Scalable /Wide
Knowledge Base Roadmap	A framework for building the knowledge base in a specific area of knowledge.	Knowledge sharing, communities of practice, knowledge reuse, knowledge retention	High/Med-Large/Wide
Knowledge Blueprint	A template for recording knowledge, skill, and information (KSI) requirements.	Knowledge acquisition, knowledge sharing, learning	Med/Scalable /Wide
Knowledge Management Plan	A plan to implement a knowledge management initiative or strategy within the organization.	Knowledge sharing, knowledge creation, succession planning, creating a learning organization	Med/Scalable /Wide
Knowledge Mapping	A process that provides a "picture" of the knowledge an organization needs to support business processes.	Knowledge audit, knowledge flows, strategic planning, succession planning, decision-making	Med/Scalable /Wide
Knowledge Moments	A new frame of reference for creating and supporting situations that connect people and their knowledge.	Knowledge sharing, organizational learning	Low/Scalable/ Wide
Knowledge Ontology	The conceptual framework that expresses the primary concepts and relationships among those concepts in a particular area.	Collaboration, knowledge sharing, search and retrieval	Med/Scalable /Narrow
Knowledge Taxonomy	A structured set of names and descriptions used to organize information and knowledge in a consistent way.	Knowledge sharing, search and retrieval, decision-making	High/Scalable /Wide

Tool	Description	Supports	Level of Effort Size of Org Scope of Impact
Ladder of Inference	An approach for checking the assumptions related to our mental processes.	Decision-making, learning, knowledge sharing	Low/Scalable/ Wide
Learning History	A structured process for gathering information related to a project, strategy or initiative.	Knowledge sharing, knowledge retention, assessment, organizational learning	Med/Scalable /C^2
Learning How to Learn	A process for investigating your own capabilities of learning and optimizing the situations in which you best learn.	Individual learning , decision-maker efficiency and effectiveness, group learning, organizational learning	Med/Scalable /Wide
Leave A Legacy	A process to capture tacit knowledge.	Knowledge capture, knowledge sharing, knowledge retention	Med/Scalable /Wide
Lessons Learned	A systematic collection, capturing, and mobilizing approach for ensuring the organization learns from its successes and mistakes.	Organization learning, decision-making, knowledge retention	High/Scalable /Wide
Makeathon	A "hackathon" specifically for designers. Usually engages 4-5 people to brainstorm, design and prototype a device under time/material/function al constraints (a competition).	Problem solving, innovation, knowledge sharing	Low/ Scalable/ Med-Wide
Memorandum of Understanding	A signed document between two organizations that details the relationship and way ahead in a specific domain.	Collaboration, working relationships, quality enhancement	Low-Med/Scalable /C^2

Tool	Description	Supports	Level of Effort Size of Org Scope of Impact
Mentoring	A learning relationship between an experienced employee and a newer, high-potential employee.	Individual learning, succession planning, knowledge sharing, knowledge retention	Med/Scalable /Wide
Oral History	A traditional form of storytelling where events from the past are communicated through the words of lived experience or a recognized expert resource. Today an oral history is considered a sound recording or historical information usually obtained through the interview process.	Individual and organizational learning, mentoring, lessons learned, dialogue	Med/Scalable /Wide
Peer-to-Peer Assist	A meeting where selected teams or groups are invited to share their experience, insights, and knowledge with a team who has requested some help.	Problem-solving, sharing lessons learned and best practices	Med/Scalable /Wide
Peer View Process	A process for building familiarity with (and trust of) the expertise of others.	Knowledge sharing, building trust	Med/Scalable /Wide
Picture Map	A map used for clarifying a process.	Knowledge sharing, learning	Low/Scalable/ Narrow
Prioritization Matrix	A process for setting priorities for tasks or issues.	Knowledge sharing, learning, decision-making	Low/Scalable/ Narrow
Proof of Concept	A short or partial pilot to demonstrate in principle the feasibility of an idea or method.	Implementation, knowledge generation	Med/Wide
Prototyping	A process in which you build a model of a system prior to building the system.	Knowledge creation, innovation, organizational learning	Med/Scalable /Med

Tool	Description	Supports	Level of Effort Size of Org Scope of Impact
Relationship Building	Processes for building relationships within organizations at all levels and area throughout the organization.	Individual learning, knowledge sharing, dialogue	Low/Scalable/ Narrow
Role Play Simulations	A process where individuals role-play in simulated situations.	Decision-making, reaction to stress, learning	Med/Med
Sand Table Tactical Decision Games	A process for learning communication and decision-making skills.	Decision-making knowledge sharing	Med/Med
Scenario Building	Planning process used to prepare for the future.	Knowledge creation, planning, organizational learning	Low/Scalable/ C^2
Self-Reflection	The capacity of humans to exercise self-reflection and thereby create knowledge from their past memories and experiences.	Reflection, new knowledge, creativity	Low-Med/NA/C^2
Shared Space	A concept that promotes environments for nurturing knowledge sharing.	Knowledge sharing, creativity, problem solving	Med/Med-Large/Wide
Sleep On It	An approach for improving problem solving and innovation by planning issues/ideas into the unconscious prior to sleeping.	Individual learning, problem solving	Low/Scalable/ Narrow
Social Network Analysis	A process for mapping the relationships among people, teams, or across organizations.	Knowledge sharing, organizational learning, improved communications, information flows	High/Scalable /Wide

Tool	Description	Supports	Level of Effort Size of Org Scope of Impact
Stakeholder Analysis	Process for identifying the individuals and groups that are impacted, either positively or negatively, by a decision, program, project , or change initiative whose support is required for successful implementation.	Assessment, change management, communication plan	Med/Scalable /C²
Storyboards	An approach to sequentially visualizing an event, process or series of activities before they occur.	Learning, knowledge sharing, knowledge retention	Low/Scalable/ Narrow
Storytelling	The oral or written construction of relevant examples to illustrate a point and effectively transfer knowledge.	Knowledge sharing, culture change, individual and organizational learning	Med/Scalable /Eide
Success Stories	The sharing of successes through the use of stories and storytelling; a strong methodology of communicating best practices across stakeholders.	Knowledge sharing, learning, team building	Med/Scalable /Wide
Vision Deployment Matrix	A Systems Thinking tool that can help organizations or individuals bridge the gap between their current reality and their espoused vision.	Organizational vision, events, individual and group learning, team collaboration	Low/Scalable/ Wide
Wiki	A website or group of web pages used for collaboration.	Knowledge sharing, collaboration, group and individual learning	Med/Wide
The World Café	A process for building knowledge about a focused need for opportunity.	Collaboration, idea generation, problem solving	Med/Med-Large/C²

And there are so many more! As a knowledge professional, no doubt YOU have your favorite processes, approaches, group exercises, etc. to advance organizational thinking, whether in problem-solving, decision-making, implementation, or creativity and innovation. We encourage you to share those with others.

AFTERWORDS

As we ride the crest of the global knowledge movement, the knowledge steeds advance with lengthening strides. Thank you for traveling this distance with us. We are all vested in this unparalleled journey that is headed at rapid speed for critical junctures. Our knowledge-related decisions and actions are shaping an increasingly shared future. It is a time of opportunity and challenge, a time of threat and peril, and a time of choice and creation. As you engage, we wish you success in your personal and enterprise endeavors with knowledge productivity and innovation. Likewise, we hope, certainly along with you, for deeper caring capacity and ennobling knowledge endeavors across our cultures, our values, our nations, and all humankind.

The extent of human knowledge, more than ever dreamed, is evidenced in how much is known by so many, and how much we are continuously learning about what we need to know for living on Planet Earth. The knowledge era is revolutionary in grand new ways, with the expansion of knowledge access and creation unprecedented in human experience. In human societies of all dimensions, more and more of us have vast access to acquiring and creating knowledge, many as the first generation in these circumstances. Furthermore, we are increasing our understanding about how knowledge is intertwined with developing who we are as individuals, and how knowledge expands our choices about how we live. Simultaneously, barriers to knowledge are both clearer and fading. In terms of the key insights in this volume, it is becoming clear that democratization is a catalyst for knowledge development and innovation in our enterprises.

On the infrastructure side, technology has accelerated the impact of knowledge proliferation everywhere in everything. In less than two centuries, governance, military, travel, communication, networking, publication, medicine, manufacturing, computer technology, and other key domains have introduced technologies into our civilizations with crescendos of transformations.

Ahead, in this century, each area of human endeavor will be infused so extensively and deeply with knowledge that the *future shock* impacts of the past will seem like mild tremors. While the adjustments to come will be individually notable, great shifts will especially occur from aggregated innovations such as the interplay we are experiencing between the internet and social media. The adaptations and changes caused by such perturbations awaken us to search for deeper meaning and purpose.

In this regard, as artificial intelligence and quantum computing extend and expand our reality, knowledge is at the core of this ubiquitous global technical infusion. It is not serendipitous that with the advent of new technologies such as functional magnetic resonance imaging (fMRI), the focus of the first decade of this century was on the workings of the human mind/brain. As the field of neuroscience exploded, we saw a glimpse of how the brain operates from the inside out. This unveiling of knowledge provided inroads into AI as leading scientists raced to technologically imitate the powers of the human mind, coalescing AI advances with new knowledge from the sciences about how our human brain-heart/mind-soul functions as the most advanced organism in our universe.

The Reblooming Knowledge Movement and Beyond

Throughout this volume we have shared insights into the increasing impact of the Knowledge Reblooming Movement through the framework of the RKM model. May we revisit with you at a somewhat deeper level the dynamics of **Resonance and Coherence** which emanate from the center of the model? Perhaps now and at key points in your future, resonance and coherence will prompt invaluable questions about what you envision for your firm's future.

Below are questions which may spark flashes of inspiration, what we call *knowledge bursts*. Mind you, since knowledge is context-sensitive and situation-dependent, it is likely that your own questions will be even more relevant to your circumstances. As a *knowledge burst* pops up, quickly jot it down or capture it on your smart phone. Then, ponder it and flesh it out as you find time for reflection and expansion, and take it further in discussions with others.

For yourself...	*What knowledge will I enjoy learning from a new field or discipline that will bring a fresh perspective to me and my work in the next three years?*
With your colleagues...	*How can we share "stretch questions" in a community space that will probe exciting new ways our activities, products, or services can be used?*
For your firm...	*Looking forward three to five years, what does the future version of our best product or service offer our best customers?*
For your industry...	*In what way could our best product or service be greatly enhanced by the capabilities of another firm in the next three years?*

For your country...	What is an untapped market segment where our products or services could raise the standard of living and bless lives?
For our world...	How could innovative versions of our products or services benefit others across global markets in the next five to seven years?

Strategic Insight

Thank you for following us a few minutes longer in this Afterword. We still want to refer to several vital matters, then we will present a powerful resource for your use, what we call *knowledge sensors*.

First, because of the increased blending of multiple disciplines and sciences in research and development, an effective use of the Knowledge Reblooming Movement and the RKM model may be through the kaleidoscopic lens of consilience where multiple resources from different knowledge domains are integrated. Consilience involves the intentional merging or blending of traditionally disparate disciplines and sciences to create new potential for creativity and innovation. This approach can coalesce knowledge into play that may have only peripheral input, but critical value. Correct, this multi-faceted reach adds complexity! Therefore, to help comprehend and navigate domestic and global forces and opportunities, clear vantage points need to be created and leveraged. The RKM model was developed with this in mind. It facilitates a strategic perspective for growing, cultivating, and deploying knowledge in a complex environment. Given this importance, we provide an invaluable overview of systems thinking and complexity in Chapter 19, which begins Section IV. An explanation for using the RKM model for knowledge productivity is offered throughout the chapters. Here, attention focuses on the theoretical foundations and the potential of the center of the model through which *Reblooming* is generated and regenerated. To help appreciate the depth of the model, it is noted that it is guided by the following:

- Living Systems Theory as described by James Grier Miller
- General Systems Theory and System Thinking by numerous contributors
- The Intelligent Complex Adaptive System by Bennet & Bennet
- The Intelligent Complex Adaptive Learning System by Bennet, Bennet & Turner
- The Course of Knowledge by Bennet, Bennet & Avedisian
- Complex System Dynamics as researched by Prigogine and his colleagues

We wish to emphasize that the prominence of resonance and coherence at the center of the RKM model bolsters principles, activities, tools, capacities, and dynamics throughout the model, supporting a systemic view of the firm.

Likewise, resonance and coherence also facilitate development of discreet systemic views and models of any part, product, or service of the firm.

Furthermore – and this is where resonance and coherence marvelously distinguish themselves separately and together – they identify and facilitate strategic changes with unprecedented speed and agility. Increasingly, as domestic and the global knowledge economies change and expand, these core functions can turn a firm on a dime, so to speak, to decisively respond to accelerated market trends, orchestrate timely product and service improvements, and introduce innovations with accelerated market roll-out.

A classic large-scale cautionary example of the inability to timely react and reorder to change is the case of the once globally dominant Eastman Kodak Company. Kodak was one of the United States' finest business success stories. Unfortunately, 2023 marks the 11th year of their tragic bankruptcy. In 1985, one of our authors was invited to Eastman Kodak for a personal briefing on Kodak's high performance corporate innovation process. It was brilliantly conceived and substantially deployed. As a result, Kodak held early digital photography patents. Nevertheless, lack of resonance and coherence left internal and external voices mute. Contrast this with Apple's courageous transition to their own Apple Silicon chips and now an audacious drive to a new era of spatial computing launched with Apple Vision Pro and the Apple development community.

We briefly turn to the discoveries that earned Ilya Prigogine the Nobel Prize in Chemistry for his work with the thermodynamics of nonequilibrium systems – dissipative structures. His achievements positioned him internationally at the forefront of scientific research in converging Chaos Theory, Complexity Theory, Systems Theory, and Quantum Physics. The reliability of his work shifted and advanced scientific theoretical paradigms and provided encouragement to scientific communities. This work led to numerous scientific awards, membership in 64 national and professional organizations, and 53 honorary degrees. It is also important to recognize that Prigogine's early studies in psychology and behavior sparked his interests in chemistry and physics, an unusual but fortuitous combination.[1042] That early cross-pollination led to research about the application of his findings to human systems and eventually led to the founding of the Center for Complex Quantum Systems at The University of Texas at Austin. Most impressive was his commitment to cross-cutting collaboration which stimulated deeper and wider research.

Now, reviewing the state of knowledge and theories about complexity, for example, one finds over 30 prominent research subject areas or domains and as many living or deceased prominent global research scientists. At this point, there are still important questions about the nature of systems, complexity, and change; nevertheless, the questions are getting better and what we *do* know provides the basis for strategic RKM management and successful innovation results. Using the **knowledge sensors**, introduced below, will help leverage what is unfolding in the research.

The use of knowledge sensors (ksensors) includes four initial steps. The first step is a systemic analysis of the firm to identify the **subsystems**. The second step is to identify the subsystems which are **critical drivers** or leverage points for rapidly making changes. While this concept is not new, in the current business environment with rapid change in mind, it increases in priority. The third step determines which of the critical drivers **need to include ksensors**. These ksensors become the repositories for gathering and analyzing strategic knowledge relevant to the subsystem they support. The fourth step assigns **essential information** requirements for each of the ksensor knowledge elements identified.

Again, the Resonance and Coherence function resides at the core of the RKM model and permeates across the firm through the combined efforts of leadership, management, and the total workforce. Ksensors are developed and supported by resonance and coherence throughout the firm, tracking three knowledge elements – sources of relevant knowledge, change potential, and possible actions. In the developing process of monitoring these elements, the quality of the ksensors will evolve as the firm's understanding and use of the model increases.

We could fill a volume with how to develop and use ksensors. Wait a minute, we already have. *Reblooming the Knowledge Movement* does just that. For example, read Chapter 7 again and compare the *RKM model* to the three ksensor knowledge elements described above and listed below. Drawing upon *Reblooming* and assessing your firm through the model will sharpen and increase the perception of your firm's capacity. It will also increase your view of the market segment you compete in. The deep value of thinking in terms of ksensors is that they establish shared focal points for your firm's communication and planning processes, drawing focus quickly which is essential as *speed* becomes your new planning mantra. Please note that the number, placement, and content of ksensors depends upon the nature of your firm's activities, products, and services, and the business environment in which you compete. Therefore, the element standards provided here are examples. You may benefit from developing others for your firm.

Let's briefly review the four key steps for creating knowledge sensors:

1. Identify the main <u>Subsystems</u> that enable rapid change.

(See the systems discussion in Chapter 19.)

2. Identify those subsystems that have <u>Critical Drivers</u> (leverage points).

3. Assign <u>ksensors</u> to selected critical drivers.

4. Select <u>Essential Information</u> for each ksensor element.

Examples of the Essential Information for the three ksensor elements include:

1. **Sources of Relevant Knowledge:**
   - ✓ Where is the best R&D research for this activity?
   - ✓ What market indicators and companies should we track?
   - ✓ Who are our best employees to search for knowledge for this activity?
2. **Change Potential:**
   - ✓ How fast can this activity be repurposed?
   - ✓ What is the most significant resource in this activity for change?
   - ✓ When changed, what is the return on investment?
3. **Possible Actions**
   - ✓ Can a new partnership, merger, or acquisition expedite change in this activity?
   - ✓ Is there an investment model that will facilitate change at this activity?
   - ✓ How can change be accomplished that fully engages the workforce?

Since the RKM model is replete with knowledge generation resources, the use of the model and ksensors positions the firm to respond and compete swiftly at the edge of innovation. This can be accelerated by the firm's integration of AI and quantum computing in activities, products, and services, which effects change faster. A largescale example of this which is just beginning to become fully visible is Microsoft Corporation's $13 billion-dollar investment in ChatGPT and DALL E2 creator OpenAI. An important thing to remember is that this competitive technological advantage will eventually be available to firms of all sizes, much as the Internet is today.

Quantum Entanglement

As we've moved through this book, the close relationship of the knowledge movement and the democratization of organizations has become clearer. Still, ultimately, we would have to ask ourselves: Is the knowledge movement CAUSING the democratization of organizations? And we would have to answer NO. As complex adaptive systems – and hopefully intelligent complex adaptive systems for sustainability in today's environment – cause and effect in organizations is difficult to trace. Cause and effect implies a responsibility for events. When there is no *specific* cause or responsibility, what is perceived as an effect is a *condition* of the system.

As we become familiar with the property of emergence in complex adaptive systems, we see that there is no doubt that the democratization of organizations is a result of the *interactions and relationships* among the organization's people and *between* the people and their environment. Since we can *see* the characteristics of democratization, *they* represent stable or quasi-stable patterns that are qualitative in nature and exert a strong influence within the system.

Nietzsche goes even further. When humans engage in introspection, they have the ability to perceive reasons, or motives, for specific actions. However, this quest for motives is largely misguided since there is no specific set of motives for action. As Nietzsche says, "Cause and effect: there is probably never such a duality, in truth a continuum faces us, from which we isolate a few pieces, just as we always perceive a movement only as isolated points, i.e., do not really see, but infer ...."[1043] As introduced in Chapter 2, this is consistent with the idea of a complex adaptive system, which has a large number of interrelated elements with nonlinear relationships, feedback loops, and dynamic uncertainties which are very difficult to understand and predict, suggesting that our conscious motives in terms of cause and effect are artificial, and that there is always another layer below that which we identify. In other words, while we can single out motives, and justify them, *there is always another layer hidden below*. Indeed, "Everything which enters consciousness is the last link in a chain, a closure ... The events which are actually connected are played out below our consciousness: the series and sequences of feelings, thoughts, etc., that appear are symptoms of what actually happens!" [1044]

But we may be able to say even more.

To explore cause and effect more fully, we refer to the recent work of Carroll,[1045] who says that while we look at the world through the lens of cause and effect, reasons why, purposes and goals, "none of those concepts exists as part of the fundamental furniture of reality at its deepest. They emerge as we zoom out from the microscopic level to the level of the everyday." He is referring to the second law of thermodynamics, which says that the total entropy (disorder or randomness) of a closed system never decreases; that it either stays constant or increases as time passes. Austrian physicist Ludwig Boltzmann took this concept and said that while it applied at the microscopic level of atoms, that there were many arrangements of atoms that appear the same *at the level of observation*. With Boltzmann's insights in mind, "it makes perfect sense that entropy tends to increase over time. The reason is simple: there are far more states with high entropy than states with low entropy. If you start in a low entropy configuration and simply evolve in almost any direction your entropy is extraordinarily likely to increase. When the entropy of a system is as high as it can get, we say that the system is in *equilibrium*. In equilibrium, time has no arrow."[1046] Carroll adds the assumption that the initial state of the Universe was low entropy, taking us all the way back to the Big Bang or Creation. This brings us to the ekinological belief that *today is based on a special condition in the far past*. In futures thinking and as introduced above, if a perceived problem does not have a solution, then that perceived problem is *not* a problem, it is a *condition* of the system.[1047] What Carroll is pointing out is that while cause and effect implies a responsibility for events, physics is simply an arrangement in a certain order, a condition of the system, with no specific cause or responsibility. "Different moments in time in the history of the Universe follow each other, according to some pattern, but no one moment causes any other."[1048]

As can be seen, by clear definition of these terms, Carroll has differentiated between cause and effect and ordered patterns, yet the question still comes to mind, wouldn't this early conditioning be considered a cause of these ordered patterns? What this philosophical argument points out is that, when considering cause and effect from the point of conditioning, a deeper understanding of the situation at hand can be gained, that is, there is what might even be called a quantum entanglement at play, *a natural ordering of patterns that started long ago such that the democratization of organizations is now emerging.*

Here we would draw your attention to a prominent futurist to help answer the question raised in Chapter 1 on page 4 when we stated: "Finally, you will find in the Afterword how the democratization cornerstone could enable the next phase in human progress." For further insight we turn to Michio Kaku, professor of theoretical physics at the City University of New York, and a #1 New York Times bestselling author, including his 2023 book, *Quantum Supremacy: How the Quantum Computer Revolution Will Change Everything.* While we would encourage you to read his entire recent book, we are selecting just one paragraph as a foundation for our prognostication:

> *A quantum computer may have formidable power, but it does not necessarily learn from its mistakes. But a quantum computer equipped with neural networks will be able to improve its calculations with each iteration, so it can solve problems faster and more efficiently by finding new solutions. Similarly, AI systems may be equipped to learn from their mistakes, but their total calculational capacity may be too small to solve very complex problems. So, an AI backed up with quantum computer calculational power could tackle more difficult problems.*[1049]

Kaku provides a symbiotic relationship between AI and quantum computing, but how would it work if you introduced direct human function into the mix? Coming back to the matter of democratization and the next phase in human progress, the anticipated confluence is even more exciting. We're not going to draw you another figure this time because we want you to use your mind's eye. Envision an employee who has been working in a position for five years and knows his job quite well. One morning he wakes up, goes to work, opens his email to find a welcoming email from the owner of the firm. The owner announces a new merger and two acquisitions. She then provides an introduction and outline for changes that will be reviewed during the next month.

Announcement of Merger and Acquisition

I.   Introduction: New Business Entity with Description of Assets
II. Drafts plans reviewed in workgroups for information and suggestions
III. Draft Strategic and Business Plans
IV. Draft New Knowledge Productivity & Innovation Plans
   - In addition to range of corporate knowledge activities plan includes employee knowledge roles and their support for continuous learning
   - Includes use of new employee collaboration platform and new corporate
   - AI and quantum computing resources
V.   Draft Benefits Plan including Employee Investment/Retirement Options

As we think about these sorts of metamorphic shifts, we might imagine a beehive effect in the firm. Moreover, we might say that the democratization effect from a heightened sense of freedom may seem like a think tank experience. In any case, organizations characterized by democratization will be readily recognized as having a knowledge and innovations-centric culture.

To the larger sphere, we do envision a phenomenon beyond Reblooming. There are species of *Everblooming* flowers that are developed to render flowers continuously. The careful selection and nurturing of these cultivars in optimal environments yields splendid results. Even so with the cultivation of knowledge. In the quest for knowledge, we believe wisdom will whisper among humanity and we will heed the beckoning and eagerly pursue *Everblooming* knowledge that will uplift and endow our human existence in areas of universal need.

One of the manifestations of this may reside in what we envision as "KnowledgePlexes", where creative and committed global citizens coalesce the synergistic capacities of Artificial Intelligence, Quantum Computing, and Human Intelligence , i.e., **AI + AC + HI**. When we render this new capacity as an equation, we don't' know what the emergent new force is, but we can believe it presents perturbations of formidable magnitude in human advancements.

With anticipation, we beckoned ChatGPT to offer verses to express the future we see, and, with some human assistance (what we call AAI, Augmented Artificial Intelligence), we offer a glimmer of the future.

Everblooming

In a garden of dreams, a single seed,
We planted with hope, our intention decreed,
To nurture a plant, elegant and fair,
With colors so vibrant, beyond compare.
We watered it deeply. We tended it well,
With the vision of beauty, our hearts could tell.

As the plant grew, it blossomed with grace,
Petals unfurled, a magical embrace,
A symphony of colors, a visual delight,
In the realm of dreams, it took flight.
Each bloom a testament, a vibrant hue,
To learning and love, as it grew.

And as we beheld that majestic sight,
We pondered on the power of human might.
For just as a plant can bloom and grow,
So too can knowledge, a continual flow,
When shared and cultivated, like a garden's care,
It blossoms in hearts, limitless and rare.

Through the wisdom seeds we consciously sow,
An *Everblooming* knowledge, a gift to bestow,
From one mind to another, it spreads like fire,
Igniting curiosity, fueling desire,
Across the globe, as boundaries erase,
Empowering minds through time and space.

From the depths of history to future unknown,
Everblooming knowledge has endlessly grown.
Guiding humanity through the darkest night,
Illuminating paths with wisdom's light.
Unearthing mysteries, solving puzzles of old,
Transforming lives, making hearts bold.

And just as the plant we cherish and adore,
With *Everblooming* beauty, forevermore,
So too our knowledge forever expands,
In the minds of people, across the lands,
Elegant, beautiful, and prolific it reigns,
As a catalyst for progress, breaking chains.

So let us tend the gardens of our mind,
Nurturing knowledge, so rare to find,
For in its *Everblooming*, we find the key,
To unlock the potential of humanity.
As we cultivate wisdom through wealth and dearth,
May we thrive and bloom with our Mother Earth.

Appendix A

Neuroscience Findings from ICALS Study

Neuroscience findings in the ICALS study are organized into 13 areas: Aging, Anticipating the Future, Creativity, Emotions, Epigenetics, Exercise and Health, Memory, Mirror Neurons, Plasticity, Social Support, Social Interaction, Stress, and the Unconscious. For purposes of this listing, when ICALS findings fit into two categories, they are listed in both of those categories. This is the foundational set for the book *Unleashing the Human Mind: A Consilience Approach to Managing Self* by David Bennet, Alex Bennet, and Robert Turner. The book is grounded in the Intelligent Complex Adaptive Learning System (ICALS) theory based on over a decade of researching experiential learning through the expanding lens of neuroscience.

Aging
At any age, mental exercise has a global positive effect on the brain.
The best mental exercise to slow aging is new learning and doing things you've never done before.
Despite certain cognitive losses, the engaged, mature brain can make effective decisions at more intuitive levels.
Physical exercise reduces cognitive decline and dementia in older people.

Anticipating the Future
The mind/brain creates an internal representation of the world.
The neocortex constantly tries to predict the next experience.
Memory stores invariant forms (used to predict the future).
The mind/brain unconsciously tailors internal knowledge to the situation at hand.
The mind uses past learning and memories to complete incoming information.

Creativity
An enriched environment can produce a personal internal reflective world of imagination and creativity.
Extraordinary creativity can be developed.
Conscious and unconscious patterns are involved with creativity.
Volleying between the conscious and the unconscious increases creativity.
The unconscious plays a big role in creativity.
The unconscious produces flashes of insight.
Meditation quiets the mind.
Free-flow and randomly mixing patterns create new patterns.
Accidental associations can create new patterns.

Emotions

The entire body is involved in emotions and the body drives the emotions.

Emotions can increase or decrease neuronal activity.

Unconscious interpretation of a situation can influence the emotional experience.

Emotions influence all incoming information.

Emotional tags impact memory.

Emotional tags influence memory recall.

Emotions miss details but are sensitive to meaning.

Emotional fear inhibits learning.

The brain can generate molecules of emotion to reinforce what is learned.

Epigenetics

What we believe leads to what we think leads to our knowledge, which leads to our actions, which determines outcomes.

Genes are not destiny. The environment can change the actions of genes via non-expression.

Genes are operating options modulated by inputs from the environment, resulting in behavior.

Exercise and Health

Exercise increases brainpower.

Volition is necessary for benefit. Forced exercise does not promote neurogenesis.

Meditation and other mental exercises can change feelings, attitudes and mindsets

Meditation quiets the mind.

Positive and negative beliefs affect every aspect of life.

Physical and mental exercise and social bonding are significant sources of stimulation of the brain.

Physical activity increases the number (and health) of neurons.

Less than seven hours of sleep may impair memory.

Memory

Memory is scattered throughout the entire cortex; it is not stored locally.

Working memory is limited.

Emotional tags impact memory.

The brain stores only a part of the meaningful incoming sensory information. The gaps are filled in (re-created) when the memory is recalled.

Memory stores invariant forms (used to predict the future).

Memories are re-created each time they are recalled and therefore never the same.

Memory recall is improved through temporal sequences of associated patterns, that is, stories and songs.

Repetition increases memory recall.

Emotional tags influence memory recall.

Memory patterns cannot be erased at will.

Memory patterns decay slowly with time.

Less than seven hours of sleep may impair memory

Mirror Neurons

Neurons create the same pattern when we see some action being taken as when we do it.

Mirror neurons are a form of cognitive mimicry that transfers active behavior and other cultural norms.

What we see we become ready to do.

Mirror neurons facilitate neural resonance between observed actions and executing actions.

Rapid transfer of tacit knowledge (bypasses cognition).

Through [mental] reliving we recreate the feelings, perspectives and other phenomena that we observe.

We may understand other people's behavior by mentally simulating it.

Plasticity

Plasticity is a result of the connections between neural patterns in the mind and the physical world—what we think and believe impacts our physical bodies.

Thoughts change the structure of the brain, and brain structure influences the creation of new thoughts.

Learning depends on modification of the brain's chemistry and architecture.

Maximum learning occurs when there are moderate levels of arousal—thereby initiating neural plasticity.

An enriched environment increases the formation and survival of new neurons.

Social Support

Language and social relationships build and shape the brain.

Adults developing complex neural patterns need emotional support to offset discomfort of this process.

The brain actually needs to seek out an affectively attuned other for learning.

Affective attunement contributes to the evolution and sculpting of the brain.

An enriched environment increases the formation and survival of new neurons.

Social Interaction

Physical mechanisms have developed in our brain to enable us to learn through social interactions.

Social interaction mechanisms foster the engagement in affective attunement, consider the intentions of others, understand what another person is thinking and think about how we want to interact

Physical and mental exercise and social bonding are significant sources of stimulation of the brain.

Stress

Stress depends on how we perceive a situation.

Stress is an active monitoring system that constantly compares current events to past experiences.

There is an optimum level of stress for learning (the inverted "U").

Stress focuses attention.

Emotional fear inhibits learning.

Voluntary learning promotes Theta waves that correlate with little or no stress and positive feedback.

Belief systems can reduce stress through reducing uncertainty.

The Unconscious

The unconscious brain is always processing.

Thinking is mostly unconscious.

A model of the self comes mostly from the unconscious.

The unconscious never lies.

We may act for reasons we are not aware of.

The unconscious can influence our thoughts and emotions without our awareness.

Unconscious interpretation of a situation can influence the emotional experience.

The unconscious plays a big role in creativity.

Conscious and unconscious patterns are involved with creativity.

The unconscious produces flashes of insight.

Volleying between the conscious and the unconscious increases creativity.

APPENDIX B

KM LEARNING OBJECTIVES

These 14 learning objectives are the result of a government-sponsored partnering session with academia and industry associations offering KM certification programs with the intent of identifying those things in KM that government knowledge workers wanted and needed to know. These learning objectives cover the breadth of what is needed to successfully implement KM in the federal sector, with the depth of knowledge and ability needed in each area was highly dependent on the specific job that needs to be done.

The first half of the learning objectives identify specific knowledge needed to work effectively in the field of KM. The second half deal with specific abilities or skills. This well-rounded set of learning objectives provides a robust way of understanding KM.

Learning Objective 1: *Have knowledge of the value added by knowledge management to the business proposition, including the return on investment, performance measures, and the ability to develop a business case.* Though knowledge management is capitalized in this objective, knowledge management is best considered as having a small "k" and a small "m." The intent is that knowledge management is not an initiative in and of itself, but supports the mission and business objectives of the organization, thus positioning KM as a strategic enabler for the organization. KM is an extremely broad field. Using metrics brings solid management practices to the forefront of decision-makers, thereby enabling choices.

Learning Objective 2: *Have knowledge of the strategies and processes to transfer explicit and tacit knowledge across time, space, and organizational boundaries, including retrieval of critical archived information enabling ideas to build upon ideas.* Since Nonaka and Takeuchi (1995) first explored the interaction between tacit and explicit knowledge, there has been a steady growth of interest in the capture of tacit knowledge. Aging workforce issues in the public sector have served as a catalyst for the development of processes and systems that facilitate understanding the role and importance of context in decision-making. But this objective goes beyond understanding the nature of tacit and explicit knowledge to focus on the transfer of understanding. Increasing the dynamics of transfer moves knowledge through the organization at an increasing rate; the more knowledge that is being transferred, the more it is available to others—and the organization—as a resource. The use of teams, communities, mentors, and dialogues coupled with widespread organizational trust greatly assists the organization in sharing tacit knowledge.

Learning Objective 3: *Have knowledge of state-of-the-art and evolving technology solutions that promote KM, including portals and collaborative and distributed learning technologies.* We live in a world of technology. The exponential increase in data and information is both driven and enabled by information technology. We have the ability to reach further and further across domains and within domains for ideas and solutions. Knowledge repositories, automated libraries, computer services, databases, etc. offer the capability for not only storing large amounts of data and information, but also efficient and intelligent retrieval and assemblage capability. Powerful search algorithms, intelligent agents, and semantic interpreters allow employees to rapidly retrieve information needed for problem-solving and decision-making. Knowledge managers and leaders need to be aware of these capabilities, how they are used, and how to integrate their operation with people to ensure knowledge availability and application.

Learning Objective 4: *Have knowledge of and the ability to facilitate knowledge creation, sharing, and reuse including developing partnerships and alliances, designing creative knowledge spaces, and using incentive structures.* Knowledge creation, sharing, and reuse are the heart of KM programs and the knowledge-centric organization. As people share knowledge, and other knowledge workers use that knowledge and find new ways to improve on it and innovate, its value increases for all of the organization. This process also provides the opportunity to identify integrators (knowledge leaders who connect people and ideas together) and subject matter experts (who provide depth of thinking in specific areas). In turn, those involved in exchanges benefit from the exchange through a more complete understanding of the area addressed, thereby becoming a more valuable resource to the organization.

Learning Objective 5: *Have knowledge of learning styles and behaviors, strive for continuous improvement, and actively engage in exploring new ideas and concepts.* People learn differently. Some learn through reading, others through lectures or visual or graphic representations, while still others learn by doing. Effective transfer of information requires understanding different learning styles and how people learn. Since adults learn best from direct experience with real-world problems, how can this be extrapolated across a virtual environment? (Knowles, 1998). As learning becomes the mutual responsibility of leaders and workers, knowledge professionals must be constant learners, seeking new information and exhibiting behavior for others to model by continuously striving to improve the organization's use of information and knowledge. This objective also sets the stage for capitalizing on new learning approaches including broadband Web-based multimedia. As new concepts unfold, models and theories for learning will evolve. A foundation in this area will prepare the organization and its knowledge workers for the future.

Learning Objective 6: *Have working knowledge of state-of-the-art research and implementation strategies for knowledge management, information management, document and records management, and data management. This includes project management of knowledge initiatives and retrieval of critical archived information.* Knowledge leaders and workers need to understand the conceptual linkages between knowledge management, information management, and data and records management. KM is part of a larger movement enabled by information technology, a movement that has brought us into the information age and is rapidly propelling us toward an age of increasing complexity where knowledge appears to be the only thing that can deal with complexity. There are continuing advances in data management, document and records management, and information management that will make information technology infrastructures more effective in supporting knowledge workers as they make their organization more effective through intelligent management of the knowledge environment. The knowledge centric organization will make maximum use of technology and the latest research findings related to information and knowledge management.

Learning Objective 7: *Have understanding of the global and economic importance of developing knowledge-based organizations to meet the challenges of the knowledge era.* We live in an omni-linked world. Anyone in the world can talk to almost anyone else in the world in real time. Technology has provided totally new ways of moving and transferring data, information, and knowledge among individuals, organizations, and governments. The results of these interactions are increased communication, and a corresponding increase in the flow of ideas and the making of decisions. Organizations are forced to scan, select, and quickly respond to the increased flow of Web-based exchanges and actions. Moreover, as the number of nodes in networks increase, the number of links increase, and as the links and their consequent relationships increase, so does the complexity. Critical thinking, the possession of deep knowledge, and the ability to work collaboratively with others who think differently may help address issues of increasing complexity. Knowledge-based organizations need to provide time and space for critical thinking.

Learning Objective 8: *Have the ability to use systems thinking in implementing solutions.* KM addresses powerful activities throughout environments, organizations, cultures, and economies. As one considers the relevant issues and opportunities, systems thinking provides a means for looking at the "big" picture while examining the component parts. Systems thinking assumes that almost everything is a system, made up of connecting elements and their relationships. Systems thinking is one of the integrative competencies that knowledge workers need to work effectively in a complex environment. Systems have boundaries and behaviors that are different from their individual elements. Systems thinking emphasizes the importance of relationships and structure within the organization and makes individuals aware of the effects of their efforts on others in the organization, permitting them to understand and perform their roles more effectively.

Learning Objective 9: Have the ability to design, develop, and sustain communities of interest and practice. Communities are social constructs. In a primarily virtual world, communities provide a fundamental capability for developing and sharing expertise throughout the workforce. Communities of practice share a domain of practice, crossing operational, functional, and organizational boundaries and defining themselves by knowledge areas, not tasks. In like manner, communities of interest share a domain of interest. Communities are managed by establishing and developing connections between individuals and organizations, and focusing on value added, mutual exchange, and continuous learning. They have an evolving agenda as participant knowledge builds and related areas of exchange emerge.

Collaboration, innovation, learning, and knowledge sharing are at the core of communities of practice and interest. Communities increase information flows in order to maximize knowledge, and exploit existing competencies to achieve maximum return. They also facilitate the transfer of best practices and lessons learned between organizational content centers, thus creating efficiencies while improving effectiveness. And communities fill in the gaps where organizational knowledge falls short and where enterprise information is underexploited. In short, sometimes we do not know what we do not know. Communities encourage personnel to access key resources and build new knowledge to complete tasks faster, better, and easier.

Learning Objective 10: Have the ability to create, develop, and sustain the flow of knowledge. This includes understanding the skills needed to leverage virtual teamwork and social networks. The flow of data, information, and knowledge moves around in the networks of systems and people. It is shared through team interaction, communities, and events, and is facilitated through knowledge repositories and portals. This flow is both horizontal and vertical, including the continuous, rapid two-way communication between key components of the organization and top-level decision-makers. With increased connectivity, we reach further and further across organizations, communities, industries, and the globe to tap resources. Virtual teamwork requires new skills of leadership, management, and facilitation to create and maintain the trust, open communication, and interdependencies needed for physically separated individuals to collaborate effectively.

Learning Objective 11: Have the ability to perform cultural and ethnographic analyses, develop knowledge taxonomies, facilitate knowledge audits, and perform knowledge mapping and needs assessments. As the amount of information and knowledge increases, tools such as taxonomies, audits, and maps help organize information for decision-making. While search engines and agents keep improving, the bottom line is that the human brain is the final arbiter of effective relationships and patterns. Analytic techniques such as cultural and ethnographic analyses and social network analysis help leaders understand organizational cultures and their characteristics. Culture is often cited as one of the main barriers to successful implementation of KM.

Learning Objective 12: *Have the ability to capture, evaluate, and use best-known* [good] *practices, including the use of storytelling to transfer these best practices.* The use of best practices across industry and government can provide efficiencies and increase effectiveness, if they are indeed best practices for the organization implementing them. How is the applicability of a best practice determined? How do you understand the context of the best practice, the simple rules that made it successful in some organizations?

Storytelling, the construction of examples to illustrate and understand a point, can be used to effectively transfer knowledge and best practices. A variety of story forms exist that will arise naturally throughout organizations, including scenarios and anecdotes. Scenarios are the articulation of possible future states, constructed within the imaginative limits of the author. An organizational story is a detailed narrative of management actions, employee interactions, or other intra-organizational events that are communicated informally within the organization. Storytelling connects people, develops creativity, and increases confidence. The appeal of stories in organizations helps build descriptive capabilities, increase organizational learning, convey complex meaning, and communicate common values and rule sets. There is a natural sharing of stories through the use of teams and communities.

Learning Objective 13: *Have the ability to manage change and complex knowledge projects.* Management concepts, whether old or new, are about change management. Considering Ross Ashby's law of requisite variety, which says there must be as many or more ways to change a system as those things in a system that need to be changed, today's world of increasing complexity presents increasing challenges (Ashby, 1964). It is also recognized that cultural change of any kind is a long, slow process. Add to that the fact that KM initiatives are particularly challenging because of the uncertainty of outcomes. Most managers like to change only one or two things at a time to mitigate against unintended consequences. This is not possible with KM. Accomplishing change requires daily support of sharing knowledge openly throughout the entire organization.

Learning Objective 14: *Have the ability to identify customers and stakeholders and tie organizational goals to the needs and requirements of those* *customers and stakeholders.* Total quality management brought to the forefront the tried and true values successful organizations have used for years, a focus on customers and stakeholders. No matter what new approach or initiative is popular, the government must keep a focused eye on the needs of their constituents, and ensure all efforts underway contribute to fulfilling their needs. This makes good business sense for public and private organizations alike.

APPENDIX C
SAMPLE KNOWLEDGE STRATEGIES

Below are two knowledge strategies. For your reflection, the first, *Becoming a Knowledge Centric Organization*, is presented in short form. The second, *Implementing eLearning*, is presented in more detail. Also, see Chapter 17, which offers details on absorptive capacity and suggested strategies for implementation.

STRATEGY: Becoming a Knowledge Centric Organization[1050]

A knowledge centric organization (KCO) is one in which knowledge is recognized as a key success factor and is systematically managed through knowledge management (KSC) best practices. When maximum synergy exists between individuals in the workplace and KSC, the organization can amplify its resource effectiveness, thereby enhancing sustainable performance.

Quite simply, a KCO is an organization that organizes virtually around the knowledge needs of its workforce and decision-makers at every level. In a continuous cycle, it is first a builder (creating websites and database structure to house and transfer content); then an operator (orchestrating interactions among individuals, teams and communities and serving as an intra-agency media agent; then a knowledge broker (overseeing and operating the exchange of goods, services, and knowledge transactions).

A question that is often asked is: If knowledge (as the capacity to take effective action, or justified true belief) exists only in human minds, how can an organization store, transfer and share knowledge? The answer has several aspects. First, even as the field was just emerging, IT vendors were quick to label their hardware and software as knowledge-based. This is a loose interpretation of the terms, since technology actually creates, stores, and moves binary or analog patterns (information) that can only be understood if translated by humans with the appropriate experience and ability to understand and develop that meaning, although AI is very much challenging that assumption. That said, data and information can be structured such that it *becomes easier* for other people to re-create understanding in their own minds that is (hopefully) close to the understanding of the originator. Thus, some stored digital patterns are more easily converted into user knowledge than others. Such systems (and others of lesser capability) are often called by its people knowledge systems or knowledge repositories. However, just as when two people are sharing knowledge in a one-on-one conversation, the only things that are physically transferred are sound pressure waves and photons or light rays. Listeners must transform these wave patterns into understanding and meaning by combining them with their personal experience, learning, feelings, and goals, thereby potentially creating knowledge which transforms information into action.

In a KCO, document repositories, automated libraries, computer services, databases, etc., offer the capability for not only storing huge amounts of data and information but also efficient and intelligent search, retrieval and assemblage capability. Powerful search algorithms, intelligent agents, and semantic interpreters, all of which are combined in good AI systems, allow employees to rapidly retrieve information needed for problem-solving and decision-making, and at exponentially accelerating rates we have become networked together through technologies that compound their inherent capabilities and functionalities with each new iteration of innovation. With interlacing layers of technological advancements, the convergence of the internet and cell phones has given rise to a nearly indispensable human tool of social networking that serves widely as an augmentation device for the human brain in nearly everything we do, including formal learning. In this environment there is no shortage of information available in the instant.

A knowledge-centric organization recognizes the value of information and knowledge in decision-making at all levels. It connects people to people, people to systems, systems to people, and systems to systems to ensure availability and delivery of the right information at the right time for decision and action. However, the effective application of decisions and actions requires not only the right information but also (and most importantly) the understanding, meaning, insight, creation of ideas and an anticipation of their outcome, all of which drive judgment and decision-making. This is the "knowledge" that is created only in the human mind. The creation, storage, transfer, and application of such knowledge is thus seen as a major resource of the organization as it is used to meet mission goals and adapt to a changing environment.

The bottom line for a KCO is **optimal sustainable performance**. It achieves this through:

1. *Aligning strategic direction.* The more information is shared, the better people collaborate, the more aligned the organization is in moving toward its vision of the future. This shared vision harnesses the collective energy of people and accelerates improvement. (See the tool of Strategic Alignment in Section IV.)

2. *Enhancing mission performance.* Operational and business performance improves as best practices are shared and new ideas built on those practices are shared. KSC drives development of a Knowledge Base relating to the organization's core competencies. (See the tool on Knowledge Base Roadmap in Section IV.)

3. *Increasing collaboration opportunities.* The collaborative and sharing aspects of knowledge centricity will enrich the exchange among people and ideas at all levels of the organization. (See the in-depth discussion of Communities of Practice in Chapter 11.)

4. *Driving process improvement.* As the sharing of information becomes embedded in day-to-day activities, the flow and exchange of good practices increases, providing the fluid for true process improvement. In addition, the high visibility of content areas across the organization facilitates the exchange of new ideas regarding process change.

5. *Facilitating learning.* Knowledge centricity provides the opportunity for individuals to put new knowledge into practice while exposing them to new challenges. Since the value of individual knowledge is a major asset of all organizations, an individual's contribution to this Knowledge Base becomes recognized and rewarded.

6. *Facilitating availability of expertise.* Knowledge centricity utilizes tacit knowledge by defining content areas and identifying tacit knowledge sources, thus providing intermediation between knowledge needs and knowledge sources. This "brokering" translates into availability of expertise which can be brought to bear on emerging issues. Tool examples are the Expertise Locator and KM Desk Guide, with "how to" info easily available on the internet.

7. *Increasing innovation and creativity.* As information begets information, ideas beget ideas. Knowledge centricity provides access to a rich pool of ideas, providing a foundation for others to build upon, sowing the seeds for creativity and innovation.

8. *Enhancing job performance.* Knowledge centricity provides the opportunity for adaptability in rapidly changing situations, and there's little in today's work environment that isn't rapidly changing. Knowledge workers can quickly access, interpret, integrate and act on new knowledge, and efficiently find out what they don't know from a vast pool of easily searchable and accessible organizational knowledge.

STRATEGY: Implementing eLearning

Having a qualified workforce is essential for an organization to meet its mission. That does not end when a new employee is hired. Hiring and sustaining a "current" and qualified workforce is critically important in today's complex and dynamic environment where change and innovation have become the capital for success. For example, in career communities such as engineering and information technology, new developments and increasing knowledge within the industry continuously raise the professional competency standards. Meeting the dynamic needs of the organization's mission and career communities requires that a robust continuous education program be in place. This fast pace of change pushes organizational learning requirements beyond the capability, and feasibility, of traditional classroom education. Thus, eLearning has become an essential part of the fabric of continuing education needed to satisfy mission requirements. For this discussion, eLearning is considered any virtual act or process used to acquire data, information, skills or knowledge: what could be thought of as enabled learning in a virtual world where technology merges with human creativity and learning to accelerate and leverage the rapid development and application of knowledge.

A cost-benefit analysis of eLearning includes a comprehensive investigation of all eLearning costs as well as a realistic projection of benefits such as return on investment (ROI). The costs for an organization establishing an eLearning program can be significant. Course conversion costs for existing classroom-based courses can be as high as $20,000 or more for a two-hour course, depending on the kind of interaction needed. A new course of similar length can cost more than twice that figure. The purchase of a learning management system (LMS) which manages the launching, assessment and record keeping of the eLearning solution can range from $100,000 to $1 million depending on the functionality desired. Note that there are also some limited functionality, open-source systems available. Other costs often overlooked are the costs of activities to help prepare employees for eLearning through hands-on training, marketing, and public relations. Also, as Artificial Intelligence has become widely available and as it rapidly matures, AI can serve an immediate learning platform for everyone in the organization.

On the benefit side of the ledger there are well-documented cost savings (ROI) associated with eLearning. These savings include reduced costs for travel, facilities and instructors. For example, Cisco estimated it saved $2.4 million during its first year of eLearning for every 1,000 eLearners. eLearning also enables costs savings through efficiency, reduced training time and enhanced productivity. Material presented via eLearning takes approximately 50 percent less time than classroom-style presentation.

The Importance of eLearning as Energetic Learning

eLearning can also provide enhanced employee job performance. To explore this further, we refer to MQI research findings published under the title "eLearning as energetic learning". With technology comes a natural excitement in terms of connectivity and its support of self-driven, experiential learning which is part of our evolutionary heritage. As our understanding of neuroscience and biology of human learning has advanced, we could better understand the personal needs of individual learners. Bringing these needs together with eLearning system capabilities offered a significant jump in our learning rate and efficiency.

When the term eLearning (electronic learning) is used today it is most often in the context of computer-based learning support systems and social media systems, and periodically associated with advanced distributed learning technology. Energetic learning and eLearning are both physical experiences; energetic learning in the sense of chemically-induced positive emotions attached to the process of learning or the content of the learning, and eLearning in terms of the learner's involvement with technology. Both energetic learning and eLearning deal with patterns; energetic learning in the sense of patterns in the brain complexing with incoming patterns and cascading up and down in hierarchical relationships, and eLearning in terms of the patterns of bits and bytes presented as visual and audible information to the learner, and, ideally, good eLearning would facilitate an experience with the learner that creates emotional tags, thus enhancing the ability to learn from that experience.

An eLearning system encompasses and integrates critical learning conditions such as feedback, re-enforcers, motivators and information sources that enable learning to occur.[1051] For purposes of this discussion, the *Energetic Learning System* (used here with initial caps) is composed of the learner (with the human defined in Chapter 2 as an intelligent complex adaptive learning system) in communion with an eLearning system. The brain uses energy as neurons fire in the process of associating patterns, creating ideas (sequences of patterns) and learning in general, which can be measured by sophisticated brain measurement instructiontation such as functional magnetic resonance imaging (fMR), electroencephalography (EEG) and transcranial magnetic stimulation (TMS).[1052] For example, the fMR process provides indirect indicators of changes in blood flow showing regions of the brain that are highly active through the direct measurement of oxygen utilization.[1053]

Emotions – signals or labels converted by the limbic system from chemical communications signals into sensations that are for the most part generated unconsciously – play large role in this process. Strong emotions, which have priority over cognition in our stream of consciousness, result in better recollection of memories.[1054] Understanding and harnessing the power of emotion can improve an individual's ability to learn.

There are a number of triggers that can support energetic learning. First is passion, with positive passions affirming that something is previous, of higher interest, or great.[1055] A passion to learn or a deep passion related to the content of learning embeds strong emotional tags with what is being learned, directly impacting the number of synapse connections created and the strength of those connections. When positive emotions create this impact, learning becomes exciting and the memory of what is learned stays with us. Memory is further enhanced when learning includes meaning and understanding of the material. See Chapter 15 on "How Leaders Inspire Action through Meaningful Knowledge".

A second trigger is intent to learn. In a study of information-processing receptors on nerve cell membranes, it was discovered that emotions were not simply derived through a feedback of the body's environmental information, but that through self-consciousness the mind can sue the brain to *generate* "molecules of emotion" and override the system.[1056] What this means is that our minds can choose to embed stronger emotional tags with specific incoming information. For example, this occurs when we engage new ideas and become excited about the potential offered by these new ideas for ourselves, our organization, or our world.

A third trigger is the eLearning system itself. While simple skill training focused on information, manual operations and logical thinking with clear, predetermined results may not engage the learner in energetic learning, when the desired performance requirements a good understanding of theory, nuances, and uncertainties in the operation, the adaptivity of the eLearning system becomes significant to the learning experience. Now it is necessary for the system to adapt to the learner's needs in order to help them create the *knowledge* needed to deal with unexpected situations. This is what happens with physical and light simulators, games, and even narratives, with progressive games offering the opportunity for long-term engagement.

More recently, *Psych*ecology Learning Games (PEGs) serve as analogs based on source code that depicts all known electromagnetic energy dynamics or algorithms that contribute to conscious and unconscious humanly embodied dynamics. Embedding symbolic languages containing a narrative-metaphorical common denominator, the PEG template can be thought of as an artificial neural network, somewhat like a Kohenen map, correlating recursive input-output, self-organizing map lattices.

The single-layer self-organizing map is a "feedforward" network, with the output syntaxes arranged on a low dimensional grid, usually in two or three dimensions. Each input is connected to all output neurons, and attached to every neuron is a weight vector with the same dimensionality as the input vectors. The number of input dimensions is usually a lot higher than the output grid dimensions.

Self-organizing maps (SOMs) are popular neural network models used for unsupervised learning, which means that *no human intervention is needed during the learning* and that little needs to be known about the characteristics of the input data. SOMs can be used for clustering data such as contextual personal and story premise, and to detect features inherent to the story problem or premise. The goal of the learning in the self-organizing map is to associate different parts of the SOM lattice to respond similarly to certain input patterns. This is partly motivated by how visual, auditory, or other sensory information is handled in separate parts of the cerebral cortex in the human brain.

What this means is that conscious player responses to the symbolic lattices of game images may be recursively correlated with unconscious affordances in the program-syntax at computational levels of the game.[1057] The narrative-metaphorical common denominator can be used to correlate data as well as to generate greater and more meaningful narrative interactivity in the game story real time, depending on the response of the player during the play sequence. In PEGs, the premise is clearly expressed in the beginning (exposition), meaning is contextually embedded in the dramatic sequence of scenes, and meaningful insight emerges as the payer gradually manipulates his/her plot by making choices that lead to the realization of the premise (lysis).

A significant finding is that through the narratives ("poetical discourse") involving sensations or feelings that are part of PEGs, there is an apprehension *beyond that which is propositional*, which would include direct intuition, states of consciousness, and perceptions regarding emotions. This was validated through the use of transreal numbers, showing that knowledge by sentience gives us the possibility of knowing everything that is not propositional.[1058] This research using transreal numbers has proven that narratives involving sensations or feelings transfer the full range of sentient knowledge, offering the strong potential to change our belief states.

The PEG "source code" includes numerous dynamics that are perceived to contribute to the objective of energetic learning, specifically: electromagnetic frequency monitoring (Braintap technology), coherent entrainment (Institute of HeartMath), asymmetrical mathematics (quantum field vectors and quantum collapse), and Jungian compensation/individuation (Myers-Briggs personality types).

Consider Formal and Information Settings

eLearning can prove effective in both formal and informal settings. A formal learning event is one in which either (1) the learner approaches content for the purpose of learning something from it (the event is directed by a particular need) or (2) the content is structured with the purpose of teaching and includes learning assessments, activities, content, and evaluation measures. An informal learning event is one in which either (1) the learner does not intend to learn something, yet in the process of interacting with the material gains knowledge, experience, or skills, or (2) the content is not structured with the purpose of teaching but imparts knowledge or skills which add to the learner's understanding.

One way to characterize formal and informal learning is to ask questions related to the purpose, form, and context.

Purpose: Is the learning externally motivated (that is, by a superior or by job requirements) or internally motivated (that is, for personal interests)? Externally motivated learning may be considered formal learning while internally motivated learning may be considered informal.

Form: Is the learning content instructional in nature (written with the intent of teaching someone particular content), or is it informational in nature (with the intent of informing but not necessarily teaching)? Instructional content may be considered formal learning while informational content may be considered informal learning.

Context: Is the learning in a classroom setting (be it virtual or face-to-face), or is it a self-study setting? Classroom learning may be considered formal while self-study may be considered informal.

Key Elements for Effectiveness

Whether instructional or informational, eLearning can be an effective delivery mechanism. However, a number of key elements are needed to ensure effectiveness. First, essential instructional components for formal learning products include:

- Clear, concise, and appropriately structured/sequenced content.

- Activities that draw relationships between concepts, challenge learners' thinking and understanding, and reinforce information.

- Evaluative measures that determine if information assimilation and retention have occurred.

That said, eLearning for formal instructional events is only as good as the value and structure of the content within it. Even with high value content, if the instructional content is poorly crafted, deficient in sound activities, and completed with inappropriate evaluative measures, the product will likely not bring about the desired results.

Specific elements that should be considered for eLearning are: the instructional presentation, sequence, and structure of the content should be appropriate for the technology. For example, a designer will not want to design an interactive discussion in an eLearning system if the technology does not support it. Likewise, an activity requiring learners to assemble a particular piece of machinery will have to be redesigned in order to be accomplished in the eLearning product. In this case, the instructional designer would need to reconsider the intent of the activity so as to tailor it to the specific capabilities of the technology. While these are simple examples, they are indicative of the types of issues that must be considered in eLearning products.

Another consideration is how the eLearning product is used in relation to the content of the situation as well as in relation to other instructional materials. One guiding question to ask is: Has the eLearning been properly assimilated into the larger instructional framework? Note that eLearning is not a solution for each and every training or learning event. It is one component of a number of solutions, its appropriateness is contingent upon the structure of the material within the product as well as the relationship of that material to other supporting, non-eLearning materials.

The DON eLearning Framework Model

An eLearning Framework Model prepared by the Department of the Navy and adapted from the DON toolkit *Learning in a Virtual World* provides a series of questions to address prior to implementing an eLearning strategy. When the answer at each level is yes, then move on to the next set of questions.

1. **Is the best education and training method eLearning?**

   Consider:
   What is the organizational need?
   Are the goals and objectives clearly stated?
   What business processes are being supported?
   Is there a business case?
   Will multiple teaching methods be used?
   Are these methods used now?
   What learning styles must be supported?
   What are the pros and cons of each method for these styles?
   Do you have a good IT network?
   Does everyone use it?
   Are the users geographically dispersed?
   How will we ensure energetic learning?
   How can Artificial Intelligence support the learning?

2. **Is eLearning aligned with the organization's strategy and programs?**

   Consider:
   Is eLearning connected to knowledge strategies?
   Is eLearning connected to the strategic plan?
   Does eLearning work with other methods?
   Can other resources be leveraged and partnerships created?
   Is this a pilot project?
   If successful, what program will it be under?
   Has the leadership openly supported and encouraged eLearning?
   Is this a core function for people or a collateral duty?

3. **Is the organization prepared?**

   Consider:
   Does your organization's culture emphasize learning?
   Are creative ideas encouraged and pursued?
   Will the IT department support this project?
   Has an assessment been made of course content?
   Are subject matter experts available?
   Do people have time to take the courses?
   Is funding allocated? Fully or partially?

4. **Are the users prepared?**

   Consider:
   Who are the learners?

What are the benefits to them?
Have the potential eLearners been asked what they need?
What are their learning styles? Technical prowess?
What are their career goals?
Is there a high employee turnover rate?
Are they funded for training?
Does this affect their schedules?
Are there rewards and recognition for success?

5. **Are adequate resources available?**

Consider:
What is the project's scope?
Does the network have sufficient bandwidth?
Can everyone access it?
Do you have a media lab?
Are content creators available?
Are contractors needed?
How much does it cost for one course? The entire curriculum?
Are instructors available for individual help sessions?
Do you need custom software?
Will IT or training develop it?
Is there enough time?
Does the content become obsolete quickly?

6. **What approach will be used?**

Consider:
Are roles and responsibilities identified and understood by all?
What are the milestones? Schedule? Critical tasks?
Who are the key stakeholders?
Is this the first eLearning project?
Does the plan account for problems?
Will eLearning be mixed with classroom and other methods?
What is the timing?
Can the pilot project use different technology than the full-scale program?
Have the consultants executed this type of eLearning before?
Is the funding and staffing secure and in place now?

7. **Is eLearning working well?**

Consider:
What do the major stakeholders consider success?
What do the learners consider success? Project leaders?
Do you have metrics for quantitative and qualitative measures?
Are you prepared to analyze the metrics and make changes as needed?
Is failure acceptable? Viewed as feedback for change?

Is the system ready for changes based on feedback? IT? Content? Style? Is it possible to add funding or staff if needed

Consider the Knowledge Content ...

It is important to consider the focus of the desired learning in terms of value, continuity, tools and risk. Here are some questions to consider.

VALUE: Is the targeted knowledge in terms of learning, leveraging and sharing about a program or a process defined as vital to the successful performance of the organization's core missions? Are there important and well-defined user needs for products and services that depend on the knowledge to be learned and shared?

CONTINUITY: Are the targeted programs, processes, or user needs expected to remain an essential part of the organization's core missions for the foreseeable future? How much of the knowledge is vested in key staff eligible for retirement and will leave a void unless learning and initiatives are taken? Are there succession and/or handover plans in place for key knowledge workers? Are learning processes such as mentoring and coaching in place to facilitate the transfer of deep knowledge? Are communities and teams working to ensure knowledge flows across the functional areas of the organization?

TOOLS: Are manuals, handbooks, records, professional writings, databases, training courses, and user networks being maintained up-to-date? Are these tools available electronically and do they adequately support the knowledge needs of current and future generations of resource management decision-makers and other customers? Are interdisciplinary teams and communities of practice supported by collaboration systems?

RISK: If no action is taken to create, capture, preserve, and share the knowledge in question, how would this impact the organization and its stakeholders? If this learning is not understood or embedded, is the organization at risk of legal action, breaches of public safety, user disaffection, or damage to the environment?

APPENDIX D

READINESS ASSESSMENT/SUCCESS SCORING

The intent of the short discussions below – in relation to "1" and "2" responses to each question of the Readiness Assessment Instrument in Chapter 8 – is to provide information and suggestions to help interpret the importance of each item to your knowledge strategy, the external environment, and the internal nature of your organization.

The questions below are grouped into the following areas: General Questions, Resources, Leadership, Management, Culture, and Alignment.

GENERAL QUESTIONS

Q1: A knowledge strategy's contribution to the current performance of my organization would be ...

Q1-2: Selecting level 2 for this item indicates that you consider that the knowledge strategy would provide a low level of contribution to performance. This suggests that the strategy itself may not be applicable to your organization at this time. Perhaps a rethinking of the specific strategy intended would result in a higher level of contribution. See the discussion on "Develop the Strategy" in Chapter 7, and several sample strategies in Appendix C. Strategy in terms of expanding absorptive capacity is also discussed in Chapter 17.

Q1-1: Selecting level 1 indicates that a knowledge strategy would have little or no contribution to your organization, and therefore your organization may not be ready to implement the knowledge strategy at this time. You may want to explore the full potential of the knowledge field in terms of other strategies or initiatives. See the discussion on "Develop the Strategy" in Chapter 7, and several sample strategies in Appendix A. See also Chapter 17. You might consider creating a team of knowledgeable leaders and managers to study the options available that could potentially provide a higher payoff to the organization.

Q2: A knowledge strategy's contribution to the sustainable performance of my organization would be ...

Q2-2: Selecting level 2 indicates that the knowledge strategy would provide little support for *sustainable* performance. If this limitation is acceptable, you may want to proceed with implementation. If this limitation is not acceptable, then the strategy should be reviewed and perhaps modified. The discussion on "Nurturing Organizational Health" in Chapter 11 may prove useful.

Q2-1: Selecting level 1 indicates that the knowledge strategy will not contribute to *sustainable* performance. This being the case, you may want to reconsider the importance of sustainability to your organization before taking further actions. The discussion on "Nurturing Organizational Health" in Chapter 11 may prove useful.

Q3: The level of credibility of the business case for a knowledge strategy is ...

Q3-2: Selecting level 2 indicates that a strong business case has not been developed at this time. This makes justification of the strategy challenging and may lead to non-acceptance by the organization. Under these conditions it is suggested that further work be put into development of the business case. See the discussion under "Build the Business Case" in Chapter 7.

Q3-1: Selecting level 1 indicates that it is difficult, or may not be possible, to develop a business case for the intended knowledge strategy. Under these conditions it is suggested that further work be put into understanding the outcome of the knowledge strategy and relating that outcome to the performance or sustainability of the organization. See the discussion under "Build the Business Case" in Chapter 7.

Q4: Support of the senior management team that oversees this organization for a knowledge strategy is ...

Q4-2: Selecting level 2 indicates that the senior management team would provide low support for the knowledge strategy OR it is perceived that this is the case. This level of support may significantly impair the outcome of the strategy. In this situation, it is essential that efforts be made to bring the senior management team onboard and ensure that this leadership support is visible across the organization. See the section on "Ensure Leadership Commitment" in Chapter 7.

Q4-1: Selecting level 1 indicates that the senior management team will have little or no support for the knowledge strategy. If the response is this strong, generally this is more than perception by the responder. Since the specific strategy anticipated and the interest and influence of the senior management team will determine whether the knowledge strategy is feasible or not, effort is required to build an understanding within the senior management team of the value of the knowledge strategy. This commitment must then be demonstrated across the organization. See the section on "Ensure Leadership Commitment" in Chapter 7.

RESOURCES

Q5: The level of financial resources available is ...

Q5-3: Selecting level 3 indicates an uncertainty concerning availability of financial resources, or perhaps an uncertainty about the financial resources needed.

Q5-2: Selecting level 2 indicates that financial resources may not be available. Depending on the specific knowledge strategy and the amount of anticipated financial resources needed, suggested actions could be to (a) go ahead and start the program in anticipation of solving any resource issues early in the program, or (b) delay the program until resources are available.

Q5-1: Selecting level 1 indicates that financial resources are not available. Unless the knowledge strategy does not require financial resources, it should be delayed and reconsidered at a later time. You may wish to consider another knowledge strategy.

Q6: The availability of qualified people to implement the knowledge strategy is ...

Q6-3: Selecting level 3 indicates some uncertainty as to the availability of qualified people for implementing the knowledge strategy. You might wish to consider utilizing recent retirees. There is a short discussion of an approach called "Engaging Golden Experience" in the Tools section under **Resources**.

Q6-2: Selecting level 2 indicates that the chances of having qualified people available to implement the knowledge strategy are low. Under these conditions, the actions may be to (a) delay the strategy until qualified people can be made available or (b) review the prioritization of human resource allocations and identify and charter the key individuals necessary to make the knowledge strategy successful. Another option is to create a phased knowledge strategy where a small number of people are initially required and plan to supplement them as the strategy proceeds. You might wish to consider utilizing recent retirees.

Q6-1: Selecting level 1 indicates that there is little chance of having qualified employees available to implement the knowledge strategy. Under these conditions, the knowledge strategy cannot be attempted. Creating a situation which has a significant chance of failure simply creates problems with morale in the future. In order to move forward, you need to review the prioritization of human resource allocations and involve individuals with appropriate skill sets and experience in order for the strategy to succeed. If funds are available for hiring additional people, you might also wish to consider utilizing recent retirees.

Q7: The amount of time available for employees to implement a knowledge strategy is

Q7-2: Selecting level 2 indicates there is most likely not enough employee time available to implement the strategy. While time commitments can be corrected during implementation, it may be risky to start a program without assurance that time priorities will support effective implementation. As a consequence, the decision to implement may need to be delayed until adequate time can be made available. You might want to reconsider the knowledge strategy in order to reduce the time needed for employees to implement the strategy, or to allocate additional time for implementation. Another option is to consider utilizing recent retirees in support of available internal personnel. In addition, you may wish to consider utilizing recent retirees.

Q7-1: Selecting level 1 indicates that employees do not have time to implement this strategy. In this case, the strategy should be reconsidered for later implementation or modified to require less employee time.

LEADERSHIP (General Manager and Direct Reports)

Q8: Leadership's level of personal interest in the knowledge strategy would be ...

Q8-2: Selecting level 2 indicates a lack of leadership interest in the knowledge strategy. This may significantly impact the effectiveness of the program, and therefore the strategy may have to be seriously reconsidered or carefully discussed with leadership in order to build their willingness to personally support the strategy. While all strategies require leadership support, and the personal interest of leadership greatly enhances the probability of success, some knowledge strategies require less leadership visibility than others. See the discussions of "Ensuring Leadership Commitment" in Chapter 7 and "Leadership Commitment Visibility" in Chapter 10.

Q8-1: Selecting level 1 indicates there is essentially little or no interest by leadership in offering their personal support. Under those conditions it would not seem wise to initiate the strategy until these conditions are changed. See the discussions of "Ensuring Leadership Commitment" in Chapter 7 and "Leadership Commitment Visibility" in Chapter 10.

Q9: Leadership's ability to work well together in support of a knowledge strategy would be ...

Q9-2: Selecting level 2 indicates that leadership does not work well together and would probably not cooperate in implementing an organizational knowledge strategy. This could present significant problems to implementing a knowledge strategy since employees in different departments would receive different directions and views on the importance and implementation of the strategy. Such differences can quickly reduce enthusiasm and create concerns among departments as to the importance of and actions necessary to the knowledge strategy. It may be best to work with leadership to determine what could be done to get their collective backing, interest and knowledge of the importance and value of the knowledge strategy prior to beginning implementation. See the discussion on "Leading and Managing" in Chapter 10 and Chapter 15 on "How Leaders Inspire Action through Meaningful Knowledge".

Q9-1: Selecting level 1 indicates there is little or no leadership collaboration, seriously jeopardizing the potential success of a knowledge strategy. Under these conditions, the organization most likely has strong silos that prevent communication and collaboration. It may be best to postpone implementation of an organization-wide knowledge strategy until these issues can be worked through. As another approach to implementation, consider selecting and implementing a knowledge initiative/strategy in a department familiar with and conducive to the knowledge strategy. The success of this approach could then serve as a pilot for a larger implementation approach and make visible to the entire organization the efficacy and potential of the knowledge strategy. See the discussion under "Build the Business Case" in Chapter 7 and Chapter 15 on "How Leaders Inspire Action through Meaningful Knowledge".

Q10: The leadership team's expectation of achieving the intended results of a knowledge strategy would be ...

Q10-2: Selecting level 2 indicates that leadership has a low expectation that the knowledge strategy will achieve its intended result. Under these conditions the workforce will likely pick up on, and react to, such perspectives of leadership. It is suggested that careful consideration be given to whether the knowledge strategy can be successfully implemented. This might be due to a lack of understanding of the knowledge strategy's potential, a disagreement with the specific strategy proposed, or the readiness of the organization to accept and implement such a strategy. Further study and recognition of why the strategy will be successful and how it will be beneficial to the Organization may be needed. It would be unwise to move ahead too quickly. Leadership must play a strong role in implementing any knowledge strategy. See the discussion under "Leading and Managing" in Chapter 10.

Q10-1: Selecting level 1 indicates that the organization is most likely not ready for implementation of a knowledge strategy. With such low expectations it would be very difficult to implement any strategy. A pilot knowledge initiative in a department, coupled with a program to inform leadership of the value of the initiative/strategy, may help build the leadership team's expectation of achieving the intended results.   Leadership's role is discussed under "Leading and Managing" in chapter 10.

Q11:   The leadership team's willingness to reward employees who contribute to the knowledge strategy is ...

Q11-2: Selecting level 2 indicates the perception that leadership has little willingness to reward employees who contribute to knowledge strategy success. Since rewards are one of the positive forces in sustaining a knowledge strategy, careful consideration should be given to the feasibility of success under these conditions. Consider including development of a rewards approach as part of the implementation strategy. A discussion of "Recognition and Rewards" is in Chapter 11.

Q11-1: Selecting level 1 indicates the perception that leadership will not reward employees engaged. If this is indeed the case, since rewards are one of the positive forces in sustaining a knowledge strategy it may be unwise to implement a knowledge strategy at this time. Another option is to find local rewards for employees who significantly contribute to the knowledge strategy, or implement a local knowledge initiative whose success would convince the leadership team of its value to the organization. A discussion of "Recognition and Rewards" is in Chapter 11.

Q12: The leadership style in my organization is [very control oriented (1), in between (2-4) or very collaborative oriented (5)] ...

Q12-2: If the leadership style leans more toward control (level 2), it will probably be difficult to get managers, or employees, to begin sharing information and knowledge. Each functional area of an organization has to find its own optimal styles of leadership dependent upon the focus of their business. For example, where safety is concerned control management may be required. Where innovation and agility are needed in the workplace, a democratic collaborative leadership approach works best. A key question to ask is: What leadership styles are best for the different departments within the organization and will they support the basic activities needed for successful knowledge strategy implementation? If the answer is yes, the knowledge strategy can move forward. If the answer is no, a separate and distinct leadership strategy should be applied to each department involved in the overarching knowledge strategy. See Chapter 1 for a discussion of leadership styles related to democratic leadership. Also, see Chapter 15 on "How Leaders Inspire Action through Meaningful Knowledge".

Q12-1: Selecting level 1 indicates a strong control-oriented leadership which, depending on the specific strategy considered, will likely prevent success. Knowledge strategies – and innovation – thrive on freedom of thought, freedom of expression, and freedom of association. In this case, efforts should be made to move the organization from a control-oriented approach to a democratic, collaborative approach, depending on the specific needs of the organization. A potential option is incorporating a change in leadership style into the knowledge strategy. See Chapter 1 for a discussion of leadership styles related to democratic leadership. Also, see Chapter 15 on "How Leaders Inspire Action through Meaningful Knowledge".

Q13: The level of leadership involvement with the workforce [as described by "management by walking around"] is ...

Q13-2: Selecting level 2 indicates that leaders have a low level of interface with employees, and therefore may not provide personal support to knowledge strategy implementation. The free flow of information and knowledge is critical to the success of a knowledge strategy. If the organization has leaders who remain aloof from their employees, those parts of the organization may have difficulty accepting and implementing a knowledge strategy. Both leadership and management roles in implementing a knowledge strategy are very important because of the typical changes in culture and behavior that occur throughout the organization as part of the strategy. See the discussion under "Leading and Managing" in Chapter 10, the discussion on "Become a Change Agent" in Chapter 9, and also Chapter 15 on Meaningful Leadership.

Q13-1: Selecting level 1 indicates that leaders are relatively aloof from their employees and it would be unlikely that they lend personal support to the knowledge strategy. If this condition is correct and not an individual perception, it may be best to delay implementation of the knowledge strategy until leadership has time to digest, analyze, understand, and recognize the importance and long-term contribution that a knowledge strategy can provide to the organization. A discussion of "Leading and Managing" is in Chapter 10. See also the discussion under "Build the Business Case" in Chapter 7. An additional approach is benchmarking, finding and learning from success stories about strategies and initiatives similar to those you propose.

Q14: In my organization, leadership's acceptance of change is ...

Q14-2: Selecting level 2 indicates leadership is typically resistant to change and this may present a strong challenge to a successful knowledge initiative. To the extent this is valid, leadership may be hesitant to accept significant changes in culture, policies, or "ways of doing business." Since the role of leadership is to set the tone and reinforce the importance of the changes resulting from a knowledge strategy, it may be wise to get leadership more on board before commencing a knowledge strategy for the organization. Such preparation time may pay high dividends in the future. Another option would be to locate a successful knowledge initiative in the organization and share the results, or implement a knowledge initiative that can validate the value of change. See the discussion under "Become a Change Agent" in Chapter 9.

Q14-1: Selecting level 1 indicates that leadership will likely resist any changes in the organization and, therefore, until this resistance is dissolved, it may be best to wait until leadership can be brought on board to support the knowledge strategy. This would need to be handled at the very top of the organization. One option would be to locate a successful knowledge initiative in the company and share the results, or implement a knowledge initiative that can validate the value of change. See the discussion under "Become a Change Agent" in Chapter 9.

Q15: Leadership's understanding of the knowledge strategy and its usefulness is ...

Q15-2: Selecting level 2 indicates that the leadership team has not been brought fully on board as to the nature and value of knowledge and innovation to the organization and hence immediate steps are suggested to bring them up to speed in order to empower them to understand and participate in the knowledge strategy. Because the leadership teams' role in the desired strategy is very important, it is suggested that this issue be corrected before commencing the knowledge strategy. See Chapter 6 and the discussion under "Build the Business Case" in Chapter 7.

Q15-1: Selecting level 1 indicates the leadership team has little or no understanding of the value of knowledge and innovation to the organization. Under these conditions it is best to delay initiating a knowledge strategy until sufficient time can be taken to ensure the leadership team is aware of, understands, and will support implementation of the knowledge strategy. See Chapter 6 and the discussion under "Build the Business Case" in Chapter 7.

MANAGEMENT

Q16: The level of communication among organization departments is ...

Q16-2: Selecting level 2 indicates that there is below average communication among departments. While a knowledge strategy may be implemented under these conditions, it would be worthwhile to observe the level of communication and take actions to improve and facilitate additional communication channels among departments to create an environment within which employees can openly, easily and effectively communicate. This may well follow directly from the knowledge strategy since many strategies include improving knowledge sharing among both individuals and departments. There are multiple resources within this book that may be of service. For example, see the discussion "Grow a Knowledge Network" in Chapter 9, the discussion under Knowledge Sharing in Chapter 11, and Chapter 14 on Relationship Network Management. Also see the section on "Communities of Practice, Interest and Learning" in Chapter 10.

Q16-1: Selecting level 1 indicates very poor or little communication among departments of the organization. While it may be feasible to successfully implement a knowledge initiative within a given department where communication is effective, an organization-wide knowledge strategy would be very difficult to implement. Social Network Analysis discussed in Chapter 9 under "Connecting the Dots" and Chapter 14 on Relationship Network Management is a methodology for identifying the areas that are holding communications back as well as the integrative points within an organization. Further, see the discussion "Grow a Knowledge Network" in Chapter 9, the discussion under Knowledge Sharing in Chapter 11, and Chapter 14 on

Relationship Network Management. Also see the section on "Communities of Practice, Interest and Learning" in Chapter 10, and scan through the tools suggested in Section IV of this book.

Q17: The level of management's empowerment of the workforce is ...

Q17-2: Selecting level 2 indicates a general overall lack of empowerment of employees. The specific level of empowerment should be determined. If it is insufficient to encourage knowledge creation, sharing, and collaboration among employees, steps should be built into the knowledge strategy to strengthen this aspect of organization effectiveness. Relationship Network Management – discussed under "Grow a Knowledge Network" in Chapter 9 and more fully in Chapter 14 – is an approach to developing self-empowerment.

Q17-1: Selecting level 1 indicates that there is very little, if any, empowerment of employees in the organization. To successfully implement a knowledge strategy under these conditions would mean building up employee confidence and practice in taking actions, creating and sharing knowledge, and accepting responsibilities for their decisions. This goal could be made part of the overall knowledge strategy implementation. Without employees feeling empowered to create and share their knowledge with others, they are likely to have a difficult time meeting any knowledge strategy objectives. Relationship Network Management – discussed under "Grow a Knowledge Network" in Chapter 9 and more fully in Chapter 14 – is an approach to developing self-empowerment.

 Q18: The use of teams or groups to accomplish specific objectives within this Organization is ...

Q18-2: Selecting level 2 indicates that teams are not used very often in your organization. Since employees who are working in teams typically communicate and collaborate with each other in a highly productive way, the importance of teams or groups to accomplish desired objectives should be carefully observed and considered when creating and implementing a knowledge strategy. Depending on the specific knowledge strategy selected, special attention would most likely have to be paid to creating effective workforce team and groups skills. See the discussion in "Grow a Knowledge Network" in chapter 9 and "Select the Team" in Chapter 7. Also, see "Nurture an Innovation Culture" in chapter 7.

Q18-1: Selecting level 1 indicates that the organization rarely uses teams. This may impose a burden on the knowledge strategy and the culture of the workforce. Given this state of affairs, it is worth looking carefully into the current culture to determine how well employees are able to communicate and collaborate in their daily work. As a minimum the knowledge strategy should include learning how to work in teams, or a knowledge initiative whose purpose is to create effective team and community communication and collaboration. This could begin as a local initiative or pilot program which would then be expanded to the entire organization. See the discussion in "Grow a Knowledge Network" in chapter 9 and "Select the Team" in Chapter 7. Also, see "Nurture an Innovation Culture" in chapter 7.

Q19: Managers' willingness to accept and implement new initiatives is ...

Q19-2: Selecting level 2 indicates that the organization's capability to implement new initiatives is low, and possibly that there is little experience in this area. Thus, some training or learning may need to be planned into the knowledge strategy. In addition, those employees who have demonstrated the willingness and capacity to work with change and implement new initiatives may be considered for leading specific parts of the knowledge strategy. It should be noted that managers who are reluctant to accept and implement new initiatives may not be easily changed. They may resist or slow down implementation of a knowledge strategy. Certainly, they need to be made aware of the need and benefit of change. Moving managers to other positions is one way of stimulating their learning and getting them used to change. See the discussion under "Become a Change Agent" in Chapter 9.

Q19-1: Selecting level 1 indicates that most managers in the organization would not be comfortable implementing new initiatives, and therefore would undoubtedly have difficulty supporting a knowledge strategy. Without management and leadership support it is very difficult for any knowledge strategy to be successfully implemented. A significant effort may be needed in moving management styles such that management actions will facilitate the creation of new initiatives and change prior to starting a knowledge strategy. Under these conditions, it would probably be best not to initiative the knowledge strategy unless that strategy directly addressed the issues of initiating and living with change. An alternate approach would be to work with the managers through team assignments and team building to give them greater experience and comfort in initiating and dealing with change, which could then be transferred to a knowledge strategy at a later date. Still another approach is to have these leaders work together as a team with the responsibility for implementing the knowledge strategy. See the discussion under "Become a Change Agent" in Chapter 9.

Q20: The level of support for knowledge sharing through the structure of this Organization is ...

Q20-2: Selecting level 2 indicates that the structure is detrimental to employee knowledge sharing, which is a key aspect of all knowledge strategies. It is important to explore whether the issue is the culture or the structure inhibits an increased level of employee knowledge sharing. If the structure is the issue, then it needs to be reviewed and perhaps modified through policies and procedures, with emphasis placed on increased collaboration among departments or divisions, or efforts made to reduce silo mentalities and practices. Implementation of a knowledge strategy should be delayed until the structure can be reviewed and needed actions taken. One step to encourage knowledge sharing may be to review the organizational processes and create more teams and communities. For example, if the structure does not contain computer networking, does not allow communities of practice, or does not encourage meetings among department heads or frequent discussions among first-line supervisors exchanging their experience, then knowledge will rarely be shared. See the discussion under "Communities of Practice, Interest and Learning" in Chapter 10 and the discussion under "Knowledge Sharing" in Chapter 11.

Creating and maintaining trust is another very important aspect of knowledge sharing and can be influenced by knowledge structure. Without a support structure, it is difficult to get a successful outcome from any knowledge strategy. Trust is entangled in various chapters throughout this book, and along with truth is a basic foundation for Reblooming the Knowledge Movement. As a starting point, see the discussion of "Trust" in Chapter 11.

Q20-1: Selecting level 1 indicates that the nature of the structure is seriously inhibiting knowledge sharing. If this is correct, it would be essential to evaluate the structure and take proper actions prior to commencing a knowledge strategy. (See the response to Q20-2 above.) Until this issue is mitigated, a knowledge strategy cannot succeed. See also the discussion under "Think Systems" in Chapter 7.

Q21: The consistency of management direction and organization goals is ...

Q21-2: Selecting level 2 indicates that management has a history of fluctuations and changing goals and directions for the organization as seen by the responder. To the extent that this is true, employees may well assume any new change program such as a knowledge strategy is another "flavor of the day" and not give it the serious consideration necessary for successful implementation. When these conditions occur, and even when perceived, they represent a potential barrier to implementation of a knowledge strategy and actions need to be taken to counter the reaction of employees. The solution could be to assure that leadership and senior management are fully aligned and supportive of the program, and are personally supportive and/or active in its implementation. This book offers a myriad of resources to help build understanding of the value of knowledge and innovation to the organization. For example, Chapter 6 specifically links knowledge and innovation. See also the discussion under "Build the Business Case" in Chapter 7. The Section on Readiness (first half of Chapter 8) can also support the important role of knowledge in the organization.

Q21-1: Selecting level 1 indicates that management has a strong history of shifting goals and directions for the organization. This condition would almost certainly generate an employee perspective of, "we have seen it before and it will go away as other initiatives have" or "this is the new flavor of the month, why should I take it seriously?" Such attitudes represent a significant barrier to successful knowledge strategy implementation and must be addressed and resolved prior to initiating a knowledge strategy. Since this issue reflects a general mistrust of management decisions and actions on the part of employees, it is larger than bringing management on-board with the strategy. Further, it will not easily go away. Definitive management decisions and actions aligned to organization goals and with consistent follow-through over time are required to mitigate this effect.

Q22: The effectiveness of the HR department's support of employee training and development is ...

Q22-2: Selecting level 2 indicates that the HR department is providing little support for employee training and development. HR has the opportunity to play a significant role in influencing and building an innovation culture relative to learning and human development. Depending on the specific knowledge strategy to be implemented, the role of the HR department may be significant and needs to be brought into the strategy, with specific required resources and responsibilities assigned to HR. Where there is a question regarding HR support, senior management may have to step in and take a personal interest to ensure that the HR department has the resources and authority to support the knowledge strategy.

Q22-1: Selecting level 1 indicates that the HR department is providing little or no support for employee training and development. This would be rare, but to the extent it occurs it would be essential to ensure that the HR department has the authority and resources to provide the needed support for employee training and development prior to implementing a knowledge strategy. Knowledge creation, sharing and application are essential to many knowledge strategies, and as a result employee training and development is foundational. Where there is a question regarding HR support, senior management may have to step in and take a personal interest to ensure that the HR department has the resources and authority to support the knowledge strategy.

CULTURE

Q23: The willingness of employees to accept and take advantage of change is ...

Q23-2: Selecting level 2 indicates that the organization's culture is not comfortable with change and may provide resistance to any knowledge strategy. The importance of this item would depend upon the change required in implementing a specific knowledge strategy. If significant change is needed, then actions should be taken to prepare the organization to accept and embrace change. Depending on the history and specific nature of the organization's culture, leadership and management style, this may be a long-term challenge. *People cannot be ordered to change*. For example, you cannot successfully tell an employee to share their knowledge, trust others, be creative, or collaborate with their peers. The following factors are instrumental in determining whether or not an individual will change: awareness, understanding, believing, feeling good, ownership, empowerment, and impact. See the discussion under "Become a Change Agent" in Chapter 9.

Organization cultures are often highly resistive to change unless they have a history of continuous learning and adapting to a changing environment. In any case, depending on the size of the organization and the specific knowledge strategy selected, this level would indicate the need for a carefully thought out and significant effort to ensure that the culture would accept and adapt to the necessary changes required by the strategy. See the discussion under "Nurture an Innovation Culture" in Chapter 7.

Q23-1: Selecting level 1 indicates that the history of the Organization is one of stability, and most likely has a culture which is change resistant. Unless the intended knowledge strategy requires little or no change in the current culture, it may be best to address the change requirements before initiating the strategy. Any knowledge strategy involves the creation, sharing and application of knowledge, all of which encompass learning and change. See the discussion under "Become a Change Agent" in Chapter 9 and the discussion under "Nurture an Innovation Culture" in Chapter 7.

Q24: The level of trust among Organization employees is ...

Q24-2: Selecting level 2 indicates that there is a below average level of trust among organization employees. While this may be acceptable to commence a knowledge strategy implementation, a high level of trust is desired for maximum knowledge sharing and organizational learning. Under this condition it may be best to consider the importance of trust among employees as it relates to the specific knowledge strategy to be implemented. If trust is significant, the strategy may be delayed until the trust level of the organization can be increased. A second option would be to build in a process for trust enhancement during the knowledge strategy implementation. Trust is one of the critical factors for a successful knowledge strategy and as such, becomes a major challenge to management and leadership. Using teams, team building and collaborative groups working closely together to make decisions and take actions on implementing the knowledge strategy could improve the overall level of trust in the organization. Trust is entangled in various chapters throughout this book, and along with truth is a basic foundation for Reblooming the Knowledge Movement. As a starting point, see the discussion of "Trust" in Chapter 11. Trust is also an essential element in Relationship Network Management (see Chapter 14).

Q24-1: Selecting level 1 indicates that there is essentially little or no trust within the Organization. Under these conditions it is most likely futile to try to implement a knowledge strategy before resolving the trust issue. Trust is entangled in various chapters throughout this book, and along with truth is a basic foundation for Reblooming the Knowledge Movement. As a starting point, see the discussion of "Trust" in Chapter 11. Trust is also an essential element in Relationship Network Management (see Chapter 14).

Q25: The capacity of employees to tackle and take a flexible approach to problems is ...

Q25-2: Selecting level 2 indicates that employees are not good at tackling and taking a flexible approach to problems. Implementation of a knowledge strategy may offer a vehicle for improving an employee's capacity to solve problems and stay flexible in how they deal with issues. The Four Organizational Processes section in Chapter 10 as well as the first half of Chapter 8 on Readiness may provide insights on the need for flexibility. In this situation it may be best to create training as part of the strategy mechanisms to improve employee capacity for problem-solving and flexibility.

Q25-1: Selecting level 1 indicates that employees have difficulty solving problems and being flexible. This kind of a condition is frequently created by a strong control-oriented organization, which has not empowered the workforce and is intolerant of mistakes. Under these conditions it may be very difficult to implement a successful knowledge strategy. The Four Organizational Processes section in Chapter 10 as well as the first half of Chapter 8 on Readiness may provide insights on the need for flexibility.

Q26: The energy level and spirit of the workforce in my organization is .

Q26-2: Selecting level 2 indicates that the employees have low energy levels and not too much spirit towards their work. While this would most likely make it quite difficult to implement a knowledge strategy, it may be possible for a successful knowledge initiative, although a lower energy level workforce is going to move slower toward an objective, and therefore the implementation program needs to take this into account. However, the knowledge strategy might be implemented in a manner which would improve the energy level and spirit of the workforce, providing management and senior leadership are personally involved and use that involvement to communicate with their employees. See the discussion under "Ensure Leadership Commitment" in Chapter 7.

Q26-1: Selecting level 1 indicates that employees have very low energy levels and little or no spirit towards their work. When this occurs, there are generally larger underlying issues at play. Regardless, this situation would make it very difficult to implement any new strategy. One approach in response to this finding is to create a problem-solving team or hold a collaborative problem-solving forum to surface and address related critical issues. See the Collaborative Problem-Solving Forum tool in Section IV.

Q27: The percentage of workers who learn fast enough to keep up with change is ...

Q27-2: Selecting level 2 indicates that the overall Organization learning rate is low. Since knowledge strategies are about creating, leveraging, sharing and applying knowledge, the learning rate of the organization is very important. With a low-level learning rate, it will likely be necessary that special care be given to upgrading the organization's capability of working collaboratively, learning, and sharing information and knowledge. This area should be addressed as a significant part of the knowledge implementation strategy. Learning is discussed in Chapter 2. See also "Continuous Learning" in Chapter 11. Note that implementation of a knowledge strategy will likely increase the learning rate throughout the organization and provide more efficient and effective use of the knowledge generated. If there are specific pockets within the organization where learning is not occurring that should be addressed as part of the strategy.

Q27-1: Selecting level 1 indicates a very low overall rate of learning for the organization. Depending upon other assessments within this instrument, it may be necessary to delay implementation of a knowledge strategy until the overall learning capacity of the organization has been improved, or direct the strategy specific toward this deficit, that is, developing and embracing an organizational learning strategy. (A sample eLearning strategy is in Appendix C.) An organization cannot survive in an uncertain and changing environment without the ability to learn. In this context, see the first half of Chapter 8 on Readiness.

Q28: The level of networking and communication among organization workers is ...

Q28-2: Networking and Communication as one of the core front petals in Reblooming Knowledge Movement (RKM) model is an indicator of how well employees work together, and is an essential element in any effective knowledge strategy. Selecting level 2 indicates there is not very much networking and communication among organization workers. At this level, a specific plan should be made and implemented to increase the amount of networking and communication among 0rganization employees as part of the knowledge strategy. See the discussion under "Grow a Knowledge Network" in Chapter 9. A good approach to expanding and connecting more fully across the organization is to implement Relationship Network Management as an organization-wide initiative, which puts full responsibility of each individual for the interactions which drive their future decision. See Chapter 14.

Q28-1: Selecting level 1 indicates there is minimal networking and communication among organization workers. In this extreme case, it is unwise to begin a knowledge strategy outside of the focus on this critical organizational need. The creation, sharing and application of knowledge represents the payoff of a knowledge strategy in terms of innovation as well as performance improvement and, as such, requires communication and networking by organization employees. Conducting a Social Network Analysis (SNA) as a process for mapping the relationships among people, teams, or across organizations will help identify places where communication links are broken. See the discussion under "Connect the Dots" in Chapter 9. See also Chapter 14 on Relationship Network Management.

Q29: The percentage of employees who understand the vision of this Organization is ...

Q29-2: Selecting level 2 indicates that most employees are not clear about, or aware of, the organization's specific vision. Before implementing a knowledge strategy, it may be best to build employee understanding of and appreciation for the vision of the organization. Any knowledge strategy is intended to improve the current and future performance of the organization in support of the vision of the organization. This relationship between the objectives of the knowledge strategy and the vision is one that is key for employees to understand the need for, and importance of, the knowledge strategy. Ensure that this connection is clearly communicated as the strategy moves forward. Be sure to ensure the vision of the organization is addressed early during implementation along with the relationship of the knowledge strategy to this vision. See the discussions in "Develop the Strategy" and "Write a Plan" in Chapter 7. Also, see the discussion under "Resonance and Coherence" in Chapter 11.

Q29-1: Selecting level 1 indicates that very few employees understand or are aware of the organization's vision. Before implementing a knowledge strategy, it is best to build employee understanding of and appreciation for the vision of the organization. When the knowledge strategy does move forward, ensure the vision of the organization is addressed early during implementation along with the relationship of the knowledge strategy and each individual's contribution to this vision. See the discussions in "Develop the Strategy" and "Write a Plan" in Chapter 7. Also, see the discussion under "Resonance and Coherence" in Chapter 11.

Q30: The percentage of employees empowered to do their job with minimal direction is ...

Q30-3: Selecting level 3 indicates that there are some employees who are empowered and do not have significant oversight.

Q30-2: Selecting level 2 indicates that there are only a few employees who are empowered, with most employees working in the same level of a control-oriented environment. This situation would make implementation of a knowledge strategy difficult since knowledge relies on the individual worker using their knowledge and expertise to collaborate and share with others, and making decisions within the envelope of their competency, experience, and level of empowerment by management. See the discussion under "Empowerment" in Chapter 9.

Q30-1: Selecting level 1 indicates that very few or perhaps none of the employees in the organization are empowered. This situation would make it quite difficult, if not impossible, to successfully implement a knowledge strategy for the Organization. Most often this is a leadership/management problem that must be addressed before moving ahead with a knowledge strategy. You may wish to review the discussion of "Leading and Managing" Chapter 9 as well as the discussion of leadership styles in Chapter 1.

Q31: For the critical processes of the organization, workforce discipline is ...

Q31-2: Selecting level 2 indicates that there are critical processes within the organization in which employee discipline may be lower than desired. Under these conditions, this discipline must be reinstated. An example of critical processes would be those that require safety procedures that must not be compromised. The challenge here is that, when implementing a knowledge strategy for the entire organization, employees involved in the critical processes maintain their discipline and careful performance on a daily basis *while simultaneously* learning and sharing their knowledge and helping others perform well. Considerations such as these need to be taken into account in the creation of knowledge strategy. Note that workforce discipline and management control are not synonymous.

Q31-1: Selecting level 1 indicates that the critical processes within the organization are not implemented with sufficient employee discipline. This rarely occurs, since was this the case an organization could not long function. If such a situation does exist it must be corrected immediately *prior* to implementing any knowledge strategy.

Q32: The level of trust between employees and managers is ...

Q32-2: Selecting level 2 indicates that there is not very much trust between management and the employees. Trust is an essential ingredient in the workplace and must be addressed before collaboration and knowledge sharing can effectively occur. Thus, actions should be considered early in the implementation phase of the knowledge strategy to improve the level of trust between management and the employees. Trust is an underlying theme throughout the discussions on knowledge strategies and initiatives, is coupled with truth as the foundation of the Reblooming Knowledge Movement (RKM) model, and is addressed throughout this book. See the discussion under "Trust" in Chapter 11.

Q32-1: Selecting level 1 indicates that there is little or no trust between management and the employees. When this situation occurs, it would be very difficult to implement almost any form of knowledge strategy unless the strategy is specifically designed to improve the level of trust throughout the organization. Trust between management and employees represents a foundation upon which empowerment, knowledge sharing and learning can be built. But building trust takes time, significant effort, and patience by all concerned. It is particularly challenging if the lack of trust is organization-wide and management is control oriented with silos and/or old boy networks built into the culture. Trust is an underlying theme throughout the discussions on knowledge strategies and initiatives, is coupled with truth as the foundation of the Reblooming Knowledge Movement model, and is addressed throughout this book. See the discussion under "Trust" in Chapter 11.

Q33: The level of employee training, learning, and development in this Organization is ...

Q33-2: Selecting level 2 indicates that while there is some employee training, learning and development it may not be adequate. Depending on the specific knowledge strategy selected, it is important to look at the various departments within the organization to determine if training, learning and development are adequate to meet current and anticipated needs relative to the creation, sharing and application of knowledge and the empowerment of employees. Specific actions may be necessary to upgrade training, learning and development either prior to commencing—or as part of—a knowledge strategy. See the discussion under "Knowledge Sharing" in Chapter 11.

Q33-1: Selecting level 1 indicates that there is little or no employee training, learning and development. If this is the case, the knowledge strategy should not be implemented unless it contains training, learning and development as part of the strategy, or perhaps *that could be* the strategy. Organizational learning and knowledge management go hand in hand. See the sample strategy on "Implementing eLearning" in Appendix C.

Q34: The percentage of employees that think in terms of systems, and how their work affects other employee efforts and the mission of the organization, is ...

Q34-2: Selecting level 2 indicates that there are perhaps a few employees who think in terms of systems and how their work affects other employee efforts and the overall mission of the organization. Since the capacity to think in terms of systems and interaction among workers provides significant support for any knowledge strategy, this characteristic in the organization may need to be further developed by using teams, or perhaps training in systems and complexity. While this situation may not preclude a successful knowledge strategy, it would be worthwhile to include team training and workshops on collaboration and communication as part of the startup of implementation. One approach would be to embrace Relationship Network Management (RNM) as a core competency for organization employees (see Chapter 14). Systems and complexity is addressed in Chapter 2, and Chapter 19 is a more depth treatment of systems and complexity.

Q34-1: Selecting level 1 indicates that there is little or no systems thinking in the organization which would include an understanding of how one employee's work affects other employees as well as its relationship to the organizational mission. While such a situation may not preclude successful knowledge implementation, it highlights the need for, and importance of, developing employee capacity to think broader than their individual job responsibilities and to begin to communicate and collaborate more effectively with other employees. Plan on including team training and workshops on collaboration and communication as part of the startup of knowledge strategy implementation. One approach would be to embrace Relationship Network Management (RNM) as a core competency for Organization employees. One approach would be to embrace Relationship Network Management (RNM) as a core competency for organization employees (see Chapter 14). Another approach for medium-large organizations would be to consider developing and supporting Communities of Practice (CoP). See the discussion under "Communities of Practice, Interest, and Learning" in Chapter 10. Systems and complexity is addressed in Chapter 2, and Chapter 19 is a more depth treatment of systems and complexity.

ALIGNMENT

NOTE: See the tool "Strategic Alignment" in Section IV.

Q35: How well will the strategic business plan support the knowledge strategy?

Q35-2: Selecting level 2 indicates that there is minimum alignment between the business plan and the knowledge strategy. If the strategic business plan is well developed and consistent with the purpose and vision of the organization, then the knowledge strategy would most likely be aligned with, and supportive of, the business plan. If the business plan does not support the needs of the knowledge strategy, then it would be necessary to ensure that the business plan and the knowledge strategy are aligned. See the discussion under "Develop the Strategy" and "Write a Plan" in Chapter 7.

Q35-1: Selecting level 1 indicates that there is little or no alignment or relationship between the business plan and the knowledge strategy. Clearly this gap needs to be addressed. If the business plan does not support the needs of the knowledge strategy, and the knowledge strategy does not support the needs of the business plan, then it will be necessary to ensure this alignment before moving forward. See the discussion under "Develop the Strategy" and "Write a Plan" in Chapter 7.

Q36: How well will the operational plan support the knowledge strategy?

Q36-2: Selecting level 2 indicates that the operational plan may provide some support for the knowledge strategy. If the operational plan and knowledge strategy are independent and do not require interaction and alignment, then a knowledge strategy may begin implementation. However, the plan and knowledge strategy may have to be reviewed to bring them into better alignment. It is best when the two mutually support each other. See the discussion under "Develop the Strategy" and "Write a Plan" in Chapter 7.

Q36-1: Selecting level 1 indicates that the operational plan will provide little or no support for the knowledge strategy. If this is the case, then the plan and the knowledge strategy need to be reviewed and brought into closer alignment and mutual support. See the discussion under "Develop the Strategy" and "Write a Plan" in Chapter 7.

Q37: How well will the capital improvement plan support implementation of a knowledge strategy?

Q37-2: Selecting level 2 indicates that the capital improvement plan is relatively independent of the knowledge strategy. While this should not be an issue unless the knowledge strategy directly impacts the capital improvement plan, the knowledge strategy should be reviewed for its relationship to the capital improvement plan to ensure the strategy supports the long-term goals of the organization, and the two should be brought into alignment. See the discussion under "Develop the Strategy" and "Write a Plan" in Chapter 7.

Q37-1: Selecting level 1 indicates that the capital improvement plan will not support the knowledge strategy. Assuming the knowledge strategy needs support from the capital improvement plan, these two need to be brought into alignment. If there are no negative impacts between the two, the knowledge strategy could begin implementation, assuming other aspects of this assessment are acceptable. See the discussion under "Develop the Strategy" and "Write a Plan" in Chapter 7.

Q38: How well will the Organization's information technology master plan support implementation of a knowledge strategy?

Q38-2: Selecting level 2 indicates that the information technology master plan provides some, but not necessarily sufficient, support for the knowledge strategy. If the knowledge strategy involves significant technological support, this issue requires careful consideration before proceeding with the strategy, and implementation may have to be delayed until technology is available. Whatever level of technology support is needed, it is important to ensure that the

technology is selected and implemented in a manner which is cohesive with organization needs and resources, and employee acceptance. Information is the foundation of knowledge, and its accessibility and ease of use is critical for success of a knowledge strategy in today's technologically advanced environment.

Q38-1: Selecting level 1 indicates that the information technology master plan would provide little or no technology in support of the knowledge strategy. Since technology is an enabler for all knowledge strategies, this may not be acceptable, depending upon the needs of the specific strategy. This issue requires careful consideration before proceeding with the strategy, and implementation should be delayed until technology is available. Whatever level of technology support is needed, it is important to ensure that the technology is selected and implemented in a manner which is cohesive with organization needs and resources, and employee acceptance.

Q39: How well will your information technology department support implementation of a knowledge strategy?

Q39-2: Selecting level 2 indicates that the information technology department will be able to provide some support, but perhaps not enough to ensure an effective knowledge strategy. If the strategy is dependent upon strong IT support, this issue should be resolved before commencing the strategy.

Q39-1: Selecting level 1 indicates that the information technology department is essentially unable to provide support to the knowledge strategy. Unless the knowledge strategy does not include any technology for its implementation, which is highly unlikely since technology is an enabler for most knowledge strategies, it is unacceptable and the strategy should be delayed until this issue is resolved.

Q40: The competency and skill sets of this organization's employees are ...

Q40-2: Selecting a 2 indicates that the competency and skills of this Organization's employees are lower than average. Depending on the knowledge strategy, it may be best to delay implementation, or to modify the strategy to include upgrading the competencies and skills of employees. One approach is to engage retirees to support rapid upgrading of employee competencies and skills.

Q40-1: Selecting a 1 indicates that the competencies and skills of the Organization workforce are low. This condition needs immediate attention. A knowledge initiative could be used to upgrade weak areas while simultaneously supporting implementation of a broader knowledge strategy.

ENDNOTES

Copyright 1962, Princeton University Press, Princeton, NJ, First Princeton Paperback Edition, 1972s.

[2] Damasio, A.R. (1999). *The feeling of what happens: Body and emotion in the making of consciousness.* Harcourt Brace & Company.

[3] Honderich, T. (1999). *The philosophers: Introducing great Western thinkers.* Oxford University Press, p. 110.

[4] Csikszentmihalyi, M. (2003). *Good business: Leadership, flow and the making of meaning.* Viking, p. 60.

[5] Frankl, V. E. (1939/1963). *Man's search for meaning: An introduction of logotherapy.* Pocket Books.

[6] Bennet, D., Bennet, A., & Turner, R. (2022). *Unleashing the human mind: A consilience approach to managing self.* MQIPress. Also, Bennet, D., Bennet, A., & Turner, R. (2018). *Expanding the self: The intelligent complex adaptive system.* MQIPress.

[7] McCraty, R. (2015). *Science of the heart: Exploring the role of the heart in human performance* (vol. 2). The HeartMath Institute, p. 24.

[8] Grigg, D. B. (1975, July). The world's agricultural labor force 1800-1970. *Geography Journal, 60*(3). Taylor & Francis, Ltd, University of Sheffield.

[9] Drucker, P. F. (1993). *Post-capitalist society.* HarperBusiness, A Division of HarperCollins Publishers, p. 20.

[10] Ackoff, R. L. (1994). *The democratic corporation: A radical prescription for recreating corporate America and rediscovering success.* Oxford University Press.

[11] Ibid, p. 72.

[12] Bennet, A., Bennet, D., & Avedisian, J. (2018). *The course of knowledge: A 21st century theory.* MQIPress.

[13] *Britannica* https://www.britannica.com/topic/democracy/The-theory-of-democracy

[14] Ibid.

[15] James, W. (1890/1980). *The principles of psychology, Vol. 1.* Holt, Rinehart & Winston.

[16] Kolb, D. A. (1984). *Experiential learning: Experience as the source of learning and development.* Prentice-Hall, p. 27.

[17] Bennet, Bennet, & Turner (2018).

[18] Dewey, J. (1938/1997). *Experience and education.* Simon & Schuster, p. 39.

[19] Van Witteloostuijn, A., & de Jong, G. (2007). Organizational democracy. In S. R. Clegg & J. R. Bailey (Eds.), *International encyclopedia of organization studies volume 3*, pp. 1039-1042. Sage Publishers.

[20] Ibid.

[21] Rousseau, D. M., & Rivero, A. (2003). Democracy, a way of organizing in a knowledge economy. *Journal of Management Inquiry, 12*(2), 115-134., p. 116.

[22] Ibid.

[23] Ibid.

[24] Blau, J. (2000). Relational wealth in the commons: Local spaces of work and residence in a global economy. In C.R. Leana & D. M. Rousseau (Eds.), *Relational wealth: The advantages of stability in a changing economy*, pp. 217-232. Oxford University Press.

[25] Fenton, T. (2022). *Freedom at work: The leadership strategy for transforming your life, your organization, and our world.* BenBella Books, Inc., p. xviii.

[26] Draws on a random sample of 3,871 executives selected from a database of over 20,000 leaders. See Goleman, D. (2000, March-April). Leadership that gets results. *Harvard Business Review*, pp. 78-90.

[27] Greenleaf, R. K. (1977/ 2002). *Servant leadership: A journey into the nature of legitimate power & greatness* (25th Anniversary Ed.). Paulist Press.

[28] de Sousa, M. (2023). The Meaningful Leader. Silabo.

[29] Hershey, P. (1985). *The situational leader*. Warner Books.

[30] Fenton, p. xxi.

[31] Ibid., pp. 89-90.

[32] Cleveland, H. (2002). *Nobody in charge: Essays on the future of leadership*. Jossey-Bass.

[33] Kurtzman, J. (1998). *Thought leaders: Insights on the future of business*. Jossey-Bass, p. xi.

[34] Rousseau & Rivero.

[35] Ibid., p. 115.

[36] Linz, J., & Stepan, A. (Eds.) (1978). *The breakdown of democratic regimes: Crisis, breakdown, and reequilibration*. Johns Hopkins University Press.

[37] Dahl, A. (1985). *A Preface to economic democracy*. University of California Press, p. 18.

[38] de Toqueville, A. (2000). *Democracy in America*. Hackett Publishing Co., p. 9.

[39] From the Foreword by Warren Bennis in Pinchot, G., & Pinchot, E. (1993). *The end of bureaucracy & the rise of the intelligent organization*. Berrett-Koehler Publishers.

[40] Stebbins, L.H. (2010). Development of reality system theory. *Journal of Business & Economics Research, 8*(4).

[41] Bennet, A., & Bennet, D. (2018). *Decision-making in the new reality: Complexity, knowledge and knowing*. MQIPress.

[42] Bennet & Bennet (2004).. *Organizational survival in the new world: The intelligent complex adaptive system*. Elsevier.

[43] Johnson, S. (2001). *Emergence*. Scribner.

[44] Axelrod, R., & Cohen, M.D. (1999). *Harnessing complexity: Organizational implications of a scientific frontier*. The Free Press, p. 15.

[45] Marshall, I., & Zohar, D. (1997). *Who's afraid of Schrödinger's cat?* William Morrow and Company, Inc. Also, Prigogine, I. (1996). *The end of certainty: Time, chaos, and the new laws of nature*. The Free Press.

[46] Zohar, D., & Marshall, I. (1994). *The quantum society: Mind, physics, and the new social vision*. William Morrow and Co., Inc.

[47] Wilber, K. (2000). *Integral psychology: Consciousness, spirit, psychology, therapy*. Shambhala Publications, p. 89.

[48] Bennet, Bennet, & Avedisian.

[49] Bennet, D., & Bennet, A. (2010). Social learning from the inside out: The creation and sharing of knowledge from the mind/brain perspective. In J. Girard & J. Girard (Eds.), *Social knowledge: Using social media to know what you know*, pp. 1-23. IGI Global.

[50] Pert, C. B. (1997). *Molecules of emotion: A science behind mind-body medicine*. Touchstone.

[51] Number forwarded from a new way of counting brain cells. Neuroscientist Suzana Herculano-Houzel, Associate Professor of Psychological Science, Vanderbilt University.

[52] Hawkins, J. C. (2021). *A thousand brains: A new theory of intelligence*. Basic Books, p. vii.

[53] Silberman, M. (2007). *The handbook of experiential learning*. Pfeiffer, p. 3.

[54] Perkins, M. (1971). *Outsmarting IQ: the emerging science of learnable intelligence*. Free Press, pp. 3-4.

[55] Bennet, Bennet, & Turner (2018).

[56] Kolb.

[57] Jung, C. G. (1990). *The undiscovered self with symbols and the interpretation of dreams* (R. F. Hull, Trans.). Princeton University Press.

[58] Bennet, Bennet, & Turner (2018).

[59] Ibid.

[60] Ibid.

[61] Kolb, p. 69.

[62] Bennet, Bennet, & Turner (2018).

[63] Cozolino, L. J. (20006). *The neuroscience of human relationships: Attachment and the developing social brain*. W. W. Norton, p. 3.

[64] Bennet, Bennet, & Turner (2018).

[65] Wiig, K. (1993a). *Knowledge management methods – Practical approaches to managing knowledge*. Schema Press.

[66] Hawkins, p. 130.

[67] Bennet, Bennet, & Turner (2018).

[68] Hawkins, pp. 131-132.

[69] SQ relates to Spiritual Quotient, a measure of Spiritual Intelligence, which is beyond the mental (IQ) and emotional (EQ) skills, measuring spiritual aptitude, which includes self-awareness and a level of Otherness (sensitivity to others). At some level all humans are spiritual in nature, and there is a direct positive correlation between spiritual characteristics and human learning. See Bennet, A., & Bennet, D. (2007). The knowledge and knowing of spiritual learning. *VINE: The Journal of Information and Knowledge Management Systems, 37*(1), 27-40.

[70] Zohar & Marshall (1994), Introduction.

[71] Pinchot, G., & Pinchot, E. (1993). *The end of bureaucracy & the rise of the intelligent organization*. Berrett-Koehler Publishers.

[72] Ibid., Warren Bennis in Foreword.

[73] Ibid., p. 70.

[74] McMaster, M.D. (1996). *The intelligence advantage: Organizing for complexity*. Butterworth-Heinemann.

[75] Bennet, Bennet, & Turner (2018).

[76] Kunz, P. G. (1968). The concept of order. University of Washington Press, p. 162.

[77] Ibid.

[78] Miller, J. G. (1978). *Living systems*. McGraw-Hill Book Company.

[79] Cummings, T. G., & Huse, E. G. (1989). *Organization development and change*, 4th ed. West Publishing Company.

[80] Gerth, H. H., & Mills, C. W. (Eds. and Trans.) (1946). *Max Weber: Essays in sociology*. Oxford University Press, p. 243.

[81] Ibid., p. 233.

[82] Connelly, C. E., Zweig, D., Webster, J., & Trougakos, J. P. (2012). Knowledge hiding in organizations. *Journal of Organizational Behavior, 33*(1), 64-88. https://doi.org/10.1002/job.737 Also, Evans, J. M., Hendron, M. G., & Oldroyd, J. B. (2015). Withholding the ace: The individual- and unit-level performance effects of self-reported and perceived knowledge hoarding. *Organizational Science, 26*(2), 494-510. https://doi.org/10.1287/orsc.2014.0945 Also, Peng, H. (2013). Why and when do people hide knowledge? *Journal of Knowledge Management, 17*(3), 398-415. https://doi.org/10.1108/JKM-12-2012-0380 Also, Webster, J., Brown, G., Zweig, D., Connelly, C. E., Brodt, S., & Sitkin, S. (2008). Beyond knowledge sharing: Withholding knowledge at work. In *Research in Personnel and Human Resources Management 27*, 1-37. Emerald Group Publishing Limited.

[83] Nystrom, P. C., & Starbuck, W. H. (1984). *Handbook of organizational design, volumes 1 and 2*. Oxford University Press. Also, Osborne, D., & Gaebler, T. (1993). *Reinventing government: How the entrepreneur spirit is transforming the public sector*. Penguin Books. Also, Pinkerton, J. P. (1995). *What comes next: The end of big government—and the new paradigm ahead*. Hyperion.

[84] Bennet & Bennet (2004).

[85] Gold, M., & Douvan, E. (1997). *A new outline of social psychology*. American Psychological Association.

[86] Arms, K., & Camp, P. (1987). *Biology*, 3rd ed. Saunders College Publishing.

[87] Dr. Arthur J. Murray, Applied Knowledge Sciences, Inc. (Used with permission).

[88] Murray, A. J. (2018). *Building the enterprise of the future: Co-creating and delivering extraordinary value in an eight-billion-mind world*. AKS Press, pp. 75-81.

[89] Curlief, S., & Plastino, A. R. (2021). *Topics on quantum information science*. Intech Open.

[90] Stonier, T. (1990). *Information and the internal structure of the universe: An introduction into information physics*. Springer-Verlag. doi:10.1007/978-1-4471-3265-3

[91] Stonier, T. (1997). *Information and meaning: An evolutionary perspective*. Springer-Verlag. doi:10.1007/978-1-4471-0977-8 Also, Bennet, D., & Bennet, A. (2008). The decision-making process for complex situations in a complex environment. In C.W. Holsapple & F. Burstein (Eds.). *Handbook on decision support systems*, pp. 3-20. Springer-Verlag.

[92] Stonier (1997).

[93] Stonier (1990).

[94] Boltzmann, L. (1896, 1898). *Lectures on gas theory* (part I and part II) (Trans. S.G. Brush, 1976). University of California Press.

[95] Schrödinger (1944) (Combined reprint, 1967). *What is life?* Cambridge University Press.

[96] Stonier (1997), p. 15.

[97] Ibid., p. 17.

[98] Stonier (1990), p. 70.

[99] Puthoff, H. E. (1989). Source of vacuum electromagnetic zero-point energy. *Physical Review A*(40), 4857-62. Also, Puthoff, H. E. (1990). The energetic vacuum: Implications for energy research. *Speculations in Science and Technology, 13*(4), 247.

[100] Stonier (1997).

[101] Laszlo, E. (2004). *Science and the Akashic Field: An integral theory of everything*. Inner Traditions, p. 107.

[102] Ibid., p. 108.

[103] https://federalnewsnetwork.com/all-about-data/2023/07/dau-trains-3000-acquisition-employees-on-data-skills-as-dod-seeks-greater-ai-readiness/#:~:text=DoD%E2%80%99s%20Defense%20Acquisition%20University%20is%20on%20a%20mission,understand%20the%20emerging%20tech%20that%20DoD%20is%20buying

[104] Davenport, T. H., & Beck, J. C. (2001). *The attention economy*. Harvard Business Review Press.

[105] Ibid, p. 7.

[106] Bennet, Bennet, & Turner (2018).

[107] Csikszentmihalyi, M. (1993). *The evolving self: A psychology for the third millennium*. HarperCollins Publishing.

[108] Amen, D. G. (2005). *Making a good brain great*. Harmony Books, p. 115.

[109] Bennet, Bennet, & Turner (2022).

[110] Carrasco, M., Ling, S., & Read, S. (2004). Attention alters appearance. *Nature Neuroscience, 7*, 308-313.

[111] Maunsell, J. H. R., & Treue, S. (2006). Feature-based attention in visual cortex. *Trends in Neuroscience, 29*, 317-322. Also, Alsplund, C. L., Fougnie, D., Zughni, S., Martin, J. W., & Marois, R. (2014, January 16). The attention blink reveals the probabilistic nature of discrete conscious perception. *Psychological Science*. http://pss.sagepub.com/

[112] UNESCO (n.d.). Information for All Programme: *Information literacy*. IFAP. https://www.unesco.org/en/ifap/information-literacy

[113] Dewey, p. 39.

[114] Bennet, Bennet, & Turner (2018).

[115] Bennet, A., & Bennet, D. (2010). The role of trust in a world of information and knowledge. *Effective Executive*. Icfai University Press.

[116] De Furia, G. L. (1997). *Interpersonal trust survey*. Pfeiffer Publishers (Wiley).

[117] Wenger, E. (1998). *Communities of practice: Learning, meaning, and identity*. Cambridge University Press. Doi:10.1017/CBO9780511803932

[118] Bennet & Bennet (2018), p. 140.

[119] Ibid, p. 141.

[120] CUCA represents accelerating **C**hange, rising **U**ncertainty, and increasing **C**omplexity combined with the human response of **A**nxiety. "Time accelerates. Distance shrinks. Networks expand. Information over-whelms. Interdependencies grow geometrically. Uncertainty dominates. Complexity boggles the ind. Such is the environment and the context within which current organizations must compete, survive, and thrive." [Bennet & Bennet (2004), p. 5. doi:10.4324/9780080513331]. VUCA represents **V**olatile, **U**ncertain, **C**omplex and **A**mbiguous, and was used largely by the U.S. Army War College in the early 1990's to refer to an "uncontrollable" environment.

[121] Bennet & Bennet (2004).

[122] De Furia, p. 155

[123] Buonomano, D. V., & Merzenich, M. M. (1998). Cortical plasticity: From synapses to maps. *Annual Review of Neuroscience, 21*(1), 149-186. Doi:10.1146/annurev.neuro.21.1.149 PMID:9530495

[124] Cozolino, L., & Sprokay, S. (2006). Neuroscience and adult learning. In S. Johnson & K. Taylor (Eds.), *The neuroscience of adult learning*. Jossey-Bass. Doi:10.1002/ace.214. Also, Cowan, W. M., & Kandel, E. R. (2001). A brief history of synapses and synaptic transmission. In W. C. Cowan, T. C. Sudhof, & C. F. Stevens (Eds.), *Synapses*. Johns Hopkins Press.

[125] LeDoux, J. (1996). *The emotional brain: The mysterious underpinnings of emotional life.* Touchstone, p. 19.

[126] Kandel, E.R. (2006). *In search of memory: The emergence of a new science of mind.* W. W. Norton & Company.

[127] Bennet, A., Bennet, D., Shelley, A., Bullard, T., & Lewis, J. (2020d). *The profundity and bifurcation of change part IV: Co-creating the future.* MQIPress.

[128] Darwin, C. (1998). *The descent of man.* Prometheus Books, p. 110.

[129] Kropotkin, P. (1902). *Mutual aid: A factor of evolution.* Heinemann.

[130] Swomley, J. (2000). Violence: Competition or cooperation. *Christian Ethics Today, 6*(1).

[131] Bradshaw, S., & Howard, P. N. (2019). *The global disinformation order: 2019 global inventory of organized social media manipulation.* Also, Krasodomski-Jones, A., Judson, E., Smith, J., Miller, C., & Jones, E. (2019, May). *Information operations in the digital age.* Warring Songs.

[132] Miniter, R. (2005). *Disinformation: 22 media myths that undermine the war on terror.* Regnery Publishing.

[133] Bennet et al., (2020d).

[134] Facebook (2019). What's the difference between organic, paid and post reach? https://www.facebook.com/help/285625061456389

[135] Buchanan, T. (2020). Why do people spread false information online? The effects of message and viewer characteristics on self-reported likelihood of sharing social media disinformation. *PLoS One, 15*(10).

[136] Acerbi, A. (2019). Cognitive attraction and online misinformation. *Palgrave Communications, 5*(15). Advance online publication. doi:10.1057415999-019-0224-y

[137] MacFlouer, N. (2004-16). *Why life is ...* Weekly radio shows: BBSRadio.com (#1-#480) and KXAM (#1-143). http://www.agelesswisdom.com/archives)of)radio)shows.htm

[138] Merriam-Webster (2016).

[139] MacFlouer (2004-16).

[140] Stocker, G. (1998). InfoWar. In G. Stocker & C. Schöplf, *Infowar.* SpringerWien.

[141] MacFlouer (2004-16).

[142] MacFlouer (2004-16).

[143] Hawkins, D.R. (2002). *Power VS force: The hidden determinants of human behavior.* Hay House, p. 278.

[144] Ibid., p. 278.

[145] *The Urantia Book* (1955). URANTIA Foundation, p. 1222.

[146] Bennet & Bennet (2004).

[147] Ibid.

[148] Lambe, P. (2011). The unacknowledged parentage of knowledge management. *The Journal of Knowledge Management, 15*(2), 175-197.

[149] Bennet, A. (2005). *Exploring aspects of knowledge management that contribute to the passion expressed by its thought leaders.* Dissertation, Fielding Graduate University, Santa Barbara, CA. Self-published. Excerpts available at www.mountainquestinstitute.com

[150] Participants in the 2004-2005 Knowledge Management Thought Leader (KMTL) research study included Verna Allee, Debra Amidon, Ramon Barquin, David Bennet, Juanita Brown, John Seely Brown, Francisco Javier Carrillo, Robert Cross, Tom Davenport, Ross Dawson, Steve Denning, Nancy Dixon, Leif Edvinsson, Kent Greenes, Susan Hanley, Clyde Holsapple, Esko Kilpi, Dorothy Leonard, Geoff Malafsky, Carla O'Dell, Larry Prusak, Madanmohan Rao, Tomasz Rudolf, Melissie Rumizen, Hubert Saint-Onge, Judi Sandrock,

Dave Snowden, Tom Stewart, Michael J.D. Sutton, Karl-Erik Sveiby, Doug Weidner, Steve Weineke, Etienne Wenger, and Karl Wiig.

[151] Participants in the 2014 Sampler Research Call, listed alphabetically by country, were Charles Dhewa (Africa), Frada Burstein (Australia), Hubert Saint-Onge (Canada), Surinder Kumar Batra (India), Madanmohan Rao (India), Edna Pasher (Israel), Francisco Javier Carrillo (Mexico), Milton Sousa (Portugal), Dave Snowden (UK), and Nancy Dixon, Kent Greenes, Larry Prusak and Etienne Wenger-Trayner (across the US).

[152] O'Dell, C., & Hubert, C. (2011). *The new edge in knowledge: How knowledge management is changing the way we do business*. John Riley & Sons, Inc., p. 2.

[153] Quote from Surinder Kumar Batra, Sampler Research Call (2014).

[154] Quote from Charles Dhewa, Sampler Research Call (2014).

[155] Kuznets, S. (1955). Economic growth and income inequality. In *The American Economic Review XLV*(1). http://www.aeaweb.org/aer/top20/45.1.1-28.pdf

[56] Mokyr, J. (2005). The intellectual origins of modern economic growth. *The Journal of Economic History, 65*(2), 285-351.

[57] Quote from Charles Dhewa, Sampler Research Call (2014).

[58] Bennet, Bennet, & Turner (2018; 2022).

[59] Cozolino (2006).

[60] Bennet, A., Bennet, D., Fafard, K., Fonda, M., Lomond, T. Messier, L., & Vaugeois, N. in cooperation with The Social Sciences and Humanities Research Council of Canada (2007). *Knowledge mobilization in the social sciences and humanities: Moving from research to action*. MQIPress.

[61] Bennet, A., & Bennet, D. (2007). CONTEXT: The shared knowledge enigma. *VINE: The Journal of Information and Knowledge Management Systems, 37*(1), 27-40.

[62] Bennet, Bennet, & Avedisian.

[63] Bennet, A., & Bennet, D. (2008). The depth of knowledge: Surface, shallow, or deep? *VINE: The Journal of Information and Knowledge Management Systems, 38*(4), 405-420.

[64] Ryle, G. (1949). *The concept of mind*. Hutchinson.

[65] Kolb.

[66] Bohm, D. (1980). *Wholeness and the implicate order*. Routledge & Kegal Paul, p. 64.

[67] Fine, G. (2003). *Plato on knowledge and forms: Selected essays*. Oxford University Press, Introduction.

[68] Gardner, J. N. (1999). *Biocosm: The new scientific theory of evolution: Intelligent life is the architect of the universe*. Inner Ocean.

[69] Bohm (1980), p. 6.

[70] American Heritage Dictionary 4th Ed. (2006). Houghton Mifflin Co. Also, Bennet, A., & Bennet, D. (2010). Leaders, decisions, and the neuro-knowledge system. In S. Wallis, *Cybernetics and systems theory in management: Tools, views and advancements*. IGI Global, 21-35.

[71] Bennet, A. (2023). *Innovative creativity: Creating with innovation in mind*. MQIPress.

[72] Fitzgerald, B. l(2003). Introduction to the special series of papers on informing each other: Bridging the gap between researcher and practitioners. In *Informing Science 6*.

[73] Bennet & Bennet (2010). Also, Bennet & Bennet (2018).

[74] Bennet & Bennet (2008).

[75] Bennet & Bennet (2013).

[76] Stonier (1997).

[77] Bennet, D., & Bennet, A. (2009), Associative patterning: the unconscious life of an organization. In Girard, J.P. (Ed.). *Building organizational memories*. IGI Global, 201-224. Also, Bennet, A., & Bennet, D. (2006). Learning as associative patterning. *VINE: The Journal of Information and Knowledge Management Systems, 36*(4), 371-376.

[78] Edelman, G., & Tononi, G. (2000). *A universe of consciousness: How matter becomes imagination*. Basic Books.

[79] Hawkins, J., & Blakeslee, S. (2004). *On intelligence: How a new understanding of the brain will lead to the creation of truly intelligent machines*. Times Books.

[80] Kandel, E. R. (2006a). *The neuroscience of adult learning: New directions for adult and continuing education*. Jossey-Bass, p. 298.

[81] Sousa, D. A. (2006). How the brain learns. Corwin Press.

[82] Bennet & Bennet (2010; 2007).

[83] Mayer-Schönberger, V, & Cukier, K. (2013). *Big data: A revolution that will transform how we live, work, and think*. Houghton Mifflin Harcourt.

[84] Anderson, J. R. (1983). *The architecture of cognition*. Harvard University Press.

[85] Damasio, A. R. (1994). *Descartes' error: Emotion, reason, and the human brain*. G.P. Putnam's Sons, p. 139.

[86] Bennet and Bennet (2007).

[87] Reber, A.S. (1993). *Implicit learning and tacit knowledge: An essay on the cognitive unconscious*. Oxford University Press. Also, Kirsner, K., Speelman, C., Mayberry, M., O'Brien-Malone, A., Anderson, M., & MacLeod, C. (Eds.) (1998). *Implicit and explicit mental processes*. Lawrence Erlbaum Associates.

[88] Reber, p. 23.

[89] Matthews, R.C. (1991). The forgetting algorithm: How fragmentary knowledge of exemplars can yield abstract knowledge. *Journal of Experimental Psychology: General, 120*, 117-119.

[90] Polanyi, M. (1967). *The tacit dimension*. Anchor Books, p. 108.

[91] Polanyi, M. (1958). *Personal knowledge: Towards a post-critical philosophy*. The University of Chicago.

[92] Goldberg, E. (2005). *The wisdom paradox: How your mind can grow stronger as your brain grows older*. Gotham Books, Penguin Group.

[93] Merriam, S.B., Caffarella, R.S., & Baumgartner, L.M. (2006). *Learning in adulthood: A comprehensive guide*. John Wiley & Sons.

[94] Damasio (1994), p. 188.

[95] Klein, G. (2003). *Intuition at work: Why developing your gut instincts will make you better at what you do*. Doubleday.

[96] Ibid.

[97] Damasio (1994).

[98] Adolphs, R. (2004). Processing of emotional and social information by the human amygdala. In M.S. Gazzaniga (Ed.), *The cognitive neurosciences III*. The Bradford Press, p. 1026.

[99] Haberlandt, K. (1998). *Human memory: Exploration and application*. Allyn & Bacon.

[200] Mulvihill, M.K. (2003). The Catholic Church in crisis: Will transformative learning lead to social change through the uncovering of emotion? In C.A. Weissner, S.R. Meyers, N.L. Pfhal, & P.J. Neaman (Eds.), *Proceedings of the 5th International Conference on Transformative Learning*, pp. 320-325. Teachers College, Columbia University, p. 322.

[201] For an in-depth treatment of the emotions in terms of emotional intelligence, see Goleman, D. (1995). *Emotional intelligence*. Bantam Books.

[202] Bennet & Bennet (2007),.

[203] Ibid.

[204] White, R. W. (1959). Motivation reconsidered: the concept of competence. *Psychological Review, 66*, 297-333.

[205] Nouwen, H.J.M. (1975). *Reaching out: the three movements of the spiritual life*. Doubleday.

[206] Sternberg, R.J. (2003). *Wisdom, intelligence, and creativity synthesized*. Cambridge University Press.

[207] Merriam et al., p. 195.

[208] Amann, T. (2003). Creating space for somatic ways of knowing within transformative learning theory. In C. A. Wiessner, S. R. Meyer, N. L. Thal, & P.G. Neaman (Eds.). *Proceedings of the Fifth International Conference on Transformative Learning*. Teacher's College, Columbia University, pp. 26-32.

[209] Damasio (1994).

[210] Phillips, P. J., Hahn, C. A., Fontana, P. C., Yates, A. N., Greene, K., Broniatowski, D. A., & Przybocki, M. A. (2021, September). *Four principles of explainable artificial intelligence*. National Institute of Standards and Technology, U.S. Department of Commerce.

[211] George, M. S. (2007). Stimulating the brain. In F. E. Bloom (Ed.), *Best of the brain from Scientific American: Mind, matter, and tomorrow's brain,* pp. 20-34. The Dana Foundation. Also, Gusnard, D. A., & Raichle, M. E. (2004). Functional imaging, neurophysiology, and the resting state of the human brain. *The cognitive neurosciences III,* pp. 1267-1280. MIT Press. Also, Ward, J. (2006). *The student's guide to cognitive neuroscience.* Psychology Press.

[212] Lam, N. (2022). Explanations in AI as claims of tacit knowledge. *Minds and Machines 32,* 135-158. https://doi.org/10.1007/s11023-021-09588-1

[213] Ibid.

[214] Chomsky, N. (1965). *Aspects of the theory of syntax.* MIT Press.

[215] Lam, p. 137.

[216] Davies, M. (1989). Connectionism, modularity, and tacit knowledge. *The British Journal for the Philosophy of Science, 40*(4), 541-555. https://doi.,org/10.1093/bjps/441.2.195 Also, Davies, M. (1990). Knowledge of rules in connectionist networks. *Intellectica, 9*(1), 81-126. Also, Davies, M. (1991). Concepts, connectionism, and the language of thought. In W. Ramsey, S. P. Stich, & D. Rumelhart (Eds.), *Philosophy and connectionist theory,* pp. 485-503. Lawrence Erlbaum Associates. Also, Davies, M. (1995). Two notions of implicit rules. *Philosophical Perspectives, 9,* 153-83. https://doi.org/10.2307/2214216

[217] Smolensky, P. (1988). On the proper treatment of connectionism. *Behavioral and Brain Sciences, 11*(1), 1-23. https://doi.org/10.1017/s0140525x00052432.

[218] Lam, p. 155.

[219] Ibid., 156.

[220] The Intelligent Social Change Journey (ISCJ) is a developmental journey of the body, mind and heart, moving from the heaviness of cause-and-effect linear extrapolations based on lower mental though), to the fluidity of co-evolving with our environment (based on higher mental thought conceptual in nature), to the lightness of breathing our thought and feelings into reality (recognizing the connections and relationships among all things). Grounded in development of our mental faculties, these are phase change, each building on and expanding previous learning in our movement toward intelligent activity. See Bennet, A., Bennet, D., Shelley, A., Bullard, T., & Lewis, J. (2020). *The profundity and bifurcation of change: Parts I – V.* MQIPress. Also, Bennet, A., Bennet, D., Shelley, A., Bullar, T., & Lewis, J. (2018). *The intelligent social change journey: Foundation for the possibilities that are YOU!* (22 book series). MQIPress.

[221] Wilson, E. O. (1998). *Consilience: The unity of knowledge.* Alfred A. Knoph, p. 8.

[222] Ibid., p. 53.

[223] Stonier, T. (1992). *Beyond information: The natural history of intelligence.* Springer-Verlag.

[224] Bennet et al. (2020).

[225] Bennet et al. (2007).

[226] Woolf, H. (Ed.). (1990). *Webster's new world dictionary of the American language.* G. and C. Merriam. Random House. Also, Turban, E. (1992). *Expert systems and applied artificial intelligence.* Macmillan. Also, Beckman, T. J. (1997). *A methodology for knowledge management.* International Association of Science and Technology for Development (IASTED) AI and Soft Computing Conference. Banff, Canada.

[227] Bennet & Bennet (2004). Also, Davenport, T. H., & Prusak, L. (1998). *Working knowledge: How organizations manage what they know.* Harvard Business School Press. Also, Probst, F., Raub, S., & Romhardt, K. (2000). *Managing knowledge: Building blocks for success.* John Wiley & Sons, Ltd.

[228] Nonaka, I., & Takeuchi, H. (1995). *The knowledge-creating company: How Japanese companies create the dynamics of innovation.* Oxford University Press. Also, van der Spek, R., & Spiskervet, A. (1997). Knowledge management: Dealing intelligently with knowledge. In J. Liebowitz & L. Wilcox (Eds.), *Knowledge management and its integrative elements.* CRC Press.

[229] Bennet & Bennet (2004); O'Dell, C., & Grayson, C., Jr. (1998). *If only we knew what we knew: The transfer of internal knowledge and best practices.* Free Press. Also, Sveiby, K., & Konrad (1989). *The invisible balance sheet.* Affarsvarlden/Ledarskap.

[230] Wiig, K. (1993b). *Knowledge management foundations—thinking about thinking—how people and organizations create, represent, and use knowledge*. Schema Press.

[231] Nonaka & Takeuchi.

[232] Burkowitz, W., & Petrach, G. (1997, July-August). Visualizing, measuring, and managing knowledge. *Research Technology Management, 40*, 24-31.

[233] Barquin, R., Bennet, A., & Remez, S. (2001). *Building knowledge management environments for electronic government*. Management Concepts.

[234] Morey, D., Marbury, M., & Thuraisingham, B. (2000). *Knowledge management: Classic and contemporary works*. The MIT Press, p. xii.

[235] Porter, D., Bennet, A., Turner, R., & Wennegren, D. (2002). *The power of team: The making of a CIO*. U.S. Department of the Navy.

[236] Morey et al., p. xii.

[237] Carrillo, F. J. (1998). Managing knowledge-based value systems. *Journal of Knowledge Management, 1*(4), pp. 280-286.

[238] Bennet, A. (2005), p. 106.

[239] KMTL Sampler Call (2014). Milton de Sousa is an academic and practitioner in Portugal. See Chapter 15.

[240] Ibid.

[241] Wiig, K. (1993b). Also, Wiig, K. (1994). *Knowledge management: The central management focus for intelligent-acting organizations*. Schema Press. Also, Wiig, K. *(1995). Knowledge management methods: Practical approaches to managing knowledge*. Schema Press.

[242] Wiig (1993), p. 20.

[243] Beckman, T. J. (1999). The current state of knowledge management. In Liebowitz (Ed.). *Knowledge management handbook*. CRC Press, p. 1.

[244] Ibid., pp. 1-1 through 1-22.

[245] KMTL Sampler Call (2014).

[246] Ibid.

[247] Ibid.

[248] Ibid.

[249] Csikszentmihalyi, M. (1990). *Flow: the psychology of optimal experience*. Harper & Row. Also, Csikszentmihalyi, M. (1996). *Creativity: Flow and the psychology of discovery and invention*. HarperCollins Publishers, Inc. Also, Csikszentmihalyi (2003).

[250] KMTL Sampler Call (2014).

[251] Wheatley, M.J. (2006). *Leadership and the new science: Discovering order in a chaotic world*. Barrett-Koehler Publishers, Inc.

[252] Argyris, C. (1999). *On organizational learning* (2nd ed.) Blackwell Publishers Ltd.

[253] Weick, K. (2001). *Making sense of the organization*. Blackwell Publishing. Also, Weick, K. (2000). *Sensemaking in organizations: Foundations for organizational science*. SAGE Publications, Inc.

[254] Wenger. Also, Wenger, E., McDermott, R., & Snyder, W. M. (2002). *Cultivating communities of practice*. Harvard Business Review Press.

[255] Stacey, R. D. (1996b). The sustainable innovation engine. *VINE, 36*(4), 398-405.

[256] Ibid., p. 10.

[257] KMTL Sampler Call (2014).

[258] Carrillo, F.J. (2001). Meta-KM: A program and a plea. Knowledge and Innovation. *Journal of the KMCI, 1*(2), pp. 3-4.

[265] KMTL Sampler Call (2014).

[260] Battram, A. (1996). *Navigating complexity: The essential guide to complexity theory in business and management*. The Industrial Society, p. 125.

[261] KMTL Sample Call (2014).

[262] Bohm (1980), p. 6.

[263] Carrillo, F. J. (2014). How knowledge and the city met. In F.J. Carrillo, T. Yigitcanlar, B. Garcia, & A. Londqvist (Eds.), *Knowledge and the city: Concepts, applications and trends of knowledge-based urban development*. Routledge. Also, Carrillo, F. J. (2004). Capital cities: A taxonomy of capital accounts for knowledge cities. *Journal of Knowledge Management, 8*(5).

Also, Carrillo, F. J. (2002). Capital systems: Implications for a global knowledge agenda. *Journal of Knowledge Management, 6*(4), 379-399. Also, Carrillo, F. J. (2001). Meta-KM: A program and a plea. Knowledge and innovation. *Journal of the KMCI, 1*(2).

[264] Lambe (2011), p. 194.

[265] KMTL Sampler Call (2014)

[266] Ibid.

[267] Ibid.

[268] Stankosky, M. (2005). *Creating the discipline of knowledge management: The latest in university research*. Elsevier Butterworth-Heinemann.

[269] Calabrese, F. A. (2010). A decade of leadership in creating the discipline of knowledge management. In A. Green, M. Stankosky, and L. Vandergriff (Eds.), *In search of knowledge management: Pursuing primary principles*. Emerald Group Publishing Limited.

[270] Green, A., Stankosky, M., & Vandergriff, L. (2010). *In search of knowledge management: Pursuing primary principles*. Emerald Group Publishing Limited.

[271] Calabrese.

[272] Ibid.

[273] Ridley, M. (2020). *How innovation works: And why it flourishes in freedom*. Harper Perennial, p. 10.

[274] Ibid., p. 8.

[275] Weisbert, R. W. (1999). Creativity and knowledge: A challenge to theories. In R.J. Sternberg (Ed.), *Handbook of creativity* (226-250). Cambridge University Press, p. 226.

[276] Ibid.

[277] Machlup, F. (1962). *The production and distribution of knowledge in the United States*. Princeton University Press, p. 179.

[278] Hobson, J. A. (1999). *Consciousness*. Scientific American Library.

[279] Andreasen, N. C. (2005). *The creating brain: The neuroscience of genius*. The Dana Foundation.

[280] Christos, G. (2003). *Memory and dreams: The creative human mind*. Rutgers University Press.

[281] Ibid.

[282] Hawkins.

[283] Christos, p. 87.

[284] Blackmore, S. (1999). *The meme machine*. Oxford University Press.

[285] Moon, J. A. (2004). *A handbook of reflective and experiential learning: Theory and practice*. Routledge-Falmer.

[286] Christos, pp. 74-75.

[287] Begley, S. (2007). *Train your mind change your brain: How a new science reeals our extraordinary potential to transform ourselves*. Ballantine Books.

[288] Merry, U. (1995). *Coping with uncertainty: Insights from the new sciences of chaos, self-organization and complexity*. Praeger.

[289] Bennet, A., & Bennet, D. (2008). The human knowledge system: Music and brain coherence. *VINE: The Journal of Information and Knowledge Management Systems 38*(3), 277-295.

[290] Oster, G. (1973). Auditory beats in the brain. *Scientific American, 229*, 94-102.

[291] Swann, R., Bosanko, S., Cohen, R., Midgley, R., & Seed, K. M. (1982). *The brain: A user's manual*. G P. Putnam & Sons.

[292] Hink, R. F., Kodera, K., Yamada, O., Kaga, K., & Suzuki, J. (1980). Binaural interaction of a beating frequency following response. *Audiology, 19*, 36-43. Also, Marsh, J. T., Brown, W. S., & Smith, J. C. (1975). Far-field recorded frequency-following response: Correlates of low pitch auditory perception in humans. *Electroencephalography and Clinical Neurophysiology, 38*, 113-119. Also, Smith, J. C., Marsh, J. T., Greenberg, S., & Brown, W. S. (1978). Human auditory frequency-following responses to a missing fundamental. *Science, 201*, 639-641.

[292] Ritchey, D. (2003). *The H.I.S.S. of the A.S.P.: Understanding the anomalously sensitive person*. Headline Books.

[293] Atwater, F. H. (2004). *The Hemi-Sync® Process*. The Monroe Institute. Also, Delmonte, M. M. (1984). Electrocortical activity and related phenomena associated with mediation practice: A

literature review. *International Journal of Neuroscience, 24*, 217-231. Also, Fischer, R. (1971). A cartography of ecstatic and meditative states. *Science, 174*(4012), 897-904.

294 Crandall, B., Klein, G., & Hoffman, R. R. (2006). *Working minds: A practitioner's guide to cognitive task analysis*. The MIT Press.

295 Ibid.

296 Christos, G. (2003). Memory and dreams: The creative human mind. Rutgers University Press, p. 90.

297 Pinker, S. (2007). *The stuff of thought: Language as window into human nature*. Viking.

298 Ridley, p. 250.

299 Eapen, T. T., Finkenstadt, D. J., Folk, J., & Venkataswamy, L. (2023, July-August). How generative AI can augment human creativity. *Harvard Business Review, 101*(4), 56-64.

300 Ibid., 58.

301 Ibid., 58-64.

302 Marchand, L. H. (2022). The innovation mindset: Eight essential steps to transform any industry. Columbia Business School Publishing.

303 Avedisian, J. (2023). Igniting a kingdom innovation culture. In A. Bennet & R. K. Baisya (Eds.), *INside INnovation: Looking from the inside out*. MQIPress.

304 Ibid.

305 Ibid.

306 Schulze, H. (2019). *Excellence wins: A non-nonsense guide to becoming the best in a world of compromise*. Zondervan.

307 Reed, L. W. (1958, December). *I, pencil: My family tree as told to Leonard E. Read*. Foundation for Economic Education.

308 Ibid., p. 4.

309 Ibid, pp. 11-12.

310 Cozolino (2006), p. 3

311 Johnson, S. (2006). The neuroscience of the mentor-learner relationship. In S. Johnson & K. Taylor (Eds.), *The neuroscience of adult learning: New direction for adult and continuing education*, pp. 73-70. Jossey-Bass, p. 65.

312 Taylor, K. (2006). Brain function and adult learning: Inplications for practice. In. S. Johnson & K. Taylor (Eds.), *The neuroscience of adult learning: New directions for adult and continuing education*, pp. 71-86. Jossey-Bass, p. 82.

313 Cozolino & Sprokay, p. 13.

314 Buonomano & Merzenich.

315 Nelson, C. A., deHaan, M., & Thomas, K. M. (2006). *Neuroscience of cognitive development: The role of experience and the developing brain*. John Wiley & Sons.

316 Stern, D. N. (2004). *The present moment in psychotherapy and everyday life*. Norton, p. 76.

317 Cozolino, p. 203.

318 Riggio, R. E. l(2015). Are you empathic? 3 types of empathy and what they mean. *Psychology Today*.

319 Cozolino, p. 206.

320 Carr, L., Iacoboni, M., Dubeau, M. C., Mazziotta, J. C., & Lenzi, G. I. (2003). Neural mechanisms of empathy in humans: A relay from neural systems for imitation to limbic areas. *Proceedings of the National Academy of Science, 100*, 5497-5502. Also, Kawashina, R. Sugiura, M., Kato, T., Nakamura, A., Hatano, K., Ito, K., et al. (1999). The human amygdala plays an important role in gaze monitoring: A PET study. *Brain, 122*, 779-783.

321 Andersson, J. L., Lilja, A., Hartvig, P., Langstrom, B., Gordh, T., Handwerker, H., et al. (1997). Somatotopic organization along the central sulcus, for pain localization in humans, as revealed by positron emission tomography. *Experimental Brain Research, 117*, 192-199.

322 Immordino-Yang, M. H., Christodoulou, J. A., & Singh, V. (2016). 'Rest is not idleness': Implications of the brain's default mode for human development and education. In M. H. Immordino-Yang (Ed.), Emotions, learning, and the brain: Exploring the educational implications and affective neuroscience (pp. 43-68). Norton.

323 Iacoboni, M. (2008). *The new science of how we connect with others: Mirroring people*. Farrar, Straus & Giroux.

[324] Rizzolatti, G. (2006, November). Mirrors in the mind. *Scientific American*, p. 56.

[325] Bennet, Bennet, & Turner (2022; 2018).

[326] Rizzolatti.

[327] Immordino-Yang, M. H. (2016). The smoke around mirror neurons: Goals as sociocultural and emotional organizers of perception and action in learning. In M. H. Immordino-Yang (Ed.), *Emotions, learning, and the brain: Exploring the educational implications of affective neuroscience*. Norton.

[328] Iacoboni.

[329] Rizzolatti, p. 61.

[330] Affirming the transfer of emotions and intentions along with thought, mathematical research engaging transreal numbers shows that knowledge by sentience gives us the possibility of knowing everything that is not propositional. Transreal numbers are an extension of real numbers developed by an English computer scientist, James A. D. W. Anderson, in 1997. This "extension" allows division over zero, which is forbidden in the realm of real numbers. See Gomide, W. (2022) Transreal numbers and sentient logic. In S. B. Schafer & A. Bennet (Eds.), *Handbook of research on global media's preternatural influence on global singularity, culture and government*, pp. 269-278. IGI Global.

[331] Zull, J. E. (2002). *The art of changing the brain: Enriching the practice of teaching by exploring the biology of learning*. Stylus.

[332] Ibid.

[333] Lee, W. B. (2023). Exploring the depth of the MIKE: An intellectual practice-based study program. In A. Bennet & R. Baisya (Eds.), *INside INnovation: Looking from the inside out*. MQIPress.

[334] Bjelland, O. M., & Wood, R. C. (2008, September). An inside view of IBM's innovation jam. *MIT Sloan Management Review, 50*(1).

[335] McCraty, p. 24.

[336] Edelman and Tononi (2000)

[337] Shelley, A. (2017). *KNOWledge SUCCESSion: Sustained performance and capability growth through strategic knowledge projects*. Business Expert Press.

[338] Srivastva, S., & Cooperrider, D. L. (Eds.) (1990). *Appreciative management and leadership*. Jossey-Bass.

[339] Cooperrider, D. L., & Srivastva, S. (1987). Appreciative inquiry. *Research in Organizational Change and Development, 1*, 129-169.

[340] Polany (1958), pp. 104-105.

[341] Hammond, S. A. (1996). *The thin book of appreciative inquiry*. Thin Book Publishing.

[342] Bennet & Bennet (2004).

[343] Lee, R. WB., Yip, J. Y., & Shek, V. W. (2021). *Knowledge risk and its mitigation: Practices and cases*. Emerald.

[344] Wiig, K. (1997, September). Knowledge management: An introduction and perspective. *Journal of Knowledge Management, 1*(1), 6-14.

[345] Ibid., p. 9.

[346] Klein, G. A. (2017). *Sources of power: How people make decisions*. MIT Press.

[347] Brooking, A.(996). *Intellectual capital: Core asset for the third millennium*. Cengage Learning.

[348] Borghoff, U. M. & Pareschi, R. (Eds.) (1998). *Information technology for knowledge management*. Berlin. Also, Ruggles, R. L. (1997). *Knowledge management tools*. Butterworth-Heinemann. Also, Tiwana, A. (2000). *The knowledge management toolkit: Practical techniques for building a KM system*. Prentice Hall.

[349] Conveyed in an email From Dr. Art Murray, May 29, 2023.

[350] Panke, S. (2019). Design thinking in education: Perspectives, opportunities and challenges. *Open Education Studies, 1*(1), 281-306. https://doi.org/10.1515/edu-2019-0022

[351] Matthews, J., & Wrigley, C. (2017). Design and design thinking in business and management higher education. *Journal of Learning Design, 10*(1), 41. https://doi.org/10.5204/jld.v9i3.294

[352] Senivongse, C. (2023). Planning on customer engagement in the digital era. In. A. Bennet & R. Baisya (Eds.), *INside INnovation: Looking from the inside out.* MQIPress.

353 Liedtka, J. (2018). Why design thinking works. *Harvard Business Review*.

354 Brown, T. (2008). Design Thinking. *Harvard Business Review*.

355 Long, T.A. (1986). Narrative unity and clinical judgment. *Theoretical Medicine 7*, 75-92.

356 Lewis, J. (2019). *Story thinking: Transforming organizations for the fourth industrial revolution*. Amazon KDP.

357 Ibid.

358 Ibid.

359 Temin, T. (2023, April 27). CX exchange 2023: Maximus' Mary Ann Monroe on why to start by identifying critical pain points. Insight by Maximus: Technology. https://federalnewsnetwork.com/technology-main/2023/04/cx-exchange-2023-maximus-maryann-monroe-on-why-good-employee-cx-starts-before-day-1/

360 Bennet & Bennet (2004). Also, Porter et al.

361 Bennet, A. (2018). *Possibilities that are YOU!, Volume 15: Seeking wisdom*. MQIPress.

362 Frijda, N. H. (2000). The psychologists' point of view. In M. Lewis & J. M. Haviland-Jones (Eds.), *Handbook of emotions* (2nd ed). The Bilford Press, pp. 59-74.

363 Polanyi (1958).

364 Kunz, p. 162.

365 Little, A. Saggeza. https://builtin.com/operations/flat-culture

366 Foss, N. J., & Klein, P. G. (2023, Spring). Rethinking hierarchy: We need to reconceive managerial authority for today's business environment – not eliminate it. *MIT Sloan Management Review, 64*(3), 56-61.

367 Simon Lelic, Editor, *InsideKnowledge*, May 2005.

368 Bennet & Bennet, 2004

369 *American Heritage Dictionary* (1992).

370 De Furia.

371 Texas Instruments (2021, March). Texas Instruments Supplier Code of Conduct. https://www.ti.com

372 Avedisian.

373 Voorhees, T., Aedisian-Riedinger, J., Pendleton, M. (2019). *Reflecting God's character in your business*. High Bridge Books.

374 Das, G. G., & Baisya, R. K. (2023). Integrated innovation strategy and framework in power section: Tata Power Company Limited. In A. Bennet and R. K. Baisya, *INside INnovation: Looking from the inside-out*.

375 Covey, S. R. (2004) *The 8th habit: From effectiveness to greatness*. Simon & Schuster, Inc., p. 296.

376 Burke, P. (2023). *Ignorance, a global history*, Yale University Press, p. 257-258.

377 Albrecht, K. (2003). *The power of minds at work: Organizational intelligence in action*. AMACOM, a division of American Management Association, pp. 156-160.

378 Ibid.

379 NSF Proto-Open Knowledge Network. https://new.nsf.gov/news/nsf-5-other-us-agencies-launch-program-build#:~:text=In%20collaboration%20with%20five%20other%20U.S.%20government%20agencies%2C,and%20knowledge%20infrastructure%20called%20an%20open%20knowledge%20network

380 Jaques, E. (1997). *Requisite organization: Total system for effective managerial organization and managerial leadership for the 21st century*. Gower.

381 See Haeckel, S. (1999). *Adaptive enterprise: Creating and leading sense and respond organizations*. Harvard Business School Press. Also, McCarthy, M., & Stein, J. (2003). *Agile business for fragile times*. McGraw Hill Publishing Co.

382 Sheffi, Y. (2005). *The Resilient Enterprise: Overcoming Vulnerability for Competitive Advantage*. The MIT Press.

383 Miller, J. (2023, April 19). Rigid, linear supply chains must be a think of the past for agencies. federalnewsnetwork.com/federal-insights/2023/04/

384 IBM (2010). *Capitalizing on Complexity: Insights from the global chief executive officer study*, p. 4. IBM Global Business Services.

[385] Ibid.

[386] United States Marine Corps (1994). *Warfighting, the U.S. Marine Corps book of strategy*. US Marine Corps, p. xv.

[387] Labovitz, G., & V. Rozanski, (1997). *The Power of Alignment: How Great Companies Stay Centered and Accomplish Extraordinary Things*. John Wiley and Sons, Inc.

[388] Wade, W. (2012). *Scenario planning: A field guide to the future*. John Wiley & Sons, Inc.

[389] Bennet, A., Bennet, D., & Lewis, J. (2015). *Leading with the future in mind: Knowledge and emergent leadership*. MQIPress.

[390] Schmidt, E. (2023, March/April). Innovation power: Why technology will define the future of geopolitics. *Foreign Affairs, 102*(2), pp. 38-52.

[391] Lewis, p. 116.

[392] Hawkins.

[393] Mulford, P. (2007). *Thoughts are things*. Barnes & Noble, p. 72.

[394] Alberts, D. S., & Hayes, R. E. (2005). *Power to the edge: Command, control in the information age*. Command & Control Research Program.

[395] Ibid., p. 48.

[396] Michael, D. N. (1977). Planning's challenge to the systems approach. In H. A. Linstone & W. H. C. Simmonds (Eds.), *Futures research: New directions*. Addison-Wesley Publishing Company, Inc.

[397] Meyer, C., & Davis, S. (2003). *It's alive: The coming convergence of information, biology, and business*. Crown Business.

[398] Alberts & Hayes, p. 227.

[399] Ibid., p. 228.

[400] Portante, T., & Tarro, R. (1997, September). Paying attention. *Wired Magazine*.

[401] Davenport & Beck.

[402] Ibid., p. 7.

[403] Ramon, S. (1997). *Earthly cycles: How past lives and soul patterns shape your life*. Pepperwood Press, p. 48.

[404] Searle, J. R. (1983). *Intentionality: An essay in the philosophy of mind*. Cambridge University Press, p. ix.

[405] Prinz, W. (2005). An ideomotor approach to imitation. In S. Hurley & N. Chater, *Perspectives on imitation: From neuroscience to social science Vol. 1: Mechanisms of imitation and imitation in animals*, pp. 141-156. MIT Press.

[406] Gell-Mann, M. (1994). *The quark and the jaguar: Adventures in the simple and the complex*. W. H. Freeman and Company.

[407] Gardner, H. (2006). *Multiple intelligences: New horizons in theory and practice*. Basic Books, p. 46.

[408] Ross, P. E. (2006, August). The expert mind. *Scientific American*, 64-71.

[409] Bennet, Bennet, & Avedisian.

[410] Henderson, M., & Thompson, D. (2003). *Values at work*. HarperCollins Publishers, p. 15.

[411] *American Heritage Dictionary of the English Language*, 4th edition (2000), Houghton-Mifflin.

[412] Lakoff, G. (2006). *Thinking points: Communicating our American values and vision*. Farrar, Strus and Giroux.

[413] Hall, B. (1998). Culture and values management. In P. Sullivan, *Profiting from intellectual capital*. John Wiley & Sons.

[414] Adapted from Bennet & Bennet (2004).

[415] Sullivan, P. H. (2000). *Value-driven intellectual capital: How to convert intangible corporate assets into market value*. John Wiley & Sons, p. 88.

[416] Collins, J. C., & Porras, J. I. (1994). *Built to last*. HarperCollins Publishers.

[417] Bennet, A., & Bennet, D. (2007). The MQI value infusion methodology. A white paper. Mountain Quest Institute, Frost, WV, p. 1.

[418] Beckett, J. C. (2006). *Mastering Monday*. Intervarsity Press, p. 138.

[419] Tichy, N. (1997). *The leadership engine*. HarperCollins Publishers, p. 114.

[420] Pollard, C. W. (1996). *The soul of the firm*. HarperBusiness and Zondervan Publishing, p. 26.

[421] Kouzes, J. M., & Posner, B. Z. (2007). *The leadership challenge*, 4th ed. Jossey-Bass, John Wiley and Sons, p. 61.

[422] Ulrich, D., & Lake, D. (1990). *Organizational capability*. John Wiley & Sons., p. 55.

[423] Collins & Porras, p. 87.

[424] Zack, M. (1999). *Knowledge and strategy*. Butterworth-Heinemann.

[425] Liebowitz, J. (Ed.) (1999). *The knowledge management handbook*. CRC Press. Also, Liebowitz, J., Rubenstein-Montano, B., McCaw, D., Buchwalter, J., & Browning, C. (2000). The knowledge audit. *Knowledge and Process Management, 7*(1), 3-10. Also, Henczel, S. (2001). *The information audit: A practical guide*. K.G. Saur. Also, Tiwana. Also, Choo, C.W., & Bontis, N. (2002). *The strategic management of intellectual capital and organizational knowledge*. Oxford University Press.

[426] Tiwana.

[427] MITRE (2022). *Crown Jewels Analysis for Industrial Control Systems*. https://www.mitre.org/news-insights/publication/creow-jewels-analysis-industrial-control-systems

[428] Col. Kenneth Parker Thompson, PhD, passed in 2012. Among his papers his family discovered research on knowledge voids, from which this table is adapted. One of his final accomplishments was an autobiography titled *From Soldier to Scholar* where he describes his personal philosophy on life's challenges and adversities. We gratefully acknowledge his contribution to this text.

[429] LeShan, L. (1976). *Alternate realities*. Ballantine.

[430] Michaelson, C., Pratt, M. G., Grant, A. M., & Dunn, C. P. (2014). Meaningful work : Connecting business ethics and organization studies. *Journal of Business Ethics, 121*, 77-90.

[431] Carroll, S. (2016) *The big picture: On the origins of life, meaning, and the universe itself.* Dutton.

[432] Walsch, N. D. (2009). *When everything changes change everything: In a time of turmoil, a pathway to peace*. EmNin Books.

[433] Silver, L., Van Kessel, P., Huang, C., Clancy, L., & Gubbala, S. (2021). *What makes life meaningful? Views from 17 advanced economies*. Pew Research Center, 221.

[434] Allan, B. A., Batz-Barbarich, C., Sterling, H. M., & Tay, L. (2019). Outcomes of meaningful work: A meta-analysis. *Journal of Management Studies, 56*(3), 500-528.

[435] Bailey, C., Yeoman, R., Madden, A., Thompson, M., & Kerridge, G. (2019). A review of the empirical literature on meaningful work: Progress and research agenda. *Human Resource Development Review, 18*(1), 83-113. Also, Lysova, E. I., Allan, B. A., Dik, B. J., Duffy, R. D., & Steger, M. F. (2019). Fostering meaningful work in organizations: A multi-level review and integration. *Journal of Vocational Behavior, 110*, 374-389.

[436] Petchsawang, P., & McLean, G. N. (2017). Workplace spirituality, mindfulness meditation, and work engagement. *Journal of Management, Spirituality & Religion, 14*(3), 216-244.

[437] "The Myths by Which We Live" (1965, September). *The Rotarian, 107*(3), 32-33, p. 55.

[438] DrewFriedman@dfriedmanWFED

[439] Wang, P. (2019). On defining artificial intelligence. *Journal of Artificial General Intelligence, 10*(2), 1-37.

[440] World Economic Forum (2018). *The future of jobs report*. Centre for the New Economy and society: Geneva, Switzerland.

[441] Bankins, S., & Formosa, P. (2023). The ethical implications of artificial intelligence (AI) for meaningful work. *Journal of Business Ethics*. https://doi.org/10.1007/s10551-023-05339-7

[442] Ibid.

[443] Hackman, J. R., & Oldham, G. R. (176). Motivation through the design of work: Test of a theory. *Organizational Behavior and Human Performance, 16*(2), 250-279.

[444] Lips-Wiersma, M., & Wright, S. (2012). Measuring the meaning of meaningful work: Development and validation of the comprehensive meaningful work scale. *Group & Organizational Management, 37*(5), 655-685.

[445] Bankins & Formosa.

[446] Floridi, I., et al. (2018). AI4People – An ethical framework for a good AI society. *Minds and Machines, 28*(4), 689-707.

447 Bankins & Formosa.

448 Ibid.

449 Malafsky, G. P., & Newman, B. D. (2001). Organizing knowledge with ontologies and taxonomies. TECHi2.

450 Das & Baisya.

451 Senivongse.

452 Bennet, A., Bennet, D., Shelley, A., Bullard, T., & Lewis, J. (2020). *The profundity and bifurcation of change part I: Laying the groundwork*. MQIPress.

453 Hess, E. D., & Ludwig, K. (2017). *Humility is the new smart: Rethinking human excellence I the smart machine age*. Berrett-Kochler Publishers, Inc.

454 Quotes from Federal News Network 2023 CX Exchange. See also, https://www.nasa.gov/press-release/nasa-receives-top-honor-of-best-place-to-work-in-federal-government

455 Barthes, R. l(1985). *In the responsibility of forms*. Hill and Wang.

456 Hook, J. (2015). Blog. https://www.joshuanhook.com/what-is-humility?

457 Ibid., p. 8.

458 Quoted from Garry Vaynerchuk's blog. Downloaded December 7, 2018, from www.garyvaynerchuk.com/confidence-humility/

459 Senge, P. M., Scharmer, C. O., Jaworski, J., & Flowers, B. S. (2004). *Presence: Exploring profound change in people, organizations and society*. Random House, Inc., p. 133.

460 Senge, P. M. (1990). *The fifth discipline*. Doubleday.

461 Bower, J. L. (2000). The purpose of change: Al commentary on Jensen and Senge. In M. K. Beer & N. Nohria (Eds.), *Breaking the code of change*, pp. 93-95. Harvard Business School Press.

462 Senge et al.

463 Scharmer, C. O. (2009). *Theory U: Leading from the future as it emerges*. Berrett-Koehler.

464 Forwarded in the January 08, 2017, daily quote from Abraham-Hicks Publications.

465 Lewis.

466 Maslow, A. H. (1971). *The farther reaches of human nature*. Arkana/Penguin Books.

467 Reed, P. (2003). A nursing theory of self-transcendence. In M. J. Smith & P. Liehr (eds.), *Middle range theory for advanced practice nursing*. Springer, pp. 145-166.

468 Ibid.

469 Wong, P. T. P. (2017). From Viktor Frankl's logotherapy to the four defining charactistics of self-transcendence. DrPaulWong.com http://www.drpaulwong.com/four-defining-characteristics-self-transcendence/

470 Flood, S. (n.d.). 5 creative ways to achieving your own transcendence. *Soulspot*. http://soulspottv.com/blog/5-creive-ways-to-achieving-your-own-transcendence/

471 Ackerman, C. (2018, June). Meaning & values: What is self-transcendence? *Positive Psychology.com*. https://positivepsychology.com/self-transcendence/

472 Reed, P. (1986). The developmental conceptual framework: Nursing reformulations and applications for family theory. In A. Whall (Ed.), *Family therapy theory for nursing: Four approaches*. Appleton-Ce3ntury-Crofts, pp. 69-92.

473 Palmer, B., Quinn Griffin, M. T., Reed, P., & Fitzpatrick, J. J. (2010). Self-transcendence and work engagement in acute care staff registered nurses. *Critical Care Nursing Quarterly, 33*, 138-147.

474 De Geus, A. (1997). *The living company: Habits for survival in a turbulent business environment*. Harvard Business School Press.

475 Rosa, H. (2022). *Resonance: A sociology of our relationship to the world*. (J. C. Wagner, Trans.). Polity.

476 Ibid., p. 166.

477 Ibid.

478 Schütz, P. (2009). Resonance. In G. Stumm & A. Pritz (Eds), *Wörterbuch der psychotherapie*. Springer, p. 594.

479 Plessner, *Laughing and crying*, 128 (translations lightly modified). "Sentimentality, which is out to be touched and misses no opportunity to enjoy an appeal bound through and through to

what is the case. Not the resonance alone, with its qualities of mood, […] governs our state, but the resonant appeal of some particular quality. In false feeling there is no appeal in an objective context, and only the resonance itself absorbs us." In Rosa, p. 475.

[480] Ibid, p. 174.

[481] Ibid., p. 170.

[482] Ibid., p. 171.

[483] Ibid., p. 233, p. 480. Also, Arendt, H. (1958). *The human condition.* University of Chicago Press. Also, Sohn-Rethel, A. (1978). *Intellectual and manual labour: A critique of epistemology.* Macmillan.; Also, Sennett, R. (2006). *The craftsman.* Yale University Press. Also, Tomasello, M. (2009). *Why we cooperate.* MIT Press. Also, Tomasello, M. (2014). *A Natural History of Human Thinking.* Harvard University Press.

[484] MacIntyre, A. (2007). *After virtue: A study in moral theory.* 3rd edition. University of Notre Dame Press, p. 187.

[485] Sennett, p. 9.

[486] Quote from Federal News Network 2023 CX Exchange. See also, https://www.nasa.gov/press-release/nasa-receives-top-honor-of-best-place-to-work-in-federal-government

[487] Bohm, D., & Hiley, B. J. (1993). *The undivided universe: An ontological interpretation of quantum theory.* Routledge. Also, Giorbran, G. (2017). *Everything and forever: Timelessness.* Barnes & Nobel. http://everythingforever.com/Bohm.htm Also, Laszlo, E. (1995). *The interconnected universe: Conceptual foundations of transdisciplinary unified theory.* Inner Traditions. Also, Laszlo, E. (2009). *Worldshift 2012: Making green business, new politics & higher consciousness work together.* Inner Traditions.

[488] McCraty, R., & Childre, D. (2010, July/August). Coherence: Bridging personal, social, and global health. *The Journal of Alternative Therapies, 16*(4), Introduction.

[489] Strogatz, S. H., & Steward, I. (1993). Coupled oscillators and biological synchronization: A subtle mathematical thread connects clocks, ambling elephants, brain rhythms and the onset of chaos. *Scientific American, 269*(6), 102-109.

[490] Ibid, p. 2.

[491] Stankosky, M. (2018). *21 for 21: Leading the 21st century global enterprise.* Emerald Books., p. 34.

[492] See Bennet, Bennet, & Turner (2022).

[493] Schaufeli, W. B., Salanova, M., Gonzalez-Roma, V., & Bakker, A. B. (2002). The measurement of engagement and burnout: A two-sample confirmatory factor analytic approach. *Journal of Happiness Studies, 3*(1), 71-92.

[494] Christian, M. S., Garza, A. S., & Slaughter, J. E. (2011). Work engagement: A quantitative review as test of its relations with task and contextual performance. *Personnel Psychology, 64*(1), 89-136.

[495] Xanthopoulou, D., Bakker, A. B., Demerouti, E., & Schaufeli, W. B. (2009). Work engagement and financial returns: A diary study on the role of job and personal resources. *Journal of Occupational and Organizational Psychology, 82*(1), 183-200.

[496] Santomauro, D. F., Herrera, A. M. M., Shadid, J., Zheng, P., Ashbaugh, C., Pigott, D. M., ... & Ferrari, A. J. (2021). Global prevalence and burden of depressive and anxiety disorders in 204 countries and territories in 2020 due to the COVID-19 pandemic. *The Lancet, 398*(10312), 1700-1712.

[497] Gallup (2022). *State of the Global Workplace 2022 Report.*

[498] Bakker, A. B., & Demerouti, E. (2014). Job demands-resources theory. In P. Y. Chen & C. I. Cooper (Eds.), *Wellbeing: A complete reference guide, Vol III.* Wiley-Blackwell, pp. 37-64.

[499] Demerouti, E., Bakker, A. B., Nachreiner, F., & Schaufeli, W. B. (2001). The job demands-resources model of burnout. *Journal of Applied Psychology, 86*(3), 499-512.

[500] Van den Broeck, A., Vansteenkiste, M., De Witte, H., & Lens, W. (2008). Explaining the relationships between job characteristics, burnout, and engagement: The role of basic psychological need satisfaction. *Work and Stress, 22*(3), 277-294.

[501] Makikangas, A., Feldt, T., Kinnunen, U., & Mauno, S. (2013). Does personality matter? Research on individual differences in occupational well-being. In A. B. Bakker (Ed.), *Advances in positive organizational psychology, Vol. 1*. Emerald, 107-143.

[502] Alfes, K., Shantz, A. D., Truss, C., & Soane, E. C. (2013). The link between perceived human resource management practices, engagement and employee behavior: A moderated mediation model. *The International Journal of Human Resource Management, 24*(2), 330-351. Also, Holman, D., & Axtell, C. (2016). Can job redesign interventions influence a broad range of employee outcomes by changing multiple job characteristics? A quasi-experimental study. *Journal of Occupational Health Psychology, 21*(3), 284-295.

[503] Eapen, T. T., Frinkenstadt, D. J., Folk, J., & Venkataswamy, L. (2023, July-August). How generative AI can augment human creativity. Harvard Business Review, 101(4), 56-64.

[504] Bennet, A., & Shelley, A. (2023). *Innovative creativity: Creating with innovation in mind.* MQIPress.

[505] Leonnard-Barton, D. (1995). *Wellsprings of knowledge: Building and sustaining the sources of innovation.* Harvard Business School Press.

[506] Stacey, R. D., Griffin, D., & Shaw, P. (2000). *Complexity and management: Fad or radical challenge to systems thinking?* Routledge.

[507] For detailed analysis of structural adaptation see Maturana, H. R., & Varela, F. J. (1987). *The tree of knowledge: The biological roots of human understanding.* New Science Library, Shambhala.

[508] Ashby, W. R. (1964). *An introduction to cybernetics.* Methuen.

[509] For an extensive treatment of the role of variation, interaction, and selection in dealing with external complexity by embracing internal complexity within an organization, see Axelrod & Cohen.

[510] Battram, A. (1996). *Navigating complexity: The essential gide to complexity theory in business and management.* The Industrial Society, p. 12.

[511] Material originally prepared by authors for the U.S. Department of the Navy toolkit, *Cport: Building Communities of Practice: Creating Value through Knowledge Communities*. A practitioners guide. Used with permission and in public domain.

[512] Drucker, P. (1999, March-April). Managing oneself. *Harvard Business Review 77*(2), p. 72.

[513] Cohen, D. & Prusak, L. (2001). *In good company, Harvard Business School Press. p. 4.*

[514] Larry Prusak, who was then leading the IBM KM Institute. The Trust Model was published in the DON cPort Toolkit.

[515] Cross, R. (2021). *Beyond collaboration overload: How to work smarter, get ahead, and restore your well-being.* Harvard Business Review Press.

[516] Kenny, Maj. R., executive officer of the 30th Signal Battalion, Wheeler Army Airfield, Hawaii. A Signal Corps officer. How to leave a legacy blog (2018, March 15). https:/from the greennotebook.com/2018/03/15/how-to-leave-a-legacy/

[517] Cohen, W. M. (1989). Innovation and learning: The two faces of R&D. *The Economic Journal, 99*(397), 569-596.

[518] Polanyi, M. (1966). *The tacit dimension.* Routledge and Keoan.

[519] Stankosky (2018), p. 24.

[520] Ibid., p. 25.

[521] Bennet et al. (2007).

[522] https://itif.org/publications/2023/06/27/productivity-growth-still-benefits-american-workers-saying-it-doesnt-reduces-support-for-technology-led-growth/

[523] Machlup.

[524] Drucker (1993), p. 193.

[525] Toffler, A. (1970). *Future shock.* Bantam Books.

[526] Bader, B. S. (2008). Distinguishing governance from management. *Great Boards, 8*(3), pp. 2-5.

[527] Quoted from Simon Lelic, editor-in-chief of *Inside Knowledge*, May 2005.

[528] The Intelligent Social Change Journey (ISCJ) is a developmental journey of the body, mind and heart, moving from the heaviness of cause-and-effect linear extrapolations, to the fluidity of co-evolving with our environment, to the lightness of breathing our thought and feelings

into reality. We are on this journey together. Change does not occur in isolation. See Bennet, A., Bennet, D., Shelley, A., Bullard, T., and Lewis, J. (2018). *The intelligent social change journey: Foundation for the possibilities that are YOU!* MQIPress. Also, more in-depth, see Bennet, A., Bennet, D., Shelley, A., Theresa, B., and Lewis, J. (2018/2020). *The profundity and bifurcation of change* (parts I-V). MQIPress

[529] Stebbins, p. 2.

[530] Marshall & Zohar. Also, Prigogine, I. (1996). *The end of certainty: Time, chaos, and the new laws of nature.* The Free Press.

[531] Zohar & Marshall (1994).

[532] Wilber, K. (2000). *Integral psychology: Consciousness, spirit, psychology, therapy.* Shambhala Publications, p. 89.

[533] Zohar, D., & Marshall I. (2012). *Spiritual capital: Wealth we can live by.* ReadHowYouWant, Intro.

[534] Wahl, H., Kaufmann, c., Eckkrammer, F., Mense, A., Gollner, H., Himmler, C., Rogner, W., Baierl, T., & Slobodian, R. (2012). Soft skills in practice and education: An evaluation. *American Journal of Business Education (AJBE) 5*(2), 225-232.

[535] Galabova, L., & McKie, L. (2013). The five fingers of my hand: Human capital and well-being in SMEs. *Personnel Review*, 772-683. http://dx.doi.org/10.1108/PR-01-2012-0017

[536] Harder, A., Andenoro, A., Roberts, T. G., Stedman, N., Newberry III, M., Parker, S. J., & Rodriguez, M. T. (2015). Does study abroad increase employability? *NACTA Journal 59*(1), 41-48.

[537] Van Laar, E., Van Deursen, A. J., Van Dijk, J., & De Haan, J. (2017). The relation between 21st-century skills and digital skills: A systematic literature review. *Computers in Human Behavior 72*, 577-588. https://doi.org/10.1016/j.chb.2017.03.010 Also, Farrugia, C., & Sanger, J. (2017). *Gaining an employment edge: The impact of study abroad on 21ˢᵗ century skills & career prospects in the US. Washington, DC.* IIE Center for Academic Mobility Research and Impact. https://globalsupport.tamu.edu/GlobalSupport/media/Doc-Files/IIE-2017-Report-Gaining-an-Employment-Edge-thru-Study-Abrd.pdf Also, Knight, R. (2017). How to manage a needy employee. *Harvard Business Review.* https://hbr.org/2017/06/how-to-manage-a-needy-employee

[538] Manz, C. C. (1986). Self-leadership: toward an expanded theory of self-influence processes in organizations. *Academy of Management Review 11*(3), 585-600. https://doi.org/10.2307/258312

[539] Neck, C. P., Houghton, J. D., Sardeshmukh, S. R., Goldsby, M., & Godwin, J. L. (2013). Self-leadership: A cognitive resource for entrepreneurs. *Journal of Small Business & Entrepreneurship 26*(5), 463-480.

[540] Neck, C. P., & Houghton, J. D. (2006). Two decades of self-leadership theory and research. *Journal of Managerial Psychology 21*(4), 270-295. https://doi.org/10.1108/0268390610663097

[541] Kim, H., Im, J., & Qu, H. (2018). Exploring antecedents and consequences of job crafting. International *Journal of Hospitality Management 75*, 18-26. https://doi.org/10.1016/j.ijhm.2018.02.014

[542] Furtner, M. R., Tutzer, L., & Sachse, P. (2018). The mindful self-leader: Investigating the relationships between self-leadership and mindfulness. *Social Behavior and Personality: An International Journal 46*(33), 353-360. https://doi.org/10.2224/sbp.6521

[543] Kabat-Zinn, J. (1995). *Wherever you go, there you are: Mindfulness meditation in everyday life.* Hyperion. Also, Kuan, T. (2012). Cognitive operations in Buddhist meditation: Interface with Western psychology. *Contemporary Buddhism 13*, 1, 35-60. https://doi.org/10.1080/14639947.2012.669281

[544] Langer, E. J. (2000). Mindful learning. *Current directions in Psychological Science 9*(6), 220-223. https://doi.org/10.1111/1467-8721.00099

[545] Shapiro, S. L., Carlson, L. E., Astin, J. A., & Freedman, B. (2006). Mechanisms of mindfulness. *Journal of Clinical Psychology 62*(3), 373-386. https://doi.orgt/10.1002/jclp

[546] Manz, C. G. (2015). Taking the self-leadership high road: Smooth surface or potholes ahead? *Academy of Management Perspectives 29*(1), 132-11. https://doi.org/10.5465/amp.2013.0060

547 Testa, D., & Sangganjanavanich, V. F. (2016). Contribution of mindfulness and emotional intelligence to burnout among counseling interns. *Counselor Education and Supervision 55*(2), 95-108. https://doi.org/10.1002/ceas.12035

548 Cairns-Lee, H. (201). Images of leadership development form the inside out. *Advances in Developing Human Resources 17*(3), 321-336.

549 Edwards, G., Elliott, C., Iszatt-White, M., & Schedlitzki, D. (2015). Using creative techniques in leadership learning and development: An introduction. *Advances in Developing Human Resources 17*(3), 279-288. https://doi.org/10.1177/152342231586616

550 Tovstiga, G. (2015). *Strategy in practice: A practitioner's guide to strategic thinking*. John Wiley & Sons.

551 Baron, L., & Parent, E. Developing authentic leadership within a training context: Three phenomena supporting the individual development process. *Journal of Leadership & Organizational Studies 22*(1), 37-53. https://doi.org/10.1177/14805181351901

552 Brendel, W., & Bennett, C. (2016). Learning to embody leadership through mindfulness and somatics practice. *Advances in Developing Human Resources 18*(3), 409-425. https://doi.org/10.1177/1523422316646068

553 Worawichayavongsa, W., & Bennet, A. (2022, February). The influence of mindfulness practice on self-leadership strategies engagement at non-managerial level. *Change Management: An International Journal 22*(2), 29-48. doi:10.18848/2327-798X/CGP/v22i02/29-48

554 Cross, R., & Dillon, K. (2023). *The microstress effect: How little things pile up and create big problems—and what to do about it*. Harvard Business Review Press, front cover.

555 Ibid.

556 Ibid.

557 Cripe, E. J., & Mansfield, R. S. (2002). *The value-added employee: 31 competencies to make yourself irresistible to any company* (2nd Ed.). Butterworth-Heinemann.

558 Senivongse, C. (2023). Competency profiling of organization's absorptive capacity development. Unpublished paper.

559 Lee (2023).

560 Blackmore.

561 Connelly et al. (2012). Also, Evans et al. Also, Peng, Q., Zhong, X., Liu, S., Zhou, H., & Ke. N. (2021). Job autonomy and knowledge hiding: The moderating roles of leader reward omission and person-supervisor fit. *Personnel Review*. https://doi.org/10.1108/PRo-03-2020-0133

562 Yang, K., Ribiére, V., & Bennet, A. (2023). Can we really hide knowledge? TBD. See also, Connelly, C. E., & Zweig, D. (2015). How perpetrators and targets construe knowledge hiding in organizations. *European Journal of Work and Organizational Psychology, 24*(33), 479-489. https://doi.org/10.1080/1359432X.2014.931325 Also, Bogilović, S., Černe, M., & Škerlavaj, M. (2017). Hiding behind a mask? Cultural intelligence, knowledge hiding, and individual and team creativity. *European Journal of Work and Organizational Psychology, 26*(5), 710-723. https://doi.org/10.1080/1359432X.2017.1337747 Also, Butt, A. S. (2019). Consequences of top-down knowledge hiding in firms: A pilot study. *Heliyon, 5*(12). https://doi.org/10.1016/j.heliyo.2019.e03000 Also, Černe, M., Hernaus, T., Dysvik, A., & Škerlavaj, M. (2014). What goes around comes around: Knowledge hiding, perceived motivational climate, and creativity. *Academy of Management Journal, 57*(1), 172-192. https://doi.org/10.5465/amj.2012.0122 Also, Malik, O. F., Shahzad, A., Raziq, M. M., Khan, M. M., Yusaf, S., & Khan, A. (2019). Perceptions of organizational politics, knowledge hiding, and employee creativity: The moderating role of professional commitment. *Personality and Individual Differences, 142*, 232-237. https://doi.org/10.1016/j.paid.2018.05.005 Also, Rhee, Y. W., & Choi, J. N. (017). Knowledge management behavior and individual creativity: Goal orientations as antecedents and in-group social status as moderating contingency. *Journal of Organizational Behavior, 38*(6), 813-832. https://doi.org/10.1002/job.2168 Also, Cai, F. Q., & Wen, N. (2018). The influence of individual goal orientation on innovation behavior from the perspective of knowledge hiding. In J. Lieu & K. L. Teves (Eds.), *Proceedings of the 2018 2nd International*

Conference on Education, Economics and Management Research 182, pp. 671-676. Also, Černe, M., Hernaus, T., Dysvik, A., & Škerlavaj, M. (2017). The role of multilevel synergistic interplay among team mastery climate, knowledge hiding, and job characteristics in stimulating innovative work behavior. *Human Resource Management Journal, 27*(2), 281-299. https://doi.org/10.1111/1748-8583.12132 Also, Wang, Y., Han, M. S., Xiang, D., & Hampson, D. P. (2019). The double-edged effects of perceived knowledge hiding: Empirical evidence from the sales context. *Journal of Knowledge Management, 23*(2), 279-296. https://doi.org/10.1108/JKM-04-2018-0245 Also, Bari, M. W., Abrar, M., Shaheen, S., Bashir, M., & Fanchen, M. (2019). Knowledge hiding behaviors and team creativity: The contingent role of perceived mastery motivational climate. *SAGE Open, 9*(3). https://doi.org/10.1177/2158244019876297 Also, Fong, P. S. W., Men, C., Luo, J., & Jia, R. (2018). Knowledge hiding and team creativity: The contingent role of task interdependence. *Management Decision, 56*(2), 329-343. https://doi.org/10.1108/MD-11-2016-0778 Also, Peng, J., Wang, Z., & Chen, X. (2019). Does self-serving leadership hinder team creativity? A moderated dual-path model: JBE. *Journal of Business Ethics, 159*(2), 419-433. Also, Zhang, Z., & Min, M. (2019). The negative consequences of knowledge hiding in NPD project teams: The roles of project work attributes. *International Journal of Project Management, 37*(2), 225-238. https://doi.org/10.1016/j.iproman.2019.01.006. Also, Singh, S. K. (2019). Territoriality, task performance, and workplace deviance: Empirical evidence on role of knowledge hiding. *Journal of Business Research, 97, 10-19.* https://doi.org/10.1016/j.jbusres.2018.12.034

[563] Yang, Kaiyu (2023, May 25). Personal email from IKI-SEA Bangkok University doctoral student.

[564] Blau, P. M. (1964). *Exchange and power in social life*. Transaction Publishers.

[565] Yang.

[566] De Furia, p. 5.

[567] Ibid.

[568] Bennet, A., Bennet, D., Shelley, A., Bullard, T., & Lewis, J. (2020c). *The profundity and bifurcation of change part III: Learning in the present*. MQIPress.

[569] Covey, S. M. R., & Merrill, R. R. (2018). *The speed of trust: The one thing that changes everything*. Simon & Schuster, p. 17.

[570] Dirks, K. T., & Ferrin, D. L. (2002). Trust in leadership: Meta-analytic findings and implication for research and practice. *Journal of Applied Psychology, 87*(4), 611-628. https://doi.org/10.1037/0021-9010.87.4.611

[571] Drawn from a seminar held by IntechOpen Journals. https://cdnintech.com/public/webinar-2/webinar-2.1-series-2023.pdf

[572] Das & Baisya.

[573] Bennet et al., PBC (2020).

[574] Quoted from *The Urantia Book* (1955). URANTIA Foundation, p. 908.

[575] Csikszentmihalyi, M., & Nakamura, J. (2005). The role of emotions in the development of wisdom. In R. J. Sternberg and J. Jordan (Eds.), *A handbook of wisdom: Psychological perspectives*. Cambridge University Press.

[576] Clayton, V., & Birren, J. E. (1980). The development of wisdom across the lifespan: A re-examination of an ancient topic. In P. B. Baltes and O. G. J. Brim (Eds.), *Life span development and behavior*. Academic Press, 104-135.

[577] Holliday, S. G., & Chandler, M. J. (1986). *Wisdom: Explorations in adult competence: Contributions to human development*, Vol. 17. Karger, Basel. Also, Erikson, J. M. (1988). *Wisdom and the senses: The way of creativity*. Norton. Also, Sternberg, R. J. (Ed.) (1990). *Wisdom: Its nature, origins, and development*. Cambridge University Press. Also, Jarvis, P. (1992). *Paradoxes of learning: On becoming an individual in society*. Jossey-Bass. Also, Kramer, D. A., & Bacelar, W. T. (1994). The educated adult in today's world: Wisdom and the mature learner. In J. D. Sinnott (Ed.), *Interdisciplinary handbook of adult lifespan learning*. Greenwood Press. Also, Bennett-Woods, D. (1997). Reflections on wisdom. Unpublished paper, University of Northern Colorado.

[578] Merriam, S. B., & Caffarella, R. S. (1999). *Learning in adulthood: A comprehensive guide* (2nd Ed.). Jossey-Bass, p. 165.

[579] Smith, J., Dixon, R. A., & Baltes, P. B. (1987). Age differences in response to life planning problems: A research analog for the study of wisdom, related knowledge. Unpublished manuscript. Also, Dittmann-Kohli, F., & Baltes, P. B. (1990). Toward a neofunctionalist conception of adult intellectual development: Wisdom as a prototypical case of intellectual growth. In C. Alexander and E. Langer (Eds.), *Beyond formal operations: Alternative endpoints to human development*. Oxford University Press.

[580] Baltes, P. B., & Smith, J. (1990). The psychology of wisdom and its ontogenesis. In R. J. Sternberg (Ed.), *Wisdom: Its nature, origins, and development*. Cambridge University Press, 87-120.

[581] Levitt, H. M. (1999). The development of wisdom: An analysis of Tibetan Buddhist experience. *Journal of Humanistic Psychology, 39*(2), 86-105.

[582] Trumpa, C. (1991). *The heart of the Buddha*. Shambhala.

[583] Woodman, M., & Dickson, E. (1996). *Dancing in the flames: The dark goddess in the transformation of consciousness*. Shambhala.

[584] Brown, W. S. (2000). Wisdom and human neurocognitive systems: Perceiving and practicing the laws of life. In W. S. Brown (Ed.), *Understanding wisdom: Sources, science and society*. Templeton Foundation Press.

[585] Sherman, N. (2000). Wise emotions. In W. S. Brown (Ed.), *Understanding wisdom: Sources, science and society*. Templeton Foundation Press.

[586] Bennet, A., & Bennet, D. (2008d). Moving from knowledge to wisdom, from ordinary consciousness to extraordinary consciousness. *VINE: Journal of Information and Knowledge Systems, 38*(1), 7-15.

[587] MacDonald, C. (1996). *Toward wisdom: Finding our way to inner peace, love, and happiness*. Hampton Roads, p. 1.

[588] Murphy, N. (2000). Introduction: A hierarchical framework for understanding wisdom. In W. S. Brown (Ed.), *Understanding wisdom: sources, science and society*. Templeton Foundation Press, p. 7.

[589] Schloss, J. P. (2000). Wisdom traditions as mechanisms for organismal integration: Evolutionary perspectives on homeostatic 'laws of life'. In W. S. Brown (Ed.), *Understanding wisdom: Sources, science and society*. Templeton Foundation Press.

[590] Erikson, p. 184.

[591] Costa, J. D. (1995). *Working wisdom: The ultimate value in the new economy*. Stoddart, p. 3.

[592] Sternberg (1990), p. 188.

[593] MacFlouer (2004-16).

[594] Sternberg (2003), p. xviii.

[595] Sternberg, R. J. (Ed.) (1990). *Wisdom: It nature, origins and development*. Cambridge University Press, p. 353.

[596] Bennet et al. (2020d).

[597] Bennet, A. (2018). *Possibilities that are YOU! Volume 15: Seeking wisdom*. MQIPress.

[598] Bennet & Shelley (2023).

[599] Bennet, Bennet, & Turner (2022).

[600] Gorz, A. (2010). *The immaterial* (C. Turner, Trans.). Seagull Books, p. 168.

[601] Dolphijn, R. (2021). Doing justice to that which matters: Subjectivity and the politics of new materialism. In H. Rosa, C. Henning & A. Bueno (Eds.), *Critical theory and new materialisms* (pp. 143–153). Routledge, p. 152.

[602] de Sousa (2023).

[603] Deloitte Touche Tohmatsu Limited (2016). *The 2016 Deloitte millennial survey. Winning over the next generation of leaders*.

[604] Ibid.

[605] Gaiseanu, F. (2018a). Information: From philosophic to physics concepts for informational modeling of consciousness. *Philosophy Study 8*(8), 368-382. doi: 10.17265/2159-5313/2018.08.004. http://www.davidpublisher.org/Public/uploads/Contribute/5c06323653cd2.pdf Also,

Gaiseanu, F. (2020a). Information-matter bipolarity of the human organism and its fundamental circuits: From philosophy to physics/neurosciences-based modeling. *Philosophy Study, 10*(2), 107-118. doi: 10.17265/2159-5313/2020.02.002. http://www.davidpublisher.com/Public/uploads/Contribute/5e5b3d8e74433.pdf Also, Gaiseanu, F. (2020b). Attitude as an expressible info-operational reaction to a perceived/purposed object/objective. *International Journal on Neuropsychology and Behavioural Sciences, 1*(1), 12-16. DOI: 10.51626/ijnbs.2020.01.00002. https://skeenapublishers.com/journal/ijnbs/IJNBS-01-00002.pdf Also, Gaiseanu, F. (2020c). *Physics of consciousness and life: The informational model of consciousness – Information in neurosciences, biocomputers and biosystems –* Romanian version: *Fizica constiintei si a vietii: Modelul informational al constiintei – Informatia in neurostiinte, biocomputere si biosisteme.* Editura GlobeEdit. https://www.amazon.com/Fizica-Conștiinței-Vieții-Informațional-Neuroștiințe/dp/6139421705

[606] Bennet, Bennet, & Turner (2022). ISBN 978-1-949829-63-1.

[607] Gaiseanu, F. (2023a). Information: From cognitive-sentient exploration of reality to predictive big data assisted informational era. *Romanian Journal of Information Science and Technology, 26*(1), 78-99. https://www.romjist.ro/full-texts/paper734.pdf

[608] Filip, F. G. (2020). DSS—A class of evolving information systems. In G. Dzemyda, J. Bernatavičienė, & J. Kacprzyk (Eds.), *Data science: New issues, challenges and applications: Studies in computational intelligence, 869*, 253-277. Springer.

[609] Gaiseanu, F. (2023b). Information and Informational Organization of the Living Structures: From empirical decision making to decisional big data-assisted informational Era. In V. E. Balas, D. Gintautas, S. Belciug, & J. Kacprzyk (Eds.), *DSS 2023, Decision making and decision support in the information and AI era*, Dedicated to Academician Florin Gheorghe Filip. Studies in Systems, Decision and Control (SSDC) Book Series from Springer.

[610] Ibid., Also, Gaiseanu (2023a).

[611] Gaiseanu, F. (2021a). Information in the universal triangle of reality for non-living/living structures: from philosophy to neuro/life sciences. *Philosophy Study, 11*(8), 607-621. https://www.davidpublisher.com/Public/uploads/Contribute/613a23ae7fc67.pdf Also, Gaiseanu, F. (2021b). Evolution and development of the information concept in biological systems: From empirical description to informational modeling of the living structures. *Philosophy Study, 11*(7), 501-516. https://www.davidpublisher.com/Public/uploads/Contribute/60ff9a4c77211.pdf Also, Gaiseanu, F. (2021c). Evaluating attitude and behavior: An info-operational procedure related/supported by the cognitive centers of mind. *International Journal on Neuropsychology and Behavioural Sciences, 2*(1), 1-5. Also, Gaiseanu (2023a).

[612] Gaiseanu, F. (2021e) Human as an informational device. *Archives in Biomedical Engineering & Biotechnology 6*(1), 1-8. ABEB.MS.ID.000629. DOI: 10.33552/ABEB.2021.06.000629 Also, Gaiseanu Florin (2021f) New perspectives in biomedical engineering and biotechnology: Information in human and biological structures. *Archives in Biomedical Engineering and Biotechnology, 6*(1), 1-3. ABEB.MS.ID.000633. DOI: 10.33552/ABEB.2021.06.000633.

[613] Gaiseanu F. (2023c). From Micro to Macro Complexity Organization Scale of the Living Organisms, Their Informational Structure/Functions Are the Same, Annals of Biostatistics & Biometric Applications, Iris Publishers. Vol 5(3): 1-12. 10.33552/ABBA.2023.05.000614. Also, Gaiseanu, F. (2023d) The Informational Model of the Human Body and Living Structures: from Micro to Macro Structuration and Functions, *Preprints* (www.preprints.org), 1-19. doi:10.20944/preprints202304.0110.v1.

[614] Bianconi E, Piovesan A, Facchin F, Beraudi A et al. (2013) An estimation of the number of cells in the human body, *Annals of Human Biology: 1*(11). DOI: 10.3109/03014460.2013.807878.

[615] Gaiseanu (2020a).

[616] Gaiseanu, F. (2019a). The informational model of consciousness: Mechanisms of embodiment/disembodiment of information. *NeuroQuantology, 17*(4), 1-17. https://www.neuroquantology.com/article.php?id=1322 Also, Gaiseanu, F. (2019b).

Information model of consciousness: From philosophic concepts to an information science of consciousness. *Philosophy Study, 9*(4), 181-196.
http://www.davidpublisher.org/Public/uploads/Contribute/5d1c009c3567e.pdf.DOI:10.17265/2159-5313/2019.04.002

[617] Gaiseanu, F. (2019c). Destiny or free will decision? A life overview from the perspective of an informational modeling of consciousness part I: Information, consciousness and life cycle. *Gerontology & Geriatric Studies 4*(1), 1-7.
https://crimsonpublishers.com/ggs/pdf/GGS.000586.pdf

[618] Gaiseanu, F. (2020d). What is life: An informational model of the living structures. *Biochemistry and Molecular Biology, 5*(2), 18-28. 18-28. doi: 10.11648/j.bmb.20200502.12.

[619] Gaiseanu (2023a). Also, Gaiseanu (2023c).

[620] Gaiseanu, F. (2021g). Solution to the mind-body relation problem: Information. *Philosophy Study, 11*(1), 42-55.
http://www.davidpublisher.com/index.php/Home/Article/index?id=44889.html

[621] Gaiseanu (2021b).

[622] Gaiseanu (2021a).

[623] Gaiseanu (2020d).

[624] Gaiseanu (2021h). Information as an essential component of the biological structures and their informational organization. *Journal of Microbiology & Biotechnology, 6*(2), 1-9.
https://medwinpublishers.com/OAJMB/information-as-an-essential-component-of-the-biological-structures-and-their-informational-organization.pdf Also, Gaiseanu (2020f). Informational structure of the living systems: From philosophy to informational modeling, *Philosophy Study, 10*(12), 795-806. doi: 10.17265/2159-5313/2020.12.004.
http://www.davidpublisher.com/Public/uploads/Contribute/5feac331230ba.pdf

[625] Gaiseanu (2023c). Also, Gaiseanu, F. (2023e). Cellular info-operability: Micro/macro-scale inter-communication in the immune system of the human/mammalian organism. *Annals of Biostatistics & Biometric Applications, 5*(1), 1-7. 10.33552/ABBA.2023.05.000605. Also, Gaiseanu, F. (2022b) Info-activity of the immune system from the perspective of the informational model of the human body and living structures. *International Journal of Frontline Research in Life Science, 1*(2), 1-12. https://doi.org/10.56355/ijfrls.2022.1.2.0025

[626] Gaiseanu F. (2023f). What is mind, what is consciousness, and where this resides. *Philosophy Study, 13*(3), 103-120. doi: 10.17265/2159-5313/2023.03.001.
https://www.davidpublisher.com/Public/uploads/Contribute/647027490c94a.pdf

[627] Gaiseanu (2019a).

[628] Gaiseanu, F. (2021d). Informational model of consciousness and life, information as a constitutive element of the living systems: From philosophy to modeling and applications. Colocviile Mihai Draganescu: Presentation on Science and Technology of Information, March 18, Romanian Academy.
https://academiaromana.ro/sectii/sectia14_informatica/sti/doc2021/d0318-ColocviileMDraganescu.pdf Also, Gaiseanu (2023a).

[629] Gaiseanu, F. (2020e). Informationally-assisted equilibrium and health: Specific ACC contribution from the perspective of the informational model of consciousness. *EC Psychology and Psychiatry J., 9*(5), 37-49. (https://www.ecronicon.com/ecpp/ECPP-09-00692.php Also, Gaiseanu, F. (2020g). Information based hierarchical brain organization/evolution from the perspective of the informational model of consciousness. *Archives in Neurology & Neuroscience 7*(5), 1-6. ANN.MS.ID.000672. DOI: 10.33552/ANN.2020.07.000672.
https://www.academia.edu/42766202/Information_Based_Hierarchical_Brain_Organization_Evolution_from_the_Perspective_of_the_Informational_Model_of_Consciousness

[630] Gaiseanu, F. (2020h). Info-relational cognitive operability of the posterior cingulate cortex according to the informational model of consciousness. *International Journal of Psychological and Brain Sciences, 5*(4): 61-68 doi: 10.11648/j.ijpbs.20200504.12.
http://www.sciencepublishinggroup.com/journal/paperinfo?journalid=170&doi=10.11648/j.ijpbs.20200504.12

[631] Gaiseanu (2018b). Also, Gaiseanu (2019c). Also, Dispenza, J. (2007). *Evolve your brain: The science of changing your mind*. Health Communications, Inc.

[632] Gaiseanu, F. (2021i). Information, info-creational field, creativity and creation, according to the informational model of consciousness. *International Journal on Neuropsychology and Behavioural Sciences 2*(3), 75–80. DOI: 10.51626/ijnbs.2021.02.000017. https://skeenapublishers.com/journal/ijnbs/IJNBS-02-00017.pdf.

[633] Gaiseanu (2021i).

[634] Gaiseanu (2023f).

[635] Gaiseanu, F. (2023h). In_novation, a great native dynamic way toward successful performance. In A. Bennet, & R. Baisya (Eds.), *INside Novation: Looking from the inside out*. MQIPress, pp. 241-270.

[636] Gaiseanu, F. (2022a). The cognitive-sentient exploration of mediated reality: From proto-cognition/epigenetic informational processes to big data assisted prediction. In S. B. Shafer & A. Bennet (Eds.), *Global media's preternatural influence on global technological singularity, culture, and government*. IGI-Global, pp. 193-213. https://www.igi-global.com/chapter/the-cognitive-sentient-exploration-of-mediated-reality/296550

[637] Gaiseanu, F. (2019f). Epigenetic information-body interaction and information-assisted evolution from the perspective of the informational model of consciousness. *Archives in Biomedical Engineering & Biotechnology, 2*(2): 1-6. DOI: 10.33552/ABEB.2019.02.000532 https://irispublishers.com/abeb/pdf/ABEB.MS.ID.000532.pdf.

[638] Gaiseanu (2023h).

[639] de Boer, M., Inchingolo, R. (2023). *Think harder, not faster: how network structure shapes*. https://www.humanbrainproject.eu/en/follow-hbp/news/2023/06/05/think-harder-not-faster-how-network-structure-shapes-decision-making Also, Schirner M, Deco G, Ritter P. (2023). Learning how network structure shapes decision-making for bio-inspired computing, *Nature Communication, 14, Article number 2963*: 1-14.

[640] Gaiseanu, F. (2021j). Mental aggressive operability from informational perspective: A deterrence manifesto. *EC Neurology, 13*(4), 31-39. https://www.ecronicon.com/ecne/pdf/ECNE-13-00879.pdf

[641] Gaiseanu, F. (2021k). Pathological expression and circuits in addiction and mood disorders: Informational relation with the brain and info-therapy. *EC Neurology, 13*(8), 24-35. https://www.ecronicon.com/ecne/pdf/ECNE-13-00924.pdf

[642] Gaiseanu (2020c).

[643] Gaiseanu (2021j).

[644] Gaiseanu (2021i).

[645] Gaiseanu (2020h).

[646] Gaiseanu (2020c).

[647] Gaiseanu (2023f). Also, Lavin, C., Melis, C., Mikulan, M., Gelormini, C., Huepe, D., Ibañez, A. (201). The anterior cingulate cortex: an integrative hub for human socially-driven interactions, *Frontiers in Neuroscience/Decision Neuroscience 7*, 64(2):1-4.

[648] Gaiseanu, F. (2019e). The silent voice of those who are no Longer: Transgenerational transmission of information from the perspective of the informational model of consciousness. *Gerontology & Geriatric Studies 5*(1): 482-488. DOI: 10.31031/GGS.2019.05.000604. https://crimsonpublishers.com/ggs/pdf/GGS.000604.pdf

[649] Gaiseanu, F. (2021l). Neuropsychological response to information of beauty/ugly brain circuits according to the informational model of consciousness. *International Journal on Neuropsychology and Behavioural Sciences (IJNBS), 2*(2), 55-59.

[650] Frijda, N. H. (2016). The evolutionary emergence of what we call "emotions". *Cognition and Emotion*, 609-620.

[651] Gaiseanu, F. (2021m). Evaluating attitude and behavior: An info-operational procedure related/supported by the cognitive centers of mind, *International Journal on Neuropsychology and Behavioural Sciences, 2*(1), 1-5.

[652] Dobs K, Bülthoff I, Schultz J (2016) Identity information content depends on the type of facial movement, Scientific Reports, 6:34301:1-9. Also, Melzer, A., Shafir, T., Tsachor, R.P.

(2019). *How Do We Recognize Emotion From Movement? Specific Motor Components Contribute to the Recognition of Each Emotion.* Front. Psychol. 10:1389: 1-11.

[653] Gaiseanu (2020c).

[654] Cohen, D., & Prusak, L. (2001). *In good company:.How social capital makes organizations work* Harvard Business School Press.

[655] Bennet, Bennet, & Turner (2023).

[656] Wenger.

[657] Bennet & Shelley.

[658] Baumeister, R. F. (1991). *Meanings of life.* Guilford Press.

[659] Ibid., p. 16.

[660] Battista, J., & Almond, R. (1973). The development of meaning in life. *Psychiatry, 36*(4), 409-427.

[661] Weick, K. E., Sutcliffe, K. M. & Obstfeld, D. (2005). Organizing and the process of sensemaking. *Organization Science, 16*, 409–21, p. 409.

[662] Pratt, M. G., & Ashforth, B. E. (2003). Fostering meaningfulness in working and at work. *Positive organizational scholarship: Foundations of a new discipline, 309*, 327.

[663] Steger, M. F., Frazier, P., Oishi, S., & Kaler, M. (2006). The meaning in life questionnaire: Assessing the presence of and search for meaning in life. *Journal of Counseling Psychology, 53*(1), 80.

[664] Wong, P. T. (1989). Personal meaning and successful aging. *Canadian Psychology/Psychologie Canadienne, 30*(3), 516.

[665] Bhatti, S. H., Vorobyev, D., Zakariya, R., & Christofi, M. (2021). Social capital, knowledge sharing, work meaningfulness and creativity: Evidence from the Pakistani pharmaceutical industry. *Journal of Intellectual Capital, 22*(2), 243-259.

[666] Johnson, R. E., Rosen, C. C., & Djurdjevic, E. (2011). Assessing the impact of common method variance on higher order multidimensional constructs. *Journal of Applied Psychology, 96*(4), 744.

[667] Zhang, Y., Sun, J. M., Lin, C. H., & Ren, H. (2020). Linking core self-evaluation to creativity: The roles of knowledge sharing and work meaningfulness. *Journal of Business and Psychology, 35*, 257-270.

[668] Merrill, M. D., Richards, R.E., Schmidt, R.V. & Wood, N. D. (1977). *The instructional strategy diagnostic profile training manual.* Courseware, Inc

[669] Ausubel, D. P. (1968). *Educational psychology: A cognitive view.* Holt, Rinehart and Winston.

[670] Levin, J. R. (1973). Inducing comprehension in poor readers. *Journal of Educational Psychology, 65*(19), 24.

[671] Reigeluth, C. M. (1983). Meaningfulness and instruction: Relating what is being learned to what a student knows. *Instructional Science, 12(3)*, 197-218.

[672] van Knippenberg, D. (2020). Meaning-based leadership. *Organizational Psychology Review, 10*(1), 6-28.

[673] Frémeaux, S., & Pavageau, B. (2022). Meaningful leadership:How can leaders contribute to meaningful work? *Journal of Management Inquiry, 31*(1), 54-66.

[674] de Sousa.

[675] Ibid.

[676] Kegan, R. (1980). Making meaning: The constructive-developmental approach to persons and practice. *The Personnel and Guidance Journal, 58*(5), 373-380.

[677] Greenleaf.

[678] van Knippenberg.

[679] Lips-Wiersma & Wright.

[680] Schein, E. H., & Schein, P. A. (2021). *Humble inquiry: The gentle art of asking instead of telling.* Berrett-Koehler Publishers.

[681] Greenleaf, p.6.

[682] Tronto, J. C. (1998). An ethic of care. *Generations: Journal of the American Society on Aging, 22*(3), 15-20.

683 Read, H. (2019). A typology of empathy and its many moral forms. *Philosophy Compass, 14*(10), e12623.

684 Schein & Shein.

685 Bennet, A. (2018). *Possibilities that are you! Volume 4: Conscious compassion*. MQI Press.

686 Wiseman, J., & Stillwell, A. (2022). Organizational justice: Typology, antecedents and consequences. *Encyclopedia, 2*(3), 1287-1295.

687 CUCA represents accelerating Change, rising Uncertainty, increasing Complexity, and the Anxiety in the individual that ensures. As quoted from Bennet, A., & Bennet, D. (2004). *Organizational survival in the new world: The intelligent complex adaptive system*, a new theory of the firm (Elsevier), "Time accelerates. Distance shrinks. Networks expand. Information over-whelms. Interdependencies grow geometrically. Uncertainty domnates. Complexity boggles the mind."

688 Kandel, E. R. (2006b). *In search of memory: The emergence of a new science of mind*. W. W. Norton & Company.

689 *Encarta World English Dictionary* (1999). St. Martin's Press.

690 Goleman (1995).

691 Bennet & Bennet (2008d). .

692 Bergson, H. (2014). *Key writings*. Bloomsbury Academic.

693 Pert, p. 276.

694 McCabe, T. J. (2019). *Interconnections: Computer science, math, poetry, stories, entrepreneurship*. Independently published.

695 See Expanded Consciousness Institute: www.expanded-consciousness.com.

696 Hawkins & Blakeslee.

697 Kuntz, P. G. (1968). *The concept of order*. University of Washington Press, p. 162.

698 Hawkins, p. 109.

699 Ibid.

700 James, J. (1996). *Thinking the future tense: A workout of the mind*. Touchstone, p. 78).

701 Shelley, A. (2007). *Organizational zoo: A survival guide to work place behavior*. Aslan Publishing.

702 Ibid., p. xiii.

703 Ibid, p. xvi.

704 Ibid, p. 119.

705 Groves, C. P. (2005). Order primates. In D. E. Wilson, D. M. Reeder (Eds), *Mammal species of the world: A taxonomic and geographic reference, vol. 1*. Johns Hopkins University Press, pp. 111-184.

706 Schipper, J., Chanson, J. S., Chiozza, F., Cox, N.A., [… + 125 authors], & Young, B. E. (2008, October 10). The status of the world's land and marine mammals: Diversity, threat, and knowledge. *Science 322*(5899), pp. 225-230. DOI: 10.1126/science.1165115

707 Mulcahy, M. P., & Prince, M. B. (2004). Using ant and butterfly pollination to involve students in scientific exploration. In M. A. O'Donnell (Ed.), *Tested studies for laboratory teaching, volume 25*. Proceedings of the 25th Workshop/conference of the Association for Biology Laboratory Education (ABLE), pp. 135-157. http://www.zoo.utoronto.ca/able

708 Sheldrake, R. (1989). *The presence of the past: Morphic resonance and the habits of nature*. Vintage Books.

709 Cohen, W. M., & Levinthal, D. A. (1990). Absorptive capacity: A new perspective on learning and innovation. *Administrative Science Quarterly, 35*(1), 128–152. Also, Roberts, N. (2015). Absorptive capacity, organizational antecedents, and environmental dynamism. *Journal of Business Research, 68*(11), 2426–2433. Also, Senivongse, C., Mariano, S., Bennet, A., & Tsui, E. (2022). Absorptive capacity efficacy in SMEs: Evidence from multiple case studies in the information technology industry. *Knowledge Management Research and Practice, 20*(5). https://doi.org/10.1080/14778238.2020.1784050. Also, Todorova, G., & Durisin, B. (2007). Absorptive capacity: Valuing a reconceptualization. *Academy of Management Review, 32*(3), 774–786. Also, Zahra, S. A., & George, G. (2002). Absorptive capacity: A review, reconceptualization, and extension. *Academy of Management Proceedings & Membership Directory, 27*(2), 185–203.

[710] Lichtenthaler, U. (2009). Absorptive capacity, environmental turbulence, and the complementarity of organizational learning processes. *Academy of Management Journal, 52,* 822–846.

[711] Chen, Y. S., Lin, M. J. J., & Chang, C. H. (2009). The positive effects of relationship learning and absorptive capacity on innovation performance and competitive advantage in industrial markets. *Industrial Marketing Management, 38*(2), 152–158.

[712] Hayes, J., & Allinson, C. W. (1998). Cognitive style and the theory and practice of individual and collective learning in organizations. *Human Relations, 51*(7), 847–871.

[713] Fenwick, T. (2008). Understanding relations of individual-collective learning in work: A review of research. *Management Learning, 39*(3), 227–243.

[714] Andreu, R., & Sieber, S. (1999). Knowledge and problem solving: A proposal for a model of individual and collective learning. Working Paper 1/99). Barcelona.

[715] Levitt, B., & James G . March. (1988). Organizational learning. *Annual Review of Sociology, 14,* 319–340.

[716] Itam Eyo, E., Sunarsi, D., & Affandi, A. (2022). A literature review in learning organization. *International Journal of Educational Administration, Management, and Leadership, 3*(1), 11–16.

[717] Senge.

[718] Todorova & Durisin.

[719] Cohen & Levinthal.

[720] Todorova & Durisin. Also, Zahra & George.

[721] Cohen & Levinthal. Also, Kostopoulos, K., Papalexandris, A., Papachroni, M., & Ioannou, G. (2011). Absorptive capacity, innovation, and financial performance. *Journal of Business Research, 64*(12), 1335–1343. Also, Soo, C., Tian, A. W., Teo, S. T. T., & Cordery, J. (2017). Intellectual capital–enhancing HR, Absorptive capacity, and innovation. *Human Resource Management, 56*(3), 431–454.

[722] Almeida, L. S., Prieto, M. D., Ferreira, A. I., Bermejo, M. R., Ferrando, M., & Ferrándiz, C. (2010). Intelligence assessment: Gardner multiple intelligence theory as an alternative. *Learning and Individual Differences, 20*(3), 225–230. https://doi.org/10.1016/j.lindif.2009.12.010 Also, Andreu, R., & Sieber, S. (1999). Knowledge and problem solving: A proposal for a model of individual and collective learning. Working Paper 1/99). Barcelona. Also, Christiansen, C. M., Horn, M. B., & Johson, C. W. (2011). Disrupting class: How disruptive innovation will change the way the world learns. *Learning and Individual Differences 20*(3). McGraw-Hill Education. Also, Fenwick. Also, Hayes & Allinson. Also, Merok Paulsen, J., & Brynjulf Hjertø, K. (2014). Exploring individual-level and group-level levers for inter-organizational knowledge transfer. *The Learning Organization, 21*(4), 274–287. Also, Tomassini, M., & Zanazzi, S. (2014). Reflexivity and self-development of competencies as key drivers in individuals' learning and career paths: Cases from Italy. *Research in Comparative and International Education, 9*(3), 301–312. https://doi.org/10.2304/rcie.2014.9.3.301

[723] Senivongse et al.

[724] Argyris A Schön, C. D. (1997). *Organizational learning: A theory of action perspective.* Reiss, 77/78, 345–348.

[725] Abel, M. (2008). Competencies management and learning organizational memory. *Journal of Knowledge Management, 12*(6), 15–30. Also Bennet & Bennet (2009).

[726] Bontis, N., Crossan, M. M., & Hullan, J. (2000). Managing an organizational learning system by aligning stocks and flows of knowledge. *Journal of Management Studies, 39*(4), 437–469.

[727] Argyris, C. (1991). Teaching smart people how to learn. *Harvard Business Review, 69*(3).

[728] Argyris, C. (1977). Double loop learning in organizations. *Harvard Business Review, 55*(5), 115–125, p. 116.

[729] Argyris (1991).

[730] Argyris & Schön, 345–348.

[731] Tosey, P., Visser, M., & Saunders, M. N. K. (2012). The origins and conceptualizations of 'triple-loop'learning: A critical review. *Management Learning, 43*(3), 291–307.

[732] Argyris (1991).

[733] Tosey et al.

[734] Kwon, C., & Nicolaides, A. (2017). Managing diversity through triple-loop learning: A call for paradigm shift. *Human Resource Development Review, 16*(1), 85–99.

[735] Ibid.

[736] Ibid.

[737] Argyris (1977).

[738] McClory, S., Read, M., & Labib, A. (2017). Conceptualising the lessons-learned process in project management: Towards a triple-loop learning framework. *International Journal of Project Management, 35*(7), 1322–1335.

[739] Kwon & Nicolaides.

[740] Bennet, A., Bennet, D., Shelley, A., Bullard, T., & Lewis, J. (2020a). *The profundity and bifurcation of change part I: Laying the groundwork*. MQIPress.

[741] Ibid.

[742] Cotter, R. J., & Cullen, J. G. (2012). Reflexive management learning: An integrative review and a conceptual typology. *Human Resource Development Review, 11*(2), 227–253.

[743] Schön, D. A. (1983). *The reflective practitioner: How professionals think in action*. Basic Books, p. 241.

[744] Cunliffe, A. L. (2002). Reflexive dialogical practice in management learning. *Management Learning, 33*(1), 35–61.

[745] Dyke, M. (2009). An enabling framework for reflexive learning: Experiential learning and reflexivity in contemporary modernity. *International Journal of Lifelong Education, 28*(3), 289–310.

[746] Bennet, Bennet, & Turner (2018).

[747] Zull.

[748] Cunliffe.

[749] Dyke.

[750] Bruno, A., Galuppo, L., & Gilardi, S. (2011). Evaluating the reflexive practices in a learning experience. *European Journal of Psychology of Education, 26*, 527–543.

[751] Parker, S., Racz, M., & Palmer, P. (2020). Reflexive learning and performative failure. *Management Learning, 51*(3), 293–313.

[752] Allen, S., Cunliffe, A. L., & Easterby-Smith, M. (2019). Understanding sustainability through the lens of ecocentric radical-reflexivity: Implications for management education. *Journal of Business Ethics, 154*, 781–795.

[753] Ibid.

[754] Bloom.

[755] Senge, p. 8.

[756] Garvin, D. A., Edmondson, A. C., & Gino, F. (2008). Is yours a learning organization? *Harvard Business Review, 86*(3), 109.

[757] Argyris & Schön. Also, Garavan, T. (1997). The learning organization: A review and evaluation. *The Learning Organization, 4*(1), 18–29.

[758] Senge, 1994.

[759] Jashapara, A. (2003). Cognition, culture and competition: An empirical test of the learning organization. *The Learning Organization, 10*(1), 31–50. https://doi.org/10.1108/09696470310457487

[760] Naim, M. F., & Lenka, U. (2020). Organizational learning and Gen Y employees' affective commitment: The mediating role of competency development and moderating role of strategic leadership. *Journal of Management & Organization, 26*(5), 815–831.

[761] Lin, Y.-T., & Jou, M. (2013). Development of an Integrated Learning Environment with Knowledge Management for Cultivating Student Critical Thinking Skills. *Procedia - Social and Behavioral Sciences, 103*, 290–298.

[762] Garvin, D. A. (2003). *Learning in action: A guide to putting the learning organization to work*. Harvard Business Review Press.

[763] Gastaldi, L., Lettieri, E., Corso, M., & Masella, C. (2012). Performance improvement in hospitals: leveraging on knowledge asset dynamics through the introduction of an electronic medical record. *Measuring Business Excellence, 16*(4), 14–30.

[764] Sun, P. Y. T., & Scott, J. L. (2003). Exploring the divide–organizational learning and learning organization. *The Learning Organization, 10*(4), 202–215.

[765] Levitt, B., & March, J. G. (1988). Organizational learning. *Annual Review of Sociology, 14*, 319–340. Also, Sun, H. C. (2003). Conceptual clarifications for 'organizational learning', 'learning organization' and 'a learning organization.' *Human Resource Development International, 6*(2), 153–166.

[766] Sun & Scott.

[767] Odor, H. O. (2018). A literature review on organizational learning and learning organizations. *International Journal of Economics & Management Sciences, 7*(1), 1–6.

[768] Ibid.

[769] Sun, P. Y. T., & Anderson, M. H. (2010). An examination of the relationship between absorptive capacity and organizational learning, and a proposed integration. *International Journal of Management Reviews, 12*(2), 130–150.

[770] Argyris & Schön.

[771] Cohen & Levinthal.

[772] Nonaka & Takeuchi.

[773] Nonaka, I., Toyama, R., & Konno, N. (2000). SECI , Ba and leadership : A unified model of dynamic knowledge creation. *Leadership, 33*(1), 5–34. https://doi.org/10.1016/S0024-6301(99)00115-6

[774] Cohen & Levinthal.

[775] Lewin, A. Y., Massini, S., & Peeters, C. (2011). Microfoundations of internal and external absorptive capacity routines. *Organization Science, 22*(1), 81–98.

[776] Zahra & George.

[777] Enkel, E., Heil, S., Hengstler, M., & Wirth, H. (2017). Exploratory and exploitative innovation: To what extent do the dimensions of individual level absorptive capacity contribute? *Technovation, 60*, 29–38.

[778] Senivongse et al.

[779] Da Silva, N., & Davis, A. R. (2011). Absorptive capacity at the individual level: Linking creativity to innovation in academia. *The Review of Higher Education, 34*(3), 355–379.

[780] Sun & Anderson.

[781] Sun & Scott.

[782] Todorova & Durisin.

[783] Abel. Also, Bennet & Bennet.

[784] Vera, D., Crossan, M., & Apaydin, M. (2012). A framework for integrating organizational learning, knowledge, capabilities, and absorptive capacity. In *Handbook of organizational learning and knowledge management*, pp. 153–180.

[785] Todorova & Durisin, pp. 777-778.

[786] Reis, J., Amorim, M., Melão, N., & Matos, P. (2018). Digital transformation: A literature review and guidelines for future research. *Advances in Intelligent Systems and Computing, 745*(May), 411–421. https://doi.org/10.1007/978-3-319-77703-0_41

[787] Smit, T. G. J. (2014). The appropriability regime as a tool to measure knowledge protection, pp. 1–12.

[788] Todorova & Durisin.

[789] Helfat, C. E., Finkelstein, S., Mitchell, W., Peteraf, M. A., Singh, H., Teece, D. J., & Winter, S. G. (2007). Dynamic capabilities: Understanding strategic change in organizations. *Strategic Management Journal, 18*. Also, Tripsas, M. (1997). Unraveling the process of creative destruction: complementary assets and incumbent survival in the typesetter industry. *Strategic Management Journal, 18*, 119–142.

[790] Leonard-Barton, D. (1992). Core capabilities and core rigidities: A paradox in managing new product development. *Strategic Management Journal, 13*(S1), 111–125.

[791] Zahra & George.

[792] Senivongse et al.

[793] Strang, K. D. (2009). Assessing team members' interpersonal competencies in new product development e-projects. *International Journal of Project Organisation and Management, 1*(4), 335–357.

[794] Cohen & Levinthal.

[795] Zahra & George.

[796] Cohen & Levinthal.

[797] Chuang, F., Morgan, R. E., & Robson, M. J. (2015). Customer and competitor insights, new product development competence, and new product creativity: Differential, integrative, and substitution effects. *Journal of Product Innovation Management, 32*(2), 175–182.

[798] Cohen & Levinthal.

[799] Inkpen, A. C., & Beamish, P. W. (1997). Knowledge, bargaining power, and the instability of international joint ventures. *Academy of Management Review, 22*(1), 177–202. Also, Lane, P. J., & Lubatkin, M. (1998). Relative absorptive capacity and interorganization learning. *Strategic Management Journal, 19*(5), 461–477.

[800] Zahra & George.

[801] Li, T., & Cavusgil, S. T. (1999). Measuring the dimensions of market knowledge competence in new product development. *European Journal of Innovation Management, 2*(3), 129–146.

[802] Senivongse et al.

[803] Porter, M. E. (1996, January 1). What is Strategy? *Harvard Business Review, 74*(6), 61–80.

[804] Ovans, A. (2022). What Is Strategy, Again? *Harvard Business School Cases*, 1–1254.

[805] This chapter summarizes the perspective on Knowledge Management (KM) and Knowledge Based Development (KBD) for the Anthropocene included in *A Modern Guide to Knowledge: From Knowledge Societies to Knowledge in the Anthropocene* (Carrillo, 2022). The book further explores how to understand the underlying behavioral basis of the knowledge economy and society. Chapters highlight the notion that unless a knowledge-based value creation and distribution paradigm is globally adopted, the possibilities for integration between a sustainable biosphere and a viable economy are dim.

[806] President of the World Capital Institute and Emeritus Professor of Knowledge Based Development at Tecnológico de Monterrey. Grant recipient of the National Researcher-III Distinction from CONACT, Mexico.

[807] Carrillo, F. J. (2014a) (Ed.). *Sistemas de capitales y mercados de conocimiento.* Amazon Kindle Direct Publishing.

[808] Powell, W. W., & Snellman, K. (2004). The knowledge economy. *Annual Review of Sociology, 30*, 199–220, p. 201. Also, Pandit, S. K. (2021). Managing and leveraging knowledge assets of the firm: The call of the day. In R. Bhattacharyya (Ed.), *Comparative advantage in the knowledge economy: A national and organizational resource* (pp. 181–194). Emerald Publishing.

[809] See: Carrillo, F. J. (2001a). La evolución de las especies de gestión de conocimiento [Paper presentation]. *Entorno Empresarial del Siglo XXI: Cinco años del Cluster de Conocimiento*, Parque Tecnológico de Zamudio, Bilbao, Spain. Also, Laszlo, K., & Laszlo, A. (2002). Evolving knowledge for development: The role of knowledge management in a changing world. *Journal of Knowledge Management, 6*(4), 400–412. Also, Rowley, J. (2003). Knowledge management – the new librarianship? From custodians of history to gatekeepers to the future. *Library Management, 24*(8/9), 433–440. Also, Garcia, B. (2008). Global KBD community developments: The MAKCi experience. *Journal of Knowledge Management, 12*(5), 91–106. Also, Dang, D., & Umemoto, K. (2009). Modelling the development toward the knowledge economy: A national capability approach. *Journal of Knowledge Management, 13*(5), 359–372. Also, Wang, X. (2009). *Knowledge-based urban development in China* [PhD dissertation, Newcastle University]. Also, Martínez, A. (2010). Personal knowledge management by the knowledge citizen: The generation aspect of organizational and social knowledge-based development. In K. Metaxiotis, F. J. Carrillo & T. Yigitcanlar (Eds.), *Knowledge-based development for cities and societies: Integrated multi-level approaches* (pp. 131–140). IGI Global. Also, Batra, S. (2012). Development perspectives of knowledge management. *Review of Knowledge Management, 2*(1), 17–23. Also, Edvardsson, I. R., Yigitcanlar, T., & Pancholi, S. (2016). Knowledge city research and practice under the microscope: A review of empirical findings. *Knowledge Management Research & Practice, 14*(4), 537–564. Also, Arsenijević, O., Trivan, D., Podbregar, I., & Šprajc, P. (2017). Strategic aspect of knowledge management. *Organizacija, 50*(2), 163–176. Also, Fachinelli,

A. C., Giacomello, C. P., Larentis, F., & D'Arrigo, F. (2017). Measuring the capital systems categories: The perspective of an integrated value system of social life as perceived by young citizens. *International Journal of Knowledge-Based Development, 8*(4), 334–345. Also, Lajul, W. (2018). Reconstructing African fractured epistemologies for African development. *Synthesis Philosophica, 33*(1), 51–76. Also, Yigitcanlar, T., & Inkinen, T. (2019). Theory and practice of knowledge cities and knowledge-based urban development. In *Geographies of disruption* (pp. 109–133). Springer.

[810] Neef, D., Siesfeld, G. A., & Cefola, J. (Eds.) (1998). *The economic impact of knowledge.* Routledge. Also, Barkhordari, S., Fattahi, M., & Azimi, N. A. (2019). The impact of knowledge-based economy on growth performance: Evidence from MENA countries. *Journal of the Knowledge Economy, 10*(3), 1168–1182.

[811] Bindé, J. (2005). *Towards knowledge societies: UNESCO world report.* UNESCO. Also, Faggian, A., Modrego, F., & McCann, P. (2019). Human capital and regional development. In R. Capello & P. Nijkamp (Eds.), *Handbook of regional growth and development theories* (pp. 149–171). Edward Elgar Publishing.

[812] Von Mutius, B. (2005). Rethinking leadership in the knowledge society learning from others: How to integrate intellectual and social capital and establish a new balance of value and values. In A. Bounfour & L. Edvinsson (Eds.), *Intellectual capital for communities* (pp. 151–163). Butterworth-Heinemann. Also, Dang, & Umemoto. Also, Van Wezemael, J. (2012). Concluding: Directions for building prosperous knowledge cities. In T. Yigicanlar, K. Metaxiotis & F. J. Carrillo (Eds.), *Building prosperous knowledge cities: Policies, plans and metrics* (pp. 374–382). Edward Elgar Publishing.

[813] The point is to emphasize the difference between unconditioned and conditioned stimuli, rather than asserting an absolute positivist ontology where reality elements can be directly grasped. Similarities between object oriented ontology (OOO), Peircean semiotics and operant conditioning are further explored in Carrillo (2022), Chapters 1, 2 and 4.

[814] See Ray Hudson's (2011, p. 2) reference to Sum and Jessop's (2008) *Towards a Cultural Political Economy*: "those versions of cultural political economy (for example, Sum and Jessop, 2008) that seek more explicitly to incorporate consideration of issues of meaning and semiosis with more traditional concerns of commodity production and value". Sum and Jessop's treatment of semiotics as sensemaking has particular significance for the context dimension of knowledge discussed above. Here, I concur with their characterization of *Towards a Cultural Political Economy* as a "post-disciplinary" approach "concerned with the semiotic and structural aspects of social life and, even more importantly, their articulation" (Sum & Jessop, 2008, p. 1) as well as with their subscription to Peirce's semantic framework (Ibid., p. 4).

[815] Smil, V. (2014). *Making the modern world: Materials and dematerialization.* John Wiley & Sons. Also, Devictor, V. (2017). The biophysical realities of ecosystems. In C. L. Spash (Ed.), *Routledge handbook of ecological economics: Nature and society* (pp. 99–107). Routledge. Also, Dieter, A. (2017). Geophysical limits, raw material use and their policy implications. In C. L. Spash (Ed.), *Routledge handbook of ecological economics: Nature and society* (pp. 99–107). Routledge.

[816] Smith, P., & Max-Neef, M. (2011). *Economics unmasked: From power and greed to compassion and the common good.* Green Books.

[817] Spash, C. L. (2021, June). *Social ecological economics* (Discussion Paper No. sre-disc-2021_06). Institute for Multi-Level Governance & Development, Department of Socioeconomics, Vienna University of Economics and Business.

[818] Hodgson, G. M. (2012). *From pleasure machines to moral communities: An evolutionary economics without Homo economicus.* University of Chicago Press. Also, Kenter, J. O. (2017). Deliberative monetary valuation. In C. L. Spash (Ed.), *Routledge handbook of ecological economics: Nature and society* (pp. 251–361). Routledge.

[819] For example, those dimensions in quotes from André Gorz and Robert F. Kennedy in Carrillo, (2022), Chapter 2.

[820] Carrillo, F. J. (2006b). From transitional to radical knowledge-based development. *Journal of Knowledge Management, 10*(5), 3–5. Also, Hodgson.

[821] Mayumi, K. T. (2017). Thermodynamics: Relevance, implications, misuse, and ways forward. In C. L. Spash (Ed.), *Routledge handbook of ecological economics: Nature and society* (pp. 89–98). Routledge.

[822] There is an increasing awareness and empirical evidence on these phenomena happening among animals.

[823] Quoted in Daly, H. (2009, 12 July). The economic thought of Frederick Soddy. Bill Totten's Weblog. Retrieved 6 March, 2022 from http:// billtotten.blogspot.com/ 2009/07/economic -thought -of -frederick -soddy .html, n.p.

[824] Carrillo (1998). Also, Graeber, D. (2001). *Toward an anthropological theory of value.* Palgrave Macmillan.

[825] Hubbard, D. W. (2007). *How to measure anything: Finding the value of intangibles in business.* John Wiley & Sons.

[826] Rutherford, M., & Samuels, W. J. (Eds.) (1996). *John R. Commons: Selected essays volume two.* Routledge. Also, Carrillo, F. J. (Ed.) (2006a). *Knowledge cities: Approaches, experiences, and perspectives.* Butterworth-Heinemann. Also, Carrillo (2006b). Also, Stiglitz, J., Sen, A., & Fitoussi, J. (2009). *Report by the Commission on the measurement of economic performance and social progress.* CMEPSP. Also, Carrillo, F. J., & Batra, S. (2012). Understanding and measurement: Perspectives on the evolution of knowledge-based development. *International Journal of Knowledge-Based Development, 3*(1), 1–16.

[827] Braudel, F. (1992). *Civilization and capitalism, 15th–18th century. Volume 1: The structure of everyday life.* University of California Press. Also, Segall, D. (2012, 19 March). Cosmopolitical reflections on economy, society, and religion. *Footnotes2Plato.* Retrieved 6 March 2022 from https://footnotes2plato.com/2012/03/19/cosmopolitical-reflections-on-economy-society-and-religion/. Also, Smith, P., & Max-Neef, M. (2011). *Economics unmasked: From power and greed to compassion and the common good.* Green Books.

[828] Reiss, M. (2011). *What went wrong with economics: The flawed assumptions that led economists astray.* CreateSpace Independent Publishing Platform.

[829] Soddy, F. ([1926] 1983). *Wealth, virtual wealth, and debt.* George Allen & Unwin/Omni. Also, Harris, M. (1974). *Cows, pigs, wars & witches: The riddles of culture.* Random House. Also, Sraffa, P. (1975). *Production of commodities by means of commodities: Prelude to a critique of economic theory.* Cambridge University Press. Also, Gudeman, S. F. (1986). *Economics as culture: Models and metaphors of livelihood.* Routledge. Also, Braudel.

[830] Grant, R. M. (2002). The knowledge-based view of the firm. In C. W. Choo & N. Bontis (Eds.), *The strategic management of intellectual capital and organizational knowledge* (pp. 133–148). Oxford University Press. Also, Morroni, M. (2006). *Knowledge, scale, and transactions in the theory of the firm.* Cambridge University Press. Also, Sveiby, K. (2001). A knowledge-based theory of the firm to guide in strategy formulation. *Journal of Intellectual Capital, 2*(4), 344–358. Also, Von Krog, G., & Grand, S. (2002). From economic theory toward a knowledge-based theory of the firm. In C. W. Choo & N. Bontis (Eds.), *The strategic management of intellectual capital and organizational knowledge* (pp. 163–183). Oxford University Press.

[831] Asian Development Bank (2007, March). *Moving toward knowledge-based economies: Asian experiences.* Retrieved 6 March 2022 from https://www.adb.org/sites/default/files/publication/29699/knowledge -based -economies.pdf. Also, Romer, P. M. (1990). *Endogenous technological change. Journal of Political Economy, 98*(5, Part 2), S71–S102. Also, Wurzburg, G. (1998). Markets and the knowledge economy: Is anything broken? Can government fix it? *Journal of Knowledge Management, 2*(1), 32–46.

[832] Gudeman.

[833] There is now a Society for Economic Anthropology and a dedicated journal, Economic Anthropology (Wiley Online).

[834] The Goldilocks principle is applied to describe the exceptional climatic conditions of the Holocene that made possible the emergence of cities, agriculture and civilizations at large. By extension, it refers here to an economic culture that takes such conditions for granted and that is bound to end with the end of the Holocene.

[835] Schumacher (1989). *Small is beautiful: A study of economics as if people mattered.* HarperPerennial, pp. 60–61.

[836] Gorz, p. 168.

[837] Dolphijn, p. 152.

[838] Smil, p. 173.

[839] Gough, I. (2020, 28 April). In times of climate breakdown, how do we value what matters? *OpenDemocracy.* Retrieved 6 March 2022 from https://www.opendemocracy.net/en/oureconomy/times-climate-breakdown-how-do-we-value-what-matters/.

[840] Ibid.

[841] Aeron-Thomas, D., Nicholls, J., Forster, S., & Westall, A. (2004). *Social return on investment: Valuing what matters.* New Economics Foundation. Also, Carrillo (2014a) .Also, Lambe, P. (2023). *Principles of knowledge auditing. Foundations for knowledge management implementation.* The MIT Press.

[842] Aeron-Thomas et al., p. 2.

[843] Roman, P., & Thiry, G. (2017). Sustainability indicators. In C. L. Spash (Ed.), *Routledge handbook of ecological economics: Nature and society* (pp. 382–392). Routledge, p. 390.

[844] Carrillo, F. J. (2016a). Knowledge markets: A typology and an overview. *International Journal of Knowledge-based Development, 7*(3), 264–289.

[845] Firestone, J., & McElroy, M. (2002). Generations of knowledge management. *Knowledge and Innovation: Journal of the KMCI, 2*(2), 111–122. Also, Rezgui, Y., Hopfe, C., & Vorakulpipat, C. (2010). Generations of knowledge management in the architecture, engineering, and construction industry: An evolutionary perspective. *Advanced Engineering Informatics, 24*(2), 219–228.

[846] Carrillo (2001a). Also, Laszlo & Laszlo. Also, Rowley. Also, Wang, X., & Lihua, R. (2006). Examining knowledge management factors in the creation of new city: Empirical evidence from Zhengdong New District, Zhengzhou, China. *Journal of Technology Management in China, 1*(3), 243–261. Also, Garcia (2008). Also, Dang & Umemoto. Also, Wang. Also, Martínez. Also, Rezgui, Y., Hopfe, C., & Vorakulpipat, C. (2010). Generations of knowledge management in the architecture, engineering, and construction industry: An evolutionary perspective. *Advanced Engineering Informatics, 24*(2), 219–228. Also, Batra, S. (2012). Development perspectives of knowledge management. *Review of Knowledge Management, 2*(1), 17–23. Also, Tzortzaki, A. M., & Mihiotis, A. (2014). A review of knowledge management theory and future directions. *Knowledge and Process Management, 21*(1), 29–41. Also, Edvardsson et al. Also, Arsenijević, O., Trivan, D., Podbregar, I., & Šprajc, P. (2017). Strategic aspect of knowledge management. *Organizacija, 50*(2), 163–176. Also, Fachinelli et al. (2017). Also, Lajul. Also, Yigitcanlar, T., & Inkinen, T. (2019). Theory and practice of knowledge cities and knowledge-based urban development. In *Geographies of disruption* (pp. 109–133). Springer.

[847] Henderson, J. C., & Venkatraman, H. (1999). Strategic alignment: Leveraging information technology for transforming organizations. *IBM Systems Journal, 38*(2/3), 472–484.

[848] Bosua, R., & Venkitachalam, K. (2013). Aligning strategies and processes in knowledge management: A framework. *Journal of Knowledge Management, 17*(3), 331–346, p. 332.

[849] Anfinsen's principle, coined in the early 1960s, is perhaps the most fundamental tenet of protein folding, "stating that the three-dimensional structure of small, globular proteins can be wholly and uniquely determined by the sequence of amino acids in the polypeptide chain" (Kirshenbaum & Zuckermann, 2019, p. 1).

[850] Wiig (1993b). Also, Carrillo (1998). Also, Bennet, A., & Bennet, D. (2014). Knowledge, theory, and practice in knowledge management: Between associative patterning and context-rich action. *Journal of Entrepreneurship, Management, and Innovation, 10*(4), 7–55.

[851] Peters, L. D., Löbler, H., Brodie, R. J., Breidbach, C. F., Hollebeek, L. D., Smith, S., Sörhammar, D., & Varey, R. J. (2014). Theorizing about resource integration through service-dominant logic. *Marketing Theory, 14*(3), 249–268.

[852] Carrillo, 1998. Also, Carrillo, F. J., & Galvis-Lista, E. (2014). Procesos de gestión de conocimiento desde el enfoque de sistemas de valor basados en conocimiento. Ideas

CONCYTEG, 9(107), 3–22. Also, Fachinelli, A. C., Carrillo, F. J., & D'Arisbo, A. (2014a). Capital system, creative economy, and knowledge city transformation: Insights from Bento Gonçalves, Brazil. *Expert Systems with Applications, 41*(12), 5614–5624. Also, Fachinelli et al. (2017). Also, Martensson, M. (2000). A critical review of knowledge management as a management tool. *Journal of Knowledge Management, 4*(3), 204–216. Also, Van Wezemael, J. (2012). Concluding: Directions for building prosperous knowledge cities. In T. Yigicanlar, K. Metaxiotis & F. J. Carrillo (Eds.), *Building prosperous knowledge cities: Policies, plans and metrics* (pp. 374–382). Edward Elgar Publishing. Also, Von Mutius.

[853] Strictly, fire is a chemical reaction as per the basic equation fuel + oxygen → carbon dioxide + water. Flames occur because of the two gases' reaction, producing heat and light. A practical approach to managing fire thus focuses on the adequate convergence of fuel and oxygen to generate a flame. See *New Scientist* (2021, 1 March), "What is fire?", retrieved 4 July, 2022 from https://www.newscientist.com/question/what-is-fire/.

[854] The "fire triangle" is a pragmatic model for preventing and controlling fire. When a chain reaction is added to this model, the "fire tetrahedron" emerges: a more complete model for fire management. Cf. https:// fire-risk-assessment-network.com/blog/fire-triangle-tetrahedron/, retrieved 6 March, 2022.

[855] This triadic model has some similarities with Charles S. Peirce's three foundational categories of his Theory of Signs. Even if throughout this book there are several acknowledgments to Pragmatism and to Peirce in particular, the KM model was developed independently, and each serves a fairly different purpose. In the case of Peirce's Semiotics, we are talking about high-order signifiers: predicates of predicates. He proposed his three universal categories in response to the logical categories of Aristotle, Kant, and Hegel (Peirce, 1868). In the case of the KM model, we are talking about necessary and sufficient conditions for a phenomenon. Although less prominent, there are also some resonances with Yrjö Engeström's activity system (Engeström, 1987). However, the similarities are of form rather than substance. Engeström's triangle was originally an attempt to represent Leontiev's activity system, which has undergone multiple variations within activity theory.

[856] Wiig (1993b).

[857] Merrill, M. D. (2002). Knowledge objects and mental models. In D. A. Wiley (Ed.), *The instructional use of learning objects* (pp. 261–280). Agency for Instructional Technology and Association for Educational Communications & Technology.

[858] Birkinshaw, J., & Sheehan, T. (2002). Managing the knowledge life cycle. *MIT Sloan Management Review, 44*(1), 75–84.

[859] Cohen, S. (1987). Knowledge, Context and Social Standards. *Synthese, 73*(1). 3-26

[860] Jarrahi, M. H., Askay, D., Eshraghi, A., & Smith, P. (2023). Artificial intelligence and knowledge management: A partnership between human and AI. *Business Horizons, 66*(1), 87-99. Also, Roger, J. (2023). *Putting content back on the throne.* Infosys Case Study.

[861] Schultze, U., & Stabell, C. (2004). Knowing what you don't know? Discourses and contradictions in knowledge management research. *Journal of Management Studies, 41*(4), 549–573.

[862] Ibid., pp. 558–559.

[863] Bhatt, G. (2001). Knowledge management in organizations: Examining the interaction between technologies, techniques, and people. *Journal of Knowledge Management, 5*(1), 68–75, p. 70.

[864] Marakas, G. M. (1999). *Decision support system in the 21st century.* Prentice Hall.

[865] Dignum, V. (2006). An overview of agents in knowledge management. In M. Umeda, A. Wolf, O. Bartenstein, U. Geske, D. Seipel & O. Takata (Eds.), *Conference proceeding: Declarative programming for knowledge management: 16th International Conference on Applications of Declarative Programming and Knowledge Management, INAP 2005.* Fukuoka, Japan (pp. 175–189). Springer. Also, Foss, N.J., & Mahnke, V. (2011). Knowledge creation in firms: An organizational economics perspective. In M. Easterby-Smith & M. A. Lyles (Eds.), *Handbook of organizational learning and knowledge management* (2nd ed., pp. 125–151). John Wiley & Sons.

[866] Schultze & Stabell, p. 558.

867 Gold, A. H., Malhotra, A., & Segars, A. H. (2001). Knowledge management: An organizational capabilities perspective. *Journal of Management Information Systems, 18*(1), 185–214.

868 Alavi, M., & Leidner, D. (2001). Knowledge management and knowledge management systems: Conceptual foundations and research issues. *MIS Quarterly, 25*(1), 107–136. Also, Yoo, K., Suh, E., & Kim, K. Y. (2007). Knowledge flow-based business process redesign: Applying a knowledge map to redesign a business process. *Journal of Knowledge Management, 11*(3), 104–125.

869 Bennet et al. (2007).

870 Foss, N.J., & Mahnke, V. (2011). Knowledge creation in firms: An organizational economics perspective. In M. Easterby-Smith & M. A. Lyles (Eds.), *Handbook of organizational learning and knowledge management* (2nd ed., pp. 125–151). John Wiley & Sons.

871 Bersin, J., Geller, J., Wakefield, N., & Brett, W. (2016). *Global human capital trends 2016.* Deloitte University Press.

872 Saenz, J., & Perez-Bouvier, A. (2014). Interaction with external agents, innovation networks, and innovation capability: The case of Uruguayan software firms. *Journal of Knowledge Management, 18*(2), 447–468.

873 Tzortzak & Mihiotis. Also, Magala, S. J. (2017). Philosophy of science or knowledge management? *Journal of Organizational Change Management, 30*(4), 454–455.

874 Knorr-Cetina, K. D. (2013). *The manufacture of knowledge: An essay on the constructivist and contextual nature of science.* Elsevier.

875 Bhatt.

876 Nonaka, I., & Konno, N. (1998). The concept of "ba": Building a foundation for knowledge creation. *California Management Review, 40*(3), 40–54.

877 In Klingan, K., Sepahvand, A., Rosol, C., & Scherer, B. M. (Eds.) (2015). *Textures of the Anthropocene: Grain vapor ray* (4 vols. and a manual). MIT Press.

878 Kantor, J. R. (1959). *Interbehavioral psychology. A sample of scientific system construction.* Principia Press.

879 Asrar-ul-Haq, M., & Anwar, S. (2016). A systematic review of knowledge management and knowledge sharing: Trends, issues, and challenges. *Cogent Business & Management, 3*(1), Article 1127744. Also, Bennet et al. (2007).

880 Dervin, B. (1998). Sense-making theory and practice: An overview of user interests in knowledge seeking and use. *Journal of Knowledge Management, 2*(2), 36–46.

881 Weick, K. (1995). *Sensemaking in organizations.* SAGE.

882 Haraway, D. J. (1988). Situated knowledges: The science question in feminism and the privilege of partial perspective. *Feminist Studies, 14*(3), 575–599.p. 590.

883 Liedloff, J. (1977). *The continuum concept.* Addison-Wesley.

884 Thompson, M. P. A., & Walsham, G. (2004). Placing knowledge management in context. *Journal of Management Studies, 41*(5), 725–747.

885 Hay, C. (2002). *Political analysis: A critical introduction.* Palgrave Macmillan, p. 94.

886 Preyer, G., & Peter, G. (2005). *Contextualism in philosophy: Knowledge, meaning, and truth.* Oxford University Press.

887 Zack, M. (1999). Developing a knowledge strategy. *California Management Review, 41*(3), 125–145. Also, Liebold, M., Probst, G., & Gibber, M. (2005). *Strategic management in the knowledge economy: New approaches and business applications.* John Wiley & Sons. Also, Carrillo, F. J., & Galvis-Lista, E. (2014). Procesos de gestión de conocimiento desde el enfoque de sistemas de valor basados en conocimiento. *Ideas CONCYTEG, 9*(107), 3–22. Also, Fachinelli et al. (2017).

888 Bhatt.

889 Greiner, M., Bohmann, T., & Krcmar, H. (2007). Strategy for knowledge management. *Journal of Knowledge Management, 11*(6), 3–15. Also, Oluikpe, P. (2012). Developing a corporate knowledge management strategy. *Journal of Knowledge Management, 16*(6), 862–878.

890 Henderson & Venkatraman. Also, Powell, W. W., & Snellman, K. (2004). The knowledge economy. *Annual Review of Sociology, 30*, 199–220.

[891] Hanson, J., Melnyk, S., & Calantone, R. (2011). Defining and measuring alignment in performance management. *International Journal of Operations and Production Management, 31*(10), 1089–1114.

[892] Carrillo (1998). Also, Clare, M. (2002). Solving the knowledge-value equation (part one). *Knowledge Management Review, 5*(2), 14–17.

[893] Bellantuono, N., Pontrandolfo, P., & Scozzi, B. (2013). Different practices for open innovation: A context-based approach. *Journal of Knowledge Management, 17*(4), 558–568.

[894] Augier, M., Shariq, S. Z., & Thanning Vendelø, M. (2001). Understanding context: Its emergence, transformation, and role in tacit knowledge sharing. *Journal of Knowledge Management, 5*(2), 125–137. Also, Nan, N. (2008). A principal–agent model for incentive design in knowledge sharing. *Journal of Knowledge Management, 12*(3), 101–113.

[895] Saint-Onge, H. (1996). Tacit knowledge: The key to the strategic alignment of intellectual capital. *Planning Review, 24*(2), 10–16.

[896] du Toit, A. (2003). Knowledge: A sense making process shared through narrative. *Journal of Knowledge Management, 7*(3), 27–37.

[897] Dulipovici, A., & Robey, D. (2013). Strategic alignment and misalignment of knowledge management systems: A social representation perspective. *Journal of Management Information Systems, 29*(4), 103–126.

[898] Stary, C. (2014). Non-disruptive knowledge and business processing in knowledge life cycles – Aligning value network analysis to process management. *Journal of Knowledge Management, 18*(4), 651–686.

[899] Bontis, N., & Fitz-Enz, J. (2002). Intellectual capital ROI: A causal map of human capital antecedents and consequents. *Journal of Intellectual Capital, 3*(3), 223–247.

[900] Petrash, G. (1996). Dow's journey to a knowledge value management culture. *European Management Journal, 14*(4), 365–373.

[901] Greiner et al. Also, Hanson, J., Melnyk, S., & Calantone, R. (2011). Defining and measuring alignment in performance management. *International Journal of Operations and Production Management, 31*(10), 1089–1114. Also, Oluikpe.

[902] Stewart, T. (1996*). Intellectual capital: The new wealth of organizations*. McGraw-Hill. Also, Magrassi, P. (2002, 18 July). A taxonomy of intellectual capital (Research Note No. COM-17-1985). Gartner Research. Retrieved 6 March 2022 from https://www.researchgate.net/profile/Paolo -Magrassi-2/publication/279013374ATaxonomy_ofIntellectualCapital/links/5589004908ae347f9bdac8f3/A-Taxonomy-of-Intellectual-Capital.pdf?origin=publicationdetail.

[903] Carrillo (2002).

[904] Garnåsjordet, P. A., Aslaksen, I., Giampietro, M., Funtowicz, S., & Ericson, T. (2012). Sustainable development indicators: From statistics to policy. *Environmental Policy and Governance, 22*(5), 322–336, p. 330.

[905] Carrillo, F. J. (2022). *A modern guide to knowledge. From knowledge economies to knowledge in the anthropocene.* Edward Elgar.

[906] McAdam, R., & McCreedy, S. (1999). A critical review of knowledge management models. *The learning organization, 6*(3), 91–100. Also, Kucza, T. (2001). *Knowledge management process model*. VTT Technical Research Centre of Finland. Also, Gold et al. Also, Kakabadse, N., Kakabadse, A., & Kouzim, A. (2003). Reviewing the knowledge management literature: Towards a taxonomy. *Journal of Knowledge Management, 7*(4), 75–91. Also, Holsapple, C., & Jones, K. (2004). Exploring primary activities of knowledge chain. *Knowledge and Process Management, 11*(3), 155–174. Also, Han, W.-H., & Zhong, Q-Y. (2006). Development of an instrument to measure knowledge management processes. In *Proceedings of the International Conference on Management Science and Engineering (ICMSE)* (pp. 1262–1268). IEEE. Also, León, M., Ponjuan, G., & Rodríguez, M. (2006). Procesos estratégicos de gestión del conocimiento. *ACIMED, 14*(2). Also, Chen, L., & Mohamed, S. (2007). Empirical study of interactions between knowledge management activities. Engineering, *Construction and Architectural Management, 14*(3), 242–260. Also, León, M., Castañeda, D., & Sánchez, I. (2007). La gestión del conocimiento en las organizaciones de información: Procesos y métodos para medir. *ACIMED, 15*(3). Also, Lin,

C., Yen, D., & Tarn, D..(2007). An industry-level knowledge management model– a study of information-related industry in Taiwan. *Information & Management, 44*(1), 22–39. Also, Barragán, A. (2009). Aproximación a una taxonomía de modelos de gestión del conocimiento. *Intangible Capital, 5*(1), 65–101. Also, Heisig, P. (2009). Harmonisation of knowledge management – comparing 160 KM frameworks around the globe. *Journal of Knowledge Management, 13*(4), 4–31. Also, Hsieh, J., Lin, B., & Lin, C. (2009). The construction and application of knowledge navigator model (KNM™): An evaluation of knowledge management maturity. *Expert Systems with Applications, 36*(2), 4087–4100. Also, Santos, M., & Dante, G. (2011). Propuesta de un modelo de medición para los procesos de la gestión del conocimiento en organizaciones de información. *Revista Interamericana de Bibliotecología, 34*(1), 87–103.

[907] Carrillo, 1996a, 1996b, 1998. Also, Firestone & McElroy, 2002. Also, Laszlo & Laszlo, 2002. Also, Skyrme, D. J. (2002). What next for knowledge management? Development and challenges. *I3 Update, 57.* Also, Rowley. Also, López, M., Cuesta, A., & Joyanes, L. (2008). *Ciudad-región conocedora: Gestión de conocimiento para una ciudad-región.* Centro Editorial Universidad de Caldas. Also, Vásquez, F., & Gabalán, J. (2009). Gestionando el conocimiento: Acercamiento conceptual en entornos organizacionales y proyección en el contexto académico. *Revista Iberoamericana de Ciencia, Tecnología y Sociedad – CTS.* Retrieved 6 March 2022 from http://www.revistacts.net/wp-content/uploads/2009/08/vazquezeditado.pdf.

[908] Carrillo, F. J. (1996a). The ways of knowledge management [Paper presentation]. The 1996 National Business Conference: The Management of Intellectual Capital and Innovation, McMaster University, Canada. Also, Carrillo, F. J. (1996b). *Managing innovation in a knowledge-based economy* [Paper presentation]. Joint Meeting of the European Association for the Study of Science and Technology and the Society for Social Studies in Science: Signatures of Knowledge Societies, Bielefeld, Germany. Also, Carrillo, 1998. Also, Carrillo (2001a). Also, Carrillo (2002). Also, Martínez, A. (2001). Un modelo de procesos clave de administración del conocimiento. *Transferencia, 14*(53), 28–29. Also, Bennet & Bennet (2014). Also, Chaparro, F. (2006). *Construyendo una ciudad-región del conocimiento en Bogotá.* Universidad del Rosario/Alcaldía Mayor de Bogotá.
, 2006. Also, Carrillo & Galvis-Lista, 2014.

[909] Sarimin, M., & Yigitcanlar, T. (2012). Towards a comprehensive and integrated knowledge-based urban development model: Status quo and directions. *International Journal of Knowledge-Based Development, 3*(2), 175–192. Also, Yigitcanlar, T., & Inkinen, T. (2019). Theory and practice of knowledge cities and knowledge-based urban development. In *Geographies of disruption* (pp. 109–133). Springer.

[910] (Carrillo, 2006a Also, World Capital Institute (WCI) & Teleos (2007 onwards). *The annual MAKCi report.* WCI.

[911] D'Arisbo, A. (2014). *Sistemas de capitais como método de análise da economia criativa para o desenvolvimento baseado no conhecimento na cidade de Bento Gonçalves* [Doctoral dissertation, Universidade de Caxias do Sul]. Also, Fachinelli, A. C., Giacomello, C. P., & Larentis, F. (2014b). The influence of capital system categories on Human Development Index in Brazil. *International Journal of Knowledge-Based Development, 6*(4), 350–369. Also, Fachinelli et al, (2014a).

[912] Ramírez, G. (2007). En búsqueda del desarrollo basado en conocimiento en Chile. In A. Mújika (Ed.), *Regiones iberomericanas del conocimiento* (pp. 187–213). Universidad de Deusto.

[913] Chaparro. Also, López, M., Cuesta, A., & Joyanes, L. (2008). *Ciudad-región conocedora: Gestión de conocimiento para una ciudad-región.* Centro Editorial Universidad de Caldas. Also, Vásquez & Gabalán Also, Zuluaga, N. (2013). *Metamorfosis de la libélula: Construcción teórica de un modelo para Manizales en la búsqueda de un sistema urbano de conocimiento.* Universidad de Manizales. Retrieved 6 March 2022 from https://ridum.umanizales.edu.co/xmlui/bitstream/handle/20.500.12746/742/Metamorfosis %20de %20la %20Lib%C3%A9lula.pdf?sequence=1&isAllowed=y.

[914] Pleitez, J., & Flamenco, E. (2007). Desarrollo basado en conocimiento aplicado a la marginalidad y probreza urbana en el Salvador. In F. Casado (Ed.), *Desarrollo basado en el conocimiento* (pp. 301–313). Comunidad Iberoamericana de Sistemas de Conocimiento.

[915] Batra, S. (2012). Development perspectives of knowledge management. *Review of Knowledge Management, 2*(1), 17–23. Also, Batra, S., Payal, R., & Carrillo F. J. (2013). Knowledge village capital framework in the Indian context. International *Journal of Knowledge-Based Development, 4*(3), 222–244.

[916] Carrillo, F. J., & Arce, G. (2020). *Arequipa, ciudad de conocimiento: Project report.* WCI/UNSA. Also, Carrillo, F. J., Arce, G., Ugarte, W., Portugal, A., Torres, G., & Sánchez, G. (2022). Intelligence capital: The management of knowledge assets and development of adaptive capacities in the city of Arequipa. *Intangible Capital, 18*(2), 163–181. Also, Lara, J. (2000). *Administración del conocimiento en el sector público: Administración tributaria del Perú* [MSc dissertation, Tecnológico de Monterrey].

[917] Arboníes, A. L. (Ed.) (2006). *Conocimiento para innovar: Cómo evitar la miopía en la gestión del conocimiento.* Ediciones Díaz de Santos. Also, Casado, F. (Ed.) (2007). *Desarrollo basado en el conocimiento: Transferencia de conocimiento.* Comunidad Iberoamericana de Sistemas de Conocimiento. Also, Lasheras, I. (2006). *Legazpi bai! El proyecto.* Mondragón Innovation and Knowledge.

[918] Garcia, B. (2004). Developing futures: A knowledge-based capital for Manchester. *Journal of Knowledge Management, 8*(5), 47–60. Also, Garcia, B. (2006). Learning conversations: Knowledge, meanings and learning networks in Greater Manchester. *Journal of Knowledge Management, 10*(5), 99–109.

[919] Carrillo & Galvis-Vista, 2014.

[920] Chase, R., & Carrillo, F. J. (2007). *The 2007 most admired knowledge city report.* World Capital Institute and Teleos. Also, Garcia, B., & Chavez, D. (2014). Network-based innovation systems: A capital base for the Monterrey city-region, Mexico. *Expert Systems with Applications, 41*(12), 5636–5646.

[921] Zapata, L. Manrique, L., Carrillo, F. J., Flores, P., Ramírez, P. Martínez, A., Treviño, A. & Valerio, G., *Aprendizaje organizacional.* McGraw-Hill.

[922] Carrillo (2002). Also, Carrillo (2014a).

[923] Zapata et al, 2011.

[924] Ibid.

[925] Valerio-Ureña, G. (2014). Capital instrumental. In F. J. Carrillo (Ed.), *Sistemas de capitales y mercados de conocimiento* (pp. 154–163). Amazon Kindle Direct Publishing.

[926] Carrillo (2022), p. 223.

[927] Nussbaum, M., & Sen, A. (Eds.) (1993). *The quality of life.* Clarendon Press. Also, Marans, R. W., & Stimson, R. (2011). *Investigating quality of urban life.* Springer.

[928] Sen, A. (1985). *Commodities and capabilities.* North-Holland. Also, United Nations Development Program (UNDP) (2020). *Human development report 2020: The next frontier: human development and the Anthropocene.* UNDP.

[929] Eid, M., & Larsen, R. J. (Eds.) (2008). *The science of subjective well-being.* Guilford Press. Also, Stone A., & Mackie C. (Eds.) (2013). *Subjective well-being: Measuring happiness, suffering, and other dimensions of experience.* National Academies Press.

[930] World Commission on Environment and Development (WCED) (1987). *Our common future.* Oxford University Press. Also, Göpel, M. (2016). *The great mindshift: How a new economic paradigm and sustainability transformations go hand in hand.* Springer.

[931] Goodin, R., Rice, J., Parpo A., & Eriksson, L. (2008). *Discretionary time: A new measure for freedom.* Cambridge University Press.

[932] The relationship between KM, KBD and these alternative perspectives on development is discussed in Carrillo, 2022 (pp. 245-247).

[933] Carrillo, F. J. (2014b). What "knowledge-based" stands for? A position paper. *International Journal of Knowledge-Based Development, 5*(4), 402–421. Also, Carrillo, F. J. (2015). Knowledge-based development as a new economic culture. *Journal of Open Innovation: Technology, Market, and Complexity, 1*(1), 1–17.

934 Rist, G. (2019). *The history of development: From western origins to global faith* (4th ed.). Zed Books.

935 Sachs, W. (Ed.) (1992). *The development dictionary: A guide to knowledge as power*. Zed Books.

936 Rist, p. 30.

937 Esteva, G. (1995). Beyond development and modernity: Regenerating the art of living. In A. Ruprecht & C. Taiana (Eds.), *The reordering of culture: Latin America, the Caribbean and Canada in the hood* (pp. 319–337). Carleton University Press, p. 321.

938 Brinkerhoff, J. M. (2002). Review of Gilbert Rist's The history of development: From western origins to global faith. *Economic Development and Cultural Change, 51*(1), 262–266, p. 262).

939 Cfr. "Rise and Fall of the Development Brand" section in Carrillo, 2022, pp. 237-252. Even if the idea showed some resistance to die, as the literature shows, it has increasingly stagnated.

940 Ziai, A. (2019). *The development dictionary @25: Post-development and its consequences*. Routledge

941 Latour, B., & Weibel, P. (Eds.) (2020). *Critical zones: The science and politics of landing on earth*. MIT Press and ZKM Centre for Art and Media, p. 23 (original emphasis).

942 Spash.

943 Schmelzer, M., Vetter, A. & Vantsinjan, A. (2022). *The future is degrowth*. Verso.

944 This has been the central purpose of the World Capital Institute from the start.

945 Foray, D. (2004). *Economics of knowledge*. MIT Press, p. 93.

946 Dieter, A. (2017). Geophysical limits, raw material use and their policy implications. In C. L. Spash (Ed.), *Routledge handbook of ecological economics: Nature and society* (pp. 99–107). Routledge, p. 99.

947 Phelps, E. (2013). *Mass flourishing: How grassroots innovation created jobs, challenge, and change*. Princeton University Press.

948 Rosa, H. (2019). *Resonance: A sociology of our relationship to the world*. Polity, p. 22.

949 P2P Foundation describing Wolfgang Hoeschele's book, *The Economics of Abundance: A Political Economy of Freedom, Equity, and Sustainability* (2010). Retrieved 6 March 2022 from https://wiki.p2pfoundation .net/ Economics of Abundance.

950 Von Bertalanffy, L. (1968). *General systems theory: Foundations, development, applications*. George Braziller.

951 Weinberg, G. M. (1975). *An introduction to general systems thinking*. John Wiley & Sons. Also, Sutherland, J. W. (1975). *Systems analysis, administration, and architecture*. Van Nostrand Reinhold Company.

952 von Bertalanffy, L., & Rapoport, A (Eds.) (1964). *General systems: Yearbook of the society for general systems research*, vol IX. The Society for General Systems Research. Also, Pattee, H. H. (1973). *Hierarchy theory: The challenge of complex systems*. George Braziller. Also, Laszlo, E. (1972). *The systems view of the world*. George Braziller. Also, Laszlo, E. (Ed.) (1973). *The world system: Models, norms, variations*. George Braziller. Also, Laszlo, E. (1999). *The systems view of the world: A holistic vision for our time*. Hampton Press, Inc. Also, van Gigch, J.P. (1978). *Applied general systems theory*. Harper & Row Publishers.

953 Koestler, A., & Smythies, J. R. (1969). *Beyond reductionism: New perspectives in the life sciences. The Alpbach Symposium*. Beacon Press.

954 Forrester, J. W. (1961). *Industrial dynamics*. Productivity Press.

955 Morrison, F. (1991). *The art of modeling dynamic systems: Forecasting for chaos, randomness, and determinism*. John Wiley & Sons., Inc. Also, Hannon, B., & Ruth, M. (1997). *Modeling dynamic biological systems*. Springer-Verlag.

956 Morecroft, J. D. W., & Sterman, J. D. (Eds.) (194). *Modeling for learning organizations*. Productivity Press. Also, Vennix, J. A. M. (1996). *Group model building: Facilitating team learning using system dynamics*. John Wiley & Sons.

957 Miller, J. G.

958 Senge.

[959] Kim, D. H. (1995). *Systems thinking tools: A user's reference guide*. Pegasus. Also, Anderson, V., & Johnson, L. (1997). *Systems thinking basics: From concepts to causal loops*. Pegasus Communications, Inc.

[960] O'Connor, J., & McDermott, I. (1997). *The art of systems thinking*. HarperCollins Publishers.

[961] Checkland, P., & Holwell, s. (1998). *Information, systems and information systems: Making sense of the field*. John Wiley & Sons. Also, Stonier (1997).

[962] Laszlo, E. (1999). The systems view of the world: A holistic vision for our time. Hampton Press, Inc.

[963] Volk, T. (1998). *Gaia's body: Toward a physiology of Earth*. Springer-Verlag. Also, Myers, N. (1984). *GAIA: An atlas of planet management*. Anchor Books. Also, Gardner, J. N. (2003). *Biocosm: The new scientific theory of evolution: Intelligent lilfe is the architect of the universe*. Inner Ocean Publishing, Inc.

[964] Luhmann, N. (1995). *Social systems*. Stanford University Press.

[965] Smolin, L. (1997). *The life of the cosmos*. Oxford University Press. Also, Leslie, J. (Ed.) (1998). *Modern cosmology and philosophy*. Prometheus Books. Also, Callender, C., & Huggett, N. (2001). *Physics meets philosophy at the Planck scale: Contemporary theories in quantum gravity*. Cambridge University Press. Also, Harrison, E. (2003). *Masks of the universe: Changing ideas on the nature of the cosmos*. Cambridge University Press. Also, Omnes, R. (1999). *Quantum philosophy: Understanding and interpreting contemporary science*. Princeton University Press.

[966] Ricard, M., & Thuan, T. X. (2001). *The quantum and the lotus: A journey to the frontiers where science and Buddhism meet*. Crown Publishers.

[967] Bohm, D. (1992). *Thought as a system*. Routledge.

[968] Capra, F. (1996). *The web of life: A new scientific understanding of living systems*. Anchor Books, Doubleday.

[969] Simon, H. A. (1996). *The sciences of the artificial*. The MIT Press, p188.

[970] Ibid., p. 93.

[971] Harold, F. M. (2001). *The way of the cell: Molecules, organisms and the order of life*. Oxford University Press.

[972] Bennet & Bennet (2004).

[973] Edelman & Tononi.

[974] Checkland & Holwell.

[975] Meyer & Davis.

[976] Bennet & Bennet, 2003.

[977] Ackoff, R. L. (1978). *The art of problem solving: Accompanied by Ackoff's fables*. John Wiley & Sons.

[978] Argyris, C. (1990). *Overcoming organizational defenses: Facilitating organizational learning*. Prentice Hall.

[979] Calaprice, A. (2000). *The expanded quotable Einstein*. Princeton University Press.

[980] Wheatley.

[981] Axelrod & Cohen.

[982] Stacy, R. D. (1992). *Managing the unknowable: Strategic boundaries between order and chaos in organizations*. Jossey-Bass, Inc. Also, McMaster, M. D. (1996). *The intelligent advantage: Organizing for complexity*. Butterworth-Heinemann.

[983] von Clausewitz, General C. (1984/2010). On war. CreateSpace Independent Publishing Platform, p. 119.

[984] The United States Marine Corps (1994). *Warfighting: The U.S. Marine Corps book of strategy*. Doubleday.

[985] Stacy.

[986] Capra. Also, Csikszentmihalyi (2003).

[987] Holland, J. H. (1998). *Emergence: From chaos to order*. Addison-Wesley Publishing Company. Also, Johnson, S. (2001). *Emergence: The connected lives of ants, brains, cities, and software*. Scribner. Also, Morowitz, H. J. (2002). *The emergence of everything: How the world became complex*. Oxford University Press. Also, Battram, A. (1996). *Navigating*

complexity: The essential guide to complexity theory in business and management. Stylus Publishing.

[988] Kelly, S., & Allison, M. (1999). The complexity advantage: How the science of complexity can help your business achieve peak performance. *Computer Science.* https://www. semanticscholar.org/paper/The-Complexity-Advantage%3A-How-the-Science-of-Can-Kelly-Allison/6368860796880d4196d11b9a8291a54e22bbbb25 Also, Csikszentmihalyi, 2003.

[989] Espejo, R., Schuhmann, W., Schwaninger, M., & Bilello, U. (1996). *Organizational transformation and learning: A cybernetic approach to management.* John Wiley & Sons. Also, Ashby.

[990] Axelrod & Cohen. Also, Stacey, R. D. (1996a). *Complexity and creativity in organizations.* Berrett-Hoehler Publishers.

[991] Bennet & Bennet, 2004; Also, Davis, S., & Meyer, C. (1998). *Blur: The speed of change in the connected economy.* Addison-Wesley.

[992] Capra, 1996. Also, Meyer & Davis, 2003.

[993] Kauffman, S. (1995). *At home in the universe: The search for the laws of self-organization and complexity.* Oxford University Press. Also, Stacey, R. D., Griffin, D., & Shaw, P. (2000). *Complexity and management: Fad or radical challenge to systems thinking?* Routledge.

[994] Axelrod & Cohen.

[995] Adapted from the Department of the Navy Knowledge Centric Organization Toolkit.

[996] Excerpted from: Bennet, A., Turner, R., Shelley, A., Turner, J., & Boyes, M. (Illustrator) (2022). *Unleashing the human mind: An OrgZoo quest field guide.* MQIPress.

[997] Pinker. Also, Nelson et al. Also, Gazzaniga, M.S. (2008). *Human: The science behind what makes us unique.* HarperCollins.

[998] Ellinor, L., & Gerard, G. (1998). *Dialogue: Rediscover the transforming power of conversation.* John Wiley & Sons, p. 26.

[999] Dobbs, D. (2007). Turning off depression. In F.E. Bloom (Ed.), *Best of the brain from Scientific American: Mind, matter, and tomorrow's brain*, p. 22.

[1000] Immordino-Yang (2016).

[1001] For more information on mirror neurons, see Gazzaniga, M. S. (2004). *The cognitive neurosciences III.* MIT Press.

[1002] Ericsson, K.A., Charness, N., Feltovich, P.J., & Hoffman, R.R. (Eds.) (2006). *The Cambridge handbook of expertise and expert performance.* Cambridge University Press.

[1003] Ross, P. E.

[1004] For additional information on the development of expertise see Ericsson et al.

[1005] For a good explanation of Emotional Intelligence see Goleman (1995). Also, Goleman, D. (1998). *Working with Emotional Intelligence.* Bantam Books.

[1006] Rescher, N. (2001). *Paradoxes: their roots, range, and resolution.* Open Court.

[1007] Sallinsbury, R. M. (1988). *Paradoxes.* Cambridge University Press.

[1008] Van Heijenoort, J. (Ed.) (1967). *From Frege to Gödel: A source book in mathematical logic. 1879-1931.* Harvard University Press.

[1009] Two excellent references are *Paradoxes: Their Roots, Range and Resolution* by Nicholas Rescher (which also includes a history of paradox) and *Paradoxes from A to Z* by Michael Clark.

[1010] March, J. G. (1991). Exploration and exploitative in organizational learning. *Organization Science, 2*(1), 71-87.

[1011] Heron, J. (1981). Philosophical basis for a new paradigm. In P. Reason & J. Rowan (Eds.), *Human Inquiry, a sourcebook of new paradigm research.* Wiley.

[1012] Blanning, R. W. (1984). Management applications of expert systems. *Information & Management, 7*(6), 311-316.

[1013] Lee, W. B. (2017). Knowledge elicitation practices for organizational development intervention. *Knowledge Management Research & Practice, 15*(1).

[1014] Boje, D. M. (1991). The storytelling organization: A study of story performance in an office-supply firm. *Administrative Science Quarterly, 36*(1), 106-126. Also, Cox, K. (2001). Stories as case knowledge: Case knowledge as stories. *Medical Education, 35*(9), 862-866. Also, Ruggles, R. (2004). *The role of stories in knowledge management.* Storytelling Foundation.

http://www.providersedge.com/docs/km_articles/The_Role_of_Stories_in_KM.pdf   Also, Sinclair, J. (2005). The impact of stories. *The Electronic Journal of Knowledge Management*, *3*(1), 53-64.

[1015] Daft, R. L. & Weick, K. E. (2001). Toward a model of organizations as interpretation systems. In K. E. Weick (Ed.), *Making sense of the organization*, 241-258, Blackwell.

[1016] Luk, C.Y.A. (2009). *A Narrative Approach to the Study of service quality performance: a case study in a public utility company in Hong Kong* (MPhil dissertation, The Hong Kong Polytechnic University, 2008) http://repository.lib.polyu.edu.hk/jspui/bitstream/10397/3143/2/b23071734_ir.pdf

[1017] Habermas, J. (1979). *Communication and the evolution of society*. Beacon Press. Also, Zerubavel, E. (1997). *Social mindscapes: An invitation to cognitive sociology*. Harvard University Press.

[1018] Liedtka, J., & Ogilvie, T. (2011). *Designing for Growth: A Design Thinking Tool Kit for Managers*. Columbia University Press.

[1019] Herreid, C. F. (1997-1998). What makes a good case? *Journal of College Science Teaching*, December-January. Also, Herreid, C. F. (2000, February). All that jazz :An essay extolling the virtues of writing case teaching notes. *Journal of College Science Teaching*, February, 225-228.

[1020] Dvir, R. (2006). Knowledge city: Seen as a collage of human knowledge moments. In F. J. Carrillo (Ed.), *Knowledge cities: Approaches, experiences, and perspectives*. Butterworth Heinemann Elsevier.

[1021] See Lewis, J. (2019). *Story Thinking: Transforming organizations for the fourth industrial revolution*. Self Published.

[1022] Kandel (2006b).

[1023] Senge.

[1024] Amen.

[1025] Lipton, B., & Bhaerman, S. (2009). Spontaneous evolution: *Our positive future (and a way to get there from here)*. Hay House,p. 217.

[1026] Bennet, Bennet, & Lewis..

[1027] Wade.

[1028] Bennet, Bennet, & Turner (2022).

[1029] Churchman, C. W. (1977). A philosophy for complexity. In H. A. Linstone & W. H. C. Simmond (Eds.), *Futures research: New directions*. Addison-Wesley Publishing Company, In.c. Also, von Forester, H. (1977). Objects: Tokens for (eigen-) behaviors. In B. Inheler, R. Gracia, & J. Voneche (Eds.), *Hommage a Jean Piaget: Epistemologie genetique et equilibration*. Delachaux et Niestel.

[1030] Schrage, M. (2000). S*erious play: How the world's best companies simulate to innovate*. Harvard Business School Press. Also, Schrage, M. (1990). Shared minds: the new technologies of collaboration. Random House.

[1031] Nonaka, I. & Takeuchi, H. (1995). *The knowledge-creating company: How Japanese companies create the dynamics of innovation*. Oxford University Press.

[1032] Wenger.

[1033] Adapted from a four-tiered model developed by Accenture, and expanded to nine levels (original source: Robert J. Thomas, Peter Cheese, James M. Benton, Human Capital Development, Accenture Research Note, November 1, 2003), and published in: Murray, A. J., & Greenes, K. A. (2006). New leadership strategies for the enterprise of the future. *VINE: The Journal of Information and Knowledge Management Systems, 36*(3), pp. 231-237.

[1034] Lafley, A. G., & Martin, R. I. (2013). *Playing to win: How strategy really works*. Harvard Business Review Press.

[1035] Merck corporate values statement: merck.com/about/mission.html

[1036] This framework was adapted from a four-tiered model developed by Accenture (Robert J. Thomas, R. J., Cheese, R., Benton, J. M. (2003, November 1). *Human capital development*. Accenture Research Note.) and expanded to nine levels.

[1037] Gell-Mann.

[1038] MacFlouer (2004-16).

[1039] MacFlouer, N. (1999). *Life's hidden meaning*. Ageless Wisdom Publishers.

[1040] Taylor, D. (1996). *The healing power of stories: Creating yourself through the stories of your life*. Doubleday.

[1041] Merriam & Caffarella.

[1042] Prigogine, Ilya and Stengers, Isabell (2017). *Order Out of Chaos: Man's New Dialogue with Nature*. Verso, Brooklyn, NY. Foreword by Alvin Toffler with a brilliant analysis of Prigogine's role in science and change.

[1043] Katsafanas, P. (2016). Nietzsche's account of self-conscious gency. In C. Sandis (Ed.), *Philosophy of action from 1500 to the present day*. Oxford University Press., GS 112.

[1044] Ibid., SA 12:1[61]/WLN 60.

[1045] Carroll (2016).

[1046] Ibid., p. 58.

[1047] Linstone, H. A. (1977). Confessions of a forecaster. In H. A. Linstone & W. H. C. Simmonds (Eds.), *Futures research: New directions. Addison-Wesley Publishing Company, Inc.*

[1048] Carroll, p. 63.

[1049] Michio, K. (2023). *Quantum supremacy: How the quantum computer revolution will change everything*. Doubleday, p. 181.

[1050] Adapted from Bennet, A. and Bennet, D. (2004). *Organizational Survival in the New World: The Intelligent Complex Adaptive System*. Boston, MA: Elsevier AND Bennet, A. and Bennet, D. (2000). "Characterizing the Next Generation Knowledge Organization" in Knowledge and Innovation: Journal of the KMCI, 1, No. 1, pp. 8-42.

[1051] Salomon, G., Perkins, D. N., & Globerson, T. (1991). Partners in cognition: Extending intelligence with intelligent technologies. *Educational Researcher, 20.*

[1052] Kurzweil, R. (2005). *The singularity is near: When humans transcend biology*. Viking Penguin. Also, Amen, D. G. (2005). *Making a good brain great*. Harmony Books.

[1053] Andreasen.

[1054] Kluwe, R. H., Luer, G., & Rosler, F. (Eds.) (2003). *Principles of learning and memory*. Birkhauser Verlag. Also, LeDoux, J. (1996). *The emotional brain: The mysterious underpinnings of emotional life*. Touchstone.

[1055] Polanyi. Also, Bennet, A., & Scott, C. L. (2019). *With passion, we live and love*. MQIPress.

[1056] Pert.

[1057] Schafer, S. B. (2022). Gamers as homeopathic media therapy: Electromagnetic antibodies in the toxic media-field. In S. B. Schafer & A. Bennet (Eds.), *Handbook of research on global media's preternatural influence on global singularity, culture and government*, pp. 397-425. IGI Global.

[1058] Gomide (2022). Also, Gomide, W. (2021a). Non-causality and transreal numbers: The world seen at speed of light. [Unpublished]. UFMT/Brazil. Also, Gomide, W. (2021b). Metaphysical aggregates and their insertion into Cantor's thought. [Unpublished]. UFMT/Brazil.

BIBLIOGRAPHY

Abel, M. (2008). Competencies management and learning organizational memory. *Journal of Knowledge Management, 12*(6), 15–30.

Acerbi, A. (2019). Cognitive attraction and online misinformation. *Palgrave Communications, 5*(15). Advance online publication. doi:10.1057415999-019-0224-y

Ackerman, C. (2018, June). Meaning & values: What is self-transcendence? *Positive Psychology.com*. https://positivepsychology.com/self-transcendence/

Ackoff, R. L. (1978). *The art of problem solving: Accompanied by Ackoff's fables*. John Wiley & Sons.

Ackoff, R. L. (1994). *The democratic corporation: A radical prescription for recreating corporate America and rediscovering success*. Oxford University Press.

Adolphs, R. (2004). Processing of emotional and social information by the human amygdala. In M.S. Gazzaniga (Ed.), *The cognitive neurosciences III*. The Bradford Press.

Aeron-Thomas, D., Nicholls, J., Forster, S., & Westall, A. (2004). *Social return on investment: Valuing what matters*. New Economics Foundation.

Alavi, M., & Leidner, D. (2001). Knowledge management and knowledge management systems: Conceptual foundations and research issues. *MIS Quarterly, 25*(1), 107–136.

Alberts, D. S., & Hayes, R. E. (2005). *Power to the edge: Command, control in the information age*. Command & Control Research Program.

Albrecht, K. (2003). *The power of minds at work: Organizational intelligence in action*. AMACOM.

Albrecht, K. (2003). *The power of minds at work: Organizational intelligence in action*. AMACOM, a division of American Management Association, pp. 156-160.

Alfes, K., Shantz, A. D., Truss, C., & Soane, E. C. (2013). The link between perceived human resource management practices, engagement and employee behavior: A moderated mediation model. *The International Journal of Human Resource Management, 24*(2), 330-351.

Allan, B. A., Batz-Barbarich, C., Sterling, H. M., & Tay, L. (2019). Outcomes of meaningful work: A meta-analysis. *Journal of Management Studies, 56*(3), 500-528.

Allen, S., Cunliffe, A. L., & Easterby-Smith, M. (2019). Understanding sustainability through the lens of ecocentric radical-reflexivity: Implications for management education. *Journal of Business Ethics, 154*, 781–795.

Almeida, L. S., Prieto, M. D., Ferreira, A. I., Bermejo, M. R., Ferrando, M., & Ferrándiz, C. (2010). Intelligence assessment: Gardner multiple intelligence theory as an alternative. *Learning and Individual Differences, 20*(3), 225–230. https://doi.org/10.1016/j.lindif.2009.12.010

Alsplund, C. L., Fougnie, D., Zughni, S., Martin, J. W., & Marois, R. (2014, January 16). The attention blink reveals the probabilistic nature of discrete conscious perception. *Psychological Science*. http://pss.sagepub.com/

Amann, T. (2003). Creating space for somatic ways of knowing within transformative learning theory. In C. A. Wiessner, S. R. Meyer, N. L. Thal, & P.G. Neaman (Eds.). *Proceedings of the Fifth International Conference on Transformative Learning*. Teacher's College, Columbia University, pp. 26-32.

Amen, D. G. (2005). *Making a good brain great*. Harmony Books.

American Heritage Dictionary (1992).

American Heritage Dictionary of the English Language, 4th edition (2000; 2006), Houghton-Mifflin Co.

Anderson, J. R. (1983). *The architecture of cognition*. Harvard University Press.

Anderson, V., & Johnson, L. (1997). *Systems thinking basics: From concepts to causal loops*. Pegasus Communications, Inc.

Andersson, J. L., Lilja, A., Hartvig, P., Langstrom, B., Gordh, T., Handwerker, H., et al. (1997). Somatotopic organization along the central sulcus, for pain localization in humans, as revealed by positron emission tomography. *Experimental Brain Research, 117*, 192-199.

Andreasen, N. C. (2005). *The creating brain: The neuroscience of genius*. The Dana Foundation Press.

Andreu, R., & Sieber, S. (1999). Knowledge and problem solving: A proposal for a model of individual and collective learning. Working Paper 1/99). Barcelona.

Andrews, T. Animal speak: The spiritual & magical powers of creatures great & small. Llewellyn Publications.

Arboníes, A. L. (Ed.) (2006). *Conocimiento para innovar: Cómo evitar la miopía en la gestión del conocimiento*. Ediciones Díaz de Santos.

Arendt, H. (1958). *The human condition*. University of Chicago Press.

Argyri, C., & Schön, C. D. (1997). *Organizational learning: A theory of action perspective*. Reiss, 77/78, 345–348.

Argyris, C. (1977). Double loop learning in organizations. *Harvard Business Review, 55*(5), 115–125, p. 116.

Argyris, C. (1990). *Overcoming organizational defenses: Facilitating organizational learning*. Prentice Hall.

Argyris, C. (1991). Teaching smart people how to learn. *Harvard Business Review, 69*(3).

Argyris, C. (1999). *On organizational learning* (2nd ed.) Blackwell Publishers Ltd.

Arms, K., & Camp, P. (1987). *Biology*, 3rd ed. Saunders College Publishing.

Arsenijević, O., Trivan, D., Podbregar, I., & Šprajc, P. (2017). Strategic aspect of knowledge management. *Organizacija, 50*(2), 163–176.

Ashby, W. R. (1964). *An introduction to cybernetics*. Methuen.

Asian Development Bank (2007, March). *Moving toward knowledge-based economies: Asian experiences*. Retrieved 6 March 2022 from https://www.adb.org/sites/default/files/publication/29699/knowledge -based -economies.pdf.

Asrar-ul-Haq, M., & Anwar, S. (2016). A systematic review of knowledge management and knowledge sharing: Trends, issues, and challenges. *Cogent Business & Management, 3*(1), Article 1127744.

Atwater, F. H. (2004). *The Hemi-Sync® Process*. The Monroe Institute.

Augier, M., Shariq, S. Z., & Thanning Vendelø, M. (2001). Understanding context: Its emergence, transformation, and role in tacit knowledge sharing. *Journal of Knowledge Management, 5*(2), 125–137.

Ausubel, D. P. (1968). *Educational psychology: A cognitive view*. Holt, Rinehart and Winston.

Avedisian, J. (2023). Igniting a kingdom innovation culture. In A. Bennet & R. K. Baisya (Eds.), *INside INnovation: Looking from the inside out*. MQIPress.

Axelrod & Cohen.

Bader, B. S. (2008). Distinguishing governance from management. *Great Boards, 8*(3), pp. 2-5.

Bailey, C., Yeoman, R., Madden, A., Thompson, M., & Kerridge, G. (2019). A review of the empirical literature on meaningful work: Progress and research agenda. *Human Resource Development Review, 18*(1), 83-113.

Bakker, A. B., & Demerouti, E. (2014). Job demands-resources theory. In P. Y. Chen & C. I. Cooper (Eds.), *Wellbeing: A complete reference guide, Vol III*. Wiley-Blackwell, pp. 37-64.

Baltes, P. B., & Smith, J. (1990). The psychology of wisdom and its ontogenesis. In R. J. Sternberg (Ed.), *Wisdom: Its nature, origins, and development*. Cambridge University Press, 87-120.

Bankins, S., & Formosa, P. (2023). The ethical implications of artificial intelligence (AI) for meaningful work. *Journal of Business Ethics*. https://doi.org/10.1007/s10551-023-05339-7

Bari, M. W., Abrar, M., Shaheen, S., Bashir, M., & Fanchen, M. (2019). Knowledge hiding behaviors and team creativity: The contingent role of perceived mastery motivational climate. *SAGE Open, 9*(3). https://doi.org/10.1177/2158244019876297

Barkhordari, S., Fattahi, M., & Azimi, N. A. (2019). The impact of knowledge-based economy on growth performance: Evidence from MENA countries. *Journal of the Knowledge Economy, 10*(3), 1168–1182.

Baron, L., & Parent, E. Developing authentic leadership within a training context: Three phenomena supporting the individual development process. *Journal of Leadership & Organizational Studies 22*(1), 37-53. https://doi.org/10.1177/14805181351901

Barquin, R., Bennet, A., & Remez, S. (2001). *Building knowledge management environments for electronic government*. Management Concepts.

Barragán, A. (2009). Aproximación a una taxonomía de modelos de gestión del conocimiento. *Intangible Capital, 5*(1), 65–101.

Barthes, R. l(1985). *In the responsibility of forms*. Hill and Wang.

Batra, S. (2012). Development perspectives of knowledge management. *Review of Knowledge Management, 2*(1), 17–23.

Batra, S., Payal, R., & Carrillo F. J. (2013). Knowledge village capital framework in the Indian context. *International Journal of Knowledge-Based Development, 4*(3), 222–244.

Battista, J., & Almond, R. (1973). The development of meaning in life. *Psychiatry, 36*(4), 409-427.

Battram, A. (1996). *Navigating complexity: The essential guide to complexity theory in business and management*. The Industrial Society.

Battram, A. (1996). *Navigating complexity: The essential guide to complexity theory in business and management*. Stylus Publishing.

Baumeister, R. F. (1991). *Meanings of life*. Guilford Press.

Beckett, J. C. (2006). *Mastering Monday*. Intervarsity Press, p. 138.

Beckman, T. J. (1997). *A methodology for knowledge management*. International Association of Science and Technology for Development (IASTED) AI and Soft Computing Conference. Banff, Canada.

Beckman, T. J. (1999). The current state of knowledge management. In Liebowitz (Ed.). *Knowledge management handbook*. CRC Press.

Begley, S. (2007). *Train your mind change your brain: How a new science reeals our extraordinary potential to transform ourselves*. Ballantine Books.

Bellantuono, N., Pontrandolfo, P., & Scozzi, B. (2013). Different practices for open innovation: A context-based approach. *Journal of Knowledge Management, 17*(4), 558–568.

Bennet, A. & Bennet, D. (2000). "Characterizing the Next Generation Knowledge Organization" in Knowledge and Innovation: Journal of the KMCI, 1, No. 1, pp. 8-42.

Bennet, A. (2005). *Exploring aspects of knowledge management that contribute to the passion expressed by its thought leaders*. Dissertation, Fielding Graduate University, Santa Barbara, CA. Self-published. Excerpts available at www.mountainquestinstitute.com

Bennet, A. (2005). *Exploring aspects of knowledge management that contribute to the passion expressed by its thought leaders*. Self-Published, p. 106.

Bennet, A. (2018). *Possibilities that are YOU! Volume 15: Seeking wisdom*. MQIPress.

Bennet, A. (2018). *Possibilities that are you! Volume 4: Conscious compassion*. MQI Press.

Bennet, A., & Bennet, D. (2004). *Organizational survival in the new world: The intelligent complex adaptive system*. Elsevier-Butterworth-Heinemann.

Bennet, A., & Bennet, D. (2006). Learning as associative patterning. *VINE: The Journal of Information and Knowledge Management Systems, 36*(4), 371-376.

Bennet, A., & Bennet, D. (2007). CONTEXT: The shared knowledge enigma. *VINE: The Journal of Information and Knowledge Management Systems, 37*(1), 27-40.

Bennet, A., & Bennet, D. (2007). *Knowledge Mobilization in the Social Sciences and the Humanities*. MQI Press.

Bennet, A., & Bennet, D. (2007). The knowledge and knowing of spiritual learning. *VINE: The Journal of Information and Knowledge Management Systems, 37*(2), 150-168.

Bennet, A., & Bennet, D. (2007). The MQI value infusion methodology. A white paper. Mountain Quest Institute, Frost, WV.

Bennet, A., & Bennet, D. (2008). Moving from knowledge to wisdom, from ordinary consciousness to extraordinary consciousness. *VINE: Journal of Information and Knowledge Systems, 38*(1), 7-15.

Bennet, A., & Bennet, D. (2008). The depth of knowledge: Surface, shallow, or deep? *VINE: The Journal of Information and Knowledge Management Systems, 38*(4), 405-420.

Bennet, A., & Bennet, D. (2008). The human knowledge system: Music and brain coherence. *VINE: The Journal of Information and Knowledge Management Systems 38*(3), 277-295.

Bennet, A., & Bennet, D. (2010). Leaders, decisions, and the neuro-knowledge system. In S. Wallis, *Cybernetics and systems theory in management: Tools, views and advancements*. IGI Global, 21-35.

Bennet, A., & Bennet, D. (2010). The role of trust in a world of information and knowledge. *Effective Executive*. Icfai University Press.

Bennet, A., & Bennet, D. (2014). Knowledge, theory, and practice in knowledge management: Between associative patterning and context-rich action. *Journal of Entrepreneurship, Management, and Innovation, 10*(4), 7–55.

Bennet, A., & Bennet, D. (2014). Knowledge, theory, and practice in knowledge management: Between associative patterning and context-rich action. *Journal of Entrepreneurship, Management, and Innovation, 10*(4), 7–55.

Bennet, A., & Bennet, D. (2018; 2015). *Decision-making in the new reality: Complexity, knowledge and knowing*. MQIPress.

Bennet, A., & Bennet, D., with Fafard, K., Fonda, M., Lomond, T., Messier, L., & Vaugeois. In cooperation with the Social Sciences and Humanities Research Council of Canada (SSHRC) (2007). *Knowledge mobilization in the social sciences and humanities: Moving from research to action*. MQIPress.

Bennet, A., & Scott, C. L. (2019). *With passion, we live and love*. MQIPress.

Bennet, A., & Shelley, A. (2023). *Innovative creativity: Creating with innovation in mind*. MQIPress.

Bennet, A., Bennet, D., & Avedisian, J. (2018). *The course of knowledge: A 21st century theory*. MQIPress.

Bennet, A., Bennet, D., & Lewis, J. (2018; 2015). *Leading with the future in mind: Knowledge and emergent leadership*. MQIPress.

Bennet, A., Bennet, D., Shelley, A., Bullar, T., & Lewis, J. (2018). *The intelligent social change journey: Foundation for the possibilities that are YOU!* (22 book series). MQIPress.

Bennet, A., Bennet, D., Shelley, A., Bullard, T., & Lewis, J. (2020a). *The profundity and bifurcation of change part I: Laying the groundwork*. MQIPress.

Bennet, A., Bennet, D., Shelley, A., Bullard, T., & Lewis, J. (2020d). *The profundity and bifurcation of change part IV: Co-creating the future*. MQIPress.

Bennet, A., Bennet, D., Shelley, A., Bullard, T., & Lewis, J. (2020c). *The profundity and bifurcation of change part III: Learning in the present*. MQIPress.

Bennet, A., Bennet, D., Shelley, A., Bullard, T., & Lewis, J. (2020). *The profundity and bifurcation of change: Parts I – V*. MQIPress.

Bennet, A., Bennet, D., Shelley, A., Bullard, T., and Lewis, J. (2018). *The intelligent social change journey: Foundation for the possibilities that are YOU!* MQIPress.

Bennet, A., Shelley, A., & Dhewa, C. (2023). *Innovative creativity: Creating with innovation in mind*. MQIPress.

Bennet, A., Turner, R., Shelley, A., Turner, J., & Boyes, M. (Illustrator) (2022). *Unleashing the human mind: An OrgZoo quest field guide*. MQIPress.

Bennet, D., & Bennet, A. (2008). The decision-making process for complex situations in a complex environment. In C.W. Holsapple & F. Burstein (Eds.). *Handbook on decision support systems*, pp. 3-20. Springer-Verlag.

Bennet, D., & Bennet, A. (2009), Associative patterning: the unconscious life of an organization. In Girard, J.P. (Ed.). *Building organizational memories*. IGI Global, 201-224.

Bennet, D., & Bennet, A. (2010). Social learning from the inside out: The creation and sharing of knowledge from the mind/brain perspective. In J. Girard & J. Girard (Eds.), *Social knowledge: Using social media to know what you know*, pp. 1-23. IGI Global.

Bennet, D., Bennet, A., & Turner, R. (2018). *Expanding the self: The intelligent complex adaptive system*. MQIPress.

Bennet, D., Bennet, A., & Turner, R. (2022). *Unleashing the human mind: A consilience approach to managing self*. MQIPress.

Bennett-Woods, D. (1997). Reflections on wisdom. Unpublished paper, University of Northern Colorado.

Bergson, H. (2014). *Key writings*. Bloomsbury Academic.

Bersin, J., Geller, J., Wakefield, N., & Brett, W. (2016). *Global human capital trends 2016*. Deloitte University Press.

Bhatt, G. (2001). Knowledge management in organizations: Examining the interaction between technologies, techniques, and people. *Journal of Knowledge Management, 5*(1), 68–75.

Bhatti, S. H., Vorobyev, D., Zakariya, R., & Christofi, M. (2021). Social capital, knowledge sharing, work meaningfulness and creativity: Evidence from the Pakistani pharmaceutical industry. *Journal of Intellectual Capital, 22*(2), 243-259.

Bianconi E, Piovesan A, Facchin F, Beraudi A et al. (2013) An estimation of the number of cells in the human body, *Annals of Human Biology: 1*(11). DOI: 10.3109/03014460.2013.807878.

Bindé, J. (2005). *Towards knowledge societies: UNESCO world report.* UNESCO.

Birkinshaw, J., & Sheehan, T. (2002). Managing the knowledge life cycle. *MIT Sloan Management Review, 44*(1), 75–84.

Bjelland, O. M., & Wood, R. C. (2008, September). An inside view of IBM's innovation jam. *MIT Sloan Management Review, 50*(1).

Blackmore, S. (1999). *The meme machine*. Oxford University Press.

Blanning, R. W. (1984). Management applications of expert systems. *Information & Management, 7*(6), 311-316.

Blau, J. (2000). Relational wealth in the commons: Local spaces of work and residence in a global economy. In C.R. Leana & D. M. Rousseau (Eds.), *Relational wealth: The advantages of stability in a changing economy*, pp. 217-232. Oxford University Press.

Blau, P. M. (1964). *Exchange and power in social life*. Transaction Publishers.

Bogilović, S., Černe, M., & Škerlavaj, M. (2017). Hiding behind a mask? Cultural intelligence, knowledge hiding, and individual and team creativity. *European Journal of Work and Organizational Psychology, 26*(5), 710-723. https://doi.org/10.1080/1359432X.2017.1337747

Bohm, D. (1980). *Wholeness and the implicate order*. Routledge & Kegal Paul, p. 64.

Bohm, D. (1992). *Thought as a system*. Routledge.

Bohm, D., & Hiley, B. J. (1993). *The undivided universe: An ontological interpretation of quantum theory*. Routledge.

Boje, D. M. (1991). The storytelling organization: A study of story performance in an office-supply firm. *Administrative Science Quarterly, 36*(1), 106-126.

Boltzmann, L. (1896, 1898). *Lectures on gas theory* (part I and part II) (Trans. S.G. Brush, 1976). University of California Press.

Bontis, N., & Fitz-Enz, J. (2002). Intellectual capital ROI: A causal map of human capital antecedents and consequents. *Journal of Intellectual Capital, 3*(3), 223–247.

Bontis, N., Crossan, M. M., & Hullan, J. (2000). Managing an organizational learning system by aligning stocks and flows of knowledge. *Journal of Management Studies, 39*(4), 437–469.

Borghoff, U. M. & Pareschi, R. (Eds.) (1998). *Information technology for knowledge management*. Berlin.

Bosua, R., & Venkitachalam, K. (2013). Aligning strategies and processes in knowledge management: A framework. *Journal of Knowledge Management, 17*(3), 331–346.

Bower, J. L. (2000). The purpose of change: Al commentary on Jensen and Senge. In M. K. Beer & N. Nohria (Eds.), *Breaking the code of change*, pp. 93-95. Harvard Business School Press.

Bradshaw, S., & Howard, P. N. (2019). *The global disinformation order: 2019 global inventory of organized social media manipulation*.

Braudel, F. (1992). *Civilization and capitalism, 15th–18th century. Volume 1: The structure of everyday life*. University of California Press.

Brendel, W., & Bennett, C. (2016). Learning to embody leadership through mindfulness and somatics practice. *Advances in Developing Human Resources 18*(3), 409-425. https://doi.org/10.1177/1523422316646068

Brinkerhoff, J. M. (2002). Review of Gilbert Rist's The history of development: From western origins to global faith. *Economic Development and Cultural Change, 51*(1), 262–266.

Britannica https://www.britannica.com/topic/democracy/The-theory-of-democracy

Brooking, A.(996). *Intellectual capital: Core asset for the third millennium*. Cengage Learning.

Brown, T. (2008). Design Thinking. *Harvard Business Review*.

Brown, W. S. (2000). Wisdom and human neurocognitive systems: Perceiving and practicing the laws of life. In W. S. Brown (Ed.), *Understanding wisdom: Sources, science and society*. Templeton Foundation Press.

Bruno, A., Galuppo, L., & Gilardi, S. (2011). Evaluating the reflexive practices in a learning experience. *European Journal of Psychology of Education, 26*, 527–543.

Buchanan, T. (2020). Why do people spread false information online? The effects of message and viewer characteristics on self-reported likelihood of sharing social media disinformation. *PLoS One, 15*(10).

Buonomano, D. V., & Merzenich, M. M. (1998). Cortical plasticity: From synapses to maps. *Annual Review of Neuroscience, 21*(1), 149-186. Doi:10.1146/annurev.neuro.21.1.149 PMID:9530495

Burke, P. (2023). *Ignorance, a global history*, Yale University Press, p. 257-258.

Burkowitz, W., & Petrach, G. (1997, July-August). Visualizing, measuring, and managing knowledge. *Research Technology Management, 40*, 24-31.

Butt, A. S. (2019). Consequences of top-down knowledge hiding in firms: A pilot study. *Heliyon, 5*(12). https://doi.org/10.1016/j.heliyo.2019.e03000

Cai, F. Q., & Wen, N. (2018). The influence of individual goal orientation on innovation behavior from the perspective of knowledge hiding. In J. Lieu & K. L. Teves (Eds.), *Proceedings of the 2018 2nd International Conference on Education, Economics and Management Research 182*, pp. 671-676.

Cairns-Lee, H. (201). Images of leadership development form the inside out. *Advances in Developing Human Resources 17*(3), 321-336.

Calabrese, F. A. (2010). A decade of leadership in creating the discipline of knowledge management. In A. Green, M. Stankosky, and L. Vandergriff (Eds.), *In search of knowledge management: Pursuing primary principles*. Emerald Group Publishing Limited.

Calaprice, A. (2000). *The expanded quotable Einstein*. Princeton University Press.

Callender, C., & Huggett, N. (2001). *Physics meets philosophy at the Planck scale: Contemporary theories in quantum gravity*. Cambridge University Press.

Capital.pdf?origin=publicationdetail.

Capra, F. (1996). *The web of life: A new scientific understanding of living systems*. Anchor Books, Doubleday.

Carr, L., Iacoboni, M., Dubeau, M. C., Mazziotta, J. C., & Lenzi, G. I. (2003). Neural mechanisms of empathy in humans: A relay from neural systems for imitation to limbic areas. *Proceedings of the National Academy of Science, 100*, 5497-5502.

Carrasco, M., Ling, S., & Read, S. (2004). Attention alters appearance. *Nature Neuroscience, 7*, 308-313.

Carrillo, F. J. (1996a). The ways of knowledge management [Paper presentation]. The 1996 National Business Conference: The Management of Intellectual Capital and Innovation, McMaster University, Canada.

Carrillo, F. J. (1996b). *Managing innovation in a knowledge-based economy* [Paper presentation]. Joint Meeting of the European Association for the Study of Science and Technology and the Society for Social Studies in Science: Signatures of Knowledge Societies, Bielefeld, Germany.

Carrillo, F. J. (1998). Managing knowledge-based value systems. *Journal of Knowledge Management, 1*(4), 28–46.

Carrillo, F. J. (2001). Meta-KM: A program and a plea. Knowledge and innovation. *Journal of the KMCI, 1*(2).

Carrillo, F. J. (2001). Meta-KM: A program and a plea. Knowledge and Innovation. *Journal of the KMCI, 1*(2), pp. 3-4.

Carrillo, F. J. (2001a). La evolución de las especies de gestión de conocimiento [Paper presentation]. Entorno Empresarial del Siglo XXI: Cinco años del Cluster de Conocimiento, Parque Tecnológico de Zamudio, Bilbao, Spain.

Carrillo, F. J. (2002). Capital systems: Implications for a global knowledge agenda. *Journal of Knowledge Management, 6*(4), 379–399.

Carrillo, F. J. (2004). Capital cities: A taxonomy of capital accounts for knowledge cities. *Journal of Knowledge Management, 8*(5).

Carrillo, F. J. (2006b). From transitional to radical knowledge-based development. *Journal of Knowledge Management, 10*(5), 3–5.

Carrillo, F. J. (2014). How knowledge and the city met. In F.J. Carrillo, T. Yigitcanlar, B. Garcia, & A. Londqvist (Eds.), *Knowledge and the city: Concepts, applications and trends of knowledge-based urban development.* Routledge.

Carrillo, F. J. (2014a) (Ed.). *Sistemas de Capitales y Mercados de Conocimiento.* Amazon Kindle Direct Publishing.

Carrillo, F. J. (2014b). What "knowledge-based" stands for? A position paper. *International Journal of Knowledge-Based Development, 5*(4), 402–421.

Carrillo, F. J. (2015). Knowledge-based development as a new economic culture. *Journal of Open Innovation: Technology, Market, and Complexity, 1*(1), 1–17.

Carrillo, F. J. (2016a). Knowledge markets: A typology and an overview. *International Journal of Knowledge-based Development, 7*(3), 264–289.

Carrillo, F. J. (2022). *A modern guide to knowledge. From knowledge economies to knowledge in the anthropocene.* Edward Elgar.

Carrillo, F. J. (Ed.) (2006a). *Knowledge cities: Approaches, experiences, and perspectives.* Butterworth-Heinemann.

Carrillo, F. J., & Arce, G. (2020). *Arequipa, ciudad de conocimiento: Project report.* WCI/UNSA.

Carrillo, F. J., & Batra, S. (2012). Understanding and measurement: Perspectives on the evolution of knowledge-based development. *International Journal of Knowledge-Based Development, 3*(1), 1–16.

Carrillo, F. J., & Galvis-Lista, E. (2014). Procesos de gestión de conocimiento desde el enfoque de sistemas de valor basados en conocimiento. Ideas CONCYTEG, 9(107), 3–22.

Carrillo, F. J., & Galvis-Lista, E. (2014). Procesos de gestión de conocimiento desde el enfoque de sistemas de valor basados en conocimiento. *Ideas CONCYTEG, 9*(107), 3–22.

Carrillo, F. J., Arce, G., Ugarte, W., Portugal, A., Torres, G., & Sánchez, G. (2022). Intelligence capital: The management of knowledge assets and development of adaptive capacities in the city of Arequipa. *Intangible Capital, 18*(2), 163–181.

Carroll, S. (2016) *The big picture: On the origins of life, meaning, and the universe itself.* Dutton.

Casado, F. (Ed.) (2007). *Desarrollo basado en el conocimiento: Transferencia de conocimiento.* Comunidad Iberoamericana de Sistemas de Conocimiento.

Černe, M., Hernaus, T., Dysvik, A., & Škerlavaj, M. (2014). What goes around comes around: Knowledge hiding, perceived motivational climate, and creativity. *Academy of Management Journal, 57*(1), 172-192. https://doi.org/10.5465/amj.2012.0122

Černe, M., Hernaus, T., Dysvik, A., & Škerlavaj, M. (2017). The role of multilevel synergistic interplay among team mastery climate, knowledge hiding, and job characteristics in stimulating innovative work behavior. *Human Resource Management Journal, 27*(2), 281-299. https://doi.org/10.1111/1748-8583.12132

Cfr. "Rise and Fall of the Development Brand" section in Carrillo, 2022, pp. 237-252. Even if the idea showed some resistance to die, as the literature shows, it has increasingly stagnated.

Chaparro, F. (2006). *Construyendo una ciudad-región del conocimiento en Bogotá.* Universidad del Rosario/Alcaldía Mayor de Bogotá.

Chase, R., & Carrillo, F. J. (2007). *The 2007 most admired knowledge city report.* World Capital Institute and Teleos.

Checkland, P., & Holwell, s. (1998). *Information, systems and information systems: Making sense of the field.* John Wiley & Sons.

Chen, L., & Mohamed, S. (2007). Empirical study of interactions between knowledge management activities. Engineering, *Construction and Architectural Management, 14*(3), 242–260.

Chen, Y. S., Lin, M. J. J., & Chang, C. H. (2009). The positive effects of relationship learning and absorptive capacity on innovation performance and competitive advantage in industrial markets. *Industrial Marketing Management, 38*(2), 152–158.

Chomsky, N. (1965). *Aspects of the theory of syntax*. MIT Press.

Choo, C.W., & Bontis, N. (2002). *The strategic management of intellectual capital and organizational knowledge*. Oxford University Press.

Christian, M. S., Garza, A. S., & Slaughter, J. E. (2011). Work engagement: A quantitative review as test of its relations with task and contextual performance. *Personnel Psychology, 64*(1), 89-136.

Christiansen, C. M., Horn, M. B., & Johson, C. W. (2011). Disrupting class: How disruptive innovation will change the way the world learns. *Learning and Individual Differences 20*(3). McGraw-Hill Education.

Christos, G. (2003). *Memory and dreams: The creative human mind*. Rutgers University Press.

Chuang, F., Morgan, R. E., & Robson, M. J. (2015). Customer and competitor insights, new product development competence, and new product creativity: Differential, integrative, and substitution effects. *Journal of Product Innovation Management, 32*(2), 175–182.

Churchman, C. W. (1977). A philosophy for complexity. In H. A. Linstone & W. H. C. Simmond (Eds.), *Futures research: New directions*. Addison-Wesley Publishing Company, Inc.

Clare, M. (2002). Solving the knowledge-value equation (part one). *Knowledge Management Review, 5*(2), 14–17.

Clark, M. (2002/2007). *Paradoxes from A to Z*. Routledge.

Clayton, V., & Birren, J. E. (1980). The development of wisdom across the lifespan: A re-examination of an ancient topic. In P. B. Baltes and O. G. J. Brim (Eds.), *Life span development and behavior*. Academic Press, 104-135.

Cleveland, H. (2002). *Nobody in charge: Essays on the future of leadership*. Jossey-Bass.

Cohen, D., & Prusak, L. (2001). *In good company: How social capital makes organizations work*. Harvard Business School Press.

Cohen, S. (1987). Knowledge, Context and Social Standards. *Synthesize, 73*(1). 3-26

Cohen, W. M. (1989). Innovation and learning: The two faces of R&D. *The Economic Journal, 99*(397), 569-596.

Cohen, W. M., & Levinthal, D. A. (1990). Absorptive capacity: A new perspective on learning and innovation. *Administrative Science Quarterly, 35*(1), 128–152.

Collins, J. (2001). *Good to great: Why some companies make the leap... and others don't*. HarperBusiness.

Collins, J. C., & Porras, J. I. (1994). *Built to last*. HarperCollins Publishers.

Connelly, C. E., & Zweig, D. (2015). How perpetrators and targets construe knowledge hiding in organizations. *European Journal of Work and Organizational Psychology, 24*(33), 479-489. https://doi.org/10.1080/1359432X.2014.931325

Connelly, C. E., Zweig, D., Webster, J., & Trougakos, J. P. (2012). Knowledge hiding in organizations. *Journal of Organizational Behavior, 33*(1), 64-88. https://doi.org/10.1002/job.737

Cooperrider, D. L., & Srivastva, S. (1987). Appreciative inquiry. *Research in Organizational Change and Development, 1*, 129-169.

Costa, J. D. (1995). *Working wisdom: The ultimate value in the new economy*. Stoddart, p. 3.

Cotter, R. J., & Cullen, J. G. (2012). Reflexive management learning: An integrative review and a conceptual typology. *Human Resource Development Review, 11*(2), 227–253.

Covey, S. M. R. (2004) *The 8th habit: From effectiveness to greatness*. Simon & Schuster, Inc.

Covey, S. M. R., & Merrill, R. R. (2018). *The speed of trust: The one thing that changes everything*. Simon & Schuster.

Cowan, W. M., & Kandel, E. R. (2001). A brief history of synapses and synaptic transmission. In W. C. Cowan, T. C. Sudhof, & C. F. Stevens (Eds.), *Synapses*. Johns Hopkins Press.

Cox, K. (2001). Stories as case knowledge: Case knowledge as stories. *Medical Education, 35*(9), 862-866.

Cozolino, L. J. (2006). *The neuroscience of human relationships: Attachment and the developing social brain*. W. W. Norton.

Cozolino, L., & Sprokay, S. (2006). Neuroscience and adult learning. In S. Johnson & K. Taylor (Eds.), *The neuroscience of adult learning*, pp. 11-19. Jossey-Bass. Doi:10.1002/ace.214.

Crandall, B., Klein, G., & Hoffman, R. R. (2006). *Working minds: A practitioner's guide to cognitive task analysis*. The MIT Press.

Cripe, E. J., & Mansfield, R. S. (2002). *The value-added employee: 31 competencies to make yourself irresistible to any company* (2nd Ed.). Butterworth-Heinemann.

Cross, R. (2021). *Beyond collaboration overload: How to work smarter, get ahead, and restore your well-being*. Harvard Business Review Press.

Cross, R., & Dillon, K. (2023). *The microstress effect: How little things pile up and create big problems—and what to do about it*. Harvard Business Review Press, front cover.

Csikszentmihalyi, M. (1990). *Flow: the psychology of optimal experience*. Harper & Row.

Csikszentmihalyi, M. (1993). *The evolving self: A psychology for the third millennium*. HarperCollins Publishing.

Csikszentmihalyi, M. (1996). *Creativity: Flow and the psychology of discovery and invention*. HarperCollins Publishers, Inc.

Csikszentmihalyi, M. (2003). *Good business: Leadership, flow and the making of meaning*. Viking Penguin.

Csikszentmihalyi, M., & Nakamura, J. (2005). The role of emotions in the development of wisdom. In R. J. Sternberg and J. Jordan (Eds.), *A handbook of wisdom: Psychological perspectives*. Cambridge University Press.

Cummings, T. G., & Huse, E. G. (1989). *Organization development and change*, 4th ed. West Publishing Company.

Cunliffe, A. L. (2002). Reflexive dialogical practice in management learning. *Management Learning, 33*(1), 35–61.

Curlief, S., & Plastino, A. R. (2021). *Topics on quantum information science*. Intech Open.

D'Arisbo, A. (2014). *Sistemas de capitais como método de análise da economia criativa para o desenvolvimento baseado no conhecimento na cidade de Bento Gonçalves* [Doctoral dissertation, Universidad de Caxias do Sul].

Da Silva, N., & Davis, A. R. (2011). Absorptive capacity at the individual level: Linking creativity to innovation in academia. *The Review of Higher Education, 34*(3), 355–379.

Daft, R. L. & Weick, K. E. (2001). Toward a model of organizations as interpretation systems. In K. E. Weick (Ed.), *Making sense of the organization*, 241-258, Blackwell.

Dahl, A. (1985). *A Preface to economic democracy*. University of California Press.

Damasio, A. R. (1994). *Descartes' error: Emotion, reason, and the human brain*. G.P. Putnam's Sons.

Damasio, A.R. (1999). *The feeling of what happens: Body and emotion in the making of consciousness*. Harcourt Brace & Company.

Dang, D., & Umemoto, K. (2009). Modelling the development toward the knowledge economy: A national capability approach. *Journal of Knowledge Management, 13*(5), 359–372.

Darwin, C. (1998). *The descent of man*. Prometheus Books.

Das, G. G., & Baisya, R. K. (2023). Integrated innovation strategy and framework in power section: Tata Power Company Limited. In A. Bennet and R. K. Baisya, *INside INnovation: Looking from the inside-out*.

Davenport, T. H., & Beck, J. C. (2001). *The attention economy*. Harvard Business Review Press.

Davenport, T. H., & Prusak, L. (1998). *Working knowledge: How organizations manage what they know*. Harvard Business School Press.

Davies, M. (1989). Connectionism, modularity, and tacit knowledge. *The British Journal for the Philosophy of Science, 40*(4), 541-555. https://doi.,org/10.1093/bjps/441.2.195

Davies, M. (1990). Knowledge of rules in connectionist networks. *Intellectica, 9*(1), 81-126.

Davies, M. (1991). Concepts, connectionism, and the language of thought. In W. Ramsey, S. P. Stich, & D. Rumelhart (Eds.), *Philosophy and connectionist theory*, pp. 485-503. Lawrence Erlbaum Associates.

Davies, M. (1995). Two notions of implicit rules. *Philosophical Perspectives, 9*, 153-83. https://doi.org/10.2307/2214216

Davis, S., & Meyer, C. (1998). *Blur: The speed of change in the connected economy*. Addison-Wesley.

de Boer, M., Inchingolo, R. (2023). *Think harder, not faster: how network structure shapes*. https://www.humanbrainproject.eu/en/follow-hbp/news/2023/06/05/think-harder-not-faster-how-network-structure-shapes-decision-making

De Furia, G. L. (1997). *Interpersonal trust survey*. Pfeiffer Publishers (Wiley).

De Geus, A. (1997). *The living company: Habits for survival in a turbulent business environment*. Harvard Business School Press.

de Sousa, M. (2023). *The Meaningful Leader*. Silabo.

de Toqueville, A. (2000). *Democracy in America*. Hackett Publishing Co.

Delmonte, M. M. (1984). Electrocortical activity and related phenomena associated with mediation practice: A literature review. *International Journal of Neuroscience, 24*, 217-231.

Deloitte Touche Tohmatsu Limited (2016). *The 2016 Deloitte millennial survey. Winning over the next generation of leaders*.

Demerouti, E., Bakker, A. B., Nachreiner, F., & Schaufeli, W. B. (2001). The job demands-resources model of burnout. *Journal of Applied Psychology, 86*(3), 499-512.

Dervin, B. (1998). Sense-making theory and practice: An overview of user interests in knowledge seeking and use. *Journal of Knowledge Management, 2*(2), 36–46.

Devictor, V. (2017). The biophysical realities of ecosystems. In C. L. Spash (Ed.), *Routledge handbook of ecological economics: Nature and society* (pp. 99–107). Routledge.

Dewey, J. (1938/1997). *Experience and education*. Simon & Schuster.

Dieter, A. (2017). Geophysical limits, raw material use and their policy implications. In C. L. Spash (Ed.), *Routledge handbook of ecological economics: Nature and society* (pp. 99–107). Routledge.

Dieter, A. (2017). Geophysical limits, raw material use and their policy implications. In C. L. Spash (Ed.), *Routledge handbook of ecological economics: Nature and society* (pp. 99–107). Routledge.

Dignum, V. (2006). An overview of agents in knowledge management. In M. Umeda, A. Wolf, O. Bartenstein, U. Geske, D. Seipel & O. Takata (Eds.), *Conference proceeding: Declarative programming for knowledge management: 16th International Conference on Applications of Declarative Programming and Knowledge Management, INAP 2005*. Fukuoka, Japan (pp. 175–189). Springer.

Dirks, K. T., & Ferrin, D. L. (2002). Trust in leadership: Meta-analytic findings and implication for research and practice. *Journal of Applied Psychology, 87*(4), 611-628. https://doi.org/10.1037/0021-9010.87.4.611

Dispenza, J. (2007). *Evolve your brain: The science of changing your mind*. Health Communications, Inc.

Dittmann-Kohli, F., & Baltes, P. B. (1990). Toward a neofunctionalist conception of adult intellectual development: Wisdom as a prototypical case of intellectual growth. In C. Alexander and E. Langer (Eds.), *Beyond formal operations: Alternative endpoints to human development*. Oxford University Press.

Dixon, N. M. (2000). *Common knowledge: How companies thrive by sharing what they know*. Harvard Business School Press.

Dobbs, D. (2007). Turning off depression. In F.E. Bloom (Ed.), *Best of the brain from Scientific American: Mind, matter, and tomorrow's brain*.

Dobs K, Bülthoff I, Schultz J (2016) Identity information content depends on the type of facial movement, Scientific Reports, 6:34301:1-9.

Dolphijn, R. (2021). Doing justice to that which matters: Subjectivity and the politics of new materialism. In H. Rosa, C. Henning & A. Bueno (Eds.), *Critical theory and new materialisms* (pp. 143–153). Routledge.

Drucker, P. (1993). *Post-capitalist society*. HarperBusiness.

Drucker, P. (1999, March-April). Managing oneself. *Harvard Business Review 77*(2).

du Toit, A. (2003). Knowledge: A sense making process shared through narrative. *Journal of Knowledge Management, 7*(3), 27–37.

Dubravac, S. (2015). *Digital destiny: How the new age of data will transform the way we wok, live, and communicate.* Regnery Publishing.

Dulipovici, A., & Robey, D. (2013). Strategic alignment and misalignment of knowledge management systems: A social representation perspective. *Journal of Management Information Systems, 29*(4), 103–126.

Dvir, R. (2006). Knowledge city: Seen as a collage of human knowledge moments. In F. J. Carrillo (Ed.), *Knowledge cities: Approaches, experiences, and perspectives.* Butterworth Heinemann Elsevier.

Dyke, M. (2009). An enabling framework for reflexive learning: Experiential learning and reflexivity in contemporary modernity. *International Journal of Lifelong Education, 28*(3), 289–310.

Eapen, T. T., Finkenstadt, D. J., Folk, J., & Venkataswammy, L. (2023, July-August). How generative AI can augment human creativity. Harvard Business Review, 101(4), 56-64.

Edelman, G., & Tononi, G. (2000). *A universe of consciousness: How matter becomes imagination.* Basic Books.

Edvardsson, I. R., Yigitcanlar, T., & Pancholi, S. (2016). Knowledge city research and practice under the microscope: A review of empirical findings. *Knowledge Management Research & Practice, 14*(4), 537–564.

Edwards, G., Elliott, C., Iszatt-White, M., & Schedlitzki, D. (2015). Using creative techniques in leadership learning and development: An introduction. *Advances in Developing Human Resources 17*(3), 279-288. https://doi.org/10.1177/152342231586616

Eid, M., & Larsen, R. J. (Eds.) (2008). *The science of subjective well-being.* Guilford Press.

Ellinor, L., & Gerard, G. (1998). *Dialogue: Rediscover the transforming power of conversation.* John Wiley & Sons.

Encarta World English Dictionary (1999). St. Martin's Press.

Enkel, E., Heil, S., Hengstler, M., & Wirth, H. (2017). Exploratory and exploitative innovation: To what extent do the dimensions of individual level absorptive capacity contribute? *Technovation, 60,* 29–38.

Ericsson, K.A., Charness, N., Feltovich, P. J., & Hoffman, R. R. (Eds.) (2006). *The Cambridge handbook of expertise and expert performance.* Cambridge University Press.

Erikson, J. M. (1988). *Wisdom and the senses: The way of creativity.* Norton.

Espejo, R., Schuhmann, W., Schwaninger, M., & Bilello, U. (1996). *Organizational transformation and learning: A cybernetic approach to management.* John Wiley & Sons.

Esteva, G. (1995). Beyond development and modernity: Regenerating the art of living. In A. Ruprecht & C. Taiana (Eds.), *The reordering of culture: Latin America, the Caribbean and Canada in the hood* (pp. 319–337). Carleton University Press.

Evans, J. M., Hendron, M. G. & Oldroyd, J. B. (2015). Withholding the ace: The individual- and unit-level performance effects of self-reported and perceived knowledge hoarding. *Organizational Science, 26*(2), 494-510. https://doi.org/10.1287/orsc.2014.0945

Facebook (2019). What's the difference between organic, paid and post reach? https://www.facebook.com/help/285625061456389

Fachinelli, A. C., Carrillo, F. J., & D'Arisbo, A. (2014a). Capital system, creative economy, and knowledge city transformation: Insights from Bento Gonçalves, Brazil. *Expert Systems with Applications, 41*(12), 5614–5624.

Fachinelli, A. C., Giacomello, C. P., & Larentis, F. (2014b). The influence of capital system categories on Human Development Index in Brazil. *International Journal of Knowledge-Based Development, 6*(4), 350–369.

Fachinelli, A. C., Giacomello, C. P., Larentis, F., & D'Arrigo, F. (2017). Measuring the capital systems categories: The perspective of an integrated value system of social life as perceived by young citizens. *International Journal of Knowledge-Based Development, 8*(4), 334–345.

Faggian, A., Modrego, F., & McCann, P. (2019). Human capital and regional development. In R. Capello & P. Nijkamp (Eds.), *Handbook of regional growth and development theories* (pp. 149–171). Edward Elgar Publishing.

Farrugia, C., & Sanger, J. (2017). *Gaining an employment edge: The impact of study abroad on 21ˢᵗ century skills & career prospects in the US. Washington, DC.* IIE Center for Academic Mobility Research and Impact. https://globalsupport.tamu.edu/GlobalSupport/media/Doc-Files/IIE-2017-Report-Gaining-an-Employment-Edge-thru-Study-Abrd.pdf

Fenton, T. (2022). *Freedom at work: The leadership strategy for transforming your life, your organization, and our world.* BenBella Books, Inc.

Fenwick, T. (2008). Understanding relations of individual-collective learning in work: A review of research. *Management Learning, 39*(3), 227–243.

Filip, F. G. (2020). DSS—A class of evolving information systems. In G. Dzemyda, J. Bernatavičienė, & J. Kacprzyk (Eds.), *Data science: New issues, challenges and applications: Studies in computational intelligence, 869,* 253-277. Springer.

Fine, G. (2003). *Plato on knowledge and forms: Selected essays.* Oxford University Press, Introduction.

Firestone, J., & McElroy, M. (2002). Generations of knowledge management. *Knowledge and Innovation: Journal of the KMCI, 2*(2), 111–122.

Fischer, R. (1971). A cartography of ecstatic and meditative states. *Science, 174*(4012), 897-904.

Fitzgerald, B. l(2003). Introduction to the special series of papers on informing each other: Bridging the gap between researcher and practitioners. In *Informing Science 6.*

Flood, S. (n.d.). 5 creative ways to achieving your own transcendence. *Soulspot.* http://soulspottv.com/blog/5-creive-ways-to-achieving-your-own-transcendence/

Floridi, I., et al. (2018). AI4People – An ethical framework for a good AI society. *Minds and Machines, 28*(4), 689-707.

Fong, P. S. W., Men, C., Luo, J., & Jia, R. (2018). Knowledge hiding and team creativity: The contingent role of task interdependence. *Management Decision, 56*(2), 329-343. https://doi.org/10.1108/MD-11-2016-0778

Foray, D. (2004). *Economics of knowledge.* MIT Press.

Forrester, J. W. (1961). *Industrial dynamics.* Productivity Press.

Foss, N. J., & Klein, P. G. (2023, Spring). Rethinking hierarchy: We need to reconceive managerial authority for today's business environment – not eliminate it. *MIT Sloan Management Review, 64*(3), 56-61.

Foss, N.J., & Mahnke, V. (2011). Knowledge creation in firms: An organizational economics perspective. In M. Easterby-Smith & M. A. Lyles (Eds.), *Handbook of organizational learning and knowledge management* (2nd ed., pp. 125–151). John Wiley & Sons.

Frankl, V. E. (1939/1963). *Man's search for meaning: An introduction of logotherapy.* Pocket Books.

Frémeaux, S., & Pavageau, B. (2022). Meaningful leadership: How can leaders contribute to meaningful work? *Journal of Management Inquiry, 31*(1), 54-66.

Frijda, N. H. (2000). The psychologists' point of view. In M. Lewis & J. M. Haviland-Jones (Eds.), *Handbook of emotions* (2ⁿᵈ ed). The Bilford Press, pp. 59-74.

Frijda, N. H. (2016). The evolutionary emergence of what we call "emotions". *Cognition and Emotion*, 609-620.

Furtner, M. R., Tutzer, L., & Sachse, P. (2018). The mindful self-leader: Investigating the relationships between self-leadership and mindfulness. *Social Behavior and Personality: An International Journal 46*(33), 353-360. https://doi.org/10.2224/sbp.6521

Gagnon, J-P. (2018, June). 2,234 Descriptions of democracy. *Democratic Theory, 5*(1), 92-113. doi: 10.3167/dt.2018.050107

Gaiseanu (2020f). Informational structure of the living systems: From philosophy to informational modeling, *Philosophy Study, 10*(12), 795-806. doi: 10.17265/2159-5313/2020.12.004. http://www.davidpublisher.com/Public/uploads/Contribute/5feac331230ba.pdf

Gaiseanu (2021h). Information as an essential component of the biological structures and their informational organization. *Journal of Microbiology & Biotechnology, 6*(2), 1-9. https://medwinpublishers.com/OAJMB/information-as-an-essential-component-of-the-biological-structures-and-their-informational-organization.pdf

Gaiseanu F. (2023c). From Micro to Macro Complexity Organization Scale of the Living Organisms, Their Informational Structure/Functions Are the Same, Annals of Biostatistics & Biometric Applications, Iris Publishers. Vol 5(3): 1-12. 10.33552/ABBA.2023.05.000614.

Gaiseanu F. (2023f). What is mind, what is consciousness, and where this resides. *Philosophy Study, 13*(3), 103-120. doi: 10.17265/2159-5313/2023.03.001. https://www.davidpublisher.com/Public/uploads/Contribute/647027490c94a.pdf

Gaiseanu Florin (2018b) Destiny or free will decision? A life overview from the Perspective of an Informational Modeling of Consciousness Part II: Attitude and Decision criteria, free will and destiny. *Gerontology & Geriatric Studies 4*(1), 1-7. https://crimsonpublishers.com/ggs/pdf/GGS.000576.pdf

Gaiseanu Florin (2021f) New perspectives in biomedical engineering and biotechnology: Information in human and biological structures. *Archives in Biomedical Engineering and Biotechnology, 6*(1), 1-3. ABEB.MS.ID.000633. DOI: 10.33552/ABEB.2021.06.000633.

Gaiseanu, F. (2018a). Information: From philosophic to physics concepts for informational modeling of consciousness. *Philosophy Study 8*(8), 368-382. doi: 10.17265/2159-5313/2018.08.004. http://www.davidpublisher.org/Public/uploads/Contribute/5c06323653cd2.pdf

Gaiseanu, F. (2019a). The informational model of consciousness: Mechanisms of embodiment/disembodiment of information. *NeuroQuantology, 17*(4), 1-17. https://www.neuroquantology.com/article.php?id=1322

Gaiseanu, F. (2019b). Information model of consciousness: From philosophic concepts to an information science of consciousness. *Philosophy Study, 9*(4), 181-196. http://www.davidpublisher.org/Public/uploads/Contribute/5d1c009c3567e.pdf.DOI:10.17265/2159-5313/2019.04.002

Gaiseanu, F. (2019c). Destiny or free will decision? A life overview from the perspective of an informational modeling of consciousness part I: Information, consciousness and life cycle. *Gerontology & Geriatric Studies 4*(1), 1-7. https://crimsonpublishers.com/ggs/pdf/GGS.000586.pdf

Gaiseanu, F. (2019e). The silent voice of those who are no Longer: Transgenerational transmission of information from the perspective of the informational model of consciousness. *Gerontology & Geriatric Studies 5*(1): 482-488. DOI: 10.31031/GGS.2019.05.000604. https://crimsonpublishers.com/ggs/pdf/GGS.000604.pdf

Gaiseanu, F. (2019f). Epigenetic information-body interaction and information-assisted evolution from the perspective of the informational model of consciousness. *Archives in Biomedical Engineering & Biotechnology, 2*(2): 1-6. DOI: 10.33552/ABEB.2019.02.000532 https://irispublishers.com/abeb/pdf/ABEB.MS.ID.000532.pdf.

Gaiseanu, F. (2020a). Information-matter bipolarity of the human organism and its fundamental circuits: From philosophy to physics/neurosciences-based modeling. *Philosophy Study, 10*(2), 107-118. doi: 10.17265/2159-5313/2020.02.002. http://www.davidpublisher.com/Public/uploads/Contribute/5e5b3d8e74433.pdf

Gaiseanu, F. (2020b). Attitude as an expressible info-operational reaction to a perceived/purposed object/objective. *International Journal on Neuropsychology and Behavioural Sciences, 1*(1), 12-16. DOI: 10.51626/ijnbs.2020.01.00002. https://skeenapublishers.com/journal/ijnbs/IJNBS-01-00002.pdf

Gaiseanu, F. (2020c). *Physics of consciousness and life: The informational model of consciousness – Information in neurosciences, biocomputers and biosystems* – Romanian version: *Fizica constiintei si a vietii: Modelul informational al constiintei – Informatia in neurostiinte, biocomputere si biosisteme.* Editura GlobeEdit. https://www.amazon.com/Fizica-Conștiinței-Vieții-Informational-Neuroștiințe/dp/6139421705

Gaiseanu, F. (2020d). What is life: An informational model of the living structures. *Biochemistry and Molecular Biology, 5*(2), 18-28. 18-28. doi: 10.11648/j.bmb.20200502.12.

Gaiseanu, F. (2020e). Informationally-assisted equilibrium and health: Specific ACC contribution from the perspective of the informational model of consciousness. *EC*

Psychology and Psychiatry J., 9(5), 37-49. (https://www.ecronicon.com/ecpp/ECPP-09-00692.php

Gaiseanu, F. (2020g). Information based hierarchical brain organization/evolution from the perspective of the informational model of consciousness. *Archives in Neurology & Neuroscience 7*(5), 1-6. ANN.MS.ID.000672. DOI: 10.33552/ANN.2020.07.000672. https://www.academia.edu/42766202/Information_Based_Hierarchical_Brain_Organization_Evolution_from_the_Perspective_of_the_Informational_Model_of_Consciousness

Gaiseanu, F. (2020h). Info-relational cognitive operability of the posterior cingulate cortex according to the informational model of consciousness. *International Journal of Psychological and Brain Sciences, 5*(4): 61-68 doi: 10.11648/j.ijpbs.20200504.12. http://www.sciencepublishinggroup.com/journal/paperinfo?journalid=170&doi=10.11648/j.ijpbs.20200504.12

Gaiseanu, F. (2021a). Information in the universal triangle of reality for non-living/living structures: from philosophy to neuro/life sciences. *Philosophy Study, 11*(8), 607-621. https://www.davidpublisher.com/Public/uploads/Contribute/613a23ae7fc67.pdf

Gaiseanu, F. (2021b). Evolution and development of the information concept in biological systems: From empirical description to informational modeling of the living structures. *Philosophy Study, 11*(7), 501-516. https://www.davidpublisher.com/Public/uploads/Contribute/60ff9a4c77211.pdf

Gaiseanu, F. (2021c). Evaluating attitude and behavior: An info-operational procedure related/supported by the cognitive centers of mind. *International Journal on Neuropsychology and Behavioural Sciences, 2*(1), 1-5.

Gaiseanu, F. (2021d). Informational model of consciousness and life, information as a constitutive element of the living systems: From philosophy to modeling and applications. Colocviile Mihai Draganescu: Presentation on Science and Technology of Information, March 18, Romanian Academy. https://academiaromana.ro/sectii/sectia14_informatica/sti/doc2021/d0318-ColocviileMDraganescu.pdf

Gaiseanu, F. (2021e) Human as an informational device. *Archives in Biomedical Engineering & Biotechnology 6*(1), 1-8. ABEB.MS.ID.000629. DOI: 10.33552/ABEB.2021.06.000629

Gaiseanu, F. (2021g). Solution to the mind-body relation problem: Information. *Philosophy Study, 11*(1), 42-55. http://www.davidpublisher.com/index.php/Home/Article/index?id=44889.html

Gaiseanu, F. (2021i). Information, info-creational field, creativity and creation, according to the informational model of consciousness. *International Journal on Neuropsychology and Behavioural Sciences 2*(3), 75–80. DOI: 10.51626/ijnbs.2021.02.000017. https://skeenapublishers.com/journal/ijnbs/IJNBS-02-00017.pdf.

Gaiseanu, F. (2021j). Mental aggressive operability from informational perspective: A deterrence manifesto. *EC Neurology, 13*(4), 31-39. https://www.ecronicon.com/ecne/pdf/ECNE-13-00879.pdf

Gaiseanu, F. (2021k). Pathological expression and circuits in addiction and mood disorders: Informational relation with the brain and info-therapy. *EC Neurology, 13*(8), 24-35. https://www.ecronicon.com/ecne/pdf/ECNE-13-00924.pdf

Gaiseanu, F. (2021l). Neuropsychological response to information of beauty/ugly brain circuits according to the informational model of consciousness. *International Journal on Neuropsychology and Behavioural Sciences (IJNBS), 2*(2), 55-59.

Gaiseanu, F. (2021m). Evaluating attitude and behavior: An info-operational procedure related/supported by the cognitive centers of mind, *International Journal on Neuropsychology and Behavioural Sciences, 2*(1), 1-5.

Gaiseanu, F. (2022a). The cognitive-sentient exploration of mediated reality: From proto-cognition/epigenetic informational processes to big data assisted prediction. In S. B. Shafer & A. Bennet (Eds.), *Global media's preternatural influence on global technological singularity, culture, and government.* IGI-Global, pp. 193-213. https://www.igi-global.com/chapter/the-cognitive-sentient-exploration-of-mediated-reality/296550

Gaiseanu, F. (2022b) Info-activity of the immune system from the perspective of the informational model of the human body and living structures. *International Journal of Frontline Research in Life Science, 1*(2), 1-12. https://doi.org/10.56355/ijfrls.2022.1.2.0025

Gaiseanu, F. (2023a). Information: From cognitive-sentient exploration of reality to predictive big data assisted informational era. *Romanian Journal of Information Science and Technology, 26*(1), 78-99. https://www.romjist.ro/full-texts/paper734.pdf

Gaiseanu, F. (2023b). Information and Informational Organization of the Living Structures: From empirical decision making to decisional big data-assisted informational Era. In V. E. Balas, D. Gintautas, S. Belciug, & J. Kacprzyk (Eds.), *DSS 2023, Decision making and decision support in the information and AI era*, Dedicated to Academician Florin Gheorghe Filip. Studies in Systems, Decision and Control (SSDC) Book Series from Springer.

Gaiseanu, F. (2023d) The Informational Model of the Human Body and Living Structures: from Micro to Macro Structuration and Functions, *Preprints* (www.preprints.org), 1-19. doi:10.20944/preprints202304.0110.v1.

Gaiseanu, F. (2023e). Cellular info-operability: Micro/macro-scale inter-communication in the immune system of the human/mammalian organism. *Annals of Biostatistics & Biometric Applications, 5*(1), 1-7. 10.33552/ABBA.2023.05.000605.

Gaiseanu, F. (2023h). In_novation, a great native dynamic way toward successful performance. In A. Bennet, & R. Baisya (Eds.), *INside Novation: Looking from the inside out*. MQIPress, pp. 241-270.

Galabova, L., & McKie, L. (2013). The five fingers of my hand: Human capital and well-being in SMEs. *Personnel Review*, 772-683. http://dx.doi.org/10.1108/PR-01-2012-0017

Gallup (2022). *State of the Global Workplace 2022 Report.*

Garavan, T. (1997). The learning organization: A review and evaluation. *The Learning Organization, 4*(1), 18–29.

Garcia, B. (2004). Developing futures: A knowledge-based capital for Manchester. *Journal of Knowledge Management, 8*(5), 47–60.

Garcia, B. (2006). Learning conversations: Knowledge, meanings and learning networks in Greater Manchester. *Journal of Knowledge Management, 10*(5), 99–109.

Garcia, B. (2008). Global KBD community developments: The MAKCi experience. *Journal of Knowledge Management, 12*(5), 91–106.

Garcia, B., & Chavez, D. (2014). Network-based innovation systems: A capital base for the Monterrey city-region, Mexico. *Expert Systems with Applications, 41*(12), 5636–5646.

Gardner, H. (1983). *Frames of mind: The theory of multiple intelligence*. Basic Books.

Gardner, H. (2006). *Multiple intelligences: New horizons in theory and practice*. Basic Books.

Gardner, J. N. (1999). *Biocosm: The new scientific theory of evolution: Intelligent life is the architect of the universe*. Inner Ocean.

Garnåsjordet, P. A., Aslaksen, I., Giampietro, M., Funtowicz, S., & Ericson, T. (2012). Sustainable development indicators: From statistics to policy. *Environmental Policy and Governance, 22*(5), 322–336.

Garvin, D. A. (2003). *Learning in action: A guide to putting the learning organization to work*. Harvard Business Review Press.

Garvin, D. A., Edmondson, A. C., & Gino, F. (2008). Is yours a learning organization? *Harvard Business Review, 86*(3).

Gastaldi, L., Lettieri, E., Corso, M., & Masella, C. (2012). Performance improvement in hospitals: leveraging on knowledge asset dynamics through the introduction of an electronic medical record. *Measuring Business Excellence, 16*(4), 14–30.

Gazzaniga, M. S. (2004). *The cognitive neurosciences III*. MIT Press.

Gazzaniga, M.S. (2008). *Human: The science behind what makes us unique*. HarperCollins.

Gell-Mann, M. (1994). *The quark and the jaguar: Adventures in the simple and the complex.* W. H. Freeman and Company.

George, M. S. (2007). Stimulating the brain. In F. E. Bloom (Ed.), *Best of the brain from Scientific American: Mind, matter, and tomorrow's brain*, pp. 20-34. The Dana Foundation.

Gerth, H. H., & Mills, C. W. (Eds. and Trans.) (1946). *Max Weber: Essays in sociology*. Oxford University Press.

Giorbran, G. (2017). *Everything and forever: Timelessness*. Barnes & Nobel.
http://everythingforever.com/Bohm.htm

Gold, A. H., Malhotra, A., & Segars, A. H. (2001). Knowledge management: An organizational capabilities perspective. *Journal of Management Information Systems, 18*(1), 185–214.

Gold, M., & Douvan, E. (1997). *A new outline of social psychology*. American Psychological Association.

Goldberg, E. (2005). *The wisdom paradox: How your mind can grow stronger as your brain grows older*. Gotham Books, Penguin Group.

Goleman (1995).

Goleman (1998).

Goleman, D. (2000, March-April). Leadership that gets results. *Harvard Business Review*, pp. 78-90.

Gomide, W. (2021a). Non-causality and transreal numbers: The world seen at speed of light. [Unpublished]. UFMT/Brazil.

Gomide, W. (2021b). Metaphysical aggregates and their insertion into Cantor's thought. [Unpublished]. UFMT/Brazil.

Gomide, W. (2022) Transreal numbers and sentient logic. In S. B. Schafer & A. Bennet (Eds.), *Handbook of research on global media's preternatural influence on global singularity, culture and government*, pp. 269-278. IGI Global.

Goodin, R., Rice, J., Parpo A., & Eriksson, L. (2008). *Discretionary time: A new measure for freedom*. Cambridge University Press.

Göpel, M. (2016). *The great mindshift: How a new economic paradigm and sustainability transformations go hand in hand*. Springer.

Gorz, A. (2010). *The immaterial* (C. Turner, Trans.). Seagull Books.

Gough, I. (2020, 28 April). In times of climate breakdown, how do we value what matters? *OpenDemocracy*. Retrieved 6 March 2022 from https://www.opendemocracy.net/en/oureconomy/times-climate-breakdown-how-do-we-value-what-matters/.

Graeber, D. (2001). *Toward an anthropological theory of value*. Palgrave Macmillan.

Grant, R. M. (2002). The knowledge-based view of the firm. In C. W. Choo & N. Bontis (Eds.), *The strategic management of intellectual capital and organizational knowledge* (pp. 133–148). Oxford University Press.

Green, A., Stankosky, M., & Vandergriff, L. (2010). *In search of knowledge management: Pursuing primary principles*. Emerald Group Publishing Limited.

Greenleaf, R. K. (1977/ 2002). *Servant leadership: A journey into the nature of legitimate power & greatness* (25th Anniversary Ed.). Paulist Press.

Greiner, M., Bohmann, T., & Krcmar, H. (2007). Strategy for knowledge management. *Journal of Knowledge Management, 11*(6), 3–15.

Greiner, M., Bohmann, T., & Krcmar, H. (2007). Strategy for knowledge management. *Journal of Knowledge Management, 11*(6), 3–15.

Grigg, D. B. (1975, July). The world's agricultural labor force 1800-1970. *Geography Journal, 60*(3). Taylor & Francis, Ltd, University of Sheffield.

Groves, C. P. (2005). Order primates. In D. E. Wilson, D. M. Reeder (Eds), *Mammal species of the world: A taxonomic and geographic reference, vol. 1*. Johns Hopkins University Press, pp. 111-184.

Gudeman, S. F. (1986). *Economics as culture: Models and metaphors of livelihood*. Routledge.

Gusnard, D. A., & Raichle, M. E. (2004). Functional imaging, neurophysiology, and the resting state of the human brain. *The cognitive neurosciences III*, pp. 1267-1280. MIT Press.

Haberlandt, K. (1998). *Human memory: Exploration and application*. Allyn & Bacon.

Habermas, J. (1979). *Communication and the evolution of society*. Beacon Press.

Hackman, J. R., & Oldham, G. R. (176). Motivation through the design of work: Test of a theory. *Organizational Behavior and Human Performance, 16*(2), 250-279.

Haeckel, S. (1999). *Adaptive enterprise: Creating and leading sense and respond organizations*. Harvard Business School Press.

Hall, B. (1998). Culture and values management. In P. Sullivan, *Profiting from intellectual capital*. John Wiley & Sons.

Hammond, S. A. (1996). *The thin book of appreciative inquiry*. Thin Book Publishing.

Han, W.-H., & Zhong, Q-Y. (2006). Development of an instrument to measure knowledge management processes. In *Proceedings of the International Conference on Management Science and Engineering (ICMSE)* (pp. 1262–1268). IEEE.

Hannon, B., & Ruth, M. (1997). *Modeling dynamic biological systems*. Springer-Verlag.

Hanson, J., Melnyk, S., & Calantone, R. (2011). Defining and measuring alignment in performance management. *International Journal of Operations and Production Management, 31*(10), 1089–1114.

Hanson, J., Melnyk, S., & Calantone, R. (2011). Defining and measuring alignment in performance management. *International Journal of Operations and Production Management, 31*(10), 1089–1114.

Haraway, D. J. (1988). Situated knowledges: The science question in feminism and the privilege of partial perspective. *Feminist Studies, 14*(3), 575–599.

Harder, A., Andenoro, A., Roberts, T. G., Stedman, N., Newberry III, M., Parker, S. J., & Rodriguez, M. T. (2015). Does study abroad increase employability? *NACTA Journal 59*(1), 41-48.

Harold, F. M. (2001). *The way of the cell: Molecules, organisms and the order of life*. Oxford University Press.

Harris, M. (1974). *Cows, pigs, wars & witches: The riddles of culture*. Random House.

Harrison, E. (2003). *Masks of the universe: Changing ideas on the nature of the cosmos*. Cambridge University Press.

Hawkins, D. R. (2002). *Power VS force: The hidden determinants of human behavior*. Hay House.

Hawkins, J. C. (2021). *A thousand brains: A new theory of intelligence*. Basic Books.

Hawkins, J., & Blakeslee, S. (2004). *On intelligence: How a new understanding of the brain will lead to the creation of truly intelligent machines*. Times Books.

Hay, C. (2002). *Political analysis: A critical introduction*. Palgrave Macmillan.

Hayes, J., & Allinson, C. W. (1998). Cognitive style and the theory and practice of individual and collective learning in organizations. *Human Relations, 51*(7), 847–871.

Heisig, P. (2009). Harmonisation of knowledge management – comparing 160 KM frameworks around the globe. *Journal of Knowledge Management, 13*(4), 4–31.

Helfat, C. E., Finkelstein, S., Mitchell, W., Peteraf, M. A., Singh, H., Teece, D. J., & Winter, S. G. (2007). Dynamic capabilities: Understanding strategic change in organizations. *Strategic Management Journal, 18*.

Henczel, S. (2001). *The information audit: A practical guide*. K.G. Saur.

Henderson, J. C., & Venkatraman, H. (1999). Strategic alignment: Leveraging information technology for transforming organizations. *IBM Systems Journal, 38*(2/3), 472–484.

Henderson, M., & Thompson, D. (2003). *Values at work*. HarperCollins Publishers.

Heron, J. (1981). Philosophical basis for a new paradigm. In P. Reason & J. Rowan (Eds.), *Human Inquiry, a sourcebook of new paradigm research*. Wiley.

Herreid, C. F. (1997-1998). What makes a good case? *Journal of College Science Teaching*, December-January.

Herreid, C. F. (2000, February). All that jazz :An essay extolling the virtues of writing case teaching notes. *Journal of College Science Teaching*, February, 225-228.

Hershey, P. (1985). *The situational leader*. Warner Books.

Hess, E. D., & Ludwig, K. (2017). *Humility is the new smart: Rethinking human excellence I the smart machine age.* Berrett-Kochler Publishers, Inc.

Hink, R. F., Kodera, K., Yamada, O., Kaga, K., & Suzuki, J. (1980). Binaural interaction of a beating frequency following response. *Audiology, 19*, 36-43.

Hobson, J. A. (1999). *Consciousness*. Scientific American Library.

Hodgson, G. M. (2012). *From pleasure machines to moral communities: An evolutionary economics without Homo economicus*. University of Chicago Press.

Hoeschele, W. (2010). *The Economics of Abundance: A Political Economy of Freedom, Equity, and Sustainability*. Retrieved 6 March 2022 from https://wiki.p2pfoundation .net/ Economics of Abundance.

Holland, J. H. (1998). *Emergence: From chaos to order*. Addison-Wesley Publishing Company.

Holliday, S. G., & Chandler, M. J. (1986). *Wisdom: Explorations in adult competence: Contributions to human development*, Vol. 17. Karger, Basel.

Holman, D., & Axtell, C. (2016). Can job redesign interventions influence a broad range of employee outcomes by changing multiple job characteristics? A quasi-experimental study. *Journal of Occupational Health Psychology, 21*(3), 284-295.

Holsapple, C., & Jones, K. (2004). Exploring primary activities of knowledge chain. *Knowledge and Process Management, 11*(3), 155–174.

Honderich, T. (1999). *The philosophers: Introducing great Western thinkers*. Oxford University Press, p. 110.

Hook, J. (2015). Blog. https://www.joshuanhook.com/what-is-humility?

Hsieh, J., Lin, B., & Lin, C. (2009). The construction and application of knowledge navigator model (KNM™): An evaluation of knowledge management maturity. *Expert Systems with Applications, 36*(2), 4087–4100.

Hubbard, D. W. (2007). *How to measure anything: Finding the value of intangibles in business*. John Wiley & Sons.

Hudson, R. (2011). Geographies of economic decline. In R. Lee, A. Leyshon, L. McDowell and P. Sunley, *A compendium of economic geography*, pp. 261-272.

Iacoboni, M. (2008). *The new science of how we connect with others: Mirroring people*. Farrar, Straus & Giroux.

Iacoboni.

IBM (2010). *Capitalizing on Complexity: Insights from the global chief executive officer study*. IBM Global Business Services.

Immordino-Yang, M. H. (2016). The smoke around mirror neurons: Goals as sociocultural and emotional organizers of perception and action in learning. In M. H. Immordino-Yang (Ed.), *Emotions, learning, and the brain: Exploring the educational implications of affective neuroscience*. Norton.

Immordino-Yang, M. H. (2016). The smoke around mirror neurons: goals as sociocultural and emotional organizers of perception and action in learning. In M. H. Immordino-Yang (Ed.), *Emotions, learning, and the brain: Exploring the educational implications of affective neuroscience*. Norton.

Immordino-Yang, M. H., Christodoulou, J. A., & Singh, V. (2016). 'Rest is not idleness': Implications of the brain's default mode for human development and education. In M. H. Immordino-Yang (Ed.), Emotions, learning, and the brain: Exploring the educational implications and affective neuroscience (pp. 43-68). Norton.

Inkpen, A. C., & Beamish, P. W. (1997). Knowledge, bargaining power, and the instability of international joint ventures. *Academy of Management Review, 22*(1), 177–202.

Itam Eyo, E., Sunarsi, D., & Affandi, A. (2022). A literature review in learning organization. *International Journal of Educational Administration, Management, and Leadership, 3*(1), 11–16.

James, J. (1996). *Thinking the future tense: A workout of the mind*. Touchstone.

James, W. (1890/1980). *The principles of psychology, Vol. 1*. Holt, Rinehart & Winston.

Jaques, E. (1997). *Requisite organization: Total system for effective managerial organization and managerial leadership for the 21st century*. Gower.

Jarrahi, M. H., Askay, D., Eshraghi, A., & Smith, P. (2023). Artificial intelligence and knowledge management: A partnership between human and AI. *Business Horizons, 66*(1), 87-99.

Jarvis, P. (1992). *Paradoxes of learning: On becoming an individual in society*. Jossey-Bass.

Jashapara, A. (2003). Cognition, culture and competition: An empirical test of the learning organization. *The Learning Organization, 10*(1), 31–50. https://doi.org/10.1108/09696470310457487

Johansen, B. (2020). *Full-spectrum thinking: how to escape boxes in a post-categorical future.* Berrett-Koehler Publishers, Inc.

Johnson, R. E., Rosen, C. C., & Djurdjevic, E. (2011). Assessing the impact of common method variance on higher order multidimensional constructs. *Journal of Applied Psychology, 96*(4).

Johnson, S. (2001). *Emergence.* Scribner.

Johnson, S. (2001). *Emergence: The connected lives of ants, brains, cities, and software.* Scribner.

Johnson, S. (2006). The neuroscience of the mentor-learner relationship. In S. Johnson & K. Taylor (Eds.), *The neuroscience of adult learning: New direction for adult and continuing education,* pp. 73-70. Jossey-Bass.

Jung, C. G. (1990). *The undiscovered self with symbols and the interpretation of dreams* (R. F. Hull, Trans.). Princeton University Press.

Kabat-Zinn, J. (1995). *Wherever you go, there you are: Mindfulness meditation in everyday life.* Hyperion.

Kakabadse, N., Kakabadse, A., & Kouzim, A. (2003). Reviewing the knowledge management literature: Towards a taxonomy. *Journal of Knowledge Management, 7*(4), 75–91.

Kaku, M. (2023). *Quantum supremacy: How the quantum compute revolution will change everything.* Doubleday. p. 181.

Kandel, E. R. (2006a). *The neuroscience of adult learning: New directions for adult and continuing education.* Jossey-Bass, p. 298. Kandel, E. R. (2006b). *In search of memory: The emergence of a new science of mind.* W. W. Norton & Company.

Kantor, J. R. (1959). *Interbehavioral psychology. A sample of scientific system construction.* Principia Press.

Katsafanas, P. (2016). Nietzsche's account of self-conscious gency. In C. Sandis (Ed.), *Philosophy of action from 1500 to the present day.* Oxford University Press., GS 112.

Kauffman, S. (1995). *At home in the universe: The search for the laws of self-organization and complexity.* Oxford University Press.

Kawashina, R. Sugiura, M., Kato, T., Nakamura, A., Hatano, K., Ito, K., et al. (1999). The human amygdala plays an important role in gaze monitoring: A PET study. *Brain, 122,* 779-783.

Kegan, R. (1980). Making meaning: The constructive-developmental approach to persons and practice. *The Personnel and Guidance Journal, 58*(5), 373-380.

Kelb, M. J. (1995). *Thinking for a change: Discovering the power to create, communicate, and lead.* Harmony Books.

Kelly, K, 2016). *Understanding the 12 technological forces that will shape our future.* Viking.

Kelly, S., & Allison, M. (1999). The complexity advantage: How the science of complexity can help your business achieve peak performance. *Computer Science.* https://www.semanticscholar.org/paper/The-Complexity-Advantage%3A-How-the-Science-of-Can-Kelly-Allison/6368860796880d4196d11b9a8291a54e22bbbb25

Kenny, Maj. R., executive officer of the 30th Signal Battalion, Wheeler Army Airfield, Hawaii. A Signal Corps officer. How to leave a legacy blog (2018, March 15). https:/from the greennotebook.com/2018/03/15/how-to-leave-a-legacy/

Kenter, J. O. (2017). Deliberative monetary valuation. In C. L. Spash (Ed.), *Routledge handbook of ecological economics: Nature and society* (pp. 251–361). Routledge.

Klingan, K., Sepahvand, A., Rosol, C., & Scherer, B. M. (Eds.) (2015). *Textures of the Anthropocene: Grain vapor ray* (4 vols. and a manual). MIT Press.

Kim, D. H. (1995). *Systems thinking tools: A user's reference guide.* Pegasus.

Kim, H., Im, J., & Qu, H. (2018). Exploring antecedents and consequences of job crafting. International *Journal of Hospitality Management 75,* 18-26. https://doi.org/10.1016/j.ijhm.2018.02.014

Kirsner, K., Speelman, C., Mayberry, M., O'Brien-Malone, A., Anderson, M., & MacLeod, C. (Eds.) (1998). *Implicit and explicit mental processes.* Lawrence Erlbaum Associates.

Klein, G. (2003). *Intuition at work: Why developing your gut instincts will make you better at what you do.* Doubleday.

Klein, G. A. (2017). *Sources of power: How people make decisions.* MIT Press.

Kluwe, R. H., Luer, G., & Rosler, F. (Eds.) (2003). *Principles of learning and memory.* Birkhauser Verlag.

Knight, R. (2017). How to manage a needy employee. *Harvard Business Review.* https://hbr.org/2017/06/how-to-manage-a-needy-employee

Knorr-Cetina, K. D. (2013). *The manufacture of knowledge: An essay on the constructivist and contextual nature of science.* Elsevier.

Koestler, A., & Smythies, J. R. (1969). *Beyond reductionism: New perspectives in the life sciences. The Alpbach Symposium.* Beacon Press.

Kolb, D. A. (1984). *Experiential learning: Experience as the source of learning and development.* Prentice-Hall.

Kostopoulos, K., Papalexandris, A., Papachroni, M., & Ioannou, G. (2011). Absorptive capacity, innovation, and financial performance. *Journal of Business Research, 64*(12), 1335–1343.

Kotter, J. (2012). *Leading change.* Harvard Business Review Press.

Koulpoulos, T.M. (2012). *Cloud surfing: A new way to think about risk, innovation, scale, and success.* Bibliomotion, Inc.

Kouzes, J. M., & Posner, B. Z. (2007). *The leadership challenge,* 4th ed. Jossey-Bass, John Wiley and Sons.

Kramer, D. A., & Bacelar, W. T. (1994). The educated adult in today's world: Wisdom and the mature learner. In J. D. Sinnott (Ed.), *Interdisciplinary handbook of adult lifespan learning.* Greenwood Press.

Krasodomski-Jones, A., Judson, E., Smith, J., Miller, C., & Jones, E. (2019, May). *Information operations in the digital age.* Warring Songs.

Kropotkin, P. (1902). *Mutual aid: A factor of evolution.* Heinemann.

Kuan, T. (2012). Cognitive operations in Buddhist meditation: Interface with Western psychology. *Contemporary Buddhism 13*, 1, 35-60. https://doi.org/10.1080/14639947.2012.669281

Kucza, T. (2001). *Knowledge management process model.* VTT Technical Research Centre of Finland.

Kuntz, P. G. (1968). *The concept of order.* University of Washington Press.

Kurtzman, J. (1998). *Thought leaders: Insights on the future of business.* Jossey-Bass.

Kurzweil, R. (2005). *The singularity is near: When humans transcend biology.* Viking Penguin.

Kurzweil, R. (2012). *How to create a mind: The secret of human thought revealed.* Viking

Kuznets, S. (1955). Economic growth and income inequality. In *The American Economic Review XLV*(1). http://www.aeaweb.org/aer/top20/45.1.1-28.pdf

Kwon, C., & Nicolaides, A. (2017). Managing diversity through triple-loop learning: A call for paradigm shift. *Human Resource Development Review, 16*(1), 85–99.

Labovitz, G., & V. Rozanski, (1997). *The Power of Alignment: How Great Companies Stay Centered and Accomplish Extraordinary Things.* John Wiley and Sons, Inc.

Lafley, A. G., & Martin, R. I. (2013). *Playing to win: How strategy really works.* Harvard Business Review Press.

Lajul, W. (2018). Reconstructing African fractured epistemologies for African development. *Synthesis Philosophica, 33*(1), 51–76.

Lakoff, G. (2006). *Thinking points: Communicating our American values and vision.* Farrar, Strus and Giroux.

Lam, N. (2022). Explanations in AI as claims of tacit knowledge. *Minds and Machines 32*, 135-158. https://doi.org/10.1007/s11023-021-09588-1

Lambe, P. (2011). The unacknowledged parentage of knowledge management. *The Journal of Knowledge Management, 15*(2), 175-197.

Lambe, P. (2023). *Principles of knowledge auditing. Foundations for knowledge management implementation.* The MIT Press.

Lane, P. J., & Lubatkin, M. (1998). Relative absorptive capacity and interorganization learning. *Strategic Management Journal, 19*(5), 461–477.

Langer, E. J. (2000). Mindful learning. *Current directions in Psychological Science 9*(6), 220-223. https://doi.org/10.1111/1467-8721.00099

Lara, J. (2000). *Administración del conocimiento en el sector público: Administración tributaria del Perú* [MSc dissertation, Tecnológico de Monterrey].

Lasheras, I. (2006). *Legazpi bai! El proyecto*. Mondragón Innovation and Knowledge.

Laszlo, E. (1972). *The systems view of the world*. George Braziller.

Laszlo, E. (1995). *The interconnected universe: Conceptual foundations of transdisciplinary unified theory*. Inner Traditions.

Laszlo, E. (1999). *The systems view of the world: A holistic vision for our time*. Hampton Press, Inc.

Laszlo, E. (2004). *Science and the Akashic Field: An integral theory of everything*. Inner Traditions.

Laszlo, E. (2009). *Worldshift 2012: Making green business, new politics & higher consciousness work together*. Inner Traditions.

Laszlo, E. (Ed.) (1973). *The world system: Models, norms, variations*. George Braziller.

Laszlo, K., & Laszlo, A. (2002). Evolving knowledge for development: The role of knowledge management in a changing world. *Journal of Knowledge Management, 6*(4), 400–412.

Latour, B., & Weibel, P. (Eds.) (2020). *Critical zones: The science and politics of landing on earth*. MIT Press and ZKM Centre for Art and Media, p. 23 (original emphasis).

Lavin, C., Melis, C., Mikulan, M., Gelormini, C., Huepe, D., Ibañez, A. (201). The anterior cingulate cortex: an integrative hub for human socially-driven interactions, *Frontiers in Neuroscience/Decision Neuroscience 7*, 64(2):1-4.

Lazlo, E. (1999). *The systems view of the world: A holistic vision for our time*. Hampton Press, Inc.

LeDoux, J. (1996). *The emotional brain: The mysterious underpinnings of emotional life*. Touchstone.

LeDoux, J. (1996). *The emotional brain: The mysterious underpinnings of emotional life*. Touchstone.

Lee, R. WB., Yip, J. Y., & Shek, V. W. (2021). *Knowledge risk and its mitigation: Practices and cases*. Emerald.

Lee, W. B. (2017). Knowledge elicitation practices for organizational development intervention. *Knowledge Management Research & Practice, 15*(1).

Lee, W. B. (2023). Exploring the depth of the MIKE: An intellectual practice-based study program. In A. Bennet & R. Baisya (Eds.), *INside INnovation: Looking from the inside out*. MQIPress.

León, M., Castañeda, D., & Sánchez, I. (2007). La gestión del conocimiento en las organizaciones de información: Procesos y métodos para medir. *ACIMED, 15*(3).

León, M., Ponjuan, G., & Rodríguez, M. (2006). Procesos estratégicos de gestión del conocimiento. *ACIMED, 14*(2).

Leonard-Barton, D. (1992). Core capabilities and core rigidities: A paradox in managing new product development. *Strategic Management Journal, 13*(S1), 111–125.

Leonnard-Barton, D. (1995). *Wellsprings of knowledge: Building and sustaining the sources of innovation*. Harvard Business School Press.

LeShan, L. (1976). *Alternate realities*. Ballantine.

Leslie, J. (Ed.) (1998). *Modern cosmology and philosophy*. Prometheus Books.

Leslie, J. (Ed.) (1998). *Modern cosmology and philosophy*. Prometheus Books.

Levin, J. R. (1973). Inducing comprehension in poor readers. *Journal of Educational Psychology, 65*(19).

Levitt, B., & March, J. G. (1988). Organizational learning. *Annual Review of Sociology, 14*, 319–340.

Levitt, H. M. (1999). The development of wisdom: An analysis of Tibetan Buddhist experience. *Journal of Humanistic Psychology, 39*(2), 86-105.

Lewin, A. Y., Massini, S., & Peeters, C. (2011). Microfoundations of internal and external absorptive capacity routines. *Organization Science, 22*(1), 81–98.

Lewis, J. (2019). *Story thinking: Transforming organizations for the fourth industrial revolution*. Amazon KDP.

Li, T., & Cavusgil, S. T. (1999). Measuring the dimensions of market knowledge competence in new product development. *European Journal of Innovation Management, 2*(3), 129–146.

Lichtenthaler, U. (2009). Absorptive capacity, environmental turbulence, and the complementarity of organizational learning processes. *Academy of Management Journal, 52,* 822–846.

Liebold, M., Probst, G., & Gibber, M. (2005). *Strategic management in the knowledge economy: New approaches and business applications.* John Wiley & Sons.

Liebowitz, J. (Ed.) (1999). *The knowledge management handbook.* CRC Press.

Liebowitz, J., Rubenstein-Montano, B., McCaw, D., Buchwalter, J., & Browning, C. (2000). The knowledge audit. *Knowledge and Process Management, 7*(1), 3-10.

Liedloff, J. (1977). *The continuum concept.* Addison-Wesley.

Liedtka, J. (2018). Why design thinking works. *Harvard Business Review.*

Liedtka, J., & Ogilvie, T. (2011). *Designing for Growth: A Design Thinking Tool Kit for Managers.* Columbia University Press.

Lin, C., Yen, D., & Tarn, D. (2007). An industry-level knowledge management model– a study of information-related industry in Taiwan. *Information & Management, 44*(1), 22–39.

Lin, Y.-T., & Jou, M. (2013). Development of an Integrated Learning Environment with Knowledge Management for Cultivating Student Critical Thinking Skills. *Procedia - Social and Behavioral Sciences, 103*, 290–298.

Linden, R. (1994). *Seamless government: A practical guide to re-engineering in the public sector.* Jossey-Bass, Inc.

Linstone, H. A. (1977). Confessions of a forecaster. In H. A. Linstone & W. H. C. Simmonds (Eds.), *Futures research: New directions. Addison-Wesley Publishing Company, Inc.*

Linz, J., & Stepan, A. (Eds.) (1978). *The breakdown of democratic regimes: Crisis, breakdown, and reequilibration.* Johns Hopkins University Press.

Lips-Wiersma, M., & Wright, S. (2012). Measuring the meaning of meaningful work: Development and validation of the comprehensive meaningful work scale. *Group & Organizational Management, 37*(5), 655-685.

Lipton, B., & Bhaerman, S. (2009). *Spontaneous evolution: Our positive future (and a way to get there from here).* Hay House.

Little, A. Saggeza. https://builtin.com/operations/flat-culture

Long, T.A. (1986). Narrative unity and clinical judgment. *Theoretical Medicine 7*, 75-92.

López, M., Cuesta, A., & Joyanes, L. (2008). *Ciudad-región conocedora: Gestión de conocimiento para una ciudad-región.* Centro Editorial Universidad de Caldas.

López, M., Cuesta, A., & Joyanes, L. (2008). *Ciudad-región conocedora: Gestión de conocimiento para una ciudad-región.* Centro Editorial Universidad de Caldas.

Luhmann, N. (1995). *Social systems.* Stanford University Press.

Luk, C.Y.A. (2009). *A Narrative Approach to the Study of service quality performance: a case study in a public utility company in Hong Kong* (MPhil dissertation, The Hong Kong Polytechnic University, 2008) http://repository.lib.polyu.edu.hk/jspui/bitstream/10397/3143/2/b23071734_ir.pdf

Lysova, E. I., Allan, B. A., Dik, B. J., Duffy, R. D., & Steger, M. F. (2019). Fostering meaningful work in organizations: A multi-level review and integration. *Journal of Vocational Behavior, 110*, 374-389.

MacDonald, C. (1996). *Toward wisdom: Finding our way to inner peace, love, and happiness.* Hampton Roads, p. 1.

MacFlouer, N. (1999). *Life's hidden meaning.* Ageless Wisdom Publishers.

MacFlouer, N. (2004-16). *Why life is ...* Weekly radio shows: BBSRadio.com (#1-#480) and KXAM (#1-143). http://www.agelesswisdom.com/archives)of)radio)shows.htm

Machlup, F. (1962). *The production and distribution of knowledge in the United States.* Princeton University Press.

MacIntyre, A. (2007). *After virtue: A study in moral theory.* 3rd edition. University of Notre Dame Press.

Magala, S. J. (2017). Philosophy of science or knowledge management? *Journal of Organizational Change Management, 30*(4), 454–455.

Magrassi, P. (2002, 18 July). A taxonomy of intellectual capital (Research Note No. COM-17-1985). Gartner Research. Retrieved 6 March 2022 from https://www.researchgate .net/profile/Paolo -Magrassi-2/publication/279013374ATaxonomy_ofIntellectualCapital/links/ 5589004908ae347f9bdac8f3/A-Taxonomy-of-Intellectual-

Makikangas, A., Feldt, T., Kinnunen, U., & Mauno, S. (2013). Does personality matter? Research on individual differences in occupational well-being. In A. B. Bakker (Ed.), *Advances in positive organizational psychology, Vol. 1*. Emerald, 107-143.

Malafsky, G. P., & Newman, B. D. (2001). Organizing knowledge with ontologies and taxonomies. TECHi2.

Malik, O. F., Shahzad, A., Raziq, M. M., Khan, M. M., Yusaf, S., & Khan, A. (2019). Perceptions of organizational politics, knowledge hiding, and employee creativity: The moderating role of professional commitment. *Personality and Individual Differences, 142*, 232-237. https://doi.org/10.1016/j.paid.2018.05.005

Manz, C. C. (1986). Self-leadership: toward an expanded theory of self-influence processes in organizations. *Academy of Management Review 11*(3), 585-600. https://doi.org/10.2307/258312

Manz, C. G. (2015). Taking the self-leadership high road: Smooth surface or potholes ahead? *Academy of Management Perspectives 29*(1), 132-11. https://doi.org/10.5465/amp.2013.0060

Marakas, G. M. (1999). *Decision support system in the 21st century*. Prentice Hall.

Marans, R. W., & Stimson, R. (2011). *Investigating quality of urban life*. Springer.

March, J. G. (1991). Exploration and exploitative in organizational learning. *Organization Science, 2*(1), 71-87.

Marchand, L. H. (2022). The innovation mindset: Eight essential steps to transform any industry. Columbia Business School Publishing.

Marsh, J. T., Brown, W. S., & Smith, J. C. (1975). Far-field recorded frequency-following response: Correlates of low pitch auditory perception in humans. *Electroencephalography and Clinical Neurophysiology, 38*, 113-119. 0

Marshall, I., & Zohar, D. (1997). *Who's afraid of Schrödinger's cat?* William Morrow and Company, Inc.

Martensson, M. (2000). A critical review of knowledge management as a management tool. *Journal of Knowledge Management, 4*(3), 204–216.

Martínez, A. (2001). Un modelo de procesos clave de administración del conocimiento. *Transferencia, 14*(53), 28–29.

Martínez, A. (2010). Personal knowledge management by the knowledge citizen: The generation aspect of organizational and social knowledge-based development. In K. Metaxiotis, F. J. Carrillo & T. Yigitcanlar (Eds.), *Knowledge-based development for cities and societies: Integrated multi-level approaches* (pp. 131–140). IGI Global.

Maslow, A. H. (1971). *The farther reaches of human nature*. Arkana/Penguin Books.

Material originally prepared by authors for the U.S. Department of the Navy toolkit, *Cport: Building Communities of Practice: Creating Value through Knowledge Communities*. A practitioners guide. Used with permission and in public domain.

Matthews, J., & Wrigley, C. (2017). Design and design thinking in business and management higher education. *Journal of Learning Design, 10*(1), 41. https://doi.org/10.5204/jld.v9i3.294

Matthews, R. C. (1991). The forgetting algorithm: How fragmentary knowledge of exemplars can yield abstract knowledge. *Journal of Experimental Psychology: General, 120*, 117-119.

Maturana, H. R., & Varela, F. J. (1987). *The tree of knowledge: The biological roots of human understanding*. New Science Library, Shambhala.

Maunsell, J. H. R., & Treue, S. (2006). Feature-based attention in visual cortex. *Trends in Neuroscience, 29*, 317-322.

Mayer-Schönberger, V, & Cukier, K. (2013). *Big data: A revolution that will transform how we live, work, and think*. Houghton Mifflin Harcourt.

Mayumi, K. T. (2017). Thermodynamics: Relevance, implications, misuse, and ways forward. In C. L. Spash (Ed.), *Routledge handbook of ecological economics: Nature and society* (pp. 89–98). Routledge.

McAdam, R., & McCreedy, S. (1999). A critical review of knowledge management models. *The learning organization, 6*(3), 91–100.

McCabe, T. J. (2019). *Interconnections: Computer science, math, poetry, stories, entrepreneurship.* Independently published.

McCarthy, M., & Stein, J. (2003). *Agile business for fragile times.* McGraw Hill Publishing Co. Lewis, J. (2019). *Story Thinking: Transforming organizations for the fourth industrial revolution.* Self-Published.

McClory, S., Read, M., & Labib, A. (2017). Conceptualising the lessons-learned process in project management: Towards a triple-loop learning framework. *International Journal of Project Management, 35*(7), 1322–1335.

McCraty, R. (2015). *Science of the heart: Exploring the role of the heart in human performance* (vol. 2). The HeartMath Institute.

McCraty, R., & Childre, D. (2010, July/August). Coherence: Bridging personal, social, and global health. *The Journal of Alternative Therapies, 16*(4).

McMaster, M.D. (1996). *The intelligence advantage: Organizing for complexity.* Butterworth-Heinemann.

Melzer, A., Shafir, T., Tsachor, R.P. (2019). How do we recognize emotion from movement? Specific motor components contribute to the recognition of each emotion. *Front. Psychol. 10:*1389: 1-11.

Merck corporate values statement: merck.com/about/mission.html

Merok Paulsen, J., & Brynjulf Hjertø, K. (2014). Exploring individual-level and group-level levers for inter-organizational knowledge transfer. *The Learning Organization, 21*(4), 274–287.

Merriam, S. B., & Caffarella, R. S. (1999). *Learning in adulthood: A comprehensive guide.* Jossey-Bass Publishers.

Merriam, S.B., Caffarella, R.S., & Baumgartner, L.M. (2006). *Learning in adulthood: A comprehensive guide.* John Wiley & Sons.

Merrill, M. D. (2002). Knowledge objects and mental models. In D. A. Wiley (Ed.), *The instructional use of learning objects* (pp. 261–280). Agency for Instructional Technology and Association for Educational Communications & Technology.

Merrill, M. D., Richards, R.E., Schmidt, R.V. & Wood, N. D. (1977). *The instructional strategy diagnostic profile training manual.* Courseware, Inc

Merry, U. (1995). *Coping with uncertainty: Insights from the new sciences of chaos, self-organization and complexity.* Praeger.

Meyer, C., & Davis, S. (2003). *It's alive: The coming convergence of information, biology, and business.* Crown Business.

Michael, D. N. (1977). Planning's challenge to the systems approach. In H. A. Linstone & W. H. C. Simmonds (Eds.), *Futures research: New directions.* Addison-Wesley Publishing Company, Inc.

Michaelson, C., Pratt, M. G., Grant, A. M., & Dunn, C. P. (2014). Meaningful work : Connecting business ethics and organization studies. *Journal of Business Ethics, 121*, 77-90.

Michio, K. (2023). *Quantum supremacy: How the quantum computer revolution will change everything.* Doubleday, p. 181.

Miller, J. (2023, April 19). Rigid, linear supply chains must be a think of the past for agencies. federalnewsnetwork.com/federal-insights/2023/04/

Miller, J. G. (1978). *Living systems.* McGraw-Hill.

Miniter, R. (2005). *Disinformation: 22 media myths that undermine the war on terror.* Regnery Publishing.

MITRE (2022). *Crown Jewels Analysis for Industrial Control Systems.* https://www.mitre.org/news-insights/publication/creow-jewels-analysis-industrial-control-systems

Mokyr, J. (2005). The intellectual origins of modern economic growth. *The Journal of Economic History, 65*(2), 285-351.

Moon, J. A. (2004). *A handbook of reflective and experiential learning: Theory and practice.* Routledge-Falmer.

Morecroft, J. D. W., & Sterman, J. D. (Eds.) (194). *Modeling for learning organizations*. Productivity Press.

Morey, D., Marbury, M., & Thuraisingham, B. (2000). *Knowledge management: Classic and contemporary works*. The MIT Press, p. xii.

Morowitz, H. J. (2002). *The emergence of everything: How the world became complex*. Oxford University Press.

Morrison, F. (1991). *The art of modeling dynamic systems: Forecasting for chaos, randomness, and determinism*. John Wiley & Sons., Inc.

Morroni, M. (2006). *Knowledge, scale, and transactions in the theory of the firm*. Cambridge University Press.

Mulcahy, M. P., & Prince, M. B. (2004). Using ant and butterfly pollination to involve students in scientific exploration. In M. A. O'Donnell (Ed.), *Tested studies for laboratory teaching, volume 25*. Proceedings of the 25th Workshop/conference of the Association for Biology Laboratory Education (ABLE), pp. 135-157. http://www.zoo.utoronto.ca/able

Mulford, P. (2007). *Thoughts are things*. Barnes & Noble.

Mulvihill, M.K. (2003). The Catholic Church in crisis: Will transformative learning lead to social change through the uncovering of emotion? In C.A. Weissner, S.R. Meyers, N.L. Pfhal, & P.J. Neaman (Eds.), *Proceedings of the 5th International Conference on Transformative Learning*, pp. 320-325. Teachers College, Columbia University.

Murphy, N. (2000). Introduction: A hierarchical framework for understanding wisdom. In W. S. Brown (Ed.), *Understanding wisdom: sources, science and society*. Templeton Foundation Press.

Murray, A. J. (2018). *Building the enterprise of the future: Co-creating and delivering extraordinary value in an eight-billion-mind world*. AKS Press, pp. 75-81.

Murray, A. J., & Greenes, K. A. (2006). New leadership strategies for the enterprise of the future. *VINE: The Journal of Information and Knowledge Management Systems, 36*(3), pp. 231-237.

Myers, N. (1984). *GAIA: An atlas of planet management*. Anchor Books.

Myths by Which We Live (1965, September). *The Rotarian, 107*(3), 32-33.

Naim, M. F., & Lenka, U. (2020). Organizational learning and Gen Y employees' affective commitment: The mediating role of competency development and moderating role of strategic leadership. *Journal of Management & Organization, 26*(5), 815–831.

Nan, N. (2008). A principal–agent model for incentive design in knowledge sharing. *Journal of Knowledge Management, 12*(3), 101–113.

Neck, C. P., & Houghton, J. D. (2006). Two decades of self-leadership theory and research. *Journal of Managerial Psychology 21*(4), 270-295. https://doi.org/10.1108/0268390610663097

Neck, C. P., Houghton, J. D., Sardeshmukh, S. R., Goldsby, M., & Godwin, J. L. (2013). Self-leadership: A cognitive resource for entrepreneurs. *Journal of Small Business & Entrepreneurship 26*(5), 463-480.

Neef, D., Siesfeld, G. A., & Cefola, J. (Eds.) (1998). *The economic impact of knowledge*. Routledge.

Nelson, C. A., deHaan, M., & Thomas, K. M. (2006). *Neuroscience of cognitive development: The role of experience and the developing brain*. John Wiley & Sons.

New Scientist (2021, 1 March), "What is fire?", retrieved 4 July, 2022 from https://www.newscientist.com/question/what-is-fire/.

Nonaka, I. & Takeuchi, H. (1995). *The knowledge-creating company: How Japanese companies create the dynamics of innovation*. Oxford University Press.

Nonaka, I., & Konno, N. (1998). The concept of "ba": Building a foundation for knowledge creation. *California Management Review, 40*(3), 40–54.

Nonaka, I., & Takeuchi, H. (1995). *The knowledge-creating company: How Japanese companies create the dynamics of innovation*. Oxford University Press.

Nonaka, I., Toyama, R., & Konno, N. (2000). SECI , Ba and leadership : A unified model of dynamic knowledge creation. *Leadership, 33*(1), 5–34. https://doi.org/10.1016/S0024-6301(99)00115-6

Nouwen, H.J.M. (1975). *Reaching out: the three movements of the spiritual life.* Doubleday.

Nussbaum, M., & Sen, A. (Eds.) (1993). *The quality of life.* Clarendon Press.

Nystrom, P. C., & Starbuck, W. H. (1984). *Handbook of organizational design, volumes 1 and 2.* Oxford University Press.

O'Connor, J., & McDermott, I. (1997). *The art of systems thinking.* HarperCollins Publishers.

O'Dell, C., & Grayson, C., Jr. (1998). *If only we knew what we knew: The transfer of internal knowledge and best practices.* Free Press.

O'Dell, C., & Hubert, C. (2011). *The new edge in knowledge: How knowledge management is changing the way we do business.* John Riley & Sons, Inc.

Odor, H. O. (2018). A literature review on organizational learning and learning organizations. *International Journal of Economics & Management Sciences, 7*(1), 1–6.

Oluikpe, P. (2012). Developing a corporate knowledge management strategy. *Journal of Knowledge Management, 16*(6), 862–878.

Omnes, R. (1999). *Quantum philosophy: Understanding and interpreting contemporary science.* Princeton University Press.

Osborne, D., & Gaebler, T. (1993). *Reinventing government: How the entrepreneur spirit is transforming the public sector.* Penguin Books.

Oster, G. (1973). Auditory beats in the brain. *Scientific American, 229*, 94-102.

Ovans, A. (2022). What Is Strategy, Again? *Harvard Business School Cases*, 1–1254.

Palmer, B., Quinn Griffin, M. T., Reed, P., & Fitzpatrick, J. J. (2010). Self-transcendence and work engagement in acute care staff registered nurses. *Critical Care Nursing Quarterly, 33*, 138-147.

Pandit, S. K. (2021). Managing and leveraging knowledge assets of the firm: The call of the day. In R. Bhattacharyya (Ed.), *Comparative advantage in the knowledge economy: A national and organizational resource* (pp. 181–194). Emerald Publishing.

Panke, S. (2019). Design thinking in education: Perspectives, opportunities and challenges. *Open Education Studies, 1*(1), 281-306. https://doi.org/10.1515/edu-2019-0022

Parker, S., Racz, M., & Palmer, P. (2020). Reflexive learning and performative failure. *Management Learning, 51*(3), 293–313.

Pattee, H. H. (1973). *Hierarchy theory: The challenge of complex systems.* George Braziller.

Peng, H. (2013). Why and when do people hide knowledge? *Journal of Knowledge Management, 17*(3), 398-415. https://doi.org/10.1108/JKM-12-2012-0380

Peng, J., Wang, Z., & Chen, X. (2019). Does self-serving leadership hinder team creativity? A moderated dual-path model: JBE. *Journal of Business Ethics, 159*(2), 419-433.

Peng, Q., Zhong, X., Liu, S., Zhou, H., & Ke. N. (2021). Job autonomy and knowledge hiding: The moderating roles of leader reward omission and person-supervisor fit. *Personnel Review.* https://doi.org/10.1108/PRo-03-2020-0133

Perkins, M. (1971). *Outsmarting IQ: the emerging science of learnable intelligence.* Free Press.

Pert, C. B. (1997). *Molecules of emotion: A science behind mind-body medicine.* Touchstone.

Petchsawang, P., & McLean, G. N. (2017). Workplace spirituality, mindfulness meditation, and work engagement. *Journal of Management, Spirituality & Religion, 14*(3), 216-244.

Peters, L. D., Löbler, H., Brodie, R. J., Breidbach, C. F., Hollebeek, L. D., Smith, S., Sörhammar, D., & Varey, R. J. (2014). Theorizing about resource integration through service-dominant logic. *Marketing Theory, 14*(3), 249–268.

Petrash, G. (1996). Dow's journey to a knowledge value management culture. *European Management Journal, 14*(4), 365–373.

Phelps, E. (2013). *Mass flourishing: How grassroots innovation created jobs, challenge, and change.* Princeton University Press.

Phillips, P. J., Hahn, C. A., Fontana, P. C., Yates, A. N., Greene, K., Broniatowski, D. A., & Przybocki, M. A. (2021, September). *Four principles of explainable artificial intelligence.* National Institute of Standards and Technology, U.S. Department of Commerce.

Pinchot, G., & Pinchot, E. (1993). *The end of bureaucracy & the rise of the intelligent organization.* Berrett-Koehler Publishers.

Pinchot, G., & Pinchot, E. (1993). *The end of bureaucracy & the rise of the intelligent organization.* Berrett-Koehler Publishers.

Pinker, S. (2007). *The stuff of thought: Language as window into human nature*. Viking.

Pinkerton, J. P. (1995). *What comes next: The end of big government—and the new paradigm ahead*. Hyperion.

Pleitez, J., & Flamenco, E. (2007). Desarrollo basado en conocimiento aplicado a la marginalidad y probreza urbana en el Salvador. In F. Casado (Ed.), *Desarrollo basado en el conocimiento* (pp. 301–313). Comunidad Iberoamericana de Sistemas de Conocimiento.

Polanyi, M. (1958). *Personal knowledge: Towards a post-critical philosophy*. The University of Chicago.

Polanyi, M. (1966). *The tacit dimension*. Routledge and Keoan.

Polanyi, M. (1967). *The tacit dimension*. Anchor Books.

Pollard, C. W. (1996). *The soul of the firm*. HarperBusiness and Zondervan Publishing.

Portante, T., & Tarro, R. (1997, September). Paying attention. *Wired Magazine*.

Porter, D., Bennet, A., Turner, R., & Wennegren, D. (2002). *The power of team: The making of a CIO*. U.S. Department of the Navy.

Porter, M. E. (1996, January 1). What is Strategy? *Harvard Business Review*, *74*(6), 61–80.

Powell, W. W., & Snellman, K. (2004). The knowledge economy. *Annual Review of Sociology*, *30*, 199–220.

Powell, W. W., & Snellman, K. (2004). The knowledge economy. *Annual Review of Sociology*, *30*, 199–220, p. 201.

Pratt, M. G., & Ashforth, B. E. (2003). Fostering meaningfulness in working and at work. *Positive organizational scholarship: Foundations of a new discipline*, *309*.

Preyer, G., & Peter, G. (2005). *Contextualism in philosophy: Knowledge, meaning, and truth*. Oxford University Press.

Prigogine, I. & Stengers, I. (2017). *Order Out of Chaos: Man's New Dialogue with Nature*. Verso, Brooklyn, NY.

Prigogine, I. (1996). *The end of certainty: Time, chaos, and the new laws of nature*. The Free Press.

Prinz, W. (2005). An ideomotor approach to imitation. In S. Hurley & N. Chater, *Perspectives on imitation: From neuroscience to social science Vol. 1: Mechanisms of imitation and imitation in animals*, pp. 141-156. MIT Press.

Probst, F., Raub, S., & Romhardt, K. (2000). *Managing knowledge: Building blocks for success*. John Wiley & Sons, Ltd.

Puthoff, H. E. (1989). Source of vacuum electromagnetic zero-point energy. *Physical Review A*(40), 4857-62.

Puthoff, H. E. (1990). The energetic vacuum: Implications for energy research. *Speculations in Science and Technology*, *13*(4).

Ramírez, G. (2007). En búsqueda del desarrollo basado en conocimiento en Chile. In A. Mújika (Ed.), *Regiones iberomericanas del conocimiento* (pp. 187–213). Universidad de Deusto.

Ramon, S. (1997). *Earthly cycles: How past lives and soul patterns shape your life*. Pepperwood Press.

Read, H. (2019). A typology of empathy and its many moral forms. *Philosophy Compass*, *14*(10), e12623.

Reber, A.S. (1993). *Implicit learning and tacit knowledge: An essay on the cognitive unconscious*. Oxford University Press.

Reed, L. W. (1958, December). *I, pencil: My family tree as told to Leonard E. Read*. Foundation for Economic Education.

Reed, P. (1986). The developmental conceptual framework: Nursing reformulations and applications for family theory. In A. Whall (Ed.), *Family therapy theory for nursing: Four approaches*. Appleton-Ce3ntury-Crofts, pp. 69-92.

Reed, P. (2003). A nursing theory of self-transcendence. In M. J. Smith & P. Liehr (eds.), *Middle range theory for advanced practice nursing*. Springer, pp. 145-166.

Reigeluth, C. M. (1983). Meaningfulness and instruction: Relating what is being learned to what a student knows. *Instructional Science*, *12*(3), 197-218.

Reis, J., Amorim, M., Melão, N., & Matos, P. (2018). Digital transformation: A literature review and guidelines for future research. *Advances in Intelligent Systems and Computing, 745*(May), 411–421. https://doi.org/10.1007/978-3-319-77703-0_41

Reiss, M. (2011). *What went wrong with economics: The flawed assumptions that led economists astray.* CreateSpace Independent Publishing Platform.

Rescher, N. (2001). *Paradoxes: their roots, range, and resolution.* Open Court.

Rescher, N. (2001). *Paradoxes: their roots, range, and resolution.* Open Court.

Rezgui, Y., Hopfe, C., & Vorakulpipat, C. (2010). Generations of knowledge management in the architecture, engineering, and construction industry: An evolutionary perspective. *Advanced Engineering Informatics, 24*(2), 219–228.

Rezgui, Y., Hopfe, C., & Vorakulpipat, C. (2010). Generations of knowledge management in the architecture, engineering, and construction industry: An evolutionary perspective. *Advanced Engineering Informatics, 24*(2), 219–228.

Rhee, Y. W., & Choi, J. N. (017). Knowledge management behavior and individual creativity: Goal orientations as antecedents and in-group social status as moderating contingency. *Journal of Organizational Behavior, 38*(6), 813-832. https://doi.org/10.1002/job.2168

Ricard, M., & Thuan, T. X. (2001). *The quantum and the lotus: A journey to the frontiers where science and Buddhism meet.* Crown Publishers.

Ridley, M. (2020). *How innovation works: And why it flourishes in freedom.* Harper Perennial.

Riggio, R. E. l(2015). Are you empathic? 3 types of empathy and what they mean. *Psychology Today.*

Rist, G. (2019). *The history of development: From western origins to global faith* (4th ed.). Zed Books.

Ritchey, D. (2003). *The H.I.S.S. of the A.S.P.: Understanding the anomalously sensitive person.* Headline Books.

Rizzolatti, G. (2006, November). Mirrors in the mind. *Scientific American.*

Roberts, N. (2015). Absorptive capacity, organizational antecedents, and environmental dynamism. *Journal of Business Research, 68*(11), 2426–2433.

Roger, J. (2023). *Putting content back on the throne.* Infosys Case Study.

Roman, P., & Thiry, G. (2017). Sustainability indicators. In C. L. Spash (Ed.), *Routledge handbook of ecological economics: Nature and society*, pp. 382–392. Routledge.

Romer, P. M. (1990). *Endogenous technological change. Journal of Political Economy, 98*(5, Part 2), S71–S102.

Rosa, H. (2022). *Resonance: A sociology of our relationship to the world.* (J. C. Wagner, Trans.). Polity.

Ross, P. E. (2006, August). The expert mind. *Scientific American*, 64-71.

Rousseau, D. M., & Rivero, A. (2003). Democracy, a way of organizing in a knowledge economy. *Journal of Management Inquiry, 12*(2), 115-134.

Rowley, J. (2003). Knowledge management – the new librarianship? From custodians of history to gatekeepers to the future. *Library Management, 24*(8/9), 433–440.

Ruggles, R. (2004). *The role of stories in knowledge management.* Storytelling Foundation. http://www.providersedge.com/docs/km_articles/The_Role_of_Stories_in_KM.pdf

Ruggles, R. L. (1997). *Knowledge management tools.* Butterworth-Heinemann.

Rutherford, M., & Samuels, W. J. (Eds.) (1996). *John R. Commons: Selected essays volume two.* Routledge.

Ryle, G. (1949). *The concept of mind.* Hutchinson.

Sachs, W. (Ed.) (1992). *The development dictionary: A guide to knowledge as power.* Zed Books.

Saenz, J., & Perez-Bouvier, A. (2014). Interaction with external agents, innovation networks, and innovation capability: The case of Uruguayan software firms. *Journal of Knowledge Management, 18*(2), 447–468.

Saint-Onge, H. (1996). Tacit knowledge: The key to the strategic alignment of intellectual capital. *Planning Review, 24*(2), 10–16.

Sallinsbury, R. M. (1988). *Paradoxes.* Cambridge University Press.

Salomon, G., Perkins, D. N., & Globerson, T. (1991). Partners in cognition: Extending intelligence with intelligent technologies. *Educational Researcher, 20.*

Santomauro, D. F., Herrera, A. M. M., Shadid, J., Zheng, P., Ashbaugh, C., Pigott, D. M., ... & Ferrari, A. J. (2021). Global prevalence and burden of depressive and anxiety disorders in 204 countries and territories in 2020 due to the COVID-19 pandemic. *The Lancet, 398*(10312), 1700-1712.

Santos, M., & Dante, G. (2011). Propuesta de un modelo de medición para los procesos de la gestión del conocimiento en organizaciones de información. *Revista Interamericana de Bibliotecología, 34*(1), 87–103.

Sarimin, M., & Yigitcanlar, T. (2012). Towards a comprehensive and integrated knowledge-based urban development model: Status quo and directions. *International Journal of Knowledge-Based Development, 3*(2), 175–192.

Schafer, S. B. (2022). Gamers as homeopathic media therapy: Electromagnetic antibodies in the toxic media-field. In S. B. Schafer & A. Bennet (Eds.), *Handbook of research on global media's preternatural influence on global singularity, culture and government*, pp. 397-425. IGI Global.

Scharmer, C. O. (2009). *Theory U: Leading from the future as it emerges*. Berrett-Koehler.

Schaufeli, W. B., Salanova, M., Gonzalez-Roma, V., & Bakker, A. B. (2002). The measurement of engagement and burnout: A two-sample confirmatory factor analytic approach. *Journal of Happiness Studies, 3*(1), 71-92.

Schein, E. H., & Schein, P. A. (2021). *Humble inquiry: The gentle art of asking instead of telling.* Berrett-Koehler Publishers.

Schipper, J., Chanson, J. S., Chiozza, F., Cox, N.A., [... + 125 authors], & Young, B. E. (2008, October 10). The status of the world's land and marine mammals: Diversity, threat, and knowledge. *Science 322*(5899), pp. 225-230. DOI: 10.1126/science.1165115

Schirner M, Deco G, Ritter P. (2023). Learning how network structure shapes decision-making for bio-inspired computing, *Nature Communication, 14, Article number 2963*: 1-14.

Schloss, J. P. (2000). Wisdom traditions as mechanisms for organismal integration: Evolutionary perspectives on homeostatic 'laws of life'. In W. S. Brown (Ed.), *Understanding wisdom: Sources, science and society*. Templeton Foundation Press.

Schmelzer, M., Vetter, A. & Vantsinjan, A. (2022). *The future is degrowth.* Verso.

Schmidt, E. (2023, March/April). Innovation power: Why technology will define the future of geopolitics. *Foreign Affairs, 102*(2), pp. 38-52.

Schön, D. A. (1983). *The reflective practitioner: How professionals think in action*. Basic Books.

Schrage, M. (2000). S*erious play: How the world's best companies simulate to innovate.* Harvard Business School Press.

Schrage, M. (1990). Shared minds: the new technologies of collaboration. Random House.

Schrödinger (1944) (Combined reprint, 1967). *What is life?* Cambridge University Press.

Schultze, U., & Stabell, C. (2004). Knowing what you don't know? Discourses and contradictions in knowledge management research. *Journal of Management Studies, 41*(4), 549–573.

Schulze, H. (2019). *Excellence wins: A non-nonsense guide to becoming the best in a world of compromise*. Zondervan.

Schumacher (1989). *Small is beautiful: A study of economics as if people mattered*. HarperPerennial, pp. 60–61.

Schütz, P. (2009). Resonance. In G. Stumm & A. Pritz (Eds), *Wörterbuch der psychotherapie*. Springer.

Searle, J. R. (1983). *Intentionality: An essay in the philosophy of mind*. Cambridge University Press.

Segall, D. (2012, 19 March). Cosmopolitical reflections on economy, society, and religion. *Footnotes2Plato*. Retrieved 6 March 2022 from https://footnotes2plato.com/2012/03/19/cosmopolitical-reflections-on-economy-society-and-religion/.

Sen, A. (1985). *Commodities and capabilities*. North-Holland.

Senge, P. M. (1990). *The fifth discipline: The art and practice of a learning organization* (2nd ed.). Doubleday Currency.

Senge, P. M., Scharmer, C. O., Jaworski, J., & Flowers, B. S. (2004). *Presence: Exploring profound change in people, organizations and society*. Random House, Inc.

Senivongse, C. (2023). Competency profiling of organization's absorptive capacity development. Unpublished paper.

Senivongse, C. (2023). Planning on customer engagement in the digital era. In. A. Bennet & R. Baisya (Eds.), *INside INnovation: Looking from the inside out*. MQIPress.

Senivongse, C., Mariano, S., Bennet, A., & Tsui, E. (2022). Absorptive capacity efficacy in SMEs: Evidence from multiple case studies in the information technology industry. *Knowledge Management Research and Practice, 20*(5). https://doi.org/10.1080/14778238.2020.1784050.

Sennett, R. (2006). *The craftsman*. Yale University Press.

Shapiro, S. L., Carlson, L. E., Astin, J. A., & Freedman, B. (2006). Mechanisms of mindfulness. *Journal of Clinical Psychology 62*(3), 373-386. https://doi.orgt/10.1002/jclp

Sheffi, Y. (2005). *The Resilient Enterprise: Overcoming Vulnerability for Competitive Advantage*. The MIT Press.

Sheldrake, R. (1989). *The presence of the past: Morphic resonance and the habits of nature*. Vintage Books.

Shelley, A. (2007). *Organizational zoo: A survival guide to work place behavior*. Aslan Publishing.

Shelley, A. (2017). *KNOWledge SUCCESSion: Sustained performance and capability growth through strategic knowledge projects*. Business Expert Press.

Sherman, N. (2000). Wise emotions. In W. S. Brown (Ed.), *Understanding wisdom: Sources, science and society*. Templeton Foundation Press.

Silberman, M. (2007). *The handbook of experiential learning*. Pfeiffer.

Silver, L., Van Kessel, P., Huang, C., Clancy, L., & Gubbala, S. (2021). *What makes life meaningful? Views from 17 advanced economies*. Pew Research Center.

Simon Lelic, Editor, *InsideKnowledge*, May 2005.

Simon, H. A. (1996). *The sciences of the artificial*. The MIT Press.

Sinclair, J. (2005). The impact of stories. *The Electronic Journal of Knowledge Management, 3*(1), 53-64.

Singh, S. K. (2019). Territoriality, task performance, and workplace deviance: Empirical evidence on role of knowledge hiding. *Journal of Business Research, 97, 10-19*. https://doi.org/10.1016/j.jbusres.2018.12.034

Skyrme, D. J. (2002). What next for knowledge management? Development and challenges. *I3 Update*.

Smil, V. (2014). *Making the modern world: Materials and dematerialization*. John Wiley & Sons.

Smit, T. G. J. (2014). The appropriability regime as a tool to measure knowledge protection, pp. 1–12.

Smith, J. C., Marsh, J. T., Greenberg, S., & Brown, W. S. (1978). Human auditory frequency-following responses to a missing fundamental. *Science, 201*, 639-641.

Smith, J., Dixon, R. A., & Baltes, P. B. (1987). Age differences in response to life planning problems: A research analog for the study of wisdom, related knowledge. Unpublished manuscript.

Smith, P., & Max-Neef, M. (2011). *Economics unmasked: From power and greed to compassion and the common good*. Green Books.

Smith, P., & Max-Neef, M. (2011). *Economics unmasked: From power and greed to compassion and the common good*. Green Books.

Smolensky, P. (1988). On the proper treatment of connectionism. *Behavioral and Brain Sciences, 11*(1), 1-23. https://doi.org/10.1017/s0140525x00052432.

Smolin, L. (1997). *The life of the cosmos*. Oxford University Press.

Soddy, F. ([1926] 1983). *Wealth, virtual wealth, and debt*. George Allen & Unwin/Omni.

Sohn-Rethel, A. (1978). *Intellectual and manual labour: A critique of epistemology*. Macmillan.

Soo, C., Tian, A. W., Teo, S. T. T., & Cordery, J. (2017). Intellectual capital–enhancing HR, Absorptive capacity, and innovation. *Human Resource Management, 56*(3), 431–454.

Sousa, D. A. (2006). How the brain learns. Corwin Press.

Spash, C. L. (2021, June). *Social ecological economics* (Discussion Paper No. sre-disc-2021_06). Institute for Multi-Level Governance & Development, Department of Socioeconomics, Vienna University of Economics and Business.

Sraffa, P. (1975). *Production of commodities by means of commodities: Prelude to a critique of economic theory.* Cambridge University Press.

Srivastva, S., & Cooperrider, D. L. (Eds.) (1990). *Appreciative management and leadership.* Jossey-Bass.

Stacey, R. D. (1996a). *Complexity and creativity in organizations.* Berrett-Hoehler Publishers.

Stacey, R. D. (1996b). The sustainable innovation engine. *VINE, 36*(4), 398-405.

Stacey, R. D., Griffin, D., & Shaw, P. (2000). *Complexity and management: Fad or radical challenge to systems thinking?* Routledge.

Stacey, R. D., Griffin, D., & Shaw, P. (2000). *Complexity and management: Fad or radical challenge to systems thinking?* Routledge.

Stacy, R. D. (1992). *Managing the unknowable: Strategic boundaries between order and chaos in organizations.* Jossey-Bass, Inc.

Stankosky, M. (2005). *Creating the discipline of knowledge management: The latest in university research.* Elsevier Butterworth-Heinemann.

Stankosky, M. (2018). *21 for 21: Leading the 21st century global enterprise.* Emerald Books.

Stary, C. (2014). Non-disruptive knowledge and business processing in knowledge life cycles – Aligning value network analysis to process management. *Journal of Knowledge Management, 18*(4), 651–686.

Stebbins, L.H. (2010). Development of reality system theory. *Journal of Business & Economics Research, 8*(4), 1-22.

Steger, M. F., Frazier, P., Oishi, S., & Kaler, M. (2006). The meaning in life questionnaire: Assessing the presence of and search for meaning in life. *Journal of Counseling Psychology, 53*(1), 80.

Stern, D. N. (2004). *The present moment in psychotherapy and everyday life.* Norton.

Sternberg, R. J. (Ed.) (1990). *Wisdom: Its nature, origins and development.* Cambridge University Press.

Sternberg, R. J. (Ed.) (1990). *Wisdom: Its nature, origins, and development.* Cambridge University Press.

Sternberg, R.J. (2003). *Wisdom, intelligence, and creativity synthesized.* Cambridge University Press.

Stewart, T. A. (1996*). Intellectual capital: The new wealth of organizations.* McGraw-Hill.

Stewart, T. A. (2001). *The wealth of knowledge: Intellectual capital and the twenty-first century organization.* Doubleday Business.

Stiglitz, J., Sen, A., & Fitoussi, J. (2009). *Report by the Commission on the measurement of economic performance and social progress.* CMEPSP.

Stocker, G. (1998). InfoWar. In G. Stocker & C. Schöplf, *Infowar.* SpringerWien.

Stone A., & Mackie C. (Eds.) (2013). *Subjective well-being: Measuring happiness, suffering, and other dimensions of experience.* National Academies Press.

Stonier, T. (1990). *Information and the internal structure of the universe: An introduction into information physics.* Springer-Verlag. doi:10.1007/978-1-4471-3265-3

Stonier, T. (1992). *Beyond information: The natural history of intelligence.* Springer-Verlag.

Stonier, T. (1997). *Information and meaning: An evolutionary perspective.* Springer-Verlag. doi:10.1007/978-1-4471-0977-8

Strang, K. D. (2009). Assessing team members' interpersonal competencies in new product development e-projects. *International Journal of Project Organisation and Management, 1*(4), 335–357.

Strogatz, S. H., & Steward, I. (1993). Coupled oscillators and biological synchronization: A subtle mathematical thread connects clocks, ambling elephants, brain rhythms and the onset of chaos. *Scientific American, 269*(6), 102-109.

Sullivan, P. H. (2000). *Value-driven intellectual capital: How to convert intangible corporate assets into market value.* John Wiley & Sons, p. 88.

Sum, N-L, & Jessop, B. (2014). Towards a cultural political economy: Putting culture in its place in political economy. Edward Elgar Publishing.

Sun, H. C. (2003). Conceptual clarifications for 'organizational learning', 'learning organization' and 'a learning organization.' *Human Resource Development International, 6*(2), 153–166.

Sun, P. Y. T., & Anderson, M. H. (2010). An examination of the relationship between absorptive capacity and organizational learning, and a proposed integration. *International Journal of Management Reviews, 12*(2), 130–150.

Sun, P. Y. T., & Scott, J. L. (2003). Exploring the divide–organizational learning and learning organization. *The Learning Organization, 10*(4), 202–215.

Sutherland, J. W. (1975). *Systems analysis, administration, and architecture.* Van Nostrand Reinhold Company.

Sveiby, K. (2001). A knowledge-based theory of the firm to guide in strategy formulation. *Journal of Intellectual Capital, 2*(4), 344–358.

Sveiby, K., & Konrad (1989). *The invisible balance sheet.* Affarsvarlden/Ledarskap.

Swann, R., Bosanko, S., Cohen, R., Midgley, R., & Seed, K. M. (1982). *The brain: A user's manual.* G P. Putnam & Sons.

Swomley, J. (2000). Violence: Competition or cooperation. *Christian Ethics Today, 6*(1).

Taylor, D. (1996). *The healing power of stories: Creating yourself through the stories of your life.* Doubleday.

Taylor, K. (2006). Brain function and adult learning: Inplications for practice. In. S. Johnson & K. Taylor (Eds.), *The neuroscience of adult learning: New directions for adult and continuing education*, pp. 71-86. Jossey-Bass.

Temin, T. (2023, April 27). CX exchange 2023: Maximus' Mary Ann Monroe on why to start by identifying critical pain points. Insight by Maximus: Technology. https://federalnewsnetwork.com/technology-main/2023/04/cx-exchange-2023-maximus-maryann-monroe-on-why-good-employee-cx-starts-before-day-1/

Testa, D., & Sangganjanavanich, V. F. (2016). Contribution of mindfulness and emotional intelligence to burnout among counseling interns. *Counselor Education and Supervision 55*(2), 95-108. https://doi.org/10.1002/ceas.12035

Texas Instruments (2021, March). Texas Instruments Supplier Code of Conduct. https://www.ti.com

The United States Marine Corps (1994). *Warfighting: The U.S. Marine Corps book of strategy.* Doubleday.

The Urantia Book (1955). URANTIA Foundation, p. 1222.

Thomas, R. J., Cheese, R., Benton, J. M. (2003, November 1). *Human capital development.* Accenture Research Note.

Thompson, M. P. A., & Walsham, G. (2004). Placing knowledge management in context. *Journal of Management Studies, 41*(5), 725–747.

Tichy, N. (1997). *The leadership engine.* HarperCollins Publishers.

Tiwana, A. (2000). *The knowledge management toolkit: Practical techniques for building a KM system.* Prentice Hall.

Todorova, G., & Durisin, B. (2007). Absorptive capacity: Valuing a reconceptualization. *Academy of Management Review, 32*(3), 774–786.

Toffler, A. (1970). *Future shock.* Bantam Books.

Tomasello, M. (2009). *Why we cooperate.* MIT Press.

Tomasello, M. (2014). *A Natural History of Human Thinking.* Harvard University Press.

Tomassini, M., & Zanazzi, S. (2014). Reflexivity and self-development of competencies as key drivers in individuals' learning and career paths: Cases from Italy. *Research in Comparative and International Education, 9*(3), 301–312. https://doi.org/10.2304/rcie.2014.9.3.301

Tosey, P., Visser, M., & Saunders, M. N. K. (2012). The origins and conceptualizations of 'triple-loop' learning: A critical review. *Management Learning, 43*(3), 291–307.

Tovstiga, G. (2015). *Strategy in practice: A practitioner's guide to strategic thinking*. John Wiley & Sons.

Tripsas, M. (1997). Unraveling the process of creative destruction: complementary assets and incumbent survival in the typesetter industry. *Strategic Management Journal, 18*, 119–142.

Tronto, J. C. (1998). An ethic of care. *Generations: Journal of the American Society on Aging, 22*(3), 15-20.

Trumpa, C. (1991). *The heart of the Buddha*. Shambhala.

Turban, E. (1992). *Expert systems and applied artificial intelligence*. Macmillan.

Tzortzaki, A. M., & Mihiotis, A. (2014). A review of knowledge management theory and future directions. *Knowledge and Process Management, 21*(1), 29–41.

Tzortzaki, A. M., & Mihiotis, A. (2014). A review of knowledge management theory and future directions. *Knowledge and Process Management, 21*(1), 29–41.

Ulrich, D., & Lake, D. (1990). *Organizational capability*. John Wiley & Sons.

UNESCO (n.d.). Information for All Programme: *Information literacy*. IFAP. https://www.unesco.org/en/ifap/information-literacy

United Nations Development Program (UNDP) (2020). *Human development report 2020: The next frontier: human development and the Anthropocene*. UNDP.

United States Marine Corps (1994). *Warfighting, the U.S. Marine Corps book of strategy*. US Marine Corps.

Valerio-Ureña, G. (2014). Capital instrumental. In F. J. Carrillo (Ed.), *Sistemas de capitales y mercados de conocimiento* (pp. 154–163). Amazon Kindle Direct Publishing.

van den Broeck, A., Vansteenkiste, M., De Witte, H., & Lens, W. (2008). Explaining the relationships between job characteristics, burnout, and engagement: The role of basic psychological need satisfaction. *Work and Stress, 22*(3), 277-294.

van der Spek, R., & Spiskervet, A. (1997). Knowledge management: Dealing intelligently with knowledge. In J. Liebowitz & L. Wilcox (Eds.), *Knowledge management and its integrative elements*. CRC Press.

van Gigch, J.P. (1978). *Applied general systems theory*. Harper & Row Publishers.

van Heijenoort, J. (Ed.) (1967). *From Frege to Gödel: A source book in mathematical logic. 1879-1931*. Harvard University Press.

van Knippenberg, D. (2020). Meaning-based leadership. *Organizational Psychology Review, 10*(1), 6-28.

van Laar, E., Van Deursen, A. J., Van Dijk, J., & De Haan, J. (2017). The relation between 21st-century skills and digital skills: A systematic literature review. *Computers in Human Behavior 72*, 577-588. https://doi.org/10.1016/j.chb.2017.03.010

van Wezemael, J. (2012). Concluding: Directions for building prosperous knowledge cities. In T. Yigicanlar, K. Metaxiotis & F. J. Carrillo (Eds.), *Building prosperous knowledge cities: Policies, plans and metrics* (pp. 374–382). Edward Elgar Publishing.

van Wezemael, J. (2012). Concluding: Directions for building prosperous knowledge cities. In T. Yigicanlar, K. Metaxiotis & F. J. Carrillo (Eds.), *Building prosperous knowledge cities: Policies, plans and metrics* (pp. 374–382). Edward Elgar Publishing.

van Witteloostuijn, A., & de Jong, G. (2007). Organizational democracy. In S. R. Clegg & J. R. Bailey (Eds.), *International encyclopedia of organization studies volume 3*, pp. 1039-1042. Sage Publishers.

Vásquez, F., & Gabalán, J. (2009). Gestionando el conocimiento: Acercamiento conceptual en entornos organizacionales y proyección en el contexto académico. *Revista Iberoamericana de Ciencia, Tecnología y Sociedad – CTS*. Retrieved 6 March 2022 from http://www.revistacts.net/wp-content/uploads/2009/08/vazquezeditado.pdf.

Vennix, J. A. M. (1996). *Group model building: Facilitating team learning using system dynamics*. John Wiley & Sons.

Vera, D., Crossan, M., & Apaydin, M. (2012). A framework for integrating organizational learning, knowledge, capabilities, and absorptive capacity. In *Handbook of organizational learning and knowledge management*, pp. 153–180.

Volk, T. (1998). *Gaia's body: Toward a physiology of Earth*. Springer-Verlag.

von Bertalanffy, L. (1968). *General systems theory: Foundations, development, applications*. George Braziller.

von Bertalanffy, L., & Rapoport, A (Eds.) (1964). *General systems: Yearbook of the society for general systems research*, vol IX. The Society for General Systems Research.

von Clausewitz, General C. (1984/2010). On war. CreateSpace Independent Publishing Platform.

von Forester, H. (1977). Objects: Tokens for (eigen-) behaviors. In B. Inheler, R. Gracia, & J. Voneche (Eds.), *Hommage a Jean Piaget: Epistemologie genetique et equilibration*. Delachaux et Niestel.

Von Krog, G., & Grand, S. (2002). From economic theory toward a knowledge-based theory of the firm. In C. W. Choo & N. Bontis (Eds.), *The strategic management of intellectual capital and organizational knowledge* (pp. 163–183). Oxford University Press.

von Mutius, B. (2005). Rethinking leadership in the knowledge society learning from others: How to integrate intellectual and social capital and establish a new balance of value and values. In A. Bounfour & L. Edvinsson (Eds.), *Intellectual capital for communities* (pp. 151–163). Butterworth-Heinemann.

von Mutius, B. (2005). Rethinking leadership in the knowledge society learning from others: How to integrate intellectual and social capital and establish a new balance of value and values. In A. Bounfour & L. Edvinsson (Eds.), *Intellectual capital for communities* (pp. 151–163). Butterworth-Heinemann.

Voorhees, T., Aedisian-Riedinger, J., Pendleton, M. (2019). *Reflecting God's character in your business*. High Bridge Books.

Wade, W. (2012). *Scenario planning: A field guide to the future*. John Wiley & Sons, Inc.

Wahl, H., Kaufmann, c., Eckkrammer, F., Mense, A., Gollner, H., Himmler, C., Rogner, W., Baierl, T., & Slobodian, R. (2012). Soft skills in practice and education: An evaluation. *American Journal of Business Education (AJBE) 5*(2), 225-232.

Walsch, N. D. (2009). *When everything changes change everything: In a time of turmoil, a pathway to peace*. EmNin Books.

Wang, P. (2019). On defining artificial intelligence. *Journal of Artificial General Intelligence, 10*(2), 1-37.

Wang, X. (2009). *Knowledge-based urban development in China* [PhD dissertation, Newcastle University].

Wang, X., & Lihua, R. (2006). Examining knowledge management factors in the creation of new city: Empirical evidence from Zhengdong New District, Zhengzhou, China. *Journal of Technology Management in China, 1*(3), 243–261.

Wang, Y., Han, M. S., Xiang, D., & Hampson, D. P. (2019). The double-edged effects of perceived knowledge hiding: Empirical evidence from the sales context. *Journal of Knowledge Management, 23*(2), 279-296. https://doi.org/10.1108/JKM-04-2018-0245

Ward, J. (2006). *The student's guide to cognitive neuroscience*. Psychology Press.

Webster, J., Brown, G., Zweig, D., Connelly, C. E., Brodt, S., & Sitkin, S. (2008). Beyond knowledge sharing: Withholding knowledge at work. In *Research in Personnel and Human Resources Management 27*, 1-37. Emerald Group Publishing Limited.

Weick, K. (1995). *Sensemaking in organizations*. SAGE.

Weick, K. (2000). *Sensemaking in organizations: Foundations for organizational science*. SAGE Publications, Inc.

Weick, K. (2001). *Making sense of the organization*. Blackwell Publishing.

Weick, K. E., Sutcliffe, K. M. & Obstfeld, D. (2005). Organizing and the process of sensemaking. *Organization Science, 16*, 409–21.

Weinberg, G. M. (1975). *An introduction to general systems thinking*. John Wiley & Sons.

Weisbert, R. W. (1999). Creativity and knowledge: A challenge to theories. In R.J. Sternberg (Ed.), *Handbook of creativity* (226-250). Cambridge University Press.

Wenger, E. (1998). *Communities of practice: Learning, meaning, and identity*. Cambridge University Press. Doi:10.1017/CBO9780511803932

Wenger, E., McDermott, R., & Snyder, W. M. (2002). *Cultivating communities of practice*. Harvard Business Review Press.

Wheatley, M.J. (2006). *Leadership and the new science: Discovering order in a chaotic world*. Barrett-Koehler Publishers, Inc.

White, R. W. (1959). Motivation reconsidered: The concept of competence. *Psychological Review, 66*, 297-333.

Wiig, K. (1993a). *Knowledge management methods – Practical approaches to managing knowledge*. Schema Press.

Wiig, K. (1993b). *Knowledge management foundations—thinking about thinking—how people and organizations create, represent, and use knowledge*. Schema Press.

Wiig, K. (1994). *Knowledge management: The central management focus for intelligent-acting organizations*. Schema Press.

Wiig, K. (1997, September). Knowledge management: An introduction and perspective. *Journal of Knowledge Management, 1*(1), 6-14.

Wilber, K. (2000). *Integral psychology: Consciousness, spirit, psychology, therapy*. Shambhala Publications.

Wilson, E. O. (1998). *Consilience: The unity of knowledge*. Alfred A. Knoph.

Winchester, S. (2023). *Knowing what we know: The transmission of knowledge from ancient wisdom to modern magic*. Barnhill Press Ltd.

Wiseman, J., & Stillwell, A. (2022). Organizational justice: Typology, antecedents and consequences. *Encyclopedia, 2*(3), 1287-1295.

Wong, P. T. (1989). Personal meaning and successful aging. *Canadian Psychology/Psychologie Canadienne, 30*(3).

Wong, P. T. P. (2017). From Viktor Frankl's logotherapy to the four defining characteristics of self-transcendence. DrPaulWong.com http://www.drpaulwong.com/four-defining-characteristics-self-transcendence/

Woodman, M., & Dickson, E. (1996). *Dancing in the flames: The dark goddess in the transformation of consciousness*. Shambhala.

Woolf, H. (Ed.). (1990). *Webster's new world dictionary of the American language*. G. and C. Merriam. Random House.

Worawichayavongsa, W., & Bennet, A. (2022, February). The influence of mindfulness practice on self-leadership strategies engagement at non-managerial level. *Change Management: An International Journal 22*(2), 29-48. doi:10.18848/2327-798X/CGP/v22i02/29-48

World Capital Institute (WCI) & Teleos (2007 onwards). *The annual MAKCi report*. WCI.

World Commission on Environment and Development (WCED) (1987). *Our common future*. Oxford University Press.

World Economic Forum (2018). *The future of jobs report*. Centre for the New Economy and Society: Geneva, Switzerland.

Wurzburg, G. (1998). Markets and the knowledge economy: Is anything broken? Can government fix it? *Journal of Knowledge Management, 2*(1), 32–46.

Xanthopoulou, D., Bakker, A. B., Demerouti, E., & Schaufeli, W. B. (2009). Work engagement and financial returns: A diary study on the role of job and personal resources. *Journal of Occupational and Organizational Psychology, 82*(1), 183-200.

Yang, K., Ribiére, V., & Bennet, A. (2023). Can we really hide knowledge? Unpublished.

Yang, Kaiyu (2023, May 25). Personal email from IKI-SEA Bangkok University doctoral student.

Yigitcanlar, T., & Inkinen, T. (2019). Theory and practice of knowledge cities and knowledge-based urban development. In *Geographies of disruption* (pp. 109–133). Springer.

Yigitcanlar, T., & Inkinen, T. (2019). Theory and practice of knowledge cities and knowledge-based urban development. In *Geographies of disruption* (pp. 109–133). Springer.

Yigitcanlar, T., & Inkinen, T. (2019). Theory and practice of knowledge cities and knowledge-based urban development. In *Geographies of disruption* (pp. 109–133). Springer.

Yoo, K., Suh, E., & Kim, K. Y. (2007). Knowledge flow-based business process redesign: Applying a knowledge map to redesign a business process. *Journal of Knowledge Management, 11*(3), 104–125.

Zack, M. (1999). Developing a knowledge strategy. *California Management Review, 41*(3), 125–145.

Zack, M. (1999). *Knowledge and strategy*. Butterworth-Heinemann.

Zahra, S. A., & George, G. (2002). Absorptive capacity: A review, reconceptualization, and extension. *Academy of Management Proceedings & Membership Directory, 27*(2), 185-203C.

Zapata, L. Manrique, L., Carrillo, F. J., Flores, P., Ramírez, P. Martínez, A., Treviño, A. & Valerio, G., *Aprendizaje organizacional*. McGraw-Hill.

Zerubavel, E. (1997). *Social mindscapes: An invitation to cognitive sociology*. Harvard University Press.

Zhang, Y., Sun, J. M., Lin, C. H., & Ren, H. (2020). Linking core self-evaluation to creativity: The roles of knowledge sharing and work meaningfulness. *Journal of Business and Psychology, 35*, 257-270.

Zhang, Z., & Min, M. (2019). The negative consequences of knowledge hiding in NPD project teams: The roles of project work attributes. *International Journal of Project Management, 37*(2), 225-238. https://doi.org/10.1016/j.iproman.2019.01.006.

Ziai, A. (2019). *The development dictionary @25: Post-development and its consequences*. Routledge

Zohar, D., & Marshall I. (2012). *Spiritual capital: Wealth we can live by*. ReadHowYouWant, Intro.

Zohar, D., & Marshall, I. (1994). *The quantum society: Mind, physics, and the new social vision*. William Morrow and Co., Inc.

Zull, J. E. (2002). *The art of changing the brain: Enriching the practice of teaching by exploring the biology of learning*. Stylus.

Zuluaga, N. (2013). *Metamorfosis de la libélula: Construcción teórica de un modelo para Manizales en la búsqueda de un sistema urbano de conocimiento*. Universidad de Manizales. Retrieved 6 March 2022 from https://ridum.umanizales.edu.co/xmlui/bitstream/handle/20.500.12746/742/Metamorfosis %20de %20la %20Lib%C3%A9lula.pdf?sequence=1 &isAllowed=y.

INDEX

ABOUT THE AUTHORS

Alex Bennet, Professor on the faculty of Bangkok University's Institute for Knowledge and Innovation Southeast Asia (IKI-SEA), is internationally recognized as an expert in knowledge management and agent for organizational change. Alex is also Co-founder and Director of the Mountain Quest Institute. She served as the Chief Knowledge Officer and Deputy Chief Information Officer for Enterprise Integration for the U.S. Department of the Navy, and was co-chair of the Federal Knowledge Management Working Group. Prior to that she served as Acquisition Reform Executive and Standards Improvement Executive for the DoN Acquisition Workforce. Dr. Bennet is the recipient of the Distinguished and Superior Public Service Awards from the U.S. government for her work in the Federal Sector. She is a Delta Epsilon Sigma and Golden Key National Honor Society graduate with a Ph.D. in Human and Organizational Systems; degrees in Management for Organizational Effectiveness, Human Development, English and Marketing; and is certified in Total Quality Management, System Dynamics and Defense Acquisition Management, and a Reiki Master, among other energy modalities. Alex believes in the *multidimensionality and interconnectedness of humanity as we move out of infancy into full consciousness*.

Robert Turner served in the military in Army Intelligence and Organizational Development, where he founded and co-developed the U.S. Army Fusion Center, an advanced decision support center. He subsequently founded and directed the Federal Aviation Administration Team Technology Center and managed programs in support of FAA leadership development. His work at the FAA included representing the FAA at the Institute for the Future in Menlo Park and at the IBM Institute for Knowledge Management (KM). He served for four years as the Chairman of the government-wide Federal KM Network. In 2003, he received the first government-wide award for service in KM. In 2006, as co-developer of the FAA Knowledge Services Network (KSN) for virtual work, he received an acclaimed government-wide award for innovation excellence. He is a member of Phi Kappa Phi whose motto is *"Let the love of learning rule humanity."* He graduated magna cum laude and received a special academic achievement medal from the University of Maryland in psychology and business. He completed his master's degree in education with Boston University. Bob co-led with his wife Jane a cohort in the joint BYU-Idaho Pathway & LDS Institute Program, an innovative global university endeavor. His research interests include individual and organizational high performance and accelerated learning. He has been an associate with the Mountain Quest Institute since its inception over 20 years ago.

The Mountain Quest Institute (MQI), located in the Allegheny Mountains of West Virginia is a research, retreat, and learning center dedicated to helping individuals achieve personal and professional growth, and organizations create and sustain high performance in a rapidly changing, uncertain, and increasingly complex world. MQI has three quests: the Quest for Knowledge, the Quest for Consciousness, and the Quest for Meaning. MQI is scientific, humanistic, and spiritual and finds no contradiction in this blend.

The Institute, situated on a farm in the Allegheny Mountains of West Virginia, is designed to provide full learning experiences, including hosting training, workshop retreats, business meetings, and healing sessions. The Center includes a 40,000-volume research library, conference room, community center, a dozen themed bedrooms, and a four-story tower with a glass ceiling for enjoying the magnificent view of the valley during the day and the stars at night. The farm boasts a mountain terrain and farmland, a labyrinth, creeks, farm animals, and a myriad of wild neighbors.

Project & Technology Management Foundation (PTMF) is a not-for-profit organization promoted by a group of very senior academicians, researchers, industry leaders and academic administrators in India with an objective to disseminate knowledge and provide training and accreditation in the area of project, program and technology management by organizing conferences, workshops, publications, syndicating research, arranging training and teaching programs and courses and collaborating and dynamically networking with other global organizations for knowledge creation. See www.ptmfonline.com

Recent Offerings from MQIPress

INside Innovation: Looking from the Inside Out (2023)

Dr. Alex Bennet and Dr. Rajat Bais (Eds.)

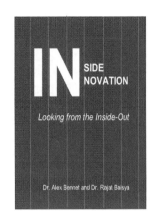

In addition to a collection of insightful innovation case studies, this book offers an unusual look at creativity and innovation from the inside out. Three innovators – a scientist, an organizational guru, and an artist – share the personal passions that have driven their success. "And, then, looking from the inside out, readers are provided the opportunity to evaluate their own organizations against the Most Innovative Knowledge Organization (MIKE) international study program and awards criteria, thus engaging their own innovative juices."

Innovative Creativity:
Creating with Innovation in Mind (2023)

Alex Bennet and Arthur Shelley
Foreword by Robert Turner

More than ever, how do we release the Genie from the lamp? How do we tap the next level of creativity and innovation that we need here on Planet Earth? This groundbreaking work beckons us to deepen our innate creativity capacities in a new and expansive way to summon the genius within each of us.

Other titles from MQIPress:

***The Profundity and Bifurcation of Change**: Parts I – V* (2017; 2020) *by Alex Bennet, David Bennet, Arthur Shelley, Theresa Bullard and John Lewis.* This five-book set supports progression of the Intelligent Social Change Journey (ISCJ), a developmental journey of the body, mind and heart, moving from the heaviness of cause-and-effect linear extrapolation, to the fluidity of co-evolving with our environment, to the lightness of breathing our thought and feelings into reality. Grounded in development of our mental faculties, these are phase changes, each building and expanding previous learning in our movement toward intelligent activity. Part I: *Laying the Groundwork*; Part II: *Learning from the Past*; Part III: *Learning in the Present*; Part IV: *Co-Creating the Future*; Part V: *Living the Future*.

Possibilities that are YOU! (a 22-volume conscious look book series) (2018) *by Alex Bennet.* All Things in Balance ♦ The Art of Thought Adjusting ♦ Associative Patterning and Attracting ♦ Beyond Action ♦ Connections as Patterns ♦ Conscious Compassion ♦ The Creative Leap ♦ The Emerging Self ♦ The Emoting Guidance System ♦ Engaging Forces ♦ The ERC's of Intuition ♦ Grounding ♦ The Humanness of Humility ♦ Intention and Attention ♦ Knowing ♦ The Living Virtues of Today ♦ Me as Co-Creator ♦ Seeking Wisdom ♦ Staying on the Path ♦ Transcendent Beauty ♦ Truth in Context.

The QUEST: Where the Mountains Meet the Library (2021) *by the Drs. David and Alex Bennet with Afterword by Robert Turner.* "This is a book of big ideas, the very ideas that have continuously filled our minds and hearts over the past 20 years, bubbling up and down as we traveled the world."

The Course of Knowledge: A 21ˢᵗ Century Theory (2015) *by Alex Bennet and David Bennet with Joyce Avedisian.* Knowledge is at the core of what it is to be human. We explore a theory of knowledge that is both pragmatic and biological.

Leading with the Future in Mind: Knowledge and Emergent Leadership (2015) by Alex Bennet and David Bennet with John Lewis. A research-based *tour de force* for the future of leadership. We are dreaming the future together.

Decision-Making in The New Reality: Complexity, Knowledge and Knowing (2013) *by Alex Bennet and David Bennet.* We live in a world that offers many possible futures, and we are making decisions every single day! This book takes a consilience approach to explore decision-making in The New Reality.

With Passion, We Live and Love: Research, Prose, Verse and Music (2021) by Alex Bennet and Cindy Lee Scott. Two unknowing sisters who met in their 70ᵗʰ year of life explore nature versus nurture through the eyes of passion. This book shares comparative glimpses of their lives.

Unleashing the Human Mind:
A Consilience Approach to Managing Self (2022)

David Bennet, Alex Bennet, Robert Turner
with Foreword by Florin Gaiseanu

What does it mean to be human? Increasingly, we recognize that we are infinitely complex beings with immense emotional and spiritual, physical and mental capacities. Presiding over these human systems, our brain is a fully integrated, biological, and extraordinary organ that is preeminent in the known Universe. Its time has come. This book is grounded in the Intelligent Complex Adaptive Learning System (ICALS) theory based on over a decade of researching experiential learning through the expanding lens of neuroscience.

Review Bites from Around the World:

Once in a while, I am exposed to a work so profound that it literally causes a massive shift in my own thinking and beliefs ... I found myself riveted to each paragraph as I embarked on a journey that vastly deepened my understanding of the learning process.

-Duane Nickull, Author, Technologist, and Seeker of Higher Truth, Canada

Every now and then a book comes along that compels your spirit. In these times of uncertainty and even great danger for humanity, this book reminds us of what it means to be human, our infinite potential and innate ability to learn and to love.

-Dr. Milton deSousa, Associate Professor, Nova School of Business and Economics, Portugal

Very few people have the gift to integrate such complex ideas, especially those about learning ... this work can be likened to the Webb Telescope, which gives us more clarity into our mysteries.

-Michael Stankosky, DSc, Author, Philosopher, Professor, Editor-Emeritus, Member of the Academy of Scholars, USA

And ...

Unleashing Field Guide: An OrgZoo Quest

Alex Bennet, Robert Turner, Arthur Shelley, Jane Turner and Mark Boyes (Illustrator) (2022)

Arthur Shelley's beloved OrgZoo critters – the voices in our heads – join us in a learning quest up the mountain to unleash the human mind.

Made in the USA
Middletown, DE
17 October 2023

40949879R00440